PUBLIC SPEAKING

A PROCESS APPROACH

Instructor's Edition

PUBLIC SPEAKING

A PROCESS APPROACH

Instructor's Edition

Deanna D. Sellnow
North Dakota State University

HARCOURT COLLEGE PUBLISHERS
Fort Worth Philadelphia San Diego New York Austin Orlando San Antonio
Toronto Montreal London Sydney Tokyo

Publisher	Earl McPeek
Acquisitions Editor	Steve Dalphin
Market Strategist	Laura Brennan
Developmental Editor	Peggy Howell
Project Editor	Rebecca Dodson
Art Director	Susan Journey
Production Manager	Holly Lewerenz

Cover design by Candice Swanson. Image provided by SuperStock, Inc., ©2002.

ISBN: 0-15-507558-6

Address for Domestic Orders
Harcourt College Publishers, 6277 Sea Harbor Drive, Orlando, FL 32887-6777
800-782-4479

Address for International Orders
International Customer Service
Harcourt, Inc., 6277 Sea Harbor Drive, Orlando, FL 32887-6777
407-345-3800
(fax) 407-345-4060
(e-mail) hbintl@harcourt.com

Address for Editorial Correspondence
Harcourt College Publishers, 301 Commerce Street, Suite 3700, Fort Worth, TX 76102

Web Site Address
http://www.harcourtcollege.com

Harcourt College Publishers will provide complimentary supplements or supplement packages to those adopters qualified under our adoption policy. Please contact your sales representative to learn how you qualify. If as an adopter or potential user you receive supplements you do not need, please return them to your sales representative or send them to: Attn: Returns Department, Troy Warehouse, 465 South Lincoln Drive, Troy, MO 63379.

Printed in the United States of America

1 2 3 4 5 6 7 8 9 0 048 9 8 7 6 5 4 3 2 1

Harcourt College Publishers

Public Speaking

A Process Approach

Deanna D. Sellnow

Introducing

A fresh and exciting new textbook for your public speaking classes!

❑ ❑ ❑ ❑

Deanna Sellnow (North Dakota State University) and Harcourt College Publishers are proud to introduce *PUBLIC SPEAKING: A PROCESS APPROACH.*

Always reflecting the latest in communication research yet fully focused on the needs of today's students, *PUBLIC SPEAKING* showcases both innovative and time-tested strategies to help readers learn and apply the skills necessary to become effective public speakers. Among these are:

- ✔ Student-friendly, conversational writing.
- ✔ Unique coverage of *learning styles* as they apply both to the speaker and the audience.
- ✔ Broad and inclusive coverage of cultural diversity.
- ✔ Sensitive and far-reaching discussion of communication apprehension and its management.
- ✔ Full coverage of public speaking ethics.
- ✔ Frequent encouragement of students to think critically.

Check out these pedagogical features!

- A variety of **sample speeches**, including extended student examples that continue across several chapters.
- **Reflective Questions.** Each chapter opens with several *Reflective Questions* that foreshadow material in the chapter. The questions are designed to encourage students to become actively engaged with the material as they read.
- ***What Do You Think?* Sidebars.** Frequently, readers are asked probing questions that prompt them to think critically and link the discussion in the text to their own life experiences and thoughts.
- **End-of-Chapter Material.** Activities that involve both group and individual work are fully described. Key words defined within the chapter are listed again at the chapter's end to ensure that the student has a grasp of the most important topics. A full glossary is found at the end of the text.

CHAPTER 4

Listening and Critiquing Communication

Reflective Questions

1. What is the difference between listening and hearing?
2. What is critical listening?
3. Why do you have trouble listening well?
4. How can you improve your listening habits?
5. What does it mean to be an ethical listener?
6. In what ways is critiquing more than listening?
7. What does it mean to be an ethical critic?

73

58 ◆ Chapter 3 Your First Speech

Kris was enrolled in public speaking fundamentals, a general education core requirement at her university. She had enrolled in the course several times before, but had always dropped it after a couple of classes, when the first speech was assigned. During a recent advising session, she confided that it seemed "unfair" to ask students to present a short speech introducing themselves before they had learned what an effective public speech looks like or how to prepare it. Kris made a lot of sense. It *is* unfair to expect students to stand up and present a speech, however short and simple, without some general guidance.

Teaching Tip
Assign one of the three speeches located in the Activities section of this chapter.

This chapter is offered in response to Kris's concerns, concerns I'm sure many of you share. You can probably identify public speakers who seem to be "good at it" and others who are "not so good at it." What you might not be able to determine, however, is why. What are the basic principles of an effective public speech? This chapter focuses on the key principles you should follow to develop and present a public speech. These principles are discussed as they relate to the three primary components of an effective public speech, as well as the "glue" that holds them together. The components are content, structure, and delivery, and the glue is being audience-centered or listener relevant. To be most helpful, consider the topic and requirements of your first speech assignment as you read the chapter. This way, you can apply the principles to your first speech as you read. Kris's first speech is offered as an example throughout our discussion to help you understand these basic principles as they work in a public speech.

What Do You Think?
Identify a public speaker you have heard who seemed to be really "good at it." Do you know why?

Teaching Tip
Refer students to the SpeechMaker CD-ROM. This software exposes them to multiple speaking scenarios and helps them with every step of the speechmaking process. Before the class, consider assigning one of the scenarios, which you discuss as you teach this chapter.

What Does It Mean to Be Audience-Centered?

Effective public speakers are continuously audience-centered. As listeners, we sense that they care about us enough to offer their ideas in ways that (a) make sense, (b) are relevant to us, (c) reflect careful research, and (d) sound interesting. Being **audience-centered** means considering who your audience members are and how your message can best be tailored to their interests, desires, and needs. Effective public speakers analyze the relationship between their audience and their message when they select their topic, as well as *throughout the speechmaking and presentation process*. This means they consider the audience when selecting a topic and developing the *content*, when organizing the *structure*, and when rehearsing the *delivery*, as well as when actually presenting the speech.

Teaching Tip
Have students write a brief paper on audience analysis. Ask them to keep the following questions in mind: What are the demographic characteristics of your peers in this class? How will you adjust your speech accordingly (topic, purpose, language, etc.)?

Kris's first speech was a "speech of self-introduction." Her audience was a group of 20 to 25 college students who were also enrolled in the course. She estimated that the other students ranged in age from 18 or 19 years old to 45 or 50 years old. Some were married. Others were not. Some had no children, some had young children, and some had grown children. The group included a single parent, a gay rights activist, a fellow who had recently returned to school to become a priest, and a migrant worker. In other words, Kris's audience was *demographically diverse*, differing in ages, experiences, attitudes, and values. However, they did have one important characteristic in common. They were all students at the same university taking the same required public speaking course.

A complete, fully integrated instructional package!

Annotated Instructor's Edition

Annotations in this volume have been provided by Stephen Hunt of Illinois State University. Four broad types of annotations appear:

Discussion Tips suggest topics for classroom discussion that relate to the material presented in the adjoining text.

❋ ❋ ❋

Teaching Tips include a wide range of suggested activities (showing videotapes, group activities, writing exercises, cross-references to other parts of the text, and so on.)

❋ ❋ ❋

Background Tips draw attention to outside research sources from which additional lecture information may be obtained.

What Does It Mean to Have Clear Structure? ◆ 61

listener relevance links are sometimes difficult to formulate, they are crucial aspects of content in an audience-centered speech.

Kris offered a general listener relevance link in her introduction by talking about how important it is to forge new friendships. In discussing her first main point, she talked about her hometown as a place her classmates might consider visiting. In discussing her second main point, she talked about how easy it can be for anyone to take family for granted. And in discussing her third main point, she talked about reasons NDSU is a good school for her and, perhaps, for others as well.

In short, content is the "stuff" of which speeches are made—their main idea and purpose, their supporting ideas or main points, their evidence to support each main point, and their listener relevance links. Good content, however, is not the only foundational component of effective public speeches: Content must be structured in a way that can easily be followed and must be delivered compellingly.

What Do You Think?

Based on the characteristics you identified about your audience members, what kinds of listener relevance links might you include in your first speech?

Technology Tip
http://www.presentations.com/deliver/speak/2000/04/30_sn_good.html
This Web page, hosted by Presentations.com, offers several tips for incorporating content.

Your First Speech

Content Checklist

1. Do your topic and purpose meet the expectations of the audience?
2. Have you limited your main points to between two and four?
3. Do you offer different kinds of evidence for each main point?
4. Do you provide listener relevance links throughout the speech?

What Does It Mean to Have Clear Structure?

The **structure** of your speech is the framework you use to organize your content. The structure guides your listeners as you talk so they can make sense of your ideas. To achieve clear structure, you should consider elements of macrostructure and of microstructure.

Macrostructure refers to the general framework for your content. In the most basic sense, the macrostructure of a public speech consists of an introduction, a body, and a conclusion. In a clearly organized speech, each of these serves a particular function:

1. *Introduction.* Tells them what you're going to tell them.
2. *Body.* Tells them.
3. *Conclusion.* Tells them what you told them.

When I explain these functions to beginning speakers, they sometimes complain that the approach seems like it would be redundant and would bore listeners. On the contrary, this approach is absolutely crucial for an effective public speech.

Teaching Tip
To illustrate how to utilize macrostructure, assign students to small groups and have them prepare a short presentation of their favorite sitcom character. Direct them to include all the elements of the introduction and conclusion, at least two main points, and transitions. This activity will help orient the students to the basic principles of speech construction and outlining. You could follow up this activity with a discussion of the microstructural choices speakers made when presenting the information.

❋ ❋ ❋

Technology Tips refer instructors to specific Web sites that will enhance lectures and provide opportunities for assigning Web exercises. In addition, technology tips show how the *SpeechMaker CD-ROM* can be used either as a lecture tool or by your students on their own.

Ethical Public Speaking ◆ 25

Conveying Your Ideas Orally

Ethical public speakers demonstrate respect for their audience when presenting a message. For example, an ethical speaker rehearses delivery, uses inclusive and tactful language, and conveys ideas in ways that address a variety of learning styles. Consider those times when you have listened to someone who was disorganized, boring, or unprepared. Did you go away feeling respected or disrespected? Ethical speakers respect their audience members' time by offering messages that are organized effectively and presented fluently.

Ethical speakers also respect their audience by using inclusive and respectful language. Terms that exclude or defame certain groups should be avoided. For example, referring to mail carriers and police officers as "mailmen" and "policemen" would exclude women, as would using the generic "he" to represent everyone. Ethical public speakers avoid racist, sexist, ageist and other kinds of abusive language, not just because avoiding such language is politically correct but, rather, because it is ethically correct.

Finally, ethical speakers respect their audience by presenting ideas in ways that address a variety of preferred learning styles. Recall that this means understanding your own preferred learning style and then preparing and presenting your public speeches so that they address the other learning styles as well. To do so, you must use a variety of different supporting material; multiple rhetorical appeals; clear, accurate, inclusive, and vivid language; vocally and visually intelligible and expressive delivery; and clear and systematic organization. To check yourself in

What Do You Think?

Consider a comedian or late-night talk show host whom you have considered to be offensive. Why were you offended? Too often, speakers fall into the trap of defaming others in the name of humor. Such speakers are not ethical because their "humor" is disrespectful to some members of their audience.

Background Tip
For an excellent discussion of the role of learning styles in the basic public speaking course, see T. Nance and A. K. Foeman, "Rethinking the Basic Public Speaking Course for African American Students and Other Students of Color," *Journal of Negro Education* 62(4) (1993), 448–458.

Even when protesting, you should use respectful language if you want to be an ethical communicator.

Additional teaching and learning tools for you and your students!

Instructor's Manual by Tamara Golish (Luther College) offers a wealth of suggestions for setting up the course, including syllabi and daily schedules. The manual is filled with speech assignments, activities, extended chapter outlines (page-referenced to the text), and sample lesson plans that include activities for all learning styles.

❋ ❋ ❋

Test Bank by Janice Stuckey (Jefferson State Community College), available both in printed form and in computerized formats, offers numerous test questions of various types—recall, conceptual, and application—for multiple cognitive levels.

❋ ❋ ❋

Interrater Reliability Training Video provides exemplary speeches to be used in training evaluators, both teachers and students, to rate speeches consistently, using reliable standards.

❋ ❋ ❋

Student Speaker Video is an hour-long videotape of representative student speeches of all types: introductory, informative, persuasive, special occasion, and extemporaneous.

❋ ❋ ❋

Overhead Transparencies by Mark Huglen (University of Minnesota–Crookston) demonstrate the resources, such as models, key charts, diagrams, and forms used in the preparation and presentation phases of public speaking.

❋ ❋ ❋

Web Site by Scott Titsworth (Minnesota State University–Moorhead) contains additional resources such as **PowerPoint Slides**, practice quizzes for students, as well as other Web links, activities, and instructor teaching tools.

❋ ❋ ❋

***SpeechMaker* CD-ROM** which may be packaged with each textbook, brings together text, full-motion video, sound, and the Internet to create a dynamic exploration of the steps involved in the speechmaking process.

SpeechMaker CD-ROM Included Free!

Reinforce the process of speechmaking with the *SpeechMaker CD-ROM!*

This interactive, multimedia software presents four speech scenarios and one additional scenario in which students may develop and record their own speeches.

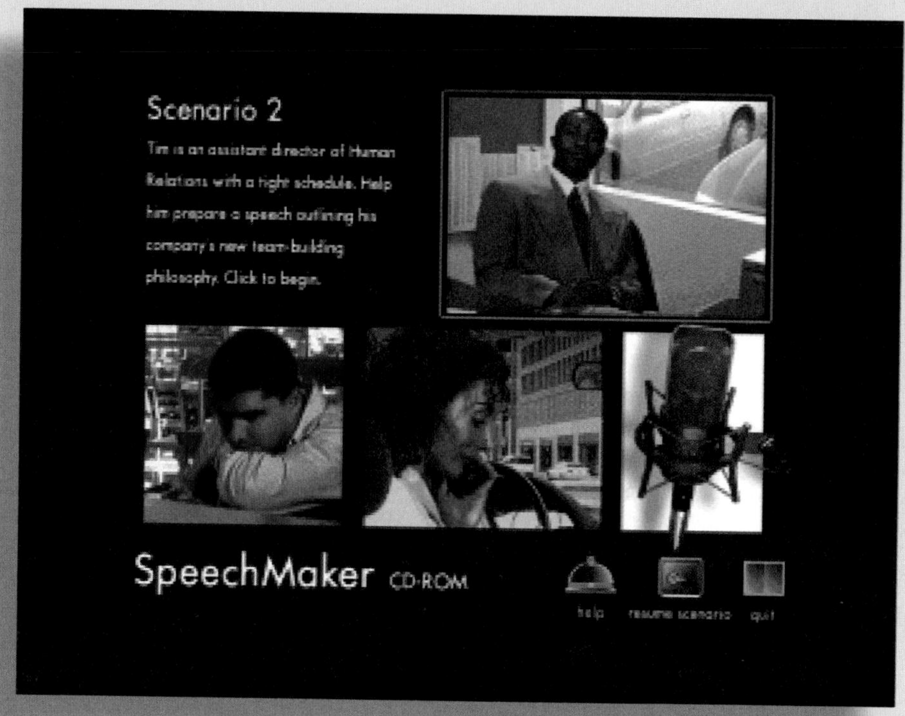

Speeches presented in the program are motivational, informative, and persuasive. Applying critical thinking skills, students work through the *SpeechMaker CD-ROM* assisting the characters in the four scenarios to develop their speeches, by evaluating twelve aspects of speech preparation, including:

- **Narrowing the topic.**
- **Analyzing the audience.**
- **Researching.**
- **Defining support.**
- **Organizing the body.**
- **Practicing delivery.**

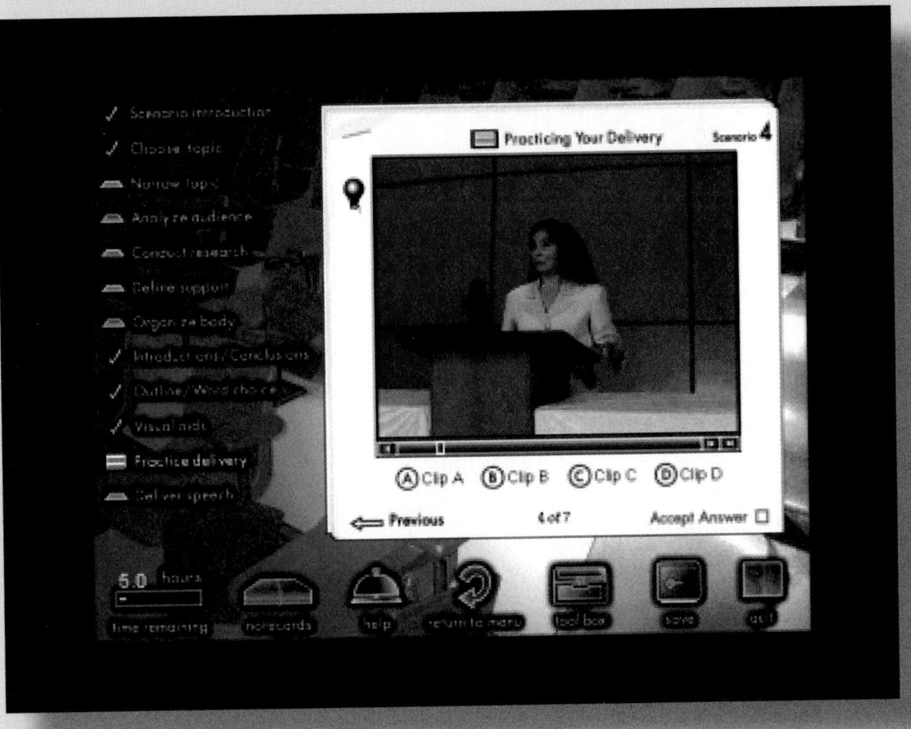

Short videos show each speaker delivering four different introductions and conclusions for his or her speech, as well as four different approaches to using the lectern, microphone, and visual aids. Students then identify the most effective approach. Finally, students critique an extended video of the full speech.

SpeechMaker includes such features as:

- **A "game" atmosphere.**
- **Multiple choice questions with feedback.**
- **A critique form for the characters' final speech.**
- **Additional information on speechmaking.**
- **Video clips.**
- **Recording functionality.**
- **Printing functionality.**
- **A link to the Internet for research.**

To order student copies of PUBLIC SPEAKING (with CD-ROM), use

ISBN: 0-15-506249-2

Here's what some reviewers said about PUBLIC SPEAKING: A PROCESS APPROACH *by Deanna Sellnow!*

"The greatest strengths of the manuscript are the focus on learning styles, inclusion of relevant classical rhetorical theory, and focus on the students' thought processes as they move through the speaking process."

Lynn Disbrow
Sinclair Community College

❋ ❋ ❋

"The writing is very student friendly. I've never met the author, but I can imagine she is an excellent, student-oriented teacher because the text is casual in tone, yet thorough . . . entertaining and also informative."

Janice Stuckey
Jefferson State Community College

❋ ❋ ❋

"I believe that Sellnow provides a more comprehensive approach to—as she envisions—the process of public speaking. Every chapter that I reviewed appears to address (in relevant, creative, and insightful ways) what other public speaking texts are currently missing."

Kelby K. Halone
Clemson University

❋ ❋ ❋

"The author's basic ideas are complemented with abundant, well-developed examples. One of the things I like about this text is the way that Sellnow illustrates important concepts by giving the reader well-developed examples from actual student speeches."

Charles J. G. Griffin
Kansas State University

❋ ❋ ❋

"The emphasis on practical suggestions for dealing with speech anxiety throughout the text is definitely the greatest strength. Chapter 2 is very strong."

Linda Anthon
Valencia Community College

❋ ❋ ❋

"Most certainly the learning theory discussion is a great strength and I really like how it is woven into all aspects of the text. Giving students the opportunity to reflect on their own learning style by taking the learning styles inventory early in the term adds a whole new dimension to what we do in the course and I imagine could set a new tone of self-discovery that could energize the classroom."

Amy Slagell
Iowa State University

I dedicate this book to Tim, Debbie (now 14), and Ricky (now 11), for tolerating this project for three long years.

Your support, your endurance, your sacrifices, and your love are absolutely appreciated by me.

I love you very much!

ABOUT THE AUTHOR

Deanna D. Sellnow is Associate Professor of Communication and Director of the Public Speaking Fundamentals Program at North Dakota State University, where she has taught since 1990. After finishing her master's degree at Wayne State University in Detroit, she completed the Ph.D. program at the University of North Dakota. She has received numerous honors for public speaking, teaching, and research, including the American Forensic Association's National Individual Events Tournament Champion in Communication Analysis, North Dakota Speech and Theatre Association's "Scholar of the Year," and "Outstanding Teacher" at North Dakota State University.

In addition to her teaching, Deanna is active in the National Communication Association, Central States Communication Association, and the North Dakota Speech and Theatre Association. She has served as Chair of the Basic Course Interest Group of the Central States Communication Association and is currently Vice-Chair Elect for the Experiential Learning Commission of the National Communication Association. She also serves as editor of the *Basic Communication Course Annual,* a publication that focuses specifically on research related to the basic course.

Deanna lives with her family in Fargo, North Dakota—husband Tim, daughter Debbie, and son Ricky, along with their golden retriever, Trini, and cat, Carl. She enjoys camping and traveling with her family, running marathons with Tim, and playing a variety of musical instruments including the saxophone, piano, and guitar.

PREFACE

I chose to write *Public Speaking: A Process Approach* because I believe that anyone can become an effective public speaker. Similarly, I believe that we can all improve our public speaking skills. In other words, I believe that effective public speaking is a process that improves as we continue to cultivate it. Effective public speakers are those who choose to work at developing their skills and ineffective speakers are those who choose not to do so. At its most fundamental level, public speaking is a process because it involves a series of steps that focus on aspects of content, structure, and delivery. That's why each chapter of this book teaches students the important concepts and then takes them step-by-step through the process of applying these concepts to their speaking activities.

Communication can be defined as the sending and receiving of verbal and nonverbal messages to create shared meaning. Public speaking is one context in which communication takes place. It is not simply a linear process, however, in which a message is sent by the speaker and received by the listener. Public speaking is a transactional process, where messages are sent and received simultaneously by both the speaker and listeners. Together, both the speaker and listeners play important roles in creating shared meaning. For this reason, *Public Speaking: A Process Approach* will consider not only the role of the speaker but also the role of the audience in effective public speaking.

Becoming effective public speakers is an evolutionary process; we must continually develop and adapt our skills to diverse audiences that change with context, society, and the times. When we operate as though the fundamentals of public speaking are a fixed set of skills, and somehow beyond our reach, we do not allow ourselves the opportunity to grow by participating in this process. This book considers public speaking skills to be fluid and adaptive, and trusts that we are all capable of developing these skills to better address the changing dynamics of diverse audiences in our society.

Features

A number of key features are designed to help students gain the skills and an appreciation for the process of public speaking.

Learning Styles

For several decades, researchers have studied the relationship between learning styles and information retention. They have found that students' retention of information is a function both of individual students' preferred learning styles and of the manner in which a teacher presents material. Furthermore, studies indicate that all students retain material best—regardless of their preferred learning style—when teachers present concepts in ways that address multiple learning styles, in other words, by "rounding the cycle of learning." (See Chapter 1 for a more complete discussion of *learning styles* and the *cycle of learning.*)

Communication researchers have only begun to consider the relationship between learning styles and effective communication. This textbook focuses on the important role that learning styles play in public speaking. Readers learn that their effectiveness as public speakers will be enhanced as they identify and understand not only their own preferred learning style, but also as they appreciate and address the diverse learning styles in their audiences. *Public Speaking: A Process Approach* presents specific strategies to help students achieve these goals.

Diversity

Since the early 1990s, public speaking textbooks have been addressing cultural diversity. Unfortunately, many have done so in ways that unintentionally marginalize or stereotype certain cultural groups. To be more inclusive and to avoid stereotyping, *Public Speaking* integrates diversity comprehensively, yet subtly, throughout the text in ways that acknowledge diversity without marginalizing and stereotyping individuals and groups. For instance, the book shows how diversity may be found in the concept of differing learning styles. Second, a somewhat different approach to demographic audience analysis is shown in Chapter 6. Third, throughout the book various examples from popular culture and from students illustrate the concepts of diversity. Finally, rather than segregating diversity in boxes or sidebars, this book integrates diversity issues and examples within the text itself.

Public Speaking Anxiety

If the research is correct, three out of four people in any classroom experience public speaking anxiety to some degree. Students need to understand why and how to manage their anxiety as it occurs throughout the speech preparation and presentation process. To that end, Chapter 2 is devoted to public speaking anxiety, offering several methods for managing it effectively. In addition, the management of speaking anxiety is discussed wherever it might occur, throughout the text.

Critical Thinking

Many textbooks offer an outline or set of learning objectives at the beginning of each chapter. Unfortunately, students rarely use these outlines or objectives as intended, that is, to focus their thinking as they read. Rather than listing objectives, each chapter opens with four to six **reflective questions.** These questions encourage students to become actively engaged with the material by seeking answers as they read. In a similar fashion, the chapters are interspersed with **What Do You Think?** boxes. These boxes ask students questions that link the text discussion to their own experiences. Doing so also encourages students to think critically about material as they read.

Examples

Students grasp ideas best when they can see examples of those ideas at work. *Public Speaking: A Process Approach* contains a wealth of examples drawn from student speakers, famous orators, and popular culture.

Ethics

Speakers make decisions at numerous points during the speechmaking process; in each decision, there are ethical considerations that affect the choice of topic, audience analysis, research, organization, language, and delivery. Listeners, too, make ethical choices in listening and evaluating. Ethics is integrated throughout the text.

Technology

This book offers practical advice for using technology effectively and ethically where appropriate. Specifically, each chapter in the *Annotated Instructor's Edition* suggests Web sites for students to visit. Chapter 7 contains abundant information on evaluating Internet resources, while Chapter 13 offers practical advice on creating effective PowerPoint presentations.

Pedagogy

In writing *Public Speaking: A Process Approach,* I have tried to remain true to the tenets of learning style theory: I explain concepts in ways that address the "feeling, watching, thinking, and doing" dimensions of the learning cycle. As they move through each chapter, students may "round the learning cycle" as they read. A list of key words for each chapter cue students on important terms that will be defined within. I have used the terminology of the communication field appropriately and have attempted always to define terms simply and completely. The Glossary at the end of the book contains all terms and definitions. At the end of every chapter are practical activities for students to do in class or on their own. Speech outlines as well as transcripts from students and professional speakers are included throughout the book.

Format

This book is organized into three units in such a way that readers can strategically follow an effective pattern for preparing and presenting public speeches for diverse situations and audiences.

Unit I: Understanding Communication Dynamics (Chapters 1–4) introduces readers to foundational components of the communication process. These concepts are relevant, not only to public speaking specifically, but to communication transactions generally. The chapters in this unit cover communication models, communication ethics, communication anxiety, listening, and evaluating.

Unit II: Preparing and Presenting Public Speeches (Chapters 5–13) sets forth the fundamental skills required to organize and deliver effective public speeches. The skills covered in these chapters include topic selection, audience analysis, research and supporting material, organization, language, delivery, and presentational aids.

Unit III: Considering Communication Contexts (Chapters 14–18) provides a basis for understanding why and in what ways content, structure, and delivery might be unique, based on the situation and the audience. The various types of speeches are included: informative, persuasive, special occasion, and speaking in small groups.

Ancillaries

The **Annotated Instructor's Edition** provides instructors with additional ideas for fostering discussion, using the Internet, and engaging students in communication activities.

The **Instructor's Manual** offers a wealth of suggestions for setting up the course, including various syllabi and daily schedules. The manual is filled with speech assignments, activities, extended chapter outlines, and sample lesson plans that include activities for all learning styles, allowing students to "round the cycle of learning."

Available both in printed form and in computerized formats, the **Test Bank** offers numerous test questions of various types: recall, conceptual, and application, in all formats for multiple cognitive levels.

The **Interrater Reliability Training Video** provides exemplary speeches to be used in training evaluators, both teachers and students, to rate consistently using reliable standards.

The ***SpeechMaker* CD-ROM,** which may be packaged with each textbook, brings together text, full-motion video, sound, and the Internet to create a dynamic exploration of the steps involved in the speechmaking process.

The ***Public Speaking* Web Site** contains additional resources such as **PowerPoint Slides,** practice quizzes for students, as well as other activities and instructor teaching tools.

The **Student Speaker Video,** a sixty-minute videotape, shows different types of speeches: self-introduction, informative, persuasive, special occasion, group symposium, and impromptu.

A collection of **Overhead Transparencies** is available to demonstrate the resources, such as models, key charts, diagrams, and forms used in the preparation and presentation phases of public speaking.

Acknowledgements

This textbook represents a process of growth and discovery for me over the past three decades as a public speaker, teacher, and director of the basic course. To thank everyone who has played a part in shaping my development as a public speaker, college teacher, and now author, I realize is impossible, but I would like to acknowledge a few: Howard Vallaincourt, my junior high school speech and debate coach; C. T. Hanson, Robert Littlefield, and Tim Sellnow who inspired me to higher levels of skill and college competition; Bernard Brock, Professor Emeritus at Wayne State University, and Ivan J. K. Dahl, Professor Emeritus at the University of North Dakota for their unrelenting belief in my abilities as a communication scholar and teacher; my father-in-law, Les Sellnow, who provided needed encouragement throughout this project; and for their unceasing, unconditional love and support, Grandpa Johnson and Grandma Miller, who were inspirational mentors who, during the writing of this book, have gone to be with the Lord.

All of the editors at Harcourt College Publishers have been marvelous to work with, providing information, encouraging me, and keeping the project on schedule. Steve Dalphin, Acquisitions Editor, provided such support since the inception of this major undertaking. Peggy Howell, Developmental Editor, is one of the most energetic and innovative people that I have had the pleasure to know and work with. Wow! Rebecca Dodson's work as project editor was both comprehensive and quick. Others from Harcourt have contributed significantly to this book: Laura Brennan, Susan Journey, Holly Lewerenz, Randee Falk, Cathy Spitzenberger, Sue Howard, Bob Tessman, and Jim Ertl.

I would also like to thank the ancillary authors who've offered their expertise and time to this project: Steve Hunt, *Illinois State University;* Janice Stuckey, *Jefferson State Community College, AL;* Tamera Golish, *Luther College, IA;* Scott Titsworth, *Minnesota State University–Moorhead;* Kimberly Cowden of *Cowden Communications* in Fargo, ND; Steve Venette, *North Dakota State University;* and Mark Huglen, University of Minnesota–Crookston.

Reviewers

Many reviewers took the time and energy to respond to drafts of some or all of the manuscript. Their careful work and thoughtful suggestions have made this book better than it otherwise would have been. A special thanks to:

Jonathan Amsbary, *University of Alabama–Birmingham*
Linda Anthon, *Valencia Community College*
Dianne Lee Blomberg, *Metropolitan State College of Denver*
Tim Borchers, *Minnesota State University–Moorhead*
Joan Butcher, *Louisiana State University*
Jim Carlson, *Jones County Community College*
Rebecca Carrier, *Cal Poly Pomona*
Leah Ceccarelli, *University of Washington*
Della Dameron Johnson, *University of Maryland, Eastern Shore*
Lisa Darnell, *University of North Alabama*
Jill Davis, *Mississippi State University*
Lynn Disbrow, *Sinclair Community College*
Cynthia Galivan, *Hudson Valley Community College*
Darla Germeroth, *University of Scranton*
Tamara Golish, *Luther College, Decora, IA*
Lisa Goodnight, *Purdue University–Calumet*
Jonathan Gray, *University of Southern Illinois*
Robert Greenstreet, *East Central University–Oklahoma*
Charles Griffin, *Kansas State University*
Mark Huglen, University of Minnesota–Crookston
Kelby Halone, *Clemson University*
Karin Hilgersom, *Spokane Community College*
Lawrence Hosman, *University of Southern Mississippi*
Steve Hunt, *Illinois State University*
Rebecca Litke, *Cal State–Northridge*

Steve Madden, *University of Southern Mississippi*
Mary Haslerud Opp, *University of North Dakota*
Nan Peck, *North Virginia Community College*
Norma Ragland, *Norfolk State University*
J. D. Ragsdale, *Sam Houston State University*
Amy Slagell, *Iowa State University*
Rick Soller, *College of Lake County*
Dick Stine, *Johnson County Community College*
Janice Stuckey, *Jefferson State Community College*
Rob Vogel, *Spokane Community College*
Beth M. Waggenspack, *Virginia Tech*

Finally, thanks to Tim and Debbie and Ricky, not just for enduring me, but also for helping and encouraging me. You have supported me, guided me and strengthened me, and will, I believe, continue to do so as we pursue our life journey together. I hope that I can do the same for each of you along the way.

To God be the glory.

DEANNA SELLNOW
NORTH DAKOTA STATE UNIVERSITY

BRIEF CONTENTS

CONTENTS

UNIT III CONSIDERING COMMUNICATION CONTEXTS

CHAPTER 1

Introduction to Communication

Reflective Questions

1. What reasons can you identify for improving your public speaking skills?
2. What are the components of a communication transaction?
3. Why does communication fail?
4. What does it mean to be an ethical communicator?

elcome! If you are reading this textbook, I assume you have just enrolled in a public speaking fundamentals course. Before starting you on the exciting process of developing your public speaking skills, I'm *congratulating* you. I'm doing so for two reasons: (a) enrolling in a public speaking course can feel very risky, and (b) taking a public speaking course can bring you enormous benefits.

Teaching Tip
Given that most students experience public speaking anxiety, it is important to provide them with opportunities early in the semester to start practicing their skills. Therefore, consider assigning a nongraded speech of introduction within the first week of class. This will give students an opportunity to start working on their communication apprehension.

If public speaking feels frightening to you, you are by no means alone. Surveys continually report that "speaking in public" is what people fear most. In other words, public speaking is feared more than flying, more than earthquakes, and more even than death! Noted television actor and comedian Jerry Seinfeld once put it this way:

> According to most studies, people's number one fear is public speaking. Number two is death. Death is number two. Does that seem right? This means to the average person, if you have to go to a funeral, you're better off in the casket than doing the eulogy (Seinfeld, 1993, p. 120).

According to recent surveys, 70 to 75 percent of the adult population fears public speaking (McCroskey, 1993; Richmond and McCroskey, 1995). This fact need not be discouraging. If you feel nervous, you can keep in mind that three out of four of your classmates do too. As many as 76 percent of *experienced* public speakers feel fearful before presenting a speech (Hahner, Sokoloff, and Salisch, 1993). Award-winning actor Meryl Streep's comments may represent the feelings of many successful public speakers:

> It's odd: I have this career that spans continents, but the pathetic thing is that I can't get up in front of people and speak. I get really, really nervous (cited in Wasserstein, 1988, p. 90).

Other successful individuals who share Streep's feelings include singer Barbra Streisand, evangelist Billy Graham, former president Ronald Reagan, and former chief executive officer of the Chrysler Corporation Lee Iacocca.

At this point, you might be wondering why people do oral presentations at all. Here is where the benefits come in. As you will soon learn, people give speeches not only because they have to, but also because it is rewarding and even fun! One of the most rewarding experiences I have in teaching this course comes from reading student responses on the end-of-semester course evaluations. Overwhelmingly, whether in the sections I teach or in the sections taught by my colleagues, students write, for example:

- I thought I'd hate this class, but I'm actually going to miss it.
- I can't believe I'm saying this, but I enjoyed this class!
- This was the *best* class I've taken. Don't change a thing.
- It was *fun!*
- I've learned so much in this class. The skills I've learned here are already benefiting me in my other classes.
- I went to a job interview last week. I applied what I've learned in this class. I know it helped. P.S. I got the job!
- I was *terrified* about taking this class, now I can't figure out why I waited so long.

By reading this book and applying what you learn to your own speeches, you too can become an effective public speaker. Consequently, you too can discover the benefits and gratification that can accompany public speaking. This book will help you to (a) control speech anxiety and use it to your advantage, (b) approach your speech topics in ways that spark and maintain listener interest, (c) organize your ideas effectively, (d) present your speeches convincingly, and (e) integrate presentational aids appropriately.

This chapter begins by presenting several compelling reasons for studying public speaking. Next, we define public speaking and situate it within the bigger picture of the communication process. Finally, the chapter addresses ethical communication as it relates to public speaking.

Discussion Tip
Encourage students to discuss their previous public speaking experiences. Ask how they prepared for these experiences. Which strategies were more helpful than others?

Why Study Public Speaking?

Over the years, I have discovered that most students who enroll in public speaking fundamentals do so not because they have a deep-seated desire to improve their public speaking skills, but because the course is required (Trank, 1990; Trank & Lewis, 1991). But even if you enrolled in the course because it is required, you will enjoy it much more and get much more out of it if you think in advance about how it can benefit you. Effective oral communication skills will improve your life in three crucial areas: in your personal relationships, in your college classes, and in your professional career (Ford & Wolvin, 1993; Kramer & Hinton, 1996; Wolvin, 1998a, 1998b; Wolvin, Berko, & Wolvin, 1999).

What Do You Think?

Why did you enroll in this course? What are two specific benefits you would like to achieve from this course by the end of the term?
(1)
(2)

Discussion Tip
Lead an in-class discussion about the benefits of oral presentation skills. Ask students to list at least three advantages of effective presentation skills. Also, have students identify how the course might be useful to their careers. This should help students make important connections between the material and their own interests.

Personal Life Benefits

Do you have a particular friend who always seems able to convince you to go to see one movie instead of another? That friend's success in persuading you is likely due, in part, to his or her effective oral communication skills. In this book, you will learn about both effective and ineffective persuasive strategies that can improve your success rate when trying to convince friends and family, as well as to evaluate the merit of their attempts to persuade you. Similarly, do you have a certain friend or friends whom you are more likely to seek out for advice instead of others? Those individuals also employ effective oral communication skills. This book also clarifies how listening is a multifaceted skill that must be tailored to particular situations to be most effective (e.g., Halone, Cunconan, Coakley, & Wolvin, 1998). The communication skills you will learn in this course can help improve your personal interactions and relationships.

What Do You Think?

Identify a recent discussion you had with a friend when you felt frustrated. Why did you feel frustrated? What are some communication skills you can focus on to improve your personal interactions?

Teaching Tip
Ask students to keep a log for a day that tracks all of their communication interactions. For example, they might note the classes they attend and the communication functions they perform, such as speaking and listening. Have students share their lists in class and encourage them to discuss what they found regarding the relevance of communication skills to everyday life.

Communication scholars often look to popular culture as a guide to understanding the values and beliefs of a society. If this guide is accurate, then what does popular culture tell us about ourselves? Just think of the number of television sitcoms, soap operas, and talk shows, as well as comic strips, movies, and books, that focus on miscommunication between people for their story lines.

> ***What Do You Think?***
> *Identify a favorite television program, comic strip, movie, or book. What skills are revealed as important for effective communication in interpersonal relationships?*

For example, miscommunication is a source of humor in television sitcoms like *Home Improvement, Ally McBeal,* and *Frasier* and a source of drama and suspense in soap operas like *Days of Our Lives, Passions,* and *All My Children* (e.g., Brinson, 1992; Douglas, 1996; Honeycutt, Wellman, & Larson, 1997; Landay, 1999; Larson, 1991; "Nineteen-nineties," 1999). Television talk shows like *Oprah, Ricki Lake,* and *Sally Jesse Raphael* often feature either guests whose personal relationships suffer from miscommunication or guests who are in some way "experts" at improving personal relationships through communication (e.g., Greenberg, Sherry, Busselle, Hnilo, & Smith, 1997; Willis, 1996; Wilson, 1996). Turning to comic strips, we see "Cathy," for example, which often focuses on miscommunication between men and women, and "Dilbert," which often deals with miscommunication in the workplace (e.g., Astor, 1999; Brown, 1997; Capowski, 1997). The fact that miscommunication is such a pervasive theme in popular culture suggests that effective oral communication skills are well worth developing.

College Education Benefits

Discussion Tip
Ask students to identify ways in which the skills taught in this course will benefit them academically. Try to help them think beyond effective oral presentation skills (e.g., how argumentation skills will help them write better essays).

The skills you learn in this class will also benefit you throughout your college career. Jake, a student of mine, avoided taking the public speaking course until the last semester of his senior year. When asked whether this class could benefit students in their education, he exclaimed, "I can't believe I waited so long to take this class. So many of the classes in my major required graded oral presentations. I realize now how much better my grades could have been. If only I'd taken this class sooner." Jake is only one of many upper-class students to have offered this kind of insight.

Two trends that emerged in the 1980s and 1990s have made effective oral communication skills even more important as an asset to college students. These trends are the speaking across the curriculum movement and the national assessment standards initiative. The speaking across the curriculum movement requires oral presentations to occur in all academic areas, not just in speech communication classes. The national assessment standards initiative requires that standardized grading criteria be employed to measure speaker effectiveness. As a result of these two movements, oral presentations are now required in many classes ranging from English to science to engineering to architecture to agriculture to economics to psychology. Simply put, it is no longer possible to earn a bachelor's degree without delivering some graded oral presentations.

In addition to teaching you important skills about preparing and presenting effective public speeches, this course will also teach you other vital communication skills—skills that are directly transferable to other academic areas. You will learn, for example, how to listen critically, take notes effectively, examine information analytically, and evaluate messages carefully. These crucial skills will empower you to succeed throughout your college education.

Professional Career Benefits

Finally, effective oral communication skills will help you succeed in whatever professional career you choose. For example, *Job Outlook 2000,* an annual forecast of hiring conducted by the National Association of Colleges and Employers, surveyed employers to find out what characteristics they sought most in new recruits. The box that follows indicates what employers identified, in rank order, from most important to least important:

Employers Seek . . .

1. **Communication skills.**
2. Motivation/initiative.
3. Teamwork skills.
4. Leadership skills.
5. **Academic achievement/GPA.**
6. Interpersonal skills.
7. Flexibility/adaptability.
8. **Technical skills.**
9. Honesty/integrity.
10. Work ethic.

Wow! If you didn't realize just how important this class would be to your professional success, you should realize it now. Notice where communication skills ranked compared to traits like academic achievement/GPA and technical skills. This startling comparison actually makes sense when you think about it: Employers know they will train their employees again and again as new technologies emerge. Communication skills, however, are foundational. Once learned, these skills will prove beneficial, regardless of your specific role in an organization.

What Do You Think?

What career do you want to pursue? What are two ways effective oral communication skills will help you succeed in this career?

If this survey doesn't convince you, consider the fact that communication training provides preparation for any entry-level position—that is, not only in fields like education, advertising, sales, and broadcasting, but also in fields like accounting, computer science, and engineering (e.g., Bakos, 1997; Kramer & Hinton, 1996; Maes, 1997; Nagle, 1987; Peterson, 1997; Stinson & Asquith, 1997; Weitzel, 1987; Wolvin, 1998a, 1998b). In other words, public speaking skills are important, even in fields where you wouldn't expect them to be.

The bottom line is that these skills are important not just for success and promotion, but for getting a job in the first place. As we all know, employers receive numerous applications for each job vacancy they post. They typically interview three or four applicants whose resumes and supporting materials identify them as most qualified for

Technology Tip
http://www.natcom.org/InstrResour/Pathways/5thEd.htm

This Web page, hosted by the National Communication Association, offers an excellent discussion of pathways to careers in communication.

Teaching Tip
Refer students to the Activities section at the end of this chapter. Have them interview a professional about the career benefits of oral communication training.

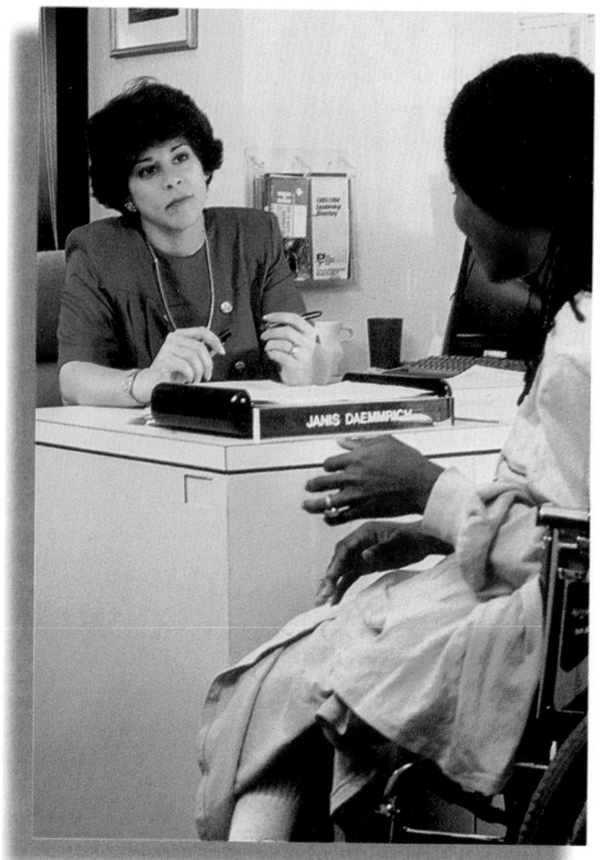

Effective public speaking skills will improve your communication skills when interviewing for jobs.

the job. Based on the interviews, which person do these employers ultimately decide to hire? Right! They hire the person who communicates most effectively in the interview.

Effective oral communication skills, then, will benefit you on many levels: They will enhance the quality of your personal relationships, increase your success in college, and improve your chances for professional success, whether you choose to enter a communication-related career or some other career.

What Is Communication?

We communicate with others in a variety of ways. For example, we mail cards and write letters, we send e-mail, and we talk on the telephone. Sometimes we communicate orally and other times we communicate in writing. To understand the dynamics of public speaking as a form of communication, you must first understand what communication is.

Teaching Tip
Before defining communication in the classroom, have students write a one-page paper in which they define communication and justify their definition. Use this written assignment as the springboard for your discussion of the definition of communication.

Communication is defined for our purposes as *the process of sending and receiving verbal and nonverbal messages to create shared meaning.* Let's look at each part of this definition in turn.

Communication is a dynamic process. By that I mean that both senders and receivers are continuously formulating, sending, and interpreting numerous messages during a particular interaction. A **message** is simply any signal sent by one person **(sender)** and interpreted by another **(receiver).** Essentially, successful communication occurs when the sender and receiver achieve mutual understanding regarding the topic discussed. This is not to say that sender and receivers agree about the merit of a topic, but rather that they agree about the meaning of the message. For example, if you are talking with your friend about *South Park* as your favorite television program, your friend need not *agree* that it is the *best* program. She or he will, however, *understand* that *South Park* is *your* favorite program.

Moreover, communication consists of both verbal and nonverbal messages. **Verbal messages** are made up of the words we use. **Nonverbal messages** are the signals we send using any other means, such as with our hands, body, face, and eyes. To clarify, you might clench your fists as you talk about an issue that angers you. Or you might smile as you recount a pleasant experience you've had. These signals are examples of nonverbal messages that accompany the ideas themselves.

Finally, our prior experiences and cultural background, as well as our expectations, influence the meaning we attach to a particular message. For example, if you decide to present a speech about the local rape and abuse crisis center and one of your audience members is a former victim of abuse (which is quite possible, given the fact that one of every eight college women will be raped by the time she graduates), her prior experiences would influence the way she hears your speech (Jhally, 1995).

Discussion Tip
Consider leading a discussion in which students are required to identify the key components of the communication process. This conversation will form a bridge to a deeper discussion of competing definitions of communication. Given that most students adopt all-inclusive definitions of communication, ask them to identify what communication is not.

Communication Contexts

Public speaking is actually only one context where communication occurs. After all, we also communicate in small groups, in one-to-one relationships, on the telephone, over the Internet, and on radio and television, as well as in newspapers, magazines, and newsletters. Communication research reveals five identifiable communication contexts: (1) intrapersonal, (2) impersonal, (3) interpersonal, (4) small group, and (5) public (Littlejohn, 1989). Public speaking occurs within the public communication context. To select the most appropriate strategies for communicating in a public context, it is important to understand public speaking as it relates to the other communication contexts.

Although these contexts differ in unique ways, they are also similar as well as interrelated in that each context operates as a forum within which communication occurs. They differ in terms of how formally you deliver your message. They also differ in terms of the kinds of information you typically share and with regard to the means by which the information is transferred from one person to another. Finally, these contexts are interrelated in that they sometimes appear to blend together in certain ways. That said, let's look more closely at each of them.

Discussion Tip
Have students discuss the relative amount of communication time they devote to each of the five discernible communication contexts listed in the text (intrapersonal, impersonal, interpersonal, small group, and public). Ask them to identify key differences in the nature of communication in these contexts. Also, ask them to consider how context influences communication.

Intrapersonal communication is simply communicating with yourself. Intrapersonal communication rarely occurs orally but rather happens in our heads as we think through our choices, our strategies, and the possible consequences of our actions. When you consider whether to tell your roommate that you are the one who broke his or her desk lamp, you are communicating intrapersonally. When you decide to replace the lamp before your roommate realizes it was broken, you are communicating intrapersonally. A good deal of our intrapersonal communication occurs subconsciously. In other words, we are often not aware of the communication choices we make intrapersonally (Kellermann, 1992). You are, in fact, communicating intrapersonally even when you don't fully realize it. When you drive into your driveway "without thinking," for example, you are communicating intrapersonally on a subconscious level. Intrapersonal communication might occur within the public speaking context, for example, if you begin to wonder how you sound to your listeners while you're presenting your speech. Or you might notice confused looks on your listeners' faces as you explain a complex process and decide to rephrase your explanation in a different way.

Impersonal communication is communication between two people about general information (Adler & Towne, 1996; Trenholm & Jenson, 1992). It is more intentional than intrapersonal communication but is still fairly informal. Usually, we communicate impersonally with people whom we know relatively little about. When you say "hi" to a stranger you pass on the sidewalk, you are communicating impersonally. When you talk about the weather with the checker at the grocery store, you are communicating impersonally. Impersonal communication might occur within the public speaking context, for example, if you share introductory remarks related to current events or the weather or the occasion before you begin your actual speech. Although these impersonal comments don't relate directly to your speech, they can act as a signal to your audience to get ready to listen.

Discussion Tip
Have students discuss ways in which new communication technologies like electronic mail have changed the nature of interpersonal communication. Discuss whether mediated communication is as "rich" as face-to-face communication.

Interpersonal communication is communication between two people who already have an identifiable relationship with each other (DeVito, 1993). In other words, we know things about the other person that distinguish her or him from other people we meet on the street. When you stop to chat with a friend between classes about weekend plans, how the kids are, or what you did last night, you are engaging in interpersonal communication. When you have a heart-to-heart talk with a close friend or family member, you are engaging in interpersonal communication.

Interpersonal communication sometimes occurs within a public communication context, for example, when speakers tell personal stories about experiences they've had as evidence to support their main points. This sharing of personal information that is not generally known by others is known as **self-disclosure.** Self-disclosure functions to establish and maintain personal relationships and can act as a similar bond in a public communication context. For example, one speaker may talk about his reasons for returning to college as part of his recent calling to become a priest. Another speaker might use self-disclosure during her speech about female bronco riders when she shows her own bruised knee (which she got as a result of being bucked off a horse the night before). Both speakers have integrated interpersonal communication within the public communication context of presenting their public speeches.

Discussion Tip
Ask students to identify a small group that they have interacted in recently. Have them identify what communication issues were rewarding or frustrating. Also, ask them to speculate about the extent to which they will have to interact in small groups in their future careers.

Small group communication is generally defined as communication occurring in a group of about three to ten people (Poole, 1998, p. 94). The group might be meeting to perform a specific task, reach a common goal, share ideas, or simply engage in a social experience. There are many kinds of small groups, for example, your family, a group of friends, a group of classmates who work together on a class project, or a small group management team in the workplace (Ancona, 1990). In small group communication, the individuals interact with each other in such a way that "each person influences and is influenced by [the] other[s]" (Shaw, 1981, p. 10). Since more people are involved, small group communication is more complex than impersonal or interpersonal communication. Yet because small groups are so important in both our personal and professional lives, we need to be able to understand and deal with these complexities. In fact, some research suggests that there are more small groups in the United States than there are people!

What Do You Think?

Identify a small group you've interacted in recently. It can be a family group, service group, social group, or business group. What communication oriented issues can you identify that made interacting in that group rewarding or frustrating for you?

Small group communication occurs within a public communication context when groups of people are asked to make public presentations. When you are asked to do so, how effectively members work together throughout the process of developing your ideas as well as how effectively your group functions together to present them reflects directly on your own success.

Public communication is communication to audiences of more than about ten people. Public speaking is, of course, one form of public communication. **Public speaking** can be defined as a sustained formal presentation made by a speaker to an audience. When you give oral presentations in this classroom, you are engaging in public speaking. Teachers engage in public speaking when they lecture to their classes. A master of ceremonies also engages in public speaking. Actors who introduce award winners and who accept awards are engaged in public speaking. Likewise, corporate managers engage in public speaking when they run large meetings. Presiding officers of various clubs engage in public speaking when they conduct meetings. When parents present their ideas about educational issues to school boards or other officials, they are engaging in public speaking. And the list goes on. Public speaking is much more prevalent in our day-to-day lives than most of us actually realize. Improving our ability to speak effectively in public is crucial to achieving important goals for ourselves, our families, and our communities.

Discussion Tip
Ask students to identify a public speaker they have seen recently. If they have not seen a public speaker, ask them what public speaking situations they have experienced. Have them identify the positive and negative behaviors of the speaker. This discussion can illuminate many of the elements of good oral style. In addition, by identifying what students fear most about the public speaking experience, you can tailor your discussion of communication apprehension to your students' specific concerns.

Parents who speak up at community meetings are engaged in public speaking.

> **What Do You Think?**
> *Identify the occasions when you've spoken to a group of more than ten people? Were you effective? Why or why not?*

Another form of public communication is mass communication. **Mass communication** can be defined as communication produced and transmitted via media to large audiences. Newspaper and magazine journalists present written articles to large publics via mass communication. Television news anchors present information via mass communication using a public speaking format. Radio disc jockeys who offer morning shows in groups of three or four at a time share ideas via mass communication using a small group communication format. Likewise, a televised debate between two presidential candidates is a mass communication form that utilizes elements of public speaking and interpersonal communication within it.

The various contexts of communication are identifiably unique. Speakers ought to understand these differences in order to formulate and articulate messages that are appropriate for a particular context. Yet more than one communication form can be used simultaneously and effectively as long as it is adapted to function within a particular context.

Models of Communication

Linear

> **Teaching Tip**
> Assign students to groups and instruct them to develop a model of the communication process. Encourage them to be both creative and critical thinkers (they could construct a visual representation of the process, produce a short skit to highlight components of communication, etc.).

Over time, scholars have developed various models of communication. Some of the earliest models were linear in nature. In other words, communication was conceived as a one-way process (see Figure 1–1). According to a **linear model of communication,** a speaker sends a message to a listener who receives the message. A speaker's role, then, is to encode the message, whereas the listener's role it to decode it. **Encoding** is the process of putting ideas into symbols, in this case, into words that the listener ought to understand. Conversely, **decoding** is the process of attaching meanings to the symbols we see

FIGURE 1–1 Linear Model of Communication

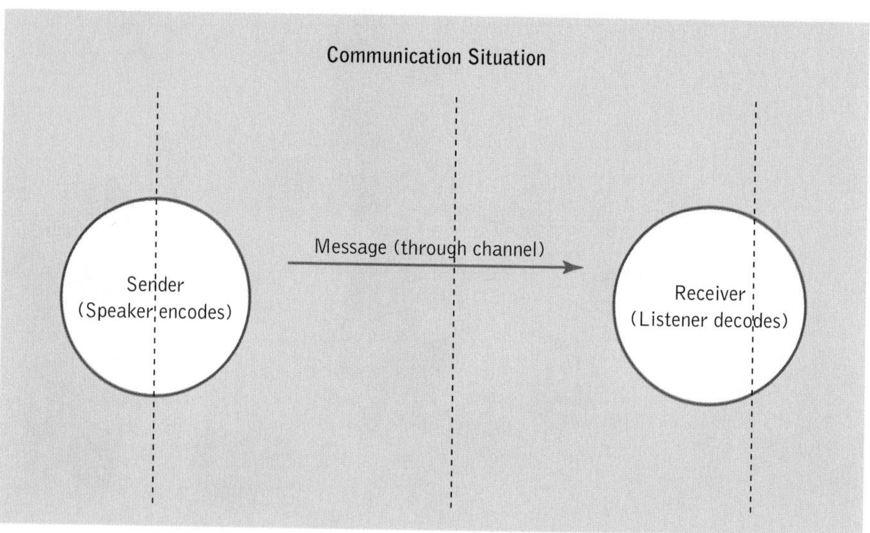

or hear. For example, a child who tells his mother he is hungry is the sender of the message: "I am hungry." The mother is the receiver of that message. Although the communication occurs within a particular context, or **communication situation,** early scholars did not consider the situation to influence the interaction in any significant way.

Technology Tip
http://www.sfc.keio.ac.jp/~masanao/Mosaic_data/com_model.html
This Web page explores several models of communication.

Interactive

As communication scholars continued to study communication, they developed an interactive model of communication. An **interactive model of communication** improves on the ideas expressed in the linear models, first, by accounting for the feedback receivers (listeners) return to senders, so that meaning is created by senders and receivers (see Figure 1–2). **Feedback** consists of all those verbal and nonverbal messages receivers send back to senders during a communication interaction. Consider the hungry child and his mother again. If the mother responds to the child's statement about being hungry with a comment like, "Oh, I didn't realize it was time for lunch already," her comment could be considered verbal feedback. Likewise, if she responded by shrugging her shoulders, this could be considered nonverbal feedback.

In addition to the inclusion of messages sent both verbally and nonverbally, an interactive model also accounts for internal and external interference that can block successful communication. **Internal interference** is any distraction that originates in the thoughts of either participant. If the mother in the earlier scenario was worried about why her other child has such a high fever, that internal interference might distract her. **External interference** is any distraction that originates in the communication situation. If the telephone begins to ring during the conversation between the mother and her child, the ringing would serve as external interference. The communication situation is considered important in the interactive model primarily because external interference can arise in it. This two-way model of communication is more complete than the linear models. But it is still limited because (a) it does not account for the simultaneous sending and receiving of messages as they result in shared meaning creation and

Teaching Tip
Ask students to list examples of internal and external interference that they have experienced in past interactions. Encourage them to identify the implications of interference on successful communication.

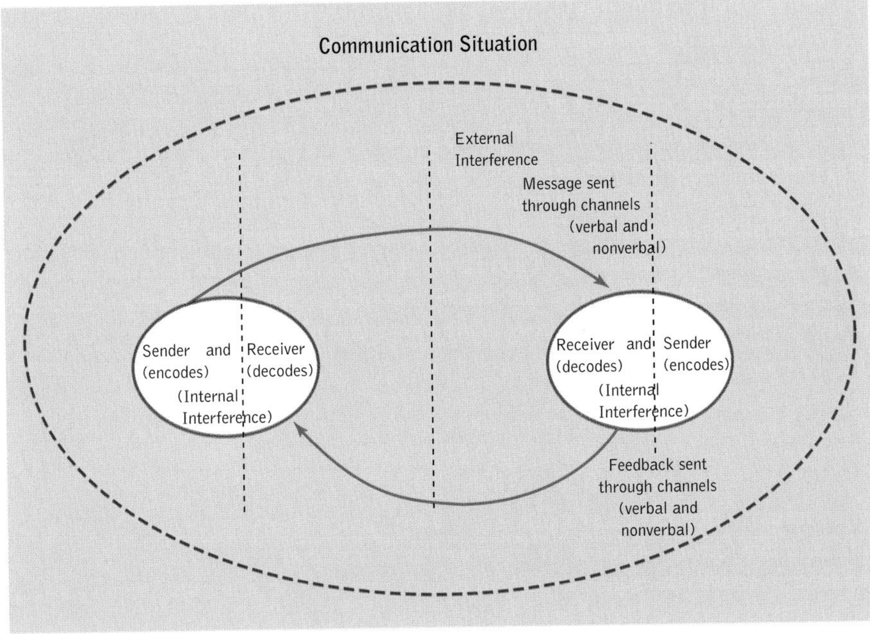

FIGURE 1–2
Interactive Model of Communication

(b) it does not consider the multifaceted ways in which the communication situation influences the communication process.

Transactional

Most recently, scholars have developed a **transactional model of communication** to understand the communication process. This model expands on the earlier models by accounting for the simultaneous sending and receiving of messages during a communication interaction, as well as the numerous ways in which the communication situation might influence the interaction. During the conversation between the mother and her hungry child, for example, the mother's lack of eye contact and stern-looking facial expressions communicate messages at the same time as her son is professing his hunger. Likewise, her son might stomp his foot or pull on her arm while telling her he is hungry. All of these messages occur simultaneously. A transactional model accounts for this complexity in communication interactions.

To better understand the dynamics of the communication process, let's dissect this transactional model to discuss more fully each of its seven basic elements. These elements are the situation, the sender(s), the message(s), the receiver(s), the channel(s), the feedback, and the interference. Figure 1–3 illustrates the transactional model of communication. We'll look at each element as it operates generally in any communication interaction, as well as within the public speaking context specifically. Finally, we'll highlight specific goals public speakers ought to strive for based on the potential implications each element might have on the success of their message.

Situation

The situation is essentially the place, time, occasion, and cultural context of the communication. Communication always occurs in some situation. The *place* of the communication might be your home, your office, your car or a bus, the park, a restaurant, or a classroom. The *time* might be early in the morning, late at night, right before class, or right after lunch. Likewise, the time might be Monday morning, Friday

FIGURE 1–3 Transactional Model of Communication

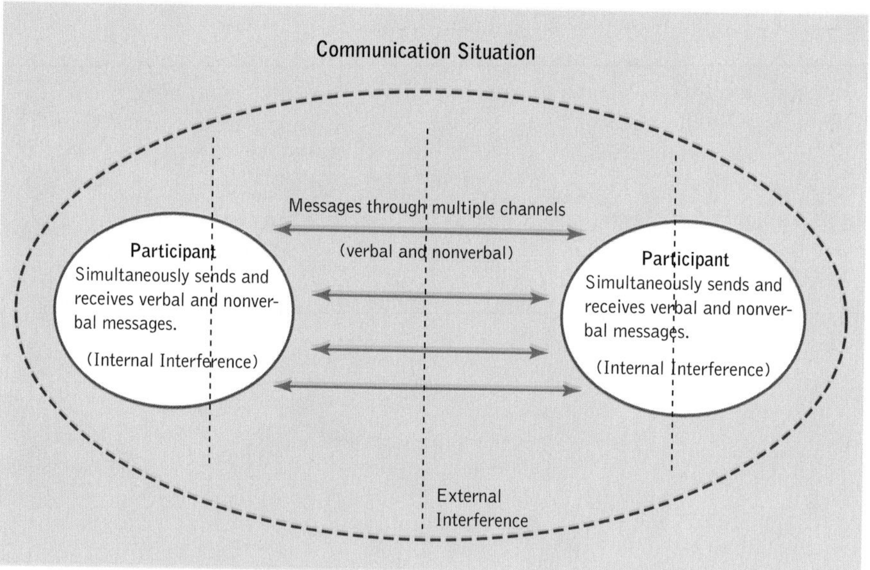

evening, or Saturday afternoon. And the *occasion* might be a board meeting, a social gathering, a special occasion like a birthday or anniversary, or a ceremonial occasion like a wedding, graduation, or funeral. These situational factors are all influenced by the *cultural context.* Culture has to do with the attitudes, beliefs, and values shared by a group, as well as their informal rules for behavior. The cultural context is important for public speakers to consider because it governs certain communication rules for us as we speak. We'll discuss cultural context in more detail in Chapter 6.

Considering the Situation. The communication situation is important because it can either help your message or hurt it. In terms of public speaking, the kind of speech that would be most appropriate for a graduation ceremony is not the same kind of speech that ought to be presented at a funeral. Likewise, the way you ought to deliver a public speech in an outdoor amphitheater or large auditorium would probably differ from the way you will deliver your speeches in the classroom. Even in the classroom, the arrangement of the furniture; number of listeners; time of day, week, or year; and context of recent events may all potentially affect your success. How? Consider delivering your speech to a group of classmates sitting in a circle rather than in a conventional classroom seating arrangement. How might they become more easily distracted from the message? How might a small and overcrowded classroom affect the attention span of listeners? The situation is an important element to consider for effective oral communication.

Considering Communication Rules. In addition to these general communication situation concerns, it is also important to speculate about communication rules that govern different situations. Essentially, you need to determine what are the communication rules for a particular situation and then modify your message or the situation in ways that allow you to adhere to the rules. **Communication rules** are guides for what is appropriate in a situation based on place, time, occasion, and cultural context. These rules are implicit rather than explicit and thus are best determined by considering how you would react if you were the receiver of the communication.

Discussion Tip
Have students discuss the ways in which communication rules vary from culture to culture. Ask them to describe instances where they have violated implicit or explicit rules. How could they avoid such an experience in the future?

Technology Tip
http://www.fit.edu/CampusLife/clubs-org/sccr/resources.html

The Society for Cross-Cultural Research Web site offers several links to intercultural communication resources.

Keep in mind that communication rules differ in different cultures. For example, I was recently introduced to a colleague from Kenya during a social gathering at a friend's home. As a friendly gesture, I asked him how many children he had. I later learned that in his culture my question was not appropriate, because referring to children in numbers devalues them as the unique God-given gifts they are believed to be. Certainly, cultural context can be globally conceived as in this example. It can also be conceived within the boundaries of a nation. A cultural group can be defined by dimensions such as age, race, ethnicity, gender, ability/disability, sexual orientation, geographic location, socioeconomic status, marital status, career, and religious beliefs, when those dimensions shape an identifiable worldview. Given this definition, the U.S. population can best be characterized as multicultural. To clarify, let me offer another example. Upon graduating with my bachelor's degree, I landed a position that took me from a rural community in Minnesota to live and work in inner-city Detroit. I learned quickly that the communication rules that were appropriate in rural Minnesota were not necessarily appropriate in this urban setting. Rather than smiling and saying "hi" to everyone I passed on the street, for example, I learned to avoid eye contact when passing people I did not know.

It is important to consider the communication rules inherent in a situation in order to ensure that they help your message rather than hurt it. To do so, you might decide to modify the situation or modify the message. For example, in the context of our culture, you probably wouldn't want to talk with a close friend or family member about a serious personal conflict while having dinner in a restaurant with a group of casual friends or business associates. You might, instead, modify the situation by waiting until you and your partner are alone to discuss the issue that was bothering you at the restaurant. Or if you felt compelled to address the issue while at the restaurant, you might modify the message in a way that depersonalizes it, making it a general statement that is not obviously connected to your partner.

> **What Do You Think?**
>
> *Identify a time when you "put your foot in your mouth." Why did you wish you hadn't said what you said? Instances like these are usually a result of not following communication rules for a particular situation or cultural context.*

When giving a public speech, you might also decide to modify the situation or your message in order to adhere to communication rules. For example, if you are asked to present an informative speech introducing yourself to the class, you ought to avoid attempting to persuade the class that your lifestyle or personal background is better than any other. I once had a student who chose to tell the class about his recent suicide attempt during this introductory speech. Doing so did not adhere to the communication rules for that situation. He could have modified the speech by talking about his personal background and lifestyle in a more general sense. If he was compelled to talk about the suicide attempt as a plea for counseling, he could have modified the situation by talking with me individually after class or during my office hours.

Sender

The sender is the person who initiates the communication. Although both sender and receiver(s) send verbal and nonverbal messages simultaneously, in public speaking contexts, the sender is the person who presents the actual speech. To be an effective public speaker, the sender must convey ethos. **Ethos,** a term meaning speaker credibility based on perceived competence and character, was originally conceived more than 2,000 years ago by the Greek philosopher Aristotle. Because listeners often have a difficult time separating the message from the sender, good ideas can easily be discounted if the sender does not establish ethos via content, delivery, and structure. By the same token, weak ideas can seem more compelling when they are offered by a speaker who conveys ethos. For example, some critics argue that Ronald Reagan's ethos allowed him to make any idea sound like a good idea, whether or not it actually was. On the contrary, Jesse Ventura, who was elected governor of Minnesota, was unwisely disregarded as a viable opponent by both the Republican candidate and the Democratic candidate because they thought he lacked ethos. In the classroom, a student who presents a well-researched, structured, and delivered speech is likely to be more successful than one who does not, simply due to the amount of ethos each exhibits.

> **What Do You Think?**
>
> *Identify a speaker you heard who was really good. What did that speaker look like and act like? How did this contribute to your perception of the speaker's credibility? (Competence? Character?)*

Your goal as a public speaker is to convince listeners of your credibility. You can do this by stating your purpose clearly, conveying relevant knowledge about the topic, and portraying a positive self-concept while speaking. Simply put, do what it takes to look good (dress up), feel good (get plenty of rest and nutrition), and sound good (research and rehearse) if you want to be good.

Technology Tip
http://www.historychannel.com/historychannel/gspeech/archieve.html

The History Channel Web site contains several historically significant speeches. Have students select a speaker and evaluate her or his credibility.

Message

The message consists of the ideas the sender (speaker) conveys to the receiver (listener). This message is actually multifaceted. Listeners combine what they hear and see to determine what the message is. In other words, your message is not only what you say, but also how you say it. The words you choose, the way you arrange them, the inflection of your voice, your posture and gestures, your facial expressions, your eye contact, and the presentational aids you integrate all are important contributors to the message.

Your goal for effective public speaking is to make sure that all of these messages fit together—that they all say what you want to say. More specifically, make sure that your nonverbal messages either emotionally or structurally reinforce your intended verbal message, making it more compelling to your listeners. Hence, you must not send nonverbal messages that distract from the verbal message, such as fidgeting, pacing, or playing with your glasses, hair, or notes. If listeners begin to watch your distracting nonverbal messages rather than listen to what you have to say, your intended message is likely to be blocked. Likewise, you must avoid sending nonverbal messages that contradict the intent of your verbal message, such as slouching, sounding or looking bored, or keeping your eyes focused on the floor in front of you or on your notes. If speakers send nonverbal messages like these that contradict the verbal message, listeners will likely believe the nonverbal messages rather than the verbal one. Consequently, your message will fail.

Technology Tip
http://www.houckassociates.com/hint6.htm

The Houck Associates Web site summarizes research findings regarding nonverbal communication.

Receiver(s)

The receiver is the person to whom the sender is communicating (the listener). For public speakers, the receiver is the audience. The intended message sent by the speaker is not always the same as the message received by the listeners. We've already learned how nonverbal messages can influence the message received. The message is also influenced by the receiver's frame of reference. Everything the speaker says and does is filtered through the listener's frame of reference. A listener's **frame of reference** is made up of his or her goals, knowledge, experiences, values, and attitudes.

Technology Tip
http://www.presentations.com/deliver/speak/2000/03/31_sn_conn.html
This Web page, hosted by Presentations.com, offers several suggestions for building rapport with the audience.

No two people can have identical frames of reference, but sometimes members of an audience tend to share certain characteristics. Thus, effective public speakers must do two things: They must try to appeal to the range of diversity represented in any audience and they must adapt their messages to each particular audience. This is accomplished by employing audience analysis and being audience centered. **Audience analysis** is the process of finding out who your listeners are and then adapting your speech to make it relevant to their interests and desires. For example, if you were to present a speech about fire safety to a group of second graders, you might focus on the concept of stop, drop, and roll. If you were to talk about fire safety with the tenants in your apartment complex, however, you might talk instead about where to place smoke alarms and fire extinguishers, how to test them, and how to use them effectively. Both speeches are on the topic of fire safety, but the topic is adapted so that it's relevant to each audience.

What Do You Think?

Were you raised in a city, in a suburb, in a small town, or on a farm?
Are you married? single? divorced?
Do you have children? grandchildren? If not, do you plan to have them someday?
What are your religious beliefs?
What are your career aspirations?
Do you belong to a political party? Why or why not?
Your answers to these questions will begin to reveal your personal frame of reference, which influences how you interpret messages.

The first goal cannot be emphasized enough. The United States is becoming ever more culturally diverse, to the point that it has been called the "first universal nation" (Wattenberg, 1991). To be on the safe side, assume that it is. In this way, you will make sure you're not appealing to too narrow a range and, more important, you will avoid the possibility of unintentionally offending or marginalizing listeners. Marginalization occurs when speakers discuss a topic from a majority perspective as though that perspective is the only legitimate one. Doing so excludes some audience members from the exchange, because their perspective is ignored as irrelevant or even nonexistent. As you prepare your speech, do not assume listeners' customs and beliefs are the same as yours. Show respect for other cultures and beliefs, and avoid **ethnocentrism,** the tendency to assume the values and beliefs of one's own culture are somehow better than those of other cultures.

Teaching Tip
Bring enough pennies to class to distribute one to each student. Have each student draw one penny and study it carefully. After two or three minutes, collect the pennies, mix them up in the front of the classroom, and ask the students to pick out the penny each initially selected. Next, lead a discussion in which you ask students how they were able to identify their pennies. Focus on similarities (date, Lincoln, color, etc.) as well as differences (unique markings, different dates, etc.). Conclusion: Although their pennies do have identifiable differences, they are all worth the same.

Audience diversity is, of course, not just cultural. It is just as important, for example, to take into account diversity in sex, gender, and sexual preference to avoid marginalizing listeners on any of these grounds. Consider Jim, for example, who gave a speech on Elton John. At several points during the speech, Jim sheepishly commented that Elton John was his role model because of his musical talent, *not* because of his sexual preference. It is quite likely that Jim's repeated comment offended or marginalized someone in his audience (*New York Times,* 1994). Or consider Luke, who gave a speech about collecting baseball cards. During the introduction, he exclaimed, "I don't know if many of the gals will be interested in this hobby, but I'll bet most of you guys will find it interesting." This unnecessary comment offended some of the women in the class. Sexist language can also serve to exclude. When Sari talked about the importance of fire fighters but repeatedly referred to them as *firemen,* she inadvertently excluded women and offended some listeners. Effective public speakers strive to use inclusive language, avoid ethnocentrism, and respect diversity.

There is yet another kind of diversity that you as a speaker should keep in mind: People have different learning styles. A **learning style** is a preferred way of receiving information. If you vary the ways you present your ideas to an audience, you will address the diverse learning styles represented in your audience and thus be more effective. A number of scholars across disciplines have developed models for understanding these different learning styles (e.g., Barbe & Swassing, 1979; Canfield, 1980; Dunn, Dunn, & Price, 1975; Gardner, 1983; Kolb, 1984; McCarthy, 1980; Renzulli & Smith, 1978). One comprehensive model that is easily adapted to the public speaking process is Kolb's (1984) cycle of learning, which combines experience, perception, cognition, and behavior (see Figure 1-4).

Background Tip
For more information on learning styles, see D. Jonaseen and B. Grabowski, *Handbook of Individual Differences, Learning, & Instruction* (Hillsdale, NJ: Erlbaum, 1993).

To clarify, the learning process can be conceived as a four-stage cycle of feeling, watching, thinking, and doing. People learn best when they move through all four of these stages because they are able to understand, retain, and apply the ideas and concepts offered. What this means is that you should address all four stages in each public speech you present. In other words, you should consider how your speech addresses each stage when organizing your ideas, developing your content, choosing supporting material, preparing your presentational aids, and rehearsing your delivery. Effective public speakers round the entire cycle of learning because doing so increases their likelihood for success.

In addition, each of us tends to prefer grasping ideas in a particular way, relying more heavily on one particular stage than the others. This tendency reflects your preferred learning style. Your preferred learning style is likely to differ from that of many of your audience members. By addressing each learning style during your speech, you can reach the diverse preferences represented in your audience as you round the cycle of learning for all. This model identifies four distinct learning styles as they reflect certain stages in the cycle: convergers, divergers, assimilators, and accommodators.

People who rely heavily on some combination of thinking and doing are referred to as **convergers.** If this is your preferred learning style, your strengths are problem solving, decision making, and the practical application of ideas. You like to find the single correct answer to problems and prefer to find these answers through deductive reasoning. You would rather deal with technical tasks than social or interpersonal issues. You also enjoy testing theories to see if they really work. In terms of public speaking, you are likely to prefer speeches that are organized using a deductive pattern and

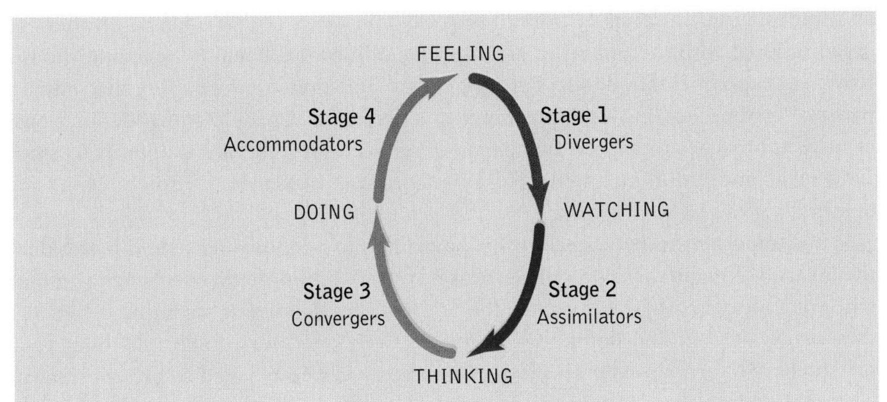

FIGURE 1–4 Kolb's Cycle of Learning

that use deductive reasoning. You probably prefer clearly articulated plans for applying concepts and theories to real-life situations. Likewise, you probably prefer supporting material and presentational aids that focus on hands-on experiences, practical applications, experimentation, and results; rhetorical appeals to logic; language that strives for accuracy and clarity; and intelligible delivery.

People who rely heavily on feeling and watching are referred to as **divergers.** This learning style has the opposite strengths from the converger. If this is your preferred learning style, your strengths are your imagination and your ability to view concrete situations, experiences, and examples from many different perspectives. You enjoy brainstorming ideas, social interactions, discussions, collaboration, and lots of concrete examples. You probably have broad cultural interests and like to gather information. You enjoy making personal connections with ideas and concepts. In terms of public speaking, you are likely to prefer inductive organizational patterns and reasoning; content that provides clear listener relevance links; supporting material that focuses on vivid descriptions, examples, and testimonies; visual aids; rhetorical appeals to emotions; vivid and emotionally charged language; and vocally and visually expressive delivery.

People who rely heavily on thinking and watching are referred to as **assimilators.** If this is your preferred learning style, you are best at understanding a wide range of information and putting it into logical, orderly form. Your greatest strength is the ability to create a logically sound and systematically precise model from abstract ideas and concepts. You enjoy critiquing the ideas of others. Unlike the converger, you are less concerned with the practical value of ideas than the logical soundness of them. Unlike the diverger, you are less concerned about people and personal connections than ideas and abstract concepts. In terms of public speaking, you are likely to prefer very clear deductive organizational patterns and parallel structure; supporting material and visual aids that focus on facts, statistics, definitions, expert opinions, and detailed explanations; rhetorical appeals to logic; language that focuses on accuracy and clarity; and intelligible delivery.

People who rely heavily on doing and feeling are referred to as **accommodators.** This learning style has the opposite strengths from the assimilator. If this is your preferred learning style, your greatest strengths lie in carrying out plans and tasks, in discovering hidden possibilities and creative approaches, in taking risks, and getting involved in new experiences. In contrast to the assimilator, you're more likely to act on intuition than systematic analysis. You prefer to rely on input and information from other people to help solve problems and are good at synthesizing such input and information. In terms of public speaking, you are probably open to a variety of organizational patterns and types of reasoning. You probably enjoy opportunities for hands-on experimentation; supporting material and presentational aids that rely on personal testimonies and examples from a variety of real people and real situations; creative approaches to and unique perspectives on topics; rhetorical appeals to emotion; vivid and emotionally charged language; and vocally and visually expressive delivery.

It is important to remember at this point that no one learning style is better than the others. Consequently, as a public speaker, you will be most effective when you present your ideas in ways that round the entire cycle of learning in terms of feeling, thinking, watching, and doing. To do so effectively, you must first understand your own preferred learning style. This is necessary because speakers tend to present ideas in ways that address their own preferred style at the expense of the other styles, particularly the opposite learning style. If you do not know your preferred learning style, take a few moments to complete the Learning Style Quiz included in the Activities section at the end of this chapter. Then you will be able to consider more accurately how you can address other learning styles in your speeches.

Let's look now at how Barry rounded the cycle of learning in his informative speech about shamans (medicine men among certain North American Indians). He offered testimonials and true stories to appeal to those who prefer to learn through feeling (accommodators and divergers). He engaged the group in a simple massage technique used to eliminate headaches to appeal to those who prefer to learn by doing (accommodators and convergers). He showed some of the herbs used in healing to appeal to those who prefer to learn by watching (divergers and assimilators). And he organized his speech systematically, using a clear preview, transitions, and summary to appeal to those who prefer to learn by thinking (assimilators and convergers). By taking into account different learning styles, Barry made it possible for listeners to grasp more fully and retain longer the ideas he offered in his speech. Finally, doing so benefited all of Barry's listeners, regardless of their preferred learning style, because his approach took the audience through the entire four-stage cycle of learning.

Teaching Tip
Have students complete the Learning Styles Quiz included in the Activities section at the end of this chapter. Lead an in-class discussion of the communicative implications of learning style diversity. Also, encourage students to utilize this discussion as they analyze their audience.

Channels

Channels are the pathways through which messages are communicated between sender and receiver. Oral communication uses multiple channels; however, the most common channels used are the auditory channel and the visual channel. The **visual channel** is what the receivers see. Messages sent via the visual channel include eye contact, facial expressions, posture, gestures, and appearance, as well as visual aids like objects, diagrams, charts, graphs, and sketches. Madeleine, who brought her dreamcatcher to show the class as she discussed its construction, used the visual channel when showing her visual aid. The **auditory channel** is what the listeners hear—that is, the words you choose to convey your message, as well as the manner in which you say them (i.e., inflection, rate, voice quality, and tone). When Martin Luther King, Jr., repeated the phrase, "I have a dream," in slightly different ways throughout his now famous speech, he was using the auditory channel. Your goal as a public speaker is to use these channels in ways that complement and reinforce each other to better ensure that listeners interpret the meaning in the same way as you intended.

Feedback

Teaching Tip
Because feedback is more difficult to get in public speaking compared to interpersonal or small group communication, emphasize to students that they will have to work hard on audience analysis.

As we discussed earlier, an effective communication transaction is a process whereby sender and receiver create shared meaning. The creation of shared meaning would not be possible without feedback. Because the communication transaction consists of the simultaneous sending and receiving of multiple messages, feedback can come from both the sender and the receiver. In the public speaking context, however, feedback is generally conceived as going from receiver to sender—that is, those messages that listeners send back to a speaker about the clarity and acceptability of the speech. Feedback might come in written or oral form; however, it is usually conveyed via facial expression, eye contact, and body language.

Your goal as a public speaker is to interpret the feedback you get from listeners and adjust your message accordingly. Sometimes your general purpose is to inform your listeners about a topic. In that case, you might adjust your message based on feedback that seems to indicate a lack of understanding. For example, as Jack tries to explain how to complete a financial aid application, he notices quizzical looks on the faces of several listeners. Before moving on, he explains the procedure again in another way. Jack interpreted the feedback (quizzical looks) and rephrased his ideas before moving on. Other times, your general purpose is to persuade others to agree with you about an issue or a course of action to be taken. If you are attempting to convince your listeners to join a fraternity, you might watch for encouraging facial expressions and head nods as you proceed. Such feedback would probably indicate that your attempt to persuade is succeeding with some listeners.

Interference

Interference is anything that acts as a barrier to the communication of a message. Interference impedes communication because it distracts listeners from the message. A communication transaction can be hurt by external or internal interference.

External interference refers to those potential barriers occurring outside the speaker or listener. External interference may be auditory or visual. For example, your stereo may act as external auditory interference when it distracts you from what your roommate is saying. In the classroom, external *auditory* interference may be a result of loud fans, classmates whispering among themselves, traffic outside, an airplane flying overhead, or people talking in the hallway. External *visual* interference, on the other hand, may occur when a classmate enters the room while you are presenting your speech, when a police officer makes an arrest outside your classroom window, or when audience members are passing notes.

Although it is not always possible to eliminate external interference, effective public speakers attempt to reduce its potential impact. You might, for example, close the classroom door to reduce the level of noise coming from people in the hallway. You might speak louder to be heard above the noise of the fans. Or you might pause for a moment during your speech as the airplane flies overhead. Effective public speakers modify their delivery in ways that reduce the potential for interference to impede the success of the transaction.

Internal interference may be physical or psychological and may occur within the speaker as well as within the listeners. Perhaps one of your listeners has a pounding headache that distracts her from listening to your speech. Maybe another listener is worried about the test he has to take next period. If you are presenting your speech right before lunch, some listeners may be thinking about what they are going to eat. As the speaker, you may also experience internal interference. You may have stayed up late rehearsing the speech and your resulting fatigue may cause you to lose your concentration. Or you may be worrying about what you look or sound like to your listeners instead of focusing on your message. This too can interfere with the communication process.

Effective public speakers consider each element of the transactional model of communication and how it might help or hurt their presentation. They seek to adapt their message to the communication situation and audience, offer their ideas using multiple channels, read and adjust to feedback, and limit the potential of external and internal interference, which can impede listeners' understanding.

Ethical Public Speaking

Kathie Lee Gifford is a generally respected television celebrity. Through the years, her popularity has resulted in other kinds of recognition, as well. For example, she has sponsored different products, such as Carnival Cruise Line and Wal-Mart clothing. Recently, however, she was scorned by many of her fans because she endorsed Wal-Mart clothing with her own line of apparel. Why? Because her adoring public learned that Wal-Mart clothing was being produced in sweatshops, a practice considered by many to be unfair and morally wrong. By endorsing the clothing, many of Kathie Lee's fans believed she also endorsed Wal-Mart's "unfair" business practices. Although Kathie Lee announced publicly that she was unaware of Wal-Mart's use of sweatshops, she had already been labeled "unethical." Consequently, she would spend years proving to her fans that, in fact, she is ethical and worthy of their respect.

Discussion Tip
Ask students to define "ethical" communication. Investigate the cultural values that influence these definitions. Often, communication behaviors preferred by the American mainstream culture are not universally held throughout all cultures. Discuss the implications of these relative judgments for the American mainstream culture's communication choices. You can also link this discussion to notions of effective communication skills, audience analysis, and ethnocentrism.

This question of what constitutes ethical behavior also pervades popular culture. Movies like *The Truman Show* ask viewers to consider the degree of "rightness" or "wrongness" in controlling someone's life experiences beyond the person's knowledge when doing so is somehow deemed to be for the individual's own good. Television cartoons like *The Simpsons* and *South Park* also focus on ethical issues, such as when it is okay to lie, to harass someone in the name of humor, or even to kill (as happens to Kenny in each episode of *South Park*). But what is ethical behavior?

An effective public speaker must do more than sound good and be convincing. An effective public speaker also makes wise ethical choices. Adolf Hitler, for example, was a very successful public speaker. After all, he succeeded in convincing a large group of followers to fight for a particular cause. Few would contend, however, that he was ethical. Why? Because the cause he convinced his followers to fight for was reprehensible (ethnic cleansing and world domination), and the tactics he persuaded them to employ were despicable. More recently, the NATO leaders' decision to use military force to stop Slobodan Milosevic's efforts toward ethnic cleansing in Yugoslavia was rooted in similar concerns. Obviously, achieving your goal is not all there is to being an effective public speaker. You must also be ethical.

What Do You Think?

Consider a time when you chose to tell a close friend only part of the story about something you had experienced. If "honesty is the best policy," then why did you decide not to tell everything?

Ethics refers to our principles about what is right and wrong, moral and immoral, honest and dishonest, fair and unfair (Johannesen, 1990; Nilsen, 1974; Wallace, 1955). To better understand the meaning of ethics, let's consider how ethical choices differ from legal choices. Whereas laws are rules by which we *must* abide, ethics are rules by which we *ought to* abide. In other words, we all realize that breaking different laws warrants certain punishments. If you are pulled over by a police officer for driving faster than the speed limit, for example, you understand that you will have to pay a fine or go to court. A speed limit is a law. If you choose to break the law, you know that you may be punished for your actions.

Discussion Tip
To initiate a discussion about the First Amendment, have students conduct a brief Internet or library search using the keywords "first amendment" and bring in one article or book to share with the rest of the class. Discuss the standards students use for assessing ethical issues surrounding communication about any issue and consider differences between legal and ethical issues.

Ethical choices, on the other hand, have no legal ramifications tied directly to them. Instead, ethical decisions are guided by your values, your conscience, your sense of justice, and your sense of fairness. Moreover, credible arguments usually exist on both sides of the ethical issue. In other words, you must choose between options that may result in both positive and negative implications for you and for others involved. In essence, my interpretation about the degree of ethical rightness or wrongness in a certain behavior might differ from yours, as well as from others in the room. Whether or not to spank children is a question of ethics. Whether or not we should clone living beings is also a question of ethics. Whether or not television violence should be censored is a question of ethics. Whether or not to tell the whole truth is also a question of ethics.

Since ethical judgments focus on degrees of rightness or wrongness in human behavior, no universal list of ethical standards exists. There are, however, general ethical codes of conduct based on some basic virtues. These virtues can be summarized as, first, demonstrating respect for ourselves and for others. In other words, we *ought to* conduct ourselves in ways that are tactful, civil, and sensitive to the needs, concerns, and beliefs of others. The second basic virtue that guides most ethical decisions is honesty. This means we ought to be truthful about our opinions, be truthful in reporting information, and be truthful about our feelings. Sometimes, however, demonstrating respect and honesty seem to be in conflict with one another. For example, my daughter once baked me a birthday cake. She forgot to include a couple of ingredients, so it didn't really taste good. When she asked me how it tasted, how was I to respond? I really wanted her to know that I respected her efforts. But could I do that if I was completely honest?

What Do You Think?

Has a friend or loved one ever asked you how a favorite outfit looks on them when it doesn't really look too good? How did you respond? Were you able to be both honest and respectful?

Teaching Tip
Have students apply the principles of ethical communication to advertising. Ask them to bring an example of an advertisement that they think is unethical and to share the ad with the rest of the class.

These virtues also provide a basis for making ethical judgments as a public speaker and listener. We will focus here on several strategies for ethical public speaking. Strategies for ethical listening will be addressed in Chapter 4, "Listening and Critiquing Communication." Essentially, you can measure yourself as an ethical public speaker by considering five key criteria throughout the speechmaking process:

- Considering your topic and goals.
- Acknowledging personal biases.
- Choosing evidence.
- Reporting sources of information.
- Conveying your ideas orally.

Considering Your Topic and Goals

You need to think carefully about your topic, both in relation to yourself and to your listeners. What are you hoping to accomplish in your speech? Do you have a thorough knowledge of the subject and relevant issues related to it? How is it relevant to your listeners? What are the potential implications of your message? Is it something you believe in strongly yourself?

Ethical speakers select topics that matter to them. If you are going to persuade listeners to recycle, for example, you ought to care about recycling and participate in recycling yourself. Ethical speakers also select topics that will matter to listeners. You need to make sure your speech will be *relevant* to your listeners and will give them new insight on the topic. In other words, talking about how to bake chocolate chip cookies is probably not an ethically sound choice if your audience consists of college students. Why? Most of them already know how to bake cookies, so your information isn't new for them. Ethical speakers strive to ensure that listeners will go away from the speech better off for having heard it. Finally, you ought to have a *thorough knowledge* of your topic. This means that you need to have researched and thought thoroughly about your topic and the issues related to it. To check the completeness of your knowledge, ask yourself, "Can I answer honestly, without evasion, any relevant question a listener might ask?" If you are able to answer yes to this question, you have satisfied this criterion of an ethical public speaker.

Acknowledging Personal Biases

Ethical public speakers acknowledge their own motivations or biases with regard to the topic. For example, if you are to present a speech about drunk driving and have been the victim of a drunk driving accident yourself, it would be most ethical to acknowledge that experience up front. Or if you plan to persuade listeners that Chevrolet makes a better truck than Ford and you work for Chevrolet, you ought to acknowledge that in your speech. Listeners ought to know if you have a personal bias or a personal investment in your topic. Acknowledging personal bias demonstrates respect and honesty. Likewise, if you share a personal testimony from someone whose opinion may influence the way listeners should consider the information, you ought to admit that openly and honestly. Don't fall victim to the assumption that not telling listeners won't hurt anything. If listeners are left to figure out these biases on their own, they will lose respect for you as an honest and, consequently, ethical public speaker.

Choosing Evidence

Ethical public speakers select and present facts and opinions related to the topic fairly and accurately. In other words, you should not distort or conceal information that the audience ought to know in order to make a fair judgment. Consider, for example, the tobacco industry. The industry chose to conceal facts about the addictive nature of nicotine in cigarettes by framing their arguments in terms of individual rights to exercise free choice, avoiding the issue of whether choice can exist with regard to an addictive additive. This ambiguous message strategy born of the industry's decision to place profit over social responsibility is an example of unethical communication with regard to the fair and accurate reporting of information (Ulmer & Sellnow, 1997).

It is also important to consider the credibility of the sources of your information. You can determine source credibility by asking yourself if the source is relevant, impartial, and recent. If your speech is about smoking and health, the *American Journal of Medicine* would probably be more relevant than *Consumer Reports.* This is not to say you cannot cite *Consumer Reports* if it published an article about smoking and health; however, it is not a publication closely tied to health issues. Conversely, if you were attempting to persuade your listeners to purchase the best-quality appliance for the price, *Consumer Reports* would be more relevant than the *American Journal of Medicine.*

If you are attempting to convince listeners that smoking is *not* addictive, the tobacco industry would not be the most credible source on which to rely. Why? Because the industry has a vested interest in sales and profit, which may mean its information about this issue is biased. To be ethical, consider the sources you select in terms of how impartial they may or may not be with regard to your topic.

Also consider how recent the publication is as it may impact the accuracy of the information. Let us again consider smoking and health. Citing a source published in 1976 may not be as accurate as citing a document published in 1999. Depending on the topic, recency may be an important consideration when choosing your evidence.

To be ethical, you also ought to demonstrate respect for diverse opinions and opposing arguments raised in the research. Essentially, this means that you acknowledge opposing evidence and opinions, while advocating your argument. In this way, ethical communication fosters free and informed choice. In a speech about the ethics of spanking, for example, a speaker can acknowledge the research that suggests spanking can harm a parent-child bond. Rather than avoid mentioning these opposing arguments, the speaker can talk about them (a) in relation to age appropriateness (i.e., confined to children between the ages of eighteen months and six years old) and (b) in addition to other methods of discipline.

To check your fairness in reporting information, ask yourself, "In the selection and presentation of materials, am I giving my audience the opportunity to make fair judgments?" If you can answer yes, then you have satisfied this criterion of an ethical speaker.

What Do You Think?

Consider a news report you have heard that seemed to leave you with more questions than answers. In what ways might knowing those answers have been important to you?

Reporting Sources of Information

Discussion Tip
Discuss your school's plagiarism policy with students. How is this policy relevant to public speaking? What constitutes plagiarism? What are the sanctions for plagiarism?

Ethical public speakers reveal the sources of information or opinions drawn from others. One of your most important ethical obligations is to avoid plagiarism. **Plagiarism** occurs when you present another person's ideas as your own. Plagiarism is still plagiarism whether it is intentional or unintentional. In other words, claiming that you didn't realize you were plagiarizing does not change the fact that you were doing so. In its most blatant form, plagiarism occurs when you present a speech constructed by someone else, passing it off as though it were your own. For example, two students once presented the same speech in different sections of a public speaking fundamentals course. Only one student composed the speech. The other student had plagiarized. Both students had acted unethically.

More often, however, speakers employ plagiarism by presenting paragraphs, sentences, or even phrases as their own ideas in a speech, or by summarizing or paraphrasing someone else's ideas without citing them. Plagiarism, in these forms, can also damage your character as a student, as well as harm you in your life beyond the classroom walls. During the 1987 presidential primaries, for example, it was discovered that Democratic senator Joseph Biden had plagiarized passages from speeches by John F. Kennedy, and Hubert Humphrey, among others. As a result, Biden eventually withdrew from the primary (Coffey, 1987; Kaus, 1987).

At this point, you might be wondering how you can avoid plagiarizing when your speech requires the use of external sources. Ethical speakers cite the sources of their information in the form of oral footnotes during the presentation and as internal references and in a reference list accompanying a written formal outline. **Oral footnotes** are brief references to the original source of particular information, cited at the point in the speech where the information is given. Just as you cite information within the text of a written composition (footnotes) as well as in the reference list at the end of the manuscript (references), you also cite reference material orally during your speech as well as in the text of the formal outline you develop. A formal outline is available to the audience upon request, and the attached reference list provides full bibliographic information on the sources cited in the oral presentation. Together the oral footnotes and reference list function just like the footnotes and reference list you would include in a written paper. They give listeners enough information to look up the sources themselves.

To make sure that you have not plagiarized, ask yourself, "Have I acknowledged the sources of my information throughout the speech?" If you can answer yes, then you have satisfied this criterion of an ethical public speaker.

Conveying Your Ideas Orally

Ethical public speakers demonstrate respect for their audience when presenting a message. For example, an ethical speaker rehearses delivery, uses inclusive and tactful language, and conveys ideas in ways that address a variety of learning styles. Consider those times when you have listened to someone who was disorganized, boring, or unprepared. Did you go away feeling respected or disrespected? Ethical speakers respect their audience members' time by offering messages that are organized effectively and presented fluently.

Ethical speakers also respect their audience by using inclusive and respectful language. Terms that exclude or defame certain groups should be avoided. For example, referring to mail carriers and police officers as "mailmen" and "policemen" would exclude women, as would using the generic "he" to represent everyone. Ethical public speakers avoid racist, sexist, ageist and other kinds of abusive language, not just because avoiding such language is politically correct but, rather, because it is ethically correct.

> ### *What Do You Think?*
> *Consider a comedian or late-night talk show host whom you have considered to be offensive. Why were you offended? Too often, speakers fall into the trap of defaming others in the name of humor. Such speakers are not ethical because their "humor" is disrespectful to some members of their audience.*

Finally, ethical speakers respect their audience by presenting ideas in ways that address a variety of preferred learning styles. Recall that this means understanding your own preferred learning style and then preparing and presenting your public speeches so that they address the other learning styles as well. To do so, you must use a variety of different supporting material; multiple rhetorical appeals; clear, accurate, inclusive, and vivid language; vocally and visually intelligible and expressive delivery; and clear and systematic organization. To check yourself in

Background Tip
For an excellent discussion of the role of learning styles in the basic public speaking course, see T. Nance and A. K. Foeman, "Rethinking the Basic Public Speaking Course for African American Students and Other Students of Color," *Journal of Negro Education 62*(4) (1993), 448–458.

Even when protesting, you should use respectful language if you want to be an ethical communicator.

terms of conveying your ideas orally, ask yourself, "If I were a member of my audience, would I be compelled to listen to my speech?" If you are able to answer yes to this question, you have satisfied this criterion of an ethical speaker.

Ethical communication is, at the very core, a simple concept. It essentially means respecting the other participants in the communication transaction. In practice, however, ethical communication requires conscious effort and strategic choices with regard to the five key criteria we have discussed here. Ethical communication is simple, but it is not necessarily easy.

SUMMARY

Teaching Tip
Ask students to keep a record of changes they notice in themselves while they are in this course. Are they more willing to speak out in other classes? Are they less apprehensive when speaking in public? This could also be incorporated into the public speaking portfolio assignment described in the Activities section of this chapter.

In this chapter, we have explored a number of reasons for improving your public speaking skills, defined and explained the process of communication as it relates to public speaking, and illustrated what it means to be an ethical public speaker. This chapter provides grounding for the remaining chapters as you continue to refine your skills in developing and presenting effective public speeches.

First, we answered the question, "Why study public speaking?" We did so by considering benefits to you in your personal relationships, in your college education, and in your professional career. Your ability to communicate effectively will help you develop and nurture positive relationships with others. You will also find this skill to be transferable to your other courses when you are asked to present your reports orally. Also, your effective public speaking skills will help you land a job by enhancing your abilities during the interview, as well as on the job. We learned that effective oral communication skills constitute one of the most desired skills sought by employers, whether or not the field is communication related.

Second, we defined communication as the process of sending and receiving verbal and nonverbal messages to create shared meaning. We explored how communication occurs in different contexts, such as intrapersonal, impersonal, interpersonal, small group, and public. We considered how the strategies you choose may differ according to context in order to be most effective. We also discussed the evolution of the models of communication as they explain this dynamic process. The process was originally conceived as linear. By this we thought of it as one-way: a sender encodes a message, which is decoded by a receiver. Eventually, this linear model was expanded and renamed as an interactive model, which accounted for the feedback offered by a receiver as well as for the interference that can arise externally and internally during the encounter. Today, we understand the communication process via what we call the transactional model of communication. This model expands on the concepts set forth in the linear and interactional models to also consider both the situational and cultural context as players in the process, as well as the simultaneous sending and receiving of multiple messages by sender and receivers during a communication encounter.

Finally, we explored what it means to be an ethical public speaker. We defined ethics as our principles about what is right and wrong, moral and immoral, honest and dishonest, fair and unfair. These principles are based on our conceptions of human virtues such as respect and honesty. We focused on five key criteria that must be considered in order to be ethical. These include (a) considering the topic and goal, (b) acknowledging personal biases, (c) choosing evidence, (d) reporting sources of information, and (e) conveying ideas orally. We concluded that ethical public speakers demonstrate respect for other participants in the communication transaction. Ethical communication is essentially a simple concept, but it is not easy.

Activities

1. **Public Speaking Portfolio.** Purchase a composition notebook and begin documenting your experiences and growth as a public speaker throughout the course. Start by developing a one- to two-page paper articulating your communication goals for this semester. Eventually, your portfolio will include (a) speech outlines, instructor evaluations, self and peer critiques for each speech you present in class; (b) a reflective question journal responding to the questions posed at the beginning of each chapter; and (c) other written assignments you complete throughout the semester.
2. **Interview a Professional.** Set up an interview with a personnel director from a company in your community. Ask the personnel director what the company looks for most in job applicants. What does the company look for on a resume, in a cover letter, during an interview? How important is oral communication skill compared to other skills, including proficiency in one's field of study, technical skill, and academic achievement?
3. **Communication Process Analysis.** After having a conversation with a friend or family member, take a few minutes to write about it in your journal or draw a picture of what occurred using the transactional model of communication as a framework. What messages and feedback were being sent? What channels were employed? What forms of interference occurred? How did these elements influence the ultimate success of shared message creation?
4. **Professional Speaker Critique.** Go to hear a professional speaker make an oral presentation. Critique the speaker's performance based on the following questions. How is the speaker dressed? How dynamic is his or her delivery style? Does the speaker use reinforcing nonverbal cues? Can you follow the speaker's organizational structure? Does he or she cite sources? How do these things influence your perception of his or her effectiveness as a speaker?
5. **Determining Your Learning Style.** As was discussed in the chapter, everyone learns best by moving through all four stages of the learning cycle. Yet each of us tends to prefer one stage over the others (Kolb, 1984). This is what is referred to as your preferred learning style. To determine your preferred learning style, complete this twelve-point learning styles quiz. (If you'd like to do a more detailed analysis, the Learning Styles Inventory can be found in the *Public Speaking Applications* workbook available from Harcourt College Publishers.)

Learning Styles Quiz

Step 1

For each question, circle the letter next to the response that is most like you. Remember there are *no wrong answers.* Work quickly. Record your first thought.

I. When I purchase a kit that requires some assembly, I am likely to begin by
- **A.** soliciting advice and possibly help from someone who has put together a similar item in the past.
- **B.** studying the pieces, diagrams, and picture on the package or box.
- **C.** reading through all of the directions.
- **D.** putting the item together, referring to the directions only when I get stuck.

II. When I try making a new recipe, I usually like to
- **A.** taste it myself first.
- **B.** see a picture of it.
- **C.** follow the recipe carefully.
- **D.** use the recipe as a general guide, modifying it as I go along.

III. When I make decisions, I usually rely most on my
- **A.** feelings.
- **B.** observations.
- **C.** thoughts.
- **D.** actions.

IV. I tend to enjoy classes most where
- **A.** students interact with each other often.
- **B.** professors use a lot of visual aids.
- **C.** professors lecture most of the time.
- **D.** Students actively apply concepts themselves.

V. I tend to be persuaded most when
- **A.** I am presented with actual examples and experiences of people.
- **B.** I have time to reflect about what I hear.
- **C.** I am presented with specific facts and statistics related to the issue.
- **D.** I experience issues firsthand.

VI. If I were asked to choose only one, I'd say I am
- **A.** intuitive.
- **B.** careful.
- **C.** logical.
- **D.** responsible.

VII. I am most likely to enjoy participating in extracurricular activities and functions
- **A.** that are new and different.
- **B.** that allow me to observe for awhile before joining in.
- **C.** that require logical analysis.
- **D.** that let me be actively involved.

VIII. I prefer working in an environment where
- **A.** I can interact with others.
- **B.** I am able to take time to reflect.
- **C.** I am challenged to analyze logically.
- **D.** I have opportunities to apply concepts and try things out.

IX. I especially dislike classes where the main focus is
- **A.** professors lecturing about abstract concepts.
- **B.** students doing lots of activities.
- **C.** students engaging in open-ended discussions.
- **D.** students taking lots of notes.

X. When discussing ideas with others, I am best at
- **A.** considering a variety of points of view.
- **B.** taking time to reflect before responding.
- **C.** using logic to analyze and evaluate.
- **D.** getting things done and accomplishing goals.

XI. When learning a new computer software program, I am most likely to begin by
- **A.** asking for advice from people who've used the program before.
- **B.** following the directions carefully.
- **C.** reading through the manual.
- **D.** experimenting with the program and using the manual only when I get stuck.

XII. When I take a vacation, I particularly enjoy
- **A.** getting to know the people who live in the place I am visiting and learning from them about their customs and experiences.
- **B.** taking time to plan each day carefully.
- **C.** reading as much as possible about each place while I'm there.
- **D.** experimenting with and trying out new customs, foods, and experiences.

Step 2

Count up the number of "A," "B," "C," and "D" responses you circled and record them in the space provided:

A = __________ B = __________ C = __________ D = __________

If you circled mostly As, you tend to prefer to learn by **feeling.**

If you circled mostly Bs, you tend to prefer to learn by **watching.**

If you circled mostly Cs, you tend to prefer to learn by **thinking.**

If you circled mostly Ds, you tend to prefer to learn by **doing.**

Step 3

Add your scores from Step 2 as follows:

A + B =

B + C =

C + D =

A + D =

Step 4

Circle the highest of the four sums from Step 3.

If you circled the A + B score: You tend to be a **diverger.** You prefer to learn by some combination of watching and feeling.

If you circled the B + C score: You tend to be an **assimilator.** You prefer to learn by some combination of watching and thinking.

If you circled the C + D score: You tend to be a **converger.** You prefer to learn by some combination of thinking and doing.

If you circled the A + D score: You tend to be an **accommodator.** You prefer to learn by some combination of doing and feeling.

Step 5

Consider how you will approach the speech preparation and presentation process in ways that address all of these learning styles. Remember, each learning style represents one stage on the cycle.

Diverger (Stage 1 preference). You probably want to know *why* you are learning things. You seek a personal connection with the content. So one of your public speaking strengths is the ability to articulate *listener relevance links.* You also like to consider things from many points of view. Another public speaking strength is your use of *examples, testimonies,* and quotations from *interviews* with real people in your speeches. (If you're a converger, you'll need to be sure to include these elements in your speeches as well.)

Assimilator (Stage 2 preference). You are likely to enjoy absorbing lots of information and strive for an understanding of *what* it means. Your public speaking strengths lie in providing clear *facts, statistics, definitions,* and *explanations* and in arranging them in a logical and orderly fashion. (If you're an accommodator, you'll need to be sure to include these elements in your speeches as well.)

Converger (Stage 3 preference). You probably like to see if the facts you learn actually work in daily life. You want to know *how* an idea, strategy, or method works by trying it out. Your public speaking strengths lie in providing *practical applications* for using information to improve current situations, as well as in conceptualizing a *workable solution* to a problem. (If you're a diverger, you'll need to be sure to include these elements in your speeches as well.)

Accommodator (Stage 4 preference). You like to take what you've discovered and figure out *where else* you can use it to *make a difference* in your life and the lives of others. Your public speaking strengths lie in your ability to come up with *new solutions* to old problems. You enjoy interacting with others and probably excel at *delivering* your speech dynamically. (If you're an assimilator, you'll need to be sure to include these elements in your speeches as well.)

Key Terms

Accommodators	Communication rules	Ethics
Assimilators	Communication situation	Ethnocentrism
Audience analysis	Convergers	Ethos
Auditory channel	Decoding	External interference
Channels	Divergers	Feedback
Communication	Encoding	Frame of reference

Impersonal communication
Interactive model of communication
Interference
Internal interference
Interpersonal communication
Intrapersonal communication
Learning style
Linear model of communication
Mass communication
Message
Nonverbal messages
Oral footnotes
Plagiarism
Public communication
Public speaking
Receiver
Self-disclosure
Sender
Small group communication
Transactional model of communication
Verbal messages
Visual channel

CHAPTER 2

Coping Effectively with Public Speaking Anxiety

Reflective Questions

1. What sorts of thoughts come to your mind when you think about giving a public speech?
2. Why might changing your self-talk help you control your public speaking anxiety?
3. What method will you try outside of class to help control your anxiety?
4. What method will you try right before you get up to give your next speech to help control your anxiety?
5. What will you do during the speech to deal effectively with anxiety?
6. What will you do right after your next speech to deal more effectively with your anxiety?

Linda hates to give speeches. It's not that she's a poor public speaker; she just gets so nervous while she's giving them that she feels like she's going to explode. Even when she speaks for only a minute or two, time seems to stand still. She can't even recall the first time she experienced public speaking anxiety. She says she has always felt this way. While she speaks, her voice gets tight and her palms sweat. It is so embarrassing. Consequently, she dreads the speaking experience from the moment the assignment is made until the entire "ordeal" is over. In fact, Linda is only one class away from earning her college degree—and she has been one class away for two years now. That class is public speaking fundamentals. If you're like Linda, you believe that you're more nervous than anyone else about public speaking and believe that your fear is insurmountable. You probably tell yourself, "That's just the way I am. I'm just not good at speaking in public." This chapter is designed to dissolve those myths. You can overcome your speech anxiety.

Teaching Tip
Before you begin this chapter, have students write a one- to two-page paper describing how afraid they are about giving a speech. Ask them to evaluate why they are afraid (if they are) and what they intend to do to make the speech go smoothly. This assignment allows students to evaluate their approach to public speaking before facing it.

To better understand this, let's look more closely at the experience of others. First, they're nervous too. In fact, more than half of all *experienced public speakers* feel nervous or fearful before presenting a speech (Hahner, Sokoloff, & Salisch, 1993). Here's what one such speaker, *Boston Globe* columnist Diane White, told her readers:

> There should be a public speaking horror movie—*Speechless in Seattle,* maybe, or *The Night of the Sweaty Palms.* I could write the screenplay. I have actually lied to avoid making speeches, and I hate to lie. But I hate public speaking

Many successful professionals like Diane White have learned to control their anxiety.

DILBERT reprinted by permission of United Feature Syndicate, Inc.

even more. It makes me nervous. How nervous? Once, when called upon to introduce a speaker, I forgot my own name. Luckily, I remembered the name of the woman I was introducing (White, 1998, p. 94).

Second, many people, regardless of how nervous they feel, have found ways to cope effectively with their public speaking anxiety. Consider Roberta Perry, who was once so nervous about public speaking that "she made wild hand gestures as she spoke—with her hands jammed in her pockets!" After learning techniques like the ones you will read about in this chapter, she controlled her anxiety—and eventually went from being a secretary to cofounding an audiovisual company and serving as its senior vice president (Griffin, 1995, p. 65).

Teaching Tip
Students often have a difficult time judging how much time it will take to research, write, and rehearse a speech. Therefore, you should reinforce the importance of careful planning, which will also help alleviate their fear of public speaking.

Perhaps you have feared public speaking for as long as you can remember. Perhaps your fear feels incredibly intense. Perhaps you even tried techniques to reduce anxiety and didn't succeed. The bottom line is that public speaking fear is natural and *can be overcome.* You simply need to read the chapter carefully and apply the techniques described—techniques designed to effectively manage that fear.

This chapter begins by giving you the background you'll need to understand public speaking anxiety. Public speaking anxiety is a form of communication apprehension, so we will look at what communication apprehension is. Then we'll discuss the reasons why people experience public speaking anxiety. After that, you will read about various techniques proven to control anxiety. To use this chapter most effectively, take notes as you read. Focus your notes on the forms of communication apprehension that plague you most, the reasons for public speaking anxiety that sound most similar to yours, and the anxiety-reducing techniques that might work best for you. By doing this, you will make this chapter a practical resource you can use each time you prepare and present public speeches.

What Is Communication Apprehension?

Over the years, the fear of public speaking has been given various names, including "speech fright," "speech anxiety," "stage fright," and "public speaking anxiety." Regardless of what you've heard it called, it is essentially the same thing—anxiety associated with giving a public speech. As the research on public speaking anxiety has developed over the past forty years, scholars have discovered that the fear of public speaking is actually only one type of anxiety housed within a general condition called communication apprehension. **Communication apprehension** (CA) can be defined as "the fear or anxiety associated with real or anticipated communication with others" (McCroskey, 1977, p. 78). Unfortunately,

Discussion Tip
Have the students discuss their previous public speaking experiences. How did they prepare for the speech? What strategies did they use to overcome communication apprehension? How have they handled nervousness in other contexts (e.g., preparing for a sporting event)?

uncontrolled communication apprehension can make life miserable for the individual who experiences it and can limit one's potential for success in both personal relationships and professional settings.

Thanks to the research that has been done, however, communication apprehension can be managed effectively. The first step, however, is to understand the various forms of communication apprehension and, subsequently, the types of anxiety that fall within each form. Understanding the different forms will help you identify what situations are most problematic for you and why. You will then be able to focus your reading and thinking effectively as we discuss specific anxiety-reduction techniques. Essentially, there are four different forms of communication apprehension: traitlike, audience-based, situational, and context based.

If you experience **traitlike communication apprehension,** you tend to feel anxious about speaking in most situations. In other words, you feel anxious about talking with others, whether the talking occurs in a one-to-one, small group, or public speaking context. About 20 percent of all people experience this type of CA (Richmond & McCroskey, 1995). Even this form of CA, which affects so many of a person's interactions, can be overcome.

Technology Tip
http://www.presentersuniversity.com/courses/cs_delivery.cfm
This Web page, hosted by Presenter's University, offers several tips for coping with speech anxiety. Have students visit this site and prepare a short list of tips to share with the rest of the class.

What Do You Think?

Identify three or four specific communication situations where you felt particularly anxious. Are the situations you have identified in some way similar to one another or is each quite different? If you identified very different situations, you may experience trait apprehension.

If you experience **audience-based communication apprehension,** you feel particularly anxious only about communicating with a certain person or group of people. For example, you might feel noticeably uncomfortable speaking to a certain professor or to your boss. Perhaps, you feel anxious about presenting speeches for your public speaking class, because the focus is specifically on speechmaking, but do not feel anxious in nongraded public speaking situations. Most of us can identify someone we feel anxious about communicating with, so this form of CA is quite common (McCroskey, 1984).

Situational communication apprehension, which is also quite common, is a short-lived feeling of anxiety that occurs during a specific encounter (McCroskey, 1984). For example, you may have felt particularly anxious while interviewing for a position you really wanted, while speaking with your professor about an assignment you thought you failed, or while telling your spouse that you wrecked the car.

Teaching Tip
Relate some of your own personal experiences with communication apprehension to your students (for example, your apprehension on the first day of class). Sharing these experiences should help the students feel more at ease as they come to understand that such nervousness is normal.

If you experience **context-based communication apprehension,** you may feel anxious whenever you have to communicate in a particular setting (McCroskey, 1984). Four such settings have been identified: the public speaking environment, meetings, group discussion situations, and one-to-one conversations. Of the settings, the public speaking environment is the one most strongly associated with communication apprehension (Richmond & McCroskey, 1995). Thus, you may feel anxious about public speaking, but not about speaking in any of the other settings. To learn more about your own anxiety, you can complete the Personal Report of Communication Apprehension (PRCA) or the Personal Report of Public Speaking Anxiety (PRPSA), both located in the Activities section at the end of this chapter.

The rest of this chapter focuses specifically on context-based CA in public speaking situations. The anxiety-reducing techniques that will be presented, however, can help you deal with other forms of communication apprehension as well.

Why Do We Experience Public Speaking Anxiety?

Researchers have discovered a number of causes for public speaking anxiety. The causes are different for different people, so to develop a personalized plan for managing your anxiety effectively, you'll need to think about which causes are relevant for you. These causes center around three factors: socialized patterns of thinking and feeling, preferred learning styles, and self-talk.

Teaching Tip
Have students complete the Personal Report of Communication Apprehension (PRCA) and Personal Report of Public Speaking Anxiety (PRPSA) contained in the Activities section of this chapter. Create and share with the group a master chart of the class distribution in terms of each level of apprehension (anonymously, of course). This shows students that they aren't the only ones experiencing anxiety.

Socialized Patterns of Thinking and Feeling

Socialized patterns of thinking and feeling are those we learned while growing up. **Socialization,** the process of learning to "fit" within the rules of a society, is crucial to a society and its members. Unfortunately, not all the patterns an individual learns are useful ones. Thus, some of us learned to be fearful of public speaking. In fact, researchers contend that most communication apprehension is primarily a result of socialization (Richmond & McCroskey, 1995). The good news here is that socialized behaviors can be unlearned. Diane White, the *Boston Globe* columnist mentioned earlier in this chapter, explained how childhood socialization contributed to her public speaking anxiety: "In my family, looking for attention was one of the worst sins a child could commit. 'Don't make a spectacle of yourself' was a familiar phrase around our house" (White, 1998, p. 94). Research has revealed that there are two main ways in which we learn in the process of socialization: modeling and reinforcement. These are primary ways in which public speaking anxiety is learned—and they are also primary ways in which it can be unlearned. We will talk more specifically about these techniques later in the chapter.

Discussion Tip
Ask students to speculate about the rules of public speaking. What general societal norms inform public speaking? How are specific public speaking behaviors rewarded and sanctioned in this culture? Do these norms differ based on gender?

Take a few minutes to write down your recollections. What was oral communication like in your home when you were a child? Did your parents talk freely with each other in your presence? Did family members talk with each other a great deal or was your family quiet and reserved? Now write down anything you remember about public speaking experiences of members of your family. Did your parents or siblings engage in public speaking? What were their experiences? Did they avoid communicating orally in public speaking situations? If your family tended to avoid speaking in public or exhibited fears about it, your own fears may stem from modeling. **Modeling** is the process by which we learn by watching and then imitating the behaviors and reactions of those whom we admire (Bandura, 1973).

Can you identify some occasions in elementary school or junior high school when you presented a speech in front of your classmates? How did they respond? How did the teacher react? Did they laugh at you or with you? Did they clap? Did they appear bored? How did you feel after presenting the speech? If the experience was one in which you felt your audience responded negatively, your public speaking fear may stem from reinforcement.

Teaching Tip
Have students write a brief essay in which they explore how they have modeled the speaker behaviors of others. Ask them to speculate about whether the behaviors they have modeled are positive or negative.

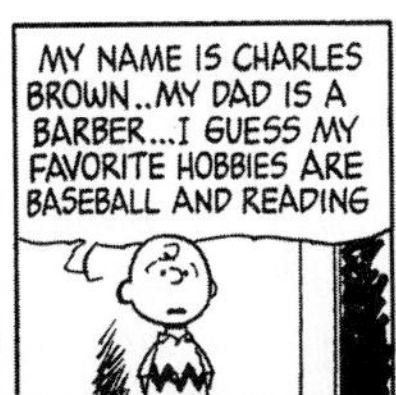

PEANUTS reprinted by permission of United Feature Syndicate, Inc.

Discussion Tip
Ask students to identify specific examples of reinforcement. How have these experiences shaped students' perceptions of public speaking?

What Do You Think?

Are there children in your life who may view you as a role model? In what ways might they be learning to imitate your behaviors and reactions about public speaking?

Reinforcement is the learning process in which the responses we get shape our expectations and thus our behavior (Daly & Stafford, 1984; McCroskey, 1982). If the responses you received after giving a speech were positive, you probably came to expect to succeed and learned to feel calm when speaking to others. If the responses you received were negative, on the other hand, you may have learned to expect failure and embarrassment and learned to feel anxious. As a result, you may be talking yourself into failure whenever you anticipate a public speaking situation. I'm happy to report that just as reinforcement can train you to feel more anxious about public speaking, so too can it be used to train you to feel less anxious. We will talk about specific strategies later in this chapter.

Preferred Learning Style

Technology Tip
http://wolf.its.ilstu.edu/CAT/online/tips/learns.html
This Web page, hosted by the Center for the Advancement of Teaching at Illinois State University, offers several excellent learning style links. Have students visit this site and write a short paper on the implications of learning styles for communication.

Your public speaking anxiety might also be connected to your preferred learning style. If you tend to prefer to learn by watching and thinking (assimilator), you might be more likely to experience high public speaking anxiety. If you prefer to learn by doing and feeling (accommodator), you might be more likely to experience low public speaking anxiety (Bourhis & Berquist, 1990; Bourhis & Stubbs, 1991; Dwyer, 1998a). This relationship between high anxiety and learning style preference is particularly true for women (Bello, 1995; Dwyer, 1998a). If your high anxiety stems from your preferred learning style, you can reduce it by approaching the public speaking process in ways that round the cycle of learning and by making extra efforts to understand clearly the requirements and grading criteria before you begin to prepare your speech (Dwyer, 1998a; McCarthy, 1987; Neer & Kircher, 1991). The good news here is that this cause of anxiety, like the others, can be overcome.

Self-Talk

Teaching Tip
Virtually any segment of the popular movie *Forrest Gump* contains examples of positive self-talk.

When we feel increased anxiety in a public speaking situation, negative self-talk is most commonly the culprit (Ayres, 1986; Behnke & Beatty, 1981; Daly & Buss, 1984; Desberg & Marsh, 1988; Pucel & Stocker, 1983; Richmond & McCroskey, 1995). **Self-talk** consists of those thoughts that go through our minds about our success or failure in a particular situation. Self-talk is, then, a form of intrapersonal communication. Negative self-talk—self-talk that focuses on being unsuccessful—increases anxiety. In other words, when you tell yourself self-defeating stories like "I can't possibly get through this presentation" or "I'm bound to fail," you are actually increasing your anxiety.

What Do You Think?

When you think about delivering a speech in front of a group, what thoughts run through your mind? Are they generally positive or negative? How might these thoughts be influencing your anxiety?

We engage in negative self-talk because of our fears. Four major fears in particular can lead to negative self-talk in public speaking situations: the fear of being stared at, the fear of the unknown, the fear of failure, and the fear of becoming fearful. By recognizing these fears and dealing with them in practical ways, we can reduce the negative self-talk and, thus, our anxiety.

It is human nature to enjoy being recognized for things we've done well; however, it is *not* human nature to enjoy being the center of attention all the time (Richmond & McCroskey, 1995). Yet when we are placed in a public speaking situation, this is exactly what happens: All eyes are focused only on us and we feel conspicuous. Fear of being stared at in this way leads to feelings of anxiety and to negative self-talk. Negative self-talk rooted in this fear of being stared at further perpetuates the anxiety. And the cycle continues. As one hesitant public speaker proclaimed, "Of course my anxiety will go up; everyone will be staring at me."

There are several ways you can deal with this fear. For example, use presentational aids with your speech, so your audience will have something else to look at. Or, if possible, arrange the room in a way that will allow audience members to divert their eyes some of the time. You might choose to arrange the seats into a semicircle or horseshoe pattern rather than in rows if you can. This way, audience members can naturally look at each other as well as at you. Sometimes this fear of being stared at has to do with audience members seeing our nervous bodily reactions. If this is the case for you, plan to cover it up. You can wear a long skirt or baggy slacks to hide shaky knees. Or you can wear a high-necked shirt or sweater to cover a blushing neck.

Discussion Tip
Should all speeches utilize visual aids? What are the advantages and disadvantages of using visual aids? How can you use presentation aids to cope with communication apprehension?

The fear of being stared at arises because we *know* what will occur: All audience members will be looking at us. *Not knowing* what is going to occur can also increase anxiety. Speakers sometimes engage in negative self-talk about possible catastrophes that may occur during the speech. If you have never seen the room, met the audience members, or delivered the speech to anyone, or if you don't know how large the audience will be or how they will react to your ideas, a fear of the unknown can easily lead to negative self-talk and increased anxiety. You can deal with this fear by reducing the number of unknowns. For example, prepare adequately in advance. Do this by researching and organizing your speech thoroughly, practicing with your presentational aids, rehearsing the speech for a few close friends, and practicing with an audio recorder or video recorder so you can hear and see yourself before you get in front of the audience. You can also check the room where you will be speaking and even meet some audience members before the day of the speech.

A third fear that can lead to negative self-talk is a fear of failure. Fear of failure does not mean you are literally worried about flunking an assignment. Negative self-talk arising from a fear of failure has to do, instead, with worrying about how your audience will react to your speech and about whether you will be able to meet their expectations. Examples include worrying that listeners will be bored, that they won't laugh at your jokes, or that they won't understand what you are trying to say. For some speakers, negative self-talk focused on worrying about making even one small mistake means failure. Speakers whose anxiety rises from a fear of failure tend to view public speaking from a performance orientation. That is, they see themselves as performing before a hypercritical audience and feel that they must create a perfect speech and deliver it flawlessly (Motley, 1991). Through negative self-talk, these speakers convince themselves that the audience will evaluate them poorly if they make any mistakes.

Teaching Tip
If you have access to a speech laboratory, instruct students to utilize this resource to work on reducing uncertainty about the process of public speaking. If you do not have access to a speech laboratory, consider providing classroom time for students to practice speaking in front of others.

But public speaking is a process of *communicating* rather than *performing;* so these fears are irrational and can be overcome. For example, deliver your speech from limited notes as opposed to either a complete manuscript or a memorized style. Doing so will help keep your focus on communicating, not performing. Also, try out your ideas on a few close friends. Ask them what they think about your jokes and about your speech in general. Getting feedback like this in advance can provide you with examples from which to create positive self-talk statements that can reduce anxiety arising from a fear of failure.

Teaching Tip
It is a good idea to assuage students' fears about public speaking by reminding them that only a small fraction of the turmoil they are feeling on the inside is visible on the outside.

The three fears discussed here can all lead to negative self-talk about the fear of becoming fearful. That is, you convince yourself that these other fears are inevitable and that, consequently, you'll be overwhelmed by fear. You may find yourself worrying that your nervousness is going to show, or that you could hyperventilate, or that you will look stupid. Speakers who worry about becoming fearful tend to engage in negative self-talk in all three areas, convincing themselves that doing a public speech at all is impossible. You can deal with the anxiety that rises from this fear by realizing that most nervous bodily reactions are not visible to audience members. Your listeners cannot see your heart pounding. If you are concerned about the bodily reactions that can be seen, plan to cover them up by dressing strategically. You can also dress up a bit more than usual, as well as stop in a bathroom and check your face, hair, and clothing before entering the room where you will be speaking to ensure that you don't look stupid. You might even rehearse your speech in front of a mirror or videotape yourself for similar reasons.

I don't know how you are feeling after reading these paragraphs about negative self-talk, but I do know that after writing each of them, I felt more anxious than before. However, several techniques are available, which you can easily learn and employ, that will effectively reduce your public speaking anxiety. Consequently, you can learn to not only be an effective public speaker, but also feel like one.

> ***What Do You Think?***
>
> *On what basis do you evaluate your success or failure as a public speaker? Do you think more about* how *you performed or* what *you communicated? How might this perspective affect your anxiety?*

What Can Be Done to Reduce Anxiety?

Teaching Tip
Have students interview someone who regularly speaks in public about how the speaker handles communication apprehension. When does the person experience anxiety? What specific methods does the individual use to overcome apprehension? What recommendations does the person offer for overcoming apprehension? Have the students present their findings in class.

Researchers have been studying communication apprehension and treatment methods for more than forty years. As a result, we know of various effective methods for controlling public speaking anxiety regardless of how the anxiety developed. Most of these methods consist of techniques designed to be performed on a daily basis, as well as right before and during a speech. These methods are systematic desensitization, cognitive restructuring, and skills training.

Systematic Desensitization

Originally developed in 1958, **systematic desensitization** focuses on relaxation and visualization (Wolpe, 1958). Research indicates that systematic desensitization is the most widely used and most effective method of treating communication apprehension (Hoffman & Sprague, 1982; McCroskey, 1972; McCroskey, Ralph, & Barrick, 1970; Richmond & McCroskey, 1995; Rolfson, 1995). In fact, over 80 percent of those who try this method reduce their level of anxiety. Systematic desensitization is essentially a three-step process that trains you to relax and to

The Process of Systematic Desensitization

1. Progressive relaxation activities.
2. Progressive visualization activities.
3. Progressive experiential activities.

maintain a state of relaxation, first while visualizing yourself in and then while participating in increasingly stressful speaking situations.

You can practice systematic desensitization on your own with the help of an audiotape, or you can practice this technique with the help of a friend. The important element of this method, however, is to begin with *daily practice* (twenty to thirty minutes) for about two weeks. You need to schedule it into your day like you might schedule exercise or some other activity that is important to you. After about two weeks of consistent practice, most people will have trained themselves to reach a relaxed state in a matter of minutes and remain there during their speech. Hence, you can imitate this state during the moments before you get up to give your speech.

Step 1: Progressive Relaxation Activities

Teaching Tip
Have students experiment with the breathing, muscle relaxation, and visualization exercises contained in the Activities section of this chapter.

The use of relaxation exercises is a technique that has proved to reduce anxiety levels. Relaxation exercises can help you in and of themselves, as well as in Step 1 of systematic desensitization. For the exercises to be effective, however, you must dedicate yourself to doing them regularly. As with aerobic activity, inconsistent exercise is unlikely to have much lasting effect. Two kinds of relaxation exercises can be particularly helpful: breathing techniques and progressive muscle relaxation therapy.

Take a moment to focus on your breathing. When you inhale, do your shoulders rise? If so, you are engaging in shallow, or chest, breathing. Shallow breathing actually contributes to anxiety, depression, and fatigue (Bourne, 1990). To see why shallow breathing contributes to anxiety, think of your lungs as balloons that fill up with air and then release it. Shallow breathing is like filling only the top half of the balloon with air. In order to keep air from entering the bottom half of the balloon, you have to close it off with your hand. The same thing happens to your lungs when you engage in shallow breathing. Like your hand on the balloon, your internal muscles must tighten in order to stop air from filling the bottom half of your lungs. When these muscles contract, you add unnecessary tension to your body—tension that contributes to anxiety.

What Do You Think?

Imagine you are about to get up to deliver a public speech. Does your breathing change and, if so, how? Do any specific parts of your body get tense and, if so, which ones?

We were all born breathing naturally from the abdomen, but many of us learned to breathe unnaturally, from the chest. For example, I remember my childhood doctor asking me to breathe deeply, saying, "I want to see your shoulders rise." He didn't realize that he was helping me learn to breathe incorrectly. I began to believe that big breaths should make my shoulders rise. Unfortunately, after years of practice, shallow breathing can begin to feel natural. Through breathing techniques, you can retrain yourself to breathe from the abdomen and thus reduce your anxiety.

FIGURE 2–1
Deep Breathing

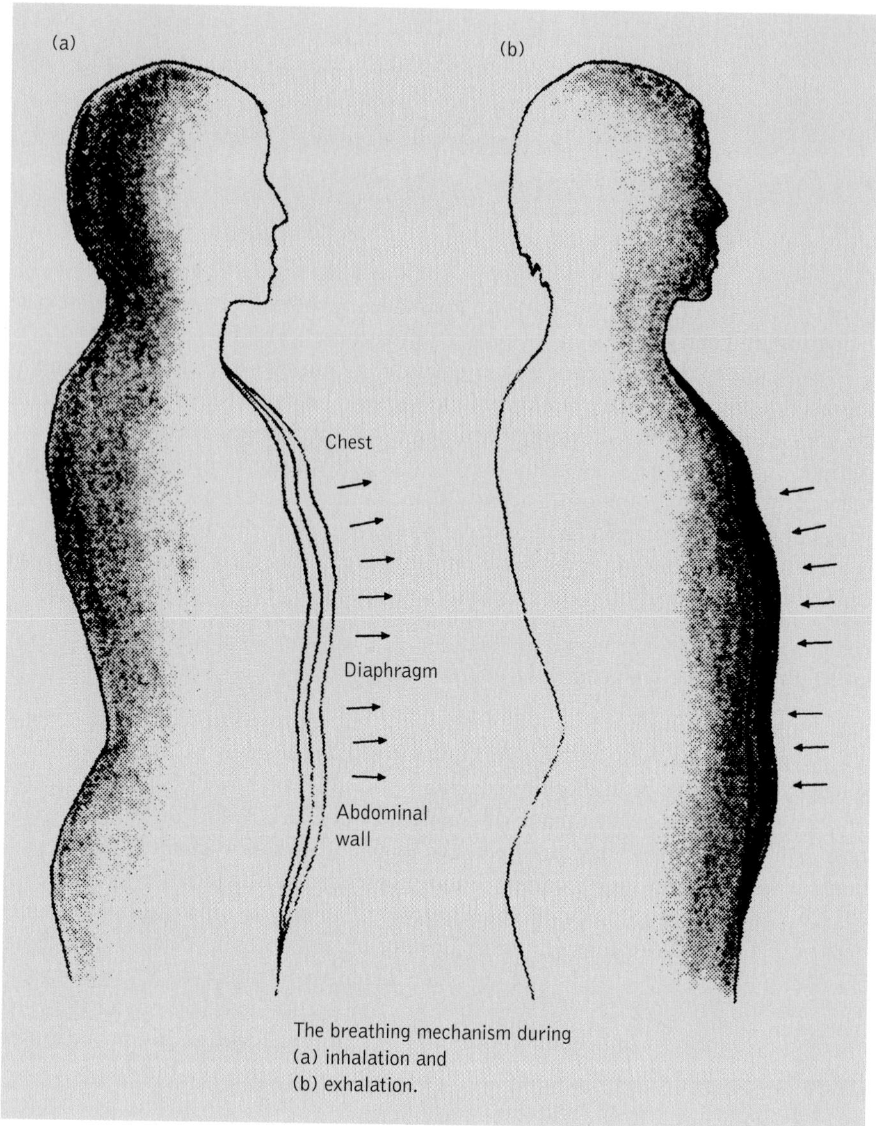

The breathing mechanism during
(a) inhalation and
(b) exhalation.

If you are breathing deeply and your lungs are filling completely, your diaphragm will move down and will push your stomach out of the way (see Figure 2–1). You can practice and monitor deep breathing by breathing so that you see your stomach expand as you inhale and return to its normal resting position as you exhale (see Activities 3 and 4 at the end of this chapter).

Another breathing exercise can be used immediately before giving a speech. It is natural to feel a sudden rush of adrenaline right before it is your turn to speak. This phenomenon, commonly referred to as nervous energy, can actually improve performance. Unfortunately, this adrenaline rush can harm you if you misinterpret it as anxiety and, consequently, your muscles tense up and you start taking shallow chest breaths. An effective response to that adrenaline rush is a sigh. Physicians and psychologists have discovered that sighing is your body's way to release tension (Davis, Echelon, & McKay, 1988). By sighing right before it is your turn to speak,

Progressive muscle relaxation therapy is one technique that can help reduce public speaking anxiety.

you can lower your anxiety level (see Activity 5 at the end of this chapter). Then that inevitable rush of adrenaline can work for you, not against you.

Along with teaching yourself to breathe deeply, you'll need to teach your body to relax. This is where **progressive muscle relaxation therapy** comes in. Although this technique was developed more than sixty years ago, it is still the most effective method for training one's body and muscles to relax (Jacobson, 1938). Progressive muscle relaxation therapy involves systematically tensing certain muscle groups for about ten seconds, and then relaxing them for another ten seconds while focusing on what this relaxed state feels like (Friedrich & Goss, 1984). Usually, each group is tensed and relaxed twice before the person moves on to the next group. The fifteen muscle groups isolated in this therapy are hands, biceps and triceps, shoulders, neck, lips, tongue, mouth, eyes and forehead, abdomen, back, midsection, thighs, stomach, calves and feet, and toes (see Activity 6 at the end of this chapter). You will probably go through this process several times before you can successfully maintain a state of deep relaxation. Once you are able to do so, you will be ready to add the visualization step of systematic desensitization.

Step 2: Progressive Visualization Activities

The second step of systematic desensitization is to visualize yourself in progressively more threatening communication situations. Once you are in a relaxed state, you may be asked to envision yourself talking with your best friend on the telephone, introducing yourself to a new acquaintance, and, ultimately, giving a public speech (see Activity 7 at the end of this chapter). Your goal is to maintain a relaxed state while envisioning yourself in each of these types of communication situations. Initially, as you visualize yourself in a particular situation, you may feel that the relaxed state is replaced with a feeling of tension and anxiety. Your goal is to learn to maintain the relaxed state in that situation, then move on to a more anxiety-arousing situation and repeat the process.

Teaching Tip
Have students complete the progressive visualization exercise contained in the Activities section of this chapter.

Step 3: Progressive Experiential Activities

The final step is to actually engage in progressively more threatening communication situations. Over several sessions, for example, you may be asked to talk to a friend about yourself, then to introduce yourself to someone you don't know well, and,

Teaching Tip
Have students complete the progressive experiential activity contained in the Activities section of this chapter.

Teaching Tip
Have students complete the progressive experiential activity contained in the Activities section of this chapter.

ultimately, to introduce yourself to a small group and then to a larger group. Your goal is to learn to maintain a relaxed state while engaging in these progressively more threatening communication situations (see Activity 8 at the end of this chapter).

Systematic desensitization can help you in two ways. First, it reduces communication apprehension in general, including fear of public speaking. That is, you train yourself to relax in public speaking and other situations. Second, you can use many of the techniques to help yourself relax when you actually give a speech. For example, just before you get up to speak, take several deep breaths while focusing on your abdomen. You should feel yourself relax. Then close your eyes and visualize yourself giving a strong speech. When you walk to the front of the room, take three more deep breaths right before beginning your speech. While doing so, look at the first couple sentences to get them firmly in mind. Finally, jot down a few prompts on your notes to remind you to breathe deeply during the speech. Keep in mind, though, that this second use of systematic desensitization will help you only if it reinforces, rather than replaces, regular systematic desensitization training.

Cognitive Restructuring

Cognitive restructuring is a four-step process designed to help you systematically rebuild your thoughts about public speaking. More specifically, cognitive restructuring is designed to eliminate your anxiety-arousing negative self-talk and replace it with anxiety-reducing positive self-talk.

The Process of Cognitive Restructuring

1. *Create a negative self-talk list.* What are my fears?
2. *Identify the irrational belief or cognitive distortion embedded in each thought.* Why are these fears irrational?
3. *Develop a coping statement for each irrational belief or distortion.* What can I tell myself instead?
4. *Practice coping statements until they become second nature.*

Step 1: Create a Negative Self-Talk List

To change your negative thoughts, you must first identify those thoughts. Take a moment to write down all of the fears that come to mind when you know you must give a public speech. List as many as you can, regardless of what they are. Karna, a student in a public speaking fundamentals class, put together a list that looked like this:

Negative Self-Talk List

I'm afraid I'll forget my speech and then I'll look foolish.

I'm afraid everyone will be able to tell that I'm nervous.

I'm afraid my voice will crack.

I'm afraid my audience won't believe me.

I'm afraid I'll sound boring.

What Do You Think?

What are the negative thoughts and fears that go through your head when you know you have to present a speech?

Step 2: Identify Irrational Beliefs and Cognitive Distortions That May Be Guiding Your Fears

Most of our fears about public speaking are rooted in irrational beliefs (Ellis & Dryden, 1987). **Irrational beliefs** project harm and danger onto an event that is neither harmful nor dangerous. Since public speaking is clearly not a life-threatening event, your fears of it are rooted in irrational beliefs. Let's look at Karna's list of negative self-talk again. She was worried that she would forget her speech and look foolish. Is that life-threatening? No. She was also concerned that people would be able to tell that she was nervous. Although listeners may or may not be able to tell she is nervous, this, too, is not life-threatening. Likewise, even if her voice does crack, and if some audience members don't believe her, and if she sounds boring, she is not likely to die as a result. She might tell herself, "I'll just die if this happens," but she won't. Hence, every negative thought she identified in her list is actually rooted in an irrational belief that the event is in some way life-threatening.

> ***What Do You Think?***
>
> *Look at the list you generated in Step 1. If any of your fears actually comes true during your public speech, will it be life-threatening? If not, then these fears are based on irrational beliefs.*

Now that you realize how most negative self-talk about public speaking is actually rooted in irrational beliefs, we can move on to discuss how most negative self-talk about public speaking is essentially a cognitive distortion. **Cognitive distortions** about public speaking are unrealistic, negative statements about yourself that lead you to judge your public speaking experience harshly, even if it goes well (Ellis & Dryden, 1987). Like the irrational beliefs themselves, cognitive distortions increase anxiety and keep you from achieving your goals. As you read through this list, consider which of them influence your self-talk about public speaking.

> **Cognitive Distortions**
>
> 1. *The perfectionist.* "If I make even one mistake, I'll be a failure."
> 2. *The self-effacing phony.* "If someone compliments me, they're just being nice. That wasn't really me because I'm not that good."
> 3. *The thin skinned.* "They looked bored; I must be bad."
> 4. *The overgeneralizer.* "I got nervous. Getting nervous is bad. So I was bad."
> 5. *The psychic.* "My audience will be bored, so I'll be bad." "I always forget my speech, so I'll forget and be bad again." "I always get nervous, so I'll get nervous and be bad."
> 6. *The negativist.* "Even though I got many compliments, I forgot one part so I'm unworthy."

Negative self-talk that stems from a cognitive distortion is often rooted in "must thoughts" that demand perfection (Dwyer, 1998b). Must thoughts may include (a) believing you *must* never make a mistake or people will think you are incompetent, (b) telling yourself that everyone in your audience *must* like your speech or you will fail, and (c) convincing yourself that you *must* not give a speech unless you feel perfectly calm. As you can probably tell, the goals implied are impossible for any human being to achieve. By allowing yourself to believe must thoughts, you set yourself up for inevitable failure.

These perfectionistic ideals stem from a performance orientation to public speaking. As we discussed earlier in the chapter, a **performance orientation** requires you to present your speech using flawless and eloquent oratorical skills to be effective (Motley, 1991). Instead, effective public speaking operates from a communication orientation. A **communication orientation** focuses on the message and helping your audience understand it.

Consider Karna's list of negative self-talk once again. Notice how the items in her negative self-talk list stem from cognitive distortions like the perfectionist, the thin skinned, and the psychic. She is not likely to forget the entire speech, but she might forget to mention something that she planned to say. Her negative self-talk, however, says doing so will mean she is a failure. This is an example of the perfectionist cognitive distortion being played out. The thin-skinned cognitive distortion is guiding her self-talk about boring her listeners and the psychic is represented in several of her statements. No public speaker is perfect. We all make mistakes. We can all learn from our mistakes. Yet cognitive distortions act as barriers keeping you from attaining your public speaking goals. They set you up for failure by feeding your negative self-talk and increasing anxiety.

What Do You Think?

Refer to the list of negative self-talk you identified in Step 1. What specific cognitive distortion is fueling each statement?

Step 3: Develop Positive Coping Statements

Once you have analyzed and understood your negative self-talk, you can develop a list of positive coping statements to replace each negative statement. It is important that you generate coping statements that fit *your* concerns. In other words, I cannot provide a list of coping statements that will work for everyone. Only you can determine what your negative self-talk statements are, why each statement is irrational, what cognitive distortion guides it, and what positive coping statement you can use to replace it. Psychologist Richard Heimberg of the State University of New York at Albany approaches this step by asking clients to list all the things they are afraid listeners will think (negative self-talk list). He then asks them to estimate how many listeners in an audience of one hundred would even notice, for example, sweaty palms or shaky knees (cognitive distortion identified). Next, how many would even care (again, cognitive distortion identified)? He concludes by helping them generate a positive coping statement to replace the negative self-talk: "By the time we get to the end, it comes down to: Can you cope with the one or two people who [notice or criticize or] get upset?" (Griffin, 1995, p. 64).

Here is how Karna worked through the process of replacing her negative self-talk statements with positive coping statements. (a) Rather than telling herself that she would forget the speech and look foolish, she began telling herself that forgetting a few details would not ruin her speech as long as she focused on getting the main points across to her audience. (b) She also reminded herself that most of her nervousness signs would not be noticeable, like sweaty palms and racing heartbeat. Moreover, most listeners wouldn't focus on her shaky knees or a crack in her voice, and those who might do so are really the ones with the problem, not her. (c) Perhaps some listeners would not believe her. However, she conducted thorough research and believed in the speech, so she would convey her thoughts honestly. She can't control the beliefs of others. (d) As for sounding boring, she probably won't sound boring as long as she focuses on the message and not the performance. After all, she rehearsed out loud a lot. If a few listeners appear bored, that is really not her problem, but theirs.

What Do You Think?

Refer to your list of negative self-talk statements, as well as the irrational beliefs and cognitive distortions that guide them. Create a positive coping statement for each negative self-talk statement you identified.

Step 4: Practice Your Coping Statements Until They Become Second Nature

Finally, you need to memorize and practice your coping statements until they replace the old script of negative self-talk in your mind. Don't become discouraged when you begin to work on this step. It may feel awkward and even phony at first. Realize, though, that this restructuring process takes time and energy, because the negative self-talk has become a part of you. The more you read your list of coping statements, memorize them, and say them to yourself silently and aloud, the more natural they will become and the more unnatural the negative thoughts will seem.

Teaching Tip
Collect your students' irrational beliefs and coping statements lists, compile them, and report the anonymous results to the entire class. This strategy should help students understand that others share similar concerns about public speaking and expose them to multiple ideas for coping with communication apprehension.

Start by reading your coping statements at least once every day. In addition, keep the list with you (in a pocket, purse, or wallet). Then, when a negative self-talk statement comes to your mind during the day, refer to your list and replace the old negative self-talk with the new positive coping statement. Also, set public speaking goals for yourself two or three times per week, so you can practice your coping statements before speaking. These goals may include asking a question during class, introducing yourself to someone you don't know, or sharing a story with acquaintances between classes or during lunch. Any speaking situation that tends to make you nervous is appropriate. Review your list right before you give each speech. Finally, practice positive coping statements after presenting each speech. Cognitive restructuring may sound almost too simple to be effective, but research proves it works. All that's required is committed practice on your part. Your fear and nervousness about public speaking will diminish.

Skills Training

The final method is based on a simple principle: The better you know something, the less anxious about it you feel. If you learn the skills involved in effective public speaking, you'll greatly reduce your fear of failure. Simply put, then, in **skills training** the speechmaking process is broken into specific skills that can be mastered, first in isolation and then together.

This entire book is designed as a skills training method. Each chapter introduces you to a specific component of the speechmaking process. Each chapter also asks you to practice the component through activities. By the time you finish reading this book, you will have completed a session of public speaking skills training and should, as a result, feel less anxiety about presenting public speeches.

To be successful, however, set specific goals for yourself as you work each skill, practice each skill in isolation, and reward yourself for achieving the goals you set. For example, you might set a goal to use transitions that verbally tie the two main points together. When you achieve that, reward yourself with positive self-talk rather than employing negative self-talk about something you hadn't yet set out to achieve. Upon achieving the goal and rewarding yourself for it, you might then set a goal of also using colorful language choices in your transitions. After doing so, reward yourself again with positive self-talk before setting a higher goal. What is important in skills training is to set attainable goals, achieve them, and reward yourself with positive self-talk *before* aspiring to a new goal. Too often, anxiety is fostered because speakers employ negative self-talk for not achieving a certain skill they hadn't even set for themselves yet, and they do so while ignoring the skills they had achieved.

Summary

In this chapter, we talked about the nature of communication apprehension, why it exists, and how you can work strategically to overcome it. We discussed how public speaking anxiety is only one type of communication apprehension; however, it affects more people than any of the other types. Likewise, most people fear public speaking more even than death. We learned that public speaking anxiety stems from socialization, learning style preference, and self-talk. If you experience public speaking anxiety, it probably stems from negative experiences you have had in the past, negative role models, or negative self-talk.

We also learned that public speaking anxiety can be reduced, and we explored three methods that have proved effective in reducing it. Systematic desensitization focuses, first, on learning to become relaxed. Then you strive to maintain a relaxed state while visualizing yourself in progressively more threatening communication situations. Ultimately, you strive to maintain a relaxed state while participating in increasingly more threatening communication situations. Cognitive restructuring is a process of replacing negative self-talk with positive self-talk. To do so, you must identify what negative self-talk statements shape your thinking about public speaking. Then you analyze those statements to discover the irrational beliefs and cognitive distortions that perpetuate them. This allows you to create alternative coping statements to replace each negative statement—coping statements that can be memorized and employed throughout the day, as well as right before and right after giving a speech. Finally, skills training breaks the speechmaking process into specific skills that can be mastered incrementally to, ultimately, reduce the fear of failure.

Ideally, public speakers will employ all of these methods in some form as they work to reduce public speaking anxiety. Although it is not possible to overcome public speaking anxiety overnight, it *can* be overcome by committing yourself to practicing relaxation and systematic desensitization, cognitive restructuring, and skills training in isolation as well as together.

Activities

These exercises are designed to reduce public speaking anxiety. To be effective, they must be practiced regularly outside of the public speaking classroom. Then they can be effectively adapted to help you during the minutes before you get up to speak, while you are speaking, and during the moments right after you finish your public speech.

1. **Personal Report of Communication Apprehension (PRCA-24).** Please indicate your level of agreement with each statement.

Personal Report of Communication Apprehension (PRCA-24)

DIRECTIONS: This instrument is composed of twenty-four statements concerning feelings about communicating with other people. Please indicate the degree to which each statement applies to you by marking whether you (1) strongly agree, (2) agree, (3) are undecided, (4) disagree, or (5) strongly disagree. Work quickly; record your first impression.

_____ 1. I dislike participating in group discussions.
_____ 2. Generally, I am comfortable while participating in group discussions.
_____ 3. I am tense and nervous while participating in group discussions.
_____ 4. I like to get involved in group discussions.
_____ 5. Engaging in a group discussion with new people makes me tense and nervous.
_____ 6. I am calm and relaxed while participating in group discussions.
_____ 7. Generally, I am nervous when I have to participate in a meeting.
_____ 8. Usually I am calm and relaxed while participating in meetings.
_____ 9. I am very calm and relaxed when I am called upon to express an opinion at a meeting.
_____ 10. I am afraid to express myself at meetings.
_____ 11. Communicating at meetings usually makes me uncomfortable.
_____ 12. I am very relaxed when answering questions at a meeting.
_____ 13. While participating in a conversation with a new acquaintance, I feel very nervous.
_____ 14. I have no fear of speaking up in conversations.
_____ 15. Ordinarily I am very tense and nervous in conversations.
_____ 16. Ordinarily I am very calm and relaxed in conversations.
_____ 17. While conversing with a new acquaintance, I feel very relaxed.
_____ 18. I'm afraid to speak up in conversations.
_____ 19. I have no fear of giving a speech.
_____ 20. Certain parts of my body feel very tense and rigid while I am giving a speech.
_____ 21. I feel relaxed while giving a speech.
_____ 22. My thoughts become confused and jumbled when I am giving a speech.
_____ 23. I face the prospect of giving a speech with confidence.
_____ 24. While giving a speech, I get so nervous I forget facts I really know.

SCORING: The PRCA permits computation of one total score and four subscores. The subscores are related to communication apprehension in each of four common communication contexts: group discussions, meetings, interpersonal conversations, and public speaking. To compute your scores merely add or subtract your scores for each item as indicated on the following page.

Subscore Desired	*Scoring Formula*
Group discussion	18 + scores for items 2, 4, and 6; − scores for items 1, 3, and 5.
Meetings	18 + scores for items 8, 9, and 12; − scores for items 7, 10, and 11.
Interpersonal conversations	18 + scores for items 14, 16, and 17; − scores for items 13, 15, and 18.
Public Speaking	18 + scores for items 19, 21, and 23; − scores for items 20, 22, and 24.

To obtain your total score for the PRCA, simply add your four subscores together. Your score should range between 24 and 120. If your score is below 24 or above 120, you have made a mistake in computing the score.

Scores on the four contexts (groups, meetings, interpersonal conversations, and public speaking) can range from a low of 6 to a high of 30. Any score above 18 indicates some degree of apprehension. If your score is above 18 for the public speaking context, you are like the overwhelming majority of Americans.

2. Personal Report of Public Speaking Anxiety (PRPSA).

Personal Report of Public Speaking Anxiety (PRPSA)

DIRECTIONS: This instrument is composed of thirty-four statements concerning feelings about communicating with other people. Indicate the degree to which the statements apply to you by marking whether you (1) strongly agree, (2) agree, (3) are undecided, (4) disagree, or (5) strongly disagree with each statement. Work quickly; record your first impression.

_____ 1. While preparing for giving a speech, I feel tense and nervous.

_____ 2. I feel tense when I see the words *speech* and *public speech* on a course outline when studying.

_____ 3. My thoughts become confused and jumbled when I am giving a speech.

_____ 4. Right after giving a speech I feel that I have had a pleasant experience.

_____ 5. I get anxious when I think about a speech coming up.

_____ 6. I have no fear of giving a speech.

_____ 7. Although I am nervous just before starting a speech, I soon settle down after starting and feel calm and comfortable.

_____ 8. I look forward to giving a speech.

_____ 9. When the instructor announces a speaking assignment in class, I can feel myself getting tense.

_____ 10. My hands tremble when I am giving a speech.

_____ 11. I feel relaxed while giving a speech.
_____ 12. I enjoy preparing for a speech.
_____ 13. I am in constant fear of forgetting what I prepared to say.
_____ 14. I get anxious if someone asks me something about my topic that I do not know.
_____ 15. I face the prospect of giving a speech with confidence.
_____ 16. I feel that I am in complete possession of myself while giving a speech.
_____ 17. My mind is clear when giving a speech.
_____ 18. I do not dread giving a speech.
_____ 19. I perspire just before starting a speech.
_____ 20. My heart beats very fast just as I start a speech.
_____ 21. I experience considerable anxiety while sitting in the room just before my speech starts.
_____ 22. Certain parts of my body feel very tense and rigid while giving a speech.
_____ 23. Realizing that only a little time remains in a speech makes me very tense and anxious.
_____ 24. While giving a speech I know I can control my feelings of tension and stress.
_____ 25. I breathe faster just before starting a speech.
_____ 26. I feel comfortable and relaxed in the hour or so just before giving a speech.
_____ 27. I do poorer on speeches because I am anxious.
_____ 28. I feel anxious when the teacher announces the date of a speaking assignment.
_____ 29. When I make a mistake while giving a speech, I find it hard to concentrate on the parts that follow.
_____ 30. During an important speech I experience a feeling of helplessness building up inside me.
_____ 31. I have trouble falling asleep the night before a speech.
_____ 32. My heart beats very fast while I present a speech.
_____ 33. I feel anxious while waiting to give my speech.
_____ 34. While giving a speech, I get so nervous I forget facts I really know.

SCORING: To determine your score on the PRPSA, complete the following steps:

Step 1. Add the scores for items, 1, 2, 3, 5, 9, 10, 13, 14, 19, 20, 21, 22, 23, 25, 27, 28, 29, 30, 31, 32, 33, and 34.
Step 2. Add the scores for items 4, 6, 7, 8, 11, 12, 15, 16, 17, 18, 24, and 26.
Step 3. Complete the following formula:

$$\text{PRPSA} = 132 - \text{Total from Step 1} + \text{Total from Step 2.}$$

Your score should range between 34 and 170. If your score is below 34 or above 170, you have made a mistake in computing the score.

Score	Anxiety about Public Speaking
120–170	Very high
111–119	Moderately high
93–110	Moderate
85–92	Moderately low
34–84	Low

3. **Controlled Deep Breathing Exercise.** If possible, lie on your back on the floor. Place a book on your stomach and take a breath. As you breathe in through your nose, watch for the book to rise. As you exhale through your mouth, watch for the book to lower. You may feel at first as though you are forcing the book to rise. With consistent practice this breathing process will become more natural. You can practice deep breathing when you watch television or listen to the radio. Remember though, this retraining exercise must be practiced every day for about twenty minutes to be successful.
4. **Breathing in Transit Exercise.** You can also practice deep breathing while you're walking to and from class. As you walk, be sure that you are standing tall. Then practice deep breathing in four-count intervals. For example, take four steps while inhaling through your nose to the count of four (think "1–2–3–4" as you inhale and walk). Then take the next four steps while exhaling through your mouth to the count of four (think "1–2–3–4" as you exhale and walk). Not only will this strategy improve your ability to breathe deeply, but it will also increase the oxygen supply to your brain and muscles, which will wake you up and give you more energy.
5. **Calming Sigh Exercise.** Use this exercise to reduce stress right before you get up to give your speech. First, inhale deeply but gently through your nose. Then slowly let the air out of you lungs while saying "Ahhhh." Finally, let your body go limp for a couple of moments. Do this exercise two or three times in a row just before speaking. You will be surprised at how it relaxes you.
6. **Progressive Muscle Relaxation Exercise.** Progressive muscle relaxation therapy is a process designed to teach you to systematically train your muscles to relax. You may find it necessary to go through the exercise daily for several days before feeling noticeable improvement in your ability to relax your muscles. There are fifteen muscle groups to be isolated. Each muscle group should be tensed for ten seconds and then released for ten seconds. The same muscle group should be tensed and relaxed twice before moving on to the next group. It usually works best to lie down on a comfortable surface for this exercise. You might solicit help from a friend to do this exercise or you can order a copy of the *Conquering Speechfright* audiotape (Harcourt College Publishers, 6277 Sea Harbor Drive, Orlando, FL 32887).

Muscle Groups

1. Hands
2. Biceps and triceps
3. Shoulders
4. Neck

5. Lips
6. Tongue
7. Mouth
8. Eyes and forehead
9. Abdomen (breathing)
10. Back
11. Midsection
12. Thighs
13. Stomach
14. Calves and feet
15. Toes

7. **Progressive Visualization Exercise.** This activity requires the help of a partner. You should be lying down, in a comfortable position with your eyes closed. Before beginning, relax your body (you can use Activity 6 to achieve this relaxed state). Your partner will begin by asking you to visualize yourself engaged in the first communication activity on the list provided here. Your partner should remain silent for about fifteen seconds while you visualize yourself in the situation. If you feel your tension increase, raise your finger. If you raise your finger, your partner will ask you to put the situation out of your mind for a few moments to regain your state of relaxation. Your partner will then ask you again to envision yourself in the situation. Once you can do so for fifteen seconds without feeling tension, your partner will ask you to put the situation out of your mind for a few moments. Then your partner will increase the visualization time to twenty seconds. After a few moments of relaxation, your partner will increase the time to twenty-five seconds and, finally, to thirty seconds. Once you can envision yourself in the situation for thirty seconds without feeling increased tension, your partner will move on to the second item on the list. You and your partner should attempt to complete no more than three or four visualization experiences per session. Subsequent sessions should begin with relaxation, followed by visualization of the last item you'd successfully completed.

Nonthreatening to Threatening Communication Situations

1. You are talking to your best friend on the telephone.
2. You are talking to your best friend in person.
3. You are introducing yourself to a new acquaintance.
4. You are talking to a clerk in a department store.
5. You are talking to a small group of people, all of whom you know well.
6. You are talking to a teacher about a problem at school.
7. You are at a social gathering where you don't know anyone but are expected to mingle.
8. You are going to ask someone out on a date with you.
9. You are going to a job interview.
10. You have been asked to introduce yourself to a group of people.
11. You have been asked to give a speech to a large group of people.

12. You are giving a speech to a large group of people.
13. You are getting ready to give a speech, but you left your notes at home.
14. You have been asked to debate another person in front of a group of people.
15. You are debating another person in front of a group of people.

8. **Progressive Experiential Activity.** As with progressive visualization, your goal is to maintain a fairly relaxed state while engaging in progressively more threatening communication situations. You should not attempt to complete more than one or two activities during one session.

Progressively More Threatening Experiential Activities

1. Talk to a friend about yourself.
2. Talk about yourself to someone you don't know well.
3. Introduce yourself to a small group.
4. Introduce yourself while standing in front of the group.
5. Introduce yourself to a large group.
6. Talk to a friend about your speech.
7. Talk about your speech to a small group.
8. Present your speech while standing in front of a small group.
9. Present your speech while standing in front of a large group.
10. Answer questions about your speech in front of a large group.
11. Discuss both sides of your topic with a friend.
12. Debate your topic with an acquaintance.
13. Debate your topic with an acquaintance in a small group.
14. Debate your topic while standing in front of a large group.
15. Answer questions about your position in front of a large group.

9. **Cognitive Restructuring Journals.** Cognitive restructuring journal entries occur in two phases. (a) Use the journal to identify communication situations where your anxiety level increases. Take it with you wherever you go so you can make a note when a particular situation increases your anxiety. Simply jot down the situation and the fears that immediately come to mind. Put the journal away until later. When you have some quiet time to reflect, complete the second phase. (b) Read the entry you completed earlier that day or week. Generate irrational beliefs and cognitive distortions linked to each fear. Finally, create a positive coping statement to replace each negative thought.

10. **Coping Statement Chart.** Create a list of (a) public speaking negative self-talk fears and the (b) irrational beliefs and cognitive distortions associated with each. Then develop a chart that you can carry in your pocket, purse, wallet, or daily planner. Refer to this chart at least once every day in order to help yourself replace negative self-talk with positive coping statements and reduce your anxiety about public speaking.

11. **Portfolio Assignment.** Create a one- to two-page paper identifying two or three personal goals you have for coping with anxiety and why, as well as how you plan to achieve them. Finally, describe how you plan to reward yourself when you achieve them.

Key Terms

- Audience-based communication apprehension
- Cognitive distortions
- Cognitive restructuring
- Communication apprehension
- Communication orientation
- Context-based communication apprehension
- Irrational beliefs
- Modeling
- Performance orientation
- Progressive muscle relaxation therapy
- Reinforcement
- Self-talk
- Situational communication apprehension
- Skills training
- Socialization
- Systematic desensitization
- Traitlike communication apprehension

CHAPTER 3

Your First Speech

Reflective Questions

1. What can you do to make the content of your speech interesting to your audience?
2. Why is it so important to look audience members in the eye while giving your public speech?
3. Why is clear structure so crucial to effective public speaking?
4. At what point(s) during the speechmaking and presentation process should you consider your audience?

ris was enrolled in public speaking fundamentals, a general education core requirement at her university. She had enrolled in the course several times before, but had always dropped it after a couple of classes, when the first speech was assigned. During a recent advising session, she confided that it seemed "unfair" to ask students to present a short speech introducing themselves before they had learned what an effective public speech looks like or how to prepare it. Kris made a lot of sense. It *is* unfair to expect students to stand up and present a speech, however short and simple, without some general guidance.

Teaching Tip
Assign one of the three speeches located in the Activities section of this chapter.

This chapter is offered in response to Kris's concerns, concerns I'm sure many of you share. You can probably identify public speakers who seem to be "good at it" and others who are "not so good at it." What you might not be able to determine, however, is why. What are the basic principles of an effective public speech? This chapter focuses on the key principles you should follow to develop and present a public speech. These principles are discussed as they relate to the three primary components of an effective public speech, as well as the "glue" that holds them together. The components are content, structure, and delivery, and the glue is being audience-centered or listener relevant. To be most helpful, consider the topic and requirements of your first speech assignment as you read the chapter. This way, you can apply the principles to your first speech as you read. Kris's first speech is offered as an example throughout our discussion to help you understand these basic principles as they work in a public speech.

> **What Do You Think?**
> *Identify a public speaker you have heard who seemed to be really "good at it." Do you know why?*

What Does It Mean to Be Audience-Centered?

Teaching Tip
Refer students to the SpeechMaker CD-ROM. This software exposes them to multiple speaking scenarios and helps them with every step of the speechmaking process. Before the class, consider assigning one of the scenarios, which you discuss as you teach this chapter.

Effective public speakers are continuously audience-centered. As listeners, we sense that they care about us enough to offer their ideas in ways that (a) make sense, (b) are relevant to us, (c) reflect careful research, and (d) sound interesting. Being **audience-centered** means considering who your audience members are and how your message can best be tailored to their interests, desires, and needs. Effective public speakers analyze the relationship between their audience and their message when they select their topic, as well as *throughout the speechmaking and presentation process.* This means they consider the audience when selecting a topic and developing the *content,* when organizing the *structure,* and when rehearsing the *delivery,* as well as when actually presenting the speech.

Teaching Tip
Have students write a brief paper on audience analysis. Ask them to keep the following questions in mind: What are the demographic characteristics of your peers in this class? How will you adjust your speech accordingly (topic, purpose, language, etc.)?

Kris's first speech was a "speech of self-introduction." Her audience was a group of twenty to twenty-five college students who were also enrolled in the course. She estimated that the other students ranged in age from eighteen or nineteen years old to forty-five or fifty years old. Some were married. Others were not. Some had no children, some had young children, and some had grown children. The group included a single parent, a gay rights activist, a fellow who had recently returned to school to become a priest, and a migrant worker. In other words, Kris's audience was *demographically diverse,* differing in ages, experiences, attitudes, and values. However, they did have one important characteristic in common. They were all students at the same university taking the same required public speaking course.

From this cursory analysis, Kris decided her audience would be a supportive group, since they were all pretty much "in the same boat," and that it would be important to respect the group's diverse perspectives and life experiences. Although her primary goal had been dictated by the instructor—to present a self-introduction speech that was true to herself, her experiences, her beliefs, and her values—audience analysis helped her tighten her focus based on her listeners. For example, she would be careful to avoid presumptions that her beliefs, values, and experiences were better than those of others. She also would try to address ways in which this particular audience of college students enrolled in public speaking might benefit from learning about her and her experiences.

> ***What Do You Think?***
>
> *Who are the members of your audience? What are some similarities and differences among them? How might knowing these similarities and differences help you develop an audience-centered speech?*

What Does It Mean to Have Good Content?

Content refers to the actual ideas in your speech: to the main topic and purpose of your speech, to the ideas and information you include to support the topic and purpose within each main point, and to the connections you make directly to listeners throughout.

The **main topic** is essentially the subject of your speech. Kris's main topic was herself, since her first speech assignment was to introduce herself to the class. An important aspect of the main topic is the purpose. The purpose is actually made up of two parts: the general purpose and the specific purpose. Simply put, the **general purpose** of any speech is to inform, persuade, or entertain. The **specific purpose** answers the question "about what?" Kris's general purpose was *to inform* and her specific purpose was to tell them a bit *about herself.*

What kind of ideas and information support your main topic and purpose? Essentially, these ideas and this information take the form of main points supporting your topic and purpose, as well as evidence supporting your main points. It is a good idea to limit your speeches to two, three, or four main points. More than four main points tend to be difficult for listeners to keep track of as they listen. Kris's instructor advised students to consider their personal backgrounds, their unique characteristics, and their professional goals to develop their first speech. To introduce herself, then, Kris decided to talk about (a) where she grew up (background), (b) what makes her unique (characteristics), and (c) why she chose North Dakota State University for her college education (professional goals). These three ideas became the main points of her speech.

Teaching Tip
Consider arranging a tour of your library's resources to show students where they can find evidence to support their ideas. During the tour, ask students to evaluate the credibility of different sources of information using the criteria presented in this chapter.

Each main point is developed with evidence. **Evidence** is any information that clarifies, explains, or supports your main point. To effectively support main points, evidence needs to have sufficient breadth and depth. **Breadth** refers to the number of pieces and different types of evidence

> ***What Do You Think?***
>
> *What are the topic and purpose of your first speech? What ideas will you focus on for your main points?*

you use. You should use many different types of evidence to appeal to the diverse learning styles represented in your audience. **Depth** refers to the level of detail you provide from each piece of evidence. Usually, you will offer two or three pieces of evidence to develop each main point. You can use things like facts, statistics, definitions, descriptions, explanations, examples, testimonies, and analogies. This evidence can come from your own personal experiences or from external research you collect from interviews or surveys, books, magazines, newspapers, journals, or the Internet.

Discussion Tip
Ask students to discuss how Kris's use of personal experiences likely affected her credibility as a speaker.

Kris used personal experiences as evidence to support each main point. For example, to support her first main point, she *described* the small town where she grew up, how long she lived there, and the school she attended and graduated from while living in that small town. Doing so added depth to her description. To support her second main point, she *explained* what growing up with a twin sister was like and how that has shaped who she is today. She offered the fact that she is exactly three minutes older than her sister and used the *analogy* of "good" and "evil" twins in her explanation, again, adding depth. To support her third main point, Kris talked about her previous academic experiences, employment experiences, and future goals and explained how they worked together to lead her to NDSU to earn her degree. She used a variety of different facts and statistics to add breadth. Ultimately, she addressed a variety of learning styles by offering personal stories, analogies, facts, statistics, explanations, and descriptions.

What Do You Think?

What pieces of evidence might you include to provide breadth and depth to each of your main points?

Finally, content should also include listener relevance links. A **listener relevance link** is a statement of how and why the ideas you offer might benefit your listeners. You should include such links when introducing your topic in general and when discussing each main point more specifically. Although

You can use analogies to support a main point, as Kris did about being a twin.

listener relevance links are sometimes difficult to formulate, they are crucial aspects of content in an audience-centered speech.

Kris offered a general listener relevance link in her introduction by talking about how important it is to forge new friendships. In discussing her first main point, she talked about her hometown as a place her classmates might consider visiting. In discussing her second main point, she talked about how easy it can be for anyone to take family for granted. And in discussing her third main point, she talked about reasons NDSU is a good school for her and, perhaps, for others as well.

In short, content is the "stuff" of which speeches are made—their main idea and purpose, their supporting ideas or main points, their evidence to support each main point, and their listener relevance links. Good content, however, is not the only foundational component of effective public speeches: Content must be structured in a way that can easily be followed and must be delivered compellingly.

What Do You Think?

Based on the characteristics you identified about your audience members, what kinds of listener relevance links might you include in your first speech?

Technology Tip
http://www.presentations.com/deliver/speak/2000/04/30_sn_good.html

This Web page, hosted by Presentations.com, offers several tips for incorporating content.

Your First Speech

Content Checklist

1. Do your topic and purpose meet the expectations of the audience?
2. Have you limited your main points to between two and four?
3. Do you offer different kinds of evidence for each main point?
4. Do you provide listener relevance links throughout the speech?

What Does It Mean to Have Clear Structure?

The **structure** of your speech is the framework you use to organize your content. The structure guides your listeners as you talk so they can make sense of your ideas. To achieve clear structure, you should consider elements of macrostructure and of microstructure.

Macrostructure refers to the general framework for your content. In the most basic sense, the macrostructure of a public speech consists of an introduction, a body, and a conclusion. In a clearly organized speech, each of these serves a particular function:

1. *Introduction.* Tells them what you're going to tell them.
2. *Body.* Tells them.
3. *Conclusion.* Tells them what you told them.

When I explain these functions to beginning speakers, they sometimes complain that the approach seems like it would be redundant and would bore listeners. On the contrary, this approach is absolutely crucial for an effective public speech.

Teaching Tip
To illustrate how to utilize macrostructure, assign students to small groups and have them prepare a short presentation of their favorite sitcom character. Direct them to include all the elements of the introduction and conclusion, at least two main points, and transitions. This activity will help orient the students to the basic principles of speech construction and outlining. You could follow up this activity with a discussion of the microstructural choices speakers made when presenting the information.

Teaching Tip
Consider providing students with a sample outline containing all of the elements of the introduction, body, and conclusion. This is a particularly good idea for watchers because they learn most effectively by modeling desired communicative behaviors.

You see, public speaking is transitory. In other words, listeners can hear the message only once. Unlike readers, they cannot go back to an idea that has confused them. Consequently, speakers must take extra care to ensure that listeners do not get lost along the way. They help their listeners out by previewing their main points in the introduction and by restating them in the conclusion. Although it may feel awkward at first, you will soon learn that listeners appreciate clearly organized macrostructural elements.

Introduction

In your **introduction,** you gain the attention of your audience, announce your topic, and provide a brief road map of how you will proceed. In other words, you "tell them what you're going to tell them." An introduction must include an **attention catcher**—something that both grabs attention and tunes listeners in to the topic. You might use a *rhetorical question* (a question that requires no direct response), a *personal anecdote* (a short story about an experience you have had), a *famous quotation* related to your speech topic, or a *humorous* (yet tactful) *story.* Since listeners tend to be apathetic unless their curiosity is aroused, it is important to take the extra time to come up with a compelling attention catcher. A **thesis statement** is a one-sentence summary of the speech. It lets listeners know your general and specific purpose. A **preview** briefly mentions the two to four main points you will explain in the body of your speech. Remember, finally, that your introduction should also include a general listener relevance link connecting your topic and purpose to your listeners. Kris's basic introduction looked like this:

I. *Attention catcher.* Have you ever looked into a mirror, seen your reflection, and then realized that the reflection in the mirror wasn't really you? (Rhetorical question) This may seem a little strange to all of you, but this has actually happened to me many times throughout my life. (Personal anecdote)

II. *Listener relevance.* As you listen to my speech today, I believe you'll begin to understand how important I believe it is to forge friendships with ourselves, with our families, and with others.

III. *Thesis statement.* Today, I'd like to inform you a little bit about who I—Kris Treinen—am. (One-sentence summary letting listeners know the general and specific purpose)

IV. *Preview.* More specifically, let's talk about where I grew up, what makes me unique, and why I chose to come to NDSU for my college degree. (Brief mention of three main points)

Body

Discussion Tip
Have the students brainstorm potential transitional phrases. Discuss which are most/least effective.

The body of your speech is the place where you explain what you mean by each main point—that is, develop each main point with sufficient evidence and a listener relevance link. Within the body of the speech, successive main points are tied together by transitions. A **transition** is a statement that ties together main points by both providing verbal closure for one main point and introducing the next. Beginning speakers sometimes neglect the closure function of a transition statement, and this hurts the fluency of their message. "Next, I'll talk about . . . ," for example, is not an effective transition statement because it does not tie the two points together. Transition statements can be very simple; however, they must serve both functions to be effective. Kris, for example, offered this transition statement between her first and second main points:

Transition. Now that you know where I grew up, let's talk about what it is about my reflection in a mirror that makes me unique.

What Do You Think?

What are the main points for your first speech? Try to generate effective transitions between each of them.

Because she mentioned the first main point and sparked curiosity about the second, Kris's transition statement was effective.

Conclusion

In the conclusion of your public speech, you give listeners a sense of closure in a way that might help them remember your main topic and ideas. Hence, the conclusion restates the thesis statement, briefly summarizes the main points, and offers a clincher. In its simplest form, a **thesis restatement** merely reiterates the thesis statement in past tense. The **main point summary** reminds listeners of the two to four main points of your speech. The **clincher** provides closure to the speech and, at the same time, ties back to the introduction. In a conclusion, you "tell them what you told them." Kris's conclusion looked like this:

Teaching Tip
Show videotapes of students presenting speeches that illustrate both good and bad conclusions. Discuss these differences in class.

I. *Thesis restatement.* Today, I've offered some insight into who I—Kris Treinen—am.

II. *Main point summary.* We've talked about where I grew up, what makes me unique, and why I chose to come to NDSU.

III. *Clincher.* So now I hope you see why I have learned to look beyond the reflection I see in the mirror to understand who I am.

You develop the macrostructure of your public speech through outlines. You will actually create three different kinds of outlines for each speech you give. You begin with a **preparation outline,** a working rough draft of your speech ideas. In this outline, you list first versions of your thesis, preview, main points, and supporting material. Preparation outlines may or may not be typed, and they usually use key phrases rather than complete sentences. You'll revise your preparation outline several times while preparing your speech as you consider breadth, depth, listener relevance, and learning styles. From that preparation outline, you develop your formal outline. A **formal outline** uses complete sentences, internal references, and a complete reference list of any external sources used to develop the speech. Kris's formal outline looked like this:

Teaching Tip
Show a video of a sample speech and have students work in groups of four to develop an outline of the speech in class.

My Self-Introduction Speech

Kris Treinen

Introduction

I. *Attention catcher.* Have you ever looked into a mirror, seen your reflection, and then realized that the reflection in the mirror wasn't really you? This may seem a little strange to all of you, but this has actually happened to me many times throughout my life.

II. *Listener relevance.* As you listen to my speech today, I believe you'll begin to understand how important I believe it is to forge friendships with ourselves, with our families, and with others.

III. *Thesis statement.* Today, I'd like to inform you a little bit about who I—Kris Treinen—am.

IV. *Preview.* More specifically, let's talk about where I grew up, what makes me unique, and why I chose to come to NDSU for my college degree.

Body

I. *First main point.* I spent most of my life before coming to NDSU growing up in the Brainerd Lakes area. Perhaps you'll want to visit this area after you hear about it today (listener relevance link).

- **A.** I grew up in a small town called Nisswa, MN.
  - **1.** I moved to Nisswa when I was three years old.
  - **2.** We lived in a house that is very special to me.
- **B.** As I grew up, I attended different schools.
  - **1.** I went to elementary school in Nisswa.
  - **2.** I then attended and graduated from Brainerd High School with four hundred twenty-four other students.

Transition: Now that you know where I grew up, let's talk about what it is about my reflection in a mirror that makes me unique.

II. *Second main point.* Well, I had a mirror image while growing up and still have her today. Her name is Karla and she is my twin sister. Every day I am away from her, I realize how easy it was to take her and my family for granted (listener relevance).

- **A.** I am exactly three minutes older than my twin sister.
  - **1.** This is when were we born.
  - **2.** This is what was it like.
- **B.** We were known as the "good" twin and the "evil" twin.
  - **1.** Here is a story about me as the "good" twin.
  - **2.** Here is a story about Karla as the "evil" twin.

Transition: Now that you know about my unique characteristic—my role as a twin and my twin sister Karla—let's talk about why I chose to come to NDSU to earn my degree.

III. *Third main point.* I chose to further my education at NDSU. NDSU is a reputable school offering a variety of reputable degrees (listener relevance).

- **A.** I earned my first degree in 1992.
    - **1.** I earned this degree from Concordia College.
    - **2.** I realized I loved to learn and knew I wanted to learn more.
- **B.** I worked in various jobs.
    - **1.** I was in customer service.
    - **2.** I did radio broadcasting.
- **C.** I knew I wanted to do something more and NDSU was right for me.
    - **1.** NDSU has a reputable program.
    - **2.** NDSU is close to home.
    - **3.** I have friends at NDSU.

Conclusion

- **I.** *Thesis restatement.* Today, I've offered some insight into who I—Kris Treinen—am.
- **II.** *Main point summary.* We've talked about where I grew up, what makes me unique, and why I chose to come to NDSU.
- **III.** *Clincher.* So now I hope you see why I have learned to look beyond the reflection I see in the mirror to understand who I am.

From your formal outline, you develop a speaking outline. A **speaking outline** is a brief outline that you'll refer to while you present your speech. You might place this outline on index cards or on paper. However, it consists of key words and phrases rather than complete sentences. It also includes delivery cue reminders. Essentially, your speaking outline provides you with only the information you need to present the speech. Kris, for example, reminded herself to "slow down," to "look up," and to "pause" on her speaking outline (see Figure 3–1). Notice how Kris was able to use the same card for both her introduction and conclusion. She merely color-coded her attention catcher and clincher. Presenting your speech from a speaking outline rather than a formal outline helps ensure that you will speak extemporaneously and communicate with your listeners rather than perform in front of them or read to them.

Microstructure refers to language and style choices you make to convey your ideas. In making these choices, you should strive for language that is *clear, inclusive,* and *vivid.*

Recall that there are no second chances with oral presentations. Oral presentations must be understood completely on the first hearing. So choose words that are familiar, concrete, and simple, rather than unfamiliar, abstract, or complex. This is not to say that you "talk down" to your audience. Rather, try to be as precise as possible—precise language is clear—but make sure that being precise doesn't mean using words that will be unfamiliar to some in your audience. Kris talked about seeing her "reflection" in the mirror rather than merely about seeing her "face" in the mirror. The word "reflection" is more precise than "face," but it is still likely to be familiar to everyone in her audience. For this same reason, avoid jargon

FIGURE 3–1
Kris's Speaking Outline

PAUSE (1-2-3) BREATHE-----SMILE!!! ☺☺ 1
ATTN C: HAVE YOU EVER LOOKED INTO A MIRROR . . .
LR: FORGE FRIENDSHIPS, FRIENDS, FAMILY . . . SLOW DOWN
TODAY, I'M—INFORM YOU—WHO I // KRIS TREINEN // AM. ///
1-WHERE I GREW UP //
2-WHAT MAKES ME UNIQUE /// SPAN ROOM
3-WHY I CHOSE NDSU ///

LOOK UP
CLINCHER: (☺☺ PAUSE) SO, / NOW I HOPE YOU SEE WHY I'VE
LEARNED TO LOOK BEYOND THE REFLECTION IN THE MIRROR . . . . WHO
I AM (PAUSE!! SMILE!!!)

I. BRAINERD LAKES AREA EYE CONTACT 2
NISSWA / SPECIAL HOUSE // DIFFERENT SCHOOLS
TRANSITION: KNOW WHERE -----→ REFLECTION IN THE MIRROR
II. KARLA -- MIRROR
BIRTH STORY /// GOOD AND EVIL TWINS
TRANSITION: KNOW UNIQUE CHARACTERISTICS // WHY NDSU? //
III. NDSU REPUTABLE SCHOOL AND DEGREES
CONCORDIA / 1992 . . . . JOBS . . . . NDSU SPAN ROOM

WAIT! PAUSE! ☺

or slang unless you need it, and if you do use it, define the words the first time you use them so all members of your audience will understand what you mean.

Since public speaking is essentially a context for communication, it is important to use language that demonstrates respect for listeners as participants in the process. Strive to use language that is inclusive. First, whenever possible, use "we" language

Teaching Tip
Students often have a difficult time incorporating inclusive language in their speech. Provide an opportunity for students to practice their speeches in small groups prior to their graded presentation. This will help alleviate communication apprehension and allow students to receive constructive criticism in a nonthreatening environment.

One strategy for expressing effective language is to paint word pictures with vivid descriptions.

rather than "I" or "you" language. "We" language acknowledges the role listeners play in creating shared understanding. Kris, for example, offered "we" language at various points in her speech. Notice, for example, how her transitions incorporate "we" language: "Now that you know where I grew up, *let's* talk about what it is about my reflection in a mirror that makes me unique." Second, avoid biased language. Your goal is to reach everyone with your message. Because biased language marginalizes some members of your audience, it will prevent you from reaching this goal.

Finally, try to paint word pictures in your speech by offering vivid descriptions. Your goal is to use descriptive language that enables listeners to see in their minds precisely what you are seeing in yours. Kris referred to her "reflection" in the mirror rather than her "face" because "reflection" is not only more precise, but it is also more vivid. At minimum, the microstructure of an effective public speech will be clear, inclusive, and vivid.

Your First Speech

Structure Checklist

1. Does your attention catcher tune listeners in to the topic?
2. Do you offer a clear preview of your main points?
3. Does each transition verbally tie the two points together?
4. Do you restate your thesis statement and summarize you main points?
5. Does your clincher tie back to the introduction?
6. Is your language clear, yet precise?
7. Are your word choices vivid?
8. Do you use inclusive language?

What Does It Mean to Have Effective Delivery?

Technology Tip
http://www.presentersuniversity.com/courses/show_deapps.cfm?RecordID595
This Web page, hosted by Presenters University, provides several delivery tips.

To be effective, a public speech must also be delivered compellingly. In fact, listeners often are more persuaded by the manner in which we deliver public speeches than they are by the actual words. **Delivery** refers to how you present your message through your voice and body—that is, through your nonverbal communication cues. Your goal is to eliminate any nonverbal communication cues that might distract listeners from your message or in some way contradict the message, as well as to integrate throughout your speech nonverbal cues that reinforce important points or clarify structure. You can achieve this goal by considering (a) use of voice and (b) use of body.

Use of Voice

To deliver your first public speech, strive to be intelligible, conversational, and expressive. Speaking intelligibly means speaking in a way that allows your ideas to be understood easily by all. To be *intelligible,* you must use a generally appropriate rate (not too fast or too slow), volume (not too loud or too soft), and pitch (not too high or too low), which will allow your ideas to be understood easily by all.

Conversational delivery occurs when you sound as though you are talking with your listeners rather than reading to them or presenting in front of them. To be *conversational,* you must *sound spontaneous*—no matter how many times you rehearsed the speech and no matter how much of it you memorized or are reading from your notes.

Expressiveness is a matter of vocal variety. To be *expressive,* you must vary your voice over the course of your speech so you sound a bit more dramatic than you would in casual conversation, without sounding melodramatic. In other words, while sounding conversational, you vary your rate, pitch, and volume to underscore your attitudes and emotional convictions; and you stress key words and phrases and pause strategically before, during, or after important ideas to make them stand out for your listeners. Kris, for example, paused during her thesis statement to help make her name stand out for her listeners. She said, "Today (pause), I'd like to inform you a little bit about who I (pause) Kris Treinen (pause) am." She also stressed key words when describing her and her sister as the "good" and the "evil" twin. She exclaimed, "*Luckily* for *me* (pause), *I* was labeled the *good* twin. Unfortunately, though, this meant my sister was saddled with the label (pause) the *evil* (pause) twin."

An intelligible, conversational, and expressive voice, then, is similar to the voice we use in casual conversation because we sound spontaneous. It differs, though in that it is *heightened* and *flexible* in ways that make your message sound more compelling to listeners.

Use of Body

Teaching Tip
Have students write a one-page paper describing why they think nonverbal communication is important. Have them consider what functions nonverbal communication serves and what problems can result when nonverbals are misunderstood.

To deliver your first public speech, you must consider how your eyes, face, stance, and hands communicate. **Eye contact**—that is, looking at the audience—is crucial. First, make sure you use your notes just as references; refer to them less than 10 percent of the time. To effectively convey commitment to your audience, you need to show them that they are more important to you than your notes. You do this by looking up from your notes at least 90 percent of the time. Second, you need to span the entire audience. Be sure to look not just at listeners in the center of the room, but also at those who are seated in far corners or in the front or the back. If you don't do this, some listeners might feel ignored or marginalized. Finally, to create a sense of connection with your listeners, look them in the eyes until your feel a sense of response coming back from them. Since much of our communication occurs with our eyes, it is important that your listeners feel this connection to you. It is generally a good idea to remind yourself in your notes to make eye contact. Kris, for example, reminded herself to "look up," to "make eye contact," and to "span the entire room" on her speaking outline.

Try to make your facial expressions reflect your conviction to the topic. As with your voice, you shouldn't exaggerate. But if you speak without much facial expression, you'll convey a lack of commitment to the topic and occasion.

You want your stance to express poise. Plant yourself firmly before you begin the speech, maintain this stance throughout the speech, and on finishing, wait a moment or two before returning to your chair. A stance that communicates poise is one with your feet about shoulder width apart, no leaning on either leg, and knees slightly bent. You might remind yourself about stance in the form of a delivery cue on your speaking outline.

Make sure any gestures you use reinforce an important point or clarify structure. Kris, for example, gestured as she previewed each main point of her speech. Doing so helped clarify her structure. Plan and practice these gestures in advance. Practice your gestures while seated at a table to make sure they extend from the elbow rather than from the wrist. Also, be sure to avoid putting your hands in your pockets, fidgeting with your notes, or playing with your hair. These behaviors distract listeners from the ideas you are trying to convey. The key is to let your hands rest on your notes or at your sides unless you are using them to emphasize an important idea.

Teaching Tip
Have students write a one-page paper describing why they think nonverbal communication is important. Have them consider what functions nonverbal communication serves and what problems can be caused when nonverbals are misunderstood.

Beginning speakers are often more anxious about delivery than they are about structure or content. This greater anxiety is usually rooted in a fear of the unknown. The only way you can eliminate it is to practice delivering your speech. You might ask a few close friends to listen and offer suggestions. You might present your speech to yourself in front of a mirror. You might even videotape yourself. But you must rehearse delivery to present an effective public speech.

Your First Speech

Delivery Checklist

1. Do you sound conversational?
2. Do you stress key words?
3. Do you incorporate pauses to reinforce the message?
4. Do you look up 90 percent of the time?
5. Do you connect with listeners?
6. Do you span the entire room?
7. Do you plant yourself firmly before beginning and throughout the speech?
8. Do your gestures extend from the elbow?

Teaching Tip
Show videos of student speeches and critique them in class. In addition, it is a good idea to ask students to evaluate the speeches using the communication concepts presented in this chapter (content, structure, effective delivery, etc.). This activity can help reduce uncertainty and anxiety about the first speech by exposing students to the criteria you will use to evaluate their speeches.

Summary

These basic elements of content, structure, and delivery are the basis upon which effective public speeches are built. As you develop your first speech, take the time to consider your listeners as they relate to each of these three elements of public speaking, and your first speech will be successful. Key principles to guide your content include selecting your topic and purpose, choosing different kinds of evidence, and providing listener relevance links throughout. The key to effective structure centers on the macrostructural elements in the introduction, the body, and the conclusion, as well as the microstructural elements of language and style. The key to effective delivery has to do with conveying your ideas in ways that reinforce the verbal message without distracting or contradicting it. You do so by considering your use of voice and use of body. The remaining chapters of the text are devoted to deeper discussions of these basic principles of effective public speaking—that is, audience-centered content, structure, and delivery.

Activities

1. **Speech of Self-Introduction.** Prepare and present a two- to three-minute speech introducing yourself to the class. Develop your main points around aspects of your personal background, some unique characteristic or experience, and professional goals. Evidence to support each main point can come from personal life experiences you've had. Deliver your speech from a speaking outline on index cards.
2. **Introduce a Classmate.** Interview a classmate to discover his or her personal background, a unique characteristic or experience, and professional goals. Evidence to support each main point can come from personal life experiences your classmate has had. Deliver an introduction speech of him or her in the form of a two- to three-minute speech using a speaking outline on index cards.
3. **Personal Significance Speech.** Prepare and present a three- to five-minute speech informing your class about an object, a person, an event, or a belief that has helped shape who you are today. Main points should focus on specific values you hold that are somehow represented by that object, person, event, or belief. Evidence to support each main point should come from personal life experiences you've had. Listeners should leave knowing why the topic is personally significant to you. Deliver your speech using a speaking outline on index cards.

Key Terms

Attention catcher
Audience-centered
Breadth
Clincher
Content
Delivery
Depth
Evidence
Eye contact
Formal outline
General purpose
Introduction

Listener relevance link
Macrostructure
Main point summary
Main topic
Microstructure
Preparation outline
Preview
Speaking outline
Specific purpose
Structure
Thesis restatement
Thesis statement
Transition

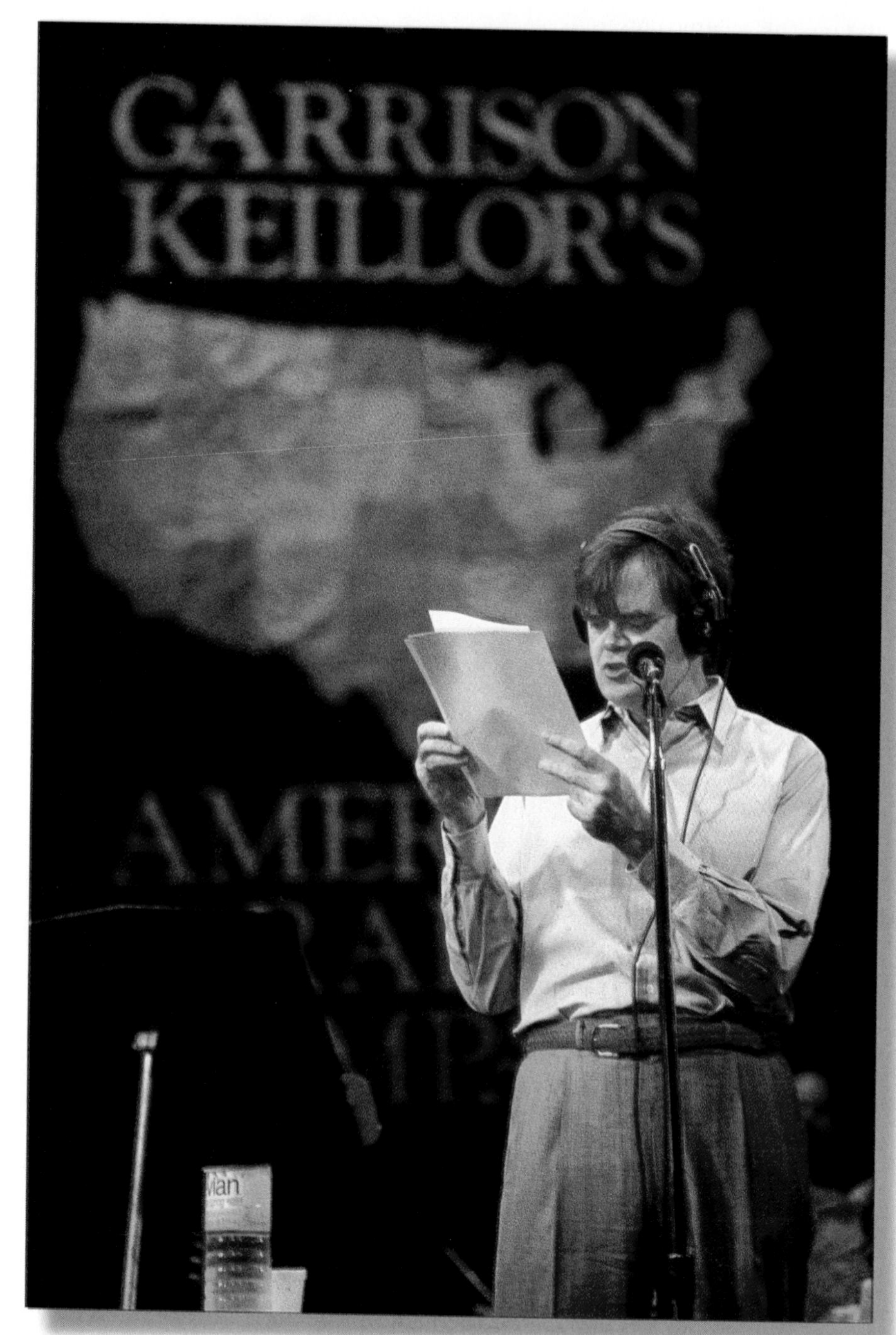
GARRISON
KEILLOR'S

CHAPTER 4

Listening and Critiquing Communication

Reflective Questions

1. What is the difference between listening and hearing?
2. What is critical listening?
3. Why do you have trouble listening well?
4. How can you improve your listening habits?
5. What does it mean to be an ethical listener?
6. In what ways is critiquing more than listening?
7. What does it mean to be an ethical critic?

Bekka was very excited to be starting her job as a public relations specialist with one of the city's most successful health care networks. Quite frankly, it was her dream job. She could hardly believe she was sitting in the corporate boardroom listening to the CEO reveal the strategy for a new marketing program. The view from the room was beautiful. She marveled at the cityscape skyline outside.

Bekka learned that she and the other five public relations specialists would be solely responsible for implementing the program. The CEO had a particularly soft voice for this large room and Bekka strained to hear. She wondered why there was no microphone in the room. Bekka decided to telephone her mother that evening to tell her how perfect this position was turning out to be.

Teaching Tip
Before a class discussion on the topic of listening, ask students to write down three to five assumptions they have about the listening process. Ask students to share their lists with the rest of the class. Discuss the textbook information about the listening process and then ask students to identify their own accurate and inaccurate assumptions about listening.

The CEO explained that each specialist would be assigned to a particular sector of the city and would be solely responsible for developing and implementing an effective public relations campaign in that sector. Bekka noticed that the CEO's speaking style was pretty poor. It reminded her of a very boring high school teacher she once had. The person sitting next to Bekka was chewing gum. It annoyed her. She made a mental note *not* to chew gum at the office. Bekka hoped she would not be assigned to Sector 3. That was traditionally a tough area for marketing health care.

As the CEO continued, Bekka felt her stomach grumble. She made another mental note. Don't skip breakfast. Suddenly, she noticed the room was quiet. She looked around to discover that all eyes were on her. The CEO was waiting for her answer. The problem, of course, was that Bekka didn't know the question. Embarrassed, Bekka felt her face flush as she replied in the only way she could: "I'm sorry. Could you repeat the question?"

Later that evening, Bekka did telephone her mother. But what she had to say wasn't so "perfect" after all.

Although Bekka had good intentions and she wanted to make a favorable first impression, she fell victim to poor listening. She is not alone. Research suggests that even when trying to listen carefully, most people remember only about 50 percent of what they have heard shortly after they have heard it and they remember only about 25 percent two days later (e.g., DeWine & Daniels, 1993; Stiel, Barker, & Watson, 1983).

There are many potential distractions in any listening situation.

Unfortunately, most people are poor listeners even though ineffective listening can hurt us personally and professionally. If we are honest with ourselves, we all can probably identify at least one time when ineffective listening caused us problems in a personal or professional relationship. If effective listening is so important to our personal and professional success, why aren't we better at it? In this chapter, we will explore answers to that question.

The chapter starts with a discussion of what listening is and why it plays such an important role in communication transactions. Then it examines the different types of listening and how understanding these types can help us become more effective listeners. The third section highlights what it means to be an ethical listener and provides specific strategies for improving listening skills. Recall from Chapter 1 that ethical decisions are rooted in the virtues of respect and honesty. These virtues provide the basis for our ethical decisions, not only as public speakers but as listeners and critics as well. The chapter ends with a discussion of the characteristics of a critique, what it means to be an ethical critic, and one method for critiquing.

Teaching Tip
Have students keep a personal journal of their listening activities for a full day. The journal should include brief descriptions of all listening situations they experienced during that day. It should also include analysis of how well the student listened in each situation, and why she or he did not listen effectively in each situation.

What Is Listening and Why Is It Important?

People sometimes make the mistake of thinking that listening and hearing are basically the same thing. They are not. **Hearing** is a physiological process, whereas listening is a psychological process. Hearing is nothing more than a biological function of our bodies. Listening, on the other hand, occurs only when we mindfully choose to attach meaning to what we hear. In other words, I can *hear* you without *listening* to you. In order to listen to you, however, I must first be able to hear you. So hearing is a necessary component of listening, but listening entails the added dimension of psychological processing (e.g., Halone, Cunconan, Coakley, & Wolvin, 1998).

Teaching Tip
List the communication skills people use, rank-ordered from most to least (listen, speak, read, write). Then list the skills taught in school, rank-ordered from most to least (write, read, speak, listen). What conclusions can you draw from this information?

Consider the following example. In the city where I live, the emergency sirens are tested at noon on the first Wednesday of each month. People can hear these sirens throughout the city. Whether I am in my home, or at the office, or outdoors, I hear the sirens. If I hear the sirens and continue doing what I'm doing without thinking about what they mean, I have merely *heard* them. But if I also consider whether they are being sounded as part of the monthly testing or as a real emergency, then I have added the dimension of mental processing. Hence, I am not only hearing but also listening. **Listening** can be defined, then, as the psychological process of receiving (hearing), attending to, constructing meaning from, and responding to spoken or nonverbal messages (International Listening Association, 1996).

Technology Tip
http://www.listen.org

Explore the International Listening Association Web site. This site contains quotes about listening, a listening bibliography, and several listening exercises.

What Do You Think?

Identify a time when you heard a message but didn't really listen. What was the result?

Listening skills are vitally important to our relationships because so much of our communication time is spent listening. Essentially, we communicate by speaking, listening, reading, and writing. As Figure 4–1 reveals, we spend more time listening than we spend engaged in all of the other forms of communication combined: 55 percent of the time we spend listening compared to 24 percent speaking, 13 percent reading, and 8 percent writing (Watson & Barker, 1984). In college, you'll spend about 90 percent of your class

FIGURE 4–1
Communication Process Breakdown

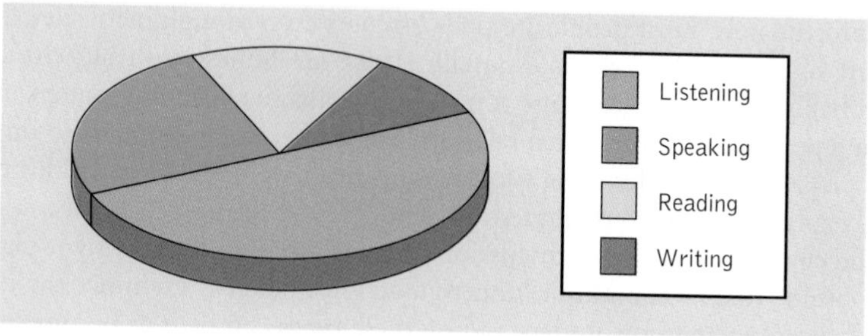

time engaged in listening (Coakley & Wolvin, 1991). Not surprisingly, studies show that students who listen more effectively learn better and, as a result, earn better grades than those who don't (Barker, Edwards, Gaines, & Holley, 1980; Hunsaker, 1991; Legge, 1971).

> ***What Do You Think?***
>
> *Consider the classes you are currently taking. How often do you speak and for how long? Do you ask questions or discuss issues? How often do other students speak? How much time is spent listening to the professor and to the other students?*

Effective listening skills are also vital for you as a professional. Research suggests that employees spend 55 to 60 percent of their time listening and that poor listening skills can add up to billion dollar mistakes. Many employers recognize this fact and offer listening training to their employees (e.g., Hiam, 1997; Linowes, 1998; Wolvin & Coakley, 1991). Moreover, a survey of top-level North American executives revealed that 80 percent believe listening is one of the most important skills needed in the corporate environment (Salopek, 1999). It simply makes sense to improve listening skills.

Types of Listening: Considering Your Purpose

Whether you are communicating with others at home, school, work, or someplace else, you can be sure that most your time will be spent listening. To listen effectively, you must consider your listening purpose for that situation. For example, you might listen to a friend give you directions to a favorite restaurant, or vent about a recent argument, or even rehearse an upcoming public speech. In each case, your listening purpose differs.

Teaching Tip
Have students bring copies of print advertisements to class. As they analyze the ads in groups, ask them to practice critical listening skills.

There are five different types of listening based on these different purposes: discriminative, comprehensive, appreciative, empathic, and critical (Wolvin & Coakley, 1992). Each type of listening demands a different degree of psychological processing. The most demanding type is critical listening. Critical listening requires us to hear, understand, evaluate, and assign worth to a message. Since we spend so much time listening, it is not feasible or necessary to engage in critical listening all the time. Hence, you ought to consider your purpose and then engage in the most appropriate type of listening for that situation. Let's look at each type as it relates to purpose.

Discriminative listening is "listening between the lines" for meaning conveyed other than through the words themselves. In other words, discriminative listening has to do with being attentive to what is said via verbal and nonverbal cues like rate, pitch, inflection, volume, quality, inflection, and so forth. Discriminative listening also includes considering the meaning behind behaviors accompanying the message, such as laughing, sighing, and yawning.

> ### *What Do You Think?*
> *Identify a time when someone lied to you. Did you suspect they were lying before you found out? What specific things about the way they talked or behaved led you to your assumption?*

Paying attention to slips of the tongue and vocalized pauses like "ums" and "uhs" as they might indicate deception are also aspects of discriminative listening. Parents trying to resolve a conflict between their children sometimes decipher meaning as much from what is *not said* as what *is said.*

Business executives also often engage in discriminative listening to determine underlying issues when dealing with their employees (Linowes, 1998). Likewise, citizens listening to political speeches sometimes make inferences about unstated matters based on what the speaker *does* offer.

Comprehensive listening is listening for understanding. It is appropriate when your purpose is to gain knowledge and retain it. You concentrate on the message in order to understand it, not to make any critical judgment of it. Realize, though, that you must physically hear as well as psychologically discriminate verbal and nonverbal messages in order to understand the meaning accurately.

We engage in comprehensive listening frequently both in our personal and professional lives. For example, in our professional lives, we listen comprehensively to speakers at seminars, conferences, and symposiums, as well as to professors when they lecture in class. In our personal lives, we listen comprehensively to radio and television news reporters talk about recent events. We listen comprehensively to family members describe their day. We listen comprehensively to physicians explain a diagnosis. And the list goes on.

> ### *What Do You Think?*
> *Do you ever turn on the radio or television in the morning to decide what to wear that day? If so, why?*

> **Discussion Tip**
> Ask students to identify several examples of contexts in which they are required to listen comprehensively. Are the types of listening discussed in this chapter mutually exclusive?

Appreciative listening is the process of listening for enjoyment through the works and experiences of others (Wolvin & Coakley, 1992). Appreciative listening can include listening to music, environmental sounds, and a public speaker's oral style. When you engage in appreciative listening, your purpose is to savor the power and beauty of well-chosen and articulated spoken words or music.

> ### *What Do You Think?*
> *Identify a public speaker who you think uses a "beautiful" oral style (a preacher, teacher, television news broadcaster, actor, professional speaker, etc.). Why do you appreciate listening to him or her?*

Listening to music is a prime example of appreciative listening. Whether you enjoy rock, pop, hip-hop, country, classical, or some other genre, the fact that you have such preferences suggests you engage in appreciative listening when you turn on the radio or play a CD. Some people also listen appreciatively to environmental sounds. I enjoy camping with my family every summer. One important reason has to do with the sounds I get to hear, like birds and crickets and even the breeze whistling through the trees. This, too, is appreciative listening. You can also listen appreciatively to the oral style of public speakers. Consider the oral style of Martin Luther King, Jr., as he delivered his famous "I Have a Dream" speech. I personally enjoy listening to the *Prairie Home Companion* radio program because I love Garrison Keillor's oral style. My friend Kathy enjoys listening to baseball games on the radio for similar reasons. She doesn't listen to understand who's winning and losing, but for the sound of a game being announced.

Empathic listening is the process of listening to support, help, and empathize with the speaker. Empathic listening is what you do when you listen to a friend vent about a problem or concern. You are essentially a sounding board for your friend as he or she sorts through an issue out loud. Usually, the goal of empathic listening is to lend support, not advice. Empathic listening requires a good deal of psychological processing on your part. This is because you must initially discriminate the verbal and nonverbal messages being sent and then comprehend those messages before you can engage in effective empathic listening.

Empathic listening occurs most often in our interpersonal relationships. Therapists, counselors, psychologists, and psychiatrists also engage in empathic listening with their clients.

Discussion Tip
Ask students to reflect upon occasions when they realized others were not listening to them. How did they come to this realization? How did it make them feel?

What Do You Think?

Have you ever vented to a close friend about someone or something that was bothering you? Were you seeking advice or seeking support? How did your friend respond and what was the result?

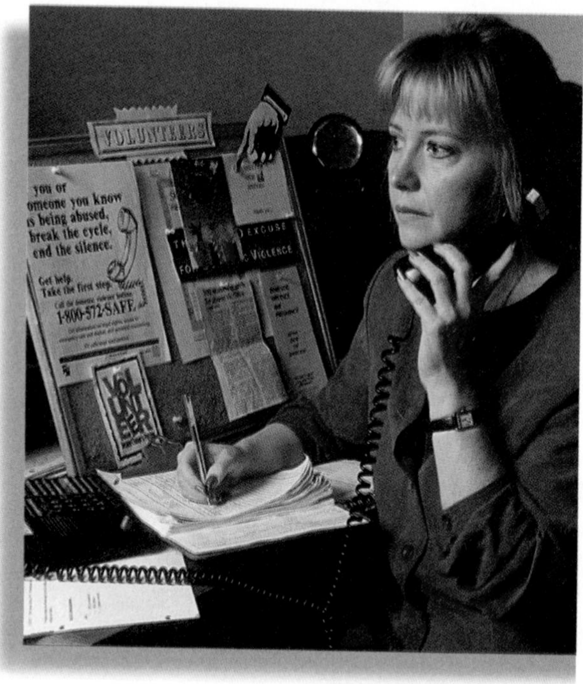

Hotline telephone volunteers engage in empathic listening.

Likewise, people who answer telephone hotlines to support troubled teens and adults also engage in empathic listening (e.g., Gunderson, 1999; Morgan, 1983).

Critical listening is the process of hearing, understanding, evaluating, and assigning worth to a message. Critical listening is appropriate when your goal is to think deeply and react analytically to a message. For example, you'll want to use critical listening when someone seeks your opinion about an issue, when you are being asked to assume a good deal of responsibility, or when you are trying to become an expert on an issue. To listen most effectively to public speakers, you should engage in critical listening. You may even want to do so when listening to your professors lecture. Why? Well, research suggests students who listen comprehensively without evaluating or reacting will forget most of the material shortly after completing the course (Luiten, Ames, & Ackerman, 1980).

Because so much time is spent listening and because critical listening demands so much effort, it is not possible to engage in critical listening all of the time. Hence, it is important to examine the situation and engage in the most appropriate type of listening for your purpose.

> ***What Do You Think?***
>
> *Identify a time in your life when you should have engaged in critical listening based on this definition. Were you successful? What was the result?*

Teaching Tip
While discussing mechanisms for improving listening, suddenly interrupt yourself and ask the class to draw a dog (any object will do). Allow approximately thirty seconds for the art work. Ask the students to place the drawings in their notebooks and resume the discussion. Students seldom ask questions about the assignment. When one does ask a question, indicate that you merely wanted to teach the class that one of the ways of improving listening is to ask questions.

The SIER Model of Critical Listening

One model that can help you understand the dimensions of critical thinking is the **SIER model** (Ross, 1983, p. 99). The SIER model shows how critical listening depends on a four-step process that begins with hearing. As Figure 4–2 highlights,

Discussion Tip
Ask students to identify potential obstacles to sensing messages. What can be done to limit these obstacles?

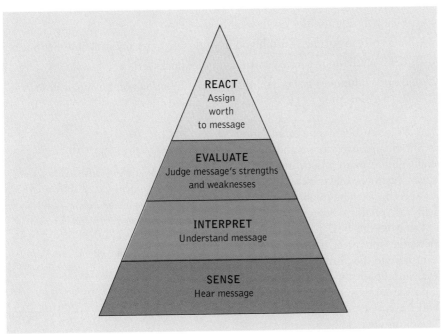

FIGURE 4–2
The SIER Model of Critical Listening

these four steps are *sense, interpret, evaluate,* and *react.* Let's discuss each of these steps and the potential obstacles you must overcome in order to ultimately achieve effective critical listening (*Active Listening,* 1997).

The first step is sensing, or simply hearing, the message. Several potential obstacles must be overcome at this level in order to proceed to the next stage. These obstacles may originate in the speaker, environment, or listener. One potential obstacle, for example, might be inadequate volume by the speaker. Debbie, although a very articulate speaker, is so quiet that only those sitting in the first few rows can make out what she is saying. Another potential obstacle might be environmental sounds, which can overpower the message, for example, loud ceiling fans, radios, or traffic noises. When one public speaking class took advantage of a nice day to go to a park, students discovered how difficult it was to be heard over the roar of traffic. Yet another obstacle might be a hearing disability in the listener. Any of these potential obstacles could prohibit you from hearing the message and, ultimately, make it impossible to listen critically.

If you can hear the message, the second step is to interpret—that is, understand it. This step involves listening comprehensively. One potential obstacle to interpretation is not knowing the language that is being spoken. Or you might know the language but not be familiar with the dialect or accent. Even unfamiliar slang or technical jargon can impede understanding. Have you ever sat through a lecture where the professor used technical jargon without defining it or assumed you understood the basic principles when you didn't? I remember being placed in a senior-level political science course as a first-year undergraduate. The professor assumed all of the students had a fundamental understanding of political science concepts, but I did not have that understanding and could not effectively interpret what he was telling us.

Sometimes a speaker's failure to enunciate clearly can act as a barrier to interpreting a message. **Enunciation** has to do with how crisply we form our vowels and consonants. For example, imagine the following conversation:

Ben: D'ja wannuh glassuh waduh?

John: Don'go'time. Gottuh goduh work 'cuz I owe my dad a hunner bucks.

Ben: Wha'duh ya' owe yer dad a hunner bucks fer?

John: I dunno. I guessee thinks I shoulduh botmah ohn fishin' license 'er somepin.

We often use sloppy enunciation in informal conversations and it generally doesn't matter. But if we were to speak this way while presenting a public speech, listeners might have problems interpreting our message.

If you can hear (sense) and understand (interpret) the message, you can move to the third step, which is to evaluate the message. When you evaluate a message, you judge its strengths and weaknesses, determine whether you agree or disagree, and decide whether you like or dislike it.

What Do You Think?

Recall a time when you tried to listen to a public speaker but couldn't understand what he or she was saying. Why couldn't you understand the speaker? Did she or he use unfamiliar jargon or slang? Did she or he use sloppy enunciation?

Critical listening sometimes breaks down at this step because we prejudge the speaker as lacking credibility. Have you ever decided a teacher was not very intelligent because he or she appeared disheveled or disorganized? If so, you encountered an obstacle at the evaluation step: Your feelings about the speaker prevented you from judging the message fairly. Strong feelings about the message can also be an obstacle. When we have strong feelings, we're often tempted to mentally argue with the speaker instead of evaluating the speaker's message. For example, Lenny disagreed with Jill's argument that alcohol should be allowed in campus dorms. While there is nothing inherently wrong with disagreeing, Lenny chose to mentally defend his own position throughout the speech rather than to listen open-mindedly to Jill's reasons and then formulate a response. Had Lenny listened to Jill and saved his judgment until the end, he could have engaged in effective evaluation.

Once you have evaluated a message, you can move to the final step in the SIER model of critical listening: react. When you react to a message, you assign worth to it. You go beyond merely judging its strengths and weaknesses to determine the ways in which you and others who may have heard the message are better off for having heard it. In other words, you answer the following questions:

1. In what way or ways am I better off for having heard this message?

And when the message is delivered to others as well as you:

2. How might this message benefit others in this room?

The potential obstacle you must overcome to react successfully is the tendency to conclude that the communication was of no value to you. If the message is in the form of public communication, you must also overcome the potential obstacle of assuming the message was of no value to others who may have heard it. You cannot tell yourself that you gained nothing from the listening experience. In other words, effective critical listeners ask themselves "What's in it for me?" and *find something.*

Often you'll discover that you've benefited from the content of the message. For example, you might have learned about some new concept, idea, or process. Or the speaker might have presented some statistics or evidence you had not been aware of or addressed a familiar topic in a new way. Sometimes, however, the content offers you no new information or insight. This happened to Wanda when she listened to Marcus talk about the process of changing a flat tire. Wanda was working her way through school as an automobile mechanic, so the content of Marcus's speech was all too familiar to her. But Wanda could also *react* by considering how the audience might benefit from the content. Wanda decided that since most of her classmates had probably never changed a flat tire, the content was worthwhile because it benefited most listeners.

You can also react to a message by assigning worth based on the speaker's delivery. For example, you can decide you're better off for having heard a speech because the delivery was effective. Marcus, for example, used eye contact and facial expressions in ways that made it seem like he was sincerely talking to each member of his audience. Wanda made a mental note to try to emulate Marcus's use of eye contact and facial expressions.

Likewise, you can decide you're better off for having heard a speaker use effective structure. Wanda also liked how Marcus tied together his attention catcher and clincher by using a hypothetical story as the opening attention catcher and offering an ending to the story in his clincher. She decided she'd try to do something just as clever with her own attention catcher and clincher.

You can also decide you're better off for having heard a speaker whose delivery or structure was ineffective. Wanda, for example, had a difficult time following Marcus's organization because his transitions did not verbally tie his points together. Wanda made a mental note to be sure to use transitions that verbally tied together her points. These kinds of reactions about a speaker's ineffective delivery or structure are also legitimate answers to the reaction questions in the SIER model of critical listening.

By representing critical listening as a four-step process, the SIER model provides several important insights: It shows how hearing is only the first step in the process of listening. It also shows how we can listen to different extents, as well as where and why our efforts to listen critically may break down.

Once you see the steps involved in critical listening, and the obstacles to critical listening, you can understand why we don't always succeed as critical listeners. When you also consider the percentage of communication time we spend listening, the task of listening might seem rather daunting. In fact, we would certainly burn out if we tried to engage in critical listening all the time. However, critical listening is not always necessary. An effective listener considers the purpose and employs the most appropriate type of listening to achieve his or her goal.

The Ethical Listener: Tips for Improving Critical Listening Skills

Research shows us that critical listening is both important and difficult—that we grasp only about 50 percent of what we hear. Fortunately, research also suggests that we can improve our ability to listen effectively by employing certain strategies. Moreover, ethical listeners constantly strive to improve their listening skills. Why? Recall our discussion in Chapter 1 where we defined an ethical choice as something we believe we "ought" to do rather than something we "have" to do. We talked about two fundamental virtues that guide our ethical decisions: respect and honesty. You must strive to improve your listening skills to honestly demonstrate respect for yourself and for the speaker.

This section discusses six of the most common bad habits that may hurt your ability to listen effectively. For each one, we'll look at reasons people fall victim to the bad habit and offer a strategy you might employ to eliminate it. As you read, consider which habits plague you most often and the types of situations where they tend to occur. Highlight at least one strategy you might use to improve your critical listening skills with regard to that habit.

Discussion Tip
Ask students to list three situations in which they experienced at least one of the poor listening habits presented in this chapter. Have students identify why they utilized these habits. In addition, encourage them to consider how they could use the strategies presented in the text to avoid poor listening habits in the future.

Bad Habits

1. Becoming distracted.
2. Faking attention.
3. Being unprepared.
4. Prejudging the speaker.
5. Mentally arguing and jumping to conclusions.
6. Listening too hard.

Bad Habit Number 1: Becoming Distracted

Becoming distracted is probably the most common bad habit that results in poor listening. Distractions may be mental, physical, auditory, or visual. Consider again the story of Bekka from the beginning of this chapter. Bekka's poor listening came as a result of becoming distracted.

While listening to the CEO, Bekka became mentally distracted when she contemplated telephoning her mother and then again when she wondered which sector she would be assigned. **Mental distractions** are simply the wandering thoughts you have when you ought to be listening to a message.

Bekka was physically distracted when she felt her stomach grumble because she had skipped breakfast. **Physical distractions** are those associated with body aches, pains, and feelings. Bekka was visually distracted by the view from the boardroom window. And Bekka experienced both a visual and auditory distraction when she became annoyed with the person who was chewing gum. **Visual distractions** are those associated with something you see, and **auditory distractions** are those associated with something you hear.

The reason we become distracted so easily has to do with the speed at which we speak and process information: Most people speak at a rate of one hundred twenty to one hundred fifty words per minute, yet our brains can process between four hundred and eight hundred words per minute (Wolvin & Coakley, 1992). What this means is that listeners usually assume we know what a speaker is going to say before she or he finishes saying it. Because you are able to comprehend so quickly what a speaker is saying, your mind has time to wander. The resulting distractions can cause you to lose your focus on the message.

Teaching Tip
Assign the "resisting distractions" exercise contained in the Activities section of this chapter.

The problem is compounded when the speaker talks more slowly than one hundred twenty words per minute (Mayer, 1996). Have you ever tried to listen carefully to someone who speaks slowly? If you are like me, you want to finish their sentences for them. In any case, with slow speakers, the chances for becoming distracted are even greater.

A Strategy: Expend Energy

Perhaps the most important strategy you can develop to improve your listening skills is to expend energy (e.g., Horowitz, 1996; Kaye, 1998; Mulvany, 1998). Expending energy means sitting up straight, leaning forward, and maintaining eye contact. Since our brains do process information more quickly than we speak, listeners must do whatever possible to stay focused. You need to expend energy at the beginning of the speech and then periodically check yourself to make sure you have not started to relax. If you've begun to drift, you need to reel yourself back in. Of course, you can engage in these behaviors and still become distracted; however, distractions are less likely when you are making a conscious attempt to remain alert than when you are slouching, leaning back, or closing your eyes.

As Marsha's classmate presented an informative speech about the Amish, for example, Marsha rested her head in her hands and closed her eyes. When the professor asked her to pay attention, she responded, "I am listening. I'm just resting my eyes." Perhaps Marsha was trying to listen; however, her lack of energy would undoubtedly encourage her mind to wander as the speech progressed.

PEANUTS reprinted by permission of United Feature Syndicate, Inc.

Bad Habit Number 2: Faking Attention

Discussion Tip
Ask your students to name three times and situations when they have the most difficulty staying focused.

Most of us have been trained to believe that as listeners we should look the speaker in the eye, nod periodically as he or she speaks, lean forward a bit in our chairs, and so forth. Our parents and teachers told us that practicing these confirming behaviors demonstrates respect for the speaker (Cissna & Sieburg, 1981). They were right. Unfortunately, however, many of us have learned to practice confirming behaviors even when we are not really listening. In other words, we fake attention. Although faking attention is useful to us on occasion, it also can cause us to miss important information and even to botch a personal or professional relationship.

Consider the following conversation between Davey and Brad. Davey had just engaged in a terrible argument with his girlfriend. In fact, she had broken off their engagement, claiming that he was insensitive and didn't respect her freedom. Davey decided to consult his best friend, Brad.

> ***What Do You Think?***
> *Think about one or more times when you slipped into the bad habit of faking attention. What was the situation? What were the consequences?*

Davey: Brad, I don't know what to do. I feel absolutely awful.

Brad: [*Nods.*]

Davey: On the one hand, I want Carol to know I respect her freedom, but on the other hand, I want her to know I can't live without her.

Brad: [*Nods again and leans forward.*]

Davey: Maybe I should just let her go. If she really cares about me, she'll come back. Or maybe I should go to her place and try to talk to her again? What do you think?

Brad: Sounds like a plan to me.

Brad was practicing confirming behaviors, but had not really listened to Davey at all.

Engaging in this bad habit also can result in missed information. Recall that this happened to Bekka who appeared to be listening to her CEO. She looked attentive and nodded as she spoke. But since she was faking attention, she was forced to ask, "Could you repeat the question?"

Teaching Tip
Extant research suggests that some learners find it particularly difficult to take structured notes as a function of their learning style. Thus, teachers may want to consider providing students with external organizational aids while presenting information (e.g., outline your lectures either on an overhead projector or a blackboard, or present students with a handout). Also, the strategies presented in this chapter will help students sharpen their note-taking skills.

A Strategy: Take Notes

One fairly effective way to avoid slipping into the bad habit of faking attention is to take notes (Bostrom, 1990; Kiewra et al., 1988; Messmer, 1998). Effective note- taking can help you in a number of other ways as well. It can reduce your tendency to

FIGURE 4–3 Outlining Method of Note-Taking

Introduction

I. Thesis: The SIER model of critical listening

II. Preview: It has four steps

Body

I. Main point number 1: First step is to sense

- **A.** Supporting material: This means you can physically hear it
- **B.** Supporting material: Obstacles occur in the speaker, listener, or environment

II. Main point number 2: Second step is to Interpret

- **A.** Supporting material: This means you understand it
- **B.** Supporting material: Obstacles include . . . etc.

become distracted from the message. It can also make you more aware of the organizational patterns of the speech. For these and other reasons, effective note-taking can increase the probability that you'll remember the information in the message.

Unfortunately, ineffective note taking can do more harm than good and few people are taught how to take effective notes. The most important thing to remember when taking notes is to be flexible in order to (a) adjust to the speaker's presentational style and (b) connect ideas to your own life experiences. If a speaker makes a claim and supports it with several examples from his or her own life, your notes might be more helpful to you if you embellish some of the speaker's examples with your own. Then when you review your notes days or weeks later, examples that relate the ideas directly to your own life might better crystallize the speech for you (Miccinati, 1988).

There are a number of methods of note taking. Because each method has its own strengths and weaknesses, you should experiment with different methods to discover which is most helpful to you. The most common method is outlining (see Figure 4–3). Outlining is effective if the structure is clear. When the speaker does not use a clear structural pattern, you might consider using the precis method (see Figure 4–4) or the organizational mapping method (see Figure 4–5). With the precis method, every few minutes you mentally summarize what you've listened to and record your summary. You should record your summaries quickly, using short phrases and incomplete sentences, so you'll be less likely to miss an important idea while you are writing. You can always go back to your notes and complete the sentences later. With the organizational mapping method, you write down each main idea as it is presented and draw a circle around it. When a significant detail,

Technology Tip
http://www.csbsju.edu/academicadvising/help/eff-list.html

This Web page contains a guide to effective note-taking using "the five R's of note taking." The site is hosted by the Department of Academic Advising Services at the College of St. Benedict/St. John's University.

FIGURE 4–4 Precis Method of Note-Taking

- Listening is more than hearing.
- SIER model (four steps).
- Sense/hear.
- Interpret/understand.
- Evaluate/judge.
- React/assign worth.

FIGURE 4–5 Organizational Mapping Method of Note-Taking

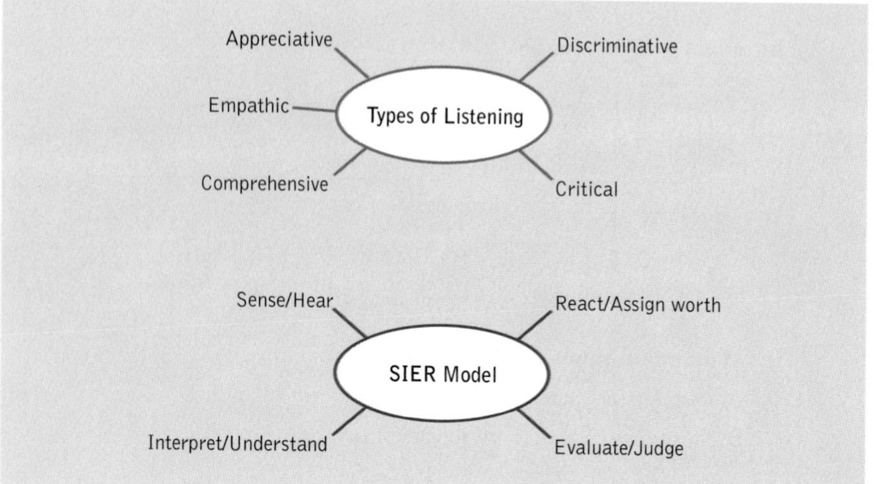

example, or piece of evidence is offered to support a main idea, you write it down on a line extending from the circled main idea.

> ***What Do You Think?***
> *Have you ever tried to take notes by outlining when a professor did not use clear structure? How helpful were your notes later on?*

Bad Habit Number 3: Being Unprepared

Discussion Tip
Ask students how much preparation they would need if they knew they were going to give a speech tomorrow. After they discuss that question, ask them how much preparation they would need if they knew they were going to critically listen to a speech tomorrow.

Good critical listening demands effort, not only during the communication event, but also before it. Specifically, good critical listening requires preparation: physical, mental, and intellectual. Unfortunately, we lead very busy lives. In other words, most people today juggle many roles and responsibilities at one time. For example, you might be a college student, employee, parent, and volunteer. Consequently, you might need to complete readings and assignments, complete your shift at work, transport children to and from after-school activities, and mail out a newsletter all on the same evening before class. In our efforts to meet all of the competing professional and personal demands on our time, we run the risk of failing to prepare adequately. If you are not prepared, you run the risk of losing your concentration, becoming distracted, failing to understand some of the information, and even falling asleep.

> ***What Do You Think?***
> *Consider a time when you went to class overtired. How much of the discussion did you remember later on?*

A Strategy: Prepare Yourself

This strategy is really quite simple; however, it is not necessarily easy to do. If you want to engage in effective critical listening, prepare physically by getting plenty of rest and eating a healthy meal. Prepare mentally by clearing your mind of competing concerns. To do this, you might even want to engage in some form of aerobic activity or meditation prior to the event. Prepare intellectually by completing any assigned reading *before* it is to be discussed so that you'll have the background you need to understand what you hear. If you are planning to attend a professional lecture, read something the speaker wrote. This will give you ideas that you can expand as you listen to the speaker. Again, this strategy of preparing is not necessarily easy. If you take it seriously, however, you will be a more effective listener on those occasions when listening to the speaker and learning about the topic are important to you.

Bad Habit Number 4: Prejudging the Speaker

As we've already seen, prejudging the speaker is an obstacle to critical listening. It's also a common bad habit. Have you ever walked into a classroom on the first day of class and, based just on the way the instructor looked, decided that the class was going to be a waste of time? Perhaps you thought the instructor looked too young, or too old, or too casual, or too formal, or too unstylish, or too eccentric. Perhaps you fell victim to inaccurate assumptions based on cultural stereotypes (Kiewitz, 1997). Once you have predetermined that you are not going to learn anything from a speaker, you will probably listen ineffectively.

Discussion Tip
Ask students to discuss ways in which they have prejudged speakers in the past. Have students identify the specific context(s) in which they have prejudged speakers. Encourage students to explain strategies for overcoming this listening habit.

According to a theory known as **impression formation and management,** we form our first impressions of people based on how they look. Research suggests, for example, that we respond more favorably to formally dressed people than to casually dressed people (Ritts, Patterson, & Tubbs, 1992). In particular, we tend to think they are more intelligent. When the speaker is a woman, such prejudgments about intelligence based on attire are especially likely (Temple & Loewen, 1993; Treinen, 1998).

What Do You Think?

Identify a speaker who you believe is really effective and one who you think is really ineffective. What role does the appearance of these speakers play in forming your impression?

A Strategy: Hear the Speaker Out

To be an effective listener, you need to consciously avoid prejudging the intelligence of speakers based on appearance or manner (Adler & Towne, 1996). Instead, listen to speakers with an open mind and don't try to evaluate the strengths and weaknesses of their messages until they have finished speaking (Gitomer, 2000). I remember learning that a former president of a national sociology association, a very reputable man in the field, always presented his formal public speeches barefooted. It would be easy to prejudge him as an eccentric fool. To do so, however, would likely result in ineffective listening.

Bad Habit Number 5: Mentally Arguing and Jumping to Conclusions

Another bad habit that we've already touched on is that of mentally arguing with the speaker and jumping to conclusions. Sometimes we find ourselves mentally arguing with speakers about particular claims they make during the speech. It might

Discussion Tip
Students often jump to conclusions when they are exposed to trigger words that strike at the core of their belief systems (e.g., a feminist who hears a speaker use exclusionary language). Have students identify their personal trigger words. Have they worked out ways to manage their reactions to such words?

even be that we notice the speaker make contradictory claims or make claims we know to be inaccurate. Even if our point is valid, by mentally arguing we fail to listen effectively to the rest of what the speaker says and the loss is ours. Sometimes we stop listening because we jump to conclusions about what the speaker's ultimate point is going to be. Whether our conclusion is right or wrong, we may miss important information.

Although humans have probably always engaged in this bad habit, modern technology has exacerbated the situation. We can get information about nearly any topic in a matter of seconds thanks to advancements such as cable television and the Internet, and we tend to know a little bit about a lot of different topics. As a result, we're more likely to run the risk of getting hung up on the details of a speech because we've learned something a bit different about the topic.

A Strategy: Find Value in Every Speech

When you mentally argue with specifics in the speech or jump to conclusions about what the speaker is going to say, you are making negative judgments about the speech and therefore cannot reach the highest level in the SIER model, which is critical listening. To fight this bad habit, consciously force yourself to find value in every speech. For example, rather than dwell on a detail that you disagree with, make a mental or written note of it and move on to find something of value in the rest of the speech.

Bad Habit Number 6: Listening Too Hard

As odd as it might sound, another bad habit that results in poor listening is listening too hard. When you try to retain every detail of a speaker's message, you experience what I call *listening overload*—you actually lose the main ideas and wind up remembering even less information than you would have if you had not tried so hard.

A Strategy: Listen Analytically

Teaching Tip
Assign students to groups of four. Have each group select a topic and discuss it (consider assigning topics for variety). Ask students to practice the listening strategies discussed in this chapter. Ask students which of the strategies were the most helpful and the most difficult and why.

To overcome the bad habit of listening too hard, try to listen analytically—that is, analyze the speech as you listen in ways that focus on the speaker's main point and general ideas. As you listen, ask yourself: What is the main point the speaker is trying to make here? What are the main ideas supporting this point? With this focused approach, you'll retain the information much better than you would if you tried to remember exact statistics or examples. Round the statistics off if this helps. To use an example from this chapter, instead of trying to remember that 55 percent of our communication time is spent listening, 24 percent speaking, 13 percent reading, and 8 percent writing, you might just try to remember that over half of our communication time is spent listening. After all, what is important to remember is the fact that more communication time is spent in listening than in all the other modes combined.

In this section, we discussed six bad habits that hurt your ability to listen critically. We also talked about six strategies you can use to avoid falling victim to each of them. These strategies will help you in any situation that requires effective critical listening, including public speaking.

Listening Tips

1. Expend energy.
2. Take notes.
3. Prepare yourself.
4. Hear the speaker out.
5. Find value in every speech.
6. Listen analytically.

The Ethical Critic: Tips for Improving Critiquing Skills

A critique is based on critical listening—that is, on hearing, comprehending, judging, and assigning worth—but goes beyond it. On the basis of your critical listening, your critique gives the speaker feedback, including suggestions for improvement. To be an ethical critic, however, your feedback must also honor the virtues of respect and honesty. You must be *honest* about what you believe the speaker did both effectively and ineffectively. You must also phrase your comments in ways that demonstrate *respect* for the speaker and his or her efforts. To be an effective critic, you'll need to be thorough—touching on content, delivery, and structure—as well as detailed and specific. You'll also need to provide both positive and negative comments. A critique that meets these criteria can be considered ethical and effective. In other words, with such a critique, you'll have done your best to make your comments fair and useful to the speaker.

Teaching Tip
Have students observe a speech and apply the tips for improving critiquing skills provided in this chapter.

Characteristics of Ethical and Effective Critiques

In an ethical and effective critique, comments are phrased as **constructive criticism.** This means that comments are positive as well as negative, are specific, are accompanied by a rationale, and are phrased in terms of the listener's perception.

Teaching Tip
Show students a sample speech and have them practice constructive criticism using the guidelines presented in this chapter. Explain to students what criteria you will employ in critiquing their speeches.

An effective critique offers specific opinions about what the speaker did not do well in terms of the content, the structure, and the delivery. These negative comments, however, must do more than merely list things the speaker did poorly. Comments like "slow down," "hard to follow," "too soft," and "confusing" are too vague to truly help the speaker improve in future speeches. To do so, the comments must be specific. What particular part of the speech was too fast, or hard to follow, or too soft, or confusing?

To be ethical, you must also explain why. The reason you cite for each statement is also known as a rationale. If you believe the preview was too soft, for example, also indicate why. Perhaps you didn't hear it, which consequently made it difficult for you to follow the speaker's structure throughout the rest of the speech.

To be ethical, you also must phrase your comments as your personal perceptions—which other listeners may or may not share—rather than as facts. One way to do so is by using "I" rather than "you" language. For example, it is more ethical to say, "I couldn't hear your preview. It would help me follow the structure of your speech better if you would speak louder when stating your preview," than to flatly state, "You need to slow down on your preview or your structure won't be clear." Offering a rationale phrased as a personal perception demonstrates that you respect the speaker's ability to decide whether or not this change will improve his or her overall effectiveness in future speeches.

Teaching Tip
Have students evaluate at least one speech given by a peer in the class. Instruct them to include at least three positive and three negative constructive comments.

A critique also includes comments about what the speaker did well in terms of the content, the structure, and the delivery. These positive comments help speakers improve by identifying specific things that work and that they ought to continue doing in future speeches. Like negative comments, these positive comments should be specific, include a rationale, and be phrased as personal opinion. Comments like "good job" and "fine" and even "great transitions" or "good

FIGURE 4–6
Sample Classmate Critique Form

Delivery	**Critique** (Identify one thing the speaker did well and why. Identify one thing the speaker could do to improve, why, and how.)
Use of Voice Intelligible? Conversational? Expressive? **Use of Body** Attire? Poise? Eye contact? Facial expressions? Gestures and movement?	
Structure	**Critique** (Identify one thing the speaker did well and why. Identify one thing the speaker could do to improve, why, and how.)
Macrostructure Introductory elements? Transitions? Concluding elements? **Microstructure** Language? Style?	
Content	**Critique** (Identify one thing the speaker did well and why. Identify one thing the speaker could do to improve, why, and how.)
Analysis Focus? Breadth? Depth? Listener relevance? Learning styles? **Support Material** Relevant? Recent? Credited? Varied? Distributed?	

eye contact" are too vague to indicate what worked for the critic. A more effective and ethical comment would be, for example, "Good eye contact. You spanned the entire room so no one seemed left out of the communication transaction." This comment lets the speaker know what the critic believes he or she should continue to do in future speeches and why. Figure 4–6 provides a sample classmate critique form.

Critique Checklist

- Did you offer specific comments about what the speaker did not do well?
- Did you offer specific comments about what the speaker did do well?
- Did you provide reasons for each comment you made?
- Did you phrase each statement as a personal perception using "I" language?

You can certainly help other speakers improve by offering effective critiques. You can also help yourself improve by completing a self-critique after each speech you give, using the same approach you use to critique others. Be sure to note things you believe you did effectively in addition to those things you believe you did ineffectively. Doing so can actually reduce public speaking anxiety because it serves as a form of cognitive restructuring. Engaging in negative self-talk after a speech increases public speaking anxiety. A self-critique forces you to temper your negative self-talk with positive criticism. If your anxiety is rooted in a fear of failure, this cognitive restructuring technique will eventually reduce your anxiety about public speaking. Figure 4–7 provides a sample self-critique form.

Evaluate your own speech performance based on these guidelines. The focus is on redefining your self-talk and offering yourself specific and constructive suggestions rather than on criticism.

Delivery **Use of Voice** **Use of Body**	**Positive Critique:** Identify one or two things you did well and why.
Structure **Macrostructure** **Microstructure**	**Positive Critique:** Identify one or two things you did well and why.
Content **Analysis** **Support Material**	**Positive Critique:** Identify one or two things you did well and why.
To improve: **Delivery:** **Structure:** **Content:**	Identify one thing you will try to do differently to improve the delivery, structure, and content of your next speech. Be sure to indicate why and how.

FIGURE 4–7
Sample Self-Critique Form

Examples of Content, Structure, and Delivery Critiques

Teaching Tip
Ask students to complete a self-critique after their first speech. Have them describe how they felt before giving it and after it was over. Was it worse/better than expected? Ask them what they will do to improve for their next speech.

Having looked at the characteristics of effective and ethical critiques, let's turn now to the content of critique comments in terms of the three major aspects of public speeches: content, structure, and delivery. You'll need to consider all three aspects as you listen to a speech. In order to critically listen as well as critique each section, it is usually most effective to jot short notes during the speech. Later you can enhance these notes to address the characteristics of effective critiques. In other words, by the time you present your critique to the speaker, make sure each comment you offer is phrased as constructive criticism.

Comments on content focus on the speaker's analysis and supporting material. You might address breadth and depth of evidence or use of listener relevance links. You might talk about how the speaker used reasoning to connect his or her evidence to the main points. Or you might talk about how relevant, recent, or credible the evidence seemed to be. Did the speaker offer a variety of evidence to support her or his main points? Did the speaker offer sufficiently detailed evidence? Did the speaker address the relevance of the topic to listeners' lives? Figure 4–8 provides some specific examples of content critique statements.

Comments on structure cover both macrostructure and microstructure. To comment on macrostructure, you focus on such elements as the attention catcher, thesis, preview, transitions, thesis restatement, main point summary, and clincher. To comment on microstructure, you focus on aspects of language and style such as accuracy, clarity, inclusion, vividness, and novelty. In other words, whereas content comments focus on the speaker's topic and supporting ideas, structure comments focus on the way the speaker puts those ideas together—in the outline, the language choices, and the style. Figure 4–9 provides examples of structure critique comments.

Comments on delivery focus on how the speaker uses his or her voice and body. When you comment on voice, for example, you might address intelligibility. How easily could you understand the message? Did the speaker's rate, volume, and enunciation help or hinder your understanding? You might address whether the speaker has a conversational style. Did the speaker sound as though he or she was talking with you rather than reading to you or presenting in front of you? You might also address emotional expression. Did the speaker vary her or his rate

FIGURE 4–8 Content Critique Examples

Content Critique Statements

Ineffective	Effective and Ethical
Interesting stories	I liked the story about your trip to the carnival. The depth of details you provided made it sound really fun.
Boring topic	The speech would have kept my interest better if I knew how each main point relates to me.
Too short	I would have liked to hear another example under each main point. This would have helped me understand why the carnival was so significant to you.

Structure Critique Statements	
Ineffective	**Effective and Ethical**
Disorganized	I had trouble knowing when a new main point was starting. It would have been helpful to me to hear clear transitions that tied the two main points together verbally.
Bad introduction	I would have tuned in to the speech quicker if you had used a creative attention catcher instead of starting immediately with the thesis statement.
Dull	I would have stayed tuned in to the speech better if you'd have used more colorful word pictures when describing the carnival.

FIGURE 4–9
Structure Critique Examples

or volume, stress key words and phrases, or incorporate pauses to reinforce an attitude?

When you comment on the speaker's use of his or her body, you might mention attire. Did the speaker's attire convey a sense of commitment to the occasion? Or you might address poise and mannerisms. Did the speaker do anything distracting, like fidgeting with notes, playing with his or her hair, or shifting her or his weight back and forth? Eye contact is another area you might address. Did the speaker look up from his or her notes at least 90 percent of the time? Did the speaker span the entire audience? Did the speaker look you in the eye? Finally, you can consider use of facial expressions and gestures. Did these nonverbal signals reinforce the verbal message? Figure 4–10 provides some delivery critique comment examples.

Constructing effective and ethical critiques is not easy. It takes a good deal of critical thinking on your part. With practice, however, you can learn to help speakers by focusing on specific things they did well and specific things they might do to improve in the areas of delivery, structure, and content and why. Doing so can help you help yourself improve as a speaker when you conduct effective and ethical self-critiques as well.

Delivery Critique Statements	
Ineffective	**Effective and Ethical**
Good rate	Rate was appropriate to easily follow your ideas. Intelligible.
Good gestures	I liked your gestures in the introduction because they helped clarify your main points for me.
Too fast	It would have helped me if you slowed down more while discussing the technical information in the first main point. I needed more time to process what you were saying.
Boring	I would have liked to hear more emotional expression in your voice. More enthusiasm when talking about the carnival would have kept my interest better.

FIGURE 4–10
Delivery Critique Examples

Summary

The psychological process of listening depends on, but is different from, the physiological process of hearing. Improved listening skills will benefit you in both your personal life and professional life. As the SIER model makes clear, critical listening involves hearing, understanding, evaluating, and assigning worth to a message.

Since it is not possible to engage in critical listening all of the time, it is important to determine which type of listening is most appropriate in a particular communication context. In addition to critical listening, these types include discriminative listening (listening "between the lines"), comprehensive listening (listening to understand), appreciative listening (listening for pleasure), and empathic listening (listening as a sounding board).

You can improve your listening skills by becoming aware of six bad habits and of strategies for dealing with these habits. To overcome the bad habit of becoming distracted, expend energy throughout the speech. To avoid faking attention, take notes. To avoid being unprepared for the speech, prepare yourself physically, mentally, and intellectually. Avoid prejudging speakers by hearing them out before evaluating their message. Avoid mentally arguing and jumping to conclusions by finding value in every speech. Finally, don't try to remember every single detail by listening too hard. Rather, listen analytically for main ideas.

A critique that is effective and ethical offers the speaker suggestions for improvement, accompanied by a rationale and phrased as a personal perception. Effective critiques can help speakers improve because they focus on the speech not the speaker, describe specific aspects of the speech, and include both strengths and weaknesses in the areas of delivery, structure, and content. In addition to critiquing other speakers, you can also critique yourself, both to improve and to replace negative self-talk with positive coping statements.

Activities

1. **Resisting Distractions.** Form a three-person group. Designate two people as "senders" and one as a "receiver." One sender is to sit on the receiver's right and the other is to sit on the receiver's left. The two senders discuss *different topics* simultaneously for three to four minutes. The listener tries to focus on one sender's message. Afterward, the receiver reports all she or he can remember.
2. **Listening Analytically.** Listen to a radio news broadcast. Summarize the main ideas in a few short sentences.
3. **Taking Notes.** Listen to a radio news report with a partner. One of you should take notes while the other just listens. Afterward, recount to each other (or to the entire class) what you can remember from the report.
4. **Effective and Ethical Critiquing.** Watch a professional speaker (a politician, a comedian, an evangelist, etc.) on television or in person. Practice writing positive and negative critique statements about delivery, structure, and content that are both effective and ethical.
5. **Sandwiching Critique Technique.** Together with two other people, attend a professional lecture or watch one on television. One person should focus on the

speaker's content, another on structure, and another on delivery. Employ the sandwiching technique for your designated aspect of the speech. To do so, simply begin by mentioning a specific thing the speaker did well and why you believe it is something the speaker should continue doing. Next, offer a suggestion for improvement, explain why the suggestion would improve the speech, and recommend how the speaker might incorporate the suggestion. Finally, provide another positive critique. This positive-negative-positive approach couches suggestions within a framework of praise, which can be more comfortable for both the beginning speaker and the beginning critic.

6. **Sandwiching Self Critique.** Critique your own speech based on content, structure, and delivery using the sandwiching technique described in Activity 5.

KEY TERMS

Appreciative listening
Auditory distractions
Comprehensive listening
Constructive criticism
Critical listening
Discriminative listening
Empathic listening
Enunciation
Hearing
Impression formation and management
Listening
Mental distractions
Physical distractions
SIER model
Visual distractions

CHAPTER 5

Selecting and Narrowing Your Topic

Reflective Questions

1. In what ways can your favorite television programs, movies, comic strips, songs, hobbies, and interests help you select a speech topic?
2. In what ways can searching the Internet help you generate potential topics?
3. How can you determine whether a particular topic could be appropriate for your speech?
4. What can you do to ensure that you'll be able to cover your ideas adequately in the allotted time frame?

hile having lunch with her friend Maria, Holly was trying to come up with a topic for the informative speech she would present in class next week. Holly had a long list of topics she'd thought of and discarded. Exasperated, she exclaimed, "Every idea I come up with seems so boring. I'm sure everybody knows about all of this stuff already! I can't think of anything I can talk about that is new and original."

Teaching Tip
Refer students to the SpeechMaker CD-ROM. This software will assist them in the topic selection process. Consider assigning one of the scenarios before the class; you can discuss it as you teach this chapter.

After glancing at Holly's list of discarded topics, Maria responded, "There are several topics on your list that I know I'd like to learn more about. For example, I see here that you worked in a day care center. I'd love to know more about that. I often wonder whether my own children are in the best environment. How do I know? And I see you took some life saving courses. I'll bet you know what to do if someone is choking. That would also be helpful for me to know. Your major in child development and family science, your experience working in day care, and your life saving experience make you an expert in some things I don't know much about at all."

"Oh," Holly said. "Maybe you're right. I do know about some things that a lot of other people don't. I wonder which of these would be most interesting to my classmates?" Holly's process of selecting a topic now began in earnest.

Teaching Tip
Have students write a one- to two-page paper on topic selection in which they answer the following questions: How did you select the topic? How did you make the topic interesting to the audience? How did you narrow the topic? If your students have not done any public speaking, instruct them to interview someone who has.

Your first task as a public speaker is to select a topic. Students often tell me that this is the most difficult part of the speechmaking process. When I ask them why, they respond that listeners are not going to be interested in anything they have to say, or that they don't know anything new and interesting to talk about. In fact, many people have this feeling when they think about selecting a topic. It's a primary reason people's anxiety level begins to rise as soon as they consider doing a public speech (Richmond & McCroskey, 1995).

> ***What Do You Think?***
> *When you think about selecting a speech topic, what thoughts typically go through your mind?*

I am happy to tell you, as I have told my students, that you *do* have

Sometimes we fail to realize that our experiences are unique and potentially interesting to our listeners.

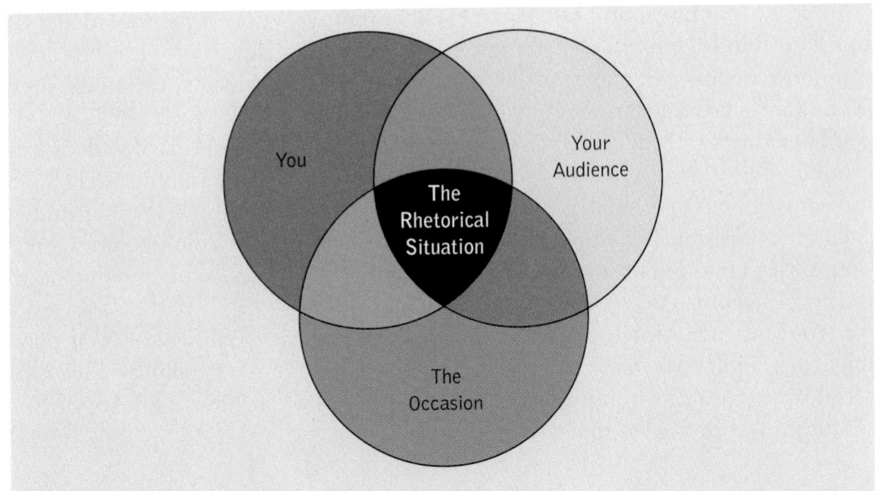

FIGURE 5–1
The Rhetorical Situation

new and interesting ideas and you *can* approach your speech in ways that will be interesting to your listeners. To succeed, however, you must (a) generate a variety of potential topics, (b) choose a topic from this list based on your interests, and (c) narrow your topic based on your audience and purpose.

Essentially, you must select and narrow your speech topic in light of the **rhetorical situation**—that is, the specific circumstances under which you will deliver the speech. As Figure 5–1 illustrates, these circumstances are the speaker (you), the audience (your classmates), and the occasion (purpose). In other words, selecting and narrowing a speech topic is based on what interests you and how that can be adapted to address audience interests and expectations. Thus, audience is a crucial factor in topic selection.

Discussion Tip
Ask students to refer to the first speeches presented in the class. What type of interaction followed the speeches? What kinds of topics would be appropriate and interesting for this audience based on that interaction?

Topic selection must include **audience analysis**—the process of understanding who your listeners are and adapting your speech to meet their needs, interests, and expectations. Because audience analysis is such an important topic in its own right, it is treated separately in Chapter 6. It is also discussed in later chapters, because audience analysis must occur throughout the speech preparation and presentation process. By following the advice laid out in this chapter and Chapter 6, you will be able to select interesting and relevant topics and, consequently, can approach topic selection with much less anxiety.

Generating Potential Topics

The first step in selecting and narrowing a topic is to generate a list of potential topic ideas. In other words, you must develop a variety of ideas from which to choose for your speech. You can generate potential topics by brainstorming and by researching.

Brainstorming

A good way to begin this process is by **brainstorming**—that is, generating as many ideas as possible (Weiten, 1986). To brainstorm, get out a sheet of paper and a pen-

Teaching Tip
Instruct the students to generate a list of speech topics by using several of the procedures discussed in this chapter. This will help familiarize students with more than one approach and facilitate the topic selection process.

cil or pen. Set a time limit of fifteen to twenty minutes. Write down every topic that comes to mind. Don't rule anything out at this point. These topics can be things you know a good deal about or they can be things about which you would like to learn more. The goal is to get as many topic possibilities on paper as possible.

Sometimes it is easier to brainstorm topics by thinking in terms of various categories—for example, places, people, events, organizations, hobbies, television programs, books, personal goals, professional goals, opinions, beliefs, attitudes, and values. Essentially, you might write these categories as column heads on a sheet of paper and brainstorm each category for five minutes before moving on to the next category.

Your instructor might assign a topic for your speech as well. For example, you might be required to talk about your professional interests, or public policies, or social issues. You can still use this approach to brainstorm different aspects or perspectives on the assigned topic.

Researching

Technology Tip
http://www.projectcensored.org/
This Web site contains information about important stories that are often overlooked by the popular press. Students can be encouraged to visit this site to explore contemporary, interesting, and challenging speech topics.

Another way to generate topic ideas is to do research. Whereas brainstorming requires you to generate potential topics based on your personal knowledge and experiences, researching allows you to look at external resources for ideas.

You might, for example, browse through several magazines and make a note of the articles that interest you. You can even add to the lists you developed while brainstorming. To generate a variety of additional topics, look through different types of magazines. *Time, Newsweek,* and *U.S. News and World Report,* for example, focus on different kinds of topics than do *People, Good Housekeeping,* or *Glamour.* And *Business Week, Forbes,* and *Consumer Reports* are likely to focus on different kinds of topics than do *Runners World, Sports Illustrated,* or *National Geographic.* Take the time to look through different kinds of magazines to expand your list most effectively.

Teaching Tip
Invite a representative from your library to visit the class and explain what resources are available for students. You might consider providing students with a list of where they can go in the library to find the specific resources listed in this chapter.

Newspapers can also be an excellent source for generating topic ideas. You might look at local newspapers as well as national publications like *USA Today, The New York Times,* and *The Wall Street Journal.* For example, one student, Jenni, got her idea for a speech about the overuse of antibacterial products from an editorial cartoon she saw in *USA Today.*

Reference books and indexes can also help you generate topic ideas. Try opening an encyclopedia, dictionary, or the *Reader's Guide to Periodical Literature* at random. Skim through the topic headings. When something catches your interest, add it to your list under the appropriate column. You can skim CD-ROM encyclopedias in a similar fashion. I tried opening my dictionary to one page at random. Here's what I came up with:

- Gravure (method of printing with etched plates or cylinders).
- Gray's Inn (one of the four legal societies forming the Inns of Court in England).
- Great Salt Lake (Utah).
- Grecism (the style or spirit of Greek culture, art, or thought).

In addition to scanning through printed materials for topics to expand your list, you can also browse the Internet. You can surf for ideas using any one of a number of search engines like *Webcrawler, Yahoo!,* or *Excite!* Each of these search engines allows you, essentially, to brainstorm a topic. Once you go to a particular site, you can continue to link to other pages that interest you. Link from site to site, jotting down ideas as they reveal themselves. If you decide to surf for additional topic possibilities, however, it is generally a good idea to limit how much time you will spend doing so (one hour should be sufficient). Otherwise, you may find yourself spending hours unnecessarily.

Technology Tip
http://www.searchenginewatch.com/

This Web site contains useful information including Web searching tips as well as search engine listings, resources, and reviews. Have students visit this site and prepare a list of sample search engines as well as search strategies to be presented in class.

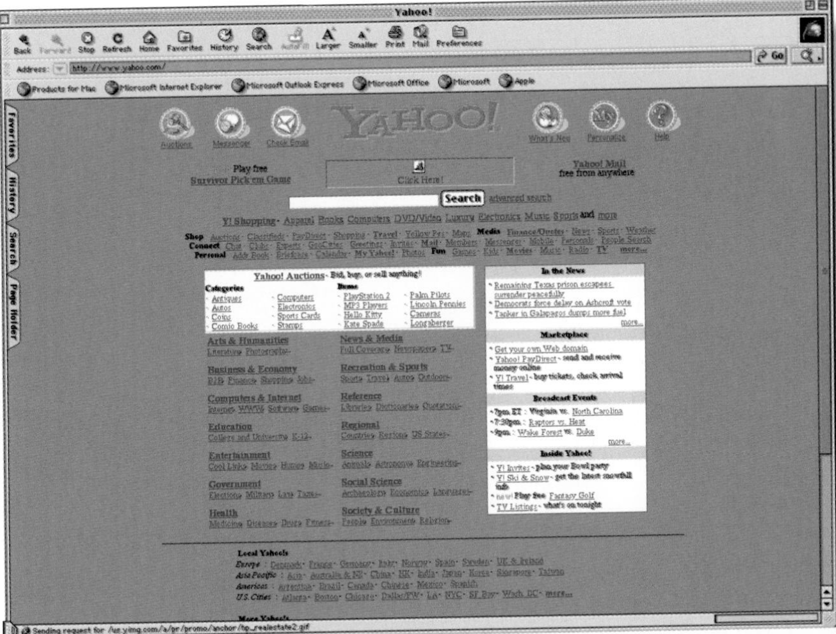

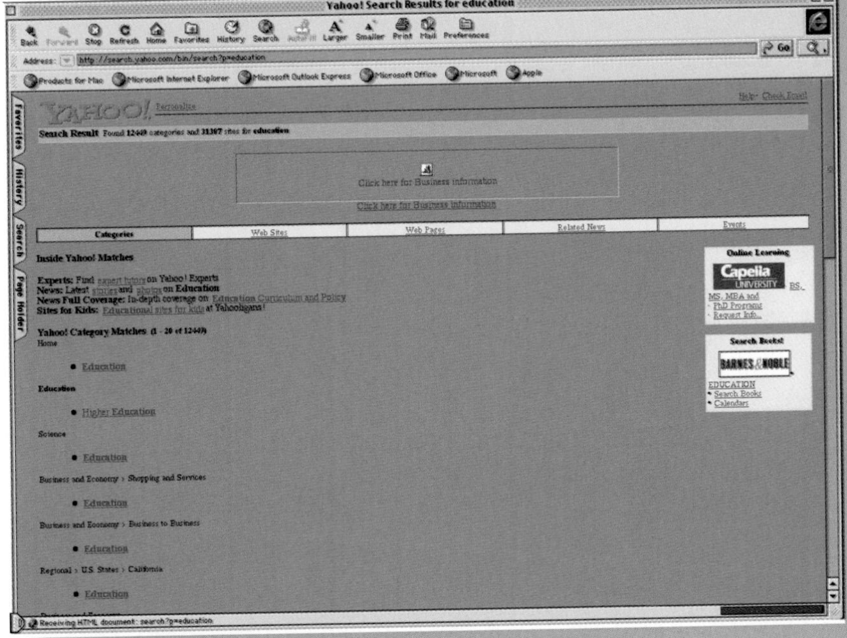

You might decide to surf the Internet to brainstorm speech topic ideas.

By the time you've finished this topic generation process by brainstorming and researching, you will have created a **personal inventory**—that is, a list of all the topics you can think of that interest you in some way. Here's Holly's personal inventory:

Holly's Personal Inventory of Topics and Ideas

Teaching Tip
To give students practice in developing a personal inventory, assign the Personal Inventory and Reaction paper included in the Activities section of this chapter.

Places	People
Bermuda Triangle	My grandmother
Trinidad	High school teacher
New Orleans	The pope
Rape and abuse crisis center	
Day care centers	
Events	**Organizations**
Shooting at Columbine High	Lion's club
My annual family reunion	Church choir
The birth of my first child	Humane society
The Stanley Cup games	
Hobbies	**TV Programs**
Playing piano	*Seinfeld*
Running	*20/20*
Going to movies	*South Park*
Swimming	*Days of Our Lives*
Books	**Personal Goals**
Backlash	Own a home
Boxcar Children	Have a dog
Bible	Graduate from college
Professional Goals	**Beliefs**
Earn at least $30,000/year	Death penalty is wrong
Managerial level	Heaven exists
Graphics industry	
Social Issues	**Public Policies**
Cost of prescription drugs	Affirmative action
Health insurance	Title 9
Teen suicide	

Opinions	Values
Women should be able to be priests.	Higher education
Elementary and secondary school day should be lengthened.	Christianity
Gun control is needed.	Family

Teaching Tip
Have students e-mail you their personal inventories. Compile a list of potential speech topics based on these reports. Distribute this list to the rest of the class to help students become more aware of their peers' interests.

The personal inventory you create actually serves two purposes. One purpose is to generate a host of diverse topic ideas, but the other equally important purpose is to begin to understand why each topic interests you. Doing so will help you determine the direction you might take for a speech on each topic.

Choosing a Topic

Once you have generated a personal inventory, you must choose a topic for your speech. There are a number of ways to explore potential topic ideas. Some of these approaches include expanding your personal inventory, creating a concept map, and doing research.

Expanding Your Personal Inventory

One way to help determine a worthy topic is to create an **expanded personal inventory** by broadening your list to include a statement as to why each of these topics interests you. Reasons usually stem from personal experiences, cultural background, religious beliefs, ethnicity, gender, socioeconomic class, birth order, and so forth. Some of the categories on Holly's expanded list look like this:

Holly's Expanded Personal Inventory

Topics/Ideas	Why?
Places	
Trinidad	Neat music
New Orleans	Love the Cajun food
Rape and abuse crisis center	My best friend was raped
Day care centers	I work at one
People	
My grandmother	She's blind and lives alone, gardens, sews, (amazing)
My high school teacher	Respected students as intelligent people

Topics/Ideas	Why?
Events	
Shooting at Columbine High	Points to a much larger problem in our society. People need to feel needed. How can we change the direction of our country?
The Stanley Cup games	I wish I could have played hockey as a kid
Hobbies	
Playing piano	I taught myself to play
Going to movies	Entertainment; helps us think about important social issues
Swimming	I'm a senior lifesaver
TV Programs	
Seinfeld	Funny; about people and relationships
20/20	Newsworthy topics; seems somewhat sensationalized
South Park	Do kids learn to be violent?
Days of Our Lives	Sex on TV—is it okay?
Personal Goals	
Have a dog	My childhood dog was my best friend
Professional Goals	
Earn at least $30,000/year	I was raised in middle-class home; hope to stay there
Graphics industry	That's my major; I love to draw
Social Issues	
Cost of prescription drugs	Seniors shouldn't have to go to Canada or Mexico for these
Health insurance	I'm bothered that some people don't have access to quality health care
Public Policies	
Affirmative action	I want to get a job because I'm most qualified
Title 9	I'm so glad young girls today have the opportunities I didn't have

Expanding your personal inventory in this way is beneficial, not only because it allows you to explore potential directions for each topic, but also because it helps you learn more about why you think and believe the way you do about different topics and

What Do You Think?

Select a topic from your personal inventory. Why does the topic interest you?

issues. A **belief** is a thing you think is true or false, an **attitude** is a predisposition to like or dislike something, and **values** are the enduring set of principles that shape your beliefs and attitudes. Understanding your own beliefs, attitudes, and values is crucial in topic selection because it is an integral component of effective audience analysis—as you will see in Chapter 6.

By expanding her personal inventory in this way, for example, Holly realized that her religious beliefs, rooted in Christianity, shape much of her thinking. She also recognized the value she places on nurturing quality interpersonal relationships with others. Hence, she might hold a negative attitude toward the animated comedy *South Park* because of the value she places on civility. Knowing what you think and believe about topics and issues ultimately provides you with a perspective by which to examine your audience and adapt your speech effectively to them. Chapter 6 explores this relationship in more detail.

Teaching Tip
Have students write a brief essay in which they explore their attitudes, beliefs, and values on a specific topic such as abortion, capital punishment, or physician-assisted suicide. How can a better understanding of your attitudes, beliefs, and values make you a better public speaker?

What Do You Think?

Look again at the items you have identified on your personal inventory and why. What beliefs, attitudes, and values does your personal inventory reveal about you?

Concept Mapping

Another strategy you might use to choose a topic is concept mapping. **Concept mapping** is a visual means of exploring connections between a topic and related ideas. To discover connections, you might ask yourself questions about the topic—questions focused on who, what, where, when, and how. Figure 5–2 is an example from Holly's list.

Teaching Tip
In order to give students practice in developing a concept map, assign the Group Concept Map activity contained in the Activities section of this chapter.

What Do You Think?

Select a topic from your personal inventory. Try creating a concept map for it. Which items on your concept map could be good speech topics?

Researching

You might choose to go to the library or visit one online to read about a particular topic in more detail and make an informed choice. Sometimes your expanded personal inventory or your concept map will lead you to the library to learn more about a possible speech topic. Holly, for example, might go to the library to learn more about tips for parents who are selecting a day care center.

Narrowing Your Topic

Once you've selected a topic, you must narrow your focus based on the rhetorical situation and purpose. As discussed earlier in the chapter, the rhetorical situation is made up of the specific circumstances under which you will deliver the speech. These circumstances are the speaker (you), the audience (your classmates), and the occasion (purpose and constraints). By now you have generated potential topic ideas based on your interests and have chosen one for your speech. Hence, you have satisfied the first circumstance of the rhetorical situation. You must also consider your audience, your purpose, and constraints. Doing so will ensure that

Teaching Tip
Assign a brief topic analysis paper in which each student conducts audience analysis, develops a specific purpose, and identifies potential sources of information for his or her speech topic. Have students complete this assignment well in advance of their scheduled speech presentations and emphasize the importance of planning ahead.

FIGURE 5–2
Holly's Concept Map

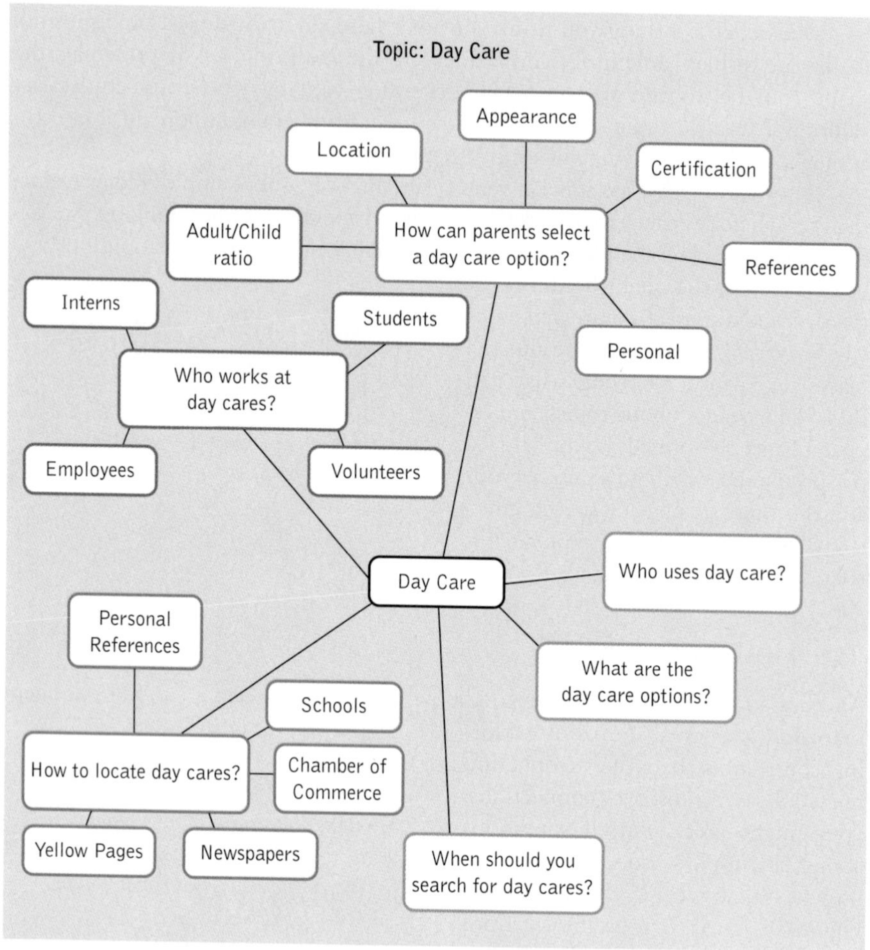

you will speak thoroughly in ways that meet the expectations of the audience and occasion. Moreover, research suggests that public speeches that make a tightly focused, simple point are most successful (Lamb, 1991; Suskind & Lublin, 1995).

The Mold Method for Narrowing Your Topic

Teaching Tip
Select a topic and demonstrate the mold method technique for narrowing a speech topic in class. To reinforce this technique, assign the Mold Method Group Exercise contained in the Activities section of this chapter.

The constraints of the rhetorical situation can be met by narrowing your focus using the mold method. This method of narrowing essentially molds your topic idea to meet the constraints of the situation by adapting to your audience and refining your purpose. Ultimately, the mold method is a five-step process that helps you formulate an effective **thesis statement**—that is, a one-sentence summary of your speech (see Figure 5–3).

Step 1: Select Your General Topic

To see how the mold method works, let's continue to use Holly as an example. In the first step, you select a general topic from your personal inventory. Holly selected day care as her general topic. Although this was not the only good topic idea her efforts generated, she chose it because she had experience working in a day care center and because she would like to make wise day care choices for her own chil-

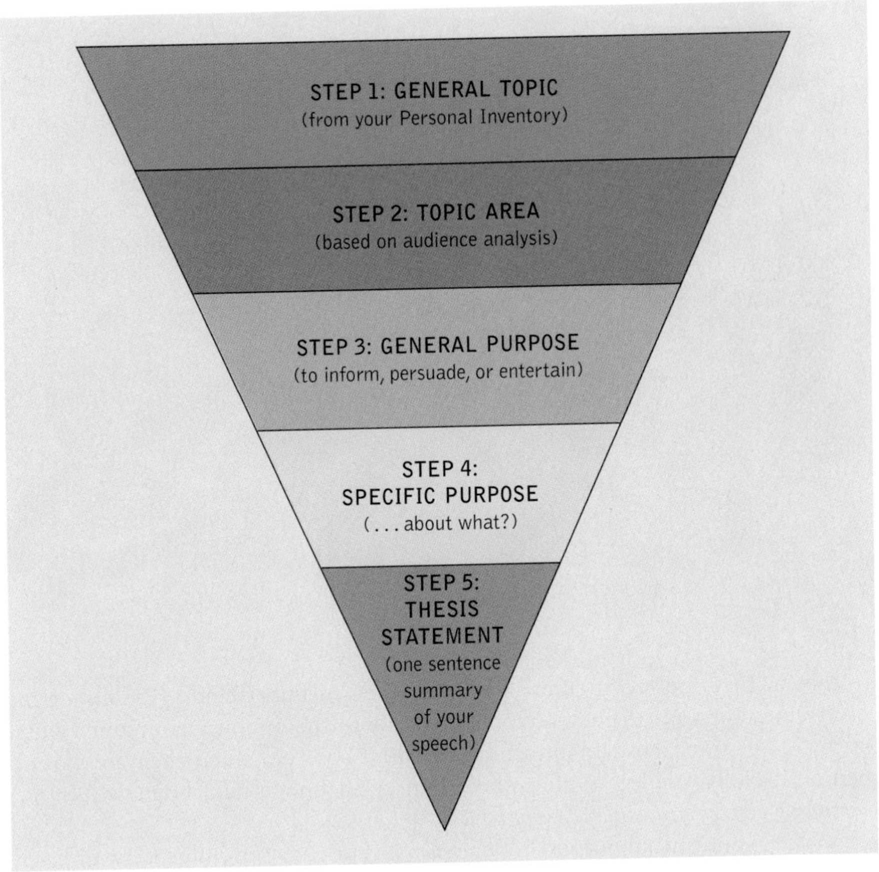

FIGURE 5–3
The Mold Method

dren. In this way, she actually completed the first step in the mold method: She chose a topic from her personal inventory.

Step 2: Determine Your Topic Area

In the second step, you narrow your general topic to a topic area based on the needs and interests of your audience. Holly discovered that most of her classmates either have children or plan to have children someday. She decided that knowing more about day care choices would benefit most listeners. Therefore, she molded her topic to focus on day care choices. This second step is based on audience analysis, which we will talk about in more detail in Chapter 6.

Step 3: Consider Your General Purpose

In the third step, you decide on the general purpose of your speech. The **general purpose** is usually specified as part of the speech requirements for assigned classroom presentations. When you are asked to present a speech in other settings, however, you must decide the general purpose yourself. There are three general purposes: to inform, to persuade, and to entertain.

When your general purpose is *to inform,* your goal is to increase your listeners' knowledge about and understanding of the topic. Chapter 14 is devoted entirely to informative speeches. When you give an informative speech, you are acting as a

Teaching Tip
Have students read a sample speech and write out the general and specific purpose as well as the thesis statement. Have them analyze the appropriateness of these elements.

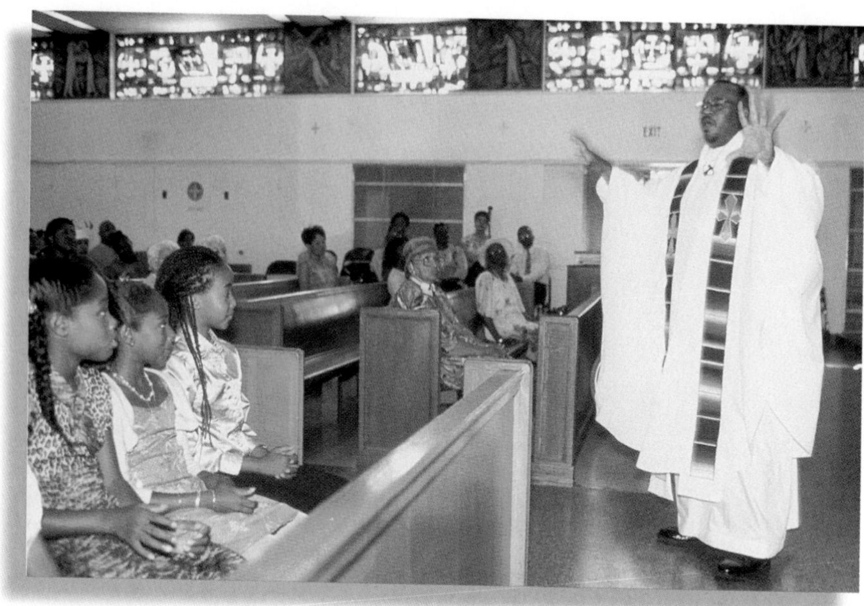

Religious leaders give persuasive speeches all the time.

teacher in that you are attempting to create shared understanding. Colleges and universities often invite guest lecturers to speak to the campus community. These invited professionals usually present informative speeches about their areas of expertise. If Holly decides to inform her listeners, she might talk about *the factors to consider when selecting a day care option.*

When your general purpose is *to persuade,* your goal is to influence your listeners' beliefs or behaviors. Although, in a persuasive speech, you *do* provide your listeners with information, your purpose in doing so is ultimately to change their beliefs or behaviors. Pastors, ministers, and rabbis often present sermons that can be classified as persuasive speeches. Television infomercials are also persuasive speeches in that they attempt to convince viewers to buy a particular product. If Holly decides to persuade her listeners, she might focus on why one day care option is better than the others. She'll talk about the major factors to consider when evaluating day care options just as she would in an informative speech, but she will do so to achieve her goal, which is *to persuade listeners that one particular option is the best.*

When your general purpose is *to entertain,* your goal is to use humor to make a point. You might share information as in an informative speech, and you might even try to win your listeners over to your point of view about something as in a persuasive speech, but above all you are entertaining your listeners through humor. Speeches to entertain also make a serious point. For example, Billy Crystal's humorous opening monologue at the 1998 Academy Awards ceremony ended with a serious point that all nominees are "winners."

If Holly decides to entertain her listeners, she might prepare a speech

What Do You Think?

Identify a time when you heard a professional speaker (a keynote address, banquet speaker, motivational speaker, preacher, etc.). Was the general purpose to inform, to persuade, or to entertain? Did it seem appropriate to you as a listener? Why or why not?

to entertain by focusing on the experiences of being a day care center employee. She might conclude, however, with a serious point about the importance of parent involvement in any kind of day care setting.

Step 4: Determine Your Specific Purpose

In the fourth step, you determine the *specific purpose* of your speech. That is, once you know whether you are going to inform, persuade, or entertain, you must answer the question "about what?" The **specific purpose** is expressed by a single phrase that identifies precisely what you hope to accomplish in your speech. When you determine your specific purpose, you select one aspect of the topic as your precise focus as well as decide what it is you hope your audience will know or feel about this aspect of the topic by the time you finish your speech.

To ensure that your specific purpose statement is precise, you must also consider the time constraints and audience expectations. In other words, you need to ask yourself questions like the following: (a) Can I cover this topic thoroughly in the time allotted? and (b) Is this specific purpose relevant to my audience—not too technical or too superficial? For Holly's informative speech, the specific purpose is to identify the factors to consider when selecting a day care option. For Holly's persuasive speech, the specific purpose is to show how and why one particular day care option is better than the others. And for Holly's speech to entertain, the specific purpose is to make her audience laugh about the experiences of a day care center employee and allude to the importance of parental involvement in any kind of day care setting.

Step 5: Create Your Thesis Statement

In the fifth and final step of the mold method, you create your *thesis statement.* As you recall, the thesis statement is a one-sentence summary of your speech. The thesis statement modifies the specific purpose from what you hope to accomplish in your speech to what you will actually say in your introduction. At this point, you may generate a thesis statement by simply combining your general purpose and your specific purpose in a way that clearly declares the main point of your speech. As you continue to work on your speech, you will probably want to modify the wording of your thesis statement. That's okay. Your goal during the narrowing process is to mold your general topic into a manageable main idea that is appropriate to the audience and the occasion.

There are three key guidelines to follow as you shape your thesis statement. Phrase your thesis statement as a complete, declarative sentence; focus on one main idea; and use concrete language and style.

Technology Tip
http://www.wisc.edu/writing/Handbook/ThesisStatements.html

This Web site, developed by The University of Wisconsin-Madison Writing Center, defines, explains, and assists in the development of a thesis. Have students visit this site before they write their next thesis statement.

Complete, Declarative Sentence. First, phrase your thesis statement as a complete, declarative sentence, not as a question or a fragment. Questions allude to the topic, but do not provide enough direction about what you hope to accomplish in the speech. Fragments are not complete thoughts, but merely ideas.

Ineffective thesis statement: How do you select a day care?

Ineffective thesis statement: Choosing a day care

Effective thesis statement: There are three key factors to consider when selecting a day care option.

Teaching Tip
Have students write out a thesis statement for a topic of their choice. Write these statements on the chalkboard and ask the class to improve them. Stress to students the importance of having clear goals for what they want to accomplish in their speeches.

Ineffective thesis statement: Why earn a college degree?

Ineffective thesis statement: Benefits of a college degree

Effective thesis statement: Earning a college degree will enhance your professional life in three particular ways.

One Main Idea. Second, narrow your thesis statement to focus concisely on one main idea. You cannot cover more than one idea thoroughly in the short time constraints of a public speech. Although your topic exploration may direct you to many interesting ideas for a speech, you need to select one idea and the specific aspect you have decided to focus on must be worded precisely in your thesis statement. Ambiguous thesis statements don't clearly reveal what dimension of a topic you plan to discuss.

Ineffective thesis statement: France is a great place to visit.

Effective thesis statement: There are three significant historical sites known for their unique architecture you'll want to see when visiting France.

Ineffective thesis statement: Choosing a day care can be difficult and there are many different options available.

Effective thesis statement: A professional day care center provides more benefits to children than any other option.

Ineffective thesis statement: The Japanese culture is very interesting.

Effective thesis statement: Traditional Japanese clothing represents three important values of the Japanese culture.

Ineffective thesis statement: We are destroying our environment.

Effective thesis statement: Water pollution is a serious environmental problem in our country.

Concrete Language and Style. Third, phrase your thesis statement using concrete language and style. Since your listeners must comprehend your main point in one sentence, that sentence must be composed concisely, using concrete terms. Inflated language and complex sentence structure might make your main point difficult to decipher on a single hearing.

Ineffective thesis statement: The growing number of violent crimes in high schools across the United States points to a problem that is embedded in our cultural values.

Effective thesis statement: The growing number of violent crimes committed in U.S. high schools is a serious problem.

Ineffective thesis statement: A social movement that is becoming stronger and growing in number throughout our country is the neo-Nazi Skinhead movement.

Effective thesis statement: Society should be alarmed by the fact that the violent hate group known as neo-Nazi Skinheads is growing rapidly.

Applying the Mold Method

Narrowing the focus of your speech using the mold method turns broad topics like those generated in your personal inventory into manageable speech topics by considering your audience, the general purpose, and the specific purpose. To test whether your thesis statement is effective based on the mold method, ask yourself the following questions:

- Does my thesis statement focus on the needs and interests of my particular audience?
- Does my thesis statement reflect the general purpose I've selected?
- Does my thesis statement address my specific purpose in a single, declarative sentence?
- Does my thesis statement focus on a single main point?
- Is my thesis statement phrased using concrete language and style?

Discussion Tip
Ask students to identify a public speaker whom they have seen recently. What did the speaker do to make the topic interesting? How did the speaker adapt the topic to the audience?

What Do You Think?

Select a topic from your personal inventory. Narrow the focus of your topic using the mold method.

Here are some examples of how Holly and others narrowed their speech topics using the mold method:

General topic:	Day care
Topic area:	Day care options
General purpose:	To inform
Specific purpose:	I want to inform my listeners about the factors they should consider when selecting a day care option.
Thesis statement:	There are three key factors to consider when selecting a day care option.
General topic:	Higher education
Topic area:	Benefits of a college degree
General purpose:	To persuade
Specific purpose:	I want to persuade high school students to attend college.
Thesis statement:	Earning a college degree will enhance your professional life in three important ways.
General topic:	Japan
Topic area:	Japanese culture
General purpose:	To inform
Specific purpose:	I want to inform listeners about how traditional Japanese clothing represents certain aspects of Japanese culture.
Thesis statement:	Traditional Japanese clothing represents three important values of the Japanese culture.

Summary

Selecting and narrowing a topic into an effective thesis statement is essentially a three-part process. You begin by brainstorming and researching to create a personal inventory—a list of places, events, people, organizations, hobbies, books, television programs, opinions, beliefs, values, and goals that interest you. Next, you choose a topic and explore the different directions you might go with it. You can do this by expanding your personal inventory with "why" statements, creating a concept map, and doing additional research. Finally, you need to narrow the focus of your topic to speak appropriately and thoroughly in the time allotted.

The mold method is a five-step process designed to effectively narrow a general topic into an appropriate thesis statement. In the first step, you choose a general topic from your personal inventory. This general topic can be anything that interests you, either because you know a lot about it or because you'd like to learn more about it. In the second step, you narrow your general topic into a topic area by considering how you might mold the topic to address your particular audience's needs and interests. This is based on audience analysis, which is the focus of Chapter 6. In the third step, you determine the general purpose for your speech—that is, to inform, to persuade, or to entertain. In the fourth step, you narrow your topic further by determining the specific purpose. The specific purpose focuses on what you hope to accomplish in the speech. In the fifth and final step, you develop your thesis statement—that is, a one-sentence summary of your speech. Your thesis statement should be phrased as a complete, declarative sentence; focus on one main idea; and use concrete language and style.

An appropriate speech topic is one that interests the speaker and is relevant to listeners. You can develop an appropriate speech topic by considering what interests you and why, and then narrowing your focus by considering your audience and purpose.

Activities

1. **Personal Inventory and Reaction Paper.** Create a list of your own interests and reasons for them. Then select one or two topics about which you feel strongly. Discuss these topics individually with two or three significant people in your life. For example, you might talk with (a) a parent, (b) a grandparent, (c) a sibling, (d) a good friend who seems very similar to you, or (e) a good friend who seems quite different from you. Based on these discussions, write a one- to two-page reaction paper highlighting the opinions and attitudes that emerged.
2. **Group Concept Map.** In groups of three or four, select a topic from one of the member's personal inventory list. Then do a concept map by passing the paper around the group. Each person adds a related idea until everyone has participated at least twice. Then talk as a group about the various directions this topic could take.
3. **Mold Method Group Exercise.** In groups of three or four, select a topic from one member's personal inventory list. Then use the mold method to narrow the general topic into a thesis statement.

Key Terms

Attitude
Audience analysis
Belief
Brainstorming
Concept mapping
Expanded personal inventory
General purpose
Personal inventory
Rhetorical situation
Specific purpose
Thesis statement
Values

CHAPTER 6

Understanding Your Audience

Reflective Questions

1. What are some characteristics you and your classmates have in common?
2. What are some characteristics you and your classmates don't have in common?
3. How might these similarities and differences be important as you prepare your speech?
4. What can you do to learn about your audience?
5. What might motivate your audience to listen to your speech?
6. How might the time of day or week impact the attention span of your listeners?
7. Why is it important to consider learning styles as a part of audience analysis?

In many ways, Duane was a local success story for the university. He worked his way through college by waiting tables at a local restaurant and typing papers for his classmates. In addition to being a full-time student and working two part-time jobs, he was active in several campus organizations. Although he was a very busy young man, he managed to graduate with a 3.8 cumulative grade point average. After earning his bachelor's degree, Duane completed medical school and was recently hired as an orthopedic specialist in a reputable medical facility in the community. Although he never thought he would end up back in this city, he was happy. His family seemed to be adjusting well too.

The university orientation organizer thought Duane would be a good role model for incoming students and asked him to present a speech during Orientation Week about "Making the Most of Your College Experience." Duane was delighted to have the opportunity to help new students learn what to do and what *not* to do. There were certainly some things he would do differently in college if he had it to do over.

Duane decided to talk about the college academic life and social life. Academically, he planned to talk about how important it is to keep up with the assignments and to attend class. Even though it is fun to be out from under the parents' thumbs, students still need to be responsible for their education. Socially, he planned to talk about the importance of becoming involved in organizations. He wanted to point out that the friendships one makes in these organizations can keep a person in school when she or he feels like dropping out. He would also caution students to avoid some of the nightlife activities around town. Although he would admit that they can be fun, too much of a good thing can hurt students academically, and it's important to remember that an education is the reason students are at the university.

Duane worked hard on his speech. He even prepared a slide show that would "speak for itself." As he walked up to the lectern, however, the "first-year students" he expected to see were not who he saw in the audience. For example, the elementary school secretary where he had just enrolled his daughter was a first-year student. The stylist who had cut his hair yesterday was a first-year student. The mechanic who changed the oil in his car the other day was a first-year student. Many of the students in the audience were at least as old as he was. Several were sitting with young children they had brought along to the event. He even recognized one student as an orderly from the medical facility where he had just been hired! First-year students sure have changed, he thought to himself. Where were the "kids" who just graduated from high school? Well, at least they would enjoy the slide show, he thought. Just then, a first-year student and his seeing-eye dog entered the auditorium. As Duane arranged his notes on the lectern, the only thought that came to him was "Help!"

Teaching Tip
Take this opportunity to emphasize to students that breakdowns in communication can be avoided if one considers the audience before speaking.

Although Duane worked hard to prepare his speech, he neglected an important step in the process—analyzing your audience. Effective public speakers are audience centered. That is, they learn who their listeners are and then adapt their speech to reflect an understanding of their listeners' interests and concerns. This aspect of understanding your audience and adapting your speech to them is known as **audience analysis** (Reinard, 1988). As you learned in Chapter 5, effective public speakers first conduct audience analysis as a part of selecting and narrowing a topic. Keep in mind, however, that it doesn't stop there. Effective public speakers employ audience analysis throughout the speechmaking process.

We begin this chapter by discussing why audience analysis is important. We then look more closely at three general areas within which you can analyze your audience. From there we offer some specific methods for doing so. Finally, we conclude with a discussion about the role of audience analysis throughout the speechmaking process, beginning with topic selection.

Why Analyze Your Audience?

Sometimes students become anxious about the concept of audience analysis. To them it can sound very technical and complex. Actually, audience analysis is one of the most important steps in the speechmaking process for *reducing* anxiety. For one thing, audience analysis will ensure you that your topic is relevant to your listeners, and this will make you feel more confident about giving your speech. Second, through audience analysis you can develop your speech so that it addresses audience expectations and motivations. This, too, should increase your confidence and reduce your anxiety. Finally, once you have analyzed your audience, your listeners are no longer total strangers to you, and research suggests that anxiety levels are highest when speaking to strangers. Speaking to people you know—even if you only know them a little bit—reduces anxiety (Richmond & McCroskey, 1995).

Teaching Tip
Make transparency masters of print ads that are targeted at different audiences. Show these ads in class and ask students to identify the target audience in each ad. Discuss how these ads would vary if they were targeted at different audiences.

Although audience analysis sounds like a difficult procedure, it really doesn't have to be. In truth, you engage in audience analysis every day, you just haven't applied the label to the process. Consider, for example, the different people with whom you interact. These people may include your parents, your children, your spouse, your coworkers, your neighbors, your close friends, and your casual acquaintances. Now, if each of these people were to ask you something as simple as how you were feeling or how your day was going, would you phrase your response in exactly the same way for each of them? If you wouldn't, the modifications you would make are essentially the result of audience analysis.

Technology Tip
http://www.presentersuniversity.com/courses/show_codefining.cfm?RecordID=118
This Web page, hosted by Presenters University, offers a simple formula for conducting audience analysis.

Why do you explain some things differently depending on whether you're talking to a young child or a parent, to a loved one or a casual acquaintance, to a group of elementary students or a group of college students? You explain things differently because you want your message to succeed—that is, you want your listener or listeners to be able to make sense of your explanation. Similarly, if you are trying to persuade different people to, say, go somewhere with you or do something, you'll phrase your argument in different ways to make it as effective as possible.

When you give speeches, you'll want to use a more formal version of the audience analysis you use in your daily life, for much the same reason: Audience analysis helps your message succeed with your listeners. In other words, it helps you achieve the goal you have set for the speech.

Another reason to engage in audience analysis during the speechmaking process is to boost your own ethos. As discussed in Chapter 1, ethos has to do with your credibility in terms of perceived competence and character. Ethos is crucial to the success of your speech because when listeners think positively of a speaker, they are more likely to think positively of the message as well.

Through audience analysis, you can understand how your listeners' attitudes, beliefs, and values are similar to and different from your own. Thus, your speech can be modified to demonstrate respect for those similarities or differences.

Even in casual conversation, we explain things differently depending on whom we're talking to.

Ultimately, adapting your speech based on this understanding can help you sound knowledgeable rather than arrogant or condescending, competent rather than naïve or misguided, and open-minded rather than intolerant. If you can keep your speech true to your own attitudes, beliefs, and values but also modify it in ways that reflect an honest understanding and respect for those of your listeners, you will likely convey ethos, making listeners more receptive to your speech.

What Is Audience Analysis?

Discussion Tip
Divide the class into small groups and have them consider the importance of demographic audience analysis. Then have each group present its findings to the class. Focus discussion on the similarities and differences in the ideas generated by the groups.

Discussion Tip
Ask students if they have ever felt marginalized by a public speaker. How did it feel? What are the implications of marginalization for speaker credibility? What can students do to avoid marginalizing or stereotyping members of the audience?

In order to fully understand what audience analysis is today, it is important to understand what it used to be. In the past, audience analysis was usually limited to making generalizations about the audience based on demographic characteristics. **Demographic characteristics** include traits like age, sex, gender, race, and sociocultural background. In other words, characteristics that can be observed or readily ascertained. The purpose of demographic analysis was for speakers to categorize listeners as belonging to a particular group, determine a profile of that group, and then make their speech relevant to that majority group. For example, if you were to speak to a group of women, you might create a profile of what you believe to be the typical needs and interests of women and then adapt the speech to address those needs and interests.

There are some inherent problems with this approach, and these problems have become more obvious with increasing diversity in our classrooms and communities. When a speaker focuses the message toward a particular group, some listeners are **marginalized**—that is, they are excluded from the communication transaction because their experiences, values, needs, and interests are essentially ignored. Moreover, the group being focused on is often **stereotyped**—that is, the speaker assumes that all members of the group behave or believe a certain way because they belong to that group. Such stereotypes can be both inaccurate and damaging. In fact, Duane's assumption that most first-year college students would be unmarried young people who had just graduated from high school led him to develop a speech that was largely irrelevant to the needs and interests of his actual audience.

Today's audiences are best described as *demographically diverse.* For example, a public speaking classroom is likely to include men and women, heterosexuals and homosexuals, students who are married and students who are single, traditional students and older students, students from many different ethnic groups and perhaps international students, and students with a range of religious beliefs. Given this diversity, the traditional approach to audience analysis not only marginalizes and stereotypes but, in most cases, is not even possible.

Teaching Tip
Have students read a sample speech and determine the target audience. Discuss how the speaker tailored the claims of the speech to demographic characteristics of the audience.

Effective audience analysis today focuses on demographic characteristics from the perspective of demographic diversity, as well as in conjunction with psychological characteristics and environmental characteristics. In other words, speakers consider demographic characteristics to discover, first, whether any demographic characteristics unite all audience members. If their analysis reveals a common demographic characteristic, however, they avoid assuming too much based on that characteristic, since doing so might result in stereotyping. If the analysis reveals no demographic characteristics shared by all, speakers try to reflect an honest understanding of and respect for the diversity of knowledge, values, and attitudes represented in the individuals who comprise the audience.

Let's consider Duane once more. One demographic characteristic shared by everyone in his audience was that they were all *first-year students at the same university.* Duane made the mistake, however, of assuming too much from this characteristic, resulting in stereotypical assumptions about their needs, interests, and expectations. His inaccurate assumptions caused him to fail in terms of adapting the speech to their actual needs and interests. Had he considered this characteristic from a perspective of demographic diversity, he might have focused on the different majors from which to choose at this institution rather than assuming students would skip classes. Likewise, he might have revealed where students can go to learn about various campus organizations and what those organizations have to offer rather than assuming students would get caught up in the nightlife unless they were persuaded to avoid doing so.

Effective audience analysis today also means going beyond an examination of demographic characteristics to also consider the psychological characteristics and the environmental characteristics of your audience. **Psychological characteristics** are those factors that motivate people to listen to and retain ideas—that is, our tendencies to respond to human needs, rhetorical appeals, and preferred learning styles. **Environmental characteristics** consist of the factors that influence why listeners attend and what they expect from a particular speech—in other words, expectations about time, setting, and occasion. Let's explore each of these general areas of audience analysis in more detail.

Analysis of Demographic Characteristics

As you've already seen, audience analysis used to focus almost exclusively on demographic characteristics. Demographic audience analysis is still important; however,

Teaching Tip
Ask students to read the "Letters to the Editor" in a Sunday paper. Have them note the major issues and the types of attitudes, values, and beliefs expressed. Discuss whether these attitudes, values, and beliefs seem representative of the community as a whole.

it takes a somewhat different form. Its goal is to help a speaker (a) determine the diversity represented in the audience and (b) discover any major patterns that could influence the speech. That is, through demographic audience analysis, you will be able to make informed inferences both about who your listeners are and about what interests they have. In both cases, your focus is on aspects that are relevant to your topic. Based on these inferences, you can shape your speech in ways that acknowledge and respect your listeners and the different values, beliefs, and attitudes they may hold. Where possible, you try to discover connections between yourself and your values and your listeners and their values—connections that you'll be able to highlight as listener relevance links throughout the speech.

Teaching Tip
Assign the Indirect Audience Analysis exercise found in the Activities section of this chapter. Compile and report the results of this analysis to the class for their consideration in the preparation of speeches. Discuss how different topics could be adapted based on class demographics.

Keep in mind that demographic analysis cannot provide you with definite answers; however, it can be the basis for useful inferences about your audience (Berko, Wolvin, & Ray, 1997; Brumfit, 1993; Iino, 1993). In other words, the only way you can know for certain what your listeners believe about a topic or expect from you as a speaker is to *ask them* before you prepare your speech. Unfortunately, it is rarely feasible or even possible to do so. Hence, speakers must rely on inferences they can draw related to their topic based on demographic audience analysis.

What, then, might your demographic audience analysis consist of and how might you use it? Your analysis can focus on a range of characteristics, including age; sex, gender, or sexual orientation; group affiliations; socioeconomic factors; and sociocultural background. You'll want to identify any characteristics that could be relevant to your topic and adapt your approach accordingly, while taking care not to stereotype your audience.

Age

Teaching Tip
Assign students to groups and provide them with the same speech topic for analysis. The students should be instructed to develop claims for the topic based on the following audiences: (a) an audience consisting primarily of seniors over the age of sixty-five, and (b) an audience consisting of eighteen- to twenty-five-year-old students in their first two years of college. Explore the ways in which students might tailor their messages to these different audiences.

Ask yourself whether your listeners will be older or younger than you are and, more specifically, what the age range of your audience is. Will your listeners include children, teenagers, young adults, middle-aged people, or seniors? Finding answers to these questions can help you shape your speech, because the age of your listeners often influences their attitudes, beliefs, and values, as well as their interests and knowledge (Caplan, 1999; Hummert, Shaner, Garstka, & Henry, 1998; Hummert, Wieman, & Nussbaum, 1994; Kemper & Harde, 1999; Nussbaum & Coupland, 1995; Thimm, 1998; Williams, 1997).

Aristotle claimed that younger listeners tend to be more optimistic and trusting, as well as easier to persuade, than older listeners (McGuire, 1985). This is a broad generalization. Older people can be very trusting and open minded, and younger people can be very distrusting and closed minded. Nonetheless, if you're giving a persuasive speech to an older audience, you might want to pay more attention than usual to making sure you have strong evidence to support your claims.

Age can also affect the basic concerns people have. At different points in life, we have different goals. To clarify, whereas a speech about career planning might be quite compelling to listeners under thirty, it would probably be less likely to interest those over fifty. They would probably be more interested in career changing or even retirement planning.

Our age clearly influences the experiences we have had, and our experiences in turn influence our knowledge and our views. Listeners who lived through, say, the Great Depression, World War II, and the Cold War are likely to view topics

The experiences of audience members can influence their attitudes about your topic.

related to economics, the military, and national security differently than those who did not experience these periods and events. Consider, for example, how your speech about the need for more U.S. military involvement in Kosovo or Indonesia might be perceived by listeners who had fought in or had lost loved ones in the Vietnam war. How might their experiences influence their attitudes regarding your topic and, ultimately, the way you might adapt your speech to demonstrate respect?

You'll therefore want to consider the age range of your audience when you develop the content of your speech. Had Duane recognized the age range of his audience when developing his speech, he could have adapted his message to demonstrate respect for the breadth of experiences and values represented. Ian, another novice public speaker, did consider the age range of his audience for his speech about fire safety. His public speaking class included students ranging in age from eighteen to forty. For the younger students, Ian offered examples of safety measures to take in residence halls and apartments. In addition, he addressed key concerns for people who own their own homes. This component added relevance for many of the older students in the class, as well as for the instructor. Because Ian had analyzed his audience in term of age, he was able to make his speech audience centered for all. Notice that, far from stereotyping his listeners, Ian demonstrated respect for the demographic diversity of his audience.

What Do You Think?

Will your audience include listeners who are older or younger than you? How might their basic concerns and life experiences influence the way they perceive your topic? What can you do to respect demographic diversity represented in your audience with regard to age?

Sex, Gender, and Sexual Orientation

Teaching Tip
Encourage interactions between cultures by pairing students with a partner who is different in terms of gender, race, age, and so on. Have students interview each other about their important attitudes, values, and beliefs. Discuss the differences and similarities in the class.

Sex is defined as the biological differences between males and females. Occasionally, a topic—for example, medical topics such as hysterectomies or prostate cancer—will seem more relevant to one sex than the other. If you're interested in such a topic, figure out how the topic may benefit both sexes. Laura, for example, presented a persuasive speech about the alarming number of unnecessary hysterectomies being performed in the United States. This topic could potentially be irrelevant to the males in her audience, since males cannot have hysterectomies. Throughout her speech, however, Laura highlighted ways in which males are also harmed by this unnecessary practice—the increases in insurance rates and the emotional trauma experienced by family members, for example. In short, effective public speakers do not discard a topic because it seems more relevant to one sex than the other, but rather they work to discover how it may be relevant to both.

Discussion Tip
What role does communication play in the socialization of individuals into masculine and feminine gender roles? How are individuals rewarded and sanctioned for adherence (or lack thereof) to these gender roles? How can speakers avoid making assumptions about the members of their audience?

A more complex concept than sex, **gender** can be defined as the socialized tendencies of men and women to perceive, believe, and behave differently in the world (Wood, 1994, pp. 21–26). Gender is not innate, as is sex, but is learned behavior. Although these tendencies cannot be universally attributed to men or women, research reveals that by the time girls and boys are four or five years old, they already understand what these "gender-appropriate" tendencies are and often act accordingly (Plotnik, 1993; Tannen, 1992).

What are these socialized tendencies of masculine and feminine gender? Essentially, "to be feminine is to be attractive, deferential, unaggressive, emotional, nurturing, and concerned with people and relationships," whereas "to be masculine is to be strong, ambitious, successful, rational, and emotionally controlled" (Wood, 1994, p. 21). Moreover, although the concept of what constitutes appropriate gender behavior changes over time, the basic blueprint continues to be fairly consistent (Faludi, 1991; Kirtley & Weaver, 1999; McAdoo, 1999; Reissman, 1990; Sellnow & Golish, 2000).

Contemporary research suggests, however, that both males and females possess these feminine and masculine tendencies (Ivy & Backlund, 1994). Your goal as a public speaker, then, is to avoid making assumptions about the males and females in your audience (Canary & Dindia, 1998; Canary & Hause, 1993; Reeder, 1996; Weatherall, 1998). You cannot presume that women are more emotional and men more logical, or that women prefer testimonials and men statistics, and so on.

It's also important to avoid gender stereotypes about the attitudes, interests, or likes and dislikes of audience members. Consider Brad, for example, who fell into

CATHY © Cathy Guisewite. Reprinted with permission of UNIVERSAL PRESS SYNDICATE. All rights reserved.

Avoid gender stereotypes about the attitudes, interests, or likes and dislikes of your audience members.

this trap when he presented an informative speech about why growing up on a farm was significant to him. Throughout the speech, he made comments like "Although the gals might not relate to the hard work of baling hay, I'm sure many of the guys know what I mean." As it turned out, several of the women in the classroom had grown up on farms and baled hay. Brad's comments stereotyped and marginalized some of his listeners and, moreover, failed to reflect and build on the reality. His ethos as a speaker was diminished and, consequently, so was the success of his speech.

As you prepare your speech, you'll also want to be sensitive to diversity of sexual orientation among audience members. Sometimes heterosexual speakers make the mistake of presuming all listeners are heterosexual. Recall from Chapter 1 that this happened when Jim presented his speech on Elton John's music. At several points during his presentation, Jim distanced himself from Elton John by making clear that it was solely for Elton John's music that he admired him. Jim had no way of knowing whether any of his listeners were homosexual and may have been offended by his remarks. And, of course, his remarks may have offended other listeners as well. Likewise, when Kari talked about the important role of fathers in raising emotionally stable children, she unknowingly marginalized Ryan who—along with his little brother—was raised by a lesbian couple. Effective public speakers, in short, respect the diversity of their audience members with regard to sexual orientation by avoiding potentially offensive remarks that assume all intimate relationships and family systems are heterosexual.

Discussion Tip
In what ways might a speaker communicate a heterosexual bias during a presentation? How can you ensure that your speech demonstrates respect in terms of sex, gender, and sexual orientation?

What Do You Think?

Consider your listeners. What can you speculate about them regarding sex? Regarding gender? Regarding sexual orientation? How can you make sure your speech demonstrates respect toward all regarding sex, gender, and sexual orientation?

Group Affiliations

Discussion Tip
Have students discuss their attitudes toward controversial topics such as abortion and capital punishment. How does group affiliation influence these attitudes? To what groups do students belong?

We belong to many groups, including, for example, political, religious, and social groups. Our group affiliations sometimes influence or reflect our views. That is, our conscious affiliation with certain groups together with the value we place on being affiliated with them affects the way we perceive experiences and events in our lives (DeSanta Ana, J., 1996; Gudykunst, Ting-Toomey, Nishida, Kim, & Heyman, 1996; Petronio, Ellemers, Giles, & Gallois, 1998; Suzuki, 1998). Therefore, you'll want to speculate about how such affiliations might influence the way listeners are likely to perceive your message. Say, for example, that you are going to present a speech about a controversial social issue. If this issue is one on which Republicans and Democrats tend to have different views, you will fare better if you know the political affiliations of your audience members. Obviously, unless you are presenting a speech at a political rally, it is highly unlikely that all your listeners will belong to the same political party. Even within a political party, not everyone is committed to the same ideals. Effective public speakers, nonetheless, attempt to learn as much as possible about the political affiliations of their listeners if political affiliation may influence listeners' perceptions about the particular speech topic.

The United States is religiously very diverse, including Protestants of many denominations, Roman Catholics, Jews, Muslims, Buddhists, Hindus, Mormons, and people who belong to numerous other religions, as well as atheists and agnostics. If your topic is one that touches on religious beliefs, you'll want to consider both how religious affiliation might influence the perception of your topic and communicate respect for diverse religions. When Dana presented her persuasive speech about a woman's right to choose whether or not to have an abortion, she would have adjusted the language and, perhaps, limited the degree to which she attempted to persuade had she realized most of her listeners were strict Roman Catholics who didn't even believe in birth control, let alone abortion.

What Do You Think?

Consider your listeners. What can you speculate about them regarding religion? Political affiliation? Social group involvement? How might your speculations influence the way in which you develop and present your speech?

Social groups include school clubs, volunteer organizations, professional groups, and the many other groups that people join to engage in their interests. Sometimes you'll give a speech to a particular group. Knowing their mission and goals can help you adapt your speech to their needs and interests. Your approach to a speech about drinking and driving, for example, is likely to differ depending on whether you are presenting it to a college fraternity, to a PTA group, or to a high school sports team. More often, you'll be presenting your speech to listeners who don't all share a social group affiliation. In such cases, you would simply approach your speech in ways that demonstrate respect for demographic diversity in terms of group affiliation.

Discussion Tip
Ask students to speculate about the importance of socioeconomic factors in audience analysis. How do these factors influence the interpretation of messages? Why is it important to avoid making assumptions about the interests of listeners based on income?

Socioeconomic Factors

Socioeconomic factors include occupation, income, and education. Each of these factors can influence the way in which your listeners may interpret your message.

Since we spend so much of our adult life working, our occupation can have a significant effect on our interests and our experiences, as well as our attitudes and beliefs. If you are speaking to a group of listeners who are in the same occupation—whether it's a group of doctors, teachers, lawyers, sales representatives, farmers, or construction workers—your listeners will have similar experiences, skills, and perspectives, and you should allude to and build on these in your speech. If you were to present a speech about gender and communication to a group of dental assistants, for example, you might try to use examples that are likely to occur in a dental office. You might talk about misinterpretations that can arise between dental assistant and patient when they are different genders.

If your listeners work for the same company, there may be even greater similarities of experiences and perspectives for you to take account of in your speech. Communication consultants, for example, often meet with employees of a company prior to presenting a speech there, so they can make their examples relate directly to the employees and their experiences.

The amount of money your listeners earn can also influence their beliefs and attitudes about your speech topic, since income pervades most other aspects of our lives. A speech about universal health care coverage, for example, is likely to be perceived differently by a group of low-income workers than by a group of high-income professionals, especially because members of the latter are far more likely to receive medical insurance from their employers. If you were giving a speech to the latter group, you might approach your speech in ways that address the comparative advantages of universal health coverage over other plans. If you were giving a speech to the former group, on the other hand, you might approach your speech in ways that reveal steps these individuals can take to make universal coverage affordable.

As with all demographic factors, however, you'll need to avoid stereotyping listeners based on their income. For example, you shouldn't assume that someone whose income level probably precludes a need to worry about health care coverage would therefore be uninterested in, or even opposed to, universal health care coverage.

The amount of education your listeners have might well affect the way you approach your topic. Very generally speaking, the more educated listeners are, the more likely they are to know something about a variety of topics. Hence, if you're speaking to a highly educated audience, you might attempt to share some unusual insight or perspective about your topic. For example, an informative speech demonstrating how to make an apple pie might provide new information to a group of elementary students; however, it would probably not teach college students anything new. To provide new insight to the college students, you might teach them how an apple pie actually can be made over a campfire.

Of course, there are many kinds of educational experiences. For example, a person might lack formal education but be widely read, as was the case with Will in the Academy Award-winning film, *Good Will Hunting.* So, as with the other areas we've looked at, it's important to avoid overgeneralizing about listeners based on educational level.

In addition, while more education may mean more knowledge about a breadth of topics, you'll need to consider how much your audience knows about your particular topic. What is their level of expertise on this topic compared to yours? For example, Susan, who was in her junior year as an engineering major, realized that however much her classmates and instructor knew about other topics, when it came to engineering, she knew more than they did. Hence, she knew that her speech on thermodynamics would likely be new to her audience.

If your audience is your classmates, it should be fairly homogeneous with regard to level of education. Even so, there is probably some variety. Some students may be in their first year; others, in their fourth or fifth year. Students' majors will differ. In short, even if you're speaking in class, you'll want to consider levels of education, especially regarding the topic of your speech. By comparing how much you and your listeners know about your topic, you can present a speech that respects your listeners for what they already know while offering them some perspective or ideas they have not considered.

> ***What Do You Think?***
>
> *What are the education levels of your classmates? What are their majors? How might these factors affect your approach to your speech topic?*

Sociocultural Background

Our **sociocultural background** is determined largely by the family and groups we grew up in — the context in which we were raised. As already discussed, the United States is a culturally diverse country. Your listeners will likely vary in ethnicity and religion, and they may be from different regions of the country and from urban, suburban, and rural areas. You'll need to be aware of your listeners' sociocultural backgrounds, especially since the context in which we are raised shapes our values, beliefs, and attitudes (e.g., Bashi & McDaniel, 1997; Donovan & Rundle, 1997; Gudykunst et al., 1996; Kim et al., 1996; Lustig & Koester, 1993; Masterson, Watson, & Cichon, 1991).

Teaching Tip
Show a videotape of a sample speech and have students identify the major values, beliefs, and attitudes of the speaker.

As you may recall from Chapter 5, *values* are broad concepts we consider important and desirable in life. They are the basis of our beliefs and attitudes. *Beliefs* are our judgments about what is true or false. *Attitudes* are our tendencies to respond negatively or positively to persons and things. All three are crucial to listeners' perceptions of our message — hence, the importance of considering listeners' sociocultural background.

A speech about gun control, for example, is likely to be perceived differently by classmates who grew up in an urban environment where gang violence was a problem than by those who grew up suburban neighborhoods where crime had not been an issue or by classmates who grew up in rural areas surrounded by ranchers and hunters. The attitudes of urban-raised listeners, for example, might reflect their belief in a need for self-protection. Likewise, the attitudes of the students raised among ranchers and hunters might be quite different from those who were raised in the suburbs. If you were advocating gun control in your speech, you might spend some time addressing alternative methods of self-protection, as a way to address those urban-raised listeners. You might also consider how your gun control plan could still respect hunters' rights and specific restrictions that would still allow hunters their rights. The point here is that you'll need to do more than just shape your speech so that it takes into account ways in which your listeners' backgrounds might differ from

> ***What Do You Think?***
>
> *What are the sociocultural backgrounds of your listeners? How might you adapt your speech to demonstrate respect for diverse values, beliefs, and attitudes?*

your own. You'll also need to make sure your speech respects the diverse backgrounds of your listeners.

Analyzing your audience based on demographic characteristics helps you realize similarities and differences among your listeners as well as between your listeners and yourself. An effective public speaker is sensitive to and respectful of the demographic diversity represented in the audience. At the very least, conducting effective demographic audience analysis will help ensure that you'll avoid making inappropriate assumptions that could marginalize or offend listeners. In all likelihood, it will also increase the impact of your speech.

Analysis of Psychological Characteristics

Effective public speakers examine the psychological characteristics of their listeners in order to make their speech relevant to them and thus motivate them to listen and retain ideas. These psychological characteristics fall into three categories: (a) human needs, (b) tendencies to respond to rhetorical appeals, and (c) preferred learning styles.

Most people have various needs, respond to various appeals, and, as discussed in Chapter 1, tend to prefer different learning styles. So the key is to be aware of the range of psychological characteristics and to draw on them when possible throughout your speech. This way, you will likely motivate your audience to listen and maintain audience interest throughout.

Maslow's Hierarchy of Needs

Advertisers use the concept of needs every day as they attempt to sell products to consumers. They claim that we'll be more attractive and popular if we buy a toothpaste that makes our teeth look whiter, a body lotion that makes our skin look younger, and, of course, a particular brand of jeans. Such advertisements are, above all, appeals to our need for love and belongingness. While public speaking and advertising are quite different, effective public speakers take the time to examine how the speech could enhance audience members' lives—how it could address their needs.

> **What Do You Think?**
>
> *Consider a television commercial that made you want to buy the product. What made the product appealing to you?*

Technology Tip
http://opax.swin.edu.au/388226/howto/it2/maslow.htm

This Web site, hosted by the Swinburne University of Technology, provides an excellent synopsis of Maslow's basic needs theory. Have students visit this site and prepare a brief report of the utility of Maslow's theory for speech construction.

You may find it useful to think in terms of A. H. Maslow's (1970) hierarchy of human needs. As shown in Figure 6–1, Maslow's hierarchy has five levels: physiological needs, safety needs, love and belongingness needs, esteem needs, and self-actualization needs, with physiological needs being the most basic. According to Maslow, we are motivated by our most basic unmet need. Applied to public speaking, this means that listeners are motivated to listen, learn, and respond to speeches that address some need they desire to have satisfied. You'll want to consider what these needs might be, and, by remembering the diversity of your audience, you might incorporate appeals focused on more than one need. Let's now look at each of the needs.

Discussion Tip
Have students relate Maslow's hierarchy of human needs to the needs identified in student speeches. How might one use Maslow's hierarchy to tailor the claims of a speech to the needs of the audience?

Physiological needs are those related to self-preservation—that is, our needs for oxygen, food, water, rest, and avoidance of pain. Can you tie your speech to

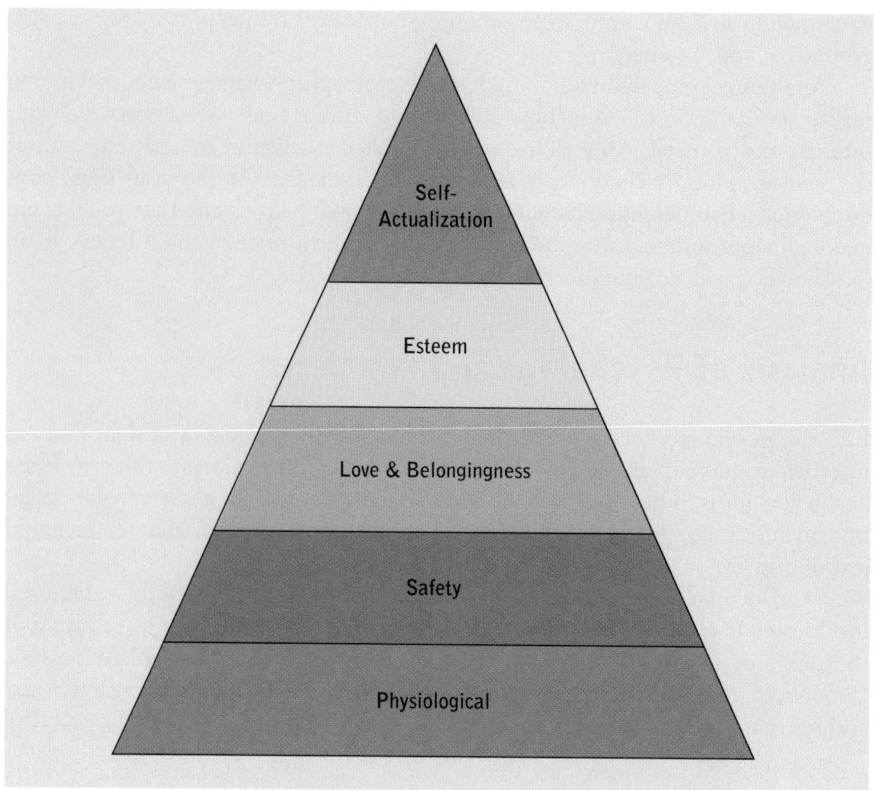

FIGURE 6–1
Maslow's Hierarchy of Human Needs

people's needs for bodily comfort, physical pleasure, sexual gratification, food, or sleep? For example, college students, who are often strapped for money, might be more likely to listen to your speech about recycling if you were to demonstrate how recycling can be used to raise some extra spending money.

Safety needs relate to our desire for order, stability, and security. We often resist change because we perceive it as violating our safety needs. To appeal to audience members' safety needs in your speech about recycling, you might talk about how, while recycling may initially seem confusing, over the long run it will enable sanitation departments to deal effectively with the increasing amount of garbage being generated.

Love and belongingness needs reflect our desire to share our lives with others. We desire approval and acceptance, and we do not like feeling isolated or alone. In your speech about recycling, suggest that your listeners join forces with neighbors or others. By talking about recycling as a group effort, you'll motivate your audience to listen and to act.

Esteem needs are related to our desire for recognition and self-respect. How might your speech appeal to listeners' desires to improve their reputation, achieve more power, gain a sense of personal achievement, and so forth? In the case of the recycling speech, you might inform listeners of a program that recognizes those who meet a certain level of recycling success.

Finally, our self-actualization needs are essentially our desire to realize our personal potential. Whereas esteem needs are most often externally defined by the perceptions others have of us, self-actualization needs are internally defined by our own perceptions of our abilities. Although the form self-actualization needs take depends very much on the individual, you might try to address these needs by thinking about what listeners might value most. For example, you might highlight where to take your recyclables in order to benefit social service organizations such as homeless shelters, rape and abuse crisis centers, or head start programs. Your listeners might not earn any formal recognition for their efforts; however, they will feel good about themselves by doing it.

> ***What Do You Think?***
>
> *In what ways can you approach your speech in order to appeal to the different need levels represented in your audience?*

Discussion Tip
Is it possible to obtain self-actualization? How do self-actualization needs differ from the other needs in Maslow's hierarchy? How can speakers target the self-actualization needs of their audience?

As you can see from the recycling example, your speech can easily address a variety of needs. While you might particularly emphasize, say, the personal financial benefits of recycling to a group of young kids who'd like pocket money, you'll improve your potential for success by addressing as many levels as possible.

Rhetorical Appeals

Ever since Aristotle explained the three rhetorical appeals—ethos, pathos, and logos—effective public speakers have been using them to motivate audience members to listen to their speeches and retain their ideas. The rhetorical appeals work because they each appeal to something humans tend to respond to psychologically.

Technology Tip
http://www.presentersuniversity.com/courses/show_deskills.cfm?RecordID=110
This Web page, hosted by Presenters University, provides an examination of the ways to balance rhetorical appeals (ethos, logos, and pathos) in presentations. Have students visit this site and prepare a brief summary of ways they might utilize these appeals in their next speech.

Ethos refers to appeals to the speaker's credibility, in the sense of competence and character. Listeners are more likely to listen seriously to a speaker who projects a competent and trustworthy image. You can foster ethos by your attire and appearance, delivery skills, and use of credible supporting material. We will talk more specifically about supporting material in Chapter 7 and about delivery skills in Chapter 12.

Pathos refers to appeals to the emotions. Listeners are more likely to retain ideas that somehow touch human emotions. Consider public service announcements that appeal for money to help starving children. Would those announcements be as effective if viewers did not *see* the starving children they could save for the price of a cup of coffee?

Logos refers to appeals to logic. Listeners are more likely to be convinced by a speaker who arranges ideas systematically and who articulates how and why particular evidence supports his or her claims—that is, by connecting each piece of evidence to the main ideas they support through reasoning.

Since different listeners are likely to be more or less compelled by each of these rhetorical appeals, you ought to employ all of them in your public speeches. In her speech about drinking and driving, for example, Karlie quoted several different sources to highlight the number of deaths that occur each year as a result of drinking and driving. Doing so boosted her ethos. Based on the statistical evidence she cited, Karlie employed logos when she calculated how many of these fatalities occur each day, as well as how likely it would be for someone in her audience to one day be a victim of a drinking-and-driving accident. Finally, Karlie shared personal testimonies

> ***What Do You Think?***
>
> *What will you do in your speech to address ethos? Pathos? Logos?*

from people who had lost loved ones to drinking-and-driving accidents. These personal stories appealed to the emotions (pathos) of her listeners. Your goal is to use a variety of rhetorical appeals throughout your speech—appeals to competence and credibility, appeals to emotions, and appeals to logic.

Learning Styles

Teaching Tip
Assign students to four groups and have them develop strategies for each of the four primary learning modes discussed in this chapter. It might be useful to assign each group a topic as well as one of the learning modes. Discuss these strategies in the class.

As you saw in Chapter 1, different people have different preferred learning styles. It follows that when your speech addresses a listener's learning style, you'll motivate that listener to pay attention (Dunn & Dunn, 1979; Magolda, 1989, Marshall, 1990; Rogers, 1983; Sprague, 1993). Moreover, research shows that all listeners—regardless of preferred learning style—grasp information best when it is presented in ways that round the entire four-stage cycle of learning (de Ciantis & Kirton, 1996; Kolb, 1984). To do so, recall that you'll need to address four primary learning modes: watching, doing, feeling, and thinking (see Figure 6–2). Hence, you'll motivate divergers who prefer to feel and watch, assimilators who prefer to watch and think, convergers who prefer to think and do, and accommodators who prefer to do and feel.

To address the watching mode, use visual aids in your speech. Your visual aids could be actual objects, photographs, and so forth. Recall that Duane offered a slide show in his speech. We will discuss visual aids in more detail in Chapter 13.

To address the doing mode, you might ask listeners to engage in an activity or to complete a computation as you speak. For example, if you were informing listeners about appropriate body fat for good physical health, you might talk them through the procedure for computing their own body fat based on height, weight, age, and body type. Better yet, you might display the formula on a visual aid as you explain it. This way you will appeal to both watching and doing.

To appeal to the feeling mode, try to use examples that place your ideas in real-life contexts. Include a range of actual examples, testimonials, and interviews from experts in the field. In your speech about appropriate body fat, you might videotape several testimonials from individuals who have successfully reduced their body fat as they talk about ways their lives have changed as a result. Showing real people speaking for themselves appeals to feeling, because the people are real, as well as to watching, because audience members can actually see them.

FIGURE 6–2
Kolb's Cycle of Learning

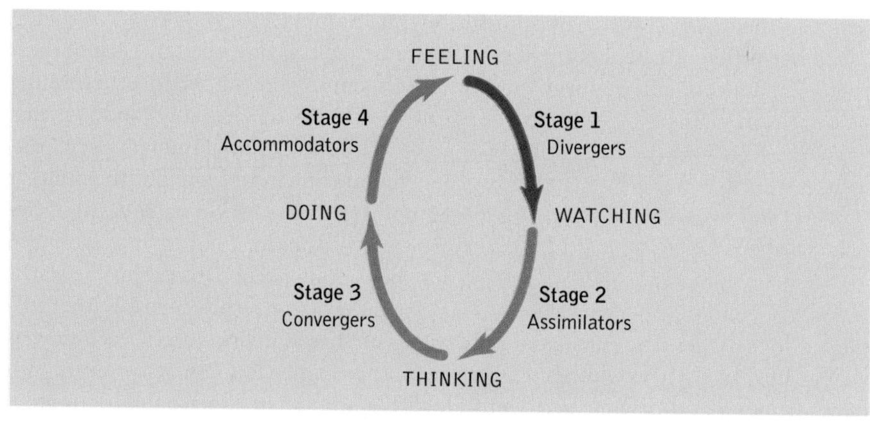

To address the thinking mode, offer facts, statistics, and detailed explanations. In the body fat speech, you might cite facts and statistics about body fat and physical health, as well as insert rhetorical questions for students to ponder later.

Let's return to the recycling speech and consider how you could address each type of learning style mentioned earlier. You might bring samples of the different types of recyclable materials—grade 1, 2, and 3 plastics and so on (watching). You might discuss examples of the kinds of recyclable products college students tend to buy (feeling). You might cite some facts and statistics pointing to the potential consequences of not recycling (thinking). And you might engage listeners in a recycling activity like proper sorting (doing). By preparing your speech in ways that address the entire learning cycle, you'll be more likely to motivate all audience members to listen to and retain the ideas you share.

What Do You Think?

How can you adapt your speech to address the different learning styles represented in your audience?

Analysis of Environmental Characteristics

As you recall, environmental characteristics consist of the factors that influence why listeners attend and what they expect from a particular speech—in other words, expectations about time, setting, and occasion. Analysis of environmental characteristics should not be overlooked. In fact, it is perhaps the easiest of the characteristics to analyze and to adapt a speech to successfully.

Chronemics

Chronemics refers to considerations related to time and our expectations about time. You need to consider how listeners might be affected by the time of the day and week when you will present the speech. For example, if you will be speaking at 8 A.M. on a Monday morning, your listeners might well be tired. You might, therefore, want to begin your speech with some sort of activity to help wake them up. This could be as simple as asking for a show of hands or to repeat some simple action after you model it. The same is true if your speech is scheduled right after lunch. If you are asked to present an eight- to ten-minute speech late on a Friday afternoon, you might consider keeping your speech closer to eight minutes to increase your chances of maintaining listener attention throughout the speech.

Teaching Tip
Ask students to write a brief essay in which they analyze the way their peers in this class orient to time. In addition, ask them to speculate about how this may vary according to one's culture.

Time constraint expectations are also important to consider. If you finish your presentation in less time than the audience anticipated, your listeners are likely to feel cheated. Suppose you'd gone to hear a favorite band play. If the concert finished in less than an hour, would you feel like you had gotten your money's worth? If you speak for more than the anticipated time, listeners may feel disrespected. I have friends, for example, who get pretty upset when the pastor's sermon takes longer than anticipated, causing them to miss a favorite pregame sports program on television.

What Do You Think?

When will you be presenting your next speech? How will you adapt your speech to adhere to time of day and week? To time constraints set forth in the assignment?

It is important to note that these examples tend to reflect the conceptions of time that predominate in our culture. Traditionally, Americans tend to view time as a commodity—something that can be bought, sold, wasted, and saved (Mirriam, 1982). This perception, however, is not universally shared. For individuals in many Native American, Mediterranean, Asian, and Middle Eastern cultures, time is not something that can be manipulated at all (DiMartino, 1989; Lee, 1990). To be an effective public speaker in our culture, however, you must adhere to these kinds of time constraints.

Physical Setting

Discussion Tip
Have students recall a time when a speech they observed seemed inappropriate for the physical setting in which it was given. Discuss how they felt on that occasion and what the speaker might have done differently.

In analyzing environmental characteristics related to physical setting, you'll look, for example, at whether the speech will be presented indoors or outdoors, in a large room or a small room, in a room with comfortable seating or uncomfortable seating, and in front of a large crowd or a small group. All of these factors can have significant repercussions for your speech.

If you will be speaking outside, you will likely have to compete with a host of distractions, such as passersby, or even traffic, wind, or heat. To compete with the distractions, you will have to speak louder and perhaps employ some novelty to maintain listeners' attention.

If you speak in a large room, you will need to speak louder and present your material in a more formal manner than if you are in a smaller room. If the room is crowded or the furniture is uncomfortable, listeners are likely to have shorter attention spans than if they are seated in a sparsely populated room with comfortable furniture. Hence, you might limit how long you will speak.

If the furniture is too comfortable, listeners may relax to the point of allowing their minds to wander from your speech. In this case, you might engage the listeners in an activity or use a variety of visual and audio aids to help them stay focused on you and your message.

What Do You Think?

What is the room like where you will be presenting your public speeches? What is the furniture like? Are there likely to be competing distractions? How might you adapt your speech to adjust to these factors?

Occasion

Discussion Tip
Ask students why it is important to know about the occasion. Ask them to speculate about how violating the expectations of the audience might affect speaker credibility.

As an effective public speaker, you also need to ask yourself, "Why have I been asked to speak on this occasion?" In other words, it is crucial to understand what the audience expects to hear and then to adhere to those expectations. For example, you may be asked to present an informative speech about a significant person in your life. If you, instead, present a persuasive speech about the need to have yearly physical examinations, your speech will not meet the expectations of the audience. And if your listeners expect to hear an informative speech about where their college tuition goes and you, instead, attempt to persuade them to boycott college until tuition gets lowered, your speech would not meet the expectations of your audience.

You also need to consider your speech topic in relation to recent speeches and events. You'll make your speech more audience centered by linking recent speeches and events where appropriate. For example, let's say you plan to present a speech about the need to eat a balanced diet. Earlier during the class period, someone spoke about the need to engage in aerobic activity. You might create a link by showing how your speech builds on the ideas offered in the earlier presentation. You might explain that aerobic activity alone is not enough to achieve good health; a balanced diet is equally important. Likewise, if you plan to persuade your classmates to use the designated driver system when drinking, you might mention an alcohol-related traffic accident that occurred recently in your community.

Methods for Audience Analysis

To this point, we have talked about analyzing your audience to discover demographic, psychological, and environmental characteristics that you can take into account as you adapt your speech to address the interests and needs of your listeners. Knowing what to analyze, however, is not enough. The question that remains is how. In this section, we talk about some direct and indirect methods you can use to effectively analyze your audience. Direct methods are approaches that solicit information from those who will actually be in your audience. While they will produce the most accurate information about your audience, sometimes time, resource, or access limitations prevent you from employing them. Hence, indirect methods must often suffice. Indirect methods are approaches that require some speculation about listeners' interests and attitudes toward your topic. In other words, you must draw inferences based on information you are able to obtain about them.

Discussion Tip
What factors determine the method of audience analysis a speaker will use? Are all of the methods possible for each speech? How much time and effort is required for each of these methods?

Direct Methods

The most common direct methods are interviews, focus groups, and surveys. In an **interview,** you ask individuals questions to obtain the information you need. You can conduct interviews with your listeners to find out about such demographic characteristics as their group affiliations and sociocultural background and about their attitudes and beliefs about your topic. Questions should be developed in advance and should include both closed-ended and open-ended questions. With a **closed-ended question,** respondents choose from a small range of specific answers supplied by the interviewer. Often these questions require just a simple yes or no answer. For her speech about unidentified flying objects (UFOs), Michelle asked the question: "Do you believe in UFOs?" With an **open-ended question,** respondents are asked to reply in their own words. Michelle also asked respondents, "What are your feelings about UFOs?" Interviews can provide a wealth of precise information about your listeners' interests and attitudes related to your topic. Unfortunately, time constraints often prevent the speaker from conducting interviews prior to developing one's speech.

Teaching Tip
Using a sample topic, break students into groups and give each a sample target audience (e.g., nontraditional students, teachers, parents, senior citizens). Students should then be required to develop a brief interview (with both open- and closed-ended questions) for analyzing the specific needs of their target audience.

The **focus group** approach differs from interviews in that you talk to a small group rather than to individuals. This approach allows you to gather information from more people in less time. The participants also talk among themselves, which can provide more descriptive information about their interests and attitudes toward your topic. However, some people may be inhibited about fully sharing their attitudes, beliefs, and values in a group setting, so the information you get might be less accurate than in individual interviews.

A **survey** is designed to gather information from a large pool of respondents in a relatively short amount of time. Respondents often complete a **questionnaire,** which may have open-ended as well as closed-ended questions. Often these responses are written. This maximizes the efficiency of the surveys, but means you don't have the opportunity to ask respondents to expand or clarify their answers.

Teaching Tip
Have students write a brief essay on audience adaptation based on the following questions: How many public presentations have you completed in the past? How did you adjust your presentation to the needs of the audience? If they have no prior public speaking experience, ask them to answer these questions based on interpersonal interactions. What direct or indirect methods of audience analysis might you use for your next speech in this class?

Sometimes your survey can be a simple poll. A **poll** is a quick method to find out where your listeners stand on your topic. Michelle could have asked her listeners whether they believed in UFOs in the form of a poll. Doing so would have surveyed her listeners in a way that would have taken much less time than interviews with each person.

> ***What Do You Think?***
>
> *What questions could you ask your listeners in order to develop a more effective and relevant speech?*

Indirect Methods

While interviews, focus groups, and surveys allow you to find out directly about your audience's characteristics, attitudes, and beliefs, you may not have the time or resources to use these methods. You can still find out a lot about your audience by using indirect methods such as observing your audience, asking other speakers, and reading written resources.

If your audience members are your classmates or another familiar group, observe them and think about who they are, what they talk about. Ask yourself questions: How many people will there be in the audience? What age range is represented? What sorts of information have they shared in previous class discussions and speeches? How might what they've talked about relate to your particular topic? Critical thinking about who your listeners are and what they have shared in the past can be a very useful method for doing audience analysis.

If you know other people who have spoken to a particular group, you might ask them for information about the group. For example, you might ask them how the audience reacted to humor, to the length of their speech, and to the kinds of stories and examples they provided. Were there any issues that seemed to make the audience uncomfortable? What were they? If you know someone who belongs to the group, you might ask that person for his or her observations and insights, especially those relevant to your topic.

Finally, in many cases you might be able to read brochures, newspaper articles, organizational bylaws, or industry abstracts to learn about the group you will be addressing. Most organizations have a Web page that can tell you a great deal about who the organization is, what its mission and goals are, how it operates, and what it has achieved.

For example, when I was asked to present a motivational speech about success to the Society of Women Engineers (SWE), a student organization on our campus, I read its Web page to learn about its purpose and membership. This way I could tailor my speech to address its members' unique goals and accomplishments. I learned that members must maintain a high GPA, volunteer to help public service organizations in the community, and act as leaders in campus government. I adapted my speech to focus on success as more than earning good grades and achieving professional goals. Being a success also means making a difference in the lives of those around you.

> ***What Do You Think?***
>
> *What do you know about your listeners based on their speeches and on conversations you've had or heard? What might this knowledge lead you to believe about how they might react to your topic?*

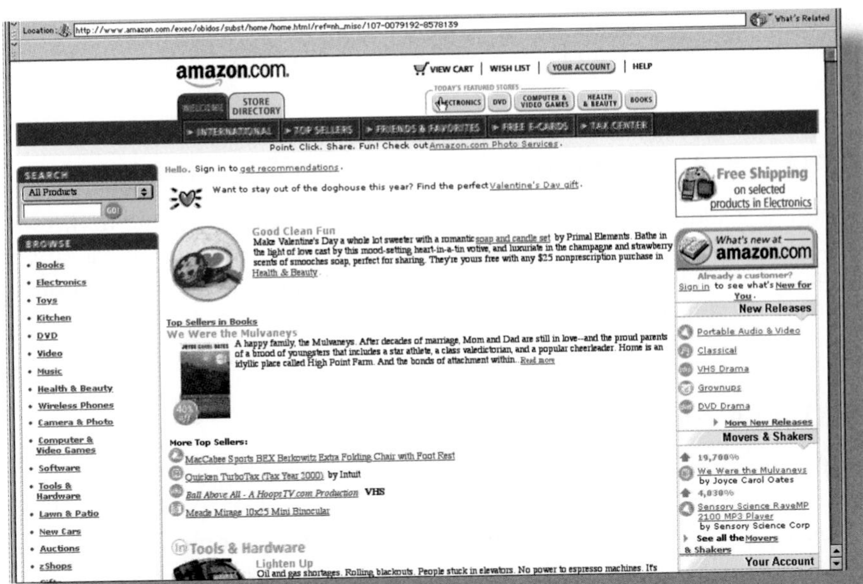

You can find out a lot about an organization by reading its company Web page.

Considering Ethics: Integrating Audience Analysis

Conducting audience analysis is a formidable but crucial task to effective public speaking. To demonstrate genuine respect for your listeners, you must integrate audience analysis throughout the speechmaking process—when you select and narrow your topic, when you choose supporting material, when you structure your ideas, and when you deliver your speech. In other words, although audience analysis begins with topic selection, it ought to be an important consideration through the preparation and presentation process (see Figure 6–3).

Discussion Tip
Ask students to differentiate between adapting to an audience and "pandering." Focus the discussion on the ethics of audience analysis.

Audience Analysis and Topic Selection

> **What Do You Think?**
>
> *What is the general topic you have selected for your next speech? How can you mold your topic into a relevant topic area based on what you have learned by analyzing your audience?*

Recall our discussion of the mold method in Chapter 5. The second step in that method is to narrow your general topic to a topic area based on the needs and interests of your listeners. Recall that Holly discovered that most of her classmates either have children or plan to have children

Teaching Tip
Place students in small groups and assign a sample speech topic (you might simply let them use one of the student's speech topics). Instruct the groups to discuss the importance of audience analysis for each topic in relation to topic selection, supporting material, structure, delivery, and presentation aids.

Direct Methods	Indirect Methods
Conduct interviews	Observe your audience
Do focus groups	Ask others
Conduct a survey	Read written resources
Do a poll	

FIGURE 6–3
Audience Analysis Method Checklist

someday. She learned this through audience analysis. Hence, she molded her general topic of day care to focus more specifically on making educated day care choices.

Audience Analysis and Supporting Material

To effectively appeal to the diverse human needs, tendencies to respond to rhetorical appeals, and preferred learning styles of your listeners, you must offer a variety of types of evidence throughout your speech—evidence such as facts, statistics, testimonies, examples, analogies, descriptions, and definitions. We will talk more about collecting and integrating effective supporting material in Chapter 7.

Audience Analysis and Structure

To effectively appeal to the diverse learning styles preferred by your listeners, you ought to structure your messages in ways that address feelers, thinkers, watchers, and doers. You can do this in your macrostructure and in your microstructure. We will talk more about these specific strategies in Chapters 8, 9, 10, and 11.

Audience Analysis and Delivery

Audience analysis ought to come into play when you rehearse your speech and when you deliver it to your audience. By addressing psychological characteristics such as human needs, rhetorical appeals, and preferred learning styles in your delivery, you will be more likely to attain and maintain listener interest throughout. Likewise, adapting your delivery to adhere to environmental characteristics regarding time of day and week, as well as setting and occasion, will improve your chances for success. We will discuss delivery strategies in light of audience analysis in more detail in Chapter 12.

Audience Analysis and Presentational Aids

Audience analysis also ought to come into play when selecting, constructing, and integrating presentational aids. By addressing diverse human needs, rhetorical appeals, and learning styles in your presentational aids, you can improve your chances for success in reaching your diverse audience. We'll talk more about this in Chapter 13.

Teaching Tip
After a round of speeches, have students write a brief essay about the speeches that demonstrated the most effective audience adaptation. Instruct them to support their arguments with examples.

Summary

Through audience analysis, a crucial step in developing and presenting successful public speeches, you examine the demographic, psychological, and environmental characteristics of your audience in order to adapt your speech to be relevant to, and effective with, your listeners.

Demographic characteristics include age; sex, gender, and sexual orientation; group affiliations; socioeconomic factors; and sociocultural background. Psychological characteristics include human needs, as expressed in Maslow's hierarchy; the rhetorical appeals of ethos, pathos, and logos; and preferred learning styles. Environmental characteristics include chronemics (i.e., time factors), the physical setting, and the occasion. Your goal is to develop and present a speech that is tailored to the needs of your specific audience while respecting its diversity.

Audience analysis may be conducted through direct and indirect methods.

Direct methods include interviews, focus groups, and surveys. Indirect methods include observation, discussion with other speakers, and use of written resources, including Web sites.

Finally, to demonstrate respect for your listeners, it is important to integrate audience analysis throughout the speech-making process. That is, you ought to consider your audience when selecting and narrowing your topic, when conducting research to collect supporting material, when structuring your ideas, when rehearsing as well as delivering your speech, and when selecting and constructing presentational aids.

The goal of audience analysis, then, is to find out who your listeners are and adapt your speech to address their interests, needs, and desires. To do so effectively, you must first understand who you are and what you value and believe. Then you can develop an understanding of and respect for the diverse knowledge, values, beliefs, and attitudes of your listeners.

Activities

1. **Focus Group Belief and Attitude Analysis.** Form a small group with three or four classmates. Each group member should select a topic from the personal inventory you created after reading Chapter 5. Each group member should select a topic about which she or he has strong feelings. Talk about each topic in terms of the beliefs and attitudes of each group member. As a group, select one topic from each list about which you all hold similar values/attitudes/beliefs and one topic from each list about which you all have different values/attitudes/beliefs. Discuss how you might approach each topic based on the environmental, demographic, and psychological characteristics of the class.
2. **Conduct a Survey.** Prepare a short questionnaire based on the topic of your next speech to discover the values, beliefs, and attitudes of your audience members regarding it. Administer the survey at the outset of the next class period.
3. **Indirect Audience Analysis.** Consider the topic you have selected for your next speech. Speculate about your listeners' interests, beliefs, and attitudes about the topic. Note your generalizations on a piece of paper with two columns next to each item you've included. Write a heading of "yes" or "no" above each column. Pass the paper around the room asking classmates to mark a slash in the appropriate column next to each generalization. Once everyone has marked the paper, review the responses and adapt your speech based on what you learn.

Key Terms

Audience analysis
Chronemics
Closed-ended question
Demographic characteristics
Environmental characteristics
Ethos
Focus group
Gender
Interview
Logos
Marginalized
Open-ended question
Pathos
Poll
Psychological characteristics
Questionnaire
Sex
Sociocultural background
Stereotype
Survey

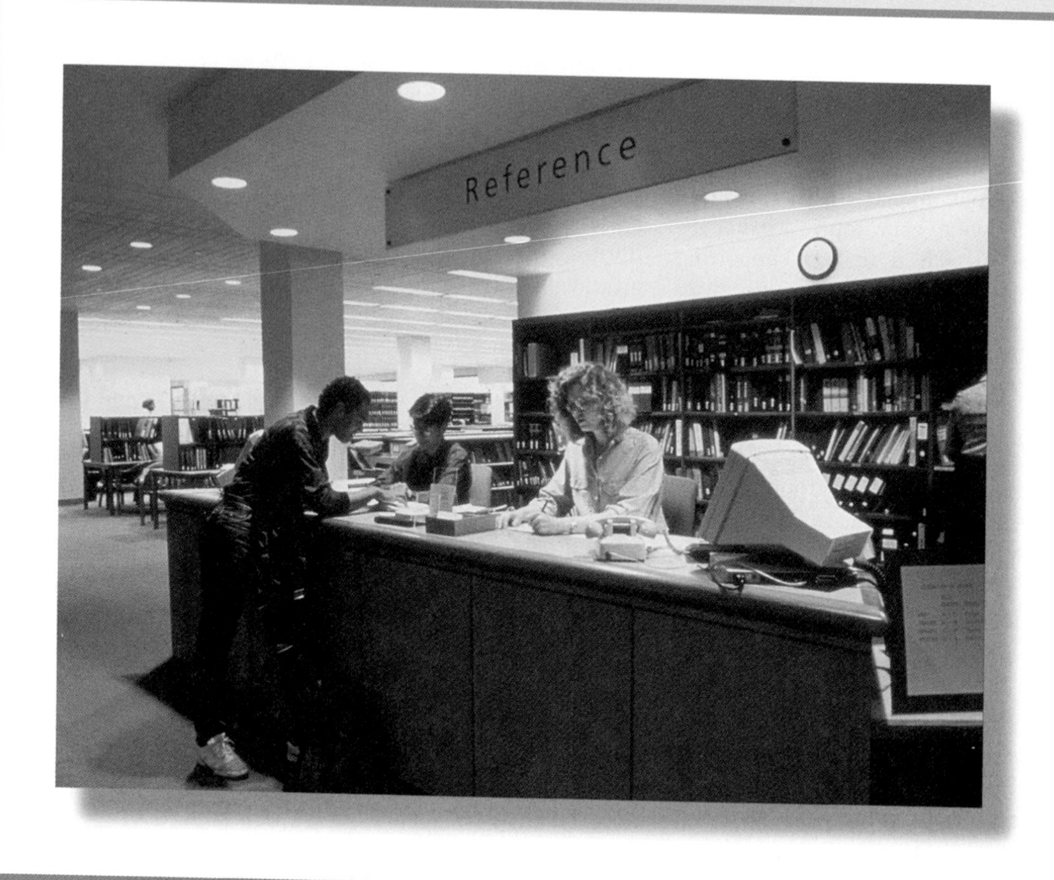
Reference

CHAPTER 7

Supporting Your Speech: Evidence and Research

Reflective Questions

1. Why is it important to use different types of supporting material when developing your main points?
2. How can you use supporting material to add breadth and depth to your speech?
3. Where can you locate evidence to support your speech?
4. What is an ethically supported speech?
5. Why is it important to cite oral footnotes during your speech?

Once you have selected and narrowed your topic, you are ready to develop it with supporting material. To beginning speakers, this often seems like a difficult task. Recall Holly from Chapter 5. After thinking she couldn't come up with a topic, Holly realized she could talk about day care options. Holly's initial doubts returned when she thought about developing her topic. "There's not that much to say about day care options. I can't possibly fill five to seven minutes with this topic." After we discussed the types of supporting material she could use to develop her speech and the research she could conduct to locate additional evidence, she left my office laughing at herself for ever having felt discouraged.

Teaching Tip
Refer students to the SpeechMaker CD-ROM. This software will assist them in developing a strategy for finding supporting material. Consider assigning one of the scenarios to be completed before the class in which you will discuss this chapter.

If you feel anything like Holly did, don't give up. This chapter is designed to help you learn—as she did—how to turn your topic and thesis statement into a speech by developing your ideas with supporting material. **Supporting material,** or **evidence,** is any information that clarifies, explains, or in some other way adds depth or breadth to your topic. You discover evidence by conducting **research,** which is the process of gathering supporting material to better understand and develop your subject. You conduct research by asking yourself questions about the topic and then seeking answers to those questions.

This chapter focuses on how to support your speech with evidence. We first talk about why supporting material is important to your public speech. Then we identify the types of supporting material available to you. From there, we move to a discussion about where to locate supporting material. We end with a discussion of what it means to do ethical research. By the time you finish reading this chapter, you will be ready to develop your main points effectively and ethically by using a variety of supporting material.

Why Is Supporting Material Important?

Discussion Tip
Ask students to brainstorm different types of supporting material. Are all of these types of supporting material appropriate? How can you determine if a source is credible? How do you cite these sources orally in your speech?

Supporting material is crucial to effective speechmaking. Essentially, without supporting material, you have no speech. You merely have a statement or opinion, which is your thesis statement. In other words, supporting material is what instills your ideas in the minds of your listeners. After all, your goal in any public speech is to get your listeners to understand and retain your message. The supporting material you select plays a primary role in achieving that goal. Hence, the supporting material you use to develop your main points can mean the difference between the success and the failure of your public speech. I tell you this not to increase your anxiety, but to instill in you the desire to consider carefully what you choose as your supporting material.

Why, then, is supporting material so important? First, supporting material is what ensures that your speech appeals to your diverse audience and to audience members with a variety of preferred learning styles. Second, supporting material gives your speech both breadth and depth and, in the process, reduces public speaking anxiety. Finally, supporting material can bolster your ethos as a speaker on your topic.

Appeal to Your Diverse Audience

To be most effective at reaching your diverse audience, your speech should offer a variety of supporting material. Recall from Chapter 6 that different listeners may be compelled by different kinds of evidence based on their preferred learning style,

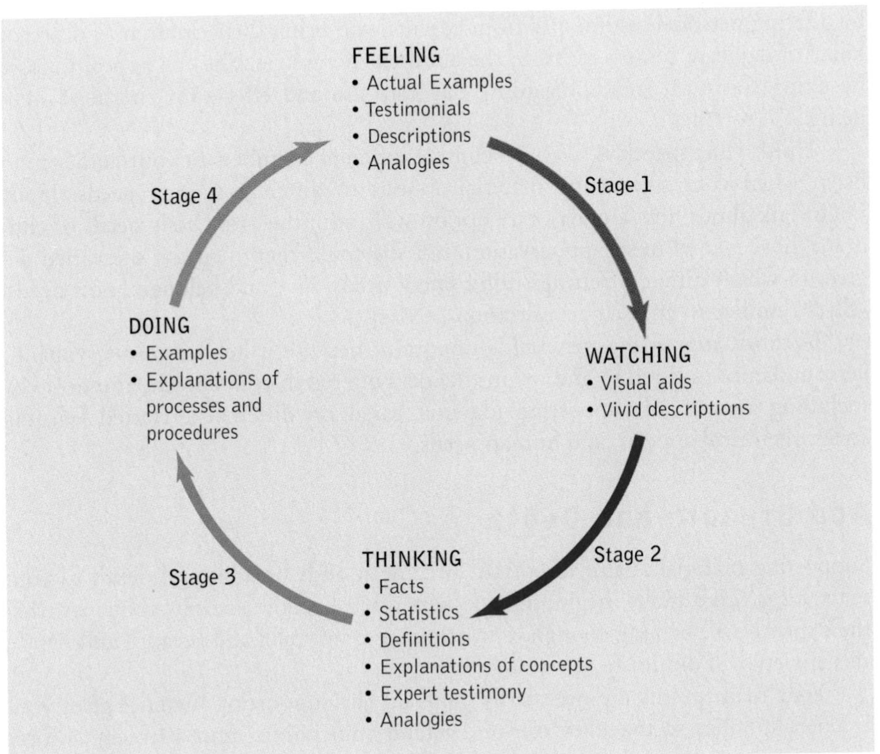

FIGURE 7–1 Supporting Material and the Learning Cycle

their tendency to respond to different rhetorical appeals, and their desire to satisfy unmet human needs (see Figure 7–1).

First, you can reach more people in your diverse audience when your supporting material appeals to doing, feeling, watching, and thinking. This point is important to remember since beginning speakers tend to rely more heavily on the types of supporting material that appeal to their own preferred learning style. However, they do so at the expense of clarity for those audience members with different preferred learning styles.

> ***What Do You Think?***
>
> *Consider a speech you heard recently that was particularly compelling. Did the speaker address your preferred learning style? How did this influence your opinion of the speech's effectiveness?*

Consider, for example, how Holly might vary the supporting material for her speech. Holly's stories about her own experiences at a day care center would appeal to the feelers in her audience. Thinkers might be more compelled by statistics on how well children do in different day care settings. Watchers would probably appreciate seeing the graphs and charts depicting these statistics, as well as pictures and diagrams of different day care settings. Finally, doers might appreciate stories related to the kinds of activities offered to children in different day care settings.

Second, your speech is likely to motivate more members of your diverse audience to listen when your supporting material offers rhetorical appeals of ethos, pathos, and logos. Holly, for example, can boost her ethos by quoting evidence based on conclusions drawn by experts in the field. She can appeal to emotions by offering personal testimonies from parents who bring their children to different kinds of day care centers, or from the children themselves. She can appeal to logic by citing statistical trends regarding day care use and effects on children's well-being.

Third, your speech is likely to compel different members of your audience to listen when your supporting material appeals to different human needs. Holly might talk about how any day care option will fulfill the most basic needs of children, those related to self-preservation, but she could then focus on the varied degrees to which different settings fulfill safety needs, love and belongingness needs, self-esteem needs, and self-actualization needs.

In short, supporting material is important because it helps motivate your diverse audience to listen to and retain the ideas offered in your speech. You do so by including a range of supporting material based on different preferred learning styles, rhetorical appeals, and human needs.

Add Breadth and Depth

Supporting material is also important because it adds breadth and depth to your main ideas. Like Holly, beginning speakers often become anxious about whether their speech will be long enough. Once you see how you'll add breadth and depth, this anxiety will diminish.

Teaching Tip
Make transparency masters of print advertisements that employ supporting materials. Show these ads in class and ask students to identify the types of supporting material in each ad. Encourage students to critique the ethical and effective use of supporting materials in these media.

Your main points are necessarily general. The supporting material gives your listeners specifics so that they can understand your points more precisely and see that your points are valid. When you clarify a point by giving different pieces of evidence to support it, you are adding **breadth.** Holly added breadth by describing several day care settings in her community rather than only the center where she is employed. When you clarify a point by offering a piece of detailed evidence, you are adding **depth.** To add depth, Holly gave an hour-by-hour schedule for a typical day at a day care center, rather than merely talking about general activities that typically occur. Offering breadth and depth helps clarify your message in ways that make your speech long enough and, consequently, reduces your anxiety.

What Do You Think?

Consider an argument you had with a friend recently. What sorts of supporting material did you use to help make your point? How did this material add breadth and depth?

Bolster Speaker Ethos

Discussion Tip
Ask students to speculate about the relationship between supporting material and speaker credibility. Can the use of qualified sources help bolster the speaker's credibility? Can unqualified or biased sources have deleterious implications for the speaker's credibility?

Supporting material is also important because it can bolster your ethos. When you offer various types of evidence drawn from a number of different sources, you convey competence and credibility. Listeners are more likely to find your speech compelling if you explain why you are an expert and how your ideas are supported by a variety of experts. Holly bolstered her ethos when she explained her own credentials as a

What Do You Think?

Consider your speech topic. In what ways are you an expert on the topic? What other resources might you draw from to further bolster your ethos on this topic?

day care center employee. She also bolstered her ethos when she quoted area providers whom she had interviewed and when she cited federal day care regulations she discovered by researching a government Web site. However, as you will learn later in this chapter, in order to bolster your ethos via external sources, you must cite their credentials.

Types of Supporting Material

You can support your ideas with (a) facts and statistics; (b) definitions, descriptions, and explanations; (c) examples; (d) testimonies; and (e) analogies. Beginning speakers sometimes make the mistake of believing that facts and statistics are the *best* forms of evidence. In reality, there is no best form. Each type has its own uses. In other words, one main point in your speech might best be supported by examples, another by statistics, and another by testimonies. Recall, too, that different audience members have different learning styles, may respond better to different rhetorical appeals, and may be motivated by addressing different human needs. Thus, different listeners tend to be persuaded by different kinds of evidence. For these reasons, the most effective public speeches use various types of supporting material.

Facts and Statistics

A **fact** is information that has been established as accurate. This means it must be documented by a credible source: for example, an eyewitness, a journalist, or a historian. Usually, facts concern events, times, people, and places. Most listeners require some factual information in order to accept a speaker's claims, although they tend to appeal most to those with a thinking learning style preference (Reinard, 1991). If a fact can't be documented in some way, it remains merely the speaker's opinion. If Holly were to talk about when the first day care centers were established, for example, her information would not be considered a fact unless she could document it. Moreover, facts become more compelling when they can be documented by more than one source. This is because different sources sometimes offer conflicting "facts." Hence, if you can cite more than one source to support a particular fact, it will be more believable. Some facts eventually become common knowledge because they have been documented as accurate over and over again. You will be most effective when using facts as supporting material in your speech, then, when you document them as accurate by citing more than one source.

Statistics are the collection and arrangement of numerical facts. Many people are swayed by numbers. Just consider, for example, how often advertisements use statistics to persuade us to buy products. We are told to use a particular toothpaste because "three out of four dentists surveyed" recommend it. We are told to eat a certain cereal because it has "100 percent" of the recommended daily allowance of essential vitamins. We are encouraged to purchase a certain brand of soup because it is "97 percent" fat free. And we are persuaded to drink a certain brand of soda pop because nationwide surveys show that "most people like it better" than the other brands.

Technology Tip
http://www.robertniles.com/stats/
This Web site, hosted by Niles Online, includes an introduction to statistical terms ("mean," "median," "mode," etc.). Have students visit this site and write a brief essay exploring the different types of statistics they could use to support ideas in their speeches.

Statistics can be used effectively as supporting material to describe quantities, to demonstrate trends, or to infer relationships. Like facts, statistics tend to appeal to the thinking dimension of the learning cycle. If Holly were to talk about the percentage of children under age five who participate in each day care option, she would be describing quantities. If she showed the percentages of children who participate in these day care options as infants, as toddlers, as preschoolers, and as school-aged children, she would be demonstrating trends. If she compared the academic achievement levels of children who had participated in each of the different day care options, she would be inferring relationships.

To use statistics effectively, follow a few simple rules:

Teaching Tip
Students often automatically equate statistics with credibility. Give students a paragraph full of statistical information and work together to analyze the statistics in light of the criteria presented in this chapter. In addition, have the students speculate about ways in which a speaker can employ statistics so the that audience easily understands them.

- *Understand what the statistics mean and explain them to your listeners.* When reading, consider not only the numbers presented, but also how those numbers relate to the whole. If Holly, for example, learned that 60 percent of children under age five participate in licensed day care, she should not assume that all 60 percent are enrolled in day care *centers,* nor should she assume that the other 40 percent receive their care from parents. She would need to do additional research to discover the breakdown of child care for both the 60 percent figure and the 40 percent figure. Not doing so would risk being misleading and unethical.
- *Round off your statistics.* At first, this suggestion might sound inaccurate and unethical. On the contrary, your goal is to help listeners retain key concepts rather than specific details. Let's say Holly's information revealed that 61.3 percent of children under age five participate in licensed day care. Later, she learned that 48.7 percent of those children participate in day care centers. The main ideas—"*about 60 percent* of the children" and "*nearly half* of those children"—are more likely to be retained by listeners than the exact percentages.
- *Limit how many statistics you offer.* Statistics should only be offered as they relate to the message you are trying to convey. You will likely find a lot of interesting statistical information as you research your topic. If you use too many statistics, however, your listeners may not remember any of them, let alone your main point. Keep in mind what your goal is and use only those statistics that help you achieve it. Holly, for example, learned about how many children under age five participate in day care today as compared to previous decades. Although these percentages were interesting, they did not relate to her specific speech goal.

Discussion Tip
Can you think of instances in which someone you were communicating with used biased statistics? How did that make you feel about the person? How can you be sure that the statistics you use in your next speech are not biased?

- *Remember that statistics are biased.* Mark Twain once said there are three kinds of lies: "lies, damned lies, and statistics." Although I wouldn't go so far as to say that all statistics are lies, I do caution you to consider the source of the information, what that source may have been trying to prove, and how that might have influenced the way the data were collected and interpreted. For example, if Holly's statistics about the relationship between day care and academic achievement had been reported by an outspoken day care center advocacy group, she might choose to discard those statistics as potentially too biased.

What Do You Think?

Consider a time when you heard a speaker who used a lot of detailed statistics. What do you remember about the speech?

Definitions, Descriptions, and Explanations

Definitions, descriptions, and explanations are forms of supporting material you may need in order to clarify your topic or some aspect of your topic. This is particularly likely when you're talking about something unfamiliar or unique.

A **definition** is simply a statement that clarifies the meaning of a word or phrase. Definitions tend to appeal to those with a thinking learning style preference, and they serve three primary purposes in public speeches. First, definitions are used to clarify the meaning of terminology that is specialized, technical, or otherwise likely to be unfamiliar. For example, when Dan talked about bioluminescence in his speech, he clarified its meaning with the following definition: "Bioluminescence is the emission of visible light by living organisms like fireflies."

Discussion Tip
Ask students to think about the use of definitions as supporting material. Why would a speaker need to use a definition? Where in the speech would definitions most likely be employed?

Second, definitions are used to clarify terminology that has more than one meaning and might be misconstrued. For example, "child abuse" is a term that encompasses a broad range of behaviors. You might define it so that your listeners will understand which behaviors you intend to talk about in your speech.

What Do You Think?

Consider a time when a speaker used unfamiliar terminology without defining it. Did you understand the message? Why or why not?

Third, especially with controversial subjects, definitions are used to reflect your stance on a subject in an attempt to draw listeners to interpret it as you do. For example, in a speech about domestic violence against women, former U.S. Secretary of Health and Human Services Donna Shalala defined such violence as "terrorism in the home" (Shalala, 1994, p. 451). She did so in an attempt to entice her listeners to interpret domestic violence against women in the same way that she does.

A **description** goes beyond a definition in that it attempts to create a picture in the minds of listeners. The best descriptions are vivid: They allow listeners to see, hear, smell, touch, or taste the thing you are describing. For these reasons, descriptions tend to appeal most to watchers and feelers. Dan described the firefly as it illuminates the pitch black night sky, darting quickly from one spot to another on an otherwise still autumn evening. By creating vivid pictures, descriptions touch on emotions, so they can be an effective way to integrate pathos into your speech. In most cases, vivid descriptions can make an otherwise dull speech come to life in the minds of listeners. Be careful, however, to avoid using vivid descriptions that are irrelevant to the topic or that may offend some listeners, such as vulgar or distastefully graphic descriptions.

Teaching Tip
Assign students to groups of four or five and ask them to write three of each of the following: descriptions, explanations, and examples. Have students discuss how each of these can be effectively and ethically used in public speaking.

An **explanation** also goes beyond a definition to provide details related to *how* and *why*—hence, appealing to the "thinking" and "doing" dimensions of the learning cycle. To explain *how* the firefly is bioluminescent, Dan talked about the way in which its abdominal organs produce a flashing light. To explain why the firefly is bioluminescent, Dan talked about its evolution to survive in its environment. As with definitions and descriptions, you should use explanations only to clarify details that are relevant to your topic and that are probably unfamiliar to your listeners.

Examples

An **example** is a specific case used to illustrate or represent a concept, condition, experience, or group of some sort. Examples tend to appeal most directly to the

Teaching Tip
Assign students to small groups and have them develop at least one brief, extended, factual, and hypothetical example. Share these examples with the entire class.

"feeling" dimension of the learning cycle. Dan used the firefly as an example of a bioluminescent organism. Examples can be *brief*, like Dan's, or they can be *extended*. A **brief example** is a short, specific instance; an **extended example** is a story or narrative developed at some length. To provide the greatest impact, brief examples are usually used in a series. This way, you can demonstrate either the magnitude or a trend. In her speech about the need to help the nation's independent farmers survive, Debbie offered a series of examples of farm foreclosures around the Midwest. "These are not isolated incidents," she concluded. "The problem is widespread and demands our attention." In her speech about day care options, Holly used an extended example to illustrate what goes on at day care centers:

> I will never forget having lunch my first day on the job at the day care center. You see, I was not familiar with what the children were expected or able to do. I watched in awe as three-year-old children poured their own milk and passed the pitcher along to the next child at the table and, likewise, dished up their own macaroni and cheese, green beans, and so on. The children visited cordially with me as we ate. When everyone was finished eating, each child at the table helped to clear the dishes away. To my amazement, these three-year-olds were behaving in a more civil manner than my roommates do! I cannot help but wonder whether my friends and I could have benefited from learning the social skills these children had mastered as a result of their experiences at a day care center.

In addition to being brief or extended, examples can be factual or hypothetical. A **factual example** is an instance that actually occurred. Holly's extended example was also factual. Factual examples can be based on events experienced by the speaker, by someone the speaker knows, or by someone the speaker learned about through research.

A **hypothetical example** is imaginary. Although hypothetical examples cannot help you prove a point, they can engage listeners by asking them to imagine themselves in a certain kind of situation. Hypothetical examples are not meant to trick your listeners into believing a fake story. Hence, you should let them know it is fictitious, yet plausible, at the outset. Hypothetical examples can enhance your speech by allowing your audience to identify with someone in a particular situation. Holly offered this hypothetical example in her speech:

> Imagine yourself in the living room of your dream home. What do you see? Perhaps you have a fireplace, or a computer, or a home entertainment system. The point is that your dream home is equipped with all the amenities you could possibly desire. Well, that's exactly what day care centers are designed to be for young children—a dream home. They have activity centers, art centers, physical recreation centers, reading centers, and the list goes on. Day care centers are dream homes for preschoolers!

Examples can be brief or extended, hypothetical or factual, based on your own experiences or the experiences of others. They can be effective supporting material when they clarify what you are talking about, help listeners grasp the magnitude of a situation, or encourage listeners to identify with someone in a particular situation. In doing so, examples can make your speech more compelling to some listeners.

Testimonies

A **testimony** is a quotation or paraphrase used to support a point. Testimonies can come from experts or from peers. **Expert testimony** is a quotation or paraphrase from a recognized professional in a field related to your topic. Since students are usually not perceived as experts in any field, citing expert testimony can add credibility to your opinions. Hence, such testimony can bolster your ethos, which will motivate those listeners who prefer learning by thinking and tend to be swayed most by ethos. Even professionals gain credibility by citing expert testimony. Holly cited testimony from her boss at the Wee Care Day Care Center, who also holds a degree in child psychology, regarding child development as it relates to different day care options.

Teaching Tip
Have students share favorite testimonials with the class. Encourage students to plan how these quotes could be used to support ideas in their speeches. Also, consider showing a sample speech that relies heavily on the use of quotes.

Peer testimony is a quotation or paraphrase from someone who has firsthand experience related to a topic. Hence, peer testimony tends to appeal to those listeners who prefer learning by feeling and tend to be swayed most by pathos. Holly also talked with some of the children and parents involved in the different day care settings to develop her speech. Likewise, Debbie talked with several farmers who had lost their farms to add credibility to her speech.

Analogies

An **analogy** is a comparison drawn between two essentially unrelated concepts or objects. Analogies highlight similarities between the unfamiliar concept or object being discussed and one that is familiar to listeners. Since analogies focus on both abstract conceptualization and concrete comparisons, they can appeal to both thinkers and feelers. Analogies help listeners understand the concept or object being discussed and may also make it more memorable. Holly introduced the hypothetical dream home example in order to compare it to a day care center. In some ways, day care centers are designed to be dream homes for preschoolers. In Holly's analogy, the two are similar in that they provide the desired amenities. Dan compared bioluminescence to a miniature flashlight. Because a flashlight is a very familiar object, this analogy helped his listeners grasp a potentially difficult concept.

Discussion Tip
How might a speaker use analogies to help the listeners better understand the topic being discussed? How can analogies be used to make a speech more memorable?

What Do You Think?

Consider the topic you selected for your next speech. What analogy could you make between some unfamiliar concept or object you will discuss and something with which your listeners are likely to be familiar? Will this help your listeners understand and remember what you are saying?

Any of these forms of supporting material can be used effectively in your public speeches. The most important thing to remember is to use a variety of supporting material. First of all, because not all listeners are swayed by the same kinds of evidence, variety helps ensure that you will reach the diverse members of your audience. Second, you need to use various types of supporting material because each point you make might be best supported by a different type of evidence. One point might best be supported with statistics, another with examples or testimonies, and another with an analogy. It is up to you to determine what types of supporting material will best clarify a particular point and then to develop the point with those types of evidence.

Locating Supporting Material: Research

Just as there are many types of supporting material, there are many places to locate supporting material. Now that you understand the need to include various types of supporting material, let's talk about the many different places you can go to find such evidence to develop your points. Supporting material can come from your own knowledge and experience, as well as from the knowledge and experience of others. You can learn about the knowledge and experience of others through methods such as interviews and surveys, through a range of library resources, and on the Internet. As stated earlier, the process of locating supporting material is called *research.*

Drawing on Personal Experience

Teaching Tip
Given that many students fail to recognize their own experiences as legitimate sources of knowledge, ask students to list their sources of personal knowledge for potential speech topics. Encourage students to recognize this knowledge as a source of credibility on the topic(s).

Begin your research by thinking about your topic in connection with yourself. You might be surprised by how productive this can be. Students often fail to give themselves credit for their own experience with a topic. Let's just consider, for example, the students whose speeches I've referred to here. Holly drew on her personal experience of working in a day care center, particularly when she developed her extended examples. Dan, a fifth-year student who had written his senior paper on bioluminescence, drew on his own academic work for evidence to develop his speech. Debbie grew up on a farm herself and witnessed her uncle's family farm foreclosure. Personal examples and stories are especially effective in adding human interest to speeches. To bolster the credibility of your personal examples, however, be sure to state your **credentials.** That is, explain what qualifies you to speak as an authority. Holly's credentials include her years of professional service in a day care center. Dan's credentials are his years of studying bioluminescence as part of his major. And Debbie's credentials lie in her experiences growing up and watching family members lose their farms.

> ***What Do You Think?***
>
> *Consider your topic again. What experiences have you had that relate to the topic? How could you cite your credentials to enhance your ethos?*

Research Interviews

Teaching Tip
Review Chapter 4 on listening skills. The research interview is an excellent context for students to practice these skills. This is also a good opportunity to reinforce the implications of poor listening.

Sometimes you may find yourself presenting a speech about which you have limited personal experience. It may be difficult or impossible to cite yourself as an expert or to offer examples from your own experiences. Yet, knowing that insights from experts and personal examples can both be extremely compelling, you want to offer some sort of personal testimony or example. You might decide to conduct an interview. An interview can also help you learn information you cannot readily learn through other resources. A **research interview,** then, is one conducted to gather information for a speech.

Beginning speakers sometimes think they won't be able to find or gain access to an expert. Don't overlook the experts who work on campus and in the community. An expert is anyone who possesses a high degree of skill in or knowledge of a certain subject. Dan's adviser, for example, has published several journal articles about bioluminescence. Dan could interview her as an expert in the field. Holly interviewed her employer at the day care center, Mr. Glass, to gain an expert's perspective. Likewise, the parents and children Holly interviewed and the farmers Debbie interviewed were also experts in that they possessed a high degree of personal experience with the topics of each woman's speech. The key to selecting someone to interview is to make sure that person is an expert on the topic of your speech. For example, Holly would not interview her public speaking teacher, who is certainly an expert in communication-related subjects, because she is not an expert in anything related to Holly's speech topic.

Teaching Tip
Help students generate sample questions for potential research interviews. Ask students to prepare five to ten questions following the guidelines presented in this chapter.

What Do You Think?

Consider your speech topic. Who might you interview as an expert on this topic? How could this expert best contribute to your speech?

Just as it is necessary to cite your credentials when offering personal experience as evidence, so must you cite the credentials of the experts you interview. Listeners will not know that Dan's adviser is an expert unless he mentions her credentials. To do so, Dan might say,

> I have the privilege of having as my adviser one of the nation's leading bioluminescence scholars. In an interview with my adviser, Dr. Susan Stromme, professor of biogenetics right here at our university, I learned that some mutant frogs have been discovered that also exhibit this ability.

Likewise, in citing her boss, Holly might say,

> In a recent interview with Mr. Bill Glass, owner and director of four Wee Care Day Care Centers right here in our community, I learned that most children who attend his day care centers on a full-time basis exhibit outstanding social skills by the time they enter kindergarten. The skills Mr. Glass has observed include empathy, cooperation, and sharing. Mr. Glass told me, "Because I have been so impressed with the skill development of children in the Wee Care Day Care Centers, I have enrolled my own children, even though they could be provided for in my own home."

You can conduct interviews with experts who have a great deal of experience related to your topic. Debbie did so when she interviewed farmers at an auction.

Discussion Tip
Why is the order of steps for preparing and conducting an interview important? What are the implications of not preparing before the interview?

If you decide to conduct an interview, there are certain guidelines you should follow. Because the person is giving you his or her time, it is important that you demonstrate respect by arriving promptly, and by being precise, courteous, and concise. To maximize the effectiveness of your interview, you must develop a plan, implement your plan appropriately, and provide closure (see Figure 7–2).

FIGURE 7–2 The Effective Research Interview Process

Before the Interview

- *Do preliminary research.* The interview should *expand on* what is available in the library and Internet resources.
- *Determine a specific purpose for the interview.* Your purpose might emerge from questions that arose while you were researching the topic.
- *Select an appropriate expert.* Choose someone who can likely answer the questions you are trying to answer.
- *Set up an interview.* You can usually do this by telephone. Introduce yourself, explain why you are asking for the interview, and if the person is willing to be interviewed, agree upon a time.
- *Prepare a list of questions.* These should consist of open-ended and closed-ended questions. Prioritize your questions so that, if you run out of time, you can make sure you asked the most important questions.

During the Interview

- *Dress professionally and bring a notebook and several pens.*
- *Arrive five to ten minutes early.*
- *Introduce yourself and repeat the purpose of the interview.*

Perhaps the most important factor determining the effectiveness of your interview is the list of questions you develop. Don't ask questions to which you already know the answer. The purpose of the interview is to learn information you could not readily find through other resources. Also, be careful to avoid **leading questions**—questions phrased in such a way as to prompt a certain response. Holly would have been guilty of asking a leading question had she asked Mr. Glass, "You *do* believe most children who participate in day care centers are well adjusted, don't you?" This could insult the person you are interviewing, and it undermines your goal as an interviewer: to learn what the expert knows and thinks.

Teaching Tip
Have students generate a list of three to four persons whom they might interview for their speech topic and help them plan the initial contact with these possible interviewees.

As you develop your questions, write both open-ended and closed-ended questions. Recall from Chapter 6 that closed-ended questions are stated so that the respondent chooses from a finite group of answers (e.g., "yes" or "no"). The benefit of closed-ended questions is that they are quick, whereas open-ended questions invite the respondent to speak freely. The benefit of open-ended questions is that they can produce a great deal of information. As an open-ended question, Holly might ask Mr. Glass, "What would you identify as benefits for children who participate in organized day care and why?"

Teaching Tip
To give students practice in conducting an interview, assign the Interview Role-Play activity included in the Activities section of this chapter.

What Do You Think?

Consider a television news program like 20/20, 60 Minutes, Dateline, Good Morning America, *or* The Today Show *where the hosts interview different "experts." In what ways do the interviewers demonstrate respect for the experts? What kinds of questions do they ask? How do they provide closure with each guest?*

Surveys

As discussed in Chapter 6, a **survey** is a research tool designed to provide information from a large number of people. Surveys, generally conducted through questionnaires, are an especially effective way of discovering the attitudes, values, and beliefs generally held by people in your community. Holly might survey a number

FIGURE 7–2 (continued)

- *Keep the interview on track.* Ask the questions on your list, departing from them as other relevant issues arise, but then returning to them.
- *Listen critically and take notes.* Use brief words and phrases while listening. If a particular quotation strikes you, ask the expert to repeat it as you transcribe it.
- *Finish within the allotted time.*
- *Thank the expert for his or her time.*

After the Interview

- *Review your notes as soon as possible.* If you wait too long, you might have trouble interpreting some of your notes and remembering what was said. Expand on ideas you jotted down. Circle quotations that may be useful in your speech.
- *Send a thank-you note to the expert.*

Teaching Tip
Have students survey the class about their speech topics. Given the amount of time necessary to prepare and complete a survey, it's a good idea to limit each survey to ten questions. Provide the students with class time to complete the surveys and then discuss the results.

of college students to see whether they believe organized day care is more harmful or helpful to child development and why they believe as they do. Depending on her purpose, she might also distribute a questionnaire to day care providers, to parents of day care children and other parents, to members of her local church, to child development professors, and so on. The data from the questionnaires might provide information about local opinions that Holly could compare to national surveys during her speech.

> ***What Do You Think?***
>
> *Consider your speech topic. What questions would help you understand where people stand on the topic? How might a survey provide information that would be useful to your speech?*

Library Resources

Teaching Tip
Consider arranging a tour of your library's resources to show students where they can find evidence to support their ideas. During the tour, ask students to evaluate the credibility of different sources of information using the criteria presented in this chapter.

Whenever I explain to my students that they must do library research for an upcoming speech, I notice the majority of them cringe, balk, or groan. I am convinced that somewhere along the way they became socialized to believe that the library is a bad place and should be avoided whenever possible. Likewise, they often look at me in disbelief when I tell them to ask a reference librarian for help when researching a topic. Consider reference librarians your friends, not your enemies. If you are having trouble finding the resources you need, it is *your responsibility* to ask a reference librarian for help. If information exists on your topic, the librarian will likely know where to find it. Remember that locating information in the library is a major part of a librarian's job.

You can find supporting material in a variety of library resources. These include (a) books, (b) reference works, (c) magazines and newspapers, and (d) government documents and academic journals.

Books

Books can be excellent sources of information, especially since they allow authors to discuss topics in depth. The disadvantage of books is that they are sometimes outdated. Since it often takes several years for a book manuscript to reach bookstore and library shelves, sometimes even books with a fairly recent copyright date can be outdated. Books about how to use the Internet are an excellent example. This technology is expanding so rapidly that the information offered in books published on the subject even as recently as 1994 are fairly outdated. For certain topics, however, this isn't a problem. For example, Dan used information gathered from books to describe how bioluminescence works. The fact that the books had been published a good number of years ago did not matter, given Dan's purpose.

Reference Works

Technology Tip
http://www.encyclopedia.com/
This Web site offers a free online encyclopedia hosted by Encyclopedia.com. Have students visit this site to find information about their speech topics.

Reference works include encyclopedias, dictionaries, yearbooks, atlases, almanacs, and biographical aids like the *Who's Who* series. They can often help you find specific descriptions and data quickly. The kinds of information they provide is limited, however, so you'll want to use them as a starting point or to supplement other kinds of resources. Debbie, for example, researched the history of farming trends by looking through *The Farmer's Almanac* year by year. Dan used a dictionary to provide an understandable definition of bioluminescence and an encyclopedia to provide a simple explanation of it. Many reference works are now available in printed and CD-ROM formats. As with books, however, keep in mind that reference works can be outdated.

Magazines and Newspapers

Magazines and newspapers are great resources for current information about a topic. Because they are published often (monthly, weekly, or daily), the information in recent issues is usually up to date. You should keep in mind, however, that authors of magazine and newspaper articles may be journalists who are drawing on the work of others, rather than being experts themselves on your particular topic. Hence, the information these periodicals provide can be useful, but they should not be used exclusively.

Technology Tip
http://www.newspapers.com/

Newspapers.com is an online resource where many of the world's leading newspapers can be found. Have students visit this site to find supporting material for their speeches.

Most libraries have printed and computerized indexes to help you search these resources efficiently. One of the most common indexes for searching magazines is the *Readers' Guide to Periodical Literature,* which is available in both printed and CD-ROM formats. Likewise, most colleges and universities also have an online catalog like WebPals or GaleNet (see Figure 7–3). Many of the major newspapers are also now specifically indexed. The *New York Times,* the *Wall Street Journal,* and *USA Today,* for example, each have their own indexes of back issues and content. Holly was able to find some interesting articles about different day care options in magazines like *Child* and *Parenting.* Moreover, these articles cited the research of some important experts, and this gave Holly a starting point for searching appropriate academic journals.

Like reference works, many popular magazines and newspapers are also available on the Internet. Most of these publications include the Web address on each hard copy. This address is usually on the front page of newspapers and inside the front cover of magazines. The online address for the local newspaper in my community, for example, is **www.in-forum.com** and for *Consumer Reports,* a popular magazine, the online address is **www.ConsumerReports.org.**

Government Documents and Academic Journals

Government documents and academic journals are valuable resources for locating supporting material because they often provide information directly from those who are doing the research. Such firsthand reporting of information can boost your credibility as a speaker on a particular topic. Some drawbacks to using these publications can be the amount of technical jargon you are forced to decipher as you read and the amount of time it takes to retrieve the resource. Many indexes are now available online via the World Wide Web, which is making it much easier and quicker to access these kinds of resources.

Technology Tip
http://www.defenselink.mil/

This Web site, hosted by the U.S. Department of Defense, offers excellent information on U.S. defense policy. Encourage students who are researching foreign policy/defense topics to visit this site.

Government documents are those published by the federal government. These documents focus on a wide range of topics. The information provided in these publications is often not available anywhere else, and citing these agencies can boost your ethos. Two indexes you might consult include the CIS/Index (published by the Congressional Information Service) and the *Monthly Catalog of United States Government Publications* (published by the Government Printing Office). These indexes are available in print and CD-ROM formats, as well as

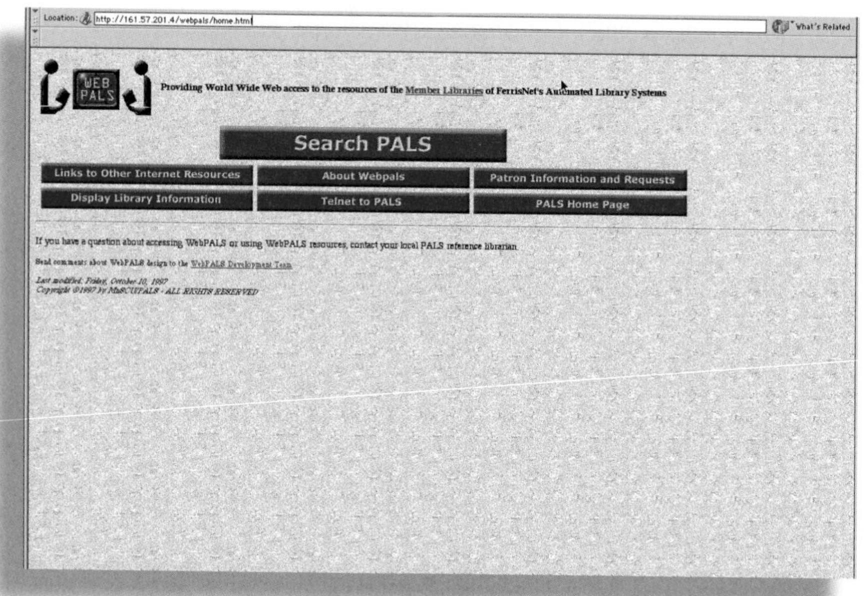

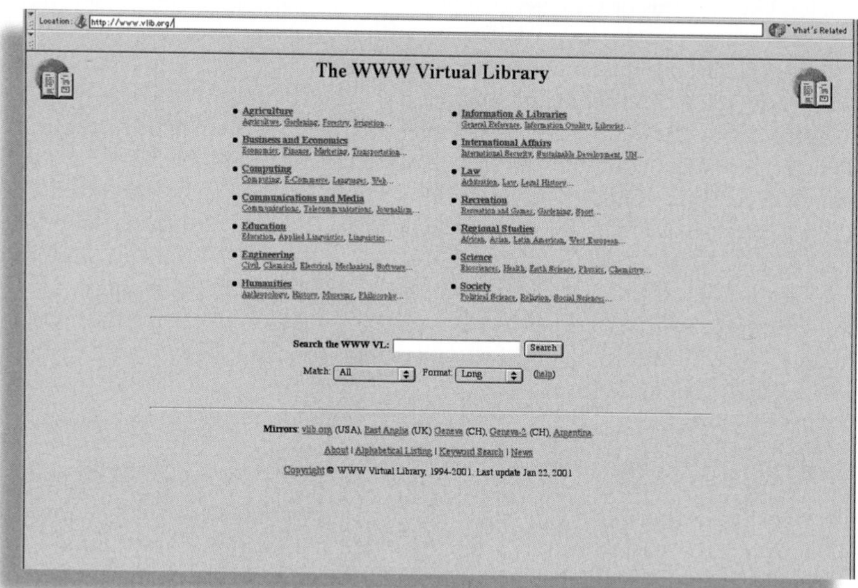

FIGURE 7–3
Popular Online Catalogs at Colleges and Universities

online (Whitely, 1994). If you choose to search online, you can get information from the Government Printing Office (**www.gpo.ucop.edu**), from federal agency indexes like FedWorld (**www.fedworld.gov**) or the Federal Web Locator (**www.infoctr.edu/fwl/**), or from the Library of Congress (**www.loc.gov**) (Basch, 1996).

Academic journals publish articles by professional researchers and educators. The focus of each academic journal is very specialized and not necessarily intended for the general public. As such, they are often riddled with technical jargon that can be difficult to decipher. However, the conclusions typically reflect the most recent research in a particular field. Indexes to academic journal articles are available in printed form, through your library's online catalog, and sometimes on CD-ROM. Some of these specialized indexes include the following:

- Education Index.
- Business Index.
- Communication Index.
- Index to Legal Periodicals.

Many specialized indexes are available on the Internet, as well. For example, *Business Sources on the Net (BSN),* which categorizes business-related sources by topics like environmental, financial, accounting, and marketing, can be accessed at **www.hbg.psu.edu/library/** (click the links labeled "Research Tools and Resources," "Web Resources," and "Business and Economic Resources").

> ### *What Do You Think?*
> *Consider your speech topic. Which library resources might be particularly useful to you? How would you conduct your library search for these materials?*

After locating the books on bioluminescence, Dan searched their authors in the *Expanded Academic Index,* his library's online index. In this way, he located some recent journal articles to update his information. Holly supplemented her interviews with additional articles she found by searching *ERIC* (Education Resources Information Center), a computerized research service focused on education-related topics, with terms like "day care," "preschool," and "early childhood education."

Teaching Tip
Select a sample of publications from each of the categories of reference material listed in this chapter and have students find them in the library. Have each student write a brief essay describing the information contained in each source as well as how that information can be used. Compile the lists and use them for future speeches.

Internet Documents

The **Internet,** often called the "information superhighway," is a worldwide network of computers that links resources and people at colleges and universities, government agencies, libraries, corporations, and homes (Quaratiello, 1997). This system essentially provides access to endless amounts of information that can support your research. For example, you can access the Internet to find the most recent information about your topic, or to communicate directly with authors of important sources or with experts in a particular field, or even to discuss your topic with others who are interested in it (Kent, 1998; Munger, Anderson, Benjamin, Busiel, & Paredes-Holt, 1999; Reddick & King, 1996; Young, 1998). The variety of resources for researchers to draw on, which was once limited by inaccessibility,

DILBERT reprinted by permission of United Feature Syndicate, Inc.

is now essentially limitless. Conducting thorough research today, then, usually includes searching the Internet.

Teaching Tip
To help students familiarize themselves with conducting research on the World Wide Web, have them complete the Internet Exploration assignment contained in the Activities section of this chapter.

Although the Internet was first created in 1969, it didn't become readily available to the general public until the 1990s. It was not until then that the World Wide Web was created. The **World Wide Web** is basically a software system that makes accessing information on the Internet as simple as using a Windows program on your personal computer. While there continue to be racial and economic inequities regarding access to and use of the Internet, such disparities are shrinking as more schools, homes, and public libraries are going online. Because the World Wide Web allows you to wander easily throughout the Internet, however, it is easy to lose sight of your purpose while "surfing." Hence, I suggest you follow seven research strategies while online. This way, the time and energy you spend researching on the Internet should provide you with valuable supporting material for your speech.

Seven Online Strategies

- Access the Internet through a BROWSER.
- Search your subject by key words using a SEARCH ENGINE.
- If the SEARCH ENGINE search was too broad, try using a DIRECTORY.
- If these searches are too narrow, try using a METASEARCH ENGINE.
- You might also access OTHER Internet resources.
- You might embellish your information by searching ELECTRONIC DISCUSSION LISTS.
- Finally, you must EVALUATE your Internet resources before including any of them in your speech.

Browsers

To access the Internet through the World Wide Web, your computer must have a browser. A **browser** is a doorway into the World Wide Web. The three most common browsers are Netscape Navigator, Internet Explorer, and Mosaic. To enter the World Wide Web, simply double-click on one of these icons.

Search Engines

Technology Tip
http://www.searchenginewatch.com/
This Web site, hosted by Internet.com, offers one of the most complete guides to using search engines available on the Internet. Have students visit this site and prepare a brief report of the types and functions of various search engines

You should search your subject by key words on a robot-generated index. A **robot-generated index,** also called a **search engine,** is a comprehensive computer program that automatically visits a multitude of Web sites and generates an index of those that match (or link to) your key words. You access these **hyperlinks** (connections between two Web documents) by double-clicking on them. Although hyperlinks can provide you with a lot of information (hits), keep aware that much of it may be irrelevant to your speech. Some of the most popular robot-generated indexes are the following:

- AltaVista—**www.altavista.com**
- Infoseek—**http://infoseek.go.com**
- Lycos—**www.lycos.com**
- Webcrawler—**www.webcrawler.com**

Directories

If you find your search on a robot-generated index is too broad and offers too many irrelevant Web sites to your topic, try searching your subject by key words on a **human-edited index,** also called a **directory**—that is, a search index that is edited by a human being who is trained in library or information sciences. Only prospective sites that pass the editor's scrutiny are added to each of these indexes. The following are two popular human-edited indexes:

- TradeWaveGalaxy—**www.einet.net**
- Yahoo—**www.yahoo.com**

Metasearch Engines

You can also search the Web using a **metasearch engine.** This tool will search for your key word through several search engines at once. The following are a few popular metasearch engines:

- Metacrawler—**www.metacrawler.com**
- Super Searcher—**www.iquest.net**
- SavvySearch—**www.savvysearch.com**

Technology Tip
http://www.dogpile.com/
This is another metasearch engine that students may find useful. Have students conduct a search using conventional and metasearch engines and compare the differences.

Other Resources

You can also access other Internet resources that are not on the World Wide Web. These include Gopher sites, Telnet sites, and Usenet news postings.

Electronic Discussion Lists

You can locate electronic discussion lists related to your topic. Perhaps the easiest way to do this is to send an e-mail message to **listserv//longman.awl.com/kennedy/**. Another is *The Online Student: Making the Grade on the Internet,* also available at **www.loyola.edu/library/table.html**.

Evaluate Resources

Finally, you need to evaluate the Internet resources you have selected for your speech. One of the most exciting strengths of the Internet is its universality. In other words, since there is no gatekeeper, anyone is allowed to create a Web site. This is exciting because previously marginalized voices can be heard. However, researchers must devise a means for evaluating the validity and reliability of the resources they locate on the Internet. Here are some key questions to ask yourself (Munger et al., 1999) before using a document from the Internet:

- Who is the author and what are his or her credentials?
- Does the author have an academic or professional affiliation?
- Is a link to the author's home page or e-mail contact information provided?
- Who is the sponsor of the resource and what are the sponsor's credentials with regard to the topic?

- Is the resource updated regularly?
- What are potential biases or hidden agendas of the author or sponsoring organization?

Some Internet documents that do not indicate an individual author nonetheless indicate an organization (e.g., a government agency, business, or nonprofit organization) as author. As long as you're sure of or can verify the organization's credentials, you can use the information in your speech. Citing the organization will add to your credibility, just as citing an individual author would. *If, however, you cannot determine the credentials of the individual author or organization responsible for the material, you should not include it as supporting material for your speech.* This is crucial advice for ethical public speakers, because the document may have been written by someone who has less expertise than you do. Citing that person's opinions would do a disservice to you and, potentially, to your listeners.

> ***What Do You Think?***
>
> *What topics might you search on the Internet? How would you conduct your search? How would you evaluate the materials you find?*

Technology Tip
http://milton.mse.jhu.edu:8001/research/education/net.html

This Web page, developed by Elizabeth Kirk at Johns Hopkins University, offers an excellent guide for evaluating information found on the World Wide Web. Ask students to visit this site before they begin conducting research.

You might also access the *Virtual Reference Desk* at **http://thorplus.lib.purdue.edu/reference/index.html.** This resource was created specifically to assist researchers in locating the credentials of Web page authors. Another resource you might access for this purpose is the *ProfNet's Expert Database,* which profiles more than two thousand authors who have been identified as experts in their fields (**www.profnet.com**). Finally, you might want to check out the *Using Cybersources* Web site at **www.devry-phx.edu** (click the links labeled "Educational Resources," "Online Writing Support Center," and "Using Cybersources"). Figure 7–4 presents several ideas for locating support material.

Conducting Ethical Research

Discussion Tip
Ask students how they might sort and arrange their evidence once they have obtained it. Ask them if it is possible to gather too much or too little information.

Effective public speakers collect various types of supporting material from diverse sources, including their own experiences, interviews, surveys, and library and Internet research. Effective public speakers also conduct ethical research. They do so by (a) evaluating their evidence and (b) documenting it appropriately. As we'll see, some of the same steps that make your speech effective also help make it ethical by demonstrating the virtues of honesty and respect.

FIGURE 7–4
Locating Support Material Checklist

- *Personal experience.*
- *Research interviews.*
- *Surveys.*
- *Library resources* (books, reference works, magazines, newspapers, government documents, academic journals).
- *Internet documents.*

Evaluating Your Evidence

Nearly any topic you might select for your public speech is likely to be discussed in numerous resources. You need to consider, therefore, whether each piece of evidence you have collected actually contributes to your purpose. You can do this by asking yourself whether the evidence is relevant, credible, and current. These questions are necessary for practical reasons (you don't want to write a speech that's unfocused or too long), but they are also necessary for ethical reasons: By using evidence that does not meet these criteria, you risk misleading your audience, which fails to demonstrate honesty or respect. You must also consider whether the evidence you have collected is thorough. You can do this by asking whether it answers all important questions, whether you've consulted a variety of resources, and whether you've used different kinds of supporting material. Again, these questions are necessary for ethical as well as practical reasons. As an ethical speaker, you must give your audience a balanced and full picture of your topic.

Is It Relevant?

As you conduct research for your speech, you will likely come across a great deal of interesting information. Some of this interesting information, however, may not be appropriate for your speech. **Relevant evidence** is information that is directly related to your topic. If you include irrelevant evidence, you'll only confuse listeners, because they'll be forced to try to figure out how it contributes to the point you are making. Information that does not address the point it is supposed to support is irrelevant and should not be included in your speech.

Teaching Tip
Develop a file of political campaign literature, rhetoric, and materials. Analyze these in class utilizing the tests of evidence presented in this chapter (relevance, timeliness, credibility, etc.).

As Dan was researching bioluminescence, for example, he learned that the bioluminescent mutant frogs have been found only near the Sheyenne River. Some researchers speculate that the polluted river in some way causes the mutation. Moreover, these frogs appear to have a significantly shorter life span than other frogs. Some environmental groups are protesting against the local power plant for continuing to pollute the river. While this information is certainly interesting, very little of it is related to Dan's main point on how bioluminescence works.

Is It Credible?

Credible evidence is information that seems both believable and reliable. Information is reliable, or generalizable, if it's true, not just in a limited number of cases, but in many similar cases. To be credible, your supporting material should come from respected sources, people who are in some way experts on your topic. However, it is important to consider whether they have direct experience with the topic. Dan's professor is a credible resource for his topic because she is an expert in the field. Holly's experience working in day care centers qualifies her as an expert of sorts on her topic. For Holly to base her speech only on her own experience, however, would not be ethical because her experience is somewhat limited and may not be reliable (generalizable). Keep in mind, especially with Internet documents, that unless the author or sponsoring organization can be identified, the source cannot be considered credible and should not be used.

Is It Current?

Since the world we live in is rapidly changing, so is the information about our world. **Current evidence** is information that is not outdated. What counts as current depends on your topic. For many topics, you'll need to locate the most recently published evidence. For others, however, research from the past continues to be valid. For example, Dan might rely on older sources to explain how bioluminescence works because there haven't been any recent relevant discoveries, whereas Holly should look for the most recent statistics about day care facilities, because these statistics are constantly changing.

Does It Answer All Important Questions?

An ethically researched speech covers the topic thoroughly in the time allotted. You ought to be able to answer the questions posed by your thesis statement. If any questions remain unanswered, you need to continue researching. Holly should be able to identify the factors to consider when selecting a day care option and why they are important before she stops researching the topic. She will likely know a good deal more about day care options than merely selection factors; however, "selection factors" is what her thesis statement says she will cover. Dan's research is not complete until he understands all aspects of how bioluminescence works.

Have You Consulted a Variety of Resources?

Teaching Tip
Have students label the types of supporting material they used on the outlines for their speeches. This should help them determine if they are using a variety of sources.

Ethical researchers use a variety of resources, including interviews, newspapers and magazines, academic journals, books, and Internet documents. Not only do different types of resources have their own strengths and weaknesses, but a combination of types enables a speaker to present a fuller picture and to address diverse learning styles by rounding the entire cycle of learning. Holly conducted interviews and surveys, consulted magazines and academic journals, and offered personal stories. Dan consulted reference books, conducted interviews, and cited Internet documents. Both speakers referenced a variety of resources to support their ideas.

Do You Use Various Types of Supporting Material?

Use of various types of supporting material is both effective and ethical. Because listeners have different learning styles, by including personal experiences and testi-

Evaluating Your Evidence Checklist

1. Is your evidence relevant?
2. Is your evidence credible?
3. Is your evidence current?
4. Does your evidence answer all important questions?
5. Have you consulted a variety of resources?
6. Do you use various types of supporting material?

monies, facts and statistics, visual representations, and practical applications, you will have the greatest impact on all your listeners.

Documenting Your Evidence

Ethical public speakers document their sources in a reference list at the end of their formal outline, internally within the text of the formal outline, and orally throughout the presentation. Failing to document your sources in these ways is considered plagiarism. Documentation is as indispensable to an oral presentation as it is to a written essay. Through documentation, you not only avoid plagiarism, but you also enhance your credibility (ethos).

Technology Tip
http://www.stylewizard.com/
This Web page, hosted by EB Communications, offers guidelines, tutorials, and worksheets to help students build a bibliography using MLA and APA formats. Have students complete at least one reference using either the MLA or APA Wizard on this site.

In the Reference List

One of the most widely used formats for documenting sources is that of the American Psychological Association (APA). The *Publication Manual of the American Psychological Association* (1994, 4th ed.) provides specific guidelines for documenting the various kinds of sources. Other widely used formats are those of the Modern Language Association (MLA) and the *Chicago Manual of Style* (University of Chicago Press). These last two formats are generally used in the humanities, whereas the APA format is generally used in the social sciences. Since the APA format has been adopted by the National Communication Association, it is illustrated here. However, you should ask your instructor whether she or he has a preference regarding citation format.

In the APA format for reference lists, certain guidelines apply to sources of all types. Alphabetize the entries by the authors' last names. Indent the first line of each entry five to seven spaces. Do not indent subsequent lines of the entry. List the author's last name, followed by a comma and one or more initials. Use "&" rather than "and" when citing multiple authors. In article and book titles, capitalize the first word, proper nouns (names of people, places, etc.), and the first word after a colon. Space once (not twice) after each period. Double-space all entries. Do not include unnecessary publishing information such as "company" or "incorporated."

The following list shows the proper citation format for some of the sources most often cited by public speaking students. For a complete listing and explanation, consult the *Publication Manual of the American Psychological Association* (4th ed.).

Books

Last name, Initial(s). (year). Title of book. City, ST: Publisher.

Sellnow, D. (2001). The process of public speaking. Fort Worth, TX: Harcourt Brace.

Journal Articles

Last name, Initial(s). (year). Title of article. Title of Journal, volume number, pages.

Ayres, J. (1991). Using visual aids to reduce speech anxiety. Communication Research Reports, 8, 73–79.

Magazines

Last name, Initial(s). (year, month). Title of article. Title of Magazine, pages.

Franklin, D. (1998, May/June). Germ crazy. Health, 95–101.

Newspapers

Last name, Initial(s). (year, month and day). Title of article. Title of Newspaper, pages.

Froslie, E. (1998, May 1). Religious addiction. The Forum, p. B1.

Television Programs

Last name, Initial(s). (Producer or Executive Producer). (year, month and day). Title of program. City, ST: Distributor.

Crystal, L. (Executive Producer). (1993, October 11). The MacNeil/Lehrer news hour. New York and Washington, DC: Public Broadcasting Service.

Music Recordings

Last name of writer, Initial(s). (Date of copyright). Title of song [Recorded by artist if different from writer]. On Title of album [Medium of recording]. Location: Label (Recording date if different from copyright date).

Brooks, M., & Peiken, S. (1997). Bitch [Recorded by M. Brooks]. On Blurring the edges [CD]. Hollywood, CA: Capitol Records.

Internet Periodicals

Last name of author, Initial(s). (date of most recent posting). Title of article [number of paragraphs]. Name of Periodical [Online], Available at: Specify path [date on which you accessed the document].

(If no author is listed, identify the organization posting the information in place of the author.)

South Dakota Lottery. (1997, September 26). Where the money goes! [4 paragraphs]. South Dakota Lottery [Online]. Available at **http://www.state.sd.us/state/executive/lottery/wherethe.htm** (version on December 1, 1997).

Other Internet Documents

Last name of author, Initial(s). (date of most recent posting). Title of article [number of paragraphs]. Sponsoring Organization [Online], Available at: Specify path [date on which you accessed the document].

(If no author is listed, identify the organization posting the information in place of the author.)

Walker, J. R. (1996, July 1996). MLA-style citations of electronic sources. [5 paragraphs]. University of South Florida [Online], Available at **http://www.cas.usf/edu/english/walker/mla.html** [October 1, 1999].

Again, the APA publication manual includes formats for many less common types of sources. When in doubt, consult the manual.

Within the Formal Outline

Like a written paper, your formal public speaking outline ought to include, along with a reference list, internal references at the points where information is based on external research. According to the APA publication manual, when summarizing results you may simply include the author and year in parentheses at the end of the last sentence. For example, Holly explained that having a grandma babysit is not always the best solution, and she based this explanation on an article she read in *Parents* magazine. Therefore, she concluded the relevant material in her outline with the following citation: (Ogintz, 1994).

If there is no author, then you should include a shortened version of the article's title and the date of the article. Holly cited several criteria for quality day care that she learned about in a newspaper article titled "Studies Identify Criteria for Better Day Care." She concluded with the following citation: ("Studies Identify," 1995).

When using a **direct quotation,** you must also indicate the page from which the quotation is drawn. This information is included in the parentheses after the year. Quotations of fewer than forty words are part of the text line; quotations of at least forty words are set off as block quotation. If you mention any citation information, such as the author's name, before the quotation, you do not need to repeat it in the parentheses. Again, see the APA manual for information on citing other kinds of sources.

Oral Citations During the Speech

To be an ethical public speaker, you must also cite your sources orally throughout your presentation. **Oral footnotes** are references to the original source made at the point in the speech where information from that source is presented.

Teaching Tip
Much of this information is new to students and they may express reservations about how to cite material orally in the speech. Therefore, it is important to facilitate their understanding of this process by asking questions and referring to the examples provided in this chapter.

Oral documentation is as necessary as the other forms if you're to avoid plagiarism, and it enhances your ethos. Beginning public speakers sometimes have difficulty understanding the reasons for citing references orally. Consider the fact that no one who hears your presentation actually sees your outline or your reference list except, perhaps, your instructor. How will the others in your audience know where your information comes from unless you tell them? Because public speaking is an oral, rather than written, form of communication, you must provide your internal references orally as well as within the text and at the end of the formal outline.

To be ethical, you must provide oral footnotes whenever you include information drawn from another source. Oral footnotes typically give listeners the name and credentials of the author and enough bibliographic information so that they could look up the source themselves. It is not necessary to include page numbers. Use of oral footnotes helps ensure that the speaker is not fabricating information or offering his or her unsubstantiated opinions. It also lets listeners know that the speaker is not plagiarizing information.

The following discussion illustrates oral footnotes for the types of sources most often cited by public speaking students. For each type, some information *should* be included and other information *may* be included, especially if it will enhance your credibility.

Books

Usually, you need to identify only the name of the author and the title of the book. You might include the date of publication or the credentials of the author, especially if doing so will enhance your credibility (e.g., if the author is well known or the date is very recent). Here are some alternative possibilities:

> In her book *Public Speaking: A Process Approach,* Sellnow argues that oral footnotes are essential because they enhance speaker credibility.
>
> In her book *Public Speaking: A Process Approach,* Sellnow, who is director of public speaking fundamentals at North Dakota State University, argues that oral footnotes are essential because they enhance speaker credibility.

Journal or Magazine Articles

For journal and magazine articles, you should include the name and date of the publication. You may also include the author and/or the title of the article.

> Ayres wrote, in a 1991 article published in *Communication Research Reports,* that using visual aids during public speaking presentations may actually reduce speech anxiety.
>
> According to a May/June 1998 article in *Health* magazine titled "Germ Crazy," not all antibacterial products actually help prevent disease. In fact, some can even make the germs more resistant.

Newspapers

For newspaper articles, include the name of the newspaper and the date of the article. Although you can also include the name of the author, citing the newspaper is more likely to boost your credibility than is citing the author.

> According to a May 1998 article published in *The Wall Street Journal,* religious addiction can be as damaging to relationships as drug or alcohol addiction.

Interviews

To cite information from an interview you conducted, include the name and credentials of the person interviewed and the date when the interview took place. If you draw on the interview more than once during the speech, you need only cite the person's name in your subsequent oral footnotes.

> In a telephone interview with Dr. Susan Nissen, physician for physical medicine at Meritcare Hospital in Fargo, conducted on January 12, 1998, I learned that most Americans will break a toe or a finger at some point during their lives.

Television Programs

For television programs, include the name of the program and the date of the original broadcast. You may also include the name of the reporter.

> According to a May 1995 CNN special broadcast called "Cry Hatred," neo-Nazi skinhead hate crimes can be linked directly to the "Oi" music skinheads listen to.

Internet Documents

For Internet documents, include the author and her or his credentials along with the date of the most recent revision. If there is no author, include the credentials of the sponsoring organization instead. Do not include the URL path as part of your oral footnote.

> North Dakota State University, a leading agricultural research institution, published a document on the Internet on December 21, 1997. According to that document, some organic fertilizers can do more to harm potato crops than their chemical counterparts.

Teaching Tip
Consider providing class time for students to practice oral citations using a few of their sources for the next speech.

The key to preparing oral footnotes is to include enough information for listeners to access the sources themselves and to offer enough credentials to enhance your credibility as a speaker on the topic. Ethical oral footnotes, then, help speakers to enhance ethos and avoid plagiarism.

Summary

Supporting material enables speakers to address diverse learning styles, reduce their public speaking anxiety by adding breadth and depth to their speech, and enhance their ethos.

In your speeches, you can and should draw on various types of supporting material. You can use facts to support your claims about events, times, and people. You can use statistics to demonstrate the significance of a problem or to highlight trends over time. Definitions, descriptions, and explanations help clarify aspects of your topic that may be somewhat unfamiliar to your listeners. Examples—whether brief or extended, hypothetical or factual—help to illustrate or represent concepts, groups, and so forth. Testimonies from peers or experts are used to provide personal support for points, increasing pathos. Analogies are used to highlight similarities between the concept or object you are discussing and something familiar to listeners.

Similarly, you can and should find supporting material in various types of sources. Draw on your own experience and expertise as well as on the experience and expertise of others. You can conduct research through interviews and surveys. You can also draw on library resources and the Internet.

It is important that your research be ethical. To evaluate your supporting material, ask yourself six key questions: Is it relevant? Is it credible? Is it current? Does it answer all important questions? Have I consulted a variety of resources? Do I use various types of supporting material? You must document your evidence in your outline and during your speech. Doing so enhances ethos and avoids plagiarism. Follow the APA format or another format to document your sources in your reference list and within your formal outline; use oral footnotes during your presentation.

Supporting material brings your speech to life for listeners and makes it compelling. By using various types of supporting material and resources, and by documenting your sources thoroughly, you'll make your use of supporting material maximally effective and ethical.

Activities

1. **Interview Role-Play:** Form a group with four of your classmates. One student is the interviewer, one is the interviewee, and the other two students critique the interview based on the information in the text and in Figure 7–1. The interviewee is an "expert" on the topic of the interviewer's upcoming speech. As a group, come up with a list of open- and closed-ended interview questions. The two critics should take notes and share their observations after the mock interview is completed. Then switch roles and repeat the process.
2. **Small Group Brainstorming.** In groups of four or five students, brainstorm a list of possible places to find supporting material for each member's upcoming speech topic. Use the categories of (a) personal experience, (b) interviews, (c) surveys, (d) library resources, and (e) Internet documents.
3. **Internet Exploration.** Alone or with a partner, spend thirty minutes surfing the Internet on a topic. Go to a variety of Web sites. Print six potentially relevant sources of information for your topic and then apply the evaluation criteria to each of them.
   - *Is it relevant?* Is it related *directly* to your topic?
   - *Is it credible?* Who is the author (or sponsoring organization) and what are his or her credentials? What are the author's potential biases or hidden agendas?
   - *Is it current?* Is the resource updated regularly? Has new information probably come out since its publication?

   Did you have to discard any items? Why or why not?

Key Terms

Academic journals
Analogy
Breadth
Brief example
Browser
Credentials
Credible evidence
Current evidence
Definition
Depth
Description
Direct quotation
Directory
Evidence
Example
Expert testimony
Explanation
Extended example
Fact
Factual example
Government documents
Human-edited index
Hyperlinks
Hypothetical example
Internet
Leading questions
Metasearch engine
Oral footnotes
Peer testimony
Relevant evidence
Research
Research interview
Robot-generated index
Search engine
Statistics
Supporting material
Survey
Testimony
World Wide Web

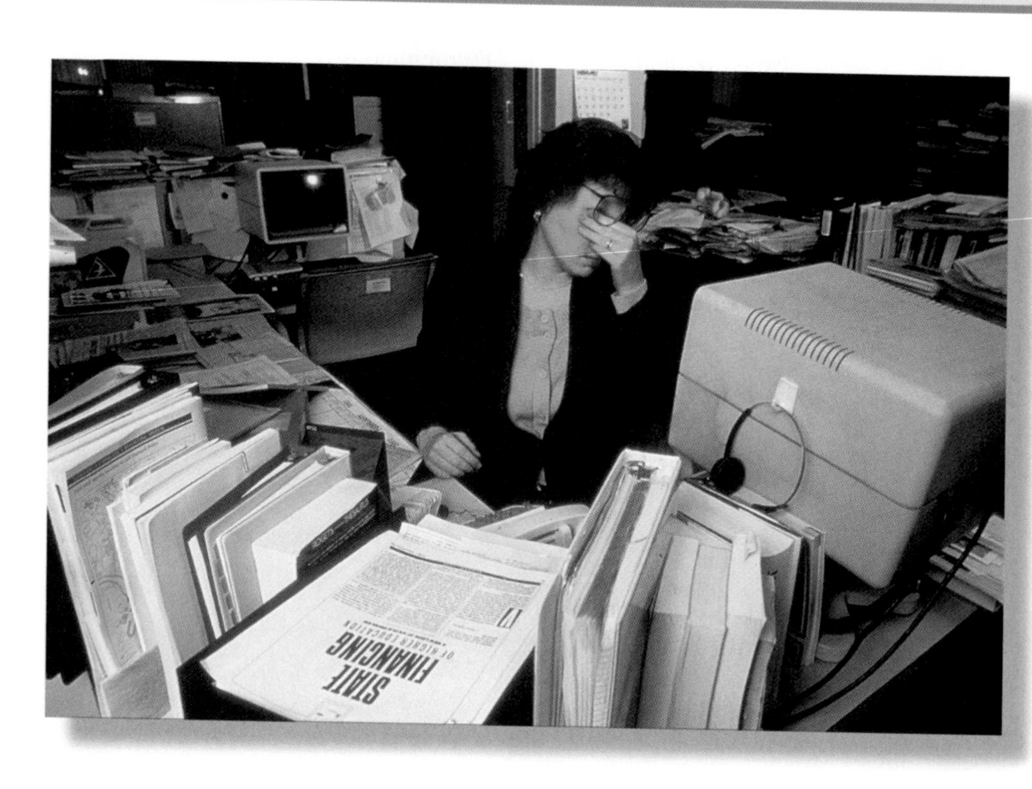
STATE
FINANCING
OF HIGHER EDUCATION

CHAPTER 8

Organizing Your Main Ideas

Reflective Questions

1. Why do your anxiety levels sometimes rise while you are organizing a public speech?
2. Why is clear organization so crucial to an effective public speech?
3. Why is it important to organize your ideas before outlining your speech?
4. Why is it important to use different types of supporting material to develop each main idea?
5. What can you do to tie your main points together?

Julie's instructor had asked students to prepare their next informative speech. Julie chose alternative methods of healing as her topic. She spent a good deal of time researching the topic and had collected a lot of supporting material. As Julie sat staring at a stack of books, journal and magazine articles, and Internet printouts, she thought, "Now what?" The more Julie read, the more anxious she became. "There are so many interesting things to say. But, how? I don't want to ramble. Where do I go from here? I need help!"

Discussion Tip
Ask students to name occasions when they have had trouble following a speaker. What specific difficulties created the confusion? What could the speaker have done differently?

Julie's anxiety was rising due to a fear of the unknown. Her negative self-talk focused on worries about not knowing how to go about organizing her ideas coherently and, as a result, of not making sense to her listeners. Julie is not alone. This concern about how to organize information effectively is one of the most common reasons for increased public speaking anxiety (Dwyer, 1998). What many people don't realize is that by following a few specific guidelines, you can organize your ideas in a way that listeners will be able to follow.

This chapter begins with an explanation of the basic elements that make up effective public speech organization, or macrostructure. Then we talk about reasons why macrostructure is so crucial to effective public speaking. From there we focus specifically on what is involved in organizing the body of your speech—that is, patterning your main points, integrating supporting material, and incorporating connectives. Doing so is the first step in organizing an effective public speech.

What Is Organization?

Teaching Tip
Refer students to the SpeechMaker CD-ROM. This software will assist them in organizing their main ideas. Consider assigning one of the scenarios to be completed before class, which you can then discuss as you teach this chapter.

Organization is the process of putting your ideas and information together in a way that will make sense to listeners. Recall our discussion in Chapter 3 about the three components of an effective public speech: content, structure, and delivery. Effective structure is achieved through clearly articulated macrostructure, which is the general framework for your ideas, and thoughtfully selected language and style, which is microstructure. The process you engage in to achieve effective structure is organization.

> ***What Do You Think?***
> *What if you asked a friend for a particular recipe and what you received was a list of ingredients? Would the recipe make sense? Why or why not?*

Teaching Tip
To illustrate how to utilize macrostructure, assign students to small groups and have them prepare a short presentation of their favorite sitcom character. Direct them to include all the elements of the introduction and conclusion, at least two main points, and transitions. This activity will help orient the students to the basic principles of speech construction and outlining. You could follow up this activity with a discussion of the microstructural choices speakers made when presenting the information.

Macrostructure consists of those elements that provide the general framework for your ideas. A speech that lacks macrostructure is like a recipe that lacks directions. Just as the list of ingredients makes no sense without directions, a string of ideas will make no sense without a general framework. Chapters 8, 9, and 10 all focus on macrostructure.

The most effective macrostructural pattern known for conveying ideas in a public speech was developed more than two thousand years ago and continues to be the most universally understood formula for presenting ideas orally today (Connor & McCagg, 1987; Darnell, 1963; Smith, 1951; Thompson, 1967). This pattern is essentially the tripartite arrangement of ideas and information into an introduction, body, and conclusion. Effective public speakers take the time to organize their main points logically, develop their introduction and conclusion thoroughly, and outline the speech comprehensively using this time-tested tripartite pattern. Doing so reduces your chances of rambling and increases your chances for "making sense" to your listeners.

Macrostructure	Microstructure
Follow the Golden Rule	*Language and Style*
Introduction Tell them what you're going to tell them	Clarity
Body Tell them	Vividness
Conclusion Tell them what you've told them	Inclusion

FIGURE 8–1
Golden Rule of Effective Structure

Microstructure, which consists of the language and style choices you make, is the other key component to structuring your message. Microstructure is discussed in detail in Chapter 11. Microstructure and macrostructure are compared in Figure 8–1.

Why Is Organization So Important to Public Speaking?

Since your goal in any communication transaction is to "make sense" to your receiver(s), clear organization is important to any message you send. The public speaking context is no exception. You will not make sense to your listeners if your ideas are not clearly organized. Since public speaking is transient (listeners must understand you based on hearing your ideas only once), it is crucial that they can follow you throughout the presentation. In a public speaking setting, listeners do not have the luxury of rereading a paragraph. Consequently, public speech organization adheres to a unique set of guidelines—guidelines we will discuss in detail throughout this chapter.

Teaching Tip
Bring to class a sample speech outline that is ineffectively organized. Assign students to groups and have them identify a more appropriate organizational pattern. In addition, have the groups revise the outline and report their results to the rest of the class.

The organizational skills you learn here will not only improve your public speeches but will also benefit your personal and professional life. For example, imagine there are two candidates for a job as public relations director for actor Jim Carey. Anita and Clarence have the same college degree and about the same level of experience. However, Anita spent a lot of time organizing what she planned to say in the interview, while Clarence stayed out late every night the week of the interview and didn't spend any time thinking about how he'd organize answers to possible interview questions. Anita's organized answers would set her apart from Clarence and would probably land her the job, leaving Clarence to continue working his college job as a checker at the deli.

Discussion Tip
How might the organizational skills presented in this chapter benefit your professional and personal life? How does clear organization help reduce public speaking anxiety?

Clear organization is also important because it helps reduce public speaking anxiety. By now you probably realize that public speaking anxiety levels can increase at any point in the speechmaking process. Knowing this, however, can actually help reduce your anxiety as long as you also know *why* anxiety levels might increase. Knowing why provides the basis for developing strategies to overcome your fear. If you find your anxiety increasing while organizing your ideas, you are probably engaged in negative self-talk centered on a fear of the unknown.

Do you find yourself worrying about "what ifs" like these? (a) What if listeners cannot figure out what it is I am trying to say? (b) What if listeners cannot follow my organization? (c) What if I ramble? (d) What if listeners cannot tell when I am finished? (e) What if I lose my place or forget what comes next? If so, then the skills you learn about organization in the next three chapters will help reduce your anxiety. Let's begin with the focus of this chapter, organizing the body of your speech.

Developing the Body of Your Speech

Your first step in the process of organizing your macrostructure is to develop the body of your speech. You actually do this before you develop your introduction and conclusion. Although this might seem a bit odd at first, it's actually something like what you do when you give someone an outfit as a gift. Before you can put the gift in a box and wrap it with a bow, you need to select the items that coordinate or "go together." Similarly, you need to develop the body of your speech before you tie it together with your introduction and conclusion. Developing the body of your speech begins with selecting a specific pattern for your main points, then integrating various types of supporting material to augment each main point, and finally creating connectives that serve as glue to hold the main points and supporting material together.

Selecting a Pattern for Your Main Points

Discussion Tip
Which of these organizational patterns is most appropriate for informative speaking? Which of these organizational patterns is most appropriate for persuasive speaking? What characteristics distinguish informative and persuasive speaking?

You might recall from Chapter 3 that listeners often have a difficult time keeping track of more than two to four main points in an oral presentation. But how do you determine what those main points ought to be? You determine your main points by considering what specific questions must be answered in order for others to understand your thesis statement. That is, you begin by asking yourself what listeners must know in order (a) *to understand* the thesis of your informative speech, (b) *to agree* with the thesis of your dispositional persuasive speech, or (c) *to act* in the way you advocate in your actuation persuasive speech. Laura, for example, had to consider what questions must be answered for listeners to understand why living a vegetarian lifestyle is such an important part of her identity. Jaime had to determine what questions must be answered for listeners to agree that cloning is good for society. For Jaime, this also meant considering reasons why people might disagree with his thesis in order to refute those beliefs as well. And for Richard, who wanted to convince listeners to try shopping online, it meant answering questions people have about the risks of online shopping as well as offering a strategic plan for doing so wisely.

> ***What Do You Think?***
> *What is the topic of your next speech? What questions will you need to answer for your audience to grasp your thesis statement?*

Technology Tip
http://owl.english.purdue.edu/handouts/general/gl_outlin.html
This Web page, hosted by the Purdue University Online Writing Lab, assists students in developing an effective outline. Have students visit this site and write a brief essay exploring the importance of effective outlining.

Once you've determined the specific questions that must be answered, you need to discover relationships among them. This way, you can select an appropriate pattern for arranging them. Two possible methods you might use are organizational mapping and card playing.

Organizational mapping is a process of brainstorming as many ideas as you can think of related to your thesis as well as to each other (see Figure 8–2). Recall that in Chapter 5 Holly used this same method during topic selection. Organizational mapping can be useful in the process of selecting main points because it provides a visual means for determining which ideas support a particular thesis statement, as well as which ideas seem to go together.

Teaching Tip
To give students practice in outlining a speech, assign the Patterning Main Points activity included in the Activities section of this chapter.

Card playing is similar to organizational mapping; however, you put each idea on a separate index card or slip of paper (see Figure 8–3). All of these separate ideas are in some way related to your thesis statement, but your goal is to discover whether some of them might be related to each other as they explain the thesis statement. Hence, you rearrange the cards as they might go together. Eventually, the relationships among some of them become clear and the tangential nature of

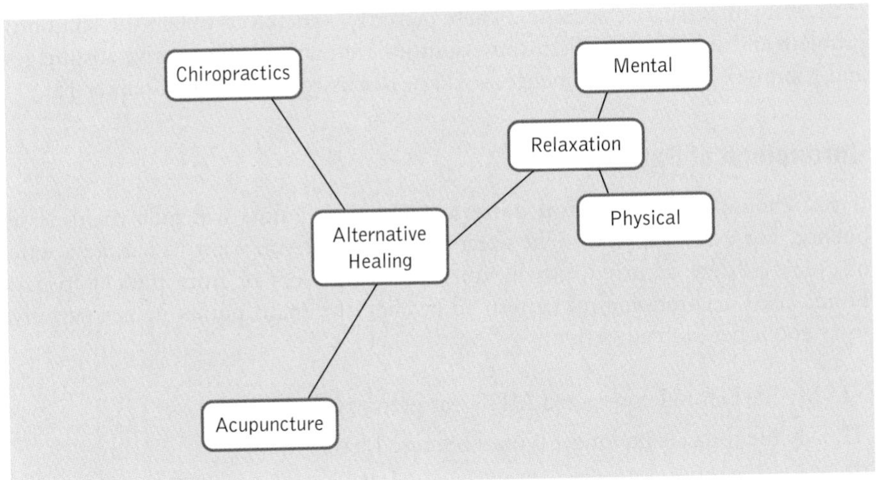

FIGURE 8–2
Organizational Mapping

others to the development of your thesis become evident. You can then discard the less relevant cards (Foss & Foss, 1994).

Whether or not you choose to use one of these methods, your ultimate goal after discovering which ideas seem to go together is to select a specific pattern for arranging your main points. Choosing a specific pattern allows you to arrange your speech in an orderly fashion, which your audience members will be able to follow as they listen. There are a number of patterns from which to choose. Some of the most common are (a) chronological, (b) causal, (c) spatial, (d) topical, and (e) comparison and contrast. There are also a number of unique patterns used

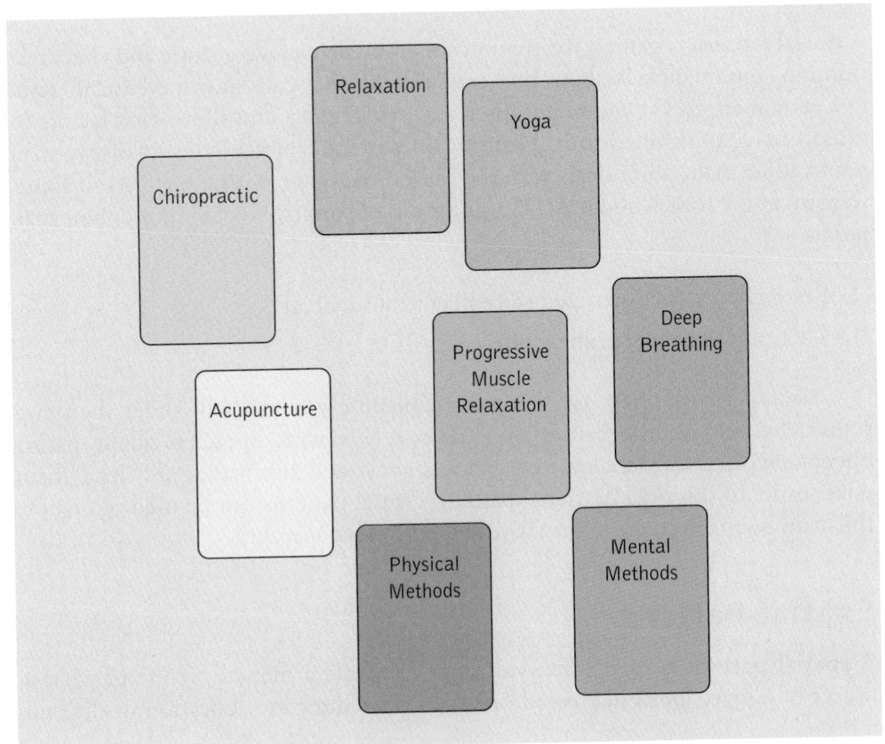

FIGURE 8–3
Relationship Cards

exclusively in persuasive speeches. These patterns—such as problem (no solution), problem and solution, problem-cause-solution, refutative, comparative advantages, and Monroe's Motivated Sequence—will be discussed in detail in Chapter 15.

Chronological Pattern

Teaching Tip
Assign students to small groups and have them discuss the advantages and limitations of the organizational patterns presented in this chapter. In addition, ask students to identify topics that are appropriate for these different patterns. Discuss each group's findings with the class.

If you choose a **chronological pattern,** your main points will follow a time sequence. For example, you might select this pattern if you want to narrate a series of events as they occurred, usually from past to present or from present to past. Lonna used a chronological pattern to arrange the main points in her narrative story about her life with AIDS:

I. My life before I contracted AIDS was pretty typical.
II. My life today is no longer typical because I have AIDS.
III. My life plans for the future are also unique because I have AIDS.

Other times, your main points might demonstrate a process or procedure. Samuel explained the process of changing a flat tire by offering a series of steps as his main points. His main points used a chronological pattern as well. Other ways to arrange your main points chronologically include seasons of the year (spring summer, fall, winter), time of day (morning, noon, night), life cycles (infant, child, teen, adult), months, years, or decades. Trace used decades for his chronological pattern about the history of rock 'n' roll music. In his four-point speech, he talked about rock music in the 1960s, the 1970s, the 1980s, and the 1990s. Chronological patterns like these are especially suited for informative speeches.

Causal Pattern

Teaching Tip
Develop a series of overheads illustrating these organizational patterns. This will help students distinguish one from the other.

A **causal pattern** organizes main points in a way that shows a cause and effect relationship. You might talk about how certain factors (or causes) will eventually result in a certain effect. Or you might discuss a certain effect and show what factors (or causes) have contributed to it. Hence, your pattern typically consists of two main points. One main point deals with the causes; the other, with the effects. If Lonna were to do the speech about AIDS using a causal pattern, she might use these main points:

I. Researchers have discovered three major causes of AIDS.
II. There are also three primary effects of AIDS.

Medical topics often use this pattern because you can talk about the symptoms (effects) and the causes of a disease. Likewise, speeches about natural phenomena like earthquakes, tornadoes, floods, and hurricanes also lend themselves easily to this organizational pattern. Causal patterns can be used to organize the main points for both informative and persuasive speeches.

Spatial Pattern

Teaching Tip
Take four or five outlines and pull them apart. Working in groups, have students reconstruct the outlines.

A **spatial pattern** is used when you want to create a mental picture of what an object or a place looks like based on location or direction. Location or direction

Speeches about natural disasters often use a causal pattern.

relates to relationships such as north to south, near to far, top to bottom, or left to right. Flight attendants use a spatial pattern when they present preflight instructions to passengers by talking about (I) where the exits are located, (II) where the flotation and oxygen devices are located, and (III) where the restrooms are located. If you wanted to explain where the library is located in relation to the rest of the campus, you might use a spatial pattern. Likewise, if you decide to talk about the components of a camera as they work when you snap a picture, your main points would employ a spatial pattern. And if you chose to talk about where various Native American Indian reservations are located throughout the United States, you would use a spatial pattern to arrange your main points. If Lonna were to use a spatial pattern for her speech on AIDS, she might talk about which parts of the world are experiencing the most rapid growth of AIDS cases and why. Spatial patterns are most often used for informative speeches.

Topical Pattern

A **topical pattern** is used when you divide a topic into subtopics or categories. If you were to inform your listeners about the qualities of a fine diamond, you might use a topical pattern. The subtopics you would use for your main points are cut, clarity, color, and carat.

You might use a topical pattern to discuss several different viewpoints on a particular concept, idea, or problem. By using this approach, you can expose your listeners to many ways of looking at an issue. Eric, for example, talked about methods of discipline using these main points:

I. One method of discipline is based on a Skinnerian perspective.
II. Another method of discipline is based on a Freudian perspective.
III. Yet another method of discipline is based on a cognitive perspective.

For the AIDS speech, Lonna could arrange the main points topically by talking about AIDS experiences from the perspective of the person with the disease, from the perspective of family and friends, and from the perspective of health care providers.

Teaching Tip
Show a videotape of a sample speech and have students develop an outline. This activity will aid in the development of both outlining and listening skills.

You can also arrange your subtopics by gradation using a topical pattern. You might discuss your main ideas from small to large, familiar to unfamiliar, simple to complex, least expensive to most expensive, and so forth (Foss & Foss, 1994). In her speech about alternative methods of healing, Julie began by talking about relaxation therapy as a fairly simple natural method of healing. She then talked about chiropractic therapy as a somewhat more complex approach

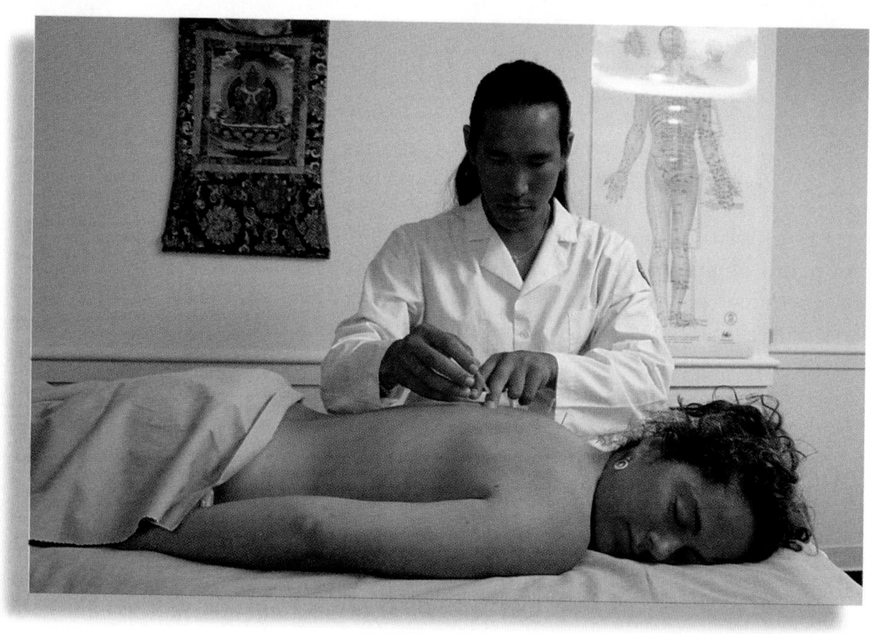

Julie used a topical pattern arranged by gradation for her speech on alternative healing methods.

to healing. And she concluded by discussing acupuncture as an even more complex form of natural healing. Her main points were arranged by gradation using a topical pattern. Because it can be used for almost any topic and for any type of speech, the topical pattern is used more often than any other (Hoffman, 1992).

Comparison and Contrast Pattern

This pattern is particularly useful for speeches about an unfamiliar concept, event, belief, or process. For example, Shannon's speech about traditional Japanese clothing used a comparison and contrast pattern. First, he compared how traditional Japanese attire was rooted in necessity much like winter outerwear, which is worn out of necessity in cold-weather climates. He then compared symbolic meanings attached to traditional Japanese clothing to the symbolic meanings for wearing certain attire in the dominant American culture. Finally, he compared the role of honor in traditional Japanese clothing to military attire in the United States today. Shannon's main points were as follows:

I. Some items of traditional Japanese attire evolved out of necessity, much like winter outerwear in cold-weather climates.

II. Some items of traditional Japanese attire have symbolic meaning as does a white wedding gown for many people in this country.

III. Some items of traditional Japanese attire represent degrees of honor or status much like military clothing, stripes, and badges in this country.

Using this pattern to arrange his main points helped make an unfamiliar topic more familiar to his listeners. For the AIDS speech, Lonna could use a comparison and contrast pattern to illustrate the experiences of AIDS victims and those of victims suffering with terminal cancer. This pattern is most useful for informative speeches about unfamiliar topics, but it is sometimes used for persuasive speeches as well.

Any of these patterns can be used to organize your main points. Selecting one pattern to arrange the ideas and information in the body of your speech increases the likelihood that listeners will be able to follow you.

Teaching Tip
Show videotapes of students presenting speeches that illustrate the organizational patterns presented in this chapter. Ask students to consider the appropriateness of these patterns given the speakers' goals.

Integrating Supporting Material

Once you have arranged your main points within a specific pattern, you are ready to integrate supporting material under each main point. You should base your selection of supporting material for each main point on four key questions.

Sort Supporting Material among the Main Points

First, ask yourself which main point each piece of supporting material you've collected relates to. Repeat this sorting process with each piece of evidence until you've considered all of them. Realize that you might discover some supporting material that doesn't really relate directly to any of your main points. Discard those pieces of evidence. Realize, too, that you might discover you need to do more research to find additional supporting material for a particular main point. Once you have discarded any extraneous evidence and collected any additional supporting material needed, you can move on to the second question.

Add Subdivisions Where Necessary

Second, ask yourself whether the supporting material lends itself to further subdivision of the main point. Recall Julie's speech on alternative forms of healing. After looking at her supporting material, she discovered that her first main point—relaxation therapy—could be subdivided according to more specific methods. She further organized her first main point into two subdivisions: (a) psychological methods and (b) physical methods. Then she organized the supporting material for her first main point once again as each piece fit under one of these subdivisions.

Consider Learning Styles

Teaching Tip
To give students an opportunity to develop claims that are sensitive to the learning styles of their listeners, assign the Addressing Learning Styles activity included in the Activities section of this chapter.

Third, ask yourself whether the supporting material you've chosen appeals to more than one learning style. Remember that the most effective retention occurs when your speech rounds the entire cycle of learning. So the supporting material you've chosen ought to address more than one learning style. That is, do you offer something for thinkers, doers, feelers, and watchers? Do you focus only on facts and statistics at the expense of personal stories and testimonies? Do you provide definitions and explanations at the expense of concrete examples? You probably won't have supporting material that addresses every stage of the cycle for each and every main point. Supporting material under each main point should, however, address more than one learning style.

Definitions, descriptions, and explanations tend to appeal to thinkers. Hypothetical or factual examples that may be brief or extended tend to appeal to feelers, as do expert and peer testimonies. Action plans, strategies, and formulas tend to appeal to doers. And any supporting material that is displayed visually or audiovisually tends to appeal to watchers. We will talk more specifically about presentational aids in Chapter 13. Ultimately, each stage of the learning cycle should be addressed in the form of supporting material somewhere in the body of your speech.

What Do You Think?

Look at the supporting material you've collected for your next speech. Which pieces address feelers? Doers? Thinkers? Watchers?

Discussion Tip
Why is it important for speakers to develop listener relevance links for each main point? How do listener relevance links sustain listener interest and motivation?

Consider Listener Relevance

Finally, ask yourself whether you provide supporting material that can serve as listener relevance links for each main point. Although your introductory comments offer a statement that relates your speech to your listeners, it is important to make such connections throughout the speech. Hence, the most effective public speeches provide clear listener relevance links for each main point. Doing so better ensures that you regain and sustain listener interest and motivation throughout the course of the speech.

Incorporating Connectives

Once you have selected a pattern for ordering your main points and integrated appropriate supporting material under each main point, you need to link these items together in ways that make your speech flow forward fluently. You achieve this by incorporating connectives. **Connectives** are words or phrases that serve as glue to hold your speech together. Connectives include transitions, internal previews and summaries, and signposts.

Transitions

Transitions are words or phrases that show the relationship between two main points and let the audience know you have completed one main point and are moving on to another. The most effective transition statements verbally tie the main point you have just completed to the one that you will talk about next in a way that clarifies the relationship between them. In the simplest sense, you are reminding your audience about where you've been and where you're going. It is as though you are saying, "Now that we've talked about (previous main point), let's discuss (upcoming main point)."

Teaching Tip
Assign students to groups and ask them to brainstorm transitional phrases. Ask them to evaluate the effectiveness and creativity of the transitional phrases. Compile the lists and use them for future speeches.

Transitions may be as short as one sentence or they may take two or three sentences to complete. As part of your macrostructure, however, they always connect two main points, or connect the introduction to the body, or connect the body to the conclusion.

You can make your transitions more creative and actually more accurate by developing them in ways that reinforce the pattern of your main points. If, for example, your main points use a chronological pattern, you might use a time change pattern when structuring your transitions. Use words like the following:

- *until, previously, later, earlier, in the past, in the future, meanwhile, before, after, at present, today, and eventually*

Lonna, for example, used this transition in her speech: "*Before* I had AIDS, my life was pretty typical, but *today* my life is definitely not typical. My life today is different because I have AIDS."

Transitions that reinforce a causal pattern use words like the following:

- *therefore, consequently, thus, so, as a result, hence, since, due to, accordingly, and because of*

In the causal speech about AIDS, Lonna might say, "Now that you realize what causes AIDS, let's look at the effects that arise *as a result* of contracting the disease."

Transitions that reinforce a spatial pattern use words like the following:

- *above, below, in front of, in back of, to the East, to the West, to the right, to the left, just behind, nearby, in the distance, next to, and furthest from*

In the preflight presentation, a transition might look like this: "Although emergency exits are located only *in the front and back of the aircraft*, oxygen and flotation devices are located *above and below* each seat."

Transitions that imply comparison use words like the following:

- *compared with, likewise, similarly, just as, much like, and in comparison*

Shannon, for example, offered this transition: "*Just as* some traditional Japanese attire carries symbolic meaning, so does some traditional attire represent degrees of honor and status *much like* military clothing does in our country."

Transitions that illustrate contrast use words like the following:

- *but, yet, however, on the other hand, in contrast, rather than, and on the contrary*

Transitions that build an argument incrementally might use words that signify additions like the following:

- *moreover, in addition, not only, also, furthermore, and besides*

In each of the three main points in Julie's speech about alternative methods of healing, for example, she used transitions that reinforced her continuum pattern:

I. Relaxation therapy

Transition: *Not only* is relaxation therapy a natural healing method you can consider, but *also* chiropractic therapy is something you might choose.

II. Chiropractic therapy

Transition: *In addition* to relaxation therapy and chiropractic therapy, another more complex natural healing method is acupuncture.

III. Acupuncture

She verbally tied her main ideas together using a strategy that reinforced the gradation approach she took using a topical pattern.

> **What Do You Think?**
>
> *What pattern do you use to arrange your main points? How can you create transitions that reinforce that pattern?*

Internal Previews and Summaries

Teaching Tip
Bring examples of both good and poor connectives to class. Have students identify the elements of effective connectives as well as the ways that poor connectives can be improved.

Internal previews and summaries essentially connect pieces of supporting material to the main point or subpoint they address. Internal previews do so before offering the supporting material, whereas internal summaries do so afterward. Essentially, you help your listeners understand how the supporting material supports the main point. You can develop these kinds of previews and summaries by answering *why* you've included the supporting material. Julie used an internal

What Do You Think?

Look at the supporting material you have selected for your main points. Where can you add internal previews and summaries to help connect your supporting material to those main points?

preview before talking about psychological methods as an alternative form of healing. She said, "I'm sure most of you have heard the concept of 'mind over matter.' Well, 'mind over matter' is actually a psychological method you can use as a form of relaxation therapy. For example . . ."

Signposts

Signposts are merely words or short phrases that mark where you are in the speech or help move the speech forward. Signposts are most commonly used to highlight numerical order—that is, "first," "second," "third," and "fourth." Signposts also can be used to focus the audience on a key idea—for example, "foremost," "most important," and "above all." Some signposts signify an explanation—for example, "to illustrate," "for instance," "in other words," "essentially," "in essence," and "to clarify." Finally, signposts are sometimes used to signal that an important idea or even the speech itself is ending: "in short," "finally," "in conclusion," "to summarize," and "in sum."

Teaching Tip
Bring to class an example of a public speech that uses few signposts. Ask students to insert signposts that will facilitate the organizational flow of the speech. Have students discuss the utility of signposts for both the speaker and the listeners.

The body houses the content of your public speech in a way that helps listeners follow along mentally with the development of your ideas as you speak. To organize the body of your speech effectively, select an appropriate pattern for the main points, integrate various types of supporting material for each main point, and tie your ideas together with connectives, which include transitions, internal previews and summaries, and signposts.

What Do You Think?

Where can you integrate signposts in your next speech?

SUMMARY

Effective public speech organization is the process of arranging the macrostructural part of speech structure. Effective organization can reduce public speaking anxiety rooted in a fear of the unknown. The macrostructural components of a public speech consist of the introduction, body, and conclusion. Because listeners must follow your organization as they listen, public speech structure must follow a specific set of guidelines. This chapter focused specifically on the first set of guidelines, those associated with organizing the body of a public speech—patterning main points, integrating supporting material, and incorporating connectives.

The body should consist of two to four main points that follow one specific pattern. Some of the most common patterns for arranging main ideas are (a) chronological, (b) causal, (c) spatial, (d) topical, and (e) comparison and

Teaching Tip
Emphasize to students why it is important that they avoid simply reading their speeches from the outline when they present the material in class. Consider limiting them to a one-page key word outline or index cards.

contrast. Each main point is developed by integrating a variety of supporting material, addressing different learning styles, and highlighting listener relevance. The elements of the body are further tied together with connectives. Transitions verbally tie together main points in ways that reinforce the pattern as well as the relationship between them. Internal previews and summaries tie together supporting material with the main point or subpoints they augment. Signposts simply mark where you are and move the speech forward with short words or phrases. The most common signposts tend to highlight numerical order. Other signposts focus the audience on a key idea, signify an explanation, or signal that the idea or the speech itself is ending.

Developing the body of a speech is the first important step in organizing macrostructure that listeners can follow. The second equally important step is creating effective introductions and conclusions, which is the focus of Chapter 9.

Activities

1. **Patterning Main Points.** Form a group with two or three classmates. Select a topic from the list that follows or come up with your own. Then create three sets of main points for the same general topic based on three different patterns. Select from chronological, causal, spatial, topical, or comparison and contrast. Topic examples for this activity should be fairly broad and could include the following:

- *Teen suicide*
- *Rugby*
- *Holidays*
- *Home schooling*
- *Sky diving*
- *Exercise*
- *Gambling*
- *Body piercing*
- *Cloning*
- *Birth control*
- *Chocolate chip cookies*
- *Restaurants*

2. **Creating Transition Statements.** Form a group with two or three classmates. Create transition statements for the main points your group arrived at in Activity 1.
3. **Addressing Learning Styles.** Form a group with two or three classmates. Now find three or four resources (e.g., magazine articles, newspaper stories, books, and Internet printouts) focused on one topic. It can be the same topic you arrived at for Activity 1. Locate supporting material for the topic that addresses each of the four learning styles: feeling, doing, watching, and thinking.

Key Terms

- Card playing
- Causal pattern
- Chronological pattern
- Connectives
- Internal previews and summaries
- Macrostructure
- Microstructure
- Organization
- Organizational mapping
- Signposts
- Spatial pattern
- Topical pattern
- Transitions

CHAPTER 9

Making Lasting Impressions: Introductions and Conclusions

Reflective Questions

1. Why is it important to devote time to developing your introduction and conclusion?
2. What should an introduction do?
3. Why is "My topic is . . ." not an effective introduction?
4. What should a conclusion do?
5. Why is it important to provide a clear preview and summary?
6. In what ways should your attention catcher and clincher work together?
7. Why is "thank you" not a clincher?

Laura had worked hard on her speech about being a vegetarian. Since she had grown up on a cattle ranch, her decision to become a vegetarian had significant implications for her and her family and she wanted to convey this in her speech. She had organized her main points chronologically: her decision, her family's reactions, and the effects of her decision on her life today. She planned to talk first about when she made her decision, then about how her family reacted, and finally about how her decision impacts her life today. She felt good about this organizational pattern and about the details and facts she'd chosen to support her main points.

Teaching Tip
Refer students to the SpeechMaker CD-ROM. This software will assist them in developing introductions and conclusions. Consider assigning one of the scenarios to be completed before the class in which you will discuss this chapter.

The body of Laura's speech was clearly organized, but her work was far from finished. Recall from Chapter 4 that listeners typically remember only about 25 percent of what they hear. Laura wanted her audience to listen to and remember her ideas. She knew she needed to create an introduction that would entice the audience to listen and a conclusion that would make her ideas memorable. The question she now needed to answer was "how?"

Once you've developed the body of your speech—that is, selected a pattern for your main points, integrated supporting material that enhances each main point, and incorporated connectives—you are ready to complete the next step in the process of organizing your speech: constructing your introduction and conclusion. This chapter presents strategies you can use to develop effective introductions and conclusions. We begin by looking at why introductions and conclusions are so crucial. Then we look specifically at introductions and conclusions in turn, based on the major functions they serve.

Why Are Introductions and Conclusions Crucial?

The way you begin and end your speech can make or break it. One key reason is what psychologists call the **primacy-recency effect:** We are more likely to remember the first and last items conveyed orally in a series than the items in between (Trenholm, 1989). Thus, your listeners are more likely to remember what you say at the beginning and the end of your speech than what you say in the body. Since your introduction and conclusion are especially likely to be remembered, you want to make sure they are strong.

Discussion Tip
Why is it important that the speaker gives listeners a framework for grasping the topic and main points in the introduction? How can speakers reinforce their main ideas in the conclusion? How can a well-developed introduction and conclusion reduce public speaking anxiety?

Another reason stems from the fact that listeners must grasp the topic and main points as they listen to the speech. They can't go back and listen to the introduction again like they can when reading an essay. You can give listeners a framework for grasping the topic and main points by clearly and precisely highlighting them in your introduction, and you can reinforce what they have grasped by clearly and precisely reminding them of your topic and main points in your conclusion.

A clearly developed introduction and conclusion can also reduce public speaking anxiety. You can give yourself positive self-talk about creating a strong first and last impression. Your introduction in particular can increase your confidence by getting you off to a good start. Likewise, since your introduction has a precise main point preview, you can always return to it as a reminder if you get stuck in the body. It can help you recall what major points you want to get across and why, getting you back on track.

> ***What Do You Think?***
> *Consider a speaker you heard who seemed really good. Did she or he say or do something in the introduction or conclusion to influence your perception?*

Developing Effective Introductions

Your introduction serves five key functions for your speech. Furthermore, effective introductions achieve all five of these functions in no more than ten to fifteen percent of your allotted speaking time. This means that the introduction of your six-minute speech should take less than one minute of your time. These functions are as follows:

- Capturing audience interest.
- Establishing a rapport with the audience.
- Establishing your credibility.
- Stating the speech topic.
- Previewing the main points.

Let's look more closely at each of these functions.

Technology Tip
http://www.presentersuniversity.com/courses/show_deapps.cfm?RecordID=531
This Web page, hosted by Presenters University, offers several tips for developing creative introductions. Have students visit this site and report their findings to the class.

Capturing Audience Interest

Use your first sentences to capture the interest of your audience. Remember, listeners are likely to be distracted by all sorts of external or internal interference. By immediately arousing your listeners' curiosity, you'll reduce the likelihood that their minds will wander to, say, what they'll be doing later, what is going on outside, or how nervous they feel about presenting their own speeches. In developing your **attention catcher,** you can draw on various possible techniques, including questions, quotations, stories or examples, startling statistics, action, and humor. Keep in mind that to be effective your attention catcher must relate to your topic; an unrelated attention catcher will confuse and distract your audience.

The attention catcher you choose for your introduction is crucial. It needs to be clever and entice listeners' curiosity about your speech. If it's not unique, you lose your attention-catching power. Advertisers are masters at creating effective attention catchers. Consider television and magazine advertisements for a moment. What do they do to grab your attention? One popular lure is sex. Why, for example, does the model in the Herbal Essences shampoo commercial act like she is having an orgasm when shampooing her hair? And why is Cindy Crawford's sweater unbuttoned to her navel in her picture on the box of Special K cereal? And why are magazine advertisements for lotions, perfumes, and makeup almost always portrayed by scantily clothed women? Although the ethical nature of such advertisements could be questioned, they do grab viewers' attention.

Another popular technique used by advertisers is humor. The "Got Milk?" advertisements are a prime example, as are the Budweiser commercials hosted by frogs. Let's look more closely at some of these attention-catching techniques.

Teaching Tip
Bring examples of both good and poor attention catchers to class. Have students identify the characteristics of effective attention catchers as well as the ways that poor attention catchers can be improved.

Teaching Tip
Make transparency masters of print ads that employ the attention-catching devices discussed in this chapter. Show these ads in class and ask students to identify the strengths and weaknesses of these devices.

Questions

One technique you might use to capture the interest of your audience is a question or series of questions. Questions are particularly useful when they are directly related to the audience and to the topic. This way they build suspense and arouse curiosity. You can use a rhetorical question or series of rhetorical questions, or a direct question or series of direct questions.

Teaching Tip
Before discussing introductions, have students write a one-page paper in which they define and provide an example for each of the attention-catching devices discussed in this chapter. Use this written assignment as the springboard for your discussion of effective introductions.

A **rhetorical question** is one that is intended to stimulate thought but not an overt response. Sonja gave a speech about the experience of moving to a new place for the first time. She began with a rhetorical question: "Have you ever packed up everything you owned, said good-bye to all of your friends, and moved to a place where you knew no one?" This question simply asked listeners to consider whether they had experienced such an event. Sometimes speakers begin with a series of rhetorical questions. For example, Sonja could have begun like this:

> Have you ever taken a trip to a place you'd never been before? How did you feel before you left? Did you travel alone? How did you feel when you arrived? Were friends or family there to greet you? Can you imagine packing up everything you own, saying good-bye to all of your friends, and moving to live someplace where you know no one? Well, that is exactly what I did.

Teaching Tip
Show a videotape of a sample speech and have students identify the elements of the introduction. Ask students to critique the introduction based on the guidelines presented in this chapter.

A series of rhetorical questions, by creating a climactic effect, can be especially effective at arousing the curiosity of the audience. They also tend to appeal to both the feeling and thinking dimensions of the learning cycle by encouraging applications to one's personal experiences in a way that stimulates critical thought. Be sure, however, that your series of rhetorical questions do, in fact, arouse curiosity. Sometimes students use ill-planned rhetorical question, as did Jennifer in her speech about the process of grooming a dog. She asked, "Have you ever had a dog?" Although this question demands no answer, it does little to arouse the curiosity of the audience.

Discussion Tip
How do direct questions differ from rhetorical questions? According to Sellnow, how might direct questions increase your public speaking anxiety?

A **direct question** differs from a rhetorical question in that it expects a response. Direct questions can be difficult to use effectively, however, for this very reason. As a result, your anxiety could increase or your speech could simply get off to a bad start. If you use a direct question, you might need to encourage your listeners to respond by saying something like "Come on now. I really want an answer," or by raising your own hand as you ask the question and pausing until listeners begin responding. This can frequently seem like a long time. Sonja could have begun her speech like this: "I'd like to see a show of hands. How many of you have ever packed up everything you owned and moved to a place where you knew no one?"

Although they pose some challenges, direct questions have the benefits of *physically* involving listeners in the communication transaction by appealing to the "doing" dimension of the learning cycle and thus making listeners more alert. This can prove particularly helpful when you must present your speech at 8 o'clock on Monday morning. Also, the responses you get might help you make the body of the speech more relevant to listeners. For example, if one of Sonja's main points was to focus on her experiences with adjusting to a new climate, she might have asked her listeners whether any of them had traveled to a new climate. If very few people had done so, she might decide to provide more detail under this main point than if many of her listeners had done so. Moreover, she might insert statements acknowledging similarities during this main point as listener relevance links.

Quotations

If you've come across a short and effective quotation, consider using it as your attention catcher. Use any kind of quotation that works well. For example, since Sonja's speech focused on the importance of courage and taking risks, she could have begun with Franklin D. Roosevelt's "The only thing we have to fear is fear itself," a well-known quotation by a famous person. Or she could have used a less well-known quotation by a famous person, like Gertrude Stein's "Considering how dangerous everything is, nothing is really very frightening." Or she could have used a quotation by someone "famous" only to her. For example:

> "No one ever said it would be easy. But you'll never know what you can do until you try." These are the words my grandmother used to tell me every time I told her I was afraid to try something new. She told me this when I was five years old and afraid to ride my bicycle without training wheels. She told me this when I was twelve years old and afraid to start junior high. And she told me this last year when I was afraid to move to a new city where I had never lived and where I would know no one.

A quotation can be a clever means of sparking the interest of listeners but only, of course, if it relates in a significant way to the topic of the speech.

Stories

Because people are naturally interested in stories, a story that serves as an example, whether actual or hypothetical, can be an effective attention catcher. Consider television advertisements again. They can be very effective at drawing listeners in when they begin with some person sharing his or her own story.

Teaching Tip
Stress the importance of ethical communication in the development of stories. Instruct students to consult with you if they are not sure whether a remark is appropriate or not.

An **actual example** may be something that happened to you; something that happened to a friend or family member; or something you learned about in a magazine, newspaper, or television news program. Actual examples tend to appeal to the feeling dimension of the learning cycle, since they focus on real people and events. Sonja elaborated on the quotation by her grandmother with actual examples from her own life.

> ***What Do You Think?***
> *Consider a television commercial that uses a story to draw you in. Does it succeed? Why or why not?*

A **hypothetical example** can take the form of your asking listeners to imagine themselves in a certain situation, or it can take the form of a story you've made up about an imaginary character in the situation. Again, this technique is particularly suited to feelers who prefer personal experiences and concrete examples. In this

Teaching Tip
Give students a topic and ask them to develop a hypothetical example that really grabs the attention of the audience. This activity should give students an excellent idea of how to develop an effective attention catcher.

case, however, you need to immediately clarify for your listeners that the story is not true. Laura used a combination of examples in her attention catcher:

> With Thanksgiving just around the corner, many of you are probably anticipating a feast complete with a flavorful, juicy turkey as the main course. I, however, plan to bring my own addition to my family dinner—a rice pilaf, with grilled vegetables and garlic-roasted tofu.

She began with a hypothetical example about her listeners and followed with an actual example from her own life.

Startling Facts or Statistics

A **startling fact or statistic** is a piece of information that is both little known and shocking. As you research your topic, you may read something that surprises you, something that you did not know was so devastating, so widespread, or so common. If so, make a note of it as a possible attention catcher. In her speech about eating disorders, for example, Marcia began her speech like this:

> Who are five of the most important women in your life? Your mother? Your sister? Your daughter? Your wife? Your best friend? Now which one of them has had or will have an eating disorder? Before you disregard my question, listen to what research tells us. One in every five women in the United States has an eating disorder.

Teaching Tip
To give students practice in developing introductions and conclusions, assign the Introductions and Conclusions activity included in the Activities section of this chapter.

Startling facts and statistics served to catch the attention of Marcia's audience much more effectively than simply stating the claim that "Eating disorders are an epidemic in this country."

Advertisers often apply this technique of startling viewers when they use sex as an attention catcher. Scantily clothed models or models engaged in some sexually illicit behavior do tend to startle and draw viewers in. Has this technique become overused and, thus, less effective? Apparently not, if based on the fact that models continue to wear more and more revealing attire, appear in more provocative positions, and behave in more illicit activities. The question this raises, of course, is one of ethics. Where should advertisers draw the line in order to demonstrate respect and honesty for themselves and their viewers?

What Do You Think?

Consider an advertisement that uses sex as an attention catcher. In your opinion, does the advertisement cross the line in terms of ethics? Why or why not?

Action

You can also use some kind of action to gain the attention of your audience. You can demonstrate the action yourself or show it on a videotaped clip, which would appeal to watchers. Or you could ask for a volunteer from the audience, or ask all audience members to participate, appealing to doers. In his speech about bungee jumping, for example, Noah show a videotaped clip of someone engaged in the activity. Juan split a stack of bricks with his hand to catch the audience's attention in his speech about karate. And in her speech about ballet, Cherise asked for a volunteer who helped her demonstrate a simple dance for her attention catcher. As with direct questions, however, asking for a volunteer or for audience participation could increase anxiety if nobody volunteers or if the audience is reluctant to participate. To reduce this possibility, you might do what Cherise did and secure your "volunteer" in advance.

Humor

Humor can also be used to catch attention. You can use a joke, and anecdote, or a story with a humorist twist. I remember a story in which a businessperson had to give a speech, for example, to an audience that was part Japanese and part American. He had learned that the Japanese always expected an apology at the beginning of the speech and that Americans expected a joke. So he apologized for not having a joke. If you use humor, however, be sure it adheres to the three R test. Your joke, anecdote, or story should be realistic, relevant, and repeatable. In other words, it can't be (a) too far-fetched, (b) unrelated to the point of your speech, or (c) potentially offensive to some listeners (Humes, 1988). If you aren't sure about whether your humor might offend someone or some group, ask several friends who belong to different racial, ethnic, gender, or special-needs groups for their opinions. Because your goal is to get through to your listeners rather than turn them off in the first sentences, follow this general rule: When in doubt, leave it out. Finally if you do choose to use humor, consider how you will handle the situation if your audience doesn't laugh. You may decide to avoid using humor in your attention catcher for either of these reasons (Slan, 1998).

Technology Tip
http://www.presentersuniversity.com/courses/show_crafting.cfm?RecordID=25

This Web page, hosted by Presenters University, offers several tips for incorporating humor in presentations. Have students visit this site and report their findings to the class.

Sometimes speakers use action to catch the attention of listeners.

All effective public speeches begin with an attention catcher. You might use a question, quotation, example, startling fact or statistic, action, or humor. Your attention catcher may be as brief as one sentence or as long as five or six sentences. Remember, however, that to be effective your attention catcher must not only arouse interest but also relate directly to the topic of your speech.

> ***What Do You Think?***
>
> *Think of a speaker who really* did *get your attention right away. What attention catcher did he or she use? Was the attention catcher connected to the topic of the speech? Was the attention catcher ethical? Why or why not?*

Establishing a Rapport with the Audience

Discussion Tip
Why is it important that you establish rapport with your audience in the introduction? What might the speaker say or do to establish rapport?

Your introduction also should help you establish a rapport—or connection—with your audience. The best way to do this is to show listeners that your speech not only will interest them, but will interest them personally. Thus, your introduction should include a **listener relevance link,** a statement of why your speech relates to or might affect listeners. This function of your introduction addresses the feeling dimension of the learning cycle. Sonja, for example, offered a statistic on how many people relocate and used it to point out that even those listeners who had never relocated before probably would someday.

Teaching Tip
To give students an opportunity to practice developing these links, assign the Listener Relevance Links activity contained in the Activities section of this chapter.

As you work on your speech, keep asking yourself questions like these: Why should listeners care about this? In what way(s) might they benefit from hearing about it? How might they be able to relate to my topic? You might focus in particular on how your speech relates to listeners' needs for health, wealth, well-being, self-esteem, success, and so forth. You can generate ideas about listener relevance by recalling what you learned about your audience's psychological and demographic characteristics during audience analysis. Levi, who spoke against the use of road salt to remove ice from streets and highways, included in his introduction a reminder that road salt rusts automobiles and thus limits how long they last. In this way, he established that his message could have a positive impact on listeners' wealth. Likewise, Marcia established rapport by talking about health and well-being when she said:

> If the research is correct, then one in every five women in this room will likely be afflicted with an eating disorder. So if it's not you, then perhaps it's the person sitting next to you. And according to a July 1998 issue of *The Washington Post,* more than 90 percent are adolescents and young women. Although the majority are women, an October 1999 news report by the British Broadcasting Company reveals that one in ten people diagnosed are men. Even children as young as three have been treated. And only 60 percent ever recover—that is, many will die.

You should, of course, include listener relevance links throughout your speech. For your introduction, choose a link that you find especially compelling and that will be general and brief enough for this point in the speech.

Establishing Your Credibility

You need to let your listeners know that you are a credible source, that they can trust what you are going to say. Doing so addresses the thinking dimension of the learning cycle. To do this, include in your introduction a **speaker credibility statement,** which is a brief statement clarifying why you are an authority on the topic of your speech. You need to answer questions like "How or why do *you* know more about the topic than your listeners probably know?" and "Why should listeners listen to *you* about this topic?"

Discussion Tip
Why is it important that you establish your credibility on the topic? How can you state your qualifications without bragging or boasting?

Students sometimes have a hard time believing that they are an authority on their topic. You do not need to be a Pulitzer Prize-winning poet to be a credible speaker on the topic of why poetry is significant to you. Nor do you have to be a well-known biotechnologist to be a credible speaker on the advantages and disadvantages of cloning. Instead, your authority can come from your academic major, as it did for Jaime, a senior majoring in biotechnology who presented a speech on cloning. Jaime simply said,

> I have been interested in the subject of cloning ever since the story about Dolly, the sheep, hit the news. As a student majoring in biotechnology, I have taken several classes related to this subject and have done a good deal of research to educate myself about this scientific breakthrough.

Or your authority can come from your personal experience, as it did for Laura, who talked about vegetarianism. Laura explained, "About five years ago, I made a decision to stop eating meat. This decision has changed my life in several ways." The amount of research you did on the topic can also make you an authority. Jaime drew on both his academic experience and research efforts for his speaker credibility statement. In short, you have to show that you are a credible source, not that you are *the* final authority or even *a* final authority.

What Do You Think?

Consider your upcoming speech topic. What personal experience, academic background, or research efforts help make you an authority on the subject?

Stating the Speech Topic

No matter how interesting your introduction is, it cannot be effective unless it gives listeners a clear sense of your topic. The introduction must include a **thesis statement,** a one-sentence summary of the speech. The thesis statement addresses the thinking dimension of the learning cycle. For maximum clarity, word your thesis statement simply and precisely. Remember that if your listeners don't grasp the thesis firmly at the outset, they will have difficulty following the rest of your speech. They do not have the luxury of rereading as in a written composition. This might also mean providing necessary background information about the topic, like short definitions or explanations. For example, in your speech about CDs, you should make it clear that you are talking about compact discs and not certificates of deposit. Likewise, depending on the topic, you might need to provide a brief historical background about it.

Laura's thesis statement was simply "Living a vegetarian lifestyle is an important aspect of who I am." Marcia's thesis statement was "Eating disorders are a serious problem in our society today." To provide necessary background, she added a short statement clarifying what she meant by eating disorders. Jaime's thesis statement was "If our scientific decisions about cloning continue to disregard ethical issues, I fear the consequences will be disastrous." He added a brief statement defining cloning as he would use it in his speech. And Sonja's thesis statement was "Relocating to a new state has taught me many lessons and, in fact, helped shape who I am today." By being both simple and precise, these statements clearly tell listeners what they will hear.

Previewing the Main Points

Discussion Tip
Why is it important that your preview be simply and precisely phrased? Can speakers provide too much or too little information in the preview statement? What suggestions does Sellnow provide for simplifying your preview statement?

By the end of your introduction, you'll have accomplished the first part of the golden rule of public speaking: Tell them what you are going to tell them. You will have done so by following the thesis statement with a **preview,** a brief statement of the main points of the speech. This preview of main points gives listeners a sense of what you will say and in what order, so that they will be able to more readily understand the body of your speech. Like the thesis statement, and for the same reasons, your preview should be simply and precisely phrased. Don't provide a lot of information. Sometimes a beginning speaker provides so much information in the preview that listeners think the speaker has already moved to the body of the speech. Keep in mind that your goal is to "tell them what you're going to tell them," *not* to actually tell them.

One strategy you might employ to keep your preview simple and clear is to condense each main point to a phrase. Marcia's preview, for example, was "To help you realize the magnitude of the eating disorder problem in our society, I'll reveal just who is at risk, how severe the effects can be, and why it has become an epidemic." You might further clarify your preview with signposts, as Sonja did: "I learned valuable life lessons: first, by facing the challenges of finding a part-time job; second, by learning to use the public transportation system; and third, by meeting new people." Or you might consider using parallelism to emphasize the content in your preview, as well as make it more simple and clear. **Parallelism** involves repeating words or grammatical structures within or across sentences. Laura, for example, used parallelism in her preview:

> **I'll talk** specifically about how I made **this choice** to live meat-free. Next, **I'll share** some of the family issues that arose as a result of **this choice.** Finally, **I'll discuss** some of the ways **this choice** affects my life today.

Notice how Laura's preview is stated simply, clearly, and precisely and that the use of parallelism emphasizes and further clarifies what her main points will be. Her preview would give listeners a clear sense of the speech's content and structure.

In short, your introduction should include the following elements, usually in this order:

- Attention catcher.
- Listener relevance link.
- Speaker credibility statement.
- Thesis statement.
- Preview.

By including each of these elements, you will fulfill each of the functions of an introduction. Moreover, you will do so in ways that round the entire cycle of learning (see Figure 9–1). You will motivate your audience to listen to what you have to say, as well as put them in a position to understand it. And remember, if you are effective, you will do all of this quickly.

Your introduction should clearly highlight the macrostructure for your speech; however, an effective introduction does much more. It also arouses the curiosity of your listeners, motivates them to listen, and establishes your credibility as a speaker on the topic. Here is what Laura's whole introduction looked like:

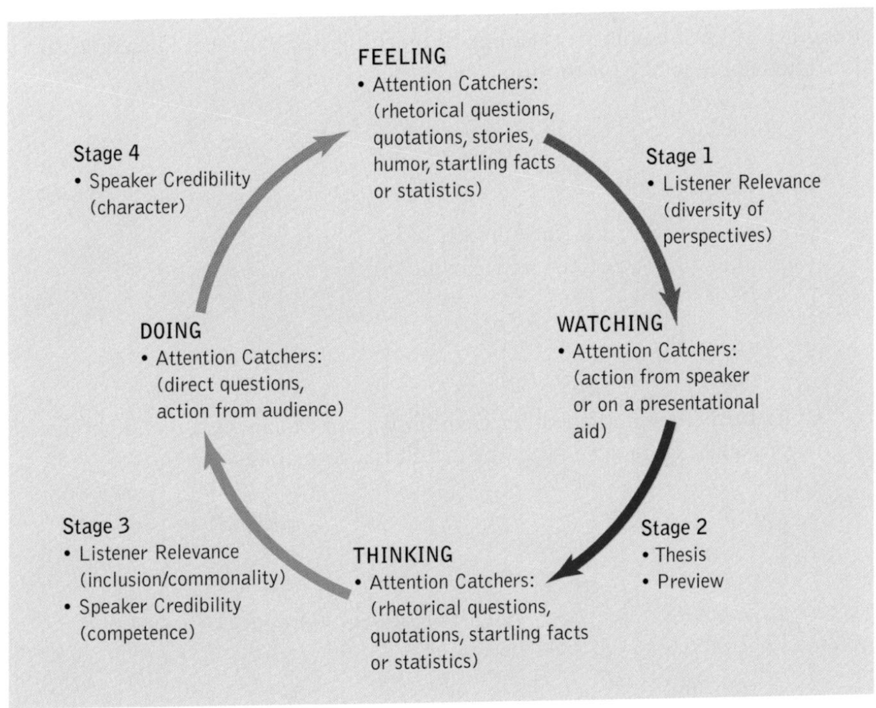

FIGURE 9–1 Introductions and the Learning Cycle

Attention catcher. With Thanksgiving just around the corner, many of you are probably anticipating a feast complete with a flavorful, juicy turkey as the main course. I, however, plan to bring my own addition to my family dinner—a rice pilaf, with grilled vegetables and garlic-roasted tofu.

Notice how Laura combined a hypothetical example with a personal example to arouse the curiosity of her listeners in a creative way.

Listener relevance link. Although a diet rich in eggs, meat, and potatoes was once the norm in our country, more and more Americans are choosing a vegetarian lifestyle, and many are doing so for health reasons. In fact, the American Dietetic Association, also known as the ADA, maintains that vegetarianism is not only healthful and adequate, but also helps in the prevention and treatment of certain diseases (**www.eatright.org**).

Here, Laura tied her topic to the basic human desire for good health as an appeal to motivate her audience members to listen to what she had to say. She strengthened the credibility of her appeal by citing the American Dietetic Association, a reputable source for this topic.

Speaker credibility statement. About five years ago, I made a decision to stop eating meat, which has changed my life in several ways.

Laura further strengthened her credibility as an expert on the topic by revealing her personal experience—that she herself is a vegetarian.

Thesis statement. Living a vegetarian lifestyle is an important aspect of who I am today.

> ### *What Do You Think?*
> *What are the main points for your next speech? What can you include for an attention catcher? Listener relevance statement? Speaker credibility statement? Thesis? Preview?*

Notice how simply and precisely Laura's thesis statement is worded. Listeners realized very easily that Laura was going to talk about the ways in which living a vegetarian lifestyle shapes who she is today.

> *Preview.* I'll talk specifically about how I made this choice to live meat-free. Next, I'll share some of the family issues that arose as a result of this choice. Finally, I'll discuss some of the ways this choice affects my life today.

Again, Laura simply and precisely highlighted what would be the three main points of her speech. She fulfilled the first step in the "golden rule" of public speaking: Tell them what you're going to tell them.

Developing Effective Conclusions

Recall that your introduction should take no more than ten to fifteen percent of your allotted speaking time. Likewise, your conclusion should be brief—it should take no more than five to ten percent of your allotted speaking time. That means the conclusion for your six-minute speech should take only twenty to forty seconds to complete! Although this might sound a bit unrealistic at first, it is crucial that you take time to develop your conclusion in a way that leaves a positive lasting impression in your listeners' minds. Hence, an effective conclusion for any type of speech serves three primary functions:

Teaching Tip
Bring examples of both good and poor conclusions to class. Have students identify the elements of effective conclusions as well as the ways that poor conclusions can be improved.

- Providing a sense of closure.
- Reinforcing the main ideas.
- Motivating listeners to remember.

Your ultimate goal is for your listeners to remember what you've discussed. Recall from our discussion in Chapter 4 that people typically retain only about twenty-five percent of what they hear. Whether you've informed, persuaded, or entertained them, you want what you said to be part of that twenty-five percent. Because of the primacy-recency effect we discussed earlier, your conclusion is a central piece of what your listeners will remember, and it's the last chance you have to reinforce your ideas. Hence, as with your introduction, you need to spend time developing your conclusion.

Providing a Sense of Closure

Teaching Tip
Have students develop at least two conclusions for their next speech and turn them in ahead of time. This will allow you to give them constructive feedback early. Although it might seem obvious that your conclusion should provide a sense of closure, few speakers have mastered the art of doing so effectively.

Some speakers simply stop when they finish the body of the speech. Listeners are left to tie the main ideas together themselves, something they may or may not be able to do on their own. Sometimes speakers will try to cover up this lack of closure by saying "thank you" or asking if there are any questions. Although there is nothing wrong with doing either, doing so should not replace providing a sense of closure with the conclusion to the actual speech.

Some speakers, on the other hand, don't know how or when to stop talking. They might signal that the speech is concluding with remarks like "In conclusion" or "In closing" or even "Let me end by saying." Hence, listeners expect to hear one or two final thoughts but instead get a conclusion that goes on and on and on, much like the Energizer bunny or the children's song "that never ends. It goes on and on my friend."

You can avoid these problems by creating conclusions that adhere to the functions described here. You can signal closure by your verbal and your nonverbal cues. Verbally, beginning your conclusion with a short phrase like those listed previously can be very effective—as long as you then stick to the five to ten percent time limit rule for your remaining remarks.

You can also provide a sense of closure nonverbally by gradually slowing down your rate and pitch as you move through your concluding remarks. You might also stress key words a bit more than you did during the body of the speech. Or you might incorporate pauses that allow time for each concluding point to sink in before moving on. Another thing you might do is allow your eye contact to rest a bit longer on each audience member before moving on to the next point. Or you can move closer to your audience by taking a step or two forward. Any of these nonverbal behaviors can help provide a sense of closure. Effective public speakers will incorporate several of them in their conclusion.

Finally, you can provide a sense of closure by accomplishing the other two functions of a conclusion: reinforcing the main ideas and motivating listeners to remember. Let's take a look at how you can achieve each of these functions in your conclusion.

Reinforcing the Main Ideas

Technology Tip
http://www.presentersuniversity.com/courses/show_archive.cfm?RecordID=72
This Web page, hosted by Presenters University, offers several tips for developing conclusions. Have students visit this site and report their findings to the class.

Your conclusion accomplishes the final part of the golden rule: Tell them what you told them. Just as the introduction contains a thesis statement and preview of main points, so the conclusion contains a thesis restatement and a main point summary. Some beginning speakers have told me that this seems redundant and even like an insult to listeners' intelligence. I remind them that public speaking is a one-time affair and that you want to be assured that listeners remember your main points. A **thesis restatement** is simply a reiteration of the thesis statement, usually offered in past tense. It is sometimes nearly verbatim, although it doesn't have to be. Laura's thesis restatement was nearly the same as her original thesis statement, but phrased in past tense, "Now you know why my vegetarian lifestyle is such an important aspect of who I am." Jaime's thesis restatement was less similar, but still restated his main thesis, "We must ground our scientific decisions about cloning in ethics or face the disastrous consequences of not doing so." Whether they are nearly verbatim or slightly modified, effective thesis restatements are still simple and precise.

A **main point summary** is a brief statement reminding listeners of the main points in the speech. This summary is usually shorter than the preview of main points. It is typically only one sentence long—and is sometimes even stated together with the thesis restatement. Marcia combined her thesis restatement and main point summary into a single sentence by stating "Now that you are aware of who is at risk and how severe the effects can be, you realize, as I do, that the eating disorder epidemic in our society cannot be ignored." Laura's main point summary was a single sentence that followed her thesis restatement:

- *Thesis restatement.* Now you know why my vegetarian lifestyle is such an important aspect of who I am.
- *Main point summary.* I talked about why I made **this choice** to be a vegetarian, how **this choice** has impacted my personal relationships, and how **this choice** continues to affect my life today.

Notice that Laura used parallelism in her main point summary. Use of parallelism further increases the likelihood that listeners will remember the main points.

As the preceding examples show, the thesis restatement and main point summary help provide closure. They do so by mirroring the introduction while signaling, through use of past tense and phrases like "Now that you realize," that the content has been presented and the speech is ending.

Motivating Listeners to Remember

A clear summary of your thesis and main points helps listeners remember them. But they will be even more likely to remember if you follow the summary with a **clincher:** a final sentence or series of sentences that reinforces your main ideas in a memorable way. Speakers who have no clincher sometimes try to provide closure by saying "thank you." Although there is nothing inherently wrong with thanking listeners for their attention, doing so does not constitute a clincher. A clincher provides closure in a memorable way without a need to say "thank you." You might motivate your listeners to remember your speech by using any of the techniques we discussed for capturing audience interest. That is, a rhetorical or direct question, a quotation, a hypothetical or actual story, a startling fact or statistic, action, or humor.

Teaching Tip
Show a videotape of a sample speech and have students identify the elements of the conclusion. Ask students to critique the conclusion based upon the guidelines presented in this chapter.

Moreover, an effective clincher often refers back to the introduction, especially to the attention catcher used there. This is what Laura did in her speech:

Teaching Tip
Before discussing conclusions, have students write a one-page paper in which they define and provide examples of clinchers. Use this assignment as the foundation for an in-class discussion of conclusions.

- *Attention catcher.* With Thanksgiving just around the corner, many of you are probably anticipating a feast complete with a flavorful, juicy turkey as the main course. I, however, plan to bring my own addition to my family dinner—a rice pilaf, with grilled vegetables and garlic-roasted tofu.
- *Clincher.* As a vegetarian, I've discovered a world of food I never knew existed. Believe me, this Thanksgiving, my mouth will water, too, as I sit down hungrily before my rice pilaf with grilled vegetables and garlic-roasted tofu.

Notice how she referred back to the attention catcher about anticipating Thanksgiving dinner by indicating that her mouth will water, too, as she sits down for her flavorful vegetarian meal. You might also use your clincher to issue a challenge based on your attention catcher as Marcia did:

Teaching Tip
To give students practice in linking the introduction and conclusion, assign the Connecting Attention Catchers and Clinchers activity contained in the Activities section of this chapter.

- *Attention catcher.* Who are five of the most important women in your life? Your mother? Your sister? Your daughter? Your wife? Your best friend? Now which one of them has had or will have an eating disorder? Before you disregard my question, listen to what research tells us. One in every five women in the United States has an eating disorder.
- *Clincher.* I urge you to do your part to stop the rapid growth of the eating disorder epidemic in our country. This problem belongs to all of us and will take the efforts of all of us to solve. Perhaps, then, you will be able to confidently respond that not a single one of those five important women in your life has had or will have an eating disorder.

Or you might simply answer the rhetorical question you posed in your attention catcher as Sonja did:

- *Attention catcher.* Have you ever packed up everything you owned, said goodbye to all of your friends, and moved to a place where you knew no one?
- *Clincher.* So, when the opportunity presents itself to pack up everything you own, say goodbye to all of your friends, and move to a place where you know no one, I hope you'll remember how my move has influenced who I am today. Perhaps, then, you'll accept the challenge and make the move!

There are a number of techniques you can use in your clincher. You can use a rhetorical question, direct question, story, startling statistic, or quotation. The most effective clinchers often tie back to the attention catcher in a way that provides a sense of closure to the speech. You might answer the question you asked or issue a challenge, but you should do so in a creative way that motivates your listeners to remember your speech.

In short, your conclusion should include the following elements, usually in this order:

- Thesis restatement.
- Main point summary.
- Clincher.

By including each of these elements, you will fulfill the functions of a conclusion. You will provide a sense of closure, remind listeners of the main ideas you offered, and motivate them to remember your speech. And, if you are effective, you will do all this quickly. Here is what Laura's whole conclusion looked like:

- *Thesis restatement.* Now you know why my vegetarian lifestyle is such an important aspect of who I am.

(Notice how Laura merely restated her thesis in past tense. Doing so made it simple and precise.)

- *Main point summary.* I talked about why I made **this choice** to be a vegetarian, how **this choice** has impacted my personal relationships, and how **this choice** continues to affect my life today.

Laura used parallelism to very clearly remind listeners of the main points of her speech.

- *Clincher.* As a vegetarian, I've discovered a world of food I never knew existed. Believe me, this Thanksgiving, my mouth will water, too, as I sit down hungrily before my rice pilaf with grilled vegetables and garlic-roasted tofu.

Laura's clincher tied back to the hypothetical and actual example she used in her attention catcher. This time, however, she talked about how her mouth would water as she anticipated her vegetarian meal just as others' mouths would water for the traditional turkey dinner. Doing so provided a sense of closure to her speech.

> ***What Do You Think?***
>
> *Consider your upcoming speech topic. How could you develop an attention catcher and clincher that tie together for this speech?*

Summary

To write effective public speeches, you must take extra care to develop strong introductions and conclusions. Strong introductions and conclusions are crucial because of the primacy-recency effect: Listeners tend to remember best the beginning and end of what they hear. They are also crucial because public speaking is a one-time affair, so listeners need the help of being told what they will hear and what they have heard. Finally, knowing you have developed a strong introduction and conclusion will reduce your speech anxiety.

Effective introductions serve five important functions: capturing your audience's interest, establishing rapport with the audience, establishing your credibility, stating your topic, and previewing the main points. The elements of an introduction that help you achieve these functions are the attention catcher, listener relevance link, speaker credibility statement, thesis statement, and preview. The most effective introductions include all of these elements briefly, taking no more than ten to fifteen percent of the allotted speaking time.

Effective conclusions serve three important functions: providing a sense of closure, reinforcing the topic and main points, and motivating listeners to remember what you've said. The elements of a conclusion that will help you achieve these functions are the thesis restatement, main point summary, and clincher. Like introductions, the most effective conclusions are brief, simple, and precise.

One of most important aspects of effective public speaking is clear structure. Your introduction, body, and conclusion combine to form the macrostructure of your speech. The

Teaching Tip
Consider assigning an impromptu speech to reinforce the concepts presented in this chapter. Have students develop the speech using each of the components of effective introductions and conclusions.

introduction and conclusion are crucial components because they reinforce for your listeners—and for you—the structure of the body of your speech. By applying what you've learned in this chapter—together with what you learned in Chapter 8 and will learn in Chapters 10 and 11—you can create clearly organized speeches that will motivate listeners to attend to and to retain your ideas.

Activities

1. **Listener Relevance Links.** Identify a favorite hobby. Form a small group of four or five students. Brainstorm to come up with a listener relevance statement for each hobby.
2. **Connecting Attention Catchers and Clinchers.** Alone or in a small group, come up with an attention catcher and a related clincher for each of the following topics:
   - Peanut butter and jelly sandwiches.
   - Spring break.
   - Depression.
   - Television violence.
   - Women in the military.
3. **Introductions and Conclusions.** In a small group of four or five students, make up an introduction and conclusion for one of the following topics. Be sure to include all five elements in your introduction and all three elements in your conclusion.
   - Oral hygiene.
   - Aerobic exercise.
   - Pet care.
   - Attitude.
4. **Video Analysis.** Watch a videotaped example of a public speech (provided by the instructor or some other source). Identify what the speaker used for each of the elements in his or her introduction and conclusion. Was each effective in your opinion? Why or why not?
   - Attention catcher.
   - Listener relevance link.
   - Speaker credibility statement.
   - Thesis statement.
   - Preview.
   - Thesis restatement.
   - Main point summary.
   - Clincher.

5. **Advertisement Analysis.** In a small group of four or five students, analyze a television or magazine advertisement. Try to locate each of the components of an introduction in your advertisement:
   - Attention catcher.
   - Listener relevance.
   - Speaker credibility.
   - Thesis.
   - Preview.

   When you've completed the task, share your discoveries with the rest of the class.

Key Terms

Actual example
Attention catcher
Clincher
Direct question
Hypothetical example
Listener relevance link
Main point summary
Parallelism
Preview
Primacy-recency effect
Rhetorical question
Speaker credibility statement
Startling fact or statistic
Thesis restatement
Thesis statement

CHAPTER 10

Outlining Your Speech

Reflective Questions

1. Why is it important to outline your public speech?
2. What is a preparation outline and why is it important?
3. Why do you prepare three different kinds of outlines?
4. Why might you give your speech a title?
5. Why include delivery cues on your speaking outline?
6. Why might you put your speaking outline on index cards?

It was late in the evening, but Laura was finished. She had chosen vegetarianism as the topic of her next speech. Based on audience analysis and guidelines posed by her teacher, she decided to talk about the ways her vegetarian lifestyle affects her life. She had collected lots of supporting material, including personal stories, definitions, explanations, facts, and statistics. And she had organized her main points and developed her introduction and conclusion. Yet as Laura looked at her notes, somehow she just didn't feel like her speech was finished. Laura was right. She wasn't finished organizing her speech. Instead, she was ready to begin the final step in the process of organizing her macrostructure: preparing her outlines.

Teaching Tip
Refer students to the SpeechMaker CD-ROM. This software will assist them in developing an outline. Consider assigning one of the scenarios to be completed before the class in which you discuss this chapter.

Notice that I said outlines, not outline. Just as an effective writer prepares a series of rough drafts on the way to completing a final manuscript, so does an effective public speaker develop a series of outlines on the way to preparing the final speech. **Outlining** is a systematic process of placing your ideas in a recognizable pattern that listeners can easily follow. This chapter begins by discussing why outlining is so important to your public speech. Then a step-by-step process of preparing effective public speaking outlines is detailed—that is, the preparation outline, the formal outline, and the speaking outline.

Why Is Outlining Important?

Outlining is important to your public speech for four important reasons:

- It places your content into a recognizable pattern for listeners to follow.
- It allows you flexibility to adjust your message as you speak.
- It provides an opportunity for you to critique your speech.
- It can reduce public speaking anxiety.

Let's look at each of these reasons in more detail.

Arranging Your Ideas within a Recognizable Pattern

Teaching Tip
Show a videotape of a sample speech and have students develop an outline. This activity will aid in the development of both outlining and listening skills.

Outlining arranges your ideas within a recognizable pattern that listeners can follow. Failing to do so increases your chances of rambling as you speak. Even if you don't ramble, listeners may perceive you in this way because they cannot decipher a logical order of your information. Over time, outlining practice will improve your ability to "think on your feet" in this way. As a result, you'll discover that it will take less time to prepare your outlines and you'll need fewer notes from which to speak. Recall our discussions of the learning cycle. To be most effective, your speech should address all four stages of the cycle. Outlining addresses the assimilator stage (watching and thinking)—that is, putting a wide range of information into concise, logical form. If you fail to outline your speech, then you will fail to reach your listeners fully because you'll fail to address one of the stages in the learning cycle.

Providing Flexibility as You Speak

It is also more effective to outline your speech than to write it out word for word. This is because an outline still provides you with some flexibility as you speak.

That is, you can take more time to develop a particular idea if you notice that listeners seem confused. Likewise, you can move more quickly through a particular definition or explanation if your listeners seem to have a firm grasp of what you mean. Thus, speaking from an outline is better than reading from a manuscript (which might also follow a recognizable pattern), because you can more fully respect the important role your listeners play in the communication transaction. You'll be more likely to communicate using a conversational style instead of sounding memorized, or mechanical, or even like you're reading.

> ***What Do You Think?***
>
> *Consider a speaker you've heard recently, for example, a teacher, a preacher, a professional speaker, or even another student. Did the speaker seem to be* talking with you or reading in front of you? *How did this affect the speaker's success or failure in reaching you?*

Providing an Opportunity to Critique Your Speech

Outlining provides you an opportunity to critique your speech and, consequently, to improve it before you actually present it in front of an audience. Outlining allows you to organize your ideas visually, and then add, delete, regroup, expand, or condense them where necessary. Once you see what you've got, you can ask yourself questions like: Am I trying to cover too much material under a particular main point? Am I repeating things my audience already knows? Do the pieces of supporting material make sense under the main points where I've placed them? Is the amount of information I include under each main point fairly balanced? In other words, will I spend a similar amount of time discussing each main point? Have I included a listener relevance link for each main point? And do I address each stage in the learning cycle somewhere in my speech? Once you can visually see what you've got, you can make adjustments that will improve the effectiveness of your speech.

Discussion Tip
How many main points should you develop in the body of your speech? Is it possible to have too few or too many main points? What might this communicate to the audience?

Reducing Public Speaking Anxiety

Finally, outlining can reduce public speaking anxiety. Recall from Chapter 2 that one of the primary reasons for increased anxiety stems from a fear of failure. That is, you might worry that listeners won't understand what it is you are trying to say. Outlining can reduce negative self-talk rooted in a fear of failure because it helps you realize that your ideas are arranged in a logical pattern, you have supporting material that makes sense under each main point, and there is a balance among your main points. Moreover, since your outline is condensed, it is harder to lose your place than when you're reading from a manuscript. This, too, can reduce anxiety rooted in a fear of failure. In essence, outlining gives you confidence that you have a thorough and well-ordered speech.

The Process of Outlining Your Public Speech

Teaching Tip
Develop a series of overheads illustrating the different types of outlines discussed in this chapter (preparation, formal, and speaking). This will help students distinguish one from another.

The process of outlining occurs in three phases. Each phase ends with the completion of a particular type of outline. In Phase 1, you construct your preparation outline. In Phase 2, you develop your formal outline. In Phase 3, you create your speaking outline.

Your Preparation Outline

Teaching Tip
Have students turn in their preparation outlines early and check to see if they have done sufficient research to develop a substantive speech.

A **preparation outline** is a working rough draft of your speech ideas. This outline may or may not be typed. If you choose to use a word processor to type your preparation outline, however, I caution you to avoid the tendency to let it pass as your formal outline. Just because your preparation outline looks good at first glance, because it is typed, doesn't necessarily mean it is good. You will need to critique and revise your preparation outline several times before you are finished with it and ready to move on to typing your formal outline. This revision process consists of six steps.

Steps 1, 2, and 3

Teaching Tip
To give students practice in developing a preparation outline, assign the Group Outline or Reformat a Message activity contained in the Activities section of this chapter.

Essentially, you've already been working on your preparation outline. You began the six-step process of putting together your preparation outline when you selected and narrowed your topic (Chapter 5), organized your main ideas (Chapter 8), and created your introduction and conclusion (Chapter 9). In other words, you completed the first step of your preparation outline when you created a thesis statement and main points. Then when you developed the body of your speech by adding supporting material to each main point, you completed Step 2. You completed Step 3 when you expanded your preparation outline by jotting down ideas for developing each element of your introduction and conclusion. Hence, at this point you have only three steps left to complete: placing your content into standard outline format (Step 4), integrating internal reference citations and a reference list (Step 5), and critiquing your outline for balance (Step 6).

What Do You Think?

What are the main points for your next speech?
What is your attention catcher?
What is your clincher?

Step 4

The fourth step in the process of generating your preparation outline is to place your ideas into a proper outline form. The most common method is the alphanumeric system. Here Roman numerals are used to identify major points; then a consistent pattern of letters and numbers follows beneath these major points. Let's break this procedure down.

First, label the introduction, body, and conclusion in the far left margin. If you do this, you'll be sure you have an introduction and a conclusion that accomplish each of the functions we discussed in Chapter 9:

Introduction.

Body.

Conclusion.

Second, use a Roman numeral and label for each of the elements in your introduction and conclusion, as well as for each main point in the body of your speech. These Roman numerals are also placed at the far left margin:

Introduction

I. Attention catcher:

II. Listener relevance link:

III. Speaker credibility statement:

IV. Thesis statement:

V. Preview:

Body

I. First main point:

II. Second main point:

III. Third main point:

Conclusion

I. Thesis restatement:

II. Main point summary:

III. Clincher:

Third, add subpoints under each main point by using capital letters. These capital letters are indented five spaces from the left margin or aligned with the first letter of the label directly above it. These subpoints typically consist of your supporting material. When preparing a speech that tells a story using a chronological pattern, you might offer an extended example for each subpoint. Although it is not necessary, you might sometimes have subpoints of the subpoints. When this is the case, use Arabic numbers:

Discussion Tip
Why is it important that you use this specific format when creating your speech outline? Why is it important that you indent and label your points and subpoints?

Body

I. First main point:

- **A.** Subpoint:
  - **1.** Sub-subpoint (if used):
  - **2.** Sub-subpoint (if used):
- **B.** Subpoint:
  - **1.** Sub-subpoint (if used):
  - **2.** Sub-subpoint (if used):

II. Second main point:

- **A.** Subpoint:
  - **1.** Sub-subpoint (if used):
  - **2.** Sub-subpoint (if used):
- **B.** Subpoint:
  - **1.** Sub-subpoint (if used):
  - **2.** Sub-subpoint (if used):

III. Third main point:
- **A.** Subpoint:
  - **1.** Sub-subpoint (if used):
  - **2.** Sub-subpoint (if used):
- **B.** Subpoint:
  - **1.** Sub-subpoint (if used):
  - **2.** Sub-subpoint (if used):

Finally, add transition statements between each main point. Align each transition label with the far left margin, since they are not actually part of the body content but rather are the structural glue that holds the main points together. Although including transitions on your outline is optional, doing so increases the likelihood that you'll remember to use them during your presentation:

Teaching Tip
Have students use the sample outline format presented in this chapter as a model for developing their speech outlines. In addition to the samples provided in this chapter, develop your own completed speech outline for students. This outline should clearly communicate your goals and expectations for this assignment.

Body

I. First main point:
- **A.** Subpoint:
  - **1.** Sub-subpoint (if used):
  - **2.** Sub-subpoint (if used):
- **B.** Subpoint:
  - **1.** Sub-subpoint (if used):
  - **2.** Sub-subpoint (if used):

What Do You Think?
Consider your next speech. What transitions will you use between each main point?

Transition

II. Second Main Point:
- **A.** Subpoint:
  - **1.** Sub-subpoint (if used):
  - **2.** Sub-subpoint (if used):
- **B.** Subpoint:
  - **1.** Sub-subpoint (if used):
  - **2.** Sub-subpoint (if used):

Transition

III. Third main point:
- **A.** Subpoint:
  - **1.** Sub-subpoint (if used):
  - **2.** Sub-subpoint (if used):
- **B.** Subpoint:
  - **1.** Sub-subpoint (if used):
  - **2.** Sub-subpoint (if used):

Step 5

Once you have arranged your ideas into this standard outline form, you are ready to integrate external source citations. Read through the outline once again, this time adding internal reference citations where appropriate throughout the outline. As you do, place the source citations in your reference list as well. This way, you'll be less likely to inadvertently leave out a source when typing your formal outline.

Teaching Tip
Remind students of the importance of using credible sources to support their claims. Also, explain that they must cite these sources orally in their speech (some students may be under the impression that it is sufficient to merely include citations in the outline).

Step 6

The final step in developing your preparation outline is to critique and revise it for balance. To complete this step successfully, you will need to examine and revise your outline several times.

Consider Sources. Begin by examining the external sources you use. Are they evenly distributed throughout the speech? If not, where might additional external sources be needed? Also consider whether you rely too heavily on one or two resources. If so, try to adjust the balance of resources used. If necessary, conduct additional research in order to rely on a variety of different sources.

Identify Listener Relevance Links. Now, go through your outline to identify **listener relevance links** under each main point. Recall from Chapter 3 that a listener relevance link is a statement that reveals how and why the ideas you offer might benefit your listeners. As you find listener relevance, label it as such. If you can't identify a listener relevance link under a particular point, take the time to add one. Remember, these links serve to maintain your listeners' interest throughout the presentation.

What Do You Think?

Consider your next speech. What will you offer as listener relevance links for each of your main points?

Discussion Tip
Why is it important to develop listener relevance links throughout the body of the speech? What will you offer as listener relevance links in your next speech?

Examine Learning Styles. Next, go through your outline to identify where you address different stages on the learning cycle. The simplest way to achieve this is by

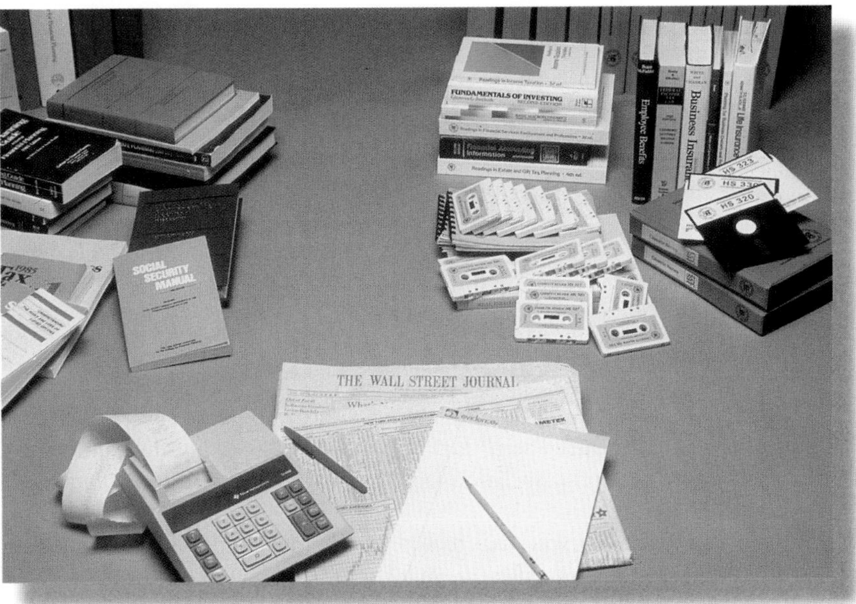

Try to rely on different kinds of sources to appeal to different learning styles.

labeling different points and subpoints as they appeal to the dimensions of watching, thinking, doing, or feeling. In doing so, you might discover that nowhere in your outline do you address a particular learning cycle stage. If so, take the time to integrate something that does. Laura realized, for example, that she needed to add something visual to her presentation. So she provided a visual aid depicting one of her favorite vegetarian recipes.

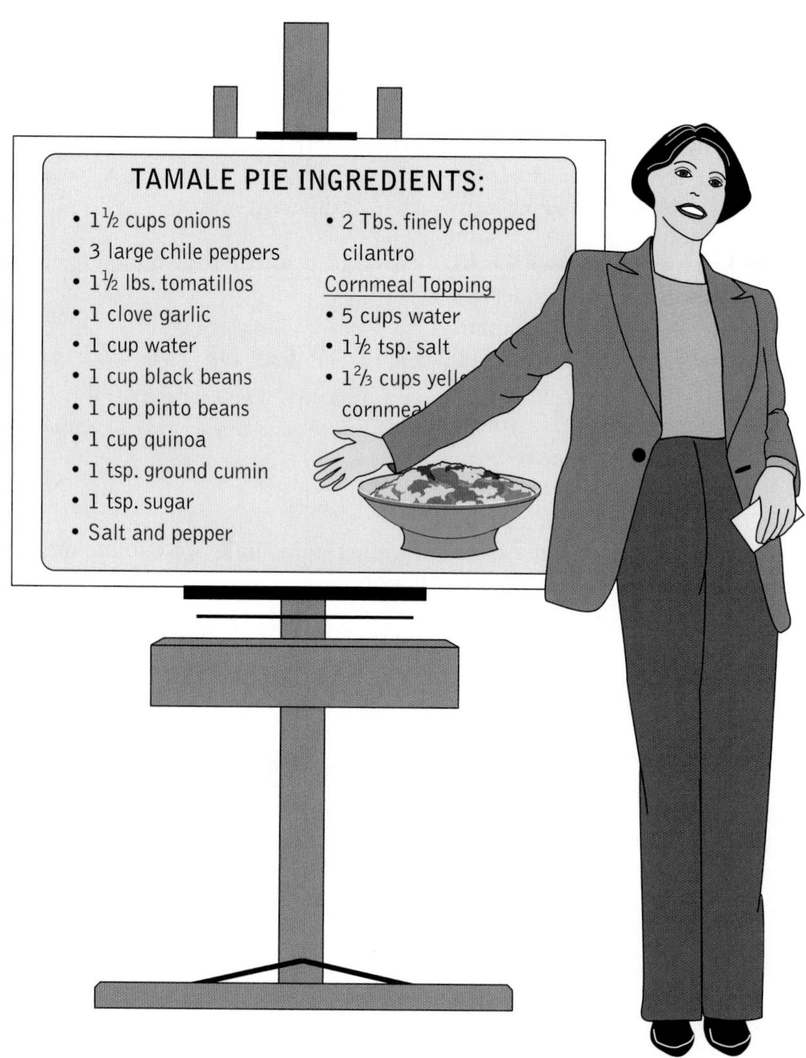

Or you might decide to add some facts or statistics in order to address the thinking dimension. Laura included some facts and statistics about healthy eating habits from the American Dietetic Association as well as a visual aid of the vegetarian food pyramid.

Perhaps you'll discover you need to add some sort of application, action plan, or activity to address the doing dimension, or some personal stories or testimonials for the feeling dimension. Laura addressed each of these dimensions by revealing

Facts and statistics are often accompanied by visual aids.

the step-by-step plan she engaged in to adjust her eating habits (doing) and sharing a story about her pet cow, Charlie, who eventually became a steak on her plate (feeling).

Remember that revising your outline to address the entire learning cycle will improve the effectiveness of your presentation. Not only will you address different preferred learning styles, but you will also enhance the degree to which all of your listeners will retain your message because you round the entire cycle of learning.

What Do You Think?

Consider your next speech. How will you address each dimension of the learning cycle? Feeling? Watching? Thinking? Doing?

Discussion Tip
How can addressing the entire learning cycle enhance the degree to which your listeners will retain your message? How does Laura address this issue?

Check Supporting Material. Now, go through your outline one more time to check for a balance of supporting material under each main point. Check to make

Discussion Tip
Why is it important for you to check your outline for symmetry? Is it always appropriate to devote the same amount of time to each main point in the body of the speech?

sure that any main point that offers one subpoint offers at least two. You cannot have an "A" without also having a "B," or a "1" without also having a "2," and so forth. If you cannot come up with a second point, revise your outline to include all that information within the main point.

Check for Symmetry. Look at your outline holistically. Will your introduction or conclusion take too much time? Will you spend about the same amount of time developing each main point? If not, you might need to delete from or add to any of these components.

Teaching Tip
Assign students to groups and have them critique each other's preparation outlines. This should help students identify problem areas that they may not catch on their own.

Technology Tip
http://www.stylewizard.com/
Remind students to visit this Web site, hosted by EB Communications, for assistance with constructing their bibliographies.

Add a Title. Finally, give your speech a title if you choose to do so. If you do add a title, make sure it is brief, no more than three to five words long. Make sure it captures the essence of your speech. Don't let it mislead the reader from the focus of your speech. And, like the attention catcher, try to use figurative language that might entice the reader to want to know more. Laura, for example, chose the title "Meat-Free and Me." Once you have critiqued and revised your outline according to this procedure, your preparation outline is complete.

> ***What Do You Think?***
> *Consider your next speech.*
> *Do you offer a "B" when you have an "A," and so forth?*
> *How much time will your introduction and conclusion take compared to your main points? Will you have a title and, if so, what will it be?*

Your preparation outline is comparable to the rough draft of a written composition. It is not the final product. Your preparation outline contains editorial comments regarding listener relevance, learning style stages, and presentational aids. Also, although all the macrostructural elements are included, rarely are they phrased as complete sentences. In addition, both internal reference citations and a reference list are included so you remember which pieces of evidence came from which sources. Figure 10–1 provides a completed preparation outline for Laura's speech on vegetarianism. A preparation outline is crucial in the process of outlining because it is the working draft, which is usually critiqued and revised several times before your ideas are thoroughly covered and logically ordered.

Discussion Tip
What is the difference between a formal outline and a speaking outline? Which one should you use when you present your speech in class?

Your Formal Outline

Once you've developed, critiqued, and revised your preparation outline to your satisfaction, you are ready to translate this working draft into a formal outline. If you have expended the effort to critique and revise your preparation outline thoroughly, the formal outline is fairly easy to prepare. A **formal outline** is a typed outline that labels and applies all of the macrostructural elements in your speech using complete sentences. Here is where you hone your language and style choices, which is the focus of Chapter 11. It also includes a speech title, your name, and internal reference citations, as well as a complete reference list. Typically, you do

> ***What Do You Think?***
> *Consider your next speech. What problems might you encounter if you deliver your speech using your formal outline as your notes?*

Technology Tip
http://owl.english.purdue.edu/handouts/general/gl_outlin.html
This Web page, hosted by the Purdue University Online Writing Lab, assists students in developing an effective outline. Have students visit this site and write a brief essay exploring the importance of effective outlining.

(Text continues on page 222.)

FIGURE 10–1
Sample Preparation Outline

Introduction

I. *Attention catcher:* Talk about anticipating typical Thanksgiving food and what I will eat (feeling) (maybe show a slide or photograph for watching).

II. *Listener relevance link:* Eating habits are changing across the country for health reasons. Cite the American Dietetic Association (ADA) (www.eatright.org) (thinking).

III. *Speaker credibility statement:* I've been a vegetarian for five years now.

IV. *Thesis statement:* Living a vegetarian lifestyle is an important aspect of who I am today.

V. *Preview:* How I made this choice, family issues as a result, ways this choice affects my life today.

Body

I. *First main point:* How I made this choice.

- **A.** *Subpoint:* Personal childhood experiences not unlike yours (listener relevance), story about my pet cow Charlie (feeling) and picture (watching).
- **B.** *Subpoint:* Book I read as a young adult thanks to my friend Amy: *Diet for a New America* (thinking).
- **C.** *Subpoint:* Steps I went through to adjust my eating habits and still be healthy, *Vegetarian Times,* Jan. 1997 (thinking and doing).

Transition:

The decision to become a vegetarian not only affected my own life, it also created some interesting issues within my family.

II. *Second main point:* Family conflicts (listener relevance—young adults separating from family to make our own decisions).

- **A.** *Subpoint:* Family felt betrayed.
    - **1.** *Sub-subpoint:* My rancher father didn't understand (feeling).
    - **2.** *Sub-subpoint:* Grandparents worried I would become anemic (feeling); myths listed in *Tufts University Health and Nutrition Letter,* April 1998 (thinking).
- **B.** *Subpoint:* Family learned more about vegetarianism.
    - **1.** *Sub-subpoint:* Some books and articles I've shared with them (*Vegetarian Times,* April 1999); *Runners World,* April 1997; *Dr. Spock's Baby and Child Care,* 1998) (thinking).
    - **2.** *Better Homes and Gardens,* June 1996 (thinking); presentational aid (watching).
    - **3.** *Sub-subpoint:* Grandma now prepares vegetarian dishes for me when I visit (feeling); show a couple of recipes to the audience on a transparency (watching and doing)(recipes in *Vegetarian Times,* Jan. 1999).

Transition:

I'm glad my family has adjusted to my choice to be a vegetarian, however, this choice continues to affect my life today.

III. *Third main point:* I deal daily with both disadvantages and advantages as a result of this choice.

A. *Subpoint:* Disadvantages.

1. *Sub-subpoint:* Limited choices at restaurants.

a. *Sub-sub-subpoint:* Menu options from popular restaurant chains (listener relevance and thinking); show items on a transparency (watching).

b. *Sub-sub-subpoint:* Personal story from Indianapolis (feeling).

2. *Sub-subpoint:* Limited choices at grocery stores.

B. *Subpoint:* Advantages.

1. *Sub-subpoint:* Low-fat diet is good for you and vegetables are natually low in fat; *NutritionAction Newsletter,* Oct. 1996 (thinking).

2. *Sub-subpoint:* Vegetables cost less than meat; *Vegetarian Times* April 1999 (thinking).

3. *Sub-subpoint:* Personal satisfaction of living a lifestyle that matches my beliefs (feeling).

Transition:

Although being a vegetarian is not always easy, it is worth the struggle because it is true to who I am.

Conclusion

I. *Thesis restatement:* This afternoon, I discussed why a vegetarian lifestyle is important to who I am.

II. *Main point summary:* How I made this choice, family issues, and impact on my life today.

III. *Clincher:* Talk about Thanksgiving dinner again to tie back to attention catcher.

References

American Dietetic Association. (2000, January 17). Position of the American Dietetic Association: Vegetarian diets [22 paragraphs]. American Dietetic Association [online]. Available at http://www.eatright.rog/adap1197.html (version on February 2, 2000).

Applegate, L. (1997, April). Vegetable matter. Runner's World, *32,* 26–27.

Beard, C. H. (1997, January). Become a vegetarian in 5 easy steps. Vegetarian Times, *223,* 74–79.

Clearing up common misconceptions about vegetarianism. (1998, April). Tufts University Health and Nutrition Letter, *16,* 4–6.

Dworkin, N. (1999). 22 reasons to go vegetarian right now. Vegetarian Times, 90–97.

Teaching Tip
To give students practice identifying the elements of a proper outline, assign the Listen and Evaluate a Message activity contained in the Activities section of this chapter.

Farell-Kingsley, K. (1999, January). Low in fat, high in flavor. Vegetarian Times, 41.

Hubbard, M. (1996, June). Scaling the vegetarian pyramid. Better Homes and Gardens, 96–98.

Robbins, J. (1998). Diet for a new America (2nd ed.). Tiburon: H. J. Kramer.

Spock, B. (1998). Dr. Spock's baby and child care (7th ed.). New York: Pocket Books.

FIGURE 10–2
Laura's Formal Outline

"Meat-Free and Me"
Laura Oster

Introduction

I. *Attention catcher:* With Thanksgiving just around the corner, many of you are probably anticipating a feast complete with a flavorful, juicy turkey as the main course. I, however, plan to bring my own addition to my family dinner—a rice pilaf, with grilled vegetables and garlic-roasted tofu.

II. *Listener relevance link:* Although a diet rich in eggs and meat was once the norm in our country, more and more Americans are choosing a vegetarian lifestyle, and many are doing so for health reasons. In fact, the American Dietetic Association, also known as the ADA, maintains that vegetarianism is not only healthful and adequate, but also helps in the prevention and treatment of certain diseases (www.eatright.org).

III. *Speaker credibility statement:* About five years ago, I made a decision to stop eating meat, which has changed my life in several ways.

IV. *Thesis statement:* Living a vegetarian lifestyle is an important aspect of who I am today.

V. *Preview:* I'll talk specifically about how I made this choice to live meat-free. Next, I'll share some of the family issues that arose as a result of this choice. Finally, I'll discuss some of the ways this choice affects my life today.

Body

I. *First main point:* I made this choice for several reasons.

A. *Subpoint:* One reason comes from my childhood. Many of my childhood experiences are probably similar to yours. I lived on a ranch with my family and my many pets. One of my pets was my cow, Charlie. His mother died giving birth to him, so I had to feed him with a bottle. As you can probably guess, Charlie and I became very close friends. We had lots of fun together. That is, until one day when my pet Charlie became the steak on my plate.

B. *Subpoint:* Another reason I made this choice comes from what I learned in a book I was given by my friend Amy. In *Diet for a New*

America, author John Robbins taught me that eating meat is not as "healthy" as we've been led to believe, nor is meat an efficient food source.

C. *Subpoint:* Finally, I was able to make this choice because I learned a simple five-step method to adjust my eating habits: (1) chart what you eat right now, (2) categorize your diet, (3) rethink the categories, (4) add new foods, and (5) make the change. (Christine Beard, Become a Vegetarian in 5 Easy Steps, 1997).

Transition:

The decision to become a vegetarian not only affected my own life, it also created some interesting issues within my family.

II. *Second main point:* I decided to become a vegetarian about the same time I moved away from home to attend college. This was tough on my family, partly because we were experiencing a number of other "growing pains" associated with my new role as an adult member of the family. These kinds of conflicts are pretty common. Perhaps you can relate.

A. *Subpoint:* My family felt I had betrayed them.

1. *Sub-subpoint:* My father, who was a rancher by trade, didn't understand.

2. *Sub-subpoint:* My grandparents tried to understand, but worried I would become anemic. They believed several myths about vegetarianism ("Clearing Up Common Misconceptions," 1998).

B. *Subpoint:* Eventually, my family learned more about vegetarianism.

1. *Sub-subpoint:* Learning about the vegetarian food pyramid helped (Hubbard, 1996).

2. *Sub-subpoint:* Since my family respects Dr. Benjamin Spock, reading about his fervent support of a vegetarian diet also helped (Spock, 1998).

3. *Sub-subpoint:* My grandma learned how to prepare several vegetarian dishes (Farell-Kingsley, 1999).

Transition:

I'm glad my family has adjusted to my choice to be a vegetarian; however, this choice continues to affect my life today.

III. *Third main point:* I deal daily with both disadvantages and advantages as a result of this choice.

A. *Subpoint:* There are some disadvantages related to being a vegetarian.

1. *Sub-subpoint:* Sometimes, my options are limited at restaurants.

a. *Sub-sub-subpoint:* My options at places like McDonald's or Burger King are limited to a garden salad and a soda.

b. *Sub-sub-subpoint:* My options at most formal restaurants are also pretty limited (Cole, 1999). Let me tell you a personal story about dining in Indianapolis with friends.

2. *Sub-subpoint:* Although it is certainly getting better, my choices are somewhat limited at grocery stores as well.

B. *Subpoint:* There are some definite advantages to being a vegetarian, advantages that—for me—outweigh the disadvantages.

1. *Sub-subpoint:* A low-fat diet is good for you and vegetables are natually low in fat.
2. *Sub-subpoint:* Vegetables cost less than meat (Dworkin, 1999).
3. *Sub-subpoint:* I feel a sense of personal satisfaction knowing that my lifestyle as a vegetarian matches my beliefs.

Transition:

Although being a vegetarian is not always easy, it is worth the struggle because it is true to who I am.

Conclusion

I. *Thesis restatement:* Now you know why a vegetarian lifestyle is such an important aspect of who I am.

II. *Main point summary:* I talked about why I made this choice, how this choice has impacted my personal relationships, and how this choice continues to affect my life today.

III. *Clincher:* As a vegetarian, I've discovered a world of food I never knew existed. Believe me, this Thanksgiving, my mouth will water, too, as I sit down hungrily before my rice pilaf with grilled vegetables and garlic-roasted tofu!

References

American Dietetic Association. (2000, January 17). Position of the American Dietetic Association: Vegetarian diets [22 paragraphs]. American Dietetic Association [online]. Available at http://www.eatright.rog/adap1197.html (version on February 2, 2000).

Applegate, L. (1997, April). Vegetable matter. Runner's World, *32*, 26–27.

Beard, C. H. (January 1997). Become a vegetarian in 5 easy steps. Vegetarian Times, *233*, 74–79.

Clearing up common misconceptions about vegetarianism. (1998, April). Tufts University Health and Nutrition Letter, *16*, 4–6.

Cole, M. R. (1999). Restaurant dining — the meatless way. Vibrant Life, *15*, 21–26.

Dworkin, N. (1999, April). 22 reasons to go vegetarian right now. Vegetarian Times, 90–97.

Farell-Kingsley, K. (1999, January). Low in fat, high in flavor. Vegetarian Times, 41.

Hubbard, M. (1996, June). Scaling the vegetarian pyramid. Better Homes and Gardens, 96–98.

Robbins, J. (1998). Diet for a new America (2nd ed.). Tiburon: H. J. Kramer.

Spock, B. (1998). Dr. Spock's baby and child care (7th ed.). New York: Pocket Books.

FIGURE 10–3
Laura's Speaking Outline

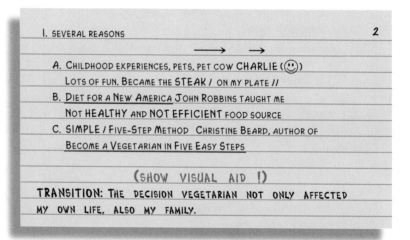

INTRO 1

PAUSE! (IN THE EYE)

I. WITH THANKSGIVING . . .
II. EGGS, MEAT, NORM . . . CHOOSING A VEGETARIAN LIFESTYLE FOR HEALTH REASONS . . . ADA MAINTAINS THAT "VEGETARIANISM IS NOT ONLY HEALTHFUL AND ADEQUATE, BUT ALSO HELPS IN THE PREVENTION OF CERTAIN DISEASES." //
III. 5 YEARS AGO
IV. VEGETARIAN WHO I AM TODAY
V. PREVIEW!!! HOW I MADE, ///FAMILY ISSUES, /// AFFECTS MY LIFE TODAY ///

I. SEVERAL REASONS 2

⟶ →

A. CHILDHOOD EXPERIENCES, PETS, PET COW CHARLIE (☺) LOTS OF FUN. BECAME THE STEAK / ON MY PLATE //
B. DIET FOR A NEW AMERICA JOHN ROBBINS TAUGHT ME NOT HEALTHY AND NOT EFFICIENT FOOD SOURCE
C. SIMPLE / FIVE-STEP METHOD CHRISTINE BEARD, AUTHOR OF BECOME A VEGETARIAN IN FIVE EASY STEPS

(SHOW VISUAL AID !)

TRANSITION: THE DECISION VEGETARIAN NOT ONLY AFFECTED MY OWN LIFE, ALSO MY FAMILY.

3

II. DECISION, COLLEGE, GROWING PAINS, CONFLICTS AS ADULT
A. FAMILY FELT BETRAYED (EYE CONTACT!!)
1. DAD, RANCHER
2. GRANDPARENTS . . . ANEMIC. BELIEVED THE MYTHS APRIL 1998 TUFTS UNIVERSITY HEALTH AND NUTRITION LETTER (SHOW AID)
B. FAMILY LEARNED
1. VEGETARIAN FOOD PYRAMID (SHOW AID)
2. DR. SPOCK 1998 EDITION OF DR. SPOCK'S BABY AND CHILD CARE: //"RAISING YOUR KIDS VEGETARIAN IS THE BEST THING YOU'LL EVER DO FOR THEM." ///

4

3. GRANDMA LEARNED RECIPES (SHOW AID: RECIPE FOR TAMALE PIE FROM JAN 99 VEGETARIAN TIMES MAGAZINE.)

TRANSITION: // I'M GLAD MY FAMILY HAS ADJUSTED TO MY CHOICE, CONTINUES TO AFFECT MY LIFE TODAY.

III. DISADVANTAGES AND ADVANTAGES

A. DISADVANTAGES

1. LIMITED AT RESTAURANT OPTIONS
   FAST FOOD AND FORMAL DINING, (INDIANAPOLIS)
2. GROCERY STORE LIMITATIONS

5

B. ADVANTAGES

1. LOW-FAT DIET = HEALTH MARION NESTLE, CHAIR, NUTRITION DEPT. AT NYU, SAYS **"THERE'S NO QUESTION THAT LARGELY VEGETARIAN DIETS ARE AS HEALTHY AS YOU CAN GET"** WALTER WILLETT, CHAIR, NUTRITION DEPT., HARVARD SCHOOL PUBLIC HEALTH **"A DIET RICH IN FRUITS & VEGETABLES PLAYS A ROLE IN REDUCING THE RISK OF ALL THE MAJOR CAUSES OF ILLNESS AND DEATH"** (NUTRITION ACTION NEWSLETTER, OCT. 1996).
2. VEGGIES COST LESS THAN MEAT. ACC. TO NORINE DWORKIN, APRIL 1999 VEGETARIAN TIMES **"REPLACING MEAT WITH VEGETABLES AND FRUITS IS ESTIMATED TO CUT FOOD BILLS BY AN AVERAGE OF // $4,000 // A YEAR."**
3. PERSONAL SATISFACTION, NOT EASY, WORTH THE STRUGGLE ///

6

CONCLUSION (PAUSE—EYE CONTACT—SLOW!!)

I. NOW YOU KNOW WHY A VEGETARIAN LIFESTYLE IS SO IMPORTANT TO WHO I AM.

II. WHY I MADE THIS CHOICE // →
   HOW THIS CHOICE HAS IMPACTED MY PERSONAL RELATIONSHIPS // →
   AND HOW THIS CHOICE CONTINUES TO AFFECT MY LIFE TODAY. /// →

III. AS A VEGETARIAN, I'VE DISCOVERED A WORLD OF FOOD I NEVER KNEW EXISTED // (SMILE) BELIEVE ME (SMILE) THIS THANKSGIVING / MY MOUTH WILL WATER TOO, AS I SIT DOWN HUNGRILY BEFORE MY RICE PILAF WITH GRILLED VEGETABLES AND GARLIC ROASTED TOFU.

(PAUSE EYE CONTACT SMILE!)

not include learning style labels or listener relevance labels on your formal outline, although you certainly can do so. Essentially, your formal outline is like your final draft of a written composition—that is, a reader could just as easily use it to develop a thorough manuscript as you can use it to deliver your speech. Figure 10–2 shows what Laura's formal outline looked like. You will also find formal outline examples at the ends of Chapters 14 and 15.

Your Speaking Outline

Teaching Tip
To give students practice in developing a speaking outline, assign the Speaking Outline activity contained in the Activities section of this chapter.

Teaching Tip
Bring to class a sample speaking outline that is ineffectively organized. Assign students to small groups and have them create a more appropriate speaking outline. Share the results with the entire class.

Discussion Tip
Why is it important that you maintain the outline format presented in this chapter when you develop your speaking outline? What kinds of delivery cues might you include in your speaking outline?

A **speaking outline** is a condensed outline used solely as a memory aid while you present your actual speech. The speaking outline is similar to both your preparation outline and your formal outline in certain ways, but it is also unique.

Like the preparation outline, your speaking outline uses key words and phrases rather than complete sentences. Your formal outline helped you shape the language you'll use to express your ideas. We'll spend more time talking about language in Chapter 11. To help you maintain a conversational style, however, your speaking outline should include only brief notes to jog your memory. Also, like the preparation outline, your speaking outline includes notes about when and where to share your presentational aids to ensure that you'll remember to share them during the speech. Figure 10–3 is Laura's speaking outline for "Meat-Free and Me."

Like the formal outline, your speaking outline includes internal references throughout. You need to include these references in your speaking notes so you don't forget to cite them orally during the presentation. Doing so avoids plagiarism and enhances ethos. The information you include in your speaking outline might differ somewhat from your formal outline. If, for example, a particular magazine or newspaper is quite well known and credible, and if the author of the article is merely reporting rather than interpreting data, you might merely cite the magazine or newspaper title orally and omit the author. It is preferable to cite both, however, along with the credentials of the otherwise unfamiliar author whenever possible.

Also, your speaking outline uses a similar outline format to the formal outline. Maintaining this format will help you see instantly where you are in the speech as you are presenting it. Since you only look momentarily at your notes periodically during the speech, you don't want to spend any more time than necessary finding your place.

Finally, your speaking outline is unique to both your preparation outline and your formal outline in four important ways. First, speaking outlines often use abbreviations. Doing so helps keep the outline as brief as possible. Laura used the ADA abbreviation on her speaking outline because she knew it stood for the American Dietetic Association. As long as you know what the abbreviation stands for and will use the complete terminology or phrase when you speak, abbreviations are fine to use in a speaking outline.

Second, speaking outlines also include delivery cues. That is, an effective speaking outline reminds you of both *what* you plan to say and *how* you plan to say it. You might jot down words like "PAUSE," "SLOW DOWN," and "GET LOUDER" at key places in the outline. You might also remind yourself to "DISPLAY THE VISUAL AID" or "PLAY THE VIDEO NOW" on your speaking outline. Rather than using actual words as reminders, you might decide to use a symbol system or color coding for your cues. For example, you could use a series of slash marks (/ / /) to indicate pauses of varying lengths. "Greater than" and "less than" symbols could be used as reminders to get louder (<) or to get softer (>). A series of arrows could remind you to gradually increase your rate (→ → → →) and a series of ellipsis points could remind you to gradually slow down (. . .). Likewise, you could underline key words or phrases that you want to stress or you could mark those words or phrases with a highlighter. Delivery cues will help you remember how to deliver your speech effectively, whether you are a beginning speaker or a professional.

Third, your speaking outline includes the actual supporting material you plan to cite during the speech. Quotations, statistics, and specific definitions or explanations are often provided in detail here so you don't inadvertently misrepresent information.

Fourth, your speaking outline is usually typed or printed in large neat letters on one side of a few three-inch by five-inch or four-inch by six-inch index cards. The number of cards you use will vary depending on the length of your speech. Index cards are better for your speaking outline than sheets of paper for a couple of important reasons. Index cards are smaller than sheets of paper, so they are less likely to distract listeners from your message. Also, you should be able to hold them in one hand, leaving the other hand free to gesture. Index cards are also stiffer than sheets of paper, making them less likely to rustle and distract listeners. Sometimes, particularly when using a lectern, you will use eight and one-half by eleven-inch paper for your speaking outline. Realize, though, that the same general rules apply. You should use a large type and a simple font, triple spacing, and clearly numbered pages. You can simply slide each sheet of paper to the side as you finish referring to it.

Teaching Tip
To give students practice identifying the elements of a proper outline, assign the Listen and Evaluate a Message activity contained in the Activities section of this chapter.

Speaking Outline Preparation Tips

- Unless you're using a lectern, use three-inch by five-inch or four-inch by six-inch index cards.
- Number your cards or pages.
- Use an outline format.
- Use abbreviations, key words, and brief phrases.
- Type or print in large, neat letters.
- Write out quotations, statistics, definitions.
- Include internal references.
- Include delivery cues.

Summary

Outlining is important to your public speech for four primary reasons: It places your content into a recognizable pattern for listeners to follow; it allows you flexibility to adjust your message as you speak; it provides an opportunity for you to critique your speech; and it can reduce public speaking anxiety.

The process of outlining actually occurs in three phases. Each phase ends with the completion of a particular kind of outline. These are the preparation outline, the formal outline, and the speaking outline.

A preparation outline is a working draft of your speech ideas. The preparation outline evolves out of a six-step process. The first step is to select and narrow a speech topic. The second step is to organize the main ideas and supporting material. The third step consists of developing the introduction and the conclusion. The fourth step is to place the major elements, main points, subpoints, and transition statements into a proper outline form. The fifth step is to integrate internal reference citations. And the final step consists of critiquing and revising the outline according to listener relevance links, learning styles, and supporting material, as well as creating a title.

A formal outline is a typed outline that labels and applies all of the content using complete sentences. It also includes a speech title, the speaker's name, internal reference citations, and a complete reference list.

A speaking outline is a condensed outline used solely as a memory aid while you present the actual speech. Like the preparation outline, a speaking outline uses key words and phrases rather than complete sentences. Like the formal outline, a speaking outline includes internal references throughout. Also like the formal outline, a speaking outline uses a proper outline format. Speaking outlines are unique in several other ways. Speaking outlines often use abbreviations. Speaking outlines also include delivery cues. Speaking outlines include the actual content of supporting material to be cited during the speech. Finally, speaking outlines are usually typed or printed in large neat letters on one side of a few numbered index cards. The exception to this rule is when speaking from a lectern. In this case, your speaking outline is usually printed or typed on eight and one-half- by eleven-inch paper.

Speakers who take the time and expend the effort to complete the entire three-phase process of outlining reap the rewards of doing so. Their speeches are clearly organized, well documented, and thorough.

ACTIVITIES

1. **Group Outline.** Form groups of four or five people per group. Make up a word like "spoophoni" or "aberambolt." Then decide as a group what it means. Create a preparation outline for a speech describing what it is.
2. **Reformat a Message.** Form groups of four or five people per group. Select an article from a magazine or a newspaper. Reformat the article into a preparation outline as described in this chapter. If the article does not offer a particular component, create one.
3. **Speaking Outline.** From the preparation outline you created in Activity 1 or 2 above, construct a speaking outline as a group and present it to the class.
4. **Listen and Evaluate a Message.** Listen to a commentary on a television or radio program. Try to identify the main points. Did the speaker offer a preview or a summary? What impact did this have on your ability to figure out the main points? Prepare a one-page critique based on your reaction.

Key Terms

Formal outline
Listener relevance link
Outlining
Preparation outline
Speaking outline

CHAPTER 11

Language and Style Choices in Your Speech

Reflective Questions

1. How can language choices foster inclusiveness?
2. Should you avoid using slang or jargon in a public speech?
3. Why is vividness important in a public speech?
4. What kinds of language can add vividness to your speech?

As her speech went on, Cindy was clearly losing her classmates. Her thesis—that anyone can use art therapy to reduce stress—was interesting and relevant. Her speech was well organized. The problem was that, in planning her speech, Cindy had never thought specifically about its language and style. Her speech included many long sentences, more appropriate to a paper than to a speech, as well as many technical terms used by art therapists. Although her content was interesting, she didn't convey it in an interesting way. She settled for abstraction instead of trying to paint vivid word pictures. Consequently, the audience found the speech both difficult and boring.

As mentioned in Chapter 8, a public speech has both macrostructure and microstructure. In other words, not only must you organize your ideas into main points that support a thesis, but you must also express the ideas in phrases and sentences. Since you can express the same idea using different language and style, these elements are essentially part of the structure—the overall framework—of your speech. The language and style choices you make, then, are the **microstructure** of your speech.

Teaching Tip
Virtually any segment of the popular movie *To Kill a Mockingbird* can be used to demonstrate the power of language.

This chapter explores effective language and style. More specifically, we look first at why language and style are so important to effective public speaking. Then we get more specific in terms of the nature of language and its implications for public speaking by looking at three major goals of language and style—clarity, vividness, and inclusion—and some specific strategies that can help you achieve these goals. Finally, we discuss when and where you should integrate language and style choices during the speech preparation process. By applying what you learn in this chapter, you can make your speeches interesting and memorable for your listeners.

Why Are Language and Style Important?

Effective microstructure is crucial because it helps maintain listener interest and, consequently, makes a speech memorable. If you think about it, speeches that have become classics are usually characterized by some language and style choices that help make them forever memorable. Consider, for example, the repetition of "I have a dream" in Martin Luther King, Jr.'s famous speech, or John Kennedy's "Ask not what your country can do for you—ask what you can do for your country." The same things that make these speeches memorable help sustain listener interest. More specifically, carefully chosen words maintain your audience's interest by increasing the clarity of your ideas, arousing emotions, and fostering a sense of inclusion with your listeners. Because you know you'll maintain listener interest, language and style can even help reduce your public speaking anxiety. Essentially, you maintain audience interest by using language and style in these ways because your language and style round the entire cycle of learning (see Figure 11–1).

Increasing Clarity

Teaching Tip
Make transparency masters of print ads that employ abstract and ambiguous language. Show these ads in class and ask students to improve them using concrete and descriptive language.

Language is important to your speech because it can either increase clarity through concrete and descriptive word choices or it can confuse listeners if it is abstract and ambiguous. That is, language is important because it makes your ideas clearer for your listeners through imagery and detail. It's like painting word pictures in the minds of listeners.

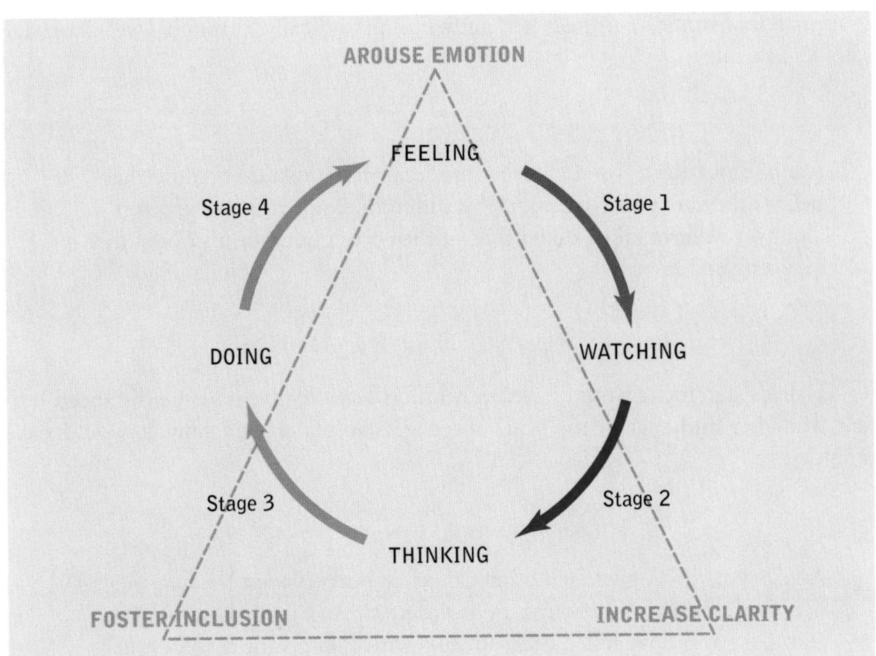

FIGURE 11–1 Language, Style, and the Learning Cycle

When you look at a beautiful painting, why does it interest you? Does it have to do with color choices, brushstrokes, attention to detail, or something else? These distinctions are what maintain your interest and ultimately make the painting memorable. Just as artists clarify their perspective of an object or a scene through detail and color, so do effective public speakers paint word pictures in the minds of listeners through carefully selected language. The descriptive words you choose add color to your ideas that sustain listener interest and, ultimately, make your ideas memorable.

> **What Do You Think?**
>
> *Consider a poem you've read and remember well. Why? How do the word choices impact your ability to remember it?*

Consider, for example, the picture you get when I describe a sunny day as "bright, warm, and friendly," compared to "blinding, scorching, and wicked." Both phrases describe the same thing, a sunny day. But the picture I've tried to paint about what that sunny day is like differs considerably in each. I've done so through descriptive words that add detail and color to my basic idea.

Fostering Inclusion

Carefully selected language and style are also important to your public speeches because it can foster inclusion with your listeners. Since public speaking is essentially a communication process, effective speakers create a sense of connection with their listeners by using "we" rather than "I" or "you" language and by avoiding biased language. Doing so serves as a subtle reminder that your listeners play an important role in the communication process, even in this public speaking context. Mary Fisher, in her "Whisper of AIDS" speech, delivered at the 1992 Republican

> **Discussion Tip**
> How can carefully selected language foster inclusion with your listeners? What will you do in your next speech to create a sense of connection with your listeners?

National Convention, united her audience periodically through "we" language choices like this:

> Adolescents don't give each other cancer or heart disease because they believe they are in love. But HIV is different. And we have helped it along—we have killed each other—with our ignorance, our prejudice, and our silence.

Fisher's statement would have been much less effective had she distanced herself from her audience with "you" language choices. Here's how it would have sounded:

> Adolescents don't give each other cancer or heart disease because they believe they are in love. But HIV is different. And [you] have helped it along—[you] have killed each other—with [your] ignorance, [your] prejudice, and [your] silence.

Teaching Tip
To give students practice in analyzing language for inclusiveness, assign the Music Lyric Analysis activity contained in the Activities section of this chapter.

Likewise, you can foster inclusion by using bias-free language. Fisher fostered inclusion in this way when she said, "It [AIDS] does not care whether you are Democrat or Republican. It does not ask whether you are black or white, male or female, gay or straight, young or old." Language choices like these can foster inclusion when integrated where appropriate in your speech.

Arousing Emotion

Language and style choices are also important because they can arouse emotions about your topic. Contrary to the childhood refrain "Sticks and stones may break my bones, but words will never hurt me," the things people tell us can make us feel miserable—or great. As our personal experiences with words make clear, words can have enormous emotional power. Effective public speakers harness that power to inspire listeners.

Teaching Tip
Show a videotape of a sample speech that contains emotionally charged words. Ask students to consider whether the speaker used language effectively and ethically.

Sometimes emotionally charged words can be used to foster a desire to know more about a topic. Geoff used language in this way in his speech about Venice by appealing to feelings of happiness, love, and romance. He began by describing Venice as "the city of love, the city of romance, and the city of my dreams." He then went on to discuss the experience of traveling through the city in gondolas rather than automobiles as being "romanticized along" as you "glide imperceptibly forward" and feeling "completely happy because life is beautiful and good."

Other times, emotionally charged words can be used to help convince listeners to agree with a position or even to take action about an issue. Your language choices can arouse feelings like adventure, companionship, curiosity, fear, guilt,

What Do You Think?

Identify an argument you've had recently. What words did the other person use that increased your anger? What words did you use for similar reasons?

loyalty, pride, or sympathy and in this way convince listeners to agree with your position and even to take action. In her speech about how students are harmed by fraternities, for example, Kris described Rutgers University student James Callahan's "untimely, unfortunate, and unnecessary death: a death that resulted from chugging Kamikazes—a nerve-numbing mixture of vodka, triple sec, and lime juice—at a college fraternity party." Kris carefully crafted this description to influence listeners' emotions by appealing to sympathy.

Teaching Tip
Develop a file of political campaign literature, rhetoric, and materials. Analyze these in class for instances of emotionally charged language.

Politicians and political activists often use emotionally charged language to arouse emotions in their listeners. Consider again, for example, the language in Mary Fisher's speech:

> The lesson history teaches is this: If you believe you are safe, you are at risk. If you do not see this killer stalking your children, look again. There is no family or community, no race or religion, no place left in America that is safe. Until we genuinely embrace this message, we are a nation at risk.
>
> Tonight, HIV marches resolutely toward AIDS in more than a million American homes. . . . One of the families is mine. If it is true that HIV inevitably turns to AIDS, then my children will inevitably turn to orphans (Fisher, 1992).

She drew listeners in by appealing to several emotions: fear, guilt, and sympathy. Her entire speech, which is an excellent example of effective language and style, is included at the end of this chapter.

Reducing Speech Anxiety

Discussion Tip
How can thinking carefully about the language and style of your next speech help reduce negative self-talk? According to Sellnow, how does the use of "I" and "you" language distance the speaker from the audience?

If you've thought carefully about the language and style of your speech and can feel confident that you'll keep your listeners interested, you'll be less likely to feel anxious or engage in negative self-talk. Most important to this is using language that fosters inclusiveness. "I" and "you" language tends to distance the speaker from the audience, while "we" language creates a sense of connection. Using "we" language reduces the perception that you as a speaker are in this transaction alone. Instead of creating a sense that you are *presenting in front of* your audience members, your language choices encourage a perception of *communicating with them*. Doing so can reduce anxiety because it helps you focus on the speech from a communication orientation rather than from a performance orientation (Motley, 1991). In addition, some figures and structures of speech—like alliteration, assonance, and onomatopoeia—can be easy to remember, thus reducing anxiety. When you carefully choose your words by considering how they increase clarity, foster inclusiveness, and arouse emotion, you will feel more confident as you speak.

The Nature of Language as Symbolic

To make wise language choices, you must first understand the nature of language. Language is symbolic. We use words as symbols to represent phenomena—objects, concepts, and so forth. For example, the word "dog" stands for a four-legged domesticated mammal many people have for a pet. "Dog," however, is not that animal. In other words, the *word* is not the *thing*.

Discussion Tip
How does language influence the way you perceive the world? Given Sellnow's argument that the *word* is not the *thing*, what can you do to reduce the risk that your audience might misinterpret your intended meaning?

Words do not have any tangible meaning in and of themselves. Rather, each of us constructs meaning based on our prior experiences with the word (Duck, 1994; Shotter, 1993)—that is, the same word might be interpreted differently by different people. For the public speaker, this means that your listeners are more likely to misinterpret your meaning unless your word choices make the intended meaning as concrete and precise as possible. Let's consider the word *dog* again. Although we both probably envision a domesticated four-legged mammal, the particular dog you pictured is probably not the same as the one I imagined or the same as the one your classmate envisioned. I pictured a fun-loving, rambunctious golden retriever. What did you envision? In other words, the word *dog* is very abstract; the phrase a "mangy hound dog whose fur was tangled and matted and whose face was graying from age" paints a more concrete picture.

Certain words are associated with certain phenomena simply because we agree to use them to do so. Language as symbolic is also arbitrary. In other words, the word *dog* does not symbolize the four-legged animal because of some inherent connection. Similarly, a pig is not called a pig because it is such a dirty animal. *Pig* could just as easily have been used to represent what makes automobiles roll *(wheel)*. Because language is arbitrary, meanings can change over time and meanings can differ across cultural groups. Hence, public speakers must make wise language choices—choices that enhance the effectiveness of their message rather than hinder it.

Denotations and Connotations

Teaching Tip
Make transparency masters of print ads and analyze them in class for examples of denotative and connotative meaning.

Let's look at it another way. If someone asked you whether you were a feminist, what would you say? Your answer likely stems from how you define "feminism." Words have both denotative and connotative meanings. A **denotation** is the dictionary definition of a word. A denotation of feminism is "a doctrine that advocates for women the same rights granted to men." Some people might agree that women should be granted the same rights as men but do not consider themselves to be feminists. The reason might lie in the connotations they attach to the word. A **connotation** is what the word suggests or implies. Different words can have similar denotations but very different connotations. In fact, for this very reason, many feminists now use the term "feminisms" rather than "feminist." Moreover, these connotations might be neutral, positive, or negative, and they may be very different for different people. Thus, some might attach negative connotations to the word "feminist," such as "male basher" or "radical" or even "femme-nazi."

Words develop connotations for us based on our experiences. Exposure to the many negative portrayals of "feminists" in the media (television, radio, film, music, etc.) might be a reason the word has certain negative connotations for some people. Others might have had negative experiences with people who called themselves feminists. Connotative meanings are important to public speakers because they often contribute to the emotional power of words. In fact, people will fight and even die for the sake of them. Public speakers can use connotative meanings to increase the emotional appeals (pathos) in their presentations. However, effective speakers need to choose words carefully by considering how potential connotations might help or hinder the message. "Feminist," "feminism," and "feminisms" are prime examples.

New Meanings

The meanings we attach to words can also change over time. The word "gay," for example, once meant "happy and lighthearted." Although this remains a definition of the word, it is now commonly understood to mean "homosexual." Today, professional speakers who supplement their speeches with "slide shows" often mean a computer-generated graphics presentation like PowerPoint, rather than a series of photographs presented via a slide projector. Likewise, "networking" once meant making personal contacts with key individuals. Today it may mean connecting your computer to others via the Internet.

Teaching Tip
Assign students to small groups and have them generate a list of at least ten new words or meanings. Share the results with the entire class.

Certainly, some words develop new meanings over time, but sometimes entirely new words are coined as needed. "Channel surfing," for example, came about with the invention of remote control devices. The development of the Internet has given rise to countless new words and phrases, for example, "surfing the Web," "punting," "scrolling," and "Wbasayc." As recently as twenty years ago, cyberspace might have been conceived of as a place where Captain Kirk took his crew on *Star Trek,* rather than the place where information is exchanged over the Internet.

Private Codes

Discussion Tip
Ask students to identify examples of slang and jargon. Discuss the differences between the cultural groups represented in the class.

Certain words also can carry unique meanings in particular cultural groups. Many groups have private codes that are not generally understood by outsiders. Slang is an example. **Slang** is simply a meaning that is arbitrarily assigned to a word by a particular social group or subculture. For example, over the years, *good* has been expressed as groovy, super, cool, rad, and bad. Public speakers should avoid using slang, since their intended meaning might not be understood by everyone in the audience. Moreover, using slang during a speech can hurt a speaker's credibility (ethos) because it doesn't sound professional.

Jargon refers to the particular terminology of a trade or profession that is not generally understood by outsiders. Different professional organizations often have their own technical jargon, used to describe phenomena that are unique to their field. Technical jargon is important because it describes specific concepts or functions precisely. To those outside the organization and to those who are new to the organization, however, technical jargon can be confusing simply because it and its meaning are unfamiliar to them.

CALVIN AND HOBBES © Watterson. Reprinted with permission of UNIVERSAL PRESS SYNDICATE. All rights reserved.

Consider professional sports. If you are unfamiliar with the jargon associated with professional football, for example, you would probably have difficulty understanding what is meant by a "hail Mary," a "blitz," a "bomb," or a "shotgun." The computer industry also has developed a host of technical jargon to describe specific concepts and functions. If you are not familiar with the terminology, however, you probably won't know what is meant by "RAM," "megabytes," or "gigabytes." Academia is no exception. Each discipline—like architecture, business, computer science, engineering, music, psychology, and so forth—has developed particular jargon that is understood by others in the field, but is usually unfamiliar to the general public. That is, you won't find these words in your standard dictionary.

Teaching Tip
Assign students to small groups and have them discuss what jargon they are likely to use in their next speech. Ask them to develop strategies for communicating these terms clearly.

Public speakers must take care when using jargon. It's okay to use some jargon as long as you define it clearly the first time you use it. In fact, doing so can be empowering to your listeners, since it lets them in on the private codes of the field—particularly when those students are working toward a degree in that field. I have tried to do that in this book: use the actual terminology of the field and define it in simple terms. My goal in doing so is to break down a potential language barrier between academicians and students. This holds true for abbreviations and acronyms as well. In my field, I can certainly talk about the NCA, for example, if I define it as the National Communication Association the first time I use the term.

Political Correctness

Teaching Tip
Have students write a brief essay in which they analyze how political correctness is discussed in the popular media. Ask them to consider whether the connotations they uncover are positive, negative, or neutral.

Finally, your language choices both reflect your **worldview**—your way of looking at the world—and attempt to shape the worldview of your listeners. Since connotations can be positively or negatively charged across groups, it is important to use language that demonstrates respect for other worldviews. This trend to reduce language bias based on worldview is often referred to as "PC" or "political correctness." **Political correctness** means simply to demonstrate through language choices a concern for fairness and respect for different groups, based on race, gender, or ethnicity, as well as different identities and worldviews (Grabmeier, 1992).

What Do You Think?

What is some of the jargon used in your field of study? What do these terms mean and how did you discover their meaning?

Do you know, for example, that many people with disabilities prefer not to be called disabled because they find the term dehumanizing (Braithwaite & Braithwaite, 1997)? Likewise, whereas words like "fireman," "mailman," and "mankind" used to refer to both men and women, they have been replaced with more inclusive terms like "firefighter," "postal carrier," and "humanity."

> **What Do You Think?**
>
> *Does the term "political correctness" have positive, neutral, or negative connotations for you? Why? Can you identify certain experiences you've had with the term that contribute to your personal connotation?*

Students sometimes tell me that political correctness seems like an overreaction to an insignificant problem, or that they do not *intend* to show disrespect by their language choices. For example, Kevin told me, "Just because I referred to medical doctors as 'he' in my speech did not mean I believe only men can be medical doctors," and Amanda remarked, "How am I supposed to know whether to call them 'Indians' or 'Native Americans.' *I* think people need to get less bent out of shape. I do not intend to be offensive." Regardless of your intent, however, to be an effective public speaker you must demonstrate respect with regard to race, ethnicity, and gender, and that means being politically correct (Strossen, 1992).

> **What Do You Think?**
>
> *Consider the recent debates about whether or not it is appropriate to call sports teams "Sioux," "Braves," "Indians," and so forth. What is your opinion and why?*

Language is symbolic. Hence, it has the potential to help or hinder your message. Your goal as a public speaker is to reduce ambiguity, demonstrate respect, and enhance vividness in the language choices you make. The next section focuses on specific strategies you can employ to ensure that you achieve these goals.

Strategies for Effective Language and Style

Now that you realize the nature of language as symbolic, you can consider specific strategies to ensure that the intent of your message will be understood and memorable. To fully understand how these strategies work in public speeches, let's start by discussing how oral style differs from written style. Then we'll discuss each strategy in detail, the strategies of accuracy, clarity, inclusion, and vividness.

Oral versus Written Style

In order to speak effectively, you need to realize that oral style differs from written style; at least it ought to. Essentially, **oral style** tends to be less formal than written style. Since a primary goal of the speaker is to establish a relationship with listeners, language choices must reflect a personal tone that encourages listeners to feel important to the speaker and the occasion. Recall that public speaking is a form of communication, not a performance. To develop this sense of relationship, then, oral style differs from written style in four important ways.

Discussion Tip
Are you more likely to use personal pronouns when you speak or when you write? Why or why not? How can public speakers use personal pronouns to acknowledge the audience as an important participant in the communication transaction?

By permission of Johnny Hart and Creators Syndicate, Inc.

First, speakers tend to use more personal pronouns. Doing so acknowledges the presence of your listeners and creates a sense of relationship with them. For example, if you were to write a paper about gun control, you might phrase your thesis statement like this: "The issue of gun control is currently being debated on a number of fronts." In an oral presentation, you might phrase it in this way: "I'd like to talk with you today about gun control, an issue that is currently being debated on a number of fronts." Notice how the audience is acknowledged as an important participant in the communication transaction. To create an even better sense of inclusion, you might even phrase it this way: "Let's talk today about gun control, an issue that is currently being debated on a number of fronts and deserves our attention." Using personal pronouns like "we," "us," and "our" creates a stronger sense of relationship. You might even mention specific audience members by name. For example:

> Last week, Georgia talked with us about teen violence and what we can do about it. Let's take that discussion further today by talking about gun control. Gun control is currently being debated on a number of fronts and deserves our attention.

Referencing listeners by name, in addition to using personal pronouns, fosters an even stronger sense of relationship between speaker and audience.

Second, speakers tend to use simple language and sentence structure. Effective oral style tends to be characterized by shorter sentences and familiar language. Because listeners must grasp meaning upon hearing your ideas only once, it is crucial to keep your sentences short and your language familiar. Also, long sentences tend to reduce the sense of relationship by sounding like you are reading from a manuscript rather than talking with your listeners. In fact, to build this sense of relationship, oral style uses more contractions than written style. For example, "let's" rather than "let us," "we'll" rather than "we will," "won't" rather than "will not," and so forth.

Teaching Tip
Show videotapes of students presenting speeches that illustrate repetition. Ask students to consider how repetition can be employed to help listeners grasp the main point(s) of the message.

Third, speakers tend to use more repetition. As we've already talked about many times, listeners don't have the luxury of stopping to reread a passage that they don't understand. Oral style uses repetition to help listeners grasp the speaker's ideas. Although repeating yourself in a written composition is discouraged, oral presentations should use redundancy in terms of previews, transitions, and summaries, as well as in terms of stating important points in more than one way. In the following passage, notice how Mary Fisher uses repetition to help listeners grasp the main point of her message:

> To the millions of you who are grieving, who are frightened, who have suffered the ravages of AIDS firsthand: Have courage and you will find comfort.
>
> To the millions who are strong, I issue this plea: Set aside prejudice and politics to make room for compassion and sound policy.

Fourth, oral style tends to use more superlatives. Since listeners cannot reread parts of a speech like they can a written passage, you need to sustain listener interest at all times. Colorful adjectives and adverbs can help draw listeners into your message. You must take care, however, not to overuse them. Doing so will reduce their effectiveness.

Finally, realize that just as writing styles vary, so do oral styles vary based on things like the personality of the speaker, the subject of the speech, and the audience. However, heeding these characteristics of oral style as you prepare and present your speech will improve your chances of effectively reaching your audience:

- Use personal pronouns.
- Use simple language and sentence structure.
- Use repetition.
- Use superlatives carefully.

It is important here to make a distinction between conversation and public speaking. Although both use the oral style, they are not quite the same. Public speaking differs from conversation in that it has fewer interruptions, is more formal in tone, has more constraints imposed on it, uses more repetition, and stays on topic longer. That said, let's look more closely at the language and style strategies of accuracy, clarity, inclusion, and vividness.

Accuracy

Accuracy means using words that most precisely convey the meaning you intend. You may recall from Chapter 1 that to be **intelligible** is to be understood. This is the most important concept for any public speaker to master. If your listeners don't understand you, your attempt to communicate effectively is doomed. There are several aspects of intelligibility. Some have to do with delivery, like pronunciation, enunciation, rate, volume, and so forth. These aspects will be discussed in Chapter 12. Others have to do with language and style. Accuracy is one of these.

Teaching Tip
Show videotapes of student speeches that do not precisely convey meaning. Assign students to small groups and have them rewrite portions of these speeches using the accuracy guidelines presented in this chapter.

Denotations

You should use words that have the right denotation. If you are not certain of the meaning of a word, look it up in a dictionary. If you are trying to think of a word that more precisely describes what you mean, use a **thesaurus.** Look up the word you've thought of and see if one of the words listed seems better for your purpose. For example, if you wanted to describe Godzilla's size and could think only of "big" and "large," you could find synonyms for "big," including "enormous," "sizable," "massive," "great," "appreciable," "bulky," "ample," "giant," "gigantic," "immense," and "extensive." Some of these words—like "enormous," "massive," and "immense"—would indeed be more precise for your purpose. Note that others—like "appreciable," "bulky," and "extensive"—would be inappropriate because they could possibly confuse listeners. A thesaurus can be a very effective tool as long as you do not fall victim to the habit of using it to look for more "sophisticated-sounding" words at the expense of intelligibility.

Connotations

Discussion Tip
Ask students to identify a situation in which they used language that aroused an unintended connotation. Encourage students to reconsider the episode from the other person's perspective.

Likewise, make sure the words you choose have the connotation you intend. Recall our discussion earlier in this chapter about the words "feminist," "feminism," and "feminisms," and the term "political correctness." Try to avoid using words that will arouse unintended connotations. If you do choose to use certain words that might arouse unintended emotional responses, be sure to define them in ways that reduce that tendency.

Standard English

Teaching Tip
Ask students to generate a list of words they frequently misuse or mispronounce. Discuss strategies for ameliorating this problem as well as the implications for speaker credibility.

Accuracy also has to do with vocabulary, pronunciation, and grammar choices. To ensure that your listeners will understand your intended meaning, use standard English. **Standard English** refers to the language preferences described in the dictionary. Take the time to discover any vocabulary or grammar tendencies you might have that result from your **dialect,** a regional variety of a language. For example, depending on dialect, an automobile "turn signal" can be called a "blinker," a "seesaw" can be called a "teeter-totter," and a "soda" can be called a "pop" or a "Coke." Sometimes speakers mispronounce certain words as a result of regional dialect. In some parts of the country, for example, many people pronounce "wash" as "warsh" and "creek" as "crick." Doing so, however, could hurt intelligibility as well as credibility. Likewise, poor grammar—for example, "he don't," "I says," "this here book," "them cars," "on account of he was sick," "beings as he was sick" and so forth—can be rooted in dialect and result in reduced intelligibility or credibility. If you know you make certain mistakes with regard to standard English, consult a handbook and then make delivery cue reminders on your speaking outline.

What Do You Think?

Based on what we've just discussed, do you think Black English is appropriate for a formal public speech? Why or why not?

Clarity

Another important aspect of intelligibility is clarity. Being clear means using familiar terms, concrete words, simple language, and the active voice, and avoiding vocalized pauses.

Use Familiar Words

Effective public speakers use words that will be familiar to their audience. Use of familiar words is especially important since listeners will not have the luxury of hearing your speech again. This is why using a thesaurus to find more sophisticated words is a mistake. Part of using familiar words is avoiding use of jargon or slang. If you do need to use jargon, be sure to define it the first time it is used. Acronyms should be introduced along with the full term they stand for. After introducing STDs in this way, Larissa was able to continue using the acronym throughout the rest of her speech:

Teaching Tip
Show students a videotape of a speaker who uses unfamiliar words (e.g., Dennis Miller's commentary on *Monday Night Football* or *Saturday Night Live*). Encourage students to consider how the use of unfamiliar terms might frustrate the audience, increase the potential for miscommunication, and damage perceived credibility.

> According to the 1996 issue of *State Legislators,* nearly two-thirds of all reported cases of sexually transmitted diseases, or STDs, occur in people under the age of twenty-five. STDs are actually bacteria and viruses that cause infections. All STDs are transmitted by sexual contact.

Slang, along with causing credibility problems, can also hurt clarity. To give an extreme example, a speaker who used "bad" in its slang sense meaning "great" might well be misunderstood as intending just the opposite.

Use Concrete Words

Recall that whereas some words are more concrete and others more abstract, **concrete words** paint a clearer, more vivid picture for listeners. The word *collie* is more concrete than *dog.* And *collie* could be made still more concrete as, for example, "the heroic, friendly, television collie we all know as Lassie." Another way to achieve greater concreteness, then, is by including modifiers like adjectives and adverbs. In her speech advocating aerobic exercise, for example, Julie made "aerobic activity" more concrete by talking about "aerobic activity like running, jogging, swimming, or bicycling."

Use Simple Language and Sentence Structure

Words that are more familiar and more concrete tend also to be simpler. Even if your ideas are complex, you should strive to express them in as simple terms as possible. To achieve simplicity, you'll need to think about the structure of your sentences. Keeping your words and sentences simple helps listeners understand and focus on the main ideas of your message. For example, in her speech about toughening environmental standards, the administrator of the U. S. Environmental Protection Agency, Carol M. Browner (1998), said this:

> And there is little doubt as to where Americans stand. They want clean air. They want the public health to come first in setting clean air standards. They want their children protected.
>
> They want the EPA to do its job—which is ensuring that the air they breathe is safe and healthy.

Notice how simple her words and sentences are and how powerfully clear her message is as a result. Contrast what she did say with what she might have said in an attempt to sound more sophisticated, and imagine that you are listening to her statement, rather than reading it:

> And there is relatively little doubt as to where Americans stand with regard to environmental issues and standards. Americans desire perfectly purified air, as well as for clean air standards that are developed by focusing first and foremost on public health. And they also yearn for protection from environmental hazards for their children.
>
> They hope that the Environmental Protection Agency will do what it was created to do, which is to ensure in every way possible that the air they breathe is both safe and healthy for them.

When presenting a public speech, simple words and sentences are often clearer and more powerful than unnecessarily complicated words and sentence structure.

Use Active Sentences

To achieve clarity, you should also use active sentences rather than passive sentences when presenting public speeches. In an **active sentence,** the subject *performs* the action, whereas in a **passive sentence,** the subject *experiences* the action (Legette, Mead, Kramer, and Beal, 1991). For example, consider how this passive sentence is made clearer as an active sentence:

Passive: "Food and clothing items were donated to the shelter by us."

Active: "We donated food and clothing items to the shelter."

Active voice is more effective for public speakers because it is clearer and more concrete.

Avoid Vocalized Pauses

Discussion Tip
Why does Sellnow refer to vocalized pauses as "verbal garbage"? Why do public speakers use vocalized pauses? How might the use of vocalized pauses damage speaker credibility?

Finally, clarity means avoiding **vocalized pauses** such as "like," "you know," "really," "well," "and," "basically," "um," and "uh," which sometimes creep in while we're formulating our next thought. I call vocalized pauses "verbal garbage" because they are unnecessary words that disrupt the fluency of your message, making your message less clear to listeners. Public speakers sometimes get into this bad habit because they fear silence. In actuality, silent pauses are less likely to disrupt the flow of ideas than are vocalized pauses.

To achieve intelligibility via language and style consider both accuracy and clarity. Use these tips to check your language and style as you prepare:

- Are your denotations accurate?
- Are your connotations intended?
- Do you use standard English?
- Do you use familiar words?
- Do you use concrete words?
- Is your sentence structure simple?
- Do you use active sentences?
- Do you avoid vocalized pauses?

Inclusion

Inclusion means making language choices that show your respect for your audience and for all types of people in general. To be inclusive, you need to use "we" language, use bias-free language, and avoid inappropriate humor.

Teaching Tip
Have students watch five television commercials or analyze five print ads and record the number of inclusive pronouns that are used. Discuss the implications of this communication strategy in class.

Use "We" Language

To make all listeners feel included and important to the communication process, demonstrate verbal immediacy, especially with "we" language. Through **verbal immediacy,** you use language to reduce the psychological distance between you and your audience. Thus, by using "we" language, instead of "you" or "they" language, you convey a sense of connection with your listeners and actively involve them in the topic and occasion. "We" language can often be incorporated into the macrostructural elements of your speech such as the thesis statement, preview, and transitions. Pete used "we" language in this way:

Thesis statement: Today we'll see why Tok Pisin of Papua New Guinea should be considered a legitimate language.

Preview: We'll do this by looking at what kind of language Tok Pisin is, some of the features of the Tok Pisin language, and why this language is necessary in New Guinea.

Transition (between the first and the second point): Since Tok Pisin is essentially a combination of languages, let's look more specifically at some of its unique features.

Used appropriately over the course of a speech, "we" language can help build verbal immediacy. The more "immediate" you are, the more likable, friendly, and understandable your listeners will find you to be (Gorham, 1988; Powell & Harville, 1990). Using "we" language is one way to create this perception.

Teaching Tip
To give students an opportunity to explore bias-free language, assign the Being Bias-Free activity included in the Activities section of this chapter.

Use Bias-Free Language

You can also foster a sense of inclusion by using bias-free language. Your goal here is to avoid stereotypes about groups based on race, ethnicity, gender, age,

Effective public speakers use inclusive language.

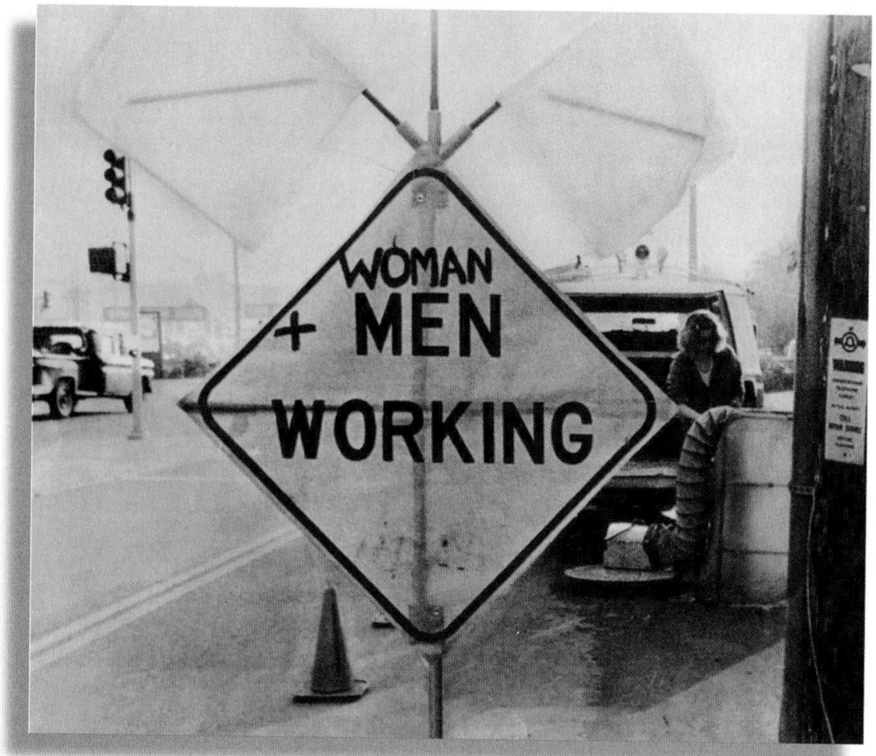

sexual orientation, or any other characteristic. Not only is biased language inaccurate and unethical, but its use is likely to marginalize, alienate, or offend some of your listeners. Thus, by using bias-free language, you'll simultaneously improve your speech and your chances of connecting with your audience. There are a number of reference books that can help you determine bias-free language alternatives (e.g., Beard & Cerf, 1993; Maggio, 1988; Miller, & Swift, 1991). Consult one of these references when you are uncertain about a word or phrase. In addition, keep the following general guidelines in mind as you work on your speech. Finally, if using bias-free language is relatively new for you, don't feel badly when you slip up occasionally. With practice it will become easier. And if you use bias-free language generally, but make an occasional mistake, listeners are less likely to become offended by it because they are more likely to realize it was not intentional.

If you follow four basic rules, you'll be well on your way to using bias-free language:

- Avoid using irrelevant descriptions related to the group a person belongs to.
- Avoid using gender-linked terms.
- Avoid using masculine pronouns to represent both men and women.
- Use parallel treatment when referring to males and females.

First, if the group a person belongs to isn't relevant to your point, don't bring it up. Concrete descriptions are useful, of course, but only when they are relevant.

In the case of people, irrelevant descriptions can be offensive. For example, if you are speaking about Sandra Day O'Connor as the first woman appointed to the Supreme Court, then the fact that she is a woman is central to your speech. If, however, you are speaking about outstanding Supreme Court justices, the fact that she is a woman is irrelevant and should not be mentioned. Similarly, if you are speaking about teachers who influenced you, you would not mention that one of these teachers was Asian American unless that fact is somehow relevant to your speech. Beginning public speakers sometimes add unnecessary descriptions when discussing people who are not white males: for example, "woman doctor." Likewise, they sometimes add unnecessary descriptions when discussing males in stereotypically female professions: for example, "male nurse." Although their intention might be to show inclusiveness by implying that group membership is somehow relevant, the actual effect can be quite the opposite (Treinen and Warren, 2001).

Second, avoid using gender-linked terms. **Gender-linked terms** are those that somehow imply exclusion of either males or females. Rather than using words like "chairman," "fireman," "mailman," "spokesman," or "mankind," which tend to exclude women, use inclusive language like "chairperson," "firefighter," "mail carrier," "speaker," or "humanity." Although students sometimes claim that they mean both men and women when they use these gender-linked terms, research reports that when people hear them, they think of men and not women (Wood, 1994). Gender-linked terms that exclude men should also be avoided. Instead of "waitress," for example, use the inclusive term "server." Instead of "stewardess," use "flight attendant." And instead of terms like "unwed mother" or "maternity leave," use "single parent" and "parental leave."

Teaching Tip
Have students bring to class a newspaper or magazine article that uses gender-linked terms. Working in groups, have students rewrite the terms using inclusive language.

Third, don't use male pronouns like "he" and "him" to represent both males and females. Doing so leads listeners to perceive that only males, and not females, are being included (e.g., Gastil, 1990; Hamilton, 1991; Switzer, 1990). Instead of "he," use "he or she." Better yet, make the sentence plural by using "they," or rephrase the sentence:

Technology Tip
http://www.chss.iup.edu/wc/resources/nonsex.html

This Web page, developed by the Indiana University of Pennsylvania Writing Center, provides several guidelines for nonsexist language usage. Have students visit this site, record examples of alternatives to male pronouns, and report their results to the class.

Problematic: Today, the typical college student knows what he wants from his education.

Preferred (use he or she): Today, the typical college student knows what he or she wants from his or her education.

Preferred (make it plural): Today, most college students know what they want from their education.

Preferred (rephrase the sentence): Today, students expect certain things from college.

Fourth, use parallel treatment when referring to males and females. **Parallel treatment** means to provide similar labels for the genders when referring to them together. Some examples are "men and women," "husband and wife," and "boys and girls." That is, avoid referring to women of all ages as "girls" if you refer to their male counterparts as "men." Also avoid statements that make assumptions about inequality. For example, the phrase "doctors and their wives" assumes that all doctors are male. A better way to phrase the statement is "doctors and their spouses."

Avoid Inappropriate Humor

Technology Tip
http://www.presentersuniversity.com/courses/show_crafting.cfm?RecordID=25

This Web page, hosted by Presenters University, offers several tips for incorporating humor in presentations. Have students visit this site and report their findings to the class.

What Do You Think?

Consider a stand-up comedian you've heard who seemed offensive. What language and style did he or she use that may have contributed to your perception?

Finally, demonstrating respect for your audience also means avoiding inappropriate humor. Unfortunately, beginning public speakers sometimes make the mistake of telling a dirty joke, making a sexist remark, or using profanity in the name of humor. Although you might not intend to be offensive or disrespectful, doing any of these things is likely to offend some listeners and should be avoided in public speeches. Being inclusive means demonstrating respect for all listeners. That means avoiding humorous comments that might offend.

Use of bias-free language is absolutely necessary for inclusive public speaking. Adhering to these strategies of using "we" language, using bias-free language, and avoiding inappropriate humor will make you a more effective public speaker.

Vividness

Teaching Tip
To give students practice in developing and utilizing vivid language, assign the Using Vivid Oral Style or Examining a Speech activity contained in the Activities section of this chapter.

Perhaps one of the most important ways you can make your speech memorable for listeners is by using vivid language and style. **Vivid language and style** evoke feelings and images in the listeners' minds and thus invites them to internalize your ideas. Recall our discussions about learning styles for a moment. By using vivid language, you can appeal to different learning styles (watching, feeling, doing, and thinking) in ways that make your ideas memorable later. You can increase vividness in your speech by appealing to the senses and by using figures and structures of speech.

Use Sensory Language

You can help your listeners internalize your ideas by appealing to the senses. These include seeing, hearing, touching, tasting, smelling, and feeling. Consider how you can re-create what something, someone, or some place *looks like*. Consider, too, how you can help listeners imagine how something *sounds*. How can you use language to convey the way something feels (textures, shapes, temperatures)? How can language re-create a sense of how something tastes or how something smells? You ought to ask yourself these kinds of questions as you formulate your speech to enhance vividness in ways that make your speech memorable.

Teaching Tip
Have students write a brief essay in which they use at least five colorful descriptors. Share the results of this activity with the entire class.

To achieve this, use colorful descriptors. In addition to making your ideas more concrete, colorful descriptors can arouse emotions by painting word pictures and appealing to the senses. They invite listeners to imagine details as you describe them. Here's how you could appeal to different senses in a speech about downhill skiing:

Sight: As you climb the hill, the bright winter sunshine glistening on the snow is blinding.

Touch and feel: Just before you take off, you gently slip your goggles over your eyes. They are bitterly cold and sting your nose for a moment.

You can help listeners remember by appealing to the senses.

Taste: You start the descent and, as you gradually pick up speed, the taste of air and ice and snow in your mouth invigorates you.

Sound: An odd silence fills the air. You hear nothing but the swish of your skis against the snow beneath your feet. At last you arrive at the bottom.

Smell and feel: You enter the warming house. As your fingers thaw in the warm air, the aroma from the wood stove in the corner comforts you. And you sleep.

By using colorful descriptors that appeal to different senses during your speech, you will maintain the interest of your listeners and make your ideas more memorable.

Use Figures and Structures of Speech

Sometimes speakers can achieve vividness by using figures of speech. **Figures of speech** are language strategies that make striking comparisons between things or ideas that are not obviously alike. In doing so, they help listeners visualize or internalize what you are saying. **Structures of speech** are sentence strategies that combine ideas in a particular way. What follows are some examples of figures and structures of speech that are commonly used to make public speeches memorable.

Teaching Tip
Assign an impromptu speech to give students practice in incorporating figures and structures of speech. Have students develop the speech using at least three of these devices.

Alliteration is the repetition of sounds at the beginnings of words that are near one another. In her speech about the history of jelly beans, Sharla used alliteration when she said, "And today, there are more than fifty fabulous fruity flavors from which to choose." As long as it's used sparingly, alliteration can catch listeners' attention and make the speech memorable. Overuse of this technique, however, can actually hurt the message because listeners might begin to focus on the technique rather than on the content of your message.

Assonance is the repetition of vowel sounds as in "she said *ouch* with an *outhouse mouth*," or "*how now brown cow.*" As with alliteration, this strategy can make your speech more memorable as long as it's not overused.

Onomatopoeia is the use of words that sound like the things they stand for. Some examples include "buzz," "hiss," "crack," and "plop." In the speech about skiing, for example, the "swish" of the skis is an example of onomatopoeia. Like alliteration, this technique can be effective when used sparingly, but can actually distract from the message when overused.

Personification attributes human qualities to a concept or to an inanimate object. When Linda talked about her car, Big Red, as her trusted friend and companion, she used personification. Likewise, when Rick talked about the flowers dancing on the front lawn, he used personification.

Repetition is achieved by restating words, phrases, or sentences for emphasis. A highly effective and famous example is Martin Luther King Jr.'s use of the phrase "I have a dream" in his speech by the same title:

> I say to you today, my friends, so even though we face the difficulties of today and tomorrow, I still have a dream. It is a dream deeply rooted in the American dream.
>
> I have a dream that one day this nation will rise up and live out the true meaning of its creed: "We hold these truths to be self-evident: that all men are created equal."
>
> I have a dream that one day on the red hills of Georgia the sons of former slaves and the sons of former slave owners will be able to sit down together at the table of brotherhood.
>
> I have a dream that one day even the state of Mississippi, a state sweltering with the heat of injustice, sweltering with the heat of oppression, will be transformed into an oasis of freedom and justice.
>
> I have a dream that my four little children will one day live in a nation where they will not be judged by the color of their skin but by the content of their character. I have a dream today (Martin Luther King, Jr., 1963).

Antithesis is combining contrasting ideas in the same sentence. John F. Kennedy used antithesis when he said, "Ask not what your country can do for you—ask what you can do for your country." Likewise, Jesse Jackson used antithesis to close his Rainbow Coalition speech powerfully when he said, "We've come from disgrace to Amazing Grace. Our time has come."

Simile is a comparison between two unlike things using the words "like" or "as." If you've seen the movie *Forrest Gump,* you might recall Forrest's use of similes throughout the film. For example, "Life is like a box of chocolates. You never know what you're going to get" and "Stupid is as stupid does." Neil used a simile in his public speech when he said, "The fireflies lit the sky like strings of thousands of holiday lights." Similes can be effective tools because they make your ideas more vivid in listeners' minds. But they should be used sparingly or they lose their appeal.

Metaphor is an implied comparison between two unlike things made without using "like" or "as." Socrates' "fame is the perfume of heroic deeds" is a metaphor because it compares fame to perfume. Metaphors can be effective because they make an abstract concept more concrete, strengthen an important point, or heighten emotions. Sometimes similes and metaphors become overused and trite. Some examples include "fit as a fiddle," "hungry as a bear," "busy as a bee," and "light as a feather." These **clichés** should be avoided because their predictability makes them ineffective for vividness.

> ***What Do You Think?***
>
> *What figures or structures of speech might you use in your next speech and where in the speech might you use them?*

Teaching Tip
Show a videotape of one of Dr. Martin Luther King, Jr.'s speeches to explore the effective use of repetition, simile, and metaphor. Ask students to discuss how these devices contribute to the style and power of the speech.

Analogy is an extended metaphor. Sometimes you can develop a story from a metaphor that makes a concept more vivid for listeners. If you were to describe a family member as the "black sheep in the barnyard," you would be using a metaphor. If you continued on to talk about other members of the family as different animals on the farm and the roles ascribed to them, you would be extending your metaphor into an analogy. An analogy can be an effective strategy for holding your speech together in a creative and vivid way.

Discussion Tip
Why is it important that public speakers avoid using clichés? How can you determine if a simile or metaphor you're considering using in your next speech has become overused and trite?

Integrating Language and Style

Recall that language and style essentially form the microstructure of your speech because effective language and style choices are crucial components of effective structure. As such, you should consider language and style choices as you develop your formal outline, the one you phrase in complete sentences. Hence, language and style choices should be considered specifically when you are transferring your ideas from the preparation outline to the formal outline.

You should also consider language and style choices when you are transferring your ideas from the formal outline to the speaking outline. That is, if you are concerned about forgetting to use certain language or style strategies during the speech, include them specifically on your speaking outline as well. Recall that Laura did this with her preview and summary. She didn't want to forget to use parallel phrasing in her actual presentation, so she worded her preview and summary quite specifically on her speaking outline.

Teaching Tip
Have students write a one- to two-page paper describing specific figures or structures of speech they might use in their next speech. This activity will help students better understand the efficacy of these devices and assist them in determining where they can be used in speeches.

Summary

Language and style choices—which are considered microstructure—are crucial to effective public speeches because they can inspire audiences to listen and make the speaker's ideas memorable. They do so by increasing clarity, fostering inclusion, and arousing emotion. Consequently, effective language and style choices can reduce public speaking anxiety rooted in a fear of failure.

Language is symbolic—that is, words do not have any tangible meaning in and of themselves. Meanings are derived from denotations, which are the dictionary definitions, and connotations, or what a word suggests or implies based on previous experiences. Meanings can also change over time and among different people or groups. Slang, for example, is a private code coined by social groups for certain words. Jargon is another kind of private code developed by professional or occupational groups. Finally, meaning is attached to words based on different worldviews. As such, it is important to make politically correct language choices.

Oral style differs from written style in four general ways: Oral style uses more personal pronouns, simpler language and sentence structure, more repetition, and more superlatives than written style. Oral style is used differently in public speaking than in conversation in that it has fewer interruptions, is more formal in tone, has more constraints imposed on it, uses more repetition, and stays on topic longer.

There are four general strategies you should consider when developing your language and style based on the nature of effective oral style. These are accuracy, clarity, inclusion, and vividness. In terms of accuracy, use correct words by considering denotations and connotations. You should also use correct grammar based on standard English.

To ensure clarity, use familiar words that make abstract ideas and concepts as concrete and precise as possible. Use simple language and sentence structure, and use active voice whenever possible. Avoid using vocalized pauses like "um," "uh," "really," "like," "you know," and "basically," which can distract listeners and disrupt the flow of your message.

Regarding inclusion, use "we" language in your structural comments as opposed to "you" or "they" language. Doing so will increase a sense of connection with your listeners. Likewise, use bias-free language. That is, avoid using irrelevant descriptions related to the group a person belongs to, gender-linked terms, or masculine pronouns to represent both men and women. Also, use parallel treatment when referring to males and females. Finally, demonstrate respect for your audience by avoiding inappropriate humor. That means refrain from telling a dirty joke, making a sexist remark, or using profanity in the name of humor. Doing any of these things is likely to offend some listeners and should be avoided in public speeches.

Being vivid means using language and style that arouse emotions. You can do so by using descriptions that appeal to the senses of seeing, hearing, tasting, touching, smelling, and feeling. You can also be vivid by using figures and structures of speech. Some effective techniques include alliteration, assonance, onomatopoeia, personification, repetition, antithesis, simile, metaphor, and analogy. Your goal is to use vivid language and style to inspire audiences to listen and remember your ideas.

Effective public speech structure is not complete until you incorporate language and style that ensure understanding and inspire listeners by painting word pictures and arousing emotions. To be an effective public speaker, integrate strategic language and style choices as you finalize your formal outline. You must consider both macrostructure and microstructure to achieve a truly effective public speech.

ACTIVITIES

1. **Music Lyric Analysis.** Select a favorite song and examine the lyrics to discover what language and style strategies are used to (a) communicate inclusion or exclusion and (b) paint vivid word pictures and arouse emotions. Ask yourself these questions:
   - Does the song use "we" language?
   - Does the song use bias-free language?
   - Does the song appeal to the senses?
   - Does the song use figures and structures of speech?
2. **Being Bias-Free.** Form pairs. With your partner, change the following terms and phrases to make them inclusive and less biased:
   - Manpower.
   - Mothering.
   - Male secretary.
   - Men and ladies.
   - Businessmen and their wives.
   - Disabled person.
   - Man (verb).
3. **Using Vivid Oral Style.** In groups of four or five students each, select an article from a magazine or newspaper. Examine where the article attempts to be vivid by appealing to sense or using figures and structures of speech. Change some sentences to make them do so more effectively. Now, rephrase the article according to the three key components of oral style: (a) Use personal pronouns, especially "we" language. (b) Use simple language and sentence structure. (c) Use repetition. Have two volunteers from the group present the two versions of the article to the class. Discuss which version is more effective and why.
4. **Examining a Speech.** In groups of four or five students each, identify and discuss the language techniques used by Mary Fisher in "Whisper of AIDS." Focus on strategies of (a) accuracy, (b) clarity, (c) inclusion, and (d) vividness. Once the groups are finished, share what was discovered with the entire class and create a master list of the strategies employed.

WHISPER OF AIDS

Mary Fisher

Less than three months ago, at platform hearings in Salt Lake City, I asked the Republican Party to lift the shroud of silence which has been draped over the issue of HIV/AIDS. I have come tonight to bring our silence to an end.

I hear a message of challenge, not self-congratulation. I want your attention, not your applause. I would never have asked to be HIV-positive. But I believe that in all things there is a good purpose, and so I stand before you, and before the nation, gladly.

The reality of AIDS is brutally clear. Two hundred thousand Americans are dead or dying; a million more are infected. Worldwide, forty million, or sixty million, or a hundred million infections will be counted in the coming few years. But despite science and research, White House meetings and congressional hearings; despite good intentions and bold initiatives, campaign slogans and hopeful promises—despite it all, it's the epidemic which is winning tonight.

In the context of an election year, I ask you—here, in this great hall, or listening in the quiet of your home—to recognize that the AIDS virus is not a political creature. It does not care whether you are Democrat or Republican. It does not ask whether you are black or white, male or female, gay or straight, young or old.

Tonight, I represent an AIDS community whose members have been reluctantly drafted from every segment of American society. Though I am white, and a mother, I am one with a black infant struggling with tubes in a Philadelphia hospital. Though I am female, and contracted this disease in marriage, and enjoy the warm support of my family, I am one with the lonely gay man sheltering a flickering candle from the cold wind of his family's rejection.

This is not a distant threat; it is a present danger. The rate of infection is increasing fastest among women and children. Largely unknown a decade ago, AIDS is the third leading killer of young-adult Americans today—but it won't be third for long. Because, unlike other diseases, this one travels. Adolescents don't give each other cancer or heart disease because they believe they are in love. But HIV is different. And we have helped it along—we have killed each other—with our ignorance, our prejudice, and our silence.

We may take refuge in our stereotypes, but we cannot hide there long. Because HIV asks only one thing of those it attacks: Are you human? And this is the right question: Are you human? Because people with HIV have not entered some alien state of being. They are human. They have not earned cruelty and they do not deserve meanness. They don't benefit from being isolated or treated as outcasts. Each of them is exactly what God made: a person. Not evil, deserving of our judgment; not victims, longing for our pity. People. Ready for support and worthy of compassion.

My call to you, my Party, is to take a public stand no less compassionate than that of the President and Mrs. Bush. They have embraced me and my family in memorable ways. In the place of judgment, they have shown affection. In difficult moments, they have raised our spirits. In the darkest hours, I have seen them reaching out not only to me, but also to my parents, armed with that stunning grief and special grace that comes only to parents who have themselves leaned too long over the bedside of a dying child.

With the President's leadership, much good has been done; much of the good has gone unheralded; as the President has insisted, "Much remains to be done."

But we do the President's cause no good if we praise the American family but ignore a virus that destroys it. We must be consistent if we are to be believed. We cannot love justice and ignore prejudice, love our children and fear to teach them. Whatever our role, as parent or policy maker, we must act as eloquently as we speak—else we have no integrity.

My call to the nation is a plea for awareness. If you believe you are safe, you are in danger. Because I was not hemophiliac, I was not at risk. Because I was not gay, I was not at risk. Because I did not inject drugs, I was not at risk.

My father has devoted much of his lifetime to guarding against another holocaust. He is part of the generation who heard Pastor Niemoeller come out of the Nazi death camps to say, "They came after the Jews and I was not a Jew, so I did not protest. They came after the Trade Unionists, and I was not a Trade Unionist, so I did not protest. They came after the Roman Catholics, and I was not a Roman Catholic, so I did not protest. Then they came after me, and there was no one left to protest."

The lesson history teaches is this: If you believe you are safe, you are at risk. If you do not see this killer stalking your children, look again. There is no family or community, no race or religion, no place left in America that is safe. Until we genuinely embrace this message, we are a nation at risk.

Tonight, HIV marches resolutely toward AIDS in more than a million American homes, littering its pathway with the bodies of the young. Young men. Young women. Young parents. Young children. One of the families is mine. If it is true that HIV inevitably turns to AIDS, then my children will inevitably turn to orphans.

My family has been a rock of support. My eighty-four-year-old father, who has pursued the healing of nations, will not accept the premise that he cannot heal his daughter. My mother has refused to be broken; she still calls at midnight to tell wonderful jokes that make me laugh. Sisters and friends, and my brother Phillip (whose birthday is today)—all have helped carry me over the hardest places. I am blessed, richly and deeply blessed, to have such a family.

But not all of you have been so blessed. You are HIV-positive but dare not say it. You have lost loved ones, but you dared not whisper the word AIDS. You weep silently; you grieve alone.

I have a message for you: It is not you who should feel shame; it is we. We who tolerate ignorance and practice prejudice, we who have taught you to fear. We must lift our shroud of silence, making it safe for you to reach out for compassion. It is our task to seek safety for our children, not in quiet denial but in effective action.

Some day our children will be grown. My son Max, now four, will take the measure of his mother; my son Zachary, now two, will sort through his memories. I may not be here to hear their judgments, but I know already what I hope they are.

I want my children to know that their mother was not a victim. She was a messenger. I do not want them to think, as I once did, that courage is the absence of fear; I want them to know that courage is the strength to act wisely when most we are afraid. I want them to have the courage to step forward when called by their nation, or their Party, and give leadership—no matter what the personal cost. I ask no more of you than I ask of myself, or of my children.

To the millions of you who are grieving, who are frightened, who have suffered the ravages of AIDS firsthand: Have courage and you will find comfort.

To the millions who are strong, I issue this plea: Set aside prejudice and politics to make room for compassion and sound policy.

To my children, I make this pledge: I will not give in, Zachary, because I draw my courage from you. Your silly giggle gives me hope. Your gentle prayers give me strength. And you, my child, give me reason to say to America, "You are at risk." And I will not rest, Max, until I have done all I can to make your world safe. I will seek a place where intimacy is not the prelude to suffering.

I will not hurry to leave you, my children. But when I go, I pray that you will not suffer shame on my account.

To all within the sound of my voice, I appeal: Learn with me the lessons of history and of grace, so my children will not be afraid to say the word AIDS when I am gone. Then their children, and yours, may not need to whisper it at all.

God bless the children, and bless us all.

Mary Fisher, Republican National Convention, Houston, Texas, August 19, 1992.

Key Terms

Accuracy
Active sentence
Alliteration
Analogy
Antithesis
Assonance
Cliché
Concrete words
Connotation
Denotation
Dialect
Figures of speech
Gender-linked terms
Inclusion
Intelligible
Jargon
Metaphor
Microstructure

Onomatopoeia
Oral style
Parallel treatment
Passive sentence
Personification
Political correctness
Repetition
Simile
Slang
Standard English
Structures of speech
Thesaurus
Verbal immediacy
Vivid language and style
Vocalized pauses
Worldview

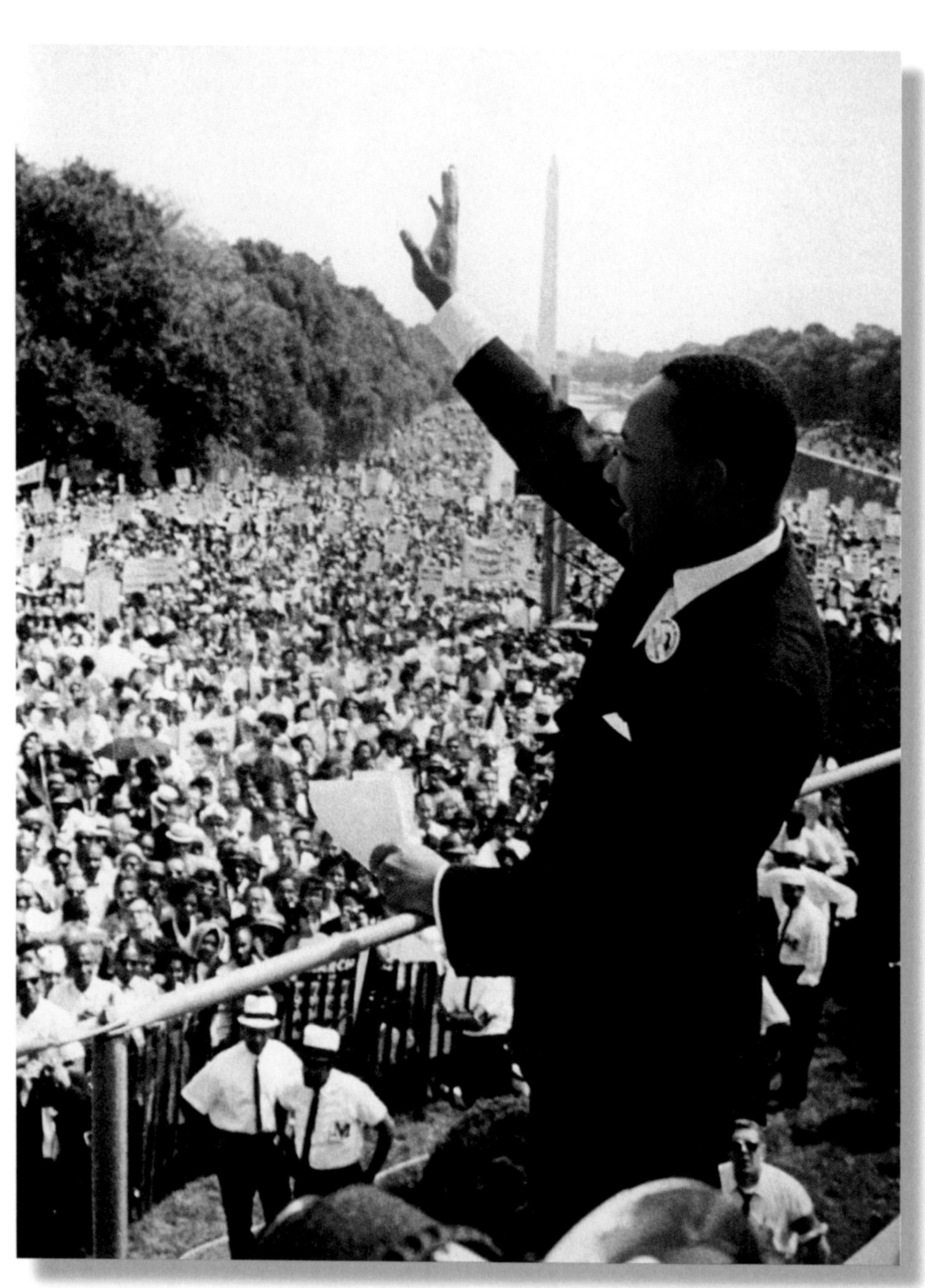

CHAPTER 12

Delivering Your Public Speech

Reflective Questions

1. What worries you most about speaking in front of a group?
2. Why is delivery so important to your message?
3. Why is it important to vary your voice when you speak?
4. Why is it important to dress up when you give a public speech?
5. How should you practice oral delivery?
6. How should you practice facial expressions? Gestures? Movement?

Trini had spent two weeks researching and preparing her speech. She drafted her speech several times before finally deciding how to organize it and had even asked several friends to offer suggestions on her outline. She was certain that her speech was thoroughly prepared. As she walked to the front of the room to deliver her speech, however, her hands began to shake. And as she began to speak, her voice quivered. It seemed to her that everyone was watching her hands shake rather than listening to her message. Her anxiety got worse as she continued. In fact, she began to have difficulty focusing on the message. Ultimately, she lost her place, skipped over most of her third main point, and finished in less time than was required. Trini returned to her seat frustrated and disgusted.

Teaching Tip
Refer students to the SpeechMaker CD-ROM. This software provides several tips for effective delivery. Consider assigning one of the scenarios to be completed before the class in which you will discuss this chapter.

Although Trini did research and structure her speech thoroughly, she wasn't thoroughly prepared. Being prepared also means practicing your delivery a number of times, including at least once in front of others. Because Trini hadn't practiced her delivery, she didn't feel comfortable with either her speech or the presence of an audience, and her fear of these unknowns increased her speech anxiety. As a result, despite all her other preparation, she was not effective when she presented her speech.

Although public speaking anxiety can occur at various points during the speech preparation process, for most people it's most strongly associated with delivery. Yet delivery practice is the step that beginning speakers most often neglect. Taking time to practice your speech is the most important strategy you can use to reduce your anxiety.

In this chapter, we'll start by looking at why delivery is so important to effective public speaking. Then we'll turn to the characteristics of delivery, the principles and types of nonverbal communication, and the methods and strategies you should use in order to deliver your speech effectively and reduce your public speaking anxiety. These tips will improve your effectiveness, not only in the classroom but also in the world beyond it.

Why Is Delivery So Important?

Technology Tip
http://www.historychannel.com/historychannel/gspeech/archieve.html
The History Channel Web site contains several historically significant speeches. Have students select a speaker and evaluate her or his delivery.

All the useful strategies we've discussed so far—for example, analyzing your audience; determining a topic and purpose; and researching, preparing, and organizing your ideas—can go to waste if you are unable to communicate those ideas effectively in your oral presentation. To be an effective public speaker, you must know what you want to say (content), organize it in a way that makes sense (structure), and communicate it in a way that is compelling (delivery). **Delivery** refers to the way you communicate your message orally and visually through your use of voice, face, and body.

Don't underestimate the importance of delivery. According to research, listeners tend to be influenced more by delivery than by the actual content of speeches (Decker, 1992). In fact, some 55 to 90 percent of the meaning listeners grasp is essentially derived from delivery. This is significant because effective delivery can make your message more compelling. You can construct an *adequate* public speech that seems *great* to your listeners simply because you delivered it effectively. It is also significant because ineffective delivery can cause listeners to miss the whole point you are trying to convey. You can construct an *excellent* public speech that *fails* to reach your listeners simply because you delivered it ineffectively.

Your goal, of course, is to construct an excellent public speech *and* to deliver it effectively. If you do so, your message is likely to be remembered by listeners well beyond the occasion of the speech.

What Are the Characteristics of Effective Delivery?

> ***What Do You Think?***
>
> *Consider a speaker you thought was really good. Why do you remember him or her? What was most inspiring to you—the ideas conveyed or the manner in which he or she conveyed them? Why?*

To understand effective delivery, we need to first look more closely at what delivery is. In contrast to the words of your speech, which are conveyed through the *verbal channel,* delivery is conveyed through the *nonverbal channel.* Hence, **nonverbal communication** consists of all those elements of your speech other than the words themselves that can contribute to the message. These nonverbal elements include characteristics of your voice, the eye contact you make, your facial expressions, gestures, body language, and even your appearance. Hence, effective delivery means effective use of these nonverbal elements.

Teaching Tip
Show videotapes of student speeches that demonstrate effective and ineffective delivery. Have students evaluate the implications of delivery for communication effectiveness.

Effective delivery has two main characteristics. First, effective delivery is listener centered—that is, the nonverbal channel is used to reinforce the verbal message, making it more compelling to listeners. A prerequisite to reinforcing your verbal message nonverbally is to avoid sending nonverbal messages that either distract from or contradict the verbal message. If listeners notice how you pace back and forth or how you periodically brush your hair from your face or even how you repeatedly gesture for no apparent reason, they are momentarily distracted from the message itself.

Second, effective delivery is conversational—that is, you sound and look as though you are talking with your listeners rather than presenting in front of them or reading to them. In other words, public speaking is communication, not performance. Although your delivery is a bit more dramatic than casual conversation, it is not theatrical. Even though you've practiced your speech strategically and have planned where and how to gesture, pause, and so forth, you still appear natural—and, thus, comfortable and sincere—to your audience.

If your delivery is both listener centered and conversational, the nonverbal elements of your speech appear spontaneous as they reinforce your verbal message. The best way to achieve this effective delivery is to practice your speech sufficiently and then, when you give it, to concentrate on the message and on whether the audience appears to be understanding it, rather than on how you look or sound.

Principles of Nonverbal Communication

To use nonverbal cues to effectively reinforce the verbal message, you need to understand four basic principles of nonverbal communication as they relate to public speaking delivery:

Teaching Tip
Remind students that it is critical that nonverbal cues are consistent with and complement verbal cues. Provide examples of how conflicting nonverbal and verbal cues may decrease the effectiveness of a speech.

- Nonverbal communication is inevitable.
- Nonverbal communication is culturally and situationally bound.

- Nonverbal cues are believed.
- Nonverbal cues are seldom isolated.

Nonverbal Communication Is Inevitable

When it comes to nonverbal communication, we cannot *not* communicate (Watzlawick, Bavelas, & Jackson, 1967). You send nonverbal messages whether you intend to or not, whether you are speaking or silent, and whether or not others perceive the messages.

Consider, for example, the first day of this class. What did you wear? What might that have communicated about you to others? Did you think the class would be fun, boring, interesting, or difficult? How might the way you walked into the room and the way you sat down have communicated your expectations? Did you look at your instructor as he or she talked? What might this eye contact or lack of it have communicated? Now consider your classmates on that first day of class. What assumptions did you make about each of them and why? Since we communicate nonverbally all the time, effective public speakers strive to make sure their nonverbal messages reinforce the verbal messages they send.

Nonverbal Communication Is Culturally and Situationally Bound

Teaching Tip
Have students write a brief essay in which they explore three examples of the similarities and differences between verbal and nonverbal communication. In addition, encourage students to examine how they might use nonverbal communication to complement their verbal cues in their next speech.

Nonverbal communication is culturally bound—that is, very few nonverbal cues mean the same thing to everyone. Although these principles apply across cultures, keep in mind that many nonverbal cues mean different things in different cultures and sometimes even in different situations. The discussion in this chapter is based mainly on the nonverbal cues used in mainstream American culture. However, if you speak to an audience that is primarily of another culture or culturally diverse, you should be aware of potential differences and adapt your speech accordingly so you don't unintentionally offend anyone.

In the mainstream American culture, for example, direct eye contact is usually interpreted as a sign of respect toward a speaker. In many Native American cultures, however, direct eye contact could be interpreted as a sign of disrespect if the speaker is a superior. Likewise, the hand gesture commonly used in the United States to signal "okay" has a vulgar meaning in Mexico and means "I'll kill you" in Tunisia.

> **What Do You Think?**
> *Have you ever felt offended or insulted by someone from another culture? Was it something you said or did? Was it something the other person said or did? Was the offense intentional?*

> **What Do You Think?**
> *Consider a time when someone misinterpreted what you meant. What sort of nonverbal cues might you have been sending to contribute to the misinterpretation?*

Teaching Tip
To give students an opportunity to practice effective nonverbal communication, assign the Nursery Rhymes or Conveying Emotions Nonverbally exercise in the Activities section of this chapter.

Nonverbal communication is also situationally bound. Because they are ambiguous, the same nonverbal cues might mean different things in different situations. In one situation a furrowed brow could mean you are confused, and in another situation the same expression could mean you are angry. That is, the meaning of a particular nonverbal cue can differ based on the situation. For example, Jesse was presenting a public speech about the civil rights movement in the United States. When he noticed that Byron had his head on his desk, Jesse assumed Byron was bored. Actually, Byron had pulled an all-nighter studying for an exam he would be taking later that day. In another part of the room, Monica was fidgeting and glancing at the clock. Jesse wondered if she was offended by his comments. Actually, Monica was worried about getting to a job interview immediately following class. Jesse became unnecessarily nervous because he misinterpreted these ambiguous nonverbal cues.

Nonverbal Cues Are Believed

When your verbal and nonverbal messages contradict each other, listeners are more likely to believe the nonverbal messages than the verbal messages. Have you ever asked a friend whether something looks good on you and gotten the response, "I think it looks good," and not believed it? Quite likely, you did not believe your friend because something in his or her tone of voice, facial expressions, or body language contradicted the verbal message.

Teaching Tip
To help students understand effective verbal and nonverbal delivery, see the Music Lyrics Interpretation assignment in the Activities section of this chapter.

What Do You Think?

Consider a time when you thought someone was lying to you. What sort of nonverbal messages contributed to your belief that they were not telling the truth?

This principle is crucial to public speaking. Timothy, for example, began his presentation by saying, "Each of us is contributing to the destruction of the planet every time we throw a soda can or a newspaper in the garbage. I'm here to convince you to do your part to save the earth by making recycling a habit in your life." But when he delivered it, he was barely audible, he shifted from foot to foot, and he never looked up from his notes. Although Timothy is an ecology major fully committed to recycling garbage and the words of his speech made this clear, his listeners were not persuaded because his voice and body language contradicted his verbal message.

In short, Timothy's message failed to reach his listeners because his nonverbal cues contradicted his verbal message and, when verbals and nonverbals contradict, listeners tend to believe the nonverbal over the verbal message.

Nonverbal Cues Are Seldom Isolated

A final principle of nonverbal communication that relates directly to public speaking is that nonverbal cues are seldom isolated. Most nonverbal messages are simultaneously conveyed by several cues. No wonder listeners tend to believe the nonverbal over the verbal when those messages contradict each other! Consider Timothy again. He sent one verbal message: We must recycle. Attached to that verbal message were several nonverbal cues, all of which contradicted the verbal message. As a result, listeners were left unconvinced.

Obviously, nonverbal communication plays a crucial role in getting your message across. That said, let's discuss the types of nonverbal communication cues as they relate to public speaking.

Types of Nonverbal Cues

Technology Tip
http://www.houckassociates.com/hint6.htm

The Houck Associates Web site summarizes research findings regarding nonverbal communication. Have students visit this site and report their findings to the class.

Six types of nonverbal cues directly relate to public speaking. These are use of (a) space, (b) time, (c) appearance, (d) eye contact, (e) body, and (f) voice. Public speakers are often trained to consider only two of these types, use of body and use of voice. Certainly, these are crucial components of effective delivery. They are also relatively complex components: Use of body includes use of facial expressions, gestures, posture, and body movement. Use of voice includes quality, rate, volume, pitch, pronunciation, enunciation, stress, and pauses. However, the other four types of nonverbal cues also impact public speech delivery. We will now look at each type and consider how it can be used to enhance effective delivery.

Space

As a public speaker, you may or may not be able to influence how far you are from your audience or how your listeners are seated. If you are able to influence these factors, you can use space in the way that is most conducive to effective delivery. The way in which space and distance communicates is also known as **proxemics** (Hall, 1968).

You'll want to stand at a distance where you and your listeners can easily and comfortably make eye contact. Basically, the more people involved in a communication transaction, the more space speakers must place between themselves and their listeners. Smaller audiences, ranging from about ten to thirty people, can be addressed most effectively from a distance of four to eight feet. For most public speaking classes, this is the ideal distance. Of course, you can move around within that range during your presentation. However, you should avoid moving farther from your audience because you could appear too formal, cold, or distant, and should avoid moving closer so that listeners in the front won't feel you've come too close. Large audiences, of forty or more people, must be addressed at a distance of more than eight feet. With a smaller audience, you need to connect with each audience member, usually through eye contact. With a large audience, such as you'd find in a lecture hall or auditorium, it is not possible to recognize audience members as individuals. Instead, you must try to create a sense of audience contact, which creates a feeling of contact without a direct meeting of the eyes between the speaker and each listener (Barker, Cegala, Kibbler, and Wahlers, 1979).

Discussion Tip
How much should you move around the room when speaking? According to Sellnow, why should speakers avoid moving farther away from the audience?

Note that these ideal distances might be different if you're speaking to an audience from another culture. For example, in many Latin American and Mediterranean countries, people tend to stand closer to one another when interacting, and the distance between a public speaker and his or her audience might be less as well (Lustig & Keoster, 1993).

> ***What Do You Think?***
>
> *Consider a class you've taken where the seats were arranged in a semicircle and one where they were arranged in a traditional lecture hall style. Which class had more discussion and interaction? What role might the seating arrangement have played?*

Two other aspects of space may influence your public speech delivery. These are group density and seating arrangement. **Group density** has to do with how crowded the room feels to the audience members. Generally, if your listeners are seated at least one and one-half feet apart from one another, they'll be best able

The effect of your speech can be influenced by how crowded the room feels.

to attend to and retain your message. Audience members who are less than one foot apart tend to be more easily distracted and have a reduced attention span. When this is the case, you might shorten your speech a bit and provide more variety in your delivery to help maintain interest throughout. For most public speeches, in or out of the classroom, audience members sit in rows and face the speaker. This arrangement is common for formal speeches, since it focuses listeners on the speaker and the speaker's message. For small group discussions, audience members are usually arranged in a semicircle in front of the speaker. Such an arrangement can encourage interaction and can even reduce speech anxiety. The speaker is not as afraid of being stared at, because listeners tend to look at each other as well as at the speaker.

Use of Space Checklist

- Consider the size of your audience.
- Consider the cultural context for your speech.
- Consider the size of the room where you'll speak.
- Consider group density.
- Consider seating arrangements.

Time

Like other nonverbal messages, the messages we send through our use of time depends on the cultural context. The meanings we attach to time are known as **chronemics.** People from Western cultures tend to be very time conscious. We carry daily planners and wear digital watches so that we can arrive and depart at precisely the "right time." In contrast, people from many other cultures are far less time conscious. Thus the two rules given here, which are based on a strict concept of punctuality, might not apply in different cultures. However, they are important to effective delivery in mainstream American culture.

Discussion Tip
Why is it important that you arrive a bit early for your next speech? What are the implications of not adhering to the time limit in terms of speaker credibility?

First, arrive a bit early to set up for your speech. Arriving at the last minute tends to send a message that you are unprepared, inconsiderate, incompetent, or uncommitted to the topic and occasion. You probably would not arrive late or even just in time for a job interview because an employer might think you did not care that much about getting the job. In the same way, listeners would be likely to think you did not care that much about sharing your message with them.

Second, adhere to the time limit your audience expects. Sometimes students argue that it's unrealistic to have time limits for their speeches. They point out that, in the real world, speakers are not penalized for speaking for more or less time than expected. That may be true in a literal sense; however, failing to adhere to time limit expectations sends the wrong message to listeners and, in this way, takes away from the success of a presentation. When a presentation is shorter than listeners expect, we tend to perceive the speaker as cheating us. When it is longer, we tend to perceive the speaker as inconsiderate of our time. You'll have a sense of this if you've ever had an instructor who repeatedly kept the class beyond the scheduled class time.

What Do You Think?

Can you think of someone you know who is perpetually late for engagements? How do you feel about your relationship with that person as a result?

Use of Time Checklist

- Arrive a bit early.
- Adhere to time limit expectations.

Discussion Tip
How should you dress for your next speech? In what ways can personal appearance be used to reinforce your message?

Appearance

Students sometimes argue that what they wear should not be a factor in determining the success of their performance. Yet studies show that a neatly groomed and professional appearance does send important messages about a speaker's commitment to the topic and occasion as well as about their credibility (Bate, 1992; Cherulnik, 1989; Lawrence & Watson, 1991; Molloy, 1975; Temple & Loewen, 1993). Appearance is only one nonverbal factor, but, like the others, it should reinforce your message and should certainly not distract from it. This concept of appearance as it communicates is known as **object language.** Looking like a professional tends to improve speaker credibility (ethos). Would you wear jeans and a sweatshirt to a job interview? Probably not. Most business professionals realize the importance of appearance to help generate respect (Blouin et al., 1982; Drogosz & Levy, 1996). Furthermore, feeling good about how you look can reduce speech anxiety by reducing tension stemming from the fear of being stared at.

What Do You Think?

Identify a time when you used clothing to create a favorable impression. What were the results? Now consider a time when you judged a speaker poorly based on appearance. What was it about that speaker's appearance that caused your negative evaluation and why?

Three general rules can help you decide how to dress and groom yourself for a presentation. First, avoid extremes. Matt's tuxedo and Angela's large, dangling ear-

"Tell me about yourself, Kugelman—your hopes, dreams, career path, and what that damn earring means."

From The Wall Street Journal —Permission, Cartoon Features Syndicate.

rings and bright red lipstick were too extreme and tended to distract listeners. This rule applies even to attire related to the speech topic. Tina, for example, wore a tutu to present her speech about ballet dancing. Although she wore the tutu to reinforce her verbal message, the tutu was so extreme a choice that it distracted listeners. Josh, on the other hand, who worked as a mail carrier, wore his uniform to deliver a speech about the U.S. postal service. His attire was novel, yet not so extreme as to prove distracting.

Second, consider the audience and occasion for the speech and dress a bit more formally than your listeners are likely to be dressed. Speakers who dress too formally tend to be perceived as untrustworthy and insincere (Phillips & Smith, 1992). Those who dress too casually are likely to appear uncommitted to the topic and occasion (Morris, Gorham, Cohen, & Huffman, 1996). An evening gown would probably be too formal for a classroom speech but quite appropriate for an after-dinner speech at an honorary society banquet. Likewise, jeans and a flannel shirt might be too casual for a classroom speech but quite appropriate for an oral presentation about fertilizers to area farmers. Dressing a bit more formally than your listeners tends to boost your credibility and communicate a sense of commitment to the topic and occasion.

Finally, consider your topic and purpose. Some topics demand a more formal appearance than others. If you are telling listeners how to succeed on a job interview, you should dress more formally than if you are telling them about co-curricular activities on campus. You might dress even more formally if you are trying to convince listeners to support an important cause. Generally, the more serious your topic and purpose, the more formally you should dress.

Appearance Checklist

- Avoid extremes.
- Consider the audience and occasion.
- Consider your topic and purpose.

Eye Contact

Discussion Tip
How can eye contact be used to include listeners in the communication transaction? What guidelines does Sellnow provide for establishing and maintaining eye contact?

Our eyes are probably our most expressive source of nonverbal communication. Moreover, eye contact is an important way to include listeners in the communication transaction. Thus, the three guidelines that follow all relate to maximizing your use of eye contact. Keep in mind, however, that, as mentioned earlier, cultural orientation shapes how we use and interpret eye contact.

First, attempt to look at your audience at least 90 percent of the time. Although you may not achieve this goal, setting your standards high will increase the likelihood you'll make sufficient audience contact. Use your notes only as a reference; don't read directly from them, and refer to them only periodically. Since our eyes express so much, the more you look at your listeners instead of your notes, the more you can support your message nonverbally with your eyes.

Second, span the entire audience with your eyes. This is important since public speaking is audience centered. Beginning speakers have a tendency to neglect listeners seated in the corners of the room. And all of us tend to favor one side of the room over the other. This tendency often corresponds to the hand we favor. I am left-handed and tend to look more to the left side than to the right side. Knowing I have this tendency, I make a conscious effort to direct my eye contact to listeners seated on the right side of the room as well.

> ***What Do You Think?***
>
> *Do you know which side you tend to favor when you speak? How might this affect your audience contact with listeners who may be seated on the other side of the room?*

Teaching Tip
Assign an impromptu speech and instruct students to attempt to look at the audience 90 percent of the time they speak. This activity will give students valuable speaking experience and assuage their anxiety about maintaining eye contact.

Finally, look listeners in the eye. Sometimes beginning speakers argue that looking listeners in the eye will increase anxiety. They say they would prefer to gaze over the heads of their listeners. Looking listeners in the eye is a much more effective strategy, for several reasons. First and foremost, most listeners will offer positive reinforcement when you look them in the eye; for example, they'll nod and smile. As a result, your anxiety is more likely to decrease when you look listeners in the eye. Second, when you look listeners in the eye, they tend to feel more like you are communicating with them and that they matter to you and your message. Third, looking listeners in the eye gives you a chance to read their feedback and adjust your message as necessary. For example, Tasha noticed that several members of her audience had quizzical looks on their faces as she explained the process of external combustion. Because she observed their feedback, she took the time to rephrase her explanation until those quizzical looks changed into affirming nods. If you are speaking in a large auditorium, you must create a sense of looking listeners in the eye even though you cannot actually do so. This is known as **audience contact.**

Eye Contact Checklist

- Look up from your notes 90 percent of the time.
- Span the entire audience.
- Look listeners in the eye.

Body

The body communicates in various ways, including through facial expressions, gestures, posture, and body movements. This form of nonverbal communication

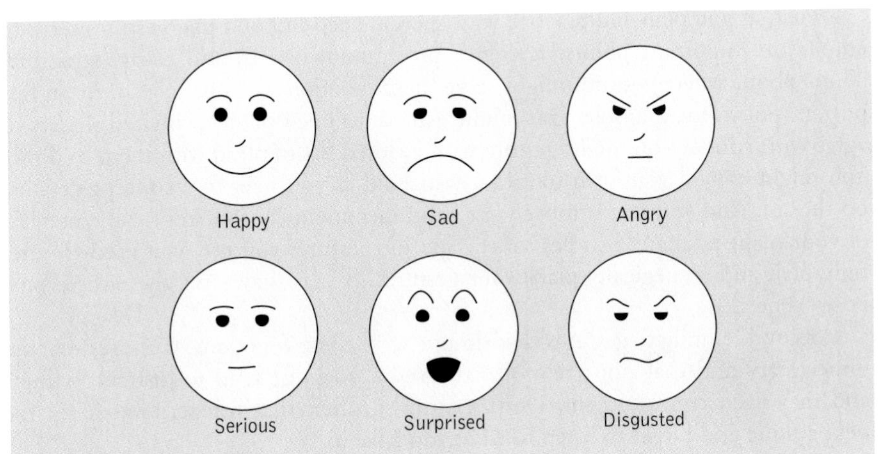

FIGURE 12–1
Using Your Face to Convey Emotions

is known as **kinesics.** Your goal as a public speaker is to use your body in a way that appears appropriate and natural, dynamic, and integrated with your verbal message.

Facial Expressions

Facial expressions can reinforce a wide range of verbal messages (see Figure 12–1). For example, Nancy furrowed her brows and pursed her lips when she told the story of two young children who were abandoned in a parking lot. Her facial expression conveyed her sense of seriousness and disgust. Thad raised his eyebrows and smiled slightly as he talked about the many new forms of entertainment a domed stadium would bring to the city. His facial expression conveyed a sense of excitement. In my experience, most beginning speakers are reluctant to include facial expressions that emotionally reinforce the verbal message. When they do, however, the increased appeal of their speech is dramatic.

Teaching Tip
Show videotapes of students presenting speeches and instruct the class to evaluate the speakers' facial expressions. Do the facial expressions reinforce or contradict the verbal messages?

The most effective facial expressions are lively and yet they appear natural and spontaneous. This is not to say, however, that they *are* natural and spontaneous. Effective facial expressions must be planned and practiced in advance. You need to go through your speech outline and determine where a facial expression could reinforce an emotional stance, decide what that facial expression might be, make a note to yourself on your speaking outline, and practice your speech using that expression. I suggest doing so in front of a mirror. This way, you can learn precisely what it feels like when you achieve the natural, yet expressive, facial expression you desire. Hence, you'll be more likely to replicate the appropriate facial expression during your actual speech.

Gestures

Discussion Tip
How can gestures be employed to emphasize an important point, reference presentational aids, and clarify structure? What guidelines does Sellnow offer for the use of gestures?

Gestures effectively reinforce the verbal message in one of three ways: They can (a) emphasize an important point, (b) reference presentational aids, or (c) clarify structure. As with facial expressions, effective gestures must appear spontaneous and natural, yet they must be carefully planned and practiced. Here are some guidelines to follow in planning and using gestures.

First, as you plan and practice your speech, keep in mind that gestures serve to emphasize important points, reference presentational aids, and clarify structure. Think about where gestures might serve these functions in your speech. At an important point, for example, you might extend an open palm to invite listeners to agree with you, or you might gesture with a closed fist to plead with them to do so. You might extend your arm toward a visual aid as you refer to a concept detailed on the aid. And you might move your hand incrementally to reinforce the preview of your main points. Regardless of the specific gestures you use, you need to carefully plan and strategically place your gestures so that they serve these three purposes as needed.

Second, eliminate gestures that do not serve these functions. Gestures that are unnecessary and that don't reinforce the verbal message tend to distract listeners and may even confuse them. Don't gesture so often that listeners watch for the next gesture and forget to listen to what you have to say.

Third, gesture from the elbow rather than from the wrist. Gestures that extend from the elbow are more natural looking. Practice gestures while sitting at a table, making your gestures above the table, not under it. This will ensure that you don't fall victim to the "penguin effect." Also, when you use a gesture to reference a presentational aid, be sure to use the hand closest to the aid in order to keep from turning your back to your audience.

Discussion Tip
How might planning and practicing your gestures help to reduce public speaking anxiety? What types of gestures will you use in your next speech?

You may find that planning and practicing your gestures has an added benefit. Some speakers claim that they get more nervous because they don't know what to do with their hands while they speak. If you work on your gestures, you will be able to use your hands purposefully. For example, Mason's speech anxiety showed because he would periodically stick his hand into his pocket and then remove it. Consequently, his listeners began watching his hand-to-pocket action rather than listening to his message. This made Mason more anxious. He knew listeners were watching his hands and yet he felt so awkward that he couldn't stop making the distracting gestures. Once Mason began planning specific gestures to reinforce certain points and practicing those gestures in advance, his awkward feelings dissipated and the distracting gesture ceased.

Posture

When you give a speech, you can convey confidence and commitment through the way you stand and carry yourself. Effective public speakers use **posture** before they begin speaking, during their speech, and as they conclude the speech.

Listeners begin to evaluate you from the moment you walk to the front of the room. To send a message of calm confidence (regardless of whether you feel calm and confident), take your time walking to the front of the room and walk with your shoulders back, not slumped. Once there, pause for a moment or two and establish eye contact with a few listeners before beginning your speech. This pause creates a sense of **initial ethos,** or credibility.

During the speech, stand firmly on both feet, keeping your feet about shoulder width apart. Do not slouch or lean on one leg. These postures tend to communicate a lack of commitment to the topic and occasion. Likewise, do not shift back and forth from one leg to the other or rock forward and backward on your heels. These postures communicate nervousness and tend to distract listeners from the message. Don't lock your knees because this could cause your knees to shake and communicate nervousness. Standing firmly on both feet while you speak communicates both confidence and commitment to the topic and occasion.

Finally, use posture to create a sense of **terminal ethos,** or closing credibility, as well. You can achieve this by pausing a moment or two and looking a few listeners in the eye upon finishing your conclusion. Although this pause might feel a bit awkward at first, it will leave your listeners believing in your commitment to the topic and occasion.

Body Movement

Some people feel more comfortable speaking when they can move around a bit. Effective movement can also help maintain listener interest by appealing to the visual dimension of the learning cycle. If you choose to move during your speech, your goal is to employ motivated movement. **Motivated movement** reinforces the verbal message by emphasizing important points, referencing presentational aids, or clarifying structure. As such, motivated movement is conducted together with a gesture to make the function even clearer. In other words, movement is not appropriate unless it embellishes a gesture.

Teaching Tip
Students are often reluctant to move while speaking. You can encourage students to move by explaining that motivated movement can reduce speaking anxiety because it presents a positive way to channel energy.

Movement in a public speech, then, operates much the same as do gestures, and the same guidelines apply. Movement that can reinforce the verbal message should be planned and practiced. Other movements should be avoided, because too much movement and movement that is not motivated distract from the verbal message.

To appear more natural, movement should be used together with some kind of gesture. For example, Leena's speech ended with a plea for more support from businesses for parental leave to care for sick children. Leena decided that, as she delivered this call to action, she would move forward and at the same time gesture with her palms up. In this way, her movement would appear natural and her call to action would come across as a sincere plea and not as a command. Leena's movement and gesture effectively bolstered her final emotional appeal to listeners.

Also, it is important to remain "open" to your audience when you move from side to side—that is, you don't want to create a sense of turning your back to anyone. If you choose to move from one side of the room to the other, lead with the foot that is nearest to the location where you are headed. In other words, if you are going to walk to the left, lead with your left foot and left hand simultaneously. If you are going to walk to the right, lead with your right foot and right hand simultaneously. This will ensure that you remain "open" to your audience while moving.

As with gestures, by using your body effectively during a presentation, you can reduce your speech anxiety. If you are a speaker who often feels like you need to move while you're speaking, motivated movement may relax you as well as reinforce your message.

Use of Body Checklist

- Use facial expressions that reinforce an emotional stance.
- Use gestures to emphasize important points, reference presentational aids, or clarify structure.
- Use posture that communicates initial and terminal ethos.
- Stand firmly on both feet during the speech.
- Use motivated movement with gestures to further reinforce the verbal message.

When moving, always remain "open" to your audience.

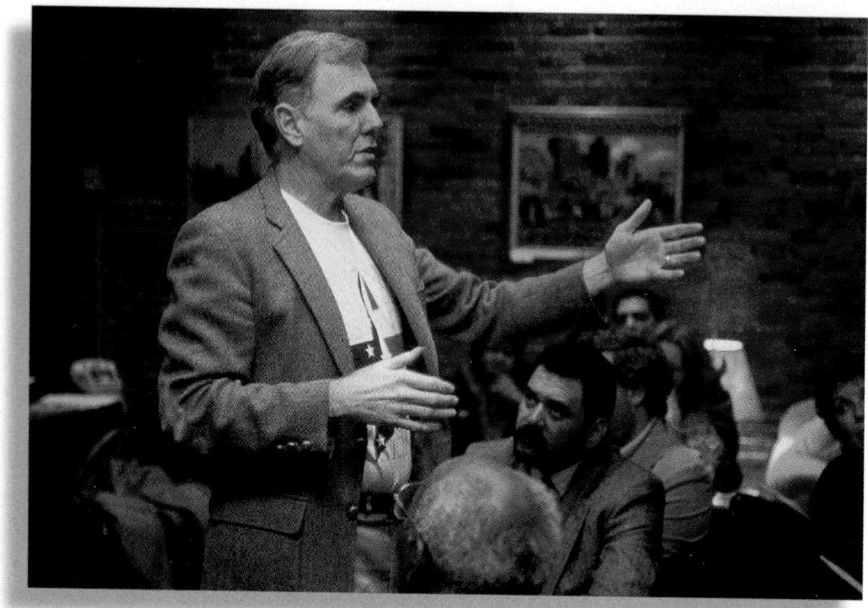

Voice

Discussion Tip
Ask students to think of the sound of different speakers' voices. Which types of voices do they perceive to be most effective? Which types of voices do they perceive to be annoying?

At the same time that you use your voice to send a verbal message, you are also using it nonverbally. Your verbal messages consist of the actual words you use—that is, of what you say. Nonverbal use of voice, in contrast, refers to all elements of voice other than the actual words—the rate, volume, pitch, quality, pronunciation, enunciation, stress, and pauses. In other words, it refers to how you say what you say. Like other aspects of nonverbal communication, nonverbal use of voice—or **paralanguage**—can contribute to meaning. For example, by changing the way I use stress in a sentence, I can convey very different meanings. Consider the sentence "Sally likes spinach." I could say "*Sally* likes spinach," meaning that Sally—not some other person—likes spinach. I could say "Sally *likes* spinach," meaning that Sally likes, rather than dislikes, spinach. I could say "Sally likes *spinach,*" meaning that Sally likes spinach rather than some other vegetable. Or I could even say "Sally likes spinach?" meaning that I didn't realize she likes spinach. Thus, when we look at use of voice as nonverbal communication, we are looking not at the words themselves, but at how we say those words.

Your goal with regard to the nonverbal elements of voice is to be intelligible, vocally varied, and, as discussed earlier, conversational. To be intelligible, you must consider quality, rate, volume, pitch, pronunciation, and enunciation. To be vocally varied, you must also consider rate, volume, and pitch, as well as stress and pauses. To be conversational, you must *sound spontaneous,* no matter how much you've practiced your speech or which delivery method you've chosen.

Intelligibility

Teaching Tip
See the Activities section of this chapter for several assignments designed to help students effectively use these nonverbal elements of voice.

Intelligibility means the capacity to be understood. If you are not intelligible, your listeners are likely to struggle with your verbal message. Moreover, intelligibility is crucial if you are to convey the message that you are a competent and credible speaker. Let's look at each aspect as it contributes to intelligibility.

Vocal quality, or **timbre,** is what distinguishes your voice from other voices. Although each voice is unique, you'll want to strive for a pleasing vocal quality. An unpleasant voice quality can hurt intelligibility because listeners tend to focus on how you sound rather than on what you're saying. To maximize the quality of your voice, you need to practice deep breathing (Activity 4) and controlled exhalation (Activity 5) and employ them whenever you give a public speech. Let's consider three of the most common problems related to vocal quality for beginning speakers: breathiness, harshness, and nasality.

If too much air escapes noticeably through the vocal folds in your throat as you speak, you'll sound feathery, fuzzy, and whispery—that is, *breathy.* The late Marilyn Monroe was famous for her breathy vocal quality, which many claim made her sound sexy. Likewise, Demi Moore, Goldie Hawn, Nicole Kidman, and Kathleen Turner have each used breathiness on occasion for this same purpose. Yet breathiness reduces ethos for public speakers because it doesn't carry well and suggests immaturity, shallowness, and a weak, frail personality (Mayer, 1994). A breathy voice comes from improper breathing habits and too little tension in the vocal folds in your throat as you speak. To reduce breathiness, in addition to deep breathing and controlled exhalation, try the cold mirror exercise (as in Activity 6).

In contrast to breathiness, if you constrict your throat too much as you speak, you'll sound *harsh.* In other words, you might sound strident, tense, and shrill like Joan Rivers or Marge Simpson or Lucille Ball and, consequently, be perceived as hypertense or abrasive. Or you might sound gravelly, gutteral, and throaty like John Wayne, Nick Nolte, or Jack Nicholson and, consequently, be perceived as cold and unsympathetic (Mayer, 1994). Either way, your intelligibility will suffer as listeners focus on the quality of your voice rather than the message you convey. If you constrict your voice while speaking for long periods of time, you'll eventually become hoarse, which will further hurt your intelligibility. To improve, in addition to deep breathing and controlled exhalation, practice speaking with a relaxed and open throat (see Activity 7).

If too much air passes through your nasal cavities as you speak, you'll sound *nasal.* Nasality is associated with immaturity, lower-than-average intelligence, and a boring personality (Mayer, 1994). Country singers like Dwight Yoakum, Dolly Parton, and George Strait are nasal. As with breathiness and harshness, nasality can hurt intelligibility as listeners focus on the sound of your voice rather than the message you are conveying. Nasality can be reduced by opening your mouth wider as you speak, relaxing your tongue in the rear of your mouth, and using crisper articulation for consonants as you speak. If you need to work on nasality, try the nasality reduction exercise described at the end of this chapter (Activity 8).

Rate refers to the speed at which the speech is delivered. Speeches should be delivered at a rate between one hundred and two hundred words per minute. Most people naturally speak at about one hundred twenty words per minute. Speaking more slowly can hurt intelligibility, because listeners might become bored and distracted from the message. Speaking more quickly directly hurts intelligibility, especially if you are presenting complex ideas and arguments.

Teaching Tip
Have students tape-record three to five minutes of their speech and calculate their speaking rate. Remind them that their rate may vary as a function of apprehension when they present in class.

Volume is how loudly or softly you speak. To be intelligible, you need to speak loudly enough to be heard easily in the back of the room but not so loudly as to bring discomfort to listeners seated near the front. This holds true whether you speak with or without a microphone. In addition to the danger of not being heard, soft-spoken speakers run the risk of losing credibility because they appear timid and unsure of themselves. Speakers who are too loud also risk losing credibility, because they may appear obnoxious or pushy.

Discussion Tip
According to Sellnow, how is volume related to perceived speaker credibility? How can you determine if you are speaking too loudly or too softly?

Pitch refers to the highness or lowness of your voice on the musical staff. Intelligible pitch is neither too high nor too low. A pitch that is too high tends to communicate nervousness; a pitch that is too low tends to sound artificial and insincere. In other words, intelligible pitch fluctuates as in normal conversation. A monotone pitch—one that does not fluctuate—can hinder intelligibility.

Pronunciation refers to how the sounds of a word are said and which parts are stressed. Think about pronunciation when you plan and practice your speech and again when you deliver it. As a general rule, use standard dictionary pronunciations, and if you are uncertain about the pronunciation of a word, look it up in a dictionary and practice saying it aloud. People mispronounce words by (a) omitting some sounds, (b) adding sounds, (c) changing the order of sounds, (d) substituting one sound for another, and (e) stressing the wrong syllables (Mayer, 1994). Some commonly mispronounced words are given in Figure 12–2, along with the correct pronunciation. Words that are mispronounced can negatively affect your credibility as well as your intelligibility.

Sometimes students argue that dialect pronunciations such as "warsh" for "wash" or "mudda" for "mother" might be more conversational than standard pronunciations if listeners are from the same region. A problem with this argument is that often there will be someone in the audience who is unfamiliar with the dialect pronunciation of a word. Wise speakers choose standard pronunciations, which everyone will recognize.

Teaching Tip
Provide class time for students to work on these aspects of delivery. Consider starting each class with one of the speaking drills contained in the Activities section of this chapter.

Enunciation is the act of speaking distinctly and clearly. In conversation we often drop sounds or run sounds together, especially when saying common combinations of words. For example, we might say "Djaeat?" for *Did you eat?* While such sloppy enunciation is common in casual conversation, a public speaker is expected to present ideas using a formal style, which includes clear enunciation. Although sloppy enunciation should not be confused with mispronunciation, it too can affect your credibility as well as intelligibility. For this reason, it is important to be

FIGURE 12–2 Commonly Mispronounced Words

Word	Correct Pronunciation	Incorrect Pronunciation
athlete	a-thlete	ath-a-lete
creek	creek	crick
environment	enviro*n*ment	enviroment
escape	e*s*cape	excape
February	Feb*r*uary	Febuary
government	gover*n*ment	goverment
hundred	hun*dred*	hunderd, hunnert
library	lib*r*ary	libary
mirror	mi*rr*or	meer
picture	pi*c*ture	pitcher
roof	roof	ruff
sandwich	san*d*wich	sanwich, samwich
wash	wash	warsh

aware of words or types of words you tend not to enunciate clearly. For example, you might have a tendency to delete the first syllable of *because* (cuz), delete the *g* in the verb ending *ing* (goin', doin', walkin', talkin'), or to combine *to* with a preceding verb (wanna, hafta, etc.). If you're aware of these patterns, you'll be better able to practice enunciating the words clearly as you practice your speech.

Vocal Variety

In addition to being intelligible, effective public speakers must strive for vocal variety. **Vocal variety** refers to changing rate, pitch, and volume—three aspects of voice discussed in the previous section—as well as stressing certain words and using pauses. Vocal variety enables speakers to reinforce the emotional meaning of their message and to be dynamic.

Discussion Tip
How does Sellnow define vocal variety? How can you use vocal variety to reinforce the emotional intent of your message?

Emotional intent can be reinforced by gradually speeding up or slowing down (varying rate), speaking higher or lower (varying pitch), or speaking louder or softer (varying volume). Generally, you might speed up your rate, raise your pitch, or increase your volume to convey emotions like joy, enthusiasm, excitement, fear, and anticipation. Conversely, you might slow down your rate, lower your pitch, or decrease your volume to communicate emotions like remorse, disgust, and sadness. For example, Dalmus exclaimed:

> Millions of Americans suffer needlessly each year. These people endure unbearable pain needlessly because, although our government is capable of helping them, it chooses to ignore their pain. Our government has no compassion, no empathy, no regard for human feeling. I'm here today to convince you to support my efforts toward legalizing marijuana as a painkiller for terminally ill patients.

To reinforce the emotional intent of his message, which had elements of anger, disgust, and seriousness in it, Dalmus chose to gradually slow down his rate, decrease his volume, and lower his pitch as he exclaimed, "Our government has no compassion, no empathy, no regard for human feeling."

In contrast, speeding your rate, raising your pitch, or increasing your volume will tend to communicate a sense of uncertainty or urgency, for example, excitement, fear, or anticipation. Generally, if you slow your rate, lower your pitch, or decrease your volume, you can communicate a sense of resolution, sadness, or even conviction—as Dalmus did in his speech—or perhaps a sense of peacefulness.

Stress refers to emphasis placed on words to indicate the importance of the ideas expressed. Stress can also be used contrastively, as in the example earlier, where "*Sally* likes spinach" is different in meaning from "Sally likes *spinach*." Let's consider a line from Dalmus's speech. Dalmus was able to give even more weight to this line by stressing the key words "compassion," "empathy," "regard," and "human feeling": "Our government has no comPASSion, no EMpathy, no reGARD for HUMan FEELing."

Pauses, too, can be used to mark important ideas. If one or more sentences express an important idea, you can pause before each sentence to signal that something important is coming up, or you can pause afterward to allow the ideas to sink in. You can pause one or more times within a sentence to add impact to a key idea. Dalmus included several short pauses within the line we've looked at, as well as a longer pause after it: "Our government has no comPASSion, / no EMpathy, / no reGARD for HUMan FEELing. / /"

Teaching Tip
Have students write a brief essay in which they employ the voice guidelines presented in this chapter to critique a speech. Also, have them elucidate how they will use these guidelines as they prepare for the next speech.

As is the case with each of the other aspects of delivery, you must plan where to vary rate, pitch, and volume, as well as to stress key words and incorporate pauses. Likewise you must place reminders on your speaking outline and practice these concepts thoroughly in order to achieve effective delivery in your actual presentation. You might even tape-record or videotape yourself practicing in order to critique whether you are actually conveying the vocal variety you intend.

Conversational Style

The third aspect of effective use of voice is being conversational. Recall from the beginning of the chapter that being conversational is so important that it can be considered a major characteristic of effective delivery. If you are **conversational,** you sound spontaneous and natural despite having thoroughly practiced your speech. If you are conversational, you talk *to* your listeners rather than *at* them; you share important ideas *with* them rather than present a speech *in front of* them. One of the best ways to achieve a conversational style is to focus on sincerely trying to get your ideas across to your listeners. This is also a great way to reduce speech anxiety, because most speakers feel less anxious when they focus on getting their message across rather than on presenting themselves as performers.

In short, effective speakers sound intelligible and conversational, and they reinforce the emotional intent of their ideas with vocal variety. As you plan and practice your speech, you must consider quality, rate, volume, and pitch, as well as pronunciation and enunciation, stresses, and pauses. Effective public speakers practice thoroughly in order to achieve these qualities in a natural-sounding way when they present their speeches.

Use of Voice Checklist

- Does your vocal quality sound pleasant?
- Do your rate, volume, pitch, pronunciation, and enunciation enhance intelligibility?
- Do you vary your rate, volume, and pitch to reinforce an emotional stance?
- Do you use pauses and stresses to convey ethos and to reinforce important points and emotions?
- Do you sound conversational?

Methods of Delivery

Understanding the components of effective delivery is certainly the first step toward developing effective oral delivery skills. At this point, however, you might be asking yourself, "How do I make my delivery meet all these criteria?" The answer, as the text has implied, is to practice your speech. We'll discuss practice, but first let's look at methods of delivery. There are four different methods of delivering a speech, and the way you practice will depend on your method of delivery.

The four methods for delivering a speech are the impromptu, manuscript, memorized, and extemporaneous methods. A public speaker might draw on elements of all four methods when delivering a speech; however, each delivery primarily follows one of the methods.

Discussion Tip
When would you be most likely to use the impromptu, manuscript, memorized, and extemporaneous methods of delivery? Which method is most appropriate for this class?

The Impromptu Method

The **impromptu method** involves speaking with limited preparation. An impromptu speech, like any other speech, focuses on one general purpose (to inform, to persuade, or to entertain) depending on the situation. Also, like any other speech, you organize your ideas using clear macrostructure as well as accurate, inclusive, and vivid language. And, like any other speech, you strive for effective delivery. Unlike other speeches, however, your preparation time for formulating and organizing your ideas is limited to a few moments. Although most beginning speakers tend to fear impromptu speaking more than any other, they have probably also engaged in this method more than any other. Have you ever been asked to tell a story on the spot, give a toast at the last minute, or even explain a concept to the entire class in response to a teacher's question? If so, you've engaged in the impromptu speaking method. We'll talk more about some of the special occasions for impromptu speaking in Chapter 17.

An advantage of speaking impromptu might be that you sound spontaneous and conversational if for no other reason than because you are forced to be. Some disadvantages are that your response won't be structured clearly and so you might sound incoherent. You might have trouble sounding fluent and expressive without much preparation. You also might find it difficult to come up with the best language and style choices in such a short amount of time. For these reasons, public speakers avoid using the impromptu method for their formal presentations.

The Manuscript Method

The **manuscript method** involves reading a speech that has been written out in its entirety. The president of the United States delivers important speeches, such as the State of the Union address, using the manuscript method. An advantage of this method is that you can carefully select your words and phrases and then use precisely these words and phrases. Hence, you are less likely to be misunderstood by listeners. This can be particularly beneficial if your speech is likely to be quoted later. One disadvantage is that, since you're reading, there will be less eye contact with your audience and, in general, less of a sense of connection. You may sound mechanical rather than conversational and sincere. It is difficult to bring a manuscript to life for the audience without a lot of practice and work because you must make formal sentences sound informal. Moreover, since your speech is written out word for word, it can be difficult to adapt to the feedback you may get from your listeners as you're speaking. For these reasons, you should avoid the manuscript method except when reading direct quotations or statistics that must be accurate.

Discussion Tip
According to Sellnow, what are the disadvantages of the manuscript method of delivery? When is it appropriate to utilize a manuscript?

What Do You Think?

Can you remember a time when you listened to a public speaker who read her or his speech to you? How did you know the speaker was reading? How did this choice impact your motivation to really listen?

The Memorized Method

The **memorized method** is similar to the manuscript method in that the entire speech is written out but differs in that the speech is presented from memory. Far from reading your speech, you don't even use notes. Professional speakers who do the same speech on different occasions and for different audiences will often do their speeches from memory. For example, public speakers who compete on a team usually use this method.

Because the memorized speech was scripted before it was memorized, this method has some of the same language and style benefits as the manuscript method. The memorized method also has the advantage of allowing you to make a great deal of eye contact. However, unexpected audience feedback may throw you off or cause you to lose your place in the speech. Since the speech is memorized, if this happens, you may find it difficult to regain your composure and continue. And because you're dealing with material that was originally written, it takes a lot of practice and hard work to get a memorized speech to sound conversational. Beginning public speakers are usually discouraged from using the memorized method for these reasons. However, you may decide to memorize some important segments of your message so you can maximize eye contact, facial expressions, and vocal variety during them. For example, speakers often memorize their attention catcher and clincher to create stronger initial and terminal ethos.

The Extemporaneous Method

Teaching Tip
If possible, have your students videotape their speeches when they practice them. This will allow them to view and correct any delivery problems. Have each student write a brief self-evaluation of his or her presentation using the criteria for effective delivery presented in this chapter.

The **extemporaneous method** requires that a speech be carefully researched and planned just like the manuscript or memorized method. However, you prepare a speaking outline, rather than writing out your speech, and speak from this speaking outline. Thus, each time you present your speech, the key concepts remain intact, but the ideas are phrased somewhat differently. This method can give you many of the advantages of the other methods while avoiding their disadvantages: You can sound spontaneous and conversational, as with the impromptu method, and yet organized and coherent, as with the memorized and manuscript methods. Precisely because it can be thoroughly planned and practiced but sound spontaneous and conversational, the extemporaneous method is usually the best approach for beginning speakers (see Figure 12–3).

FIGURE 12–3
Delivery Methods and Their Effects

+ = Potential strength of this method
− = Potential weakness of this method

METHOD	Impromptu	Manuscript	Memorized	Extemporaneous
Macrostructure	−	+	+	+
Language and style	−	+	+	+
Eye contact	+	−	+	+
Intelligibility	−	+	+	+
Vocal variety	−	−	+	+
Conversationality	+	−	−	+
Adaptability	+	−	−	+

Practicing the Speech

To gain the considerable advantages of the extemporaneous method, you need to practice your speech out loud in advance. Through practice, you refine the content of your speech and work out its delivery.

Practice will make you more effective. It gives you the opportunity to experiment with each type of nonverbal cue. You can try various facial expressions, gestures, and movement; you can try saying words and phrases in different ways in terms of rate, pitch, volume, stresses, and pauses. By experimenting strategically, you can figure out how to use your voice and body to reinforce your verbal message. Ultimately, you can make notes on your speaking outline to serve as reminders when you present the actual speech.

Practice has other important benefits, too. Most important, it reduces speech anxiety. Most of our speech anxiety is rooted in our fear of the unknown, which arises when we ask ourselves "what if" questions. By practicing out loud in advance, you eliminate some of those what-ifs because you prove to yourself that you can get from the beginning to the end. Anxiety is reduced because uncertainty is reduced. Practicing also reduces your anxiety by improving your speech delivery and thus increasing your self-confidence. Finally, practicing will enhance your ethos. The more times you practice your speech, the more fluent you will sound and the more confident you will appear. Fluency and confidence improve credibility.

Teaching Tip
To reinforce the importance of nonverbal communication, show a videotaped speech with the sound turned off. Ask students to determine the feelings portrayed through the speaker's nonverbal language.

When Should You Begin Practicing Your Speech?

Some beginning speakers fall into the procrastination trap, and practice always suffers. If you wait until the end to prepare your speech, you're going to run out of time before having a chance to actually practice the speech. Recall our discussion at the beginning of this chapter. Even the most clearly organized and thoroughly researched speech is likely to fail if your delivery is poor. Ideally, you ought to finish outlining your speech *at least three days before your assigned speaking day,* so you have the rest of the time to practice. It is a lot like taking piano lessons. The student who practices a little bit each day improves much more than the one who crams all of her or his practicing into the time right before a lesson.

Discussion Tip
How soon before your next speech should you finish outlining your speech? How many times should you practice delivering your next speech before your presentation in class?

How Should You Practice Your Speech?

As you practice, you should focus especially on nonverbal cues related to use of voice and use of body, since these are the cues where there is most to be figured out. You'll also need to work on smoothly and effectively incorporating your presentational aids.

Always practice out loud. Reading through your notes silently and thinking about how you will deliver your speech is not good enough. You need to make sure that you will be intelligible and conversational, and you need to plan how to use vocal variety effectively. Tape-record yourself, listen to the recording, and critique your vocal style. Give your speech in front of a few friends, and ask them for feedback. As you practice, look for and work on mispronunciation and sloppy enunciation. Also, practice using vocal variety like stresses, pauses, and changes in rate

Teaching Tip
If you have access to a speech laboratory, instruct students to utilize this resource before their next speech. If you do not have access to a speech laboratory, consider providing classroom time for students to practice speaking in front of others.

and volume at different points in your speech and in different ways. Choose those techniques that best support your ideas. Feedback from friends can be helpful here. Your goal is to form fluent and conversational sentences from a speaking outline. Even if you begin practicing with a manuscript, gradually reduce the sentences in the manuscript to the key words and phrases you will be limited to during the actual presentation.

Once you have decided how you want to deliver your ideas orally, mark delivery cue reminders to yourself on your speaking outline. For example, you might capitalize or highlight words you plan to stress. Recall from Chapter 10 that slash marks (/) can be used to signal pauses. Arrows pointing up or down can signal volume changes. You might also include short notes to remind yourself to SLOW DOWN or to LOOK AT THE AUDIENCE or to REFER TO THE PRESENTATIONAL AID. The coding system you devise ought to be your own. What is important is that you use delivery cues and that you have some system for coding them. Even the most accomplished speakers use cues to remind themselves about delivery.

Recall that use of body includes facial expressions, gestures, and movements. As with vocal cues, you can spot and correct problems in and develop effective use of these cues by practicing in front of friends whose opinions you trust. Practicing in front of a mirror and videotaping yourself can also be helpful. While practicing, you should focus on, for example, whether your facial expressions reinforce your verbal message, especially at important points, whether your gestures and movements appear natural and spontaneous, and whether you remain "open" to your audience rather than turning your back on them. Natural-looking use of body is, in fact, well practiced.

Incorporate your presentational aids. Practice both revealing them and concealing them at the appropriate points during the speech. Practice gesturing toward them. Try to think of the worst possible things that could happen while you're using your presentational aids—and plan what you'll do if those things do happen. What will you do if the posterboard falls to the floor, the projector malfunctions, or the visual aids are in the wrong order? Although you should try to avoid such problems, you should also have an alternative course of action ready. Chapter 13 will provide more specifics on the use of presentational aids.

Make sure you practice enough times. The more you practice, the more techniques you can try and the more likely you will be to find the ones that work and to actually incorporate them when you present your speech. Make sure, also, that you practice fully enough. The more aspects of nonverbal communication you include in your practice, the less you'll fear the unknown and the less you'll feel anxiety.

Delivery and Public Speaking Anxiety

Teaching Tip
Give students a list of tongue twisters to use as warm-ups before speeches or to practice with at home using a tape recorder.

Public speaking anxiety is difficult to fully eliminate; in fact, some degree of anxiety is useful, since it releases adrenaline, which helps you think faster and speak with more enthusiasm. Your goal, then, is to achieve **controlled nervousness**—that is, to control your anxiety and turn it into positive energy that can actually enhance your delivery. What follows are two sets of tips for this purpose; the first is for use while practicing, the second is for use when presenting your speech.

While Practicing the Speech

1. *Speak extemporaneously.* We've seen the advantages of the extemporaneous method, and to feel comfortable about using this method effectively in your speech, you need to use it in your practices as well.
2. *Concentrate on getting your ideas across.* In trying out various nonverbal cues, keep in mind that these should support your verbal message. Avoid flowery language or overly dramatic oral delivery. When all is said and done, the purpose for speaking in public is to share your message with listeners. You'll feel more relaxed about your speech if you've geared it to this purpose.
3. *Imagine yourself presenting an excellent speech.* As we've seen, negative imaging and self-talk will *most certainly hurt* you by increasing your anxiety, and positive imaging and self-talk *might help* you by reducing it. Imaging and self-talk tend to be self-reinforcing. Therefore, you should use positive imaging and self-talk throughout the process of practicing your speech.
4. *Devote extra time to practicing the introduction and conclusion.* Use practice to polish both the content and delivery of your introduction and conclusion. Not only does research tell us that listeners are most likely to remember the beginning and end of the message, but, just as important, your confidence is usually enhanced when you feel good about how the first few lines go.
5. *Practice in the room where you will present the speech.* To reduce the fear of the unknown, try to practice in the room where you'll be presenting the speech. You will have a sense of how loudly or softly you need to speak and can prepare for possible environmental distractions that might occur because of the setting.
6. *Devote extra time to gestures.* Speech anxiety rooted in the fear of being stared at escalates when speakers start worrying about what to do with their hands. For this reason, it's especially important to develop gestures that are effective and to practice them in front of a mirror or in front of friends to reassure yourself that they look natural and spontaneous.

Teaching Tip
See the Activities section of this chapter for several assignments designed to help students improve delivery.

While Presenting the Speech

1. *Employ mental and physical relaxation techniques before leaving your seat.* Use deep breathing exercises, muscular relaxation techniques, and positive self-talk to lower your pulse and help you feel calmer. Then, right before you walk to the front of the room, take three deep breaths. Tighten your muscles while holding each breath; relax your muscles while exhaling each breath. This exercise takes a short amount of time and can make a dramatic difference in lowering your anxiety.
2. *Pause before beginning the speech.* Walk to the front of the room, organize your materials, and plant your feet firmly. Then force yourself to pause for three seconds before beginning the speech. You can either count silently "one-one thousand, two-one thousand, three-one thousand" or look down at your notes and silently read the attention catcher you've prepared. This technique will help you appear confident to your audience and will help you feel more confident and calm as well. Moreover, reading over your attention catcher may

Teaching Tip
Remind students of the many relaxation techniques discussed in Chapter 2. Have them review these techniques before their next speech.

help reduce the fear of failure because you'll have the chance to get those words firmly in mind before beginning the speech.

3. *Focus on the message.* Communicate rather than perform. Public speaking is not the same as acting. You have researched and organized a message, which you believe will benefit your listeners. That is what is important, so focus on getting your message through.
4. *Remember that everyone makes mistakes.* Keep the speech in perspective. When you make a mistake, as is inevitable, don't focus on the mistake and whether anyone noticed it. Instead, remind yourself that everyone makes mistakes and move on.
5. *Remember that most bodily reactions are not visible.* As speakers, we often believe that everyone notices our wobbly knees or shaky hands. Yet most bodily reactions are not noticeable. If your knees begin to wobble, remind yourself of this, so you can stay focused on your message.
6. *Never apologize for your nervousness.* Beginning speakers sometimes make the mistake of starting out by saying how nervous they are. Saying this might actually cause listeners to focus on the potential nervous behaviors rather than the message. Hence, *never* apologize for your nervousness.

Teaching Tip
Tape segments of a variety of speakers from newscasts. Ask students to evaluate these speakers in terms of poise. In addition, discuss the relationship between poise and perceived credibility.

7. *Act poised.* Regardless of how you feel inside, act poised. Remember that everyone makes mistakes and that most nervous bodily actions aren't seen. So act poised and most people will never know how you feel.
8. *Look audience members in the eyes.* Keep in mind that avoiding eye contact usually increases anxiety, because your imagination tends to overestimate negative reactions, whereas in reality most listeners will provide positive nonverbal feedback. Looking listeners in the eye, then, will not only reduce your anxiety, but, as you perceive your listeners' smiles and nods, will increase your confidence as well.
9. *Do not let individual listeners upset you.* If, while presenting your speech, you notice someone who seems inattentive or even belligerent, remind yourself that this attitude is his or her problem, not yours. Forget about that person and focus instead on the other twenty or so listeners who *are* supportive.
10. *Always remember, it is normal to be nervous.* The most effective public speakers are nervous. They simply learn how to control their anxiety and make it work for them. You can too!

Summary

Teaching Tip
If time permits, allow a question-and-answer period after each speech. This will encourage students to speak extemporaneously and provide the speaker with an opportunity to clarify any confusing claims.

Since delivery is crucial to effective public speaking, a speech is thoroughly prepared only if it has been thoroughly practiced. Delivery is how you present your speech through your use of voice, face, and body. Thus, delivery is rooted in nonverbal communication; it has to do with *how* we say what we say. The two essential characteristics of effective delivery are being listener centered and sounding conversational. That is, your goal is to get through to your listeners in a way that acknowledges their central role in the communication process. Your delivery should be communication based, not performance based.

There are various types of nonverbal cues you need to consider as they reinforce your verbal message. These include the use of space and distance, time constraints, appearance, eye contact, use of body, and use of voice. While all six types are important, use of body and use of voice require extra attention. Use of body includes nonverbal cues related to facial expression, posture, gestures, and movement. Use of voice concerns intelligibility, vocal variety, and conversational style.

There are four methods of delivery: the impromptu, manuscript, memorized, and extemporaneous methods. Speeches may contain elements of various methods but must belong primarily to one. The extemporaneous method, which involves speaking from an outline, combines the advantages of the other methods in that an extemporaneous speech is simultaneously prepared and conversational. Hence, this method is generally the most effective choice for beginning public speakers.

You should practice your speech several times before actually giving it. You'll not only improve its effectiveness, but will also reduce your anxiety and increase your ethos. You should begin practicing at least three days before your speech. You should work on nonverbal cues related to use of voice and body and on how to incorporate your presentational aids. By following several tips given for managing speech anxiety while practicing and while presenting your speech, you'll reduce your anxiety and, instead, make it work for you.

Activities

1. **Music Lyrics Interpretation.** Bring the lyrics to a favorite song with you to class. In pairs, work to discover how to convey the emotional intent of the lyrics orally. Then consider how to further reinforce the emotional intent through use of body. Finally, read those lyrics to the group, employing the techniques for use of voice and use of body detailed in this chapter.

   Use of voice: Intelligible, vocally varied, conversational

   Use of body: Facial expressions, posture, gestures, movement

2. **Nursery Rhymes.** Form pairs. Each pair will read a nursery rhyme or short children's story to the group to demonstrate effective versus ineffective use of a particular type of nonverbal cue. For example, one partner will read using effective eye contract and the other using ineffective eye contact; other pairs will demonstrate effective/ineffective facial expressions, gestures, use of pauses, stresses, and so on. After a pair reads, discuss as a group why each partner was effective or ineffective. Talk about the consequences of each type of nonverbal cues for public speakers.

3. **Conveying Emotions Nonverbally.** Form a group with three or four classmates. As a group, identify a variety of emotions (sadness, excitement, worry, fear, etc.) and write them on index cards. Place the cards face down on a pile in the front of the room. One at a time, draw a card from the pile. Each student recites the same nursery rhyme or children's poem three times for the class, trying to convey the emotion on his or her card. The first time, the speaker should try to convey the emotion through voice alone. The second time, the speaker adds facial expression; and the third time the speaker should

add body language as well. After each recitation, the class tries to guess the emotion. When each speaker finishes, he or she should talk about what was done to convey the emotion vocally, facially, and bodily. Talk about the implications for public speakers.

4. **Deep Breathing.** First, lie flat on your back. Place a book on your abdomen, and place one hand on the upper part of your chest. Breathe in and out as naturally as possible. You should notice a slow and regular expansion and contraction in the area under the book and very little movement in the area under your hand. Practice doing this until it becomes second nature. Second, stand up and place one hand on the front of your abdomen and the other on your lower back. Breathe in and out as naturally as possible, trying to keep most of the movement in the center of your body.
5. **Controlled Exhalation.** Take a deep breath and release it slowly, making the sound "sssss." Keep it even and regular to the count of ten, then fifteen, and finally twenty. Repeat this process with the sound "fffff." Eventually, sustain the "ssssss" and the "fffff" sounds to the count of thirty.
6. **Cold Mirror Test.** Hold a very cold mirror about one and one-half inches from your mouth. Say "aaahhh." Check the mirror. If it's foggy, you're allowing too much breath to escape as you speak. Wipe the mirror off and try again, saying "aaahhh" much louder. There should be less fogging. Practice until you can keep the mirror from becoming foggy. Then repeat this activity with the sounds "oh," "ow," "ee," and "oo."
7. **Open Throat.** With your tongue on the floor of your mouth and hand placed gently around your neck, begin a gentle yawn. As you exhale, allow yourself to pronounce a gentle, easy "ah." Keep your tongue on the floor of your mouth and neck relaxed as you do. Eventually, try to say a phrase or sentence with that same open feeling in your mouth and throat and relaxed sensation in your neck.
8. **Nasality Reduction.** Pinch your nostrils shut with your thumb and forefinger. Now say this sentence: "When may I sing my song?" You should feel vibrations in your nose, especially on "m," "n," and "ng." Now pinch your nose again and say this sentence: "Those who gossip to you will also gossip about you." If you feel any vibrations in your nose, you have too much nasality. Continue saying the sentence until you feel no vibrations at all. Try to re-create this feeling whenever you speak.
9. **Audio Self-Critique.** Record your delivery of an upcoming speech on audiotape and listen to it. Critique yourself according to intelligibility, vocal variety, and conversationality. Determine what specific things you can do differently to improve your use of voice. Indicate them on your notes, and practice the speech several more times. Then audiotape yourself again, comparing the two versions to assess effective change. Include this self-critique in your portfolio.
10. **Video Self-Critique.** Videotape your delivery of an upcoming speech and then watch the video without the sound. Critique yourself according to facial expressions, posture, gestures, and movement. Determine what specific changes you can make to improve your use of body. Indicate them in your notes, and practice the speech several more times. Then videotape yourself again, comparing the two versions to assess effective change. Include this self-critique in your portfolio.

Key Terms

- Audience contact
- Chronemics
- Controlled nervousness
- Conversational
- Delivery
- Enunciation
- Extemporaneous method
- Facial expressions
- Group density
- Impromptu method
- Initial ethos
- Intelligibility
- Kinesics
- Manuscript method
- Memorized method
- Motivated movement
- Nonverbal communication
- Object language
- Paralanguage
- Pauses
- Pitch
- Posture
- Pronunciation
- Proxemics
- Rate
- Stress
- Terminal ethos
- Timbre
- Vocal quality
- Vocal variety
- Volume

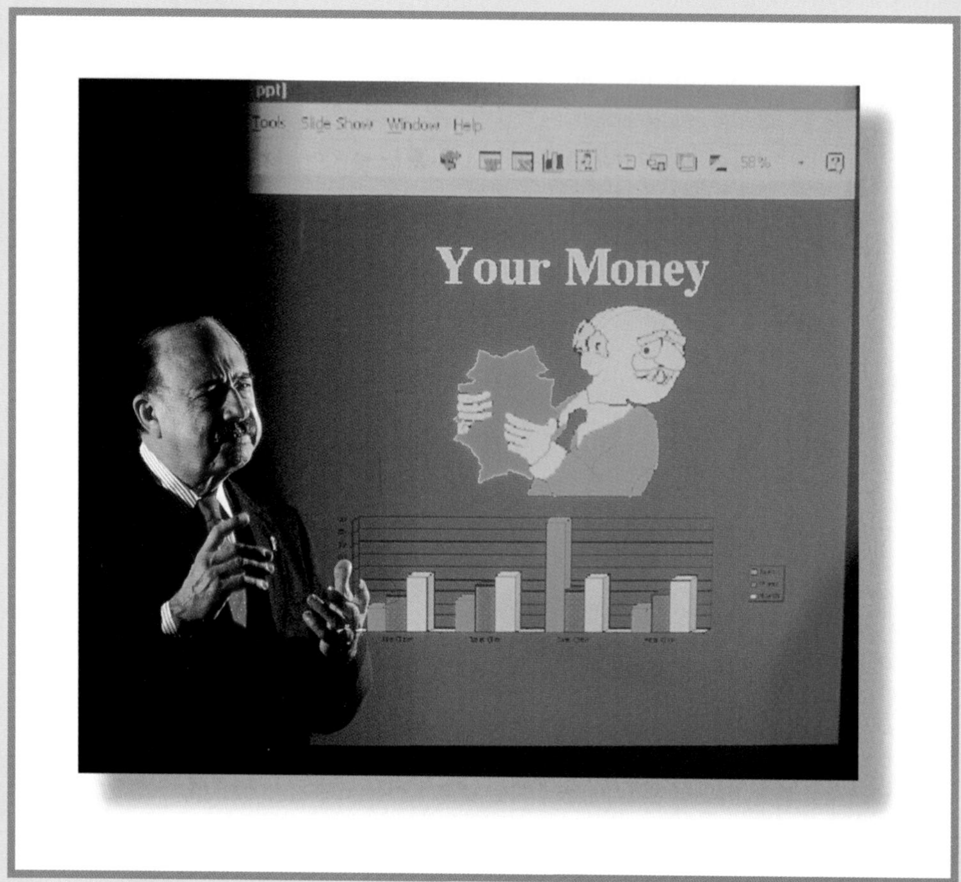

Tools Slide Show Window Help
Your Money

CHAPTER 13

Creating and Using Presentational Aids

Reflective Questions

1. Why might presentational aids enhance your credibility?
2. What different types of presentational aids could you use?
3. Why should photographs not be passed around the audience?
4. Why not use a chalkboard?
5. Why should visual aids be more than a mere list of words?
6. When might you use a video clip for a presentational aid?

Ivy gave a speech about religious rites of passage. She chose to focus on the similarities and differences between the Jewish bar mitzvah and the Christian confirmation. After her introduction, she went over to the slide projector so she could show some specific aspects of each ceremony as she spoke. She turned the switch only to discover that the light bulb had burned out. Although she had taken a great deal of time to prepare and organize her presentational aids, she had not anticipated this catastrophe. She gave the presentation without her slides, trying her best to explain in words what the slides would have shown. But she could tell by the looks on many listeners' faces that much remained unclear.

Teaching Tip
Refer students to the Speech-Maker CD-ROM. This software provides several tips for creating and using presentational aids. Consider assigning one of the scenarios to be completed before the class in which you will discuss this chapter.

Claus's speech compared the origins and rules of football and rugby. Claus had prepared charts to help listeners visualize some differences between the sports. At the appropriate point in his speech, he unrolled the first poster and placed it on an easel. Just as he was about to begin his explanation, the poster rolled back up and tumbled to the floor. Claus calmly picked it up and held it in his hands while he spoke. Because he had to hold the poster, he could not make adequate eye contact or use gestures.

Ahmad's speech was on how television sitcoms often stereotype African Americans. He had videotaped portions of three different television programs to support his three main points. After showing the first of these, Ahmad noticed that he had only one minute left to complete his speech. He had to leave out the other two videotaped examples, although his speech was less compelling as a result.

Each of these speakers would have benefited from knowing more about using presentational aids in a public speech. Ivy could have prepared for the worst by bringing an extra light bulb, preparing a handout, or even arriving early enough to check her equipment in advance. Claus could have used sturdier posterboard for his charts. And Ahmad could have timed his speech, including the videotaped examples, in advance, to ensure that he would remain within the time limit. Each speaker learned an important lesson about using presentational aids. It is unfortunate, however, that they had to learn these lessons while presenting their speeches.

What Are Presentational Aids?

Teaching Tip
Assign a brief written essay in which students analyze the graphics in an issue of *USA Today*. Ask them to evaluate whether these materials effectively facilitate understanding.

Presentational aids help explain the ideas in your speech. They are usually visual, audio, or audiovisual. **Visual aids** include actual objects, models, photographs, drawings and diagrams, graphs, and charts. Ivy's photographs made into slides and Claus's charts were visual aids. **Audio aids** focus on sound and include things like recordings of music, conversations, interviews, speeches, or environmental sounds. **Audiovisual aids,** like videotapes or computer-generated slide show presentations, combine sight and sound. Occasionally, you might use presentational aids that focus on the other senses of touch, smell, and taste.

Teaching Tip
To illustrate the communicative power of presentational aids, see the Who Can Follow Directions? assignment located in the Activities section of this chapter.

By supplementing your words, presentational aids make your ideas more concrete and clear for listeners (e.g., Mitchell, 1987). Consider some examples from everyday life. Can you recall a time when someone gave you directions that only seemed to confuse you more? If you had been given a map to look at, it's unlikely that you would have gotten confused. Imagine trying to teach a toddler how to tie shoelaces without demonstrating the process. Or imagine trying to describe what your favorite musical group sounds like without playing a bit of their music. One reason schools perform fire drills, cities sound storm alarms, and radio stations have tests of the emergency broadcast system is to give people a chance to hear what these alarms sound like so they will recognize them when they signal a real emergency. Clearly we understand things better when we can actually see or hear them.

> ***What Do You Think?***
>
> *Think of a time when you tried to explain to someone what something sounded, smelled, or tasted like. Was it easy or difficult to do? Why or why not?*

This chapter begins with a discussion of how presentational aids can enhance a public speech. We then explore the types of presentational aids from which you can choose and the advantages and disadvantages of each. We also consider various media for displaying these aids and their advantages and disadvantages. Finally, we discuss factors you need to think about in order to construct effective presentational aids and use them effectively in your speech.

Why Use Presentational Aids?

The main reason for using presentational aids is to *make verbal messages more concrete.* That is, effective presentational aids clarify the verbal message so listeners better comprehend what the speaker means. For example, John is presenting an informative speech about the proper way to groom a dog. As he talks about clipping toenails, he shows a slide. As he talks about trimming whiskers, he shows a slide. And as he talks about grooming techniques unique to dogs that shed and dogs that don't, he shows slides. Doing so makes his explanations more concrete because listeners are able to see what he is talking about as he explains it. The main purpose

Teaching Tip
Have students bring one object to class and describe what they find interesting about that object. The object should be hidden and the class should be instructed to guess what the object is based solely on the descriptions provided by the speaker. Have the speaker repeat the exercise using the object as a presentational aid.

It would be difficult or impossible to learn how to tie a shoe without the help of visual aids to demonstrate the process.

DILBERT reprinted py permission of United Feature Syndicate, Inc.

of an aid is to help make the verbal message more concrete. If a potential aid does not fulfill this purpose, it should not be used.

> ### *What Do You Think?*
> *Can you recall a time when a speaker used a visual aid that confused you? Why? What impact did it have on the effectiveness of the speech?*

Presentational aids have several additional benefits. They add variety to your speech, reduce your public speaking anxiety, increase listener retention, enhance the persuasive appeal of your speech, and reach more listeners by addressing different learning styles.

Presentational aids *add variety* to a speech by giving the audience something new to look at or listen to. Listeners whose minds begin to wander to thoughts about what they plan to eat for lunch or what the weather is like outside can be drawn back into your speech when you introduce a presentational aid. Creatively constructed presentational aids can prove especially effective for this purpose.

Stephanie used a creatively constructed visual aid to add variety to her informative speech on the rises and falls in popularity of the Rolling Stones over several decades. She presented a bar graph depicting the total sales of successive recordings. She added variety to her graph by using pictures of tongues, something lead singer Mick Jagger is known for, to represent numerical increments on the bars.

Presentational aids can *help reduce public speaking anxiety.* Visual aids can decrease anxiety stemming from the fear of being stared at, because listeners will be looking at your visual aid, not at you. All presentational aids can reduce anxiety stemming from the fear of failure, because the information they contain will help jog your memory about portions of your speech.

Discussion Tip
How can presentational aids be used to reduce public speaking anxiety? How many presentational aids should you use in your next speech?

Presentational aids *increase listener retention.* This is an important function, since listener retention is one of your main goals as a speaker. An effectively constructed and integrated presentational aid can help listeners remember key points after the speech is over. Researchers have discovered that we tend to retain only about 10 percent of what we hear, yet we are likely to remember as much as 65 percent of what we both see and hear (Zayes-Baya, 1977–1978).

By adding impact to a speech, presentational aids can *increase a speaker's credibility and, thus, persuasive appeal.* In a study by the 3M Corporation, for example, speakers who used visual aids in their presentations were 43 percent more likely to persuade their listeners than were their counterparts who did not use visual aids (Vogel, Dickson, & Lehman, 1986).

You've undoubtedly seen many examples of how the impact of presentational aids can increase persuasive appeal. Consider, for example, how much more persuasive television advertisements requesting help for needy children in developing countries are because they show the children struggling to survive. Of course, poorly constructed or poorly used presentational aids won't help and might hurt your persuasive appeal. For example, during the 1992 presidential campaign, Ross Perot's infomercials included visual aids that were unprofessionally constructed and awkwardly used. Programs like *Saturday Night Live* poked fun at these aids, which suggests that Perot would have been better off not using visual aids at all than using them ineffectively.

Finally, presentational aids can increase the number of listeners you are able to reach with your message because they *address diverse learning styles.* Recall that your audience is comprised of individuals who have different learning style preferences—of feeling, thinking, watching, and doing. Whereas some listeners might understand your message quite accurately merely by listening to it, others might better grasp your ideas if they are reinforced visually or in other ways. Moreover, by addressing all learning styles you will round the entire cycle of learning. Doing so benefits all listeners, because all will retain your message better regardless of their preferred learning style.

Discussion Tip
How can presentational aids be utilized to address diverse learning styles? What types of learners would most likely benefit from the inclusion of audio and visual aids?

Teaching Tip
To illustrate how presentational aids can be incorporated to address diverse learning styles, see the Did You See What I Saw? assignment in the Activities section of this chapter.

Consider, for example, how Andria used presentational aids in her speech on acupressure. Andria explained that acupressure is a natural method of relieving pain, similar to acupuncture, but it relies on fingertip stimulation rather than needles. As she discussed the kinds of pain acupressure can relieve, she incorporated a videotaped clip of a person experiencing a severe migraine headache. This aid was intended to appeal especially to watchers and feelers—that is, listeners who want to see real-life examples.

She later showed a diagram of the human body, depicting pressure-point locations and the specific pains associated with each point. This aid addressed the learning styles of watchers and thinkers who want to see the logical soundness of abstract concepts.

Using herself as a sort of presentational aid, Andria demonstrated the acupressure stimulation procedure for reducing headache pain by applying pressure to one hand with the thumb and forefinger of her other hand. She asked listeners to try this as well. Doing so addressed the learning style of doers in the audience who want to experiment with practical applications.

She concluded by showing another videotaped clip of the same person after her headache had been relieved through acupressure. Andria increased her chances of reaching her listeners by reinforcing her ideas with presentational aids that addressed the various learning-style stages.

Why Use Presentational Aids?

1. To make the verbal message clearer.
2. To add variety.
3. To reduce public speaking anxiety.
4. To increase listener retention.
5. To increase persuasive appeal.
6. To address diverse learning styles.

Types of Presentational Aids

Teaching Tip
Bring examples of both good and poor presentational aids to class. Have students identify the characteristics of effective presentational aids as well as the ways that poor presentational aids can be improved.

There are many different types of presentational aids. To determine what type or types to use in your speech, you need to understand the advantages and disadvantages of each. You'll then need to think about what will work best to make your particular message concrete. Presentational aids are classified as either actual objects or symbolic representations. Representations include models, photographs, drawings and diagrams, maps, graphs, charts, audio materials, audiovisual materials, and other sensory materials.

Actual Objects

Teaching Tip
Provide students with clear guidelines for evaluating the appropriateness of presentational aids (e.g., no live animals, no firearms, or no illegal substances).

Actual objects are the most concrete visual representation you can use to explain your message. Objects can be animate (people, animals, or plants) or inanimate.

As we saw with Andria, you can use yourself as a presentational aid. You might, for example, demonstrate sign language letters, ballet steps, yoga positions, or tennis strokes. Or you might dress in a Pakistani wedding gown, a postal uniform, or a tutu. You can also use a person other than yourself as a presentational aid. Isaak, for example, used his roommate to demonstrate the process of applying theatrical makeup to make actors appear old.

Using a person is often a good way to keep your audience's attention. If you're using the person to demonstrate a process, doers and feelers will definitely benefit. One possible disadvantage is that those in the back of the room might not be able to see a demonstration (for example, if you demonstrate yoga positions while seated on the floor). Another is that if you use other people, they might become a distraction before or after the points they help clarify. In other words, there might be logistical problems to overcome.

Animals have similar advantages but greater logistical problems—that is, they are interesting to the audience, but often too interesting, and they are difficult to control. You may not be able to stop your puppy from relieving its bladder or your cat from meowing or clawing in fear. If you're worrying about your animal's behavior, not only does your presentational aid become ineffective, but your public speaking anxiety is likely to increase. When Josey used her cat as a presentational aid in a speech about pet therapy, the cat was well behaved, but some listeners were more interested in observing the cat than in concentrating on Josey's speech. At best, then, the disadvantages of using animals tend to outweigh the advantages.

A wide range of inanimate objects can be effective presentational aids. For example, when Clara gave an informative speech on golf, she used golf clubs both to show listeners the differences between woods and irons and to demonstrate various drives and putts.

Discussion Tip
According to Sellnow, what are the primary advantages and disadvantages of using inanimate objects as presentational aids?

An advantage of using inanimate objects is that listeners see precisely the thing you are talking about. Potential disadvantages of using inanimate objects include size, complexity, and dangerousness. Size can be a problem in either direction. Randy's four-wheeled all-terrain vehicle was too large to fit through the doorway of the classroom; Marjie's diamond ring was too small to be seen by those at the back of the room. Sometimes the size and complexity problems are linked. For example, Shayla realized the number of miniature parts housed in her thirty-five millimeter camera made it too complex to be an effective presentational aid. Any object that could be dangerous should not even be considered. When Lana brought a twelve-

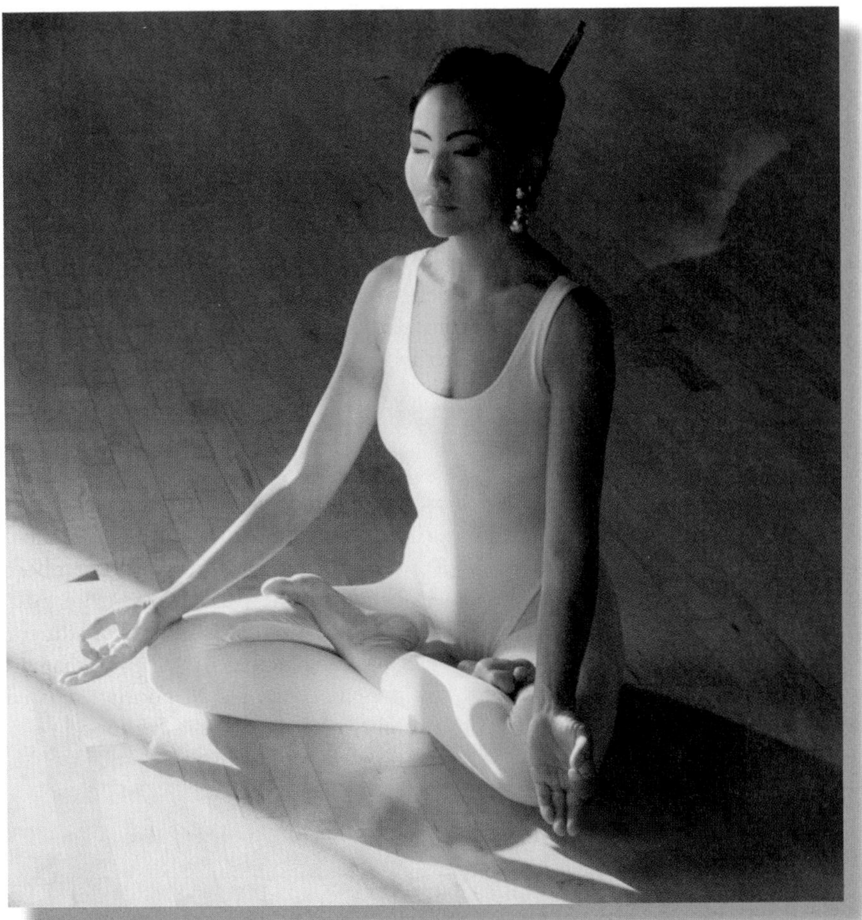

Sometimes you can use yourself as a visual aid. If you do, you'll have to consider potential logistical problems.

gauge shotgun to class, her instructor told her she could not use this presentational aid, which was not even allowed on campus.

What Randy, Marjie, and Shayla did—and what Lana should have done—was to bring a representation of the object, rather than the object itself: Randy brought a model of his vehicle; Marjie, an enlarged picture of her ring; and Shayla, a simplified diagram of her camera. Often, when it won't work to use an object as a presentational aid, you can use a representation of that object instead. Because there are so many types of representations, they have many different functions as presentational aids.

> ***What Do You Think?***
>
> *Consider a time when you observed a speaker using an actual object for a presentational aid. Was it effective? Why or why not?*

Models

Models are scaled-down or scaled-up versions of actual objects. Randy's all-terrain vehicle is an example of a scaled-down model. In a speech about ear infections, Jen used a scaled-up model of the human inner ear. Models can be very effective because they are concrete representations of the object you are talking about. Sometimes, however, obtaining or creating models can prove quite costly or time-consuming.

Photographs

Photographs are an obvious alternative when neither objects nor models are feasible. However, photographs have the disadvantage of being small. To be used effectively in a speech, they must be enlarged in some way. You might transpose the photographs into slides or transparencies, or use them in a computerized slide show program like Microsoft's PowerPoint, Lotus's Freelance Graphics, or Adobe's Persuasion, all of which are discussed later in this chapter.

Drawings and Diagrams

Drawings are yet another alternative to objects and models. A **diagram** is a type of drawing used to show a whole and its parts. Claus's representations of the football and rugby fields were diagrams, as was Andria's representation of the human body and its pressure points (see Figure 13–1). Students often use drawings and diagrams because they are relatively simple and inexpensive to construct. For students with limited artistic ability, however, creating an effective drawing or diagram might pose some difficulties. As with any presentational aid, if poorly prepared, drawings and diagrams can lessen your credibility and your persuasive appeal.

FIGURE 13–1
Pressure Points

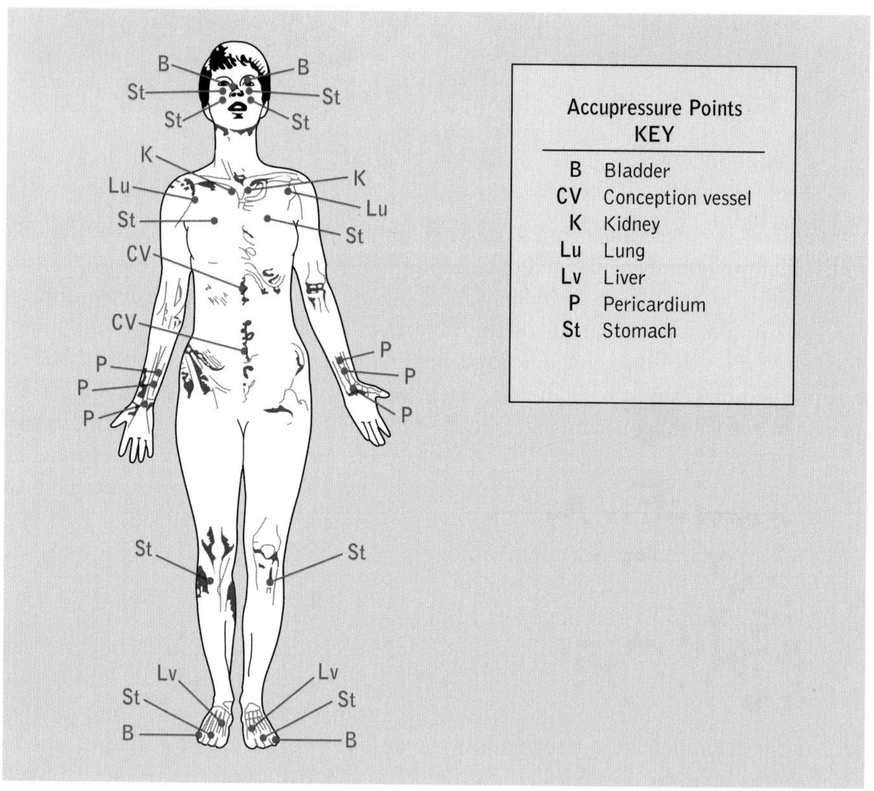

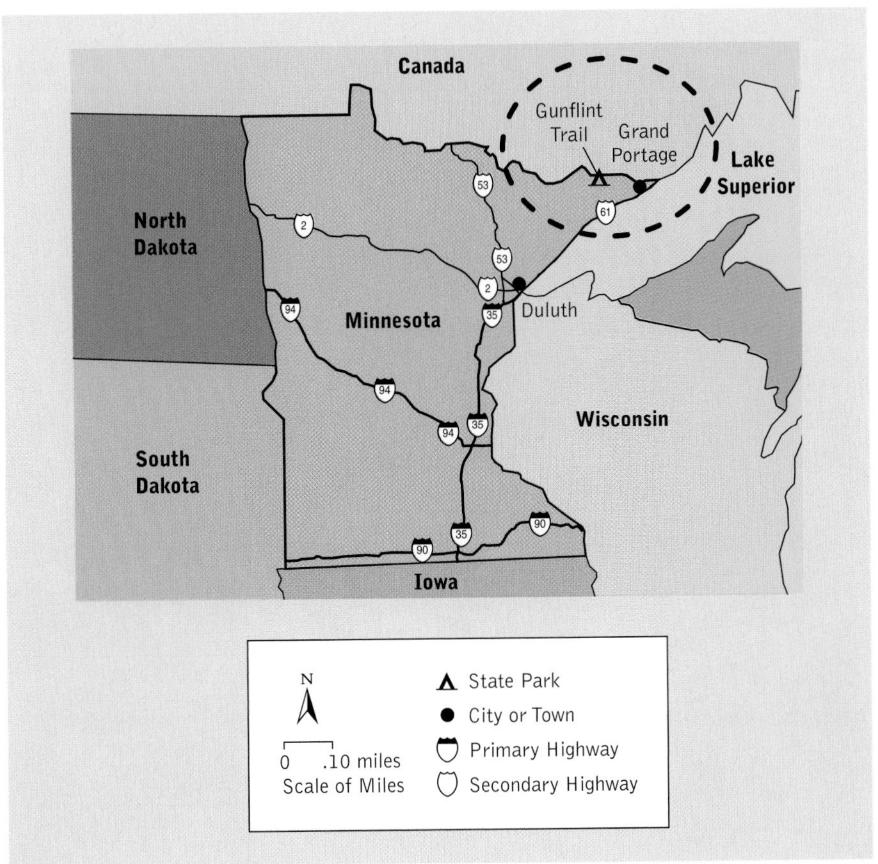

FIGURE 13–2
The Boundary Waters Canoe Area

Maps

Depending on your speech topic, you might use as a presentational aid a map of a campus or neighborhood, city, state, country, or the world. **Maps** are schematic representations of real or imaginary geographic areas. You can use a map to show a route or to show where two or more places are in relation to one another. When Brian gave a speech on the boundary waters canoe area, located between Canada and Minnesota, he used a map to show both where the area is and how big it is (see Figure 13–2). When Debbie gave a speech on her family's trip to the Grand Canyon, she used a map on which she'd outlined the route they took and highlighted the key places she discussed in her speech.

Discussion Tip
For which organizational pattern would maps be most appropriate? What are the advantages and disadvantages of using maps as presentational aids?

Graphs

Graphs are generally representations intended to make statistics, statistical trends, and statistical relationships clearer and more understandable. Graphs can make complex numerical trends and relationships more concrete because they allow numbers to be represented visually. Graphs are sometimes used unethically, however, particularly when they mislead the audience through the use of distorted units of measure. That said, there are several kinds of graphs.

Teaching Tip
Before you discuss this material, have students prepare a bar, line, and pie graph using the same data set. Ask them to evaluate which graph would most effectively communicate the data.

FIGURE 13–3
How Much Caffeine Are You Getting?

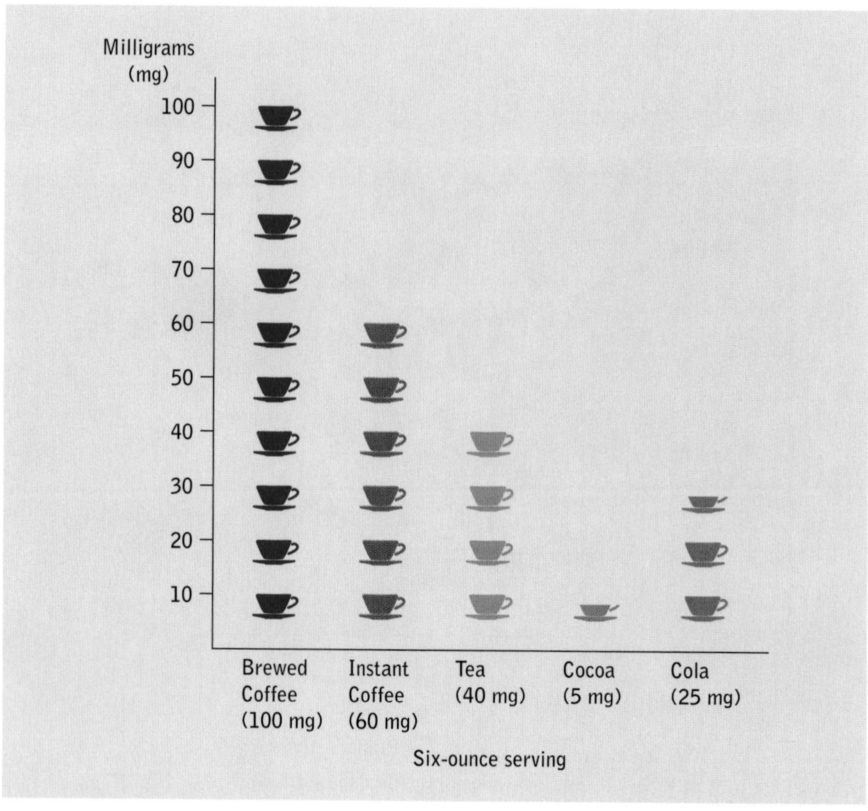

Teaching Tip
Assign students to small groups and have them brainstorm ways they might incorporate presentational aids in their next speech. Share the results with the entire class.

Bar graphs consist of parallel bars with lengths proportional to specific quantities that highlight comparisons between two or more items. For example, Libby used a bar graph to compare the amounts of garbage produced by the United States, Japan, England, Mexico, and Canada. Jaqueline used a bar graph to compare the amounts of caffeine found in one serving of chocolate, coffee, tea, and cola (see Figure 13–3). Notice how Jaqueline used coffee cups as symbols in her bars to add interest and reinforce what the numbers mean.

Line graphs are especially useful for representing trends over time. Daily reports of the Dow Jones Industrial average are usually reported with a line graph (see Figure 13–4). Glynnis used a line graph to show the reduction of people's perceived public speaking anxiety each week over the course of a six-week treatment period. A line graph can also show two or more related trends, enabling you to make comparisons. As in Figure 13–5, Rebecca used a line graph to compare projected public school enrollment trends throughout the district.

Teaching Tip
Bring examples of both good and poor graphs to class. Have students identify the elements of effective graphs as well as the ways that ineffective graphs could be improved.

Pie graphs show what proportion of a whole is represented by each of its parts. In his speech about eating a balanced diet, Tim used the pie graph in Figure 13–6 to show the maximum number of calories that should come from carbohydrates, saturated fat, unsaturated fat, and other food sources like protein. Ideally, a pie graph is divided into two to five parts. If there are more than eight items, a pie graph should not be used, as it would be too cluttered to be effective. If you have more than eight items, consider grouping several of the less important items into a category called "other," as Tim did.

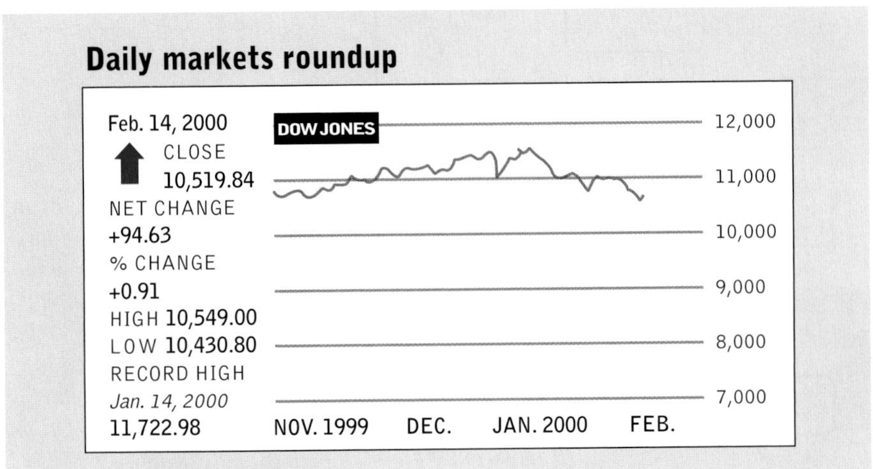

FIGURE 13–4
Dow Jones Daily Market Roundup

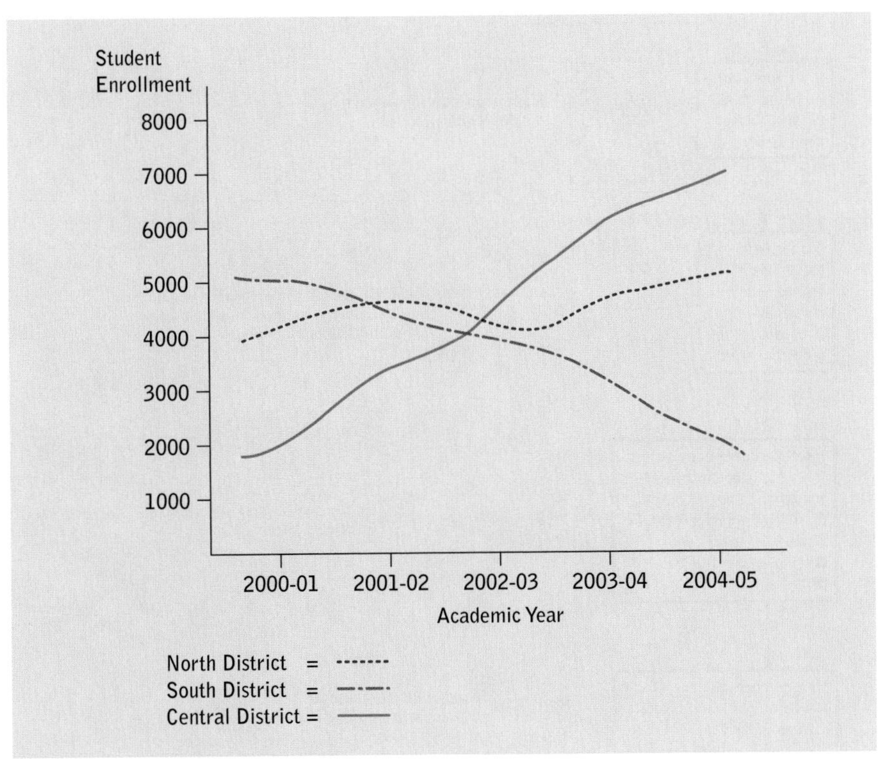

FIGURE 13–5
Projected Public School Enrollments

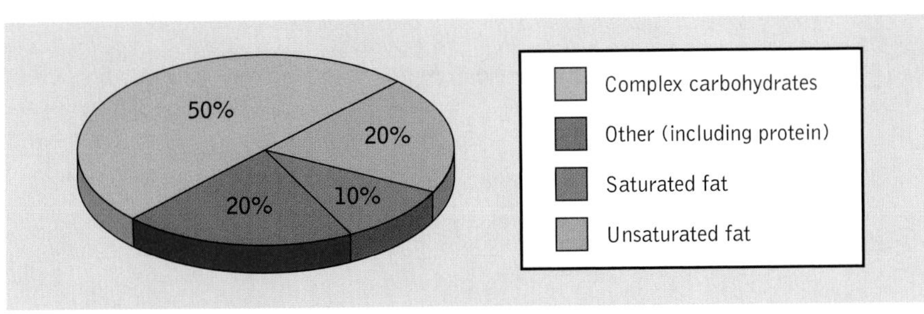

FIGURE 13–6
Fat and Complex Carbohydrates in a Balanced Diet

FIGURE 13–7
Why Are You Overweight?

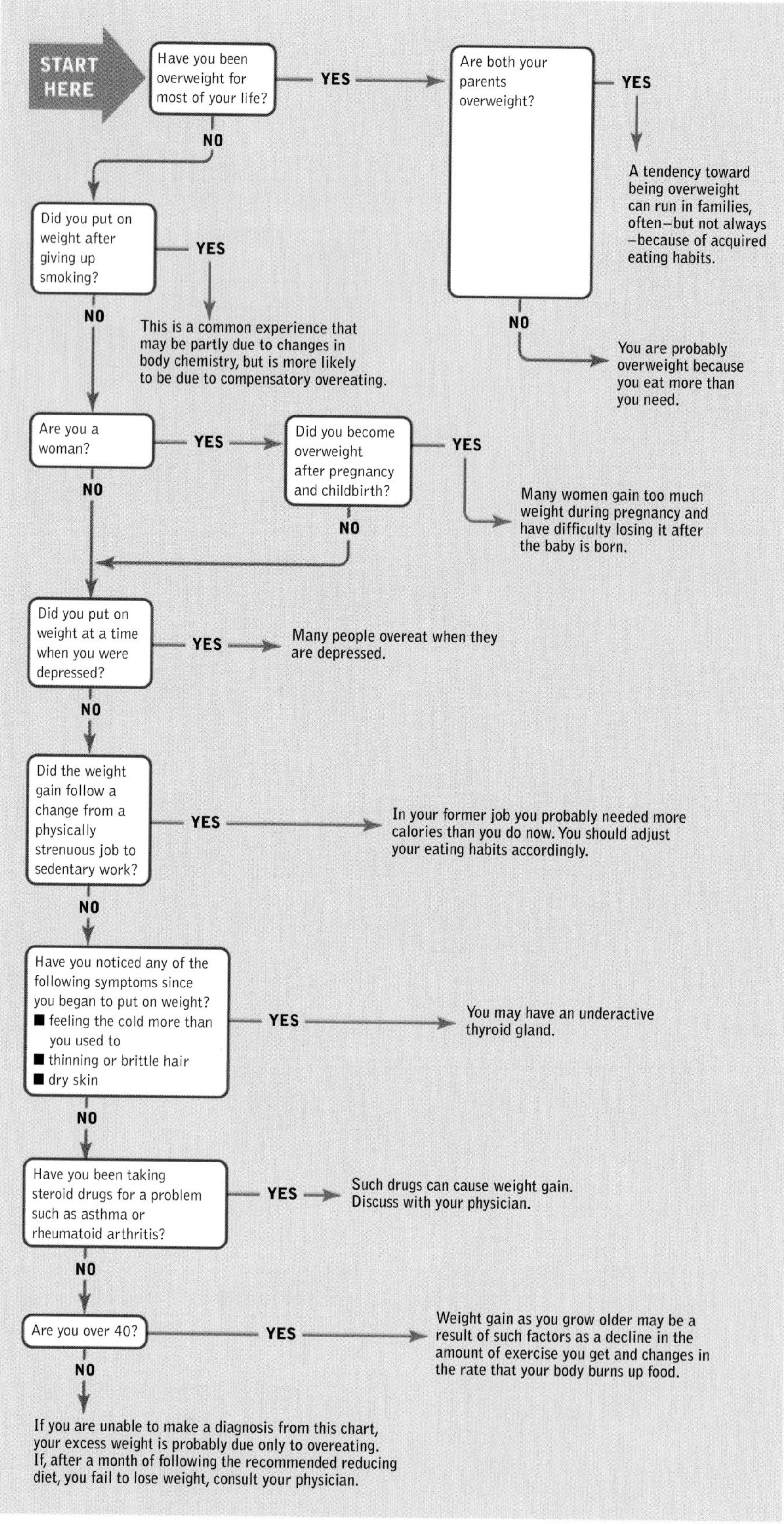

START HERE
Have you been overweight for most of your life?
YES
Are both your parents overweight?
YES
A tendency toward being overweight can run in families, often—but not always—because of acquired eating habits.
NO
You are probably overweight because you eat more than you need.
NO
Did you put on weight after giving up smoking?
YES
This is a common experience that may be partly due to changes in body chemistry, but is more likely to be due to compensatory overeating.
NO
Are you a woman?
YES
Did you become overweight after pregnancy and childbirth?
YES
Many women gain too much weight during pregnancy and have difficulty losing it after the baby is born.
NO
NO
Did you put on weight at a time when you were depressed?
YES
Many people overeat when they are depressed.
NO
Did the weight gain follow a change from a physically strenuous job to sedentary work?
YES
In your former job you probably needed more calories than you do now. You should adjust your eating habits accordingly.
NO
Have you noticed any of the following symptoms since you began to put on weight?
■ feeling the cold more than you used to
■ thinning or brittle hair
■ dry skin
YES
You may have an underactive thyroid gland.
NO
Have you been taking steroid drugs for a problem such as asthma or rheumatoid arthritis?
YES
Such drugs can cause weight gain. Discuss with your physician.
NO
Are you over 40?
YES
Weight gain as you grow older may be a result of such factors as a decline in the amount of exercise you get and changes in the rate that your body burns up food.
NO
If you are unable to make a diagnosis from this chart, your excess weight is probably due only to overeating. If, after a month of following the recommended reducing diet, you fail to lose weight, consult your physician.

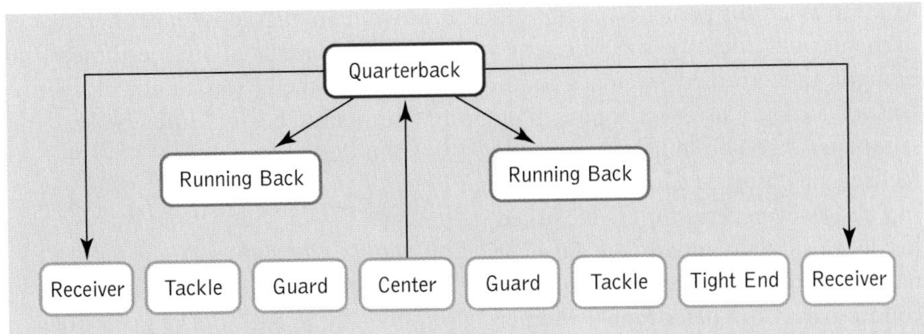

FIGURE 13–8
The Offensive Lineup

Charts

Charts can be used to clarify relationships between steps or positions. **Flowcharts** illustrate a sequence of steps. Tim also used the flowchart in Figure 13–7 to help listeners assess why they might be overweight. **Organizational charts** usually illustrate hierarchical relationships among positions in an organization. In his speech, Claus used the organizational chart in Figure 13–8 to highlight the relationships between the offensive players and the quarterback in football.

Audio Materials

There are times when an explanation or description is incomplete without sound. For example, Robert knew that his explanation of New Age music as representing a philosophy of inner peace would be clearer and more compelling if he played and discussed a sample of the music. In addition to music, audio materials include audiotaped excerpts of famous speeches, radio programs, and recordings of interviews, conversations, or environmental sounds. In her speech about whales, for example, Emily played a recording of them "singing." If you want to include audio material, make sure that you'll have enough time to present it and that you have access to a high-quality cassette or CD player.

Teaching Tip
Assign students to small groups and ask them to generate a list of potential speech topics. Have the groups evaluate which types of presentational aids would be most appropriate for each topic.

Audiovisual Materials

Materials that use both sight and sound include videotapes, films, and computer-generated slide shows. Ahmad knew that his explanation of television sitcom stereotypes of African Americans would be clearer if he showed some examples. His idea was a good one. The problem he encountered, as discussed earlier in the chapter, illustrates a disadvantage of audiovisual material: It can be hard to incorporate given the time constraints of your speech. The need for equipment can also be a disadvantage, especially for presentations before large audiences where multimedia projection units and a large screen or multiple viewing monitors might be required.

Teaching Tip
If possible, bring an audiovisual aid to class and demonstrate the use of this presentational aid in your lecture. Ask students to critique the effectiveness of this device as a presentational aid.

Other Sensory Aids

Depending on your topic, you might also choose to include other **sensory aids,** ones that focus on sound, smell, touch, or taste. For example, David brought in his trumpet and three different types of mutes to demonstrate what each one sounds like. He asked his audience to close their eyes while he played each of them to see if they could identify the different types. In her speech about perfume, Pam brought in perfumed swatches for her listeners to smell. You might also bring sensory aids for listeners to touch such as fabric swatches or different kinds of sandpaper. Or you might bring aids focused on taste, as Greg did for his speech about generic foods. He asked his listeners to compare the taste of name-brand cereals to their generic counterparts to determine whether they could tell the difference.

Certainly, there are many different types of presentational aids, including actual objects and symbolic representations. Each type has both advantages and disadvantages you'll need to consider as you determine what will be both appropriate and effective for your speech.

> ***What Do You Think?***
>
> *Consider your next speech. What types of presentational aids could you use to help make your ideas more concrete for your listeners?*

Media for Displaying Presentational Aids

Media are the equipment used to display your presentational aids. Some media are nonelectronic—for example, chalkboards, flip charts, posterboards, and handouts. Electronic media include slides and slide projectors, transparencies and overhead projectors, cassette or CD players, VCRs and LCD projectors or monitors, as well as computers and LCD panels or projectors.

Nonelectronic Media

Chalkboard

> **Discussion Tip**
> According to Sellnow, what are the primary advantages and limitations of nonelectronic media for displaying presentational aids? Which type of nonelectronic aid would be most appropriate for your next speech?

Students often ask about using the chalkboard to display their presentational aids. The chalkboard seems appealing to students because it costs nothing and requires no preparation time before the speech. I explain that the one occasion when using a chalkboard or white board is an effective choice is when the speaker wants to encourage direct listener participation. In such a case, you do not know in advance what particular ideas will be raised. The chalkboard allows for the inclusion of these ideas and facilitates any related discussion. Hence, a chalkboard should only be used under this rare circumstance. Formal public speeches seldom involve direct listener participation.

A chalkboard also has considerable disadvantages in a formal public speaking context. First, few students can draw neatly enough on the board to enhance their credibility. Second, you must turn your back to the audience while drawing on the board, which limits your ability to maintain eye contact. Third, the flow of your speech is likely to be disrupted while you are drawing on the board. Unfortunately, these disadvantages of using the chalkboard far outweigh its advantages.

Flip Charts and Posterboards

Flip charts are large pads of paper displayed on easels. Professional trainers commonly use them in business and industry. **Posterboards** are large pieces of tag board or foam core displayed on easels. Both have the advantages of being relatively inexpensive and easy to work with. They can be used to display a wide range of presentational aids, and if carefully prepared in advance, they should enhance your credibility. For all these reasons, many beginning public speakers use flip charts or posterboards to display their visual aids. To avoid Claus's dilemma, however, be sure to use sturdy posterboard that won't roll up and fall to the floor during your speech.

Handouts

Handouts are an effective medium for displaying any presentational aids you want listeners to refer to after the speech. For example, a handout might give listeners a set of steps to follow later, useful telephone numbers and addresses, or math formulas they can refer to after the speech occasion. Tim used a handout to display his flowchart about determining reasons for being overweight. Handouts should not be distributed or used before or during a speech because they can be distracting; listeners wind up reading the handout instead of listening to the speaker. If you use a handout, distribute it at the end of your presentation.

Teaching Tip
Ask students to develop a handout that could be distributed after their next speech. This activity will give students experience with handouts as presentational aids and help them refine the claims of their speech.

What Do You Think?

When you receive a handout during a public presentation, do you continue to listen to the speaker or do you focus on reading the handout? Does this seem to affect what you later remember from the speech?

Electronic Media

Electronic media can be more effective than nonelectronic media because they often appear more professional, increasing your ethos and persuasive appeal. Unfortunately, however, it is sometimes difficult or impossible to get access to this equipment. If you decide to use electronic media, it is your responsibility to make sure you can get the appropriate equipment to your room on the day you speak. As stated earlier, electronic media include slides and slide projectors, transparencies and overhead projectors, audiocassette and CD players, VCRs and LCD projectors or monitors, and computers and LCD panels or projectors.

Slides and Slide Projectors

If you decide to use photographs as visual aids, you could have your photographs made into slides and then project them onto a screen using a slide projector. Debbie had several photographs from her trip to the Grand Canyon made into slides, and she displayed them in this way. Slides make your photographs easy for all audience members to see. Recall that photographs are fairly concrete representations. However, the disadvantages of getting access to a slide projector and paying the price for turning your photographs into slides might outweigh the advantages.

Teaching Tip
If your college has a media lab, ask a representative from that lab to speak to your class about the ways the lab might be able to assist students in the development of presentational materials.

Transparencies and Overhead Projectors

You can use transparencies and an overhead projector to display many different types of visual aids—for example, photographs, drawings, diagrams, maps, graphs, and charts. Transparencies can be particularly effective for illustrating layers of complexity. For example, Rebecca used three transparencies to display her line graph about public school enrollment projections. Each transparency allowed her to superimpose an additional line to her graph as she moved into her discussion of a particular district.

Transparencies are simple and inexpensive to create. Almost any photocopier can transfer visual materials onto transparencies. Transparencies are also easy to transport and to use. Most classrooms and meeting rooms have overhead projectors in them. And the items you place on your transparencies can be made to look very professional by using computer software programs and photocopiers to create them. For these reasons, many public speakers choose to display their visual aids using transparencies and overhead projectors.

Audiocassette and CD Players

If you decide to use audio materials for presentational aids, you will need to make sure you have access to the appropriate media for displaying them. Audiocassette and CD players offer an affordable and effective way to share audio examples during a public speech. You might need to consider accessibility to the equipment as well as sound quality if you choose these media for your aids.

VCRs and LCD Projectors or Monitors

If you choose to show a videotaped clip for a presentational aid, you will need to make sure you have access to a VCR and LCD projector or monitor. Ideally, you can show your examples using an LCD multimedia projector. An **LCD projector** is a unit that can be connected to a VCR or computer, which projects the images onto a screen. The main advantage of displaying your videotaped clip using an LCD projector is that it enlarges the images so that all audience members can see them. Disadvantages include accessibility and cost. Because they are rather expensive, LCD projectors are not easily accessible to most beginning speakers. If you don't have access to an LCD projector, you can display your videotaped clip using a VCR connected to a television monitor or to multiple monitors, depending on the size of your audience.

Computer and LCD Panels or Projectors

Teaching Tip
If your college has a technology resource center, have students who are interested in using a computer in their next presentation meet with a specialist for advice on using the equipment.

Computerized slide show presentations, like those you can create using Microsoft's PowerPoint, Lotus's Freelance Graphics, or Adobe's Persuasion, are becoming increasingly popular as a means by which to both prepare and display presentational aids. When used effectively, computerized slide shows can be very effective because they can appeal to a variety of learning styles by integrating a wide range of presentational aids (Hotch, 1992). Most of the computer software programs allow you to integrate drawings, diagrams, maps, graphs, charts, lists, photographs, and video clips. Essentially, you can include nearly anything you can imagine in your slide show by creating it yourself, using the folders of clip art included in the software, downloading materials from the Internet, or scanning data you find in various print resources into the system.

A major disadvantage is the need to have access to a computer and LCD panel or projector for displaying the slide show. An **LCD panel** is a device connected to a computer and placed on top of an overhead projector that projects what is on the computer monitor to a screen in the front of the room. An LCD projector is a similar device that has its own light source. Recall that LCD projectors can also be used to project videotaped images onto a screen. LCD panels are more portable and less expensive than LCD projectors, but they require overhead projectors with very bright projection lights. A second disadvantage of these presentations is that a computer malfunction during the presentation can mean total disaster. If you elect to prepare a computerized slide show and project it with an LCD panel or projector, be sure that good quality equipment is available for the presentation and prepare backup materials in the form of overhead transparencies or handouts.

As we discussed earlier in the chapter, presentational aids can enhance your verbal message by making it more concrete, clear, understandable, interesting, credible, and memorable. However, if poorly constructed or ineffectively used, presentational aids can detract from your message, making it less clear, less credible, and less interesting. To ensure that your presentational aids enhance the verbal message, you need to follow specific guidelines when constructing and using them.

Teaching Tip
To give students practice in selecting appropriate presentational aids, see the Selecting Presentational Aids or Visual Aid Workshop assignments in the Activities section of this chapter.

Constructing Presentational Aids

Students often feel apprehensive about constructing their presentational aids, usually just because they feel unsure about what constitutes an effective presentational aid. Moreover, although computerized slide shows are becoming more popular, many people who use them neglect to follow the guidelines for effective presentational aid construction. For this reason, computerized slide shows are specifically addressed throughout the discussion that follows. The discussion is arranged according to five key guidelines: (a) The presentational aid should enhance the verbal message by presenting information in some other way, (b) the presentational aid should communicate ideas clearly, (c) the presentational aid should be worth the cost in terms of time and money, (d) the presentational aid should not take too much time to present, and (e) the media needed to display the presentational aid must be accessible and manageable.

The Aid Should Enhance the Verbal Message

To enhance the verbal message, a presentational aid should consist of more than just words. Avoid visual aids that simply list phrases used in the speech. For all presentational aids—including those like videotapes and CDs that are clearly not just words—make sure that your aid reinforces your verbal message and in some way goes beyond it.

Teaching Tip
To give students an opportunity to apply these guidelines, see the Battle of the Visual Aids assignment contained in the Activities section of this chapter.

Considering Computerized Slide Shows

One of the most common mistakes made by speakers who use computerized slide shows is to offer slides that are nothing more than a series of bulleted lists. To enhance the verbal message, your presentational aids—even when in the form of a computerized slide show—must include something other than words. Keep in mind that an advantage of computerized slide shows is that they make it possible to use a wide range of material and, in doing so, appeal to diverse learning styles. Does your slide show include, for example, charts, graphs, diagrams, and relevant clip art or pictures you've downloaded from the Internet or scanned in?

The Aid Should Communicate Ideas Clearly

Like your verbal message, your presentational aid won't be effective unless it's clear. In order to present your ideas clearly, your presentational aid must be large enough for the room and audience, be simple, and use color effectively.

Size

Your visual or audiovisual aid should be large enough so that even those in the back of the room can see it. If your photographs are too small, have them enlarged to at least ten by twelve inches. Better yet, convert them into slides or transparencies that can be projected on a screen in the front of the room, or scan them into a computerized slide show. If you display your visual aids on a flip chart or posterboard, the media should be at least two by three feet. To ensure that your videotaped clips can be easily seen, use a monitor with a twenty-five-inch screen for audiences of thirty or fewer people. For larger audiences, use multiple monitors or an LCD panel or projector that can project the images on a large screen.

For all types of visual and audiovisual aids, print titles and labels in large letters. This means they should be at least two to three inches tall. Labels should be large enough to be seen easily in the back of the room. Ideally, to check size you should place a draft of your presentational aid in the front of the room where you will be speaking and walk around to make sure it is legible from all parts of the room.

Simplicity

Discussion Tip
Why is it important that speakers convey only one idea per presentational aid? According to Sellnow, what guidelines should speakers utilize for visual clarity?

Keep your presentational aids *simple,* conceptually and visually. Remember that their purpose is to make understanding easier, not harder. Convey only one idea per presentational aid, and express that idea clearly in the title. Include no more than three or four points to support the ideas, and express those clearly with single words or short phrases. If more seems needed, divide the material between two aids.

For visual clarity, draw neatly and spell correctly. Don't use all capital letters for labels and titles. It's easier for audience members to read a combination of capital and lowercase letters. If necessary, use stencils, ask a friend to help you, or use a computer to create titles and labels. Use only one font for all titles and labels, even if you have a series of aids. Choose a strong, straight font like Arial, Helvetica, or Times New Roman (see Figure 13–9). Thin fonts, italicized fonts, and shadowed fonts are difficult to read (see Figure 13–10). Include enough information so that the presentational aid makes sense on its own, but not so much that it becomes cluttered: Remember that you'll be explaining the aid orally.

FIGURE 13–9
Good Font Choices

This is Arial.
This is Futura.
This is Helvetica.
This is Times New Roman.

This Helvetica Neue Light Condensed is too thin.

This Goudy italicized font is hard to read.

This Kuenstler cursive font is difficult to read.

FIGURE 13–10
Poor Font Choices

Color

Careful use of color can do a lot to make your presentational aids clear. Use a single background color, even if you have a series of aids. Make sure there is sufficient contrast between your background and your labels and images. Generally, light colors like white, tan, or a pastel work best for backgrounds, while bold colors like black, blue, or purple work best for titles and labels, since they can be seen more easily from a distance. Avoid using more than two or three colors in a presentational aid. In particular, avoid using red and green together, since audience members who are colorblind have difficulty distinguishing them.

Teaching Tip
Tell students to carefully consider the colors they use on posters. Neon and yellow colors can be very difficult to read from the back of the classroom. Instruct students to view their posters from a distance to be sure they are easy to read.

Considering Computerized Slide Shows

As with other presentational aids, you should use a type size that is large enough to be seen clearly from anywhere in the room. Generally, this means that for audiences of forty or more, slide titles should be in forty-four point type and labels in thirty-four point type; for audiences of twelve to forty people, titles should be in forty-point type and labels in twenty-eight point type. For smaller audiences, titles should be in thirty-six point type and labels in twenty-four point type (Currid, 1995). You should never use a point size smaller than twenty on a computer slide show slide.

As with other presentational aids, you should use a single font throughout, because mixing fonts would make your slides less clear. Likewise, it's best to stick to two or three colors on a slide, because more than that can make them less clear.

In addition, each software program offers a number of slide background designs. As with font, stick to one background design for the entire show. Some backgrounds project better on a screen than others. Typically, light text on a dark background projects most clearly. You can also use a dark text on a light background. The key is to make sure there is a distinct contrast between your background color and your texts and images. Avoid backgrounds that use pastels. This limits the contrast and makes the projections less clear. To choose an effective design, you should experiment with the designs in the room where you plan to present.

Slide show programs also offer a number of different **slide transitions,** or ways to move from one slide to the next; for example, fade in, fly in, and checkerboard. Again, choose one effect and stick to it for the entire presentation. Using many different effects tends to be both distracting and confusing.

Discussion Tip
How many different slide transitions should you incorporate in your PowerPoint presentation? According to Sellnow, why is it important to use bullets in PowerPoint presentations? How many words per bullet should you use?

Use bullets to highlight key points, but try to avoid more than one to three words per bullet. You should never use more than six words per line or six words per slide. Remember, your slide show should enhance the verbal message, not replace or repeat it.

The Aid Should Be Worth the Cost of Time and Money

Presentational aids need not take hours and hours to prepare. Consider some time-saving measures. For example, you might be able to find some useful maps, charts,

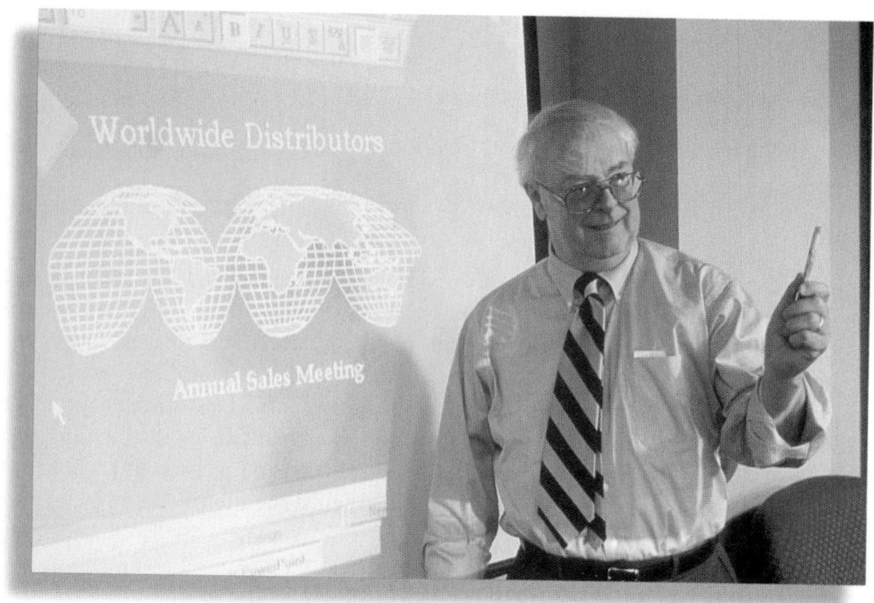

If you use computer-generated visual aids, like PowerPoint, your slide show must still enhance the verbal message, not replace or repeat it.

or graphs on the Internet or in books or articles. Such images can serve as the basis for some of your presentational aids. Of course, you'll need to cite these sources. You can cite them as a footnote on the aid or orally as you discuss the aid in your speech. Soliciting help from friends might also help with time.

You should also be able to figure out ways to keep your expenses down. For example, if you would have to pay a lot for permission to use a copyrighted aid, use a different aid instead. Likewise, rather than hire a professional graphic designer to construct diagrams, charts, or graphs, you could pay a student in a field like graphic design or art to help you.

Considering Computerized Slide Shows

Although computerized slide shows can be very professional and impressive, they can be costly in terms of time and money, especially if you're not familiar with the equipment and software. To save time, you might solicit help from a friend who is familiar with the equipment and software. Or you might pay a student in a field like computer science or communication to help you. Or you might decide that several posterboard diagrams serve the same purpose for a fraction of the cost.

The Aid Should Not Take Too Much Time to Present

As we saw earlier in the chapter, Ahmad learned his lesson the hard way. His videotaped examples consumed so much of his speaking time that he was forced to eliminate a couple of examples and part of his verbal message. Be sure to consider how long it will take to present your slides, videotaped excerpts, cassette recordings, and so on. As a general rule, your aids should be limited to at most 15 to 20 percent of your total speaking time. For a four-to-six-minute speech, then, your aids combined should take less than one minute of the speech.

Considering Computerized Slide Shows

Your computerized slide show presentational aids should also not usurp your speech. Avoid using so many slides that they overtake what you have to say. You should limit yourself to at most one slide for every two minutes of your speech. You should insert blank slides between your presentational slides, so you can control listeners' focus on them. In addition, to ensure that you don't spend too much time on a particular slide, you might elect to use the automatic time-sequencing option offered in the software. This option will automatically transition to the blank slide after a certain number of seconds, based on how you have preprogrammed it.

The Media Needed Must Be Accessible and Manageable

Before deciding on a presentational aid, you need to consider the equipment it requires. Make sure that you have access to the relevant equipment—like a slide projector, overhead, VCR, monitor, cassette player, computer, LCD panel or LCD projector—that it is in proper working order, and that you know how to operate it. As illustrated by Ivy's predicament at the beginning of the chapter, it is important to have backup equipment or backup plans. With regard to equipment, being prepared means abiding by Murphy's law: Anything that can go wrong will go wrong. If you prepare backups, you can defeat Murphy if necessary.

Discussion Tip
What should you do if your presentational aid does not function properly? Discuss options with students and make your expectations clear.

Considering Computerized Slide Shows

The equipment and its quality tend to vary from facility to facility. Plan ahead by finding out whether the computer you will be using is a Macintosh or IBM compatible and by making sure that the LCD panel or projector provides quality images and by verifying that the room you will be speaking in has a screen and dimmable lights. Save your slide show on more than one disc or CD and bring handouts or transparencies as a backup.

Technology Tip
http://www.powerpointers.com/
This Web site, developed by PowerPointers, offers a number of tips for integrating computerized slide shows in presentations. Have students visit this site and report their findings to the class.

> ***What Do You Think?***
> *Consider your next speech and the types of presentational aids you might use. What media would be best for displaying them and why?*

Using Presentational Aids

You will use your presentational aids effectively if you adhere to five specific suggestions: (a) Practice with your presentational aids, (b) position your presentational aids before beginning your speech, (c) explain and integrate your aids at appropriate points during the speech, (d) talk to your audience, not to the presentational aid, and (e) disclose and conceal your presentational aids when appropriate.

Practice With Your Presentational Aids

Because presentational aids can actually hurt your credibility if you fumble while using them, you must practice with your aids when you practice your speech. Regardless of the types of aids and media you use, practice will help you spot potential problems. Had Claus practiced with his posterboards, he would have found out that they weren't sturdy enough. When you practice, make notes on your speaking outline to remind yourself where in the speech you will present your aids.

Be aware of the challenges of each medium you use to present your aids, and practice accordingly. For example, if you have visual aids on posterboards, practice revealing and concealing them smoothly. If you have audiotaped or videotaped clips, practice to ensure that your speech can be completed within the time frame and to become comfortable with the equipment. Practice with overheads and transparencies to get used to placing them on and removing them from the projector, as well as to point to items on the screen rather than on the transparency itself. Practice with your computer-generated slide show and the LCD panel or projector you'll be using for the actual presentation so that you'll be familiar with the setup and operating procedure of that particular unit. Practicing in advance with your presentational aids reduces your anxiety because your use of the aids becomes more proficient and they are no longer an unknown to be feared.

But practice cannot fully eliminate the unknowns, so plan for the unexpected as you practice with your aids. What will you do if your equipment malfunctions or your presentational aids get lost or ruined on the way to class? By becoming aware of possible problems, you'll be fully prepared.

Position Your Presentational Aids Before Beginning Your Speech

Teaching Tip
Before the next speech, tell students how to operate any presentation equipment available to them in the classroom. Consider providing class time for students to practice with this equipment.

Before speaking, position all your presentational aids and equipment and make sure that everything is ready and in working order. This means checking that your posterboards or slides are in the proper order and positioned where all audience members can see them. It means testing to make sure that the equipment for your video or audio aids works and that the excerpts are cued to the correct spot. It also means testing your overhead projector, slide projector, computer, and LCD unit to make sure that everything works and will be visible throughout the room. Taking the time to position your presentational aids will make you feel more confident and look more professional and at ease.

Explain and Integrate Your Presentational Aids

Remember that the presentational aids cannot speak for themselves. You need to explain them and to integrate them fully and appropriately into your speech. Explaining and integrating presentational aids means helping listeners understand why and how they support and enhance the verbal message. You can achieve this goal by following a five-step process:

1. *Reveal* the aid by disclosing it to the group.
2. *Explain* what the aid is by describing its purpose.
3. *Refer* to the aid by pointing to it and then to the images or details you are talking about.
4. *Integrate* the aid by showing its connection to the point you are making in your speech.
5. *Remove* the aid by concealing it from the group.

Include reminders about these steps at the appropriate points in your speaking notes. The step of pointing to your aids and to specific items is an important one for helping listeners understand. Point with your hand or a pointer, and make sure listeners can tell what you're pointing to. Remember, if your presentational aids are projected onto a screen, point to content on the actual screen, not on the overhead projector.

Talk to Your Audience, Not to the Presentational Aid

Beginning speakers sometimes make the mistake of facing their aid as they explain it, making it seem as though they are talking to their aid rather than to their listeners. It's important not to lose your connection to the audience. When explaining a visual aid displayed on a posterboard or flip chart, stand to one side of the visual aid and gesture with the hand closest to the aid. If you do this, you cannot turn your back to the audience. Likewise, stand to one side of the VCR/monitor or cassette player and operate the controls with the hand closest to the aid. Also, stand to one side of the projection screen and gesture with the hand closest to the screen.

Technology Tip
http://www.presentations.com/

This Web site, hosted by Bill Communications, offers several suggestions for using presentational aids in speeches. Tell students to visit this site and write a brief essay summarizing their findings.

Disclose and Conceal Your Presentational Aids When Appropriate

Show each aid only when you're about to discuss it and remove it from view as soon as you've finished discussing it. An aid that is disclosed at other times can distract listeners from your speech. This principle applies to all types of aids.

With visual aids on a posterboard or flip chart, use a cover sheet that you can easily remove and replace. Or simply turn the posterboard around on the easel when you are not discussing the visual aid. Turn off the video or audio player when you are not using it; don't let a video or song play in the background while you continue your speech because this can be distracting. Likewise, if you are using transparencies, turn off the projector when you are through discussing a transparency, or use a cover sheet if you want to keep the projector on between transparencies. With computer-generated slide shows, blank slides between each presentational aid can function like a cover sheet. Recall that any handouts should be distributed after a speech, since you cannot conceal them once they are in your listeners' hands. If the handout contains material you want to discuss in the speech, consider displaying that material on a posterboard, transparency, or slide as well. This way, you can control where your listeners place their attention and then provide them with a handout at the close of the speech.

SUMMARY

Presentational aids—visual, audio, or audiovisual—are supporting material that help you explain your ideas. Visual aids include actual objects, models, photographs, drawings and diagrams, maps, graphs, and charts. Audio aids can be anything from musical recordings to excerpts from famous speeches or even taped examples of environmental sounds. The most common audiovisual aids are videotapes and films. Other sensory aids include those that appeal to taste, touch, or smell.

Technology Tip
http://www.presentationpro.com/

This Web site, hosted by PresentationPro, offers a number of free, professionally designed PowerPoint templates. Have students who are considering using PowerPoint in their next presentation visit this site.

Presentational aids enhance your speech in various ways. These benefits include clarifying the verbal message, adding variety, reducing public speaking anxiety, increasing listener retention, increasing persuasive appeal, and addressing different learning styles.

Each of the many types of presentational aids has its advantages and disadvantages. When deciding which types to use, you'll need to weigh these advantages and disadvantages. You can use actual objects, which can be animate or inanimate. Or you can use models, photographs, drawings and diagrams, maps, graphs, charts, audio materials, audiovisual materials, or other sensory materials.

There are also various types of media—or equipment—you can use for displaying your presentational aids. Nonelectronic media include chalkboards, flip charts, posterboards, and handouts. Electronic media include slides and slide projectors, transparencies and overhead projectors, audio cassette and CD players, VCRs and LCD projectors or monitors, and computers and LCD panels or projectors. Sometimes cost and accessibility factors limit your choices regarding media for displaying presentational aids.

When constructing and using presentational aids, you need to follow specific guidelines. When constructing a presentational aid, you need to consider whether (a) it enhances the verbal message, (b) it communicates ideas clearly, (c) it is worth the cost of time and money, (d) it can be used effectively within the allotted time, and (e) the equipment needed is accessible. When using presentational aids, practice in advance, position your aids before beginning your speech, explain and integrate them during the speech, talk to the audience, and disclose and conceal the aids when appropriate.

When constructed and used effectively, presentational aids can make an excellent speech even better. They do so by making the message clearer and more memorable as they address different learning styles. Following the advice offered in this chapter will ensure that your presentational aids function effectively to make your speeches all that they can be.

Technology Tip
http://cgl.microsoft.com/clipgallerylive/default.asp?nEULA=1&nInterface=0

This Web site, hosted by Microsoft, offers an excellent selection of free clip art that can be used in electronic presentations. Have students who are considering using PowerPoint in their next presentation visit this site.

ACTIVITIES

1. **Who Can Follow Directions?** Find a partner. One partner should give the other partner the directions to a familiar destination. You may not use gestures or other visual aids to clarify the directions. Once one partner has finished giving the directions, the other person should try to guess the location. Discuss what made the task simple or difficult.
2. **Battle of the Visual Aids.** Form small groups of three to five persons each. Each group will be given four or five visual aids used by former student speakers. Decide with your group members which visual aid is the best and why. This judgment should be based on the construction guidelines set forth in this chapter: (a) Does it enhance the verbal message? (b) Does it communicate ideas clearly? (c) Would it be costly to prepare in terms of time and money? (d) Would it take a long time to present? (e) Would it be difficult to access needed equipment? After all groups have selected their favorite visual aid, each group will present its "best" visual aid to the class and explain why.
3. **Did You See What I Saw?** Form an observation team with two or three of your classmates. Locate five or six visual aids in magazines, newspapers, and books.

Then critique each one based on how it addresses diverse learning styles: feelers, watchers, thinkers, and doers. Select one visual aid that seems to best address each learning style and explain to the entire class why you picked that one.

4. **Selecting Presentational Aids.** Form small groups of three or four persons each. Choose a topic that could be used for the next classroom speech and brainstorm potential presentational aids for that topic. Try to come up with at least four presentational aids. Select from actual objects, models, photographs, drawings or diagrams, maps, graphs, charts, audio materials, audiovisual materials, or other sensory materials. For each presentational aid you come up with, decide what media you would use to display it and why.
5. **Visual Aid Workshop.** Form a group with two or three classmates. Select one of the topics listed below or come up with one of your own. Construct two different visual aids clarifying the same information. Use notebook paper and markers to construct your aids. When you've finished, show and explain each of the aids to the class. Ask the class to vote for the most effective visual aid and why.

    - Your group is employed by *Rolling Stone.* Construct two possible visual aids showing the three best-selling CDs of the year.
    - Your group is employed by a travel and tourism agency for your state. Construct two possible visual aids showing places visitors should see.
    - Your group is employed by the university relations department at your college or university. Construct two possible visual aids showing the reasons students should attend your school.
    - You and your group are members of the film academy. Construct two possible visual aids showing the three best films of the year.

Key Terms

Audio aids
Audiovisual aids
Bar graphs
Diagram
Flip charts
Flowcharts
Graphs
LCD panel
LCD projector
Line graphs
Maps
Media
Models
Organizational charts
Pie graphs
Posterboards
Presentational aids
Sensory aids
Slide transitions
Visual aids

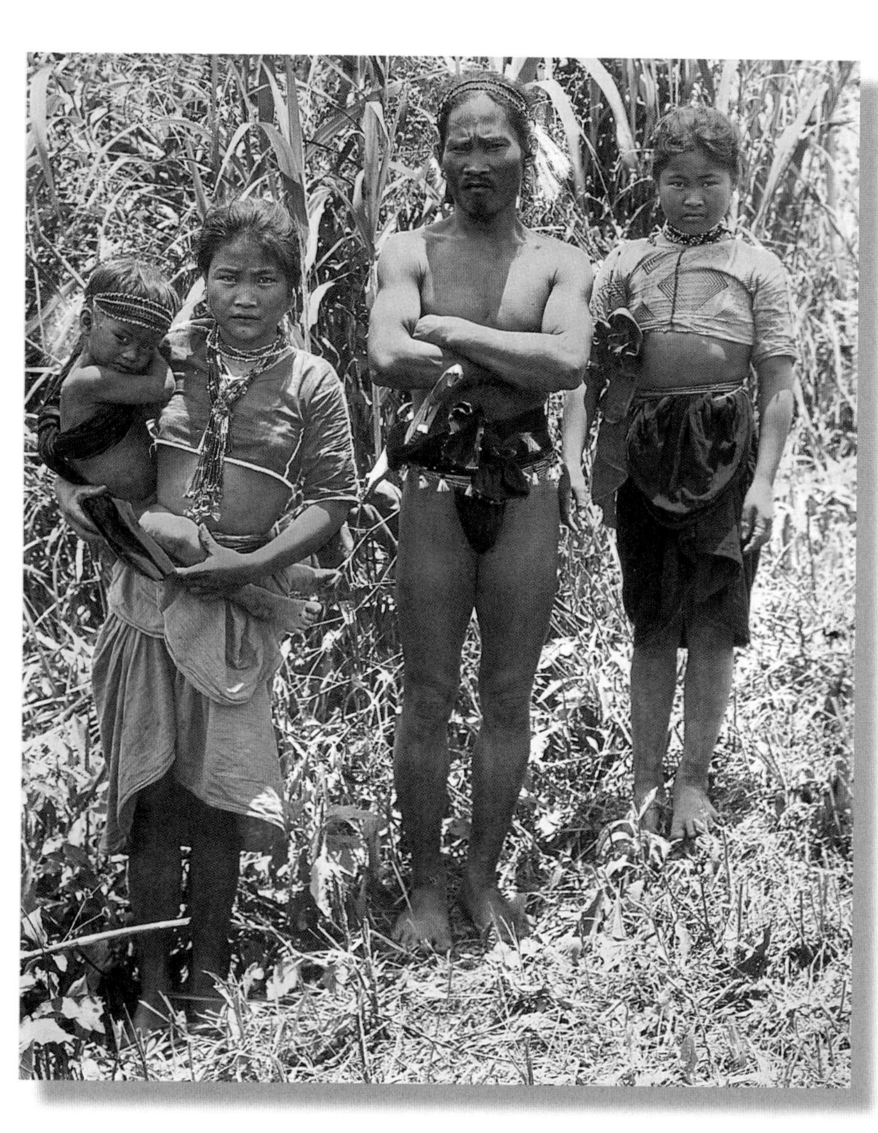

CHAPTER 14

Informative Speaking

Reflective Questions

1. Why might your public speaking anxiety increase when you are going to give an informative speech?
2. Why should you consider different learning styles while preparing your informative speech?
3. What kinds of questions do informative speakers attempt to answer and how?
4. What are some types of organization that might be relevant to an informative speech?

Eric's mom telephoned him early one morning to wish him a belated happy birthday. During the conversation, she asked him *what* he did to celebrate his special day. She asked him *where* he celebrated his birthday, *who* he celebrated it with, and *why* he did not come home to celebrate. He explained that he had celebrated his birthday in the park with his fiancé, Mandy. Mandy made a special recipe for strawberry torte handed down from her grandmother instead of a traditional birthday cake. He chose to spend the day in the park with Mandy instead of coming home because Mandy had to work that evening. Since she could not come home with him, Eric decided to stay at school with her. Eric's mom asked him *how* Mandy made the torte. She thought she might try the recipe for Eric's younger sister's graduation open house later that month. Finally, she asked Eric *what* he wanted for his birthday, since she had not yet bought his present. Eric talked about some new computer software he wanted and the special features of it. In answering his mother's questions, Eric was actually engaged in informative speaking.

Teaching Tip
Refer students to the SpeechMaker CD-ROM. This software provides several tips for effective informative speaking. Consider assigning one of the scenarios to be completed before the class in which you will discuss this chapter.

Whenever you visit with friends or family about people you know, places you've been, things you've done, or even issues you are considering, you're practicing informative speaking. In other words, you engage in informative speaking all the time, even though you don't always realize it. Not only that, you are constantly being bombarded with information, whether it comes from television, newspapers, magazines, or the Internet. In fact, more information has been published in the past thirty years than was published in the previous five thousand years, and the amount of information is doubling every two and one-half years (Banach, 1991). Thanks to the Internet, the amount of information we have access to is immeasurable. In fact, many people refer to this era as the "information age."

What Do You Think?

Consider the last conversation you had with a friend or family member. In what ways were you engaged in informative speaking?

This chapter focuses on the nature and purpose of informative speaking. We begin by discussing the unique characteristics of informative speeches as they differ from other kinds of public speeches. We also discuss the specific types of informative speeches, as well as the patterns that tend to be most appropriate for each type. Then we reveal some specific guidelines for creating effective informative speeches. The chapter ends with a sample informative speech with commentary.

Discussion Tip
Ask students to recall their most effective high school or college teachers. How did these teachers communicate information to the class? What characteristics of their teaching might be relevant to the material presented in this chapter?

What Is Informative Speaking?

Your primary purpose when speaking to inform is to share knowledge with others in order to create mutual understanding. When doing **informative speaking,** you inform your listeners by answering questions such as "who," "when," "what," "where," "why," "how to," and "how does." Informative speakers are essentially teachers, answering questions about objects, events, places, people, processes, procedures, concepts, or issues.

Teaching Tip
Lead an in-class discussion regarding the utility of informative speaking skills. Remind students that they will find themselves using these skills in and outside of the professional realm (teaching, sales, parent-teacher conferences, etc.).

All public speeches, even informative speeches, are based on goals. Your goal as an informative speaker is for your listeners to understand your topic in the same way you do. In this sense, informative speakers also shape perceptions about (a) how listeners will view things and (b) what is important to know about those things. Let's consider the goal of an informative speaker in relation to the goals of

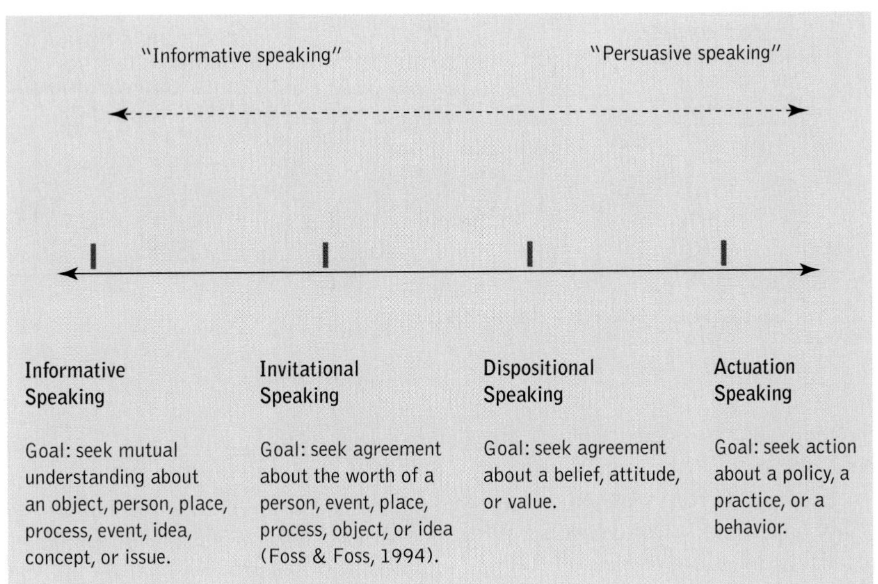

FIGURE 14–1
The Public Speaking Continuum

other kinds of speakers (see Figure 14–1). The informative speaker's goal is to help listeners learn something about a particular topic. Success or failure is ultimately measured by how well listeners *understand, retain,* and *apply* the ideas to their own lives. Notice how the goal becomes loftier as you move further to the right on the continuum. The invitational speaker seeks agreement about the worth of a person, event, place, process, object, or idea. We'll focus more specifically on invitational speeches in Chapters 15–17. The dispositional persuasive speaker seeks agreement about a belief, attitude, or value, and the actuation persuasive speaker seeks not only agreement but also action. These persuasive speech types will be discussed in detail in Chapters 15 and 16. Hence, the goal of the informative speaker is fairly modest in comparison—to achieve mutual understanding about an object, person, place, process, event, idea, concept, or issue.

Although your goal as an informative speaker is fairly modest, effective informative speaking poses a unique challenge to public speakers: It can be difficult to *gain the attention* of listeners as well as *sustain their attention* throughout a presentation. Whereas your goal as a persuasive speaker is to influence your listeners' dispositions or actions, your goal as an informative speaker is simply to get listeners to learn (i.e., understand, retain, and apply). Moreover, the consequences of not achieving mutual understanding are relatively insignificant. Hence, listeners can easily become distracted or lose interest during the speech.

For some public speakers, anxiety increases when they think about preparing and presenting an informative speech. This anxiety typically comes from the speaker's concern that she or he will be boring, that listeners will not be interested, that listeners will already know this information, and that listeners won't care about the topic. Interestingly, these fears usually stem from one's previous experiences listening to informative speakers. After all, by the time you graduate from high school, you have been exposed to dozens of informative speakers and multitudes of informative speeches.

Teaching Tip
Assign a brief written paper in which students discuss their previous informative speaking experiences. What kinds of topics did they speak about? How did they make the topics interesting for the audience? If they have no prior public speaking experience, ask them to analyze speakers they have been exposed to in the past.

To help make my point, let us focus on teachers as informative speakers. If you think about it for a moment or two, you can probably identify one or two

DILBERT reprinted by permission of United Feature Syndicate, Inc.

Discussion Tip
According to Sellnow, what are the key distinctions between informative and persuasive speaking? Are informative speeches inherently persuasive?

teachers you considered very effective and one or two you considered very ineffective. If you were to describe why some were ineffective, you would probably mention reasons like "boring," "dull," "irrelevant," "disorganized," "confusing," "condescending," and "apathetic." Whether consciously or subconsciously, you may fear that you will sound like those teachers! Fortunately, however, there are strategies for preparing and presenting effective and interesting informative speeches that will reduce anxiety rooted in a fear of failure.

What Do You Think?

Identify a former teacher you consider effective. Why? Identify some specific reasons for your opinion.

Types and Patterns of Informative Speeches

Although the goal of any informative speech is to create mutual understanding, there are three different types of informative speeches. These types are the speech of description, the speech of explanation, and the speech of demonstration. These types have different specific goals, that is, they result in different kinds of understanding. In other words, although any good speech will offer elements of all three—description, explanation, and demonstration—your primary thesis will focus on only one of them. Ultimately, then, determining which type of informative speech you will do helps shape your thesis statement.

To determine which type of speech you want to present, ask yourself what it is you are attempting to clarify. Are you trying to (a) paint a picture, (b) clarify a concept, issue, or idea, or (c) outline a process, procedure, or function? For example, let's consider an informative speech about tires. Perhaps you want listeners to learn how to change a flat tire. In this case, your primary focus would be to outline a process or procedure. Hence, you would arrange your ideas chronologically in a speech of demonstration. Or you might want listeners to understand what tires are made of. In this case, you would paint a picture in a speech of description. Or maybe you want listeners to understand why certain tire treads provide better traction in different climates. You would do so by clarifying a concept in a speech of explanation. All three of these informative speeches are about tires. Yet your specific goal is different in each one based on what you want to clarify. Hence, determining which type of informative speech you'll do—description, explanation, or demonstration—helps narrow your focus and shape your thesis statement.

Speeches of Description

What Do You Think?

Consider your next speech. What do you want to clarify? Would you do so best through a speech of description, explanation, or demonstration?

Your goal in a **speech of description** is to create *a clear picture* in the minds of your listeners. That is, your speech attempts to answer an overarching question like "who is/was? . . . " "what is/was? . . . " or "where is/was? . . . " In the tire example, the question was "What is a tire made of?" Generally, informative speeches of description are about objects, people, events, or places. Examples include Ben's speech about the items to include in a winter survival kit, Lynetta's speech about the life of Walt Disney, Lori's speech about the annual hometown potato festival, and Stephanie's speech about great places to go for spring break when you don't have a lot of money.

Teaching Tip
To provide students with an opportunity to analyze an informative speaker, see the Professional Speaker Analysis assignment in the Activities section of this chapter.

Films and television programs often take the shape of speeches of description. For example, the movie *The Messenger* tells the story of Joan of Arc. It functions like a speech of description because it attempts to create in the minds of viewers a clear picture of who Joan of Arc was. Likewise, a television program like VH1's *Behind the Music* attempts to paint a picture of who particular musicians are in the minds of viewers. Many of the programs you'll find on the Discovery Channel or the History Channel also function like speeches of description. As I perused the television guide recently, for example, I saw programs about chimpanzees in the Congo, gorillas, sharks, crocodiles, disasters in America, and military blunders—all of which focus on painting pictures in the minds of viewers.

As discussed in Chapter 8, there are many different ways to organize the body of your speech. Each speech topic is unique, so it wouldn't make sense to say that a particular type of speech should follow a certain organizational pattern. Nonetheless, some patterns lend themselves more easily to speeches of description than others.

To describe people or objects, you'll often arrange your main points using a chronological or topical pattern. When Tom gave a speech about Beethoven, he used a chronological pattern by talking first about Beethoven's experiences as a child, then about his experiences as an adult before becoming deaf, and finally about his experiences as an adult after becoming deaf. When Christina talked about her dog, Domino, she used a topical pattern to discuss what she learned from him—that is, responsibility, unconditional love, and friendship.

Teaching Tip
Have students write a brief essay analyzing the appropriateness of these organizational patterns for their speech topics. This assignment should help students focus their ideas and develop their outlines.

To describe places, you'll often use a spatial pattern. When Mike talked about the college library, he used a spatial pattern to explain where to find academic journals, books, and reference resources in relation to the main entrance and to each other.

To describe events, you might use a topical, comparative, or chronological pattern. Pam used a comparative pattern to describe certain rituals in an Amish wedding ceremony compared to rituals in a typical wedding ceremony of the dominant American culture. Lori used a chronological pattern to talk about her trip to the Holy Land.

Speeches of Explanation

Your goal in a **speech of explanation** is to generate *a clear interpretation* in the minds of your listeners. Your speech attempts to answer an overarching question like "why does/is? . . . " or "what does? . . . " Speeches of explanation often

A speech about who Joan of Arc was paints a picture for listeners, so it is a speech of description.

Teaching Tip
To give students practice in differentiating between these types of speeches, see the Brainstorming Informative Speech Types assignment contained in the Activities section of this chapter.

focus on issues, concepts, ideas, or beliefs. Examples include Laura's speech about why she chose to be a vegetarian, Ricky's speech about the advantages and disadvantages of home schooling, and Debbie's speech about the different forms of sexual harassment.

Television also provides examples of programs that function like speeches of explanation. For example, when *20/20* aired a story that focused on the differences between boys and girls, it did so as a speech of explanation. When television programs like *7th Heaven* or *Touched by an Angel* focus on complex issues like premarital sex or teen violence, they are attempting to explain what is occurring in society as a speech of explanation. When the nightly news programs offer in-depth segments about issues like women and heart disease, the effects of divorce on children, or medical ethics, they are offering information in the form of speeches of explanation.

Speeches of explanation often follow a causal, topical, or comparison and contrast pattern. When Ricky talked about the advantages and disadvantages of home schooling, for example, he employed a topical pattern. Debbie used a topical pattern arranged by gradation to talk about sexual harassment. She began by discussing the most severe forms like coercion and threats, then moved to less severe forms like bribes and propositions, and ended with the least severe forms like teasing and telling sexist jokes.

Speeches of Demonstration

In a **speech of demonstration,** your goal is to *clarify a process or procedure* in the minds of your listeners. That is, your speech attempts to answer an overarching question like "how does? . . . " or "how do? . . . " Speeches of demonstration tend to focus on how something works, functions, or is accomplished. Examples include John's speech about how to harvest wild rice, Rory's speech about how to make chocolate chip cookies, and Colleen's speech about how laser surgery corrects vision impairments.

Teaching Tip
Many hardware suppliers have videos to demonstrate how to complete a home repair project. Obtain one of these videos and show it in class. Instruct the students to analyze how well the tape works as a speech of demonstration.

Television programs like *This Old House,* which shows viewers how to remodel and repair their homes, *Sewing with Nancy,* which demonstrates the process of sewing, *Daily Workout,* which takes viewers through an exercise regime, or even *The Magic Schoolbus,* which often shows how the body functions, are essentially speeches of demonstration that attempt to clarify for their viewers how to do something or how something works.

What Do You Think?

Consider one of your favorite television programs. Would you consider it to be more like a speech of description, explanation, or demonstration? Why?

Since speeches of demonstration are about processes or procedures, they most often use a chronological pattern. These patterns allow the speaker to move through the steps in a procedure or to detail a process.

Guidelines for Effective Informative Speaking

Of course, the general principles discussed earlier in this book should be considered as you prepare and present your informative speeches. There are certain guidelines, however, that you should follow extra carefully when speaking to inform. Since your goal is essentially to teach your listeners something, you should consider how your speech relates to the learning process. Ask yourself five key questions as you prepare your speech:

Teaching Tip
Consider requiring that your students use at least one presentational aid in the informative speech. This will ensure that students get practice utilizing presentational aids, add interest to the speech, and reduce speaking anxiety.

- Is my speech new?
- Is my speech relevant?
- Is my speech clear?
- Is my speech novel?
- Does my speech address different learning styles?

Let's look at how you can answer each of these questions effectively in your informative speech.

Is My Speech New?

Since your primary goal in an informative speech is to share knowledge to create mutual understanding, the knowledge ought to be information your listeners don't already know. Recall that the content of your speech is essentially its main points and the material that supports them. With an informative speech in particular, you need to shape the content in ways that will capture and sustain the interest of your listeners. Your content must help you break through the **apathy barrier,** the tendency of listeners to be indifferent toward your speech, partly as a result of their having heard over the years some informative speeches that were not very interesting. You can make your content new and, thus, more interesting to listeners by considering the topic itself and your overall approach.

> ***What Do You Think?***
>
> *Consider a time in the past week when you became bored listening to a friend, teacher, speaker, or television or radio program. Why?*

Technology Tip
http://www.projectcensored.org/
This Web site contains information about important stories that are often overlooked by the popular press. Students can be encouraged to visit this site to explore contemporary, interesting, and challenging speech topics.

First, consider your topic. Select a topic that is new to your listeners. If your topic is one that listeners know relatively little about, they are likely to be more interested in your speech. Summer chose to inform her listeners about the Ebola virus. Since her listeners didn't know much about this virus, her topic was new.

It can be difficult, however, to come up with a topic that is new—in and of itself—to listeners. Even if your topic is one that listeners are somewhat familiar with, however, you can make it new for them. Think about your audience, using audience analysis as discussed in Chapter 6, and ask yourself the question: What is it about my topic that listeners probably don't know? Not only will this strategy help you hold listeners' interest, but it is crucial for ethical informative speaking since your primary goal is to share knowledge. You can make your topic new by your approach to it, by considering depth, breadth, or perspective.

One way to make your information new is by adding depth—that is, by looking at your topic deeply enough that you go beyond people's general knowledge of it. Jen did this when she gave an informative speech about psychics. Most listeners know that psychics claim to predict the future but know little about the actual methods they use to do so. So Jen focused on psychics' methods and on their roots in astrology, astronomy, and numerology.

> ***What Do You Think?***
>
> *What is the topic of your next speech? How can you make it new to listeners through depth, breadth, or perspective?*

Another way to make your information new is by adding breadth—that is, by looking at how the topic relates to a range of associated topics. Larissa did this when she informed listeners about the effects of hysterectomies. She discussed some of the physical and emotional consequences for the individual undergoing the operation, the emotional and relational effects on the patient's friends and family, and the financial costs these operations have on society.

Information also can be made new by presenting it from a unique perspective, from a point of view that listeners have probably never considered. Charity approached her speech about migrant workers by discussing it from the perspective of the workers themselves.

Is My Speech Relevant?

In addition to making your information new to listeners, you also need to relate your information directly to their needs and desires. Moreover, don't assume that listeners will recognize the relevance of the information. Instead, use listener relevance links to tell listeners how each main point affects them. By showing listeners how they can benefit from learning the information you offer, you'll add considerably to their interest in your speech.

Teaching Tip
Assign students to small groups and have them discuss their speech topics. Instruct them to probe for reasons why their peers might find the topic(s) relevant. This activity will assist students in the development of audience-centered relevance statements.

One way to make your speech more relevant is to compare the new information that you're presenting to things listeners are more familiar with. Andria did this when she compared the unfamiliar practice of acupressure to the more familiar practice of acupuncture. Amanda did this when she compared certain Islamic traditions with those of Judeo-Christian traditions, which were more likely to be familiar to her audience. In addition to making information more relevant to listeners, comparisons like these can also make it clearer.

Is My Speech Clear?

Since your goal is to create mutual understanding, it is important that your meaning is clear to your listeners. Sharing knowledge in an informative speech differs from doing so in a written document because listeners must understand what you mean as you tell them. They don't have the opportunity to read a particular sentence or paragraph several times until it makes sense. Hence, it is crucial to convey your message clearly. You can do so by limiting complex vocabulary and technical jargon, avoiding abstractions, and explaining everything thoroughly.

Teaching Tip
To give students practice in developing clear messages, see the Giving Clear Directions assignment located in the Activities section of this chapter.

Whenever possible, use straightforward, concrete language in your informative speech. When you must use complex or technical jargon, define it as simply as you can. Remember that your purpose is to communicate your ideas clearly, not to impress your audience with jargon. This is not to say you should never use jargon. To the contrary, when defined simply, jargon can actually make your message clearer. In his speech, "Take a Test Drive on the Information Superhighway: Unmasking the Jargon," for example, Carl S. Ledbetter (1995) clarified technical jargon about the Internet throughout his speech. In doing so, he demystified the jargon for his listeners:

Teaching Tip
Emphasize the importance of defining key terms that speakers may take for granted.

> Let's start with "National Information Infrastructure." That means pork for every state. This is the only kind of infrastructure ever invented for which the construction workers are politicians.
>
> "Multimedia" means more than one medium—a fancy way of saying "Talkies"—movies with sound. Multimedia means mixing voice, video, image, and data in a single communication system.
>
> It's the difference between the records we played as teenagers, which we could only listen to, and the music videos our kids listen to and watch (p. 567).

Being clear also means avoiding abstractions. If you're vague, listeners won't fully grasp your meaning. You can avoid abstractions by describing your examples thoroughly through vivid imagery and detail as we discussed in Chapter 11. You can also avoid abstractions by comparing unfamiliar ideas, objects, or concepts with those that your listeners might be more familiar with. Recall that Andria did this when she compared acupressure to acupuncture and Carl Ledbetter did so in the previous example by comparing multimedia to records and music videos.

Teaching Tip
Show videotapes of student speeches that lack clarity. Assign students to small groups and have them rewrite portions of the speeches using the clarity guidelines presented in this chapter.

Finally, being clear means explaining everything thoroughly. In other words, don't overestimate what your audience already knows. Beginning speakers sometimes assume that their classmates are also familiar with information that they have learned as a result of majoring in a particular field. Remember that your listeners are probably not majoring in the same subject as you are and, consequently, do not know as much about it as you do. What's common knowledge in your field is probably not generally known by all. Likewise, your personal and professional experiences outside the walls of academia are probably not common knowledge either. If you have an opportunity to survey the class before the speech, you can learn a good deal about what these students already know. If not, it is best to prepare your speech based on the assumption that your listeners will be hearing about your topic for the first time.

What Do You Think?

Consider your next speech. Will you be using any terms or concepts that you should define for your listeners? Will you be introducing any abstract ideas or concepts that you should explain clearly to your listeners?

Is My Speech Novel?

Teaching Tip
Many students find that their topic may be considered old or irrelevant to audience members. To help them develop novel approaches, assign students to small groups and give each a list of common topics. Have them brainstorm ways to make the topics more interesting and exciting.

In order to achieve your goal—mutual understanding—you need to gain and maintain the interest of your listeners throughout the speech. One way to do this is through novelty. You can add a creative flair to your speech for this purpose within your primary structural elements, your language choices, and your delivery style.

It is perhaps more important in an informative speech than in any other kind of speech to start with an attention catcher that sparks listener interest. Try to be creative in developing your attention catcher. For example, you might start with a physical activity or with a startling fact or statistic, a story, or anything else that will make listeners curious and involved. Humor can serve as an effective attention catcher for an informative speech, since it can lighten the atmosphere and make people more receptive to learning (Wallinger, 1997; Wanzer & Frymeier, 1999). As always, of course, be sure to avoid potentially offensive humor (Sev'er & Ungar, 1997; Swift & Swift, 1994). Although the attention catcher is especially important, think of ways to make each element of structure—your listener relevance links, preview, transitions, and so on, all the way to your clincher—work to sustain listener interest.

What Do You Think?

Consider a television commercial you've seen that uses humor. To what degree does the use of humor grab your attention, maintain it, and help you remember it?

Use vivid language and style in your informative speech. Appeal to listeners' senses; help them see, hear, feel, taste, and smell what you are talking about. Where relevant, use emotional appeals. Be creative by using some figures of speech (e.g., alliteration, repetition, similes, metaphors, and analogies; see Chapter 11) to reinforce some important points. As you prepare, think of yourself as an audience member listening to your informative speech. Continually ask and answer this question: What sorts of language and style choices might gain and sustain my interest and help me remember the speech if I were in my audience?

Teaching Tip
To give students practice in developing and utilizing vivid language, see the Using Vivid Oral Style assignment contained in the Activities section of Chapter 11.

Use your voice to convey enthusiasm about the information you are sharing. If you sound enthusiastic, you're more likely to interest listeners in learning the information. As you practice, think about how you might use changes in rate, pitch, and volume as well as pauses and stresses to reinforce your ideas (see Chapter 12). Likewise, your facial expressions should convey enthusiasm about your topic as well as reinforce the emotions in your verbal message. Gestures and movement can also play an important role in an informative speech. You can use them to emphasize the points you want listeners to remember so they can better grasp the information. You can also use them to help gain and sustain listener attention. Our eyes are attracted to moving objects, so by gesturing and using movement appropriately, you can draw listeners back into your speech.

What Do You Think?

Consider your next speech. How can you make the attention catcher novel? What language choices can you integrate to spark listener interest? Where can you incorporate delivery skills to help you sound and look enthusiastic about your topic?

Does My Speech Address Different Learning Styles?

Learning styles research suggests that different listeners are likely to be more and less interested in different kinds of supporting material. Some will prefer facts and statistics; some, personal examples; some, definitions and explanations; and some, presentational aids. By including different kinds of supporting material, you'll be more likely to gain and maintain the interest of all your listeners. Moreover, by including different kinds of supporting material, your speech will round the entire cycle of learning—that is, you will help all of your listeners better understand, retain, and apply the information. For this same reason, you should also present your supporting material in different ways—not just verbally, but visually and audiovisually as well (see Figure 14–2).

For listeners who prefer to learn by feeling, include some supporting material that addresses *concrete experiences*. In other words, share personal stories from people who've actually experienced what it is you're talking about. The experiences can be your own, or you can include examples involving people you've read about or even personal testimonies from people you've interviewed. In her speech about acupressure, for example, Andria shared personal testimonies from several individuals who had been helped by the practice.

Teaching Tip
Have students write a brief essay in which they analyze how supporting material can be incorporated in their next speech to round the entire cycle of learning. Encourage them to complete this assignment using the supporting material they have gathered for their next speech.

For listeners who prefer to learn by doing, include supporting material that addresses *active experimentation*. These listeners value seeing a practical approach; they like to see what applications your topic has. Give examples of such application. If relevant to your topic, provide a formula or procedure that audience

FIGURE 14–2 Informative Speaking and the Learning Cycle

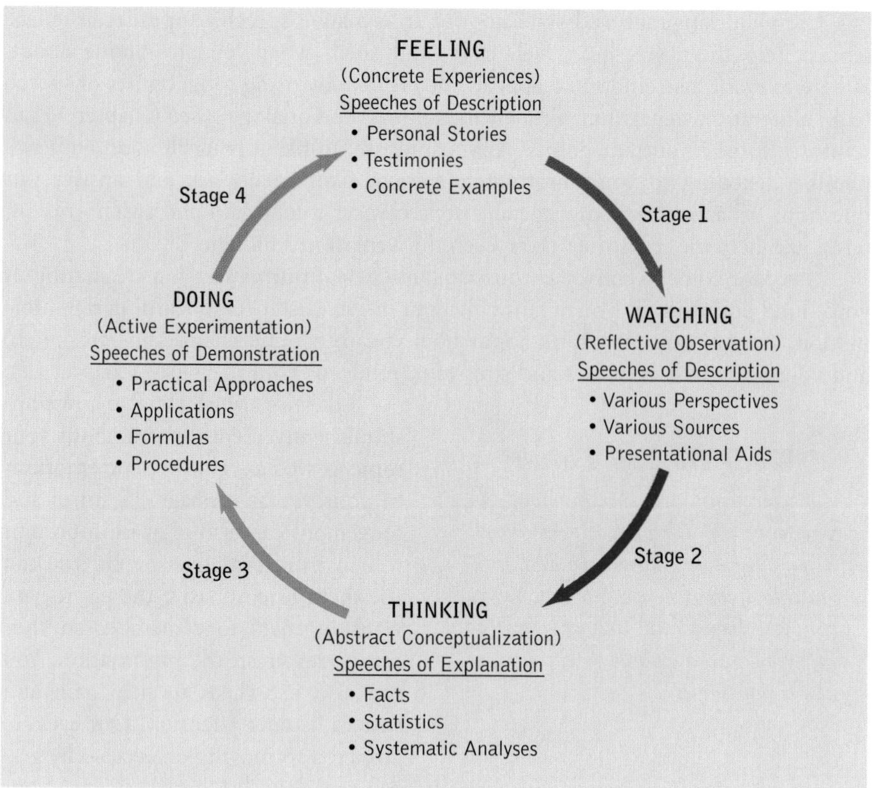

members can complete for self-assessment. Andria demonstrated one simple acupressure procedure for relieving headaches—by applying pressure between the thumb and forefinger—and asked her listeners to try it at the same time.

For listeners who prefer to learn by thinking, include supporting material that addresses *abstract conceptualization.* You might, for example, include a systematic analysis of some aspect of your topic or relevant facts and statistics. Andria shared statistics about the growing number of medical doctors who endorse acupressure as a viable option for pain relief. She also included facts that compared costs of over-the-counter pain medications with acupressure.

Finally, for listeners who prefer to learn by watching, include supporting material that addresses *reflective observation.* Since these learners rely on objectivity and careful observation before making a judgment, your supporting material should reflect a variety of perspectives. Include research from different kinds of sources (books, journals, magazines, newspapers, government documents, and so forth), and identify those sources. Try to include opinions from academics and other professionals in the field, as well as from nonspecialists. You also might conduct a survey to get the opinions of a broad range of people on some aspect of your topic.

As discussed in Chapter 13, your presentational aids, too, should address different learning styles. For example, you might include graphs and charts showing statistical relationships and trends (thinker), a videotaped clip of someone experiencing the topic firsthand (feeler), and a diagram showing the relationships among a variety of perspectives (watcher). As with the verbal part of your speech, variety in your presentational aids will help all of your listeners understand, retain, and apply the information you offer.

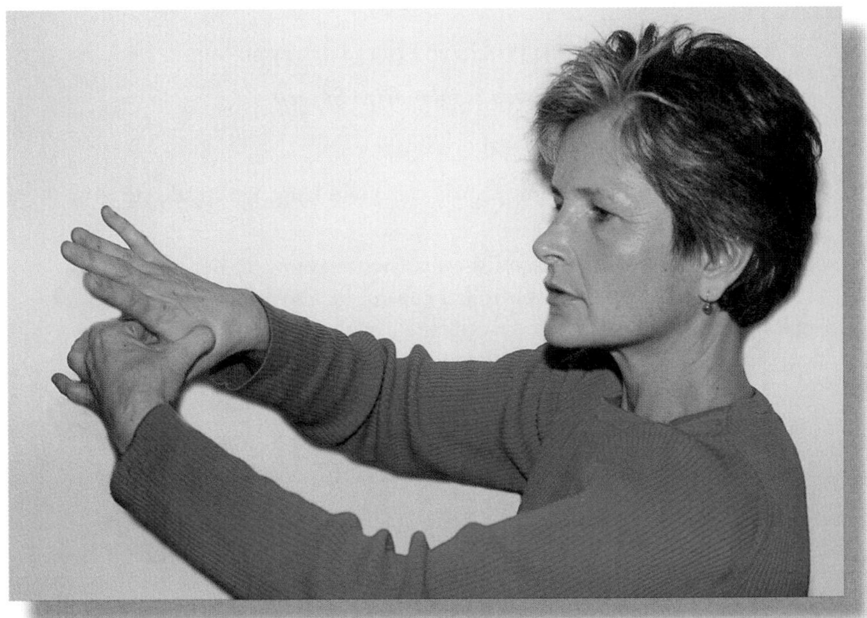

You can address doers by showing them a formula or demonstrating a procedure they can repeat themselves.

In short, you can shape the content, structure, and delivery of your informative speech in ways that will help you gain and sustain your listeners' interest. You can do so by considering how your topic or approach to your topic is new. You can also do so by relating your speech directly to your listeners' needs and desires, and you can do so by using clear language that limits complex vocabulary, defines jargon, and explains ideas fully. Likewise, your enthusiastic delivery style can maintain audience interest. Finally, you can use supporting material that addresses feelers, watchers, thinkers, and doers.

What Do You Think?

Consider your next speech. What can you do to ensure that your supporting material addresses the learning style preferences of all your listeners?

Teaching Tip
To provide students with an opportunity to practice informative speaking, see the Painting Colorful Pictures assignment located in the Activities section of this chapter.

A Sample Informative Speech

The following speech provides an example of how to apply the guidelines offered in this chapter to an informative speech. After examining these first few paragraphs and the commentary provided in the introduction, continue the process for the rest of the speech. Use these questions to guide your analysis:

- How is the speech made new?
- How is the speech made relevant?
- How are complex ideas made clear?
- How is the speech made novel?
- How does the speech address feelers, thinkers, watchers, and doers?

Teaching Tip
Have students analyze Laurie's speech using the guidelines for effective informative speaking presented in this chapter.

"The Illongot Headhunters"

Laurie's Informative Speech

Line-by-Line Analysis

Attention catcher: Notice how Laurie uses vivid language to add novelty and arouse curiosity right away.

Listener relevance: Laurie establishes listener relevance in her opening comments to draw listeners into her topic. She also appeals to fear by talking about killing people just for their heads.

Speaker credibility: Laurie establishes her credibility so listeners will be more inclined to believe that she has a degree of expertise.

Thesis: Laurie's thesis statement is somewhat blunt, reading more like a specific purpose than a thesis. Still, it very clearly identifies the topic of her speech.

Preview: Again, her preview is very clearly stated. Listeners know she is doing a speech of description. We should have a clear picture in our minds when she is finished.

Challenge yourself to continue commenting on Laurie's speech based on the guidelines offered in this chapter.

The Speech

Introduction

I. *Attention catcher:* In the spring, when the fire plant blooms, the gentle swinden farmers of the Philippines go mad with anger and turn into the ferocious headhunters of South Seas legend.

II. *Listener relevance:* Remember Robinson Crusoe, the Swiss family Robinson, or even the swashbuckling or missionary stories of childhood about island savages? Well, headhunters of the Illongot tribe were still killing people for their heads just twenty years ago and there is no guarantee they won't start again.

III. *Speaker credibility:* My interest in the Illongot grew out of an anthropology course I took and research I've done into the history and culture of this hunter/gatherer tribe.

IV. *Thesis statement:* Today, I'd like to give you a glimpse into the lives of the Illongot headhunters.

V. *Preview:* To help you understand who these people are, I'll talk about the headhunting ritual itself, some important restrictions on it, and what caused the Illongot to stop the practice.

Transition:

As I said, the Illongot are an indigenous tribe living in the jungles of the Philippine Islands subsisting on hunting, gathering, and swinden farming. "Indigenous" means original and usually tribal, and "swinden farming" is a kind of slash-and-burn agriculture where the people till the land until it doesn't produce well, and then they move on (*Microsoft Encarta,* 1995). Many jungle-dwelling tribes in the Philippines practice this kind of farming (*Vanishing People of the Earth*, 1986). But "taking heads" is a special practice that is unique to the Illongot tribe.

Body

I. *First main point:* Headhunting was done by young, unmarried men as a manhood ritual. It was essentially a rite of passage from boyhood to manhood.

Listener relevance: This rite of passage concept is not unique to the Illongot tribe. It is actually quite similar to the sort of ritual of boys who go out on their first hunting trip with their fathers in this country.

Discussion Tip
Why is it important that speeches use listener relevance links in the body of the speech? How could Laurie tailor this link to the specific concerns and interests of this class?

A. *Subpoint:* Taking the head of an enemy was required before a young man could marry.

1. *Sub-subpoint:* Young women viewed more successful men favorably.

2. *Sub-subpoint:* Tribal leaders viewed more successful men favorably.

B. *Subpoint:* Headhunting was done when the bright red fire plant bloomed.

1. *Sub-subpoint:* The blooming plant was associated with overwhelming anger.

2. *Sub-subpoint:* Some speculate that the plant actually has a chemical effect that intensifies feelings of anger when it blooms.

3. *Sub-subpoint:* Although these connections are not fully understood, they have come about, in part, because the Illongot are typically known as a close-knit tribe who rarely show anger (Rosaldo, 1980).

Transition:

Because headhunting was a rite-of-passage ritual, several restrictions governing whose heads could be taken also existed.

II. *Second main point:* The most important restriction had to do with whose heads could be hunted.

A. *Subpoint:* Only people who were members of other Philippine tribes could be headhunted.

Discussion Tip
Does Laurie sufficiently develop the main points in the body of this speech? What might she say in the speech to establish the credibility of her sources?

Listener relevance: As you can probably imagine, whether you are hunting gophers or gold or even heads, things don't always go as planned.

- **B.** *Subpoint:* Sometimes anthropologists would mistakenly be killed (Rosaldo, *Illongot Headhunting,* 1980).
- **C.** *Subpoint:* Sometimes missionaries who were trying to convert the people to Christianity would be killed (Rosaldo, *Knowledge and Passion,* 1980).

Transition:

Unfortunately, these murders of people who were not members of Philippine tribes resulted in some bad press for the Illongot and eventually led to the end of the practice.

III. *Third main point:* Why did the Illongot stop headhunting?

- **A.** *Subpoint:* Christianity actually had relatively little to do with it.
- **B.** *Subpoint:* The headhunting ritual ended primarily due to economics and politics.

Listener relevance: It seems that money plays a major role, not only in our country, but in other countries as well.

  1. *Sub-subpoint:* When the government forced the Illongot to live in permanent compounds, they could no longer engage in swinden farming, which resulted in starvation (Rosaldo, 1980, *Illongot Headhunting).*
  2. *Sub-subpoint:* In order to receive government assistance, the tribe had to agree to stop engaging in the ritualistic practice of headhunting.

- **C.** *Subpoint:* Since the practice of headhunting did not end because of a change in Illongot beliefs, it may not be permanent.
  1. *Sub-subpoint:* It might depend on the government.
  2. *Sub-subpoint:* It might depend on the church.
  3. *Sub-subpoint:* It might depend on the blooming of the fire plant.

Conclusion

I. *Thesis restatement:* Now I hope you have a clearer picture—more than just a snapshot—of who the Illongot headhunters of the Philippines are.

II. *Main point summary:* We discussed the headhunting practice as a ritual, some of its unique restrictions, and why the tribe has stopped practicing it.

III. *Clincher:* Whether they practice the ritual or not, we can assume that when spring is in the air and the fire plant blossoms are flaming red, young Illongot men continue to dream of taking heads and winning a wife. Today they dream. Tomorrow—who can tell?

References

Microsoft Corporation. (1995). Philippines. Microsoft Encarta, 1995.

National Geographic Special Publications Division. (1986). Vanishing people of the earth. Washington, D.C: National Geographic Society.

Rosaldo, M. Z. (1980). Knowledge and passion: Illongot notions of self and social life. Cambridge, England: Cambridge University Press.

Rosaldo, R. (1980). Illongot headhunting 1883(1974: A study in society and his tory. Stanford, CA: University Press.

Discussion Tip
How does Laurie relate the clincher to her attention catcher? What could she do to make this conclusion more memorable?

Summary

Informative speaking is the process of sharing knowledge to create mutual understanding. A speaker informs by answering questions such as "who," "when," "what," "where," "why," "how to," and "how does." Successful informative speakers are those who help listeners understand their perspective, retain their ideas, and apply them after the presentation is over. Informative speakers are essentially teachers, answering questions about objects, events, places, people, processes, procedures, ideas, concepts, beliefs, or issues. Public speaking anxiety sometimes increases when preparing informative speeches due to a fear of failure about boring listeners. These anxieties can be overcome.

Although the goal of any informative speech is to create mutual understanding, there are three different types of informative speeches: the speech of description, the speech of explanation, and the speech of demonstration. Any good speech will offer elements of all three; however, your primary thesis will focus on only one of them. Ultimately, determining which type of informative speech you are preparing helps narrow your topic and shape your thesis statement. To determine which type of speech you want to present, you should ask yourself what it is you are attempting to clarify. Are you trying to (a) paint a picture; (b) explain a concept, issue, or idea; or (c) outline a process, procedure, or function?

Finally, there are certain guidelines you should follow extra carefully when speaking to inform. You can meet these guidelines by answering five key questions as you prepare your speech: (a) Is my speech new? (b) Is my speech relevant? (c) Is my speech clear? (d) Is my speech novel? (e) Does my speech address different learning styles (feeling, watching, thinking, and doing)? Following these guidelines as you prepare and present will help you give an informative speech that achieves its goal of sharing knowledge to create mutual understanding, and listeners will go away able to retain and apply what they've learned.

Activities

1. **Professional Speaker Analysis.** Attend a lecture on campus. Examine the speech in terms of the aspects discussed in this chapter. Answer the following questions and provide examples from the speech.
   - Is it a speech of description, explanation, or demonstration?
   - What kinds of supporting material are offered to appeal to thinkers, doers, feelers, and watchers?
   - In what way or ways is the topic new?
   - Does the speaker define technical jargon?
   - What are some examples of vivid language?
   - How does the speaker use his or her voice and body to sustain interest?
   - What sort of presentational aids are offered and how do they address the feelers, doers, thinkers, and watchers?
2. **Brainstorming Informative Speech Types.** Form a group with two or three of your classmates. Generate several potential speech topics. Select one topic and do the following:
   - Create three different specific purpose statements: one for a speech of description, one for a speech of explanation, and one for a speech of demonstration.
   - Next, select one of the specific purpose statements and pattern the main points for it.
   - Share your results with the class.
3. **Painting Colorful Pictures.** Choose one of the following topics and describe the scene to the class as colorfully and specifically as possible. Ask your classmates to draw pictures of what is described and share their pictures with the speaker afterward. Discuss the results.
   - Your most embarrassing moment.
   - Your most memorable Fourth of July celebration.
   - Your first day of college.
   - A favorite teacher.
   - A shopping mall in December.
   - A lazy river canoeing trip in September.
   - Disneyland or Disneyworld.
   - Your most memorable childhood birthday.
   - New York City on New Year's Eve.
4. **Giving Clear Directions.** Select one of the following topics. Give the class directions to it or for it. Then ask the class to guess what your topic was.
   - Directions from the classroom to the campus library.
   - Directions from the classroom to a familiar restaurant.
   - Making a paper airplane.

- Making a piece of peanut butter toast.
- Planting a vegetable garden.
- Shampooing your hair.

KEY TERMS

Apathy barrier
Informative speaking
Speech of demonstration
Speech of description
Speech of explanation

CHAPTER 15

Persuasive Speaking: Types and Designs

Reflective Questions

1. How does persuasive speaking differ from informative speaking?
2. Why might your public speaking anxiety increase when you're preparing and presenting a persuasive speech?
3. How does your target audience influence the way you will approach your speech?
4. How can you shape your speech if you expect your audience to be hostile?
5. How might speeches aimed at influencing beliefs and attitudes differ from speeches aimed at influencing actions?

adison had had her heart set on a steak dinner for her birthday celebration. She rarely allowed herself the luxury of a good steak, and she'd been looking forward to this dinner for several weeks. As she looked over the menu, however, nothing really appealed to her. She wondered how Rick had managed to convince her to go to an Italian restaurant. She finally ordered the chicken tetrazinni, although she'd rather have had filet mignon.

Teaching Tip
Refer students to the SpeechMaker CD-ROM. This software provides several tips for effective persuasive speaking. Consider assigning one of the scenarios to be reviewed before the class in which you will discuss this chapter.

Sherry stared at her graded examination in disbelief. How could she have earned such a low grade? She answered every question correctly, but lost points on each one. What more was she supposed to have written? To make matters worse, her friend Dana had earned a higher grade with less complete answers! "Well," Sherry thought, "there's only one way to find out." She knocked on the professor's door. "Sherry, come in! What can I do for you?" "Well . . . the reason I came by . . . is . . . well I really think I deserve a better grade on this examination. I've reviewed my notes and even talked with some classmates. I'm not one to complain, but I really think I've answered the questions completely. I guess I'm asking you to look at it one more time." "Sure, Sherry," her professor responded. "I admire your courage. I'll take another look at your exam."

> ***What Do You Think?***
> *Consider a time when someone convinced you to do something you had not planned on doing. What did they say or do that changed your mind?*

Although we rarely think about it, we are constantly sending or being sent persuasive messages. Perhaps a friend tried to convince you to go to one restaurant, or movie, or sporting event instead of another. Or perhaps your children tried to convince you to let them go to the water slide, to a friend's house, or to summer camp. Undoubtedly, a salesperson has tried to convince you to purchase an outfit, an appliance, an automobile, or a house. In addition to the persuasive messages we get from other people, we are bombarded with messages from the media—for example, with television commercials and newspaper and magazine advertisements.

Teaching Tip
Assign students to small groups and have them brainstorm ways they might use persuasion in the future. Encourage them to consider applications beyond the workplace.

On the other hand, perhaps you have tried to convince a professor to change a grade, or a spouse to go out to dinner, or a client to purchase a particular product. The importance of persuasive messages in our lives is undeniable. But why do some messages successfully convince us to change our opinions or behaviors, while others do not? What exactly is persuasive speaking and what makes it effective?

This chapter focuses on the major characteristics of persuasive speaking and on the basic types and ways of organizing persuasive speeches. More specifically, we begin by looking at the nature and importance of persuasive speaking. Then we examine the relationship between persuasive speaking and public speaking anxiety. We identify some specific steps you can take to manage anxiety effectively and improve your chances for success. The rest of the chapter will help you with the process of determining your thesis statement and designing your main points in ways that function most effectively to influence listeners. Then in Chapter 16 we'll focus on specific strategies you can use throughout your persuasive speech to improve your chances for success.

What Is Persuasive Speaking?

To understand persuasive speaking, we must first define persuasion. **Persuasion** is the process of influencing other people's attitudes, beliefs, values, or behaviors.

Persuasive speaking, then, is simply the process of influencing attitudes, beliefs, values, or behaviors through a public speech. Essentially, a persuasive speaker develops an argument in support of a particular position on a topic. In a public speaking context, "argument" does not mean "quarrel," "dispute," or "disagreement." Rather, **argument** means articulating a position with the support of evidence and reasoning. It is in this sense that persuasive speakers "argue" a position (Perloff, 1993).

Teaching Tip
Students often confuse verbal aggressiveness and argumentativeness. Have students write a brief essay exploring these two concepts. In particular, have students identify ways in which they can engage in argument and avoid verbal aggressiveness.

It is sometimes easiest to understand what persuasive speaking is by comparing it to informative speaking. Recall that the goal of an informative speaker is to create mutual understanding about a topic. A persuasive speaker creates mutual understanding too, but he or she does more than that. A persuasive speaker must also influence listeners to agree with his or her position and, in some cases, even motivate them to take action as a result. For example, an informative speaker might talk about how to set up a recycling center. A persuasive speaker might include this information in the speech, but he or she will go further, seeking to convince listeners that recycling is crucial, to convince them to actually start a recycling center, or to convince them to lobby Congress in support of recycling legislation. In a sense, whereas informative speakers are *teachers,* persuasive speakers are *leaders.* That is, your role as a persuasive speaker is to lead listeners to agree with you. For this reason, persuasive speaking is the most complex and most challenging kind of public speaking but also potentially the most rewarding.

Persuasive speaking can occur only when there are two or more points of view on a topic. These points of view might be directly opposed or may differ only in degree. For example, let's say you decided to present a speech about television censorship. You could present a speech in favor of it or opposed to it. In this case, your goal is fairly lofty—to get listeners to agree with one of two directly opposite points of view. On the other hand, you could argue that television censorship should be made more accessible to parents and guardians. In this case, your persuasive position would seek to convince listeners to a degree. Persuasion occurs any time you influence a listener's position in the direction you advocate, even when it is only a matter of degree. To be effective, you'll want to discover the various points of view that exist for your topic and also, as we'll see later in the chapter, to determine where your audience stands.

Discussion Tip
Ask students to identify a persuasive speaker they have seen recently. If they have not seen a persuasive speaker, ask them to recall persuasive speaking situations they have experienced. Have them identify the positive and negative characteristics of the speaker's arguments. This discussion can be used as a springboard for helping students to identify the characteristics of effective argumentation.

Effective persuasive speaking is important for you as a speaker and as a listener. As a speaker, you'll learn to articulate your position effectively about topics that matter to you with solid logic and reasoning. Consequently, you can make a difference by fostering positive changes to improve your school, community, and even society. As a listener, persuasive speaking can make you aware of problems around you and ways to solve them. It can also force you to reevaluate your position on various topics, as well as improve your ability to defend them. Also, being able to judge how well others use persuasive speaking techniques can help you improve your own effectiveness as a persuasive speaker when called to do so.

Teaching Tip
Stress to students that the skills presented in this chapter will help them become more critical consumers of persuasive messages.

Persuasive speeches can be divided into two main types: dispositional persuasive speeches and actuation persuasive speeches (see Figure 15–1). The specific goal of each type differs depending on what you are actually trying to influence. Just as the type of informative speech you selected helped determine the thesis statement of your informative speech (recall Chapter 14), so does the type of persuasive speech you select help determine the thesis statement of your persuasive speech.

FIGURE 15–1
Types of Persuasive Speeches

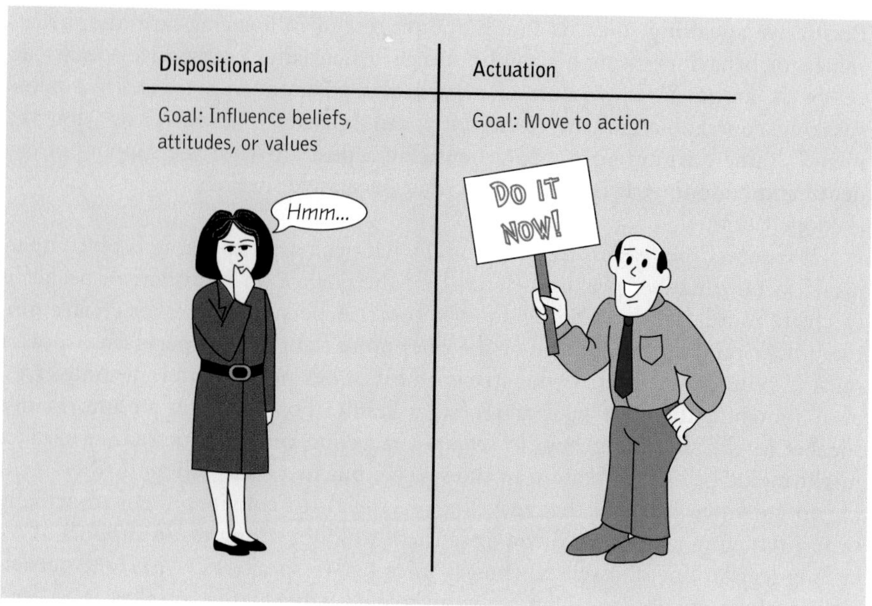

Dispositional Persuasive Speeches

A **dispositional persuasive speech** is designed to influence listeners' disposition toward your topic—that is, their beliefs, attitudes, or values. Let's look at each of these factors more closely.

Technology Tip
http://www.sasked.gove.sk.ca/docs/comm20/mod6.html
This Web page, hosted by Saskatchewan Education, provides an overview of persuasive speaking as well as several activities. Have students visit this site, complete several of the activities, and write a brief essay explaining what they found.

A **belief** is something we accept as true or false even though it has not yet been or cannot be shown to be so. For example, you might hold the belief that watching gratuitous violence or sex on television promotes teenage violence or sexual promiscuity. A speech that attempts to convince listeners of this is a dispositional persuasive speech about a belief. Notice that this is a belief because, although you can support your position with evidence, other points of view are possible and defensible. In contrast, no one can dispute the fact that some television programs do depict violence and sex. Since this is known to be true, it is not a belief.

What Do You Think?

Do you believe the gratuitous violence on television today promotes violent behavior in children and teenagers? Why or why not?

An **attitude** is our tendency to respond favorably or unfavorably to something, to like or dislike it. For example, you might strongly dislike television shows with gratuitous violence and sex. In a dispositional persuasive speech about an attitude, you might argue that such shows are vulgar or unappealing.

A **value** is a deeply held concept about what is and isn't good, right, and important with regard to conduct and existence. Values that many people hold include honesty, respect, integrity, loyalty, freedom, justice, order, love, courage, and wisdom (Johannesen, 1990). In a dispositional persuasive speech about a value, you might argue that television violence and sex are wrong because they reflect a lack of respect for human beings. In fact, Eric's speech, located on pages 346–348, is an example.

A speech arguing that so much television violence is wrong is a dispositional speech focused on a value.

Our beliefs, attitudes, and values are often closely related. For example, if we value wisdom and believe that older people are wise, we might have a favorable attitude toward older people in the workplace. Nonetheless, we need to focus on only one of these factors in our dispositional speech, as in the examples of speeches on television violence and sex. It's important to know which one you'll focus on when shaping your speech. Attitudes change fairly frequently and are thus easier to influence than beliefs or values. Beliefs can often be influenced only with a great deal of evidence. Values, because they are so deeply held, are the hardest of all to influence. Suppose, for example, that you're giving a speech arguing for capital punishment. You'd be more likely to convince someone who opposes it on the grounds that it doesn't deter crime (assuming, of course, that you can present evidence to support your position) than someone who opposes it on the grounds that it is immoral and wrong.

Teaching Tip
Assign students to small groups and give each group a sample persuasive speech topic. Instruct the students to discuss strategies for shaping the speech topic in a way that focuses on a belief, attitude, and value. Share the results with the entire class.

In sum, you can take the same speech topic and shape it in a way that focuses on a belief or an attitude or a value. Although you'll likely offer supporting material reflecting each of these factors, the primary goal of your dispositional persuasive speech should be grounded in only one.

Actuation Persuasive Speeches

Actuation persuasive speeches are designed to influence behavior. **Actuate** means move to action. So you seek to move your listeners to action in your actuation persuasive speech. An advertiser that tries to convince you to buy its product instead of a competitor's is engaged in actuation persuasive speaking. When Sherry tried to convince her professor to reconsider her grade, she was engaged in actuation persuasive speaking. The action sometimes involves politics or policy. For example, you might urge listeners to vote for a certain candidate, write to their representatives in support of a bill, or demonstrate against a tuition increase. Josh did this when he staged an all-night vigil outside the home of the college president. Or the actions might concern individual behaviors. For example, you might urge listeners to wear their seat belts, take a multivitamin, or even floss their teeth regularly.

Discussion Tip
According to Sellnow, why is actuation persuasive speaking the most challenging type of public speaking? What ethical concerns are most relevant to this type of persuasive speaking?

Actuation persuasive speaking is the most challenging type of public speaking. In order to successfully persuade listeners to act, you must be competent in all forms of public speaking. Recall the public speaking continuum discussed in Chapter 14. The further to the right you proceed on the continuum, the more you must accomplish in order to succeed. When speaking to inform, for instance, you merely share knowledge in order to achieve your goal of mutual understanding. When speaking to persuade about a disposition, you still must inform your listeners; however, you do so in ways that ultimately achieve your goal of influencing beliefs, attitudes, or values. When seeking action (actuation speaking), you must inform your listeners about various aspects of your topic. You must also seek agreement about the significance of the problem and what is causing it (belief), of the feasibility of your plan for solving the problem (attitude), and of the worthiness of your solution (value). You must do all of these things in order to achieve your ultimate goal of motivating your listeners to act.

Consider Tammy's speech about dental hygiene. Her ultimate goal was to seek action; that is, to get listeners to floss regularly so as to avoid gum disease. To do this, she had to inform her listeners about the nature of gum disease and seek agreement about how gum disease can cause life-threatening medical problems (belief), as well as about why most people don't floss (attitude). Then she could seek action by actually compelling her listeners to promote expanded dental education programs, advertising campaigns, and, of course, behavior modification on a personal level (Frisby, 1998).

Teaching Tip
Ask students to bring to class examples of persuasive materials that they believe are unethical. Discuss these in terms of the guidelines for ethical speaking presented in this text.

There is one other challenge you need to take especially seriously with persuasive speaking, particularly actuation persuasive speaking. Although ethics are important in any type of public speech, the potential consequences of a successful persuasive speech can be more significant than those of an informative speech. After all, you are attempting to convince listeners to change their thinking or behavior. It is therefore your ethical responsibility to thoroughly research your content and to accurately and fully represent your findings. Don't just rely on the sources that support your argument. If you successfully convince listeners to do something, then the consequences of their doing so is your responsibility.

Let's say you successfully convince your listeners to stop taking over-the-counter drugs. What if one of your listeners had been taking an aspirin a day to help prevent the risk of heart disease? If you were successful, this listener would stop doing so. The potential implications are your responsibility. You would have been more ethical to acknowledge that in some cases the benefits of taking over-the-counter drugs outweigh the disadvantages, particularly when they have been prescribed by a doctor. Your evidence must have sufficient breadth and depth, and you must reason ethically with your evidence. As will be discussed in Chapter 16, this means, in part, avoiding what is known as faulty reasoning.

What Do You Think?

Consider an infomercial you've seen that advocated a particular diet, dietary supplement, or piece of exercise equipment. What claims were made about what the product will do? Were potential risks addressed? Do you think the infomercial was ethical? Why or why not?

Persuasive Speaking and Public Speaking Anxiety

When you consider the challenges involved in persuasive speaking, it's not surprising to note that it can contribute to public speaking anxiety. It's one thing to talk to listeners about the safety features of seat belts. It's quite another to convince them to wear their seat belts whenever they drive or ride in a car. Likewise, it's one thing to explain how to floss your teeth, but quite another thing to convince listeners to do so on a daily basis. Clearly, it takes more to motivate listeners to change their thinking or behaviors than it does to motivate them to listen and retain information. Moreover, you're acting not just as a teacher, but also as a leader. Because the expectations you place on yourself are greater when speaking to persuade, your fear of failure can also be greater, resulting in increased public speaking anxiety.

Discussion Tip
In what ways do the challenges involved in persuasive speaking contribute to public speaking anxiety? How might you combat such anxiety?

The best way to combat this fear of failure is to make sure that the structure, language, content, and delivery of your speech are appropriate and serve your particular persuasive purpose. We'll look at strategies for effectively shaping language, content, and delivery in Chapter 16. Here we'll focus on the earlier step of structuring your speech. We'll begin with earliest step of all, the one on which the success of all the others ultimately depends: analyzing your audience. Audience analysis will itself help you with your speech anxiety: The more you know about your listeners and where they stand on your topic, the more confident you can be that you know how to go about attempting to persuade them.

Using Audience Analysis to Shape Your Speech

Effective persuasive speakers employ audience analysis, not only to speculate about what listeners may and may not know but also to speculate about where listeners stand. This speculation affects even what kind of persuasive speech they decide to give.

For most topics, even before analyzing your audience, you can safely assume that listeners will have different opinions in relation to your topic. Some listeners probably already agree with you or already behave in the manner you plan to advocate. Other listeners probably do not yet have a firm position about your topic. Yet others are probably opposed to your position. Each of these situations suggests a different persuasive aim. If listeners agree, you should attempt to *reinforce* their point of view in your speech. If they're undecided, you should attempt to help them *form* a position. If they're opposed, you should attempt to *reform* their position. But since your listeners probably have a range of positions, how do you know which aim to focus on? The answer is that you analyze your audience to figure out if there is a majority group. This majority group becomes your **target audience**—the portion of your audience you most want to persuade. You will want to tailor your message in ways that are most likely to influence them. Tailoring your speech to the majority does not mean ignoring the other audience members; however, to be effective, you must aim for a target group. Let's look more closely at how audience analysis can shape what you aim for in your speech.

Teaching Tip
To give students practice in tailoring their claims to a target audience, see the Identifying Your Target Audience assignment in the Activities section of this chapter.

If you discover that most of your listeners already agree with you, your most effective strategy would be to *seek action* in an actuation persuasive speech. Margaret, for instance, discovered that most of her listeners already believed recycling is important but that few actually recycled anything other than some newspapers and soda cans. These listeners, therefore, were her target audience, and she tailored her speech so it supported the aim of changing behaviors regarding recycling. If most of Margaret's audience had already engaged in comprehensive recycling programs, she could have aimed instead at seeking action to help change policies about recycling. She might have focused, for instance, on the need for stronger recycling regulations at the state or local level, or on practices that local businesses ought to initiate. In either case, she would have included specific steps listeners must take to help make the changes a reality. When most of your listeners—your target audience—already agree with you, seek action in your persuasive speech.

Teaching Tip
Refer to the ideas of audience analysis presented in Chapter 6. Remind students that these concepts are critical in persuasive speaking because the more a speaker knows about an audience, the more persuasive that speaker will be.

If you discover that most of your listeners are not sure where they stand on an issue, your strategy should probably be to *seek agreement* in a dispositional persuasive speech. In a classroom poll, Eric and Jen discovered that seventeen of the twenty-two students were unsure about whether or not television censorship is a good thing. They themselves supported different sides of the issue—Eric favored television censorship whereas Jen opposed it—but they each decided to give a speech focusing on the reasons for their respective position. When your target audience is unsure, your persuasive speech can help them form a position. Eric's outline is included at the end of this chapter.

If you discover that most of your listeners are opposed to your stand, your most effective strategy would be to seek **incremental change** in a dispositional persuasive speech. That is, you attempt to move them even to a small degree in the direction of your position, with the idea that further movement in that direction might then be possible at a later time. You can begin by brainstorming the objections, questions, and criticisms they might raise. Then shape your speech around your answers and responses to them. You might try using a **coactive approach,** a strategic method for confronting reluctant audiences intelligently and constructively (Simons, 1986). This method has five basic parts:

1. Establish good will early in the speech.
2. Start by talking about general areas of agreement rather than disagreement.
3. Set modest goals.
4. Cite authorities your audience will respect.
5. Acknowledge opposing arguments respectfully.

Discussion Tip
What guidelines does Sellnow offer for establishing a welcoming climate for hostile audiences? Why is it important to set modest goals when attempting to persuade hostile audiences?

First, establish a welcoming climate, one that doesn't feel confrontational. This is not the time to use a startling statistic for an attention catcher. Because your audience is reluctant, you need to ease them into your speech gently.

Second, talk about beliefs, attitudes, and values related to your topic that your audience is likely to share with you. Your goal at this point is simply to get listeners nodding their heads in agreement with you. Henrietta did this in her speech about how technology is taking away our rights when she said:

> People do it every day. They walk in an airport through an electronic device; if it beeps, they walk back around, empty their keys and change and walk through it again. We accept these modern-day intrusions on our personal liberties because we recognize the need for ever tighter security in an increasingly dangerous world and we regard the resulting inconvenience as a small price to pay for our own safety and well-being.

Video surveillance in public places is already here, and a new generation of sophisticated weapons and contraband devices is only a few years away. Today, I will be discussing this technology, how this technology can infringe on Fourth Amendment guarantees, and some solutions regarding how we can defend our constitutional rights (Lewis, 1998).

Third, set modest goals, for example, the goal of getting your audience to consider what you have to say. Such a goal might, at first, seem inappropriate to persuasive speaking. However, if you can achieve this goal through your speech, you might ultimately go beyond it. For example, because of the **sleeper effect,** change may emerge later after listeners have absorbed your ideas and incorporated them into their own beliefs. Moreover, if your speech has resulted in **raised consciousness,** you've sensitized your audience to the issue and made them more receptive to persuasion in the future (McCombs, 1981). Or you may have gained **situational acceptance**—that is, listeners agree that a certain policy, approach, or behavior is acceptable in some situations. Neil did this in his speech about abortion. After discovering in a classroom survey that most of his listeners opposed abortion, he chose to argue only that abortion might be justified when the mother's life is in danger. By limiting his argument in this way, he got his target audience to consider what he had to say and may in some cases have gained situational acceptance.

Fourth, when you are persuading a reluctant audience, it is extremely important to cite authorities they are likely to recognize and respect. Remember that in listeners' minds you are not an expert, particularly to listeners who oppose your position. The more credible external support you can offer, the greater your chances for success.

Fifth, acknowledge the arguments of the opposing side in a respectful way. You must treat opposing arguments as valid and understandable ones before going on to identify flaws in them. For example, Lori acknowledged that seat belt laws do restrict our rights—and then went on to examine the need to balance rights with responsibilities in matters of safety, life, and death.

Background Tip
For more information on responding to counterarguments, see S. E. Toulmin, *The Uses of Argument* (London: Cambridge University Press, 1958).

Identifying your target audience allows you to tailor your persuasive approach in ways that increase your potential for success and limit your anxiety. When most of your listeners already agree with you, seek action. When most of your listeners are undecided about the issue, help them form a position by seeking agreement. When most of your audience opposes your position, seek incremental agreement change, for example, by using a coactive approach. Once you have identified your target audience and thought about how best to approach your topic, determine your thesis statement and organize your main points.

What Do You Think?

What is the topic for your persuasive speech? Who is your target audience and where do they stand? If you don't know, what can you do to find out? What approach will you take and why?

Determining Your Persuasive Approach

1. When your target audience agrees with you, seek action.
2. When your target audience is undecided, seek agreement.
3. When your target audience opposes your position, seek incremental change.

Making a Claim in Your Thesis Statement

As with any speech, you must narrow your persuasive speech topic in order to arrive at a manageable thesis statement. However, you'll do this by a somewhat different process, namely, by deciding what specific claim you want to make—a claim of fact, value, or policy. Your thesis statement is essentially a claim of one of these types. Each type of claim leads to a different type of persuasive speech. You determine your claim based on what you learn through audience analysis about where your target audience stands regarding your issue.

Claim of Fact

Teaching Tip
Make transparency masters of print ads that utilize claims of fact, value, and policy. Show these ads in class and ask students to identify the different claims in each ad.

A **claim of fact** focuses on whether something is true—that is, it takes a position on something that is not known but can be argued for. Thus, a thesis statement that makes a claim of fact leads to a dispositional persuasive speech about a belief. When your thesis statement makes a claim of fact, you seek agreement from your listeners. Claims of fact can concern the past, present, or future.

Claims of fact concerning the past can be on topics as different as whether Lee Harvey Oswald acted alone in shooting President Kennedy and whether birds evolved from dinosaurs. Remember that if something is already known or accepted as the truth by all, it cannot be the basis for a claim of fact or a dispositional speech about a belief. One couldn't give a speech on whether President Nixon resigned—we all know that he did. Even though the truth of the claim of fact you're making is not known, your thesis statement is phrased as though the claim of fact is true. For example, your thesis statement might be as follows:

> Although Lee Harvey Oswald shot President Kennedy, he was actually part of a larger conspiracy.

Or you might state:

> The birds that are on earth today are the descendants of dinosaurs.

Claims of fact concerning the present are also possible. One fertile area for these kinds of claims is health, including new treatments, drugs, and substances. For example, a possible thesis statement might be as follows:

> Olestra, a fat-free chemical being used commonly in snack chips, is harmful to one's health.

Thesis statements making other claims of fact about the present include: Graphic depictions of sex and violence on television promote teenage sex and violence; growing up in a two-career family is harmful to children; sexual orientation is genetically determined; the media's depictions of "ideal" women as unnaturally thin promotes eating disorders among teenaged girls; and there is life on other planets in the universe.

Discussion Tip
What types of factual claims does Sellnow discuss in this chapter? How can predictions be considered claims of fact?

After being carefully examined and researched, many claims of fact about the present are eventually proved or disproved. At that point, a claim of fact and persuasive speech would no longer be possible. In the 1950s, for example, you might have presented a persuasive speech arguing that smoking does or does not cause lung cancer. Today, however, we know that smoking is a leading cause of lung cancer.

Claims of fact can also be focused in the future, as you know if you've ever predicted who would win the World Series, the Stanley Cup, the Super Bowl, or some other sporting event. Your prediction could have served as a thesis statement based on a claim of fact. Science fiction films and novels are often based on claims of fact focused in the future. Viewers and readers are enticed by them because they include an element of plausibility. Some examples include the following: E-mail will eventually render traditional postal service obsolete; global warming will eventually force us to live on water as well as land; and thanks to computers and the Internet, there will one day be no paperbound books.

Claims of fact provide the basis for your thesis statement in a dispositional speech about a belief. They can focus on the past by arguing that something did or did not exist or occur in a certain way. Claims of fact can focus on the present by contending that something is or is not harmful, does or does not exist, or is or is not the cause of something else. Finally, claims of fact can focus on the future by predicting what will or will not occur.

> **What Do You Think?**
>
> *Consider a Science Fiction film you've seen like* The Matrix, Waterworld, Alien, Terminator, *or some other one. What claim of fact was being argued in it?*

Claim of Value

A **claim of value** makes a judgment about whether some concept or action is good, right, moral, fair, or better than some other concept or action. Claims of value shape thesis statements for dispositional persuasive speeches about values. As with speeches based on claims of fact, you seek agreement from your listeners—but here the agreement concerns a judgment of worth.

As we saw earlier, dispositional persuasive speeches about values can be particularly difficult, because values are harder to change than beliefs. If your speech is based on a claim of value, you'll need to provide evidence that appeals to logic, as well as supporting material that appeals to emotion. This is crucial in order to foster a sense of internal commitment from your listeners. Thesis statements that make claims of value are easy to generate. After all, they are often rooted in our personal positions about things we deem important. However, preparing and presenting an effective speech focused on them often takes more effort.

> **Teaching Tip**
> A good place to find examples of fact, value, and policy claims is in the editorial section of the newspaper. You can use your school newspaper to find issues that are relevant to students. Analyze the different persuasive claims used in several editorials.

Here are some examples of thesis statements that make claims of value.

Jimmy Carter was an excellent president.
Cloning is wrong.
Spanking children is an appropriate form of discipline.
Brisk walking is a better form of aerobic exercise than running.
The Oprah Winfrey Show is better than *Sally Jesse Raphael.*
A low-fat diet is actually healthier than a fat-free diet.

> **What Do You Think?**
>
> *What is a personal position you value? What claim of value could you make as a thesis statement? What are your reasons for this claim?*

Claim of Policy

A **claim of policy** states a position about whether a specific course of action should be taken. A thesis statement that makes a claim of policy leads to an actuation persuasive speech. As already discussed, such speeches are the most complex and demanding type because you're calling for action and because you'll often need to convince listeners of dispositional claims of fact and value so that they will be ready to consider the course of action (claim of policy) you advocate. In order to argue effectively that the government should abolish the death penalty, for example, it might also be necessary to convince listeners that the death penalty causes certain problems (claims of fact) and that the death penalty is immoral (claim of value).

Technology Tip
http://debate.uvm.edu/ceda topics.html

This Web page, hosted by the Cross Examination Debate Association, explores several policy topics. Have students visit this site and write a brief essay summarizing their findings.

Here are some examples of questions that could give rise to a claim of policy. "What should be done to improve the quality of education in the United States?" "What should be done to reduce the problems associated with nuclear waste?" "Should the legal age for drinking alcohol be changed?" "What should be done to improve recycling efforts?" "What should be done to deal with the problem of domestic violence?" By brainstorming about these kinds of questions, you can come up with a claim for your thesis statement (see Figure 15–2). Here are some examples.

We must improve the quality of education in the United States.
The legal drinking age should be lowered to 18.
Government agencies, community organizations, and individuals must do more to foster the habit of recycling.
The government, professional organizations, and individuals must each do their part to tackle the problem of domestic violence in this country.

You can effectively narrow your persuasive speech topic by considering whether to focus on a claim of fact, value, or policy. Dispositional persuasive speech thesis statements make a claim of fact or a claim of value. Actuation persuasive speeches make a claim of policy. You determine your claim based on what you learn through audience analysis about where your target audience stands regarding the issue.

Organizing Your Main Points

Although some of the organizational patterns we discussed in Chapter 8 can be used in persuasive speeches (particularly topical and causal), there are also several patterns uniquely suited to building persuasive speech arguments. Four unique

FIGURE 15–2 Making a Claim in Your Thesis Statement

Fact	Value	Policy
Past	Good/Bad	Do it/Don't do it
Did/Did not occur	Moral/Immoral	Should/Shouldn't
Present	Fair/Unfair	Must/Must not
Does/Does not exist		
Cause/Doesn't cause		
Is linked/Is not linked		
Future		
Will/Will not occur		

Dispositional	Actuation
Topical	Problem/Solution
Causal	Problem/Cause/Solution
Refutative	
Comparative Advantages	Modified Comparative Advantages
Invitational	Monroe's Motivated Sequence
Problem (no solution)	

FIGURE 15–3
Persuasive Speech Main Point Patterns

patterns that work particularly well for dispositional persuasive speeches are the refutative, comparative advantages, invitational, and problem (no solution) patterns. Four patterns that are particularly appropriate for actuation persuasive speeches are problem/solution, problem/cause/solution, modified comparative advantages, and Monroe's motivated sequence (see Figure 15–3).

Organizing Dispositional Persuasive Speeches

Usually you'll find that several specific reasons emerge in support of your dispositional speech claim. In such cases, each reason will probably serve as a main point in the body of your speech. Hence, your main point pattern is essentially topical. Other times—particularly when you're preparing a dispositional speech focused on a claim of fact—you'll find that a causal design is most effective for your purpose. However, there will be times when neither of these patterns is appropriate, for example, when your target audience is opposed to your position or when the points of view surrounding your topic vary merely in degree. In these cases, you'll be more effective by choosing a refutative, comparative advantages, invitational, or problem (no solution) main point pattern.

Some experts argue that you should place each of your strongest arguments at the beginning and the end of your speech, based on the primacy-recency effect we talked about in Chapter 9 (e.g., Cook, 1989). But others say that the placement should depend on your audience, that you should place your strongest argument first when your target audience is opposed to your position and last when your target audience is neutral (e.g., Sonnenberg, 1988). It's likely you'll be most effective if you order your arguments by considering both the topic and the audience.

Discussion Tip
Where in the speech should you place your strongest argument? How might the placement of arguments be influenced by the disposition of the audience?

Refutative Pattern

The **refutative pattern** is a main point arrangement that persuades by both disproving the opposing position and bolstering your own. Essentially you counter opposing arguments by showing how they are flawed. Once your audience understands the flaws in those arguments, they are more receptive to accepting the arguments you present to support your position. The refutative pattern is particularly effective when your target audience opposes your position because you begin by acknowledging their arguments and then show the flaws in them before posing and supporting your own. You can follow this four-step strategy to develop your main points:

1. State an argument in support of the position you are refuting.
2. State and give evidence of the flaws in this argument.

3. State and give evidence to support your argument.
4. Show how your argument erodes the argument of the opposing side.

Although this is not the only refutative strategy for organizing your main points, it is an effective one. You might follow this four-step process for each main point or you might use it to develop your main points together. For example, in a speech with four main points you might combine Steps 1 and 2 for your first main point, Steps 4 and 5 for your second main point, Steps 1 and 2 for your third main point, and Steps 3 and 5 for your fourth main point. Laine used this refutative pattern for her dispositional persuasive speech about school uniforms. Her thesis statement was "School uniforms will not solve the problems in our school system." Her main points were as follows:

Teaching Tip
Remind students that it is essential to have a strong and credible information base for successful persuasion.

I. *First main point:* Some people claim that school uniforms reduce violence.
   A. *Subpoint:* This argument is based on beliefs regarding social comparison theory, child development, and socioeconomic status (explain each of these).
   B. *Subpoint:* Although these beliefs make sense to a certain degree, several studies have been conducted that show that schools that switched to uniforms actually experienced increased violence among students (cite some of the results and conclusions).
   C. *Subpoint:* When one looks at the evidence regarding school uniforms and violence, then it is obvious that school uniforms will not reduce violence and may even result in more of it.

II. *Second main point:* Some people claim that school uniforms will improve academic achievement and standardized test scores.
   A. *Subpoint:* This argument is based on beliefs regarding social comparison theory, child development, and emotional intelligence (explain each of these).
   B. *Subpoint:* Again, these perceptions tend to make sense, that is, until one considers the research conducted that shows no significant improvement in test scores by students in schools where uniforms were made mandatory (cite some of the results and conclusions).
   C. *Subpoint:* Although there may be good reasons for mandating school uniforms, improving academic achievement and test scores is not among them.

Laine concluded her speech by restating her thesis statement that "School uniforms will not solve the problems in our school systems." She summarized her main points by reminding listeners that school uniforms "won't necessarily reduce violence among students or improve academic achievement," and clinched with "I'm not here to convince you that we shouldn't adopt a school uniform policy, but let's not do so for the wrong reasons."

Comparative Advantages Pattern

The **comparative advantages pattern** is a main point arrangement that leads your audience to agree with you that one of two or more alternatives is better than the others. Your goal is to show how the advantages of the alternative you advocate outweigh the disadvantages, as well as how the advantages of this particular alternative surpass the advantages of the other options (Ziegelmueller, Kay, & Dause, 1990, p. 186). To do so, you might also show how the disadvantages of other options outweigh their advantages. Since your goal in a dispositional speech is to seek agreement, you stop short of advocating action. Instead, you leave that decision ultimately to your listeners. For this reason, the comparative advantages pattern can be very effective with target audiences that oppose your position. It can also be effective with these target audiences because, unlike the refutative pattern, you can acknowledge that both or all alternatives have merit. You are simply illustrating why one alternative is better than the others. Moreover, this is essentially the approach salespeople often use when they try to convince you that their brand is better than the competition. However, they take it a step further to convince you to actually purchase their product. In doing so, they actually modify the comparative advantages pattern to also seek action, which we'll discuss later in this chapter.

Teaching Tip
To give students an opportunity to utilize the comparative advantages pattern, see the Debating with Comparative Advantages assignment contained in the Activities section of this chapter.

Recall these thesis statement claims we mentioned earlier in the chapter: *The Oprah Winfrey Show* is better than *Sally Jesse Raphael;* brisk walking is a better form of aerobic exercise than running; and a low-fat diet is actually healthier than a fat-free diet. Each of these claims seeks agreement about one alternative over another and could be argued effectively using the comparative advantages pattern. You could also use this pattern effectively to support claims that "*The Oprah Winfrey Show* is the best daytime talk show on television today" or that "Brisk walking is the best form of aerobic exercise."

John used this pattern to develop his speech that Chevrolet trucks are better than Ford trucks. He focused on comparative advantages and disadvantages regarding cost, dependability, and special features. He found supporting material in publications like *Consumer Reports,* from interviews with local automobile mechanics and used-car dealers, by surveying a representative sample of the general population, as well as from personal experience. Dan also used the comparative advantages pattern to develop his speech about satellite television.

Thesis statement: A satellite system is better than a cable subscription for getting television programming.

Discussion Tip
Where could Dan go to find credible sources to substantiate these claims? Which of these arguments do you find most compelling? Why?

I. *First main point:* Many people have cable television subscriptions because cable offers several advantages over rooftop antenna reception.

- **A.** *Subpoint:* One advantage is its consistently clearer reception than with a rooftop antenna.
- **B.** *Subpoint:* Another advantage is the ability to access a variety of programming, as opposed to merely two, three, or four local stations.
- **C.** *Subpoint:* Finally, it is possible to select from a variety of cable subscription packages, allowing one to access specialty programming like movies and sports.

II. *Second main point:* Satellite television is now another option from which to choose.

- **A.** *Subpoint:* Advantages include its excellent picture and sound quality, access to a plethora of movie and sports programming, customer service satisfaction, and value for the money.

B. *Subpoint:* Some potential disadvantages include initial costs for the dish and installation, need for a clear southern exposure for your dish, limited access to local television stations, and the inability to watch two different satellite programs at the same time in your home.

III. *Third main point:* Comparative advantages and disadvantages illustrate that, unless your property does not have a clear view to the south, satellite is the better alternative.

A. *Subpoint:* Cost issues ultimately weigh in favor of satellite television, particularly for sports and movie enthusiasts (cite ratings from *Consumer Reports*, December 1999).

B. *Subpoint:* Picture and sound quality are better with satellite television.

C. *Subpoint:* Customer service satisfaction is better with satellite television.

D. *Subpoint:* Access to local programs can be easily obtained with a rooftop antenna, which is free to use.

E. *Subpoint:* Ability to watch different programs on different television sets at the same time can be achieved with a rooftop antenna or by purchasing an add-on receiver (about $100) and paying an additional $5 per month.

F. *Subpoint:* When all the inherent advantages and disadvantages of cable and satellite television options are compared, satellite television clearly provides the best value for your money.

Dan concluded by restating his thesis statement claim that satellite is a better alternative than cable for receiving television programming. He summarized his main points and then clinched by reminding his listeners that "I'm not here to tell you what to do. I am here, however, to help you see why the advantages of a satellite system outweigh its disadvantages, as well as any potential advantages of cable television. My only hope is that I've made that point *perfectly clear.*"

Invitational Pattern

Teaching Tip
To give students an opportunity to utilize this organizational pattern, see the Invitational Impromptu Speaking assignment in the Activities section of this chapter.

The **invitational pattern** is a main point arrangement designed to invite rather than convince listeners to agree with your position. It is particularly useful when your target audience is opposed to your position and perhaps even hostile toward it. Essentially, you approach the topic by first recognizing the presence of other positions and the validity of these perspectives. Then you search for common ground and communicate on the basis of that common ground. You also focus on positive aspects of a person or situation rather than what is wrong with that person or situation, and you encourage persistence of those positive behaviors rather than resisting or even battling negative behaviors (Foss & Foss, 1994; Foss, Foss, & Griffin,1999). You can follow this three-step strategy for arranging your main points:

1. Offer your perspective and describe how it works for you.
2. Create an atmosphere that encourages mutual understanding.
3. Focus on positive aspects of a situation and persistence of them.

Recall that Laura did this in her personal significance speech about being a vegetarian. She did not focus on the negative consequences of eating meat. Instead, she talked about her belief in a meat-free diet and why it works for her. She created common ground by telling her story about becoming a vegetarian. Finally, she focused on positive aspects of her current situation and how she manages to continue the behavior. Ultimately, her listeners might choose to become vegetarians; however, she concluded in a way that acknowledges either choice, leaving the ultimate choice to them.

Thesis statement: Living a vegetarian lifestyle is an important aspect of who I am today.

I. *First main point:* I made this choice for several reasons.

II. *Second main point:* I decided to become a vegetarian about the same time I moved away from home to attend college. Perhaps you can relate.

III. *Third main point:* I deal daily with advantages and disadvantages of this choice, but the advantages outweigh the disadvantages.

Laura concluded by restating her belief in being a vegetarian and clinched with a positive visualization about her upcoming Thanksgiving dinner, but she ultimately left the decision to choose a similar lifestyle to her listeners.

Problem (No Solution) Pattern

The **problem (no solution) pattern** is a main point arrangement that focuses on the depth and breadth of a problem in order to convince listeners that it is, in fact, a significant problem. This pattern is particularly useful for developing claim of fact speeches focused in the present or future, since your goal in these kinds of speeches is to attain agreement about whether something exists or is likely to occur. It is also a good choice when your target audience is uncertain about or opposed to your position. Luke used this pattern in his speech about binge drinking on college campuses.

Teaching Tip
Remind students that we commonly use the problem approach (along with the other approaches discussed in this chapter) in our interactions with others. Have students write a brief essay in which they reflect on previous communication encounters and analyze the persuasive strategies used.

Thesis statement: Binge drinking is becoming a serious problem on college campuses across the United States.

I. *First main point:* Binge drinking is common among college students.

II. *Second main point:* Binge drinking causes serious problems for these students.

III. *Third main point:* Binge drinking causes serious problems for society as well.

Each of these main point patterns can help you develop a convincing argument for your dispositional speech. Which one you choose depends on your topic, your claim, and your target audience.

What follows is an outline from a student's dispositional persuasive speech focused on a claim of fact focused in the future. The main points are arranged in a topical pattern.

Teaching Tip
Divide the class into small groups and have each group analyze this speech. Allow each group five minutes to present its findings to the class.

Persuasive Speech Outline Example

Television Censorship Will Save America's Children

by Eric Gustafson, North Dakota State University

Introduction

I. *Attention catcher:* According to the American Psychological Association, the average American child spends more time watching television than doing anything else besides sleeping (APA Web site). Imagine that for a moment. Kids spend more time being influenced by television than they do being influenced by their teachers, their friends, or their families.

II. *Listener relevance:* As Americans and as parents and potential parents, we should be concerned about how television is shaping our children.

III. *Speaker credibility:* I am concerned, not only because I am a future parent, but also because I grew up in a typical American household and have been exposed to television my whole life. As a result of the research I've done, I realize that . . .

IV. *Thesis:* Television censorship is necessary to save our children.

V. *Preview:* Today we will see how television censorship will soon become available to households throughout the United States. Then we will examine why television censorship is absolutely essential to modern parenting. Finally, we will explore the profound effects of current television programming on our nation's children.

Body

I. *First main point:* Let's look at how television censorship will soon be possible.

  A. *Subpoint:* Thanks to the V-chip, a device that allows users to censor what can be viewed on their personal television sets, the ability to censor programming will soon be available across the country.

    1. *Sub-subpoint:* The V-chip has become a standard feature on all new television sets built after 1999 (Geier, 1998).

    2. *Sub-subpoint:* The V-Chip can be added to television sets made before 1999.

  B. *Subpoint:* Implementing the V-chip into television sets provides parents a means by which to control what their children watch (Geier, 1998).

Transition:

Now that we've determined how feasible TV censorship is, let's examine why censorship is a necessary element of parenting in society today.

II. *Second main point:* In today's society, TV censorship is necessary to allow parents to control what kids see on television.

A. *Subpoint:* More than ever before in history, television is filled with brutal acts of violence and graphic acts of sex (Slaby, 1994).

B. *Subpoint:* Compared to the 1950s when television was first introduced into family homes, more children are being raised by two-career parents and single parents. So more children are unsupervised in the afternoon hours.

1. *Sub-subpoint:* In 1994, there were an estimated thirteen million latch-key children (Solomon, 1994).
2. *Sub-subpoint:* This means that kids can watch any show they choose to, including shows with graphic sexual and violent content.

C. *Subpoint:* The introduction and growth of cable television has led to an explosion in the number of programs to watch.

1. *Sub-subpoint:* This explosion means there are many more programs with graphic sexual and violent content available throughout the day.
2. *Sub-subpoint:* Programs with "adult content" that move into syndication and are programmed on cable don't face time-of-day restrictions.

Transition:

It is certainly obvious that TV censorship is critical for today's parents. Let's examine now why it is so important for and beneficial to children.

III. *Third Main Point:* Television has a profound effect on the value system and behavior of children.

A. *Subpoint:* TV violence can foster violent tendencies in young people.

1. *Sub-subpoint:* In 1993, a five-year-old child started a fire, killing his infant sister, after watching an episode of *Beavis and Butthead* where this type of act had been depicted ("Mother Blames," 1993).
2. *Sub-subpoint:* According to Harvard pediatrics professor Ronald G. Slaby, "viewing large quantities of TV violence as children is one of the best predictors of violent adult behavior" (Slaby, 1994).
3. *Sub-subpoint:* Violence on television is "often misportrayed; often shown as legitimate, justified, rewarded, effective, and clean" (Slaby, 1994).

B. *Subpoint:* The growth of graphic sex and violence depicted on television is promoting a moral decline among children in American society.

1. *Sub-subpoint:* Researcher Robert Maginnis discovered in a survey of Americans between the ages of eighteen and thirty that an overwhelming 63 percent of the respondents said that television encourages teenage sex (McNamara, 1998).

2. *Sub-subpoint:* Are these really the kinds of messages we want the children of this country to be learning? Is this a healthy pastime for our children to grow up on?

Conclusion

I. *Thesis restatement:* Today we have examined why television censorship is necessary to save our children.

II. *Main point summary:* Television censorship has been made possible through the V-chip, first installed as a standard television feature in 1999. Moreover, television censorship is essential for effective contemporary parenting, and it will defer the potential negative effects that programming can have on children.

III. *Clincher:* If the research is correct and children today truly spend more time watching television than doing any other activity besides sleeping, then it is our duty as parents, guardians, and shapers of the future to filter the programs children are exposed to. Television censorship is a *must* to save our children.

References

American Psychological Association Link (1998, May 24). [Online]: http://edie.cprost.sfu.ca/gcnest/ISS4-21c.html.

Geier, R. (1998, March 23). Anxious parents will get a V-chip. U.S. News and World Report, 28.

McNamara, J. (1998, January). Anything goes: Moral bankruptcy or television and Hollywood. USA Today Magazine, 62–63.

Mother blames deadly fire on MTV cartoon. (1993, October 10). The New York Times, sec. 1, p. 14.

Slaby, R. (1994, April). Closing the education gap on TV's entertainment violence. Education Digest, 4–8.

Solomon, C. M. (1994, March). Latchkey kids. Parents, 42.

Organizing Actuation Persuasive Speeches

Because your goal in an actuation persuasive speech is to seek action, you must offer a plan or solution for listeners to act on. Hence, your actuation persuasive speech likely will be arranged according to one of four possible patterns—problem/solution, problem/cause/solution, modified comparative advantages, or Monroe's motivated sequence—all of which offer precisely that.

Problem/Solution Pattern

Teaching Tip
Develop a file of political campaign literature, rhetoric, and materials. Have students identify the organizational patterns and persuasive strategies employed in these materials.

A **problem/solution pattern** is arranged into two main points. The first main point examines the problem, and the second presents a solution. The problem illustrates what you believe is wrong with present conditions and why. The problem should be examined in sufficient breadth and depth, as well as offer listener relevance. You might provide breadth, for example, by talking about the scope of the problem and the number of people it affects and by talking about trends over time, including trends likely for the future if the problem isn't addressed. You might provide depth by talking about harms—that is, those directly affected by the problem and how their lives are affected. In her speech about the problem of gang violence, for example, Karlie gave the problem breadth by talking about the wide range of people who join gangs and about the presence of gangs in communities across the country. She gave it depth by looking closely at the harmful effects of gangs on a particular community. She incorporated listener relevance by offering examples from her listeners' own community.

Thesis statement: We must do something to squelch the alarming problem of gang violence in our country.

I. *First main point:* We cannot deny the fact that gang violence is a serious problem.

- **A.** *Subpoint:* Gang violence occurs in urban, suburban, and rural communities and areas across the country. (Cite examples and statistics about growing numbers.)
- **B.** *Subpoint:* Gang violence occurs in our fine community as well. (Cite examples and statistics.)
- **C.** *Subpoint:* Contrary to what you might believe, gang members are not isolated to one ethnic or racial group, or from a particular social class. (Cite examples and statistics.)
- **D.** *Subpoint:* The consequences of gang violence include harassment, vandalism, dismemberment, and death. (Cite examples and statistics.)

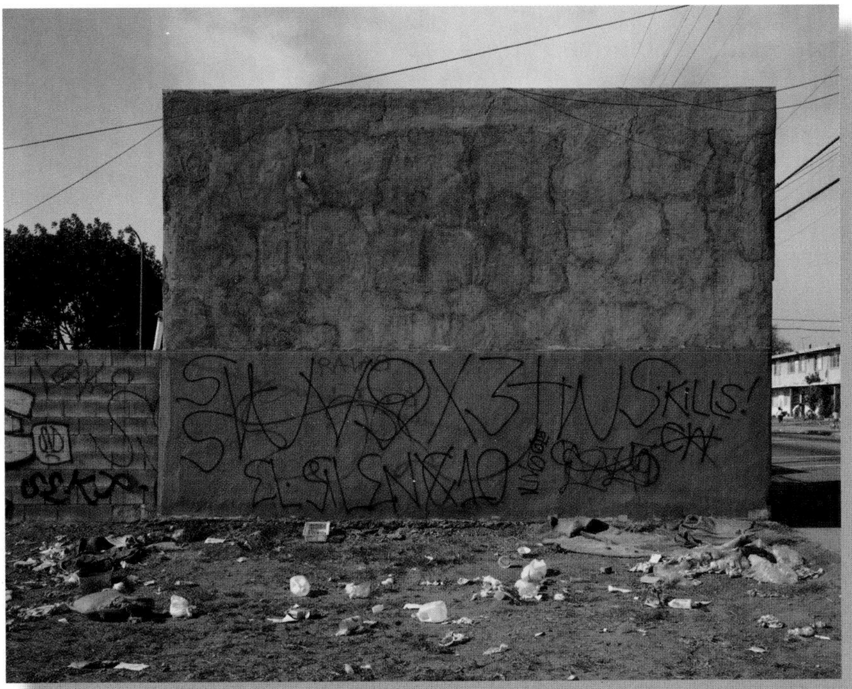

Gang violence is a problem across the United States.

Teaching Tip
Students often have difficulty developing a concrete solution to the problems they identify in persuasive speeches. Encourage students to clearly develop their advocacy in their persuasive speech. In addition, provide multiple examples of how to develop solutions.

The solution is typically multifaceted, indicating what listeners should do personally as well as what should be done on a larger scale. The solution on a larger scale might take the form of policies or regulations that different levels of government should enact and/or of strategies that businesses or local organizations could use. In any case, you ought to leave your listeners with a strategy they can implement personally to help solve the problem. Thus, in her speech about gang-related violence, Karlie posed this three-part solution:

II. *Second main point:* Although gang violence is too large a problem to eradicate with one simple solution, there are some issues that ought to be addressed to begin to deal effectively with it.

- **A.** *Subpoint:* Congress should pass gun control laws to limit gang member access to guns. (Explain the plan.)
- **B.** *Subpoint:* Schools and communities must implement programs that give kids positive alternatives to joining gangs and participating in gang activity. (Offer examples.)
- **C.** *Subpoint:* As parents and guardians, we must be accountable for the actions of our children.
  1. *Sub-subpoint:* This includes encouraging them to participate in healthy activities and taking an interest in them when they do.
  2. *Sub-subpoint:* This also means knowing where our children are and what they're doing during their free time.
  3. *Sub-subpoint:* And this means being responsible for and accepting certain consequences when they do engage in inappropriate, and perhaps harmful, activities.

Problem/Cause/Solution Pattern

Teaching Tip
To give students practice with this organizational pattern, see the Problems and Causes assignment in the Activities section of this chapter.

The **problem/cause/solution pattern** is a main point arrangement with the first main point articulating the problem, the second analyzing its causes, and the third presenting multifaceted solutions. This pattern differs from the problem/solution pattern in that the addition of a main point on causes makes it possible to analyze the problem more thoroughly with regard to some underlying reasons for its existence and then to tie the solutions directly to these causes. This pattern is particularly useful for addressing problems that have been dealt with unsuccessfully in the past. These failures often stem from lack of attention to the inherent causes of the problem. Developing a main point specifically about causes can illuminate these underlying issues and, as a result, give rise to new solutions that may in fact be more effective.

In working on her recycling speech, for example, Margaret discovered that people's failure to recycle stems mainly from their ignorance about recycling and the inconvenience of recycling. She was therefore able to present the causes of the problem and to offer solutions that directly addressed them. To address ignorance as a cause, she proposed community programs and promotional campaigns designed to clarify proper recycling procedures. To address inconvenience as a cause, she made two proposals: first, that public cafeterias and restaurants be required to have clearly labeled recycling bins wherever they have trash containers, and second, that city sanitation departments be expanded to provide curbside pickup of recyclable materials.

Thesis statement: If we don't want garbage to overcome us and our world, we must make the habit of recycling the norm rather than the exception.

I. *First main point (problem):* Waste disposal is a significant problem.

II. *Second main point (cause[s]):* Since most of us realize that waste disposal is a serious problem and recycling can be an effective solution, why aren't we better about doing it?

  A. *Subpoint:* One reason has to do with ignorance about recycling.

  B. *Subpoint:* Another reason has to do with inconvenience.

Transition: I see many of you nodding your heads in agreement with me at this point—waste disposal is a serious problem that recycling could help solve *if* it weren't difficult or inconvenient to implement. But let's not stop there.

III. *Third main point (solution):* Let me propose three solutions that will make recycling both easier and more convenient.

  A. *Subpoint:* We need to implement community programs and promotional campaigns that clarify proper recycling procedures. (Explain what these might look like and what audience members must do to make them a reality.)

  B. *Subpoint:* Public cafeterias and restaurants should be required to have clearly labeled recycling bins wherever they have trash containers. (Explain what audience members must do to make this a reality.)

  C. *Subpoint:* City sanitation departments must be expanded to provide curbside pickup of recyclable materials. (Explain what audience members must do to make this a reality.)

Teaching Tip
Use video clips from programs like *Judge Judy* or *Court TV* as teaching tools for this chapter. Have students analyze the types of appeals, organizational patterns, and persuasive strategies used by speakers.

Modified Comparative Advantages Pattern

Recall our discussion about the comparative advantages pattern as a main point arrangement that leads your audience to agree with your disposition that one of two or more alternatives is better than the others (Ziegelmueller, Kay, & Dause, 1990, p. 186). In its purest form, the comparative advantages pattern does not advocate action; however, action is often implied. Hence, this pattern is sometimes modified to offer an explicit plan and to advocate action. This is particularly true when more than one plan exists. Your goal is to illustrate both why your plan is the best and to convince listeners to act on it. In this case, you arrange your main points to, first, identify the problem and its significance, then the other plan(s) proposed to solve the problem, and finally your solution and why it's better than the others. If Dan were to modify his comparative advantages speech about satellite television, it might look like this:

Thesis statement: If you are looking for the best value and quality television reception available today, choose a satellite television system.

I. *First main point (problem):* We need to invest in some system for television reception if we want access to the information and entertainment it provides.

II. *Second main point (alternatives):* There are several options available today.
   A. *Subpoint:* Using a rooftop antenna is one option.
   B. *Subpoint:* Subscribing to cable television is another option.
   C. *Subpoint:* Installing a satellite system is another option.

III. *Third main point (best plan):* Choose satellite television.
   A. *Subpoint:* Here's why satellite television system is the best plan available.
   B. *Subpoint:* Here's what you need to do to install satellite television system in your home.

Monroe's Motivated Sequence

Teaching Tip
To give students an opportunity to experiment with Monroe's motivated sequence, see the Group Commercial assignment located in the Activities section of this chapter.

Monroe's motivated sequence is a five-step approach for arranging your main points. This pattern is particularly useful because it allows you to develop both the problem and solution, as well as illustrate in detail the consequences of implementing your plan or failing to do so. These steps are attention, need, satisfaction, visualization, and action. Typically, you'll deal with the attention step in your introductory comments, deal with the action step in your concluding remarks, and develop the other steps as your three main points.

Step 1: Attention

Teaching Tip
Tape several television commercials and have students identify the organizational patterns used in them. Instruct them to reformat one of the commercials using Monroe's motivated sequence.

Your first step is to catch the attention of your listeners. Although you should do this in any speech, you might spend a little more time on it here, because you want to start motivating listeners not only to listen but also to internalize a sense of urgency about doing something about a particular problem. Hence, you might present and explain two or three examples or startling statistics. Essentially, you capture your listeners' attention with your attention catcher and other introductory comments.

In her speech about sexual assault policies on college campuses, Maria Lucia R. Anton (1994) achieved the attention this way:

Thesis statement: Sexual assault has become a major problem on U.S. campuses today. However, in spite of increased sexual assaults on campuses, many still lack a policy to protect their students.

Attention: "If you want to take her blouse off, you have to ask. If you want to touch her breast, you have to ask. If you want to move your hand down to her genitals, you have to ask. If you want to put your finger inside her, you have to ask."

What I've just quoted is part of the freshman orientation at Antioch College in Ohio. In the sexual offense policy of this college, emphasis is given to three major points: (1) If you have a sexually transmitted disease, you

> must disclose it to a potential partner; (2) to knowingly take advantage of someone who is under the influence of alcohol, drugs, and/or prescribed medication is not acceptable behavior in the Antioch community; (3) obtaining consent is an ongoing process in any sexual interaction. The request for consent must be specific to each act.
>
> The policy is designed to create a "safe" campus environment according to Antioch President Alan Guskin. For those who engage in sex, the goal is 100 percent consensual sex. It isn't enough to ask someone if they would like to have sex; you have to get verbal consent every step of the way.
>
> This policy has been highly publicized and you may have heard it before. The policy addresses sexual offenses such as rape, which involves penetration, and sexual assault, which does not. In both instances, the respondent coerced or forced the primary witness to engage in nonconsensual sexual conduct with the respondent or another.

Step 2: Need

This step is similar to the problem portion of the problem/solution and problem/cause/solution patterns. You show listeners that there is a serious problem with the existing situation or the present conditions. Develop the need for a change with strong supporting materials; then demonstrate the depth and breadth of the problem as well as how it impacts listeners.

Discussion Tip
Ask students if they have ever been persuaded to do something as a result of a fear appeal. When is the use of fear appeals unethical?

You can develop your supporting points by illustrating the need with specific incidents. You can also highlight ramifications of the problem with facts, statistics, examples, and quotations. Finally, you can point to the direct relevance of the problem to the people seated in your audience. Maria developed the need in her speech by sharing specific instances, statistics, and effects:

> *First main point—Need:* Sexual assault has become a reality in many campuses across the nation. Carleton College in Northfield, Minnesota, was sued for $800,000 in damages by four university women. The women charged that Carleton was negligent in protecting them against a known rapist. From the June 1991 issue of *Time* magazine:
>
>> Amy had been on campus for just five weeks when she joined some friends to watch a video in the room of a senior. One by one the other students went away, leaving her alone with a student whose name she didn't even know. "It ended up with his hands around my throat," she recalls. In a lawsuit she has filed against the college, she charges that he locked the door and raped her again and again for the next four hours. "I didn't want him to kill me, I just kept trying not to cry." Only afterwards did he tell her, almost defiantly, his name. It was on top of the "castration list" posted on women's bathroom walls around campus to warn other students about college rapists. Amy's attacker was found guilty of sexual assault but was only suspended.

> Julie started dating a fellow cast member in a Carleton play. They had never slept together, she charges in a civil suit, until he came to her dorm room one night, uninvited, and raped her. She struggled to hold her life and education together, but finally could manage no longer and left school. Only later did Julie learn that her assailant was the same man who had attacked Amy.

Ladies and gentlemen, the court held that the college knew this man was a rapist. The administration may have been able to prevent this from happening if they had expelled the attacker, but they didn't. My campus has no reports of sexual assault. Is the administration waiting for someone to be assaulted before it formulates a sexual assault policy? This mistake has been made elsewhere; we don't have to prove it again.

Perhaps some statistics will help you understand the magnitude of the problem. According to *New Statesman and Society,* June 21, 1991, issue:

> A 1985 survey of sampled campuses by *Ms. Magazine* and the National Institute of Mental Health found that one in every four college women were victims of sexual assault, 74 percent knew their attackers. Even worse, between 30 to 40 percent of male students indicated they might force a woman to have sex if they knew they would escape punishment.
>
> In just one year from 1988–1989, reports of student rape at the University of California increased from two to eighty.

These numbers are indeed disturbing. But more disturbing are the effects of sexual assault: a victim feeling the shock of why something this terrible was allowed to happen; having intense fears that behind every dark corner could be an attacker ready to grab her, push her to the ground, and sexually assault her; many waking moments of anxiety and impaired concentration as she remembers the attack; countless nights of reliving the traumatic incident in her sleep; mood swings and depression as she tries to deal internally with the physical hurt and the emotional turmoil that this attack has caused.

Step 3: Satisfaction

Teaching Tip
Assign students to small groups. Instruct each group to develop a persuasive speech, using Monroe's motivated sequence, to sell an object to the class. The object can be anything in the classroom (desk, pencils, newspapers, etc.).

This step is similar to the solution portion of the problem/solution and problem/cause/solution patterns. You present your plan for solving the problem, providing enough detail so listeners have a clear understanding of how your plan will actually solve the problem. You might develop your supporting points by explaining your proposal in an easily understood fashion. You might demonstrate precisely how the solution meets the need pointed out in the need step. You might also cite actual examples of where this proposal has worked effectively. Finally, you might show how your proposal overcomes any potential objections. Maria offered her plan by indicating how her proposal is only a first step, but a necessary one, as well as laying it out very clearly:

Second main point—Satisfaction: Many campuses are open invitations for sexual assault. The absence of a policy is a grand invitation. I have never been sexually assaulted so why do I care so much about a policy? You know why—because I could be assaulted. I won't sit and wait to be among one out of every four women on my campus to be assaulted. The first step to keep myself out of the statistics is to push for a sexual assault policy on my campus. One way to do this is through a petition to the university.

Although the Antioch policy sounds a little far-fetched and has been the target of criticism in comedy routines such as those on *Saturday Night Live* and although students feel that formalizing such a policy is unnatural, many campuses are taking heed and revisiting their own policies. Campuses like mine don't have a sexual assault policy to revisit. Does yours?

By far the most controversial policy today is the one established at Antioch College. I'm not saying that we need one as specific as theirs, but every university has a responsibility to provide a safe environment for its students. Universities have an obligation to provide a sexual assault policy.

The following points are fundamental to the safety of the students and need to be addressed by universities:

1. Every campus should have a sexual assault policy that is developed with input from the students, faculty, staff, and administration. The policy then needs to be publicized in the student handbook. The school newspaper should print and campus radio broadcast the policy periodically to heighten awareness.
2. Campuses must institute programs to educate students and other campus personnel. Examples of these policies can include discussing the sexual assault policy during mandatory student orientation and conducting special workshops for faculty and other staff.
3. Campuses should outline a step-by-step written procedure to guarantee that sexual assault victims are assisted by the university. It is pertinent that they are not without support at this very critical time.

Discussion Tip
How does Maria demonstrate that her proposal will solve the problem of sexual assault? What evidence does Maria provide to substantiate her claims?

Step 4: Visualization

Your goal in this step is to visualize the future in order to intensify listeners' desire to solve the problem. You might visualize a positive future by describing what will happen if your plan is implemented. Picture your listeners enjoying the benefits that acceptance of your proposal will produce. You might visualize a negative future by describing what will happen if the situation continues on its current course. Picture listeners enduring the unpleasant effects resulting from the failure to implement your proposal. You might provide both positive and negative visualization.

The visualization step should be able to stand the test of reality—that is, the conditions you describe must seem realistic. The more vivid your visualiza-

Discussion Tip
According to Sellnow, what is the speaker's goal in the visualization step? How does Maria develop her visualization step?

tion is, the stronger the reaction it will evoke from the audience. Maria developed her visualization step first with positive visualization and then with negative visualization:

> *Third main point—Visualization:* My vision is a campus where there is no place for any sexual assault. I want to leave the classroom at night knowing that my trip from the building to the car will not be one of fear for my personal safety.
>
> You may be saying to yourself that there are laws to handle crimes like these. From *The Chronicle of Higher Education,* May 15, 1991, issue, Jane McDonnell, a senior lecturer in women's studies at Carleton, says colleges cannot turn their back on women. "We'd be abandoning victims if we merely sent them to the police," she says. "The wheels of justice tend to grind slowly and rape has one of the lowest conviction rates of any crime."
>
> Without a policy, most institutions lack specific penalties for sexual assault and choose to prosecute offenders under the general student-conduct code. At Carleton College, for example, Amy's attacker was allowed back on campus after his suspension, and consequently he raped again.
>
> Although the policy may not stop the actual assault, would-be offenders will think twice before committing sexual assault if they know they will be punished. In addition, it guarantees justice for victims of sexual assault. We need to make it loud and clear that sexual assault will not be tolerated.

Step 5: Action

Teaching Tip
To give students experience applying these concepts outside of the classroom, have them complete the Analyze an Advertisement assignment in the Activities section of this chapter.

This step provides the basis for your conclusion. By now you have convinced your audience that the problem and its consequences warrant implementing your solution. Here is where you tell each of your listeners what they should do and how they can do it. Perhaps you will provide them with addresses to write to or telephone numbers to call. Perhaps you will give them the names of organizations to join. Perhaps you will hand them a petition to sign. Once you provide them with a specific call to action, you conclude with a final appeal to reinforce their commitment to act. This comes as part of your clincher as you tie back to your attention catcher. Here are Maria's concluding remarks, including her call to action:

> *Conclusion—Action:* Yes, universities have a big task in the struggle to prevent sexual assault.
>
> You and I can actively assist in this task and can make a giant contribution to move it forward. On my campus, students have not only voiced

> their concerns, but we have also started a petition demanding that the university formulate a sexual assault policy.
>
> The bottom line is that we need to prevent sexual assault on campus. The key to prevention is a sexual assault policy. If your university does not have a policy, then you need to petition your administration to have one. I know I won't stop my advocacy until I see a policy on my campus.

Actuation persuasive speeches are unique in that they seek action from listeners. Because they advocate a plan of action, they are arranged according to a problem/solution, problem/cause/solution, modified comparative advantages, or Monroe's motivated sequence pattern.

Summary

This chapter focused on the nature of persuasion as it relates specifically to persuasive speaking. Persuasion is the process of influencing the beliefs, attitudes, values, or behaviors of others. Persuasive speaking is engaging in persuasion within a public speaking context.

Persuasive speaking differs from informative speaking in that persuasive speakers are essentially leaders rather than teachers. Hence, persuasive speakers build arguments in support of a particular position. Dispositional persuasive speeches seek agreement about a position by focusing on a belief, an attitude, or a value. Actuation persuasive speeches seek action regarding a policy or behavior.

Because persuasive speeches attempt to influence listeners, they can be more difficult to prepare than informative speeches. Consequently, public speaking anxiety might increase. One factor behind increased anxiety is not knowing where your listeners stand on the issue. By analyzing your audience, you can discover your target audience and adapt your speech to them. The result will be reduced anxiety and increased effectiveness.

In a persuasive speech, your thesis statement will make one of three kinds of claims: a claim of fact for a dispositional speech focused on a belief, a claim of value for a dispositional speech focused on an attitude or value, or a claim of policy for actuation persuasive speeches.

The most common main point arrangements for dispositional persuasive speeches are the topical, causal, refutative, comparative advantages, invitational, or problem (no solution) main point patterns. The most common main point arrangements used in actuation persuasive speeches are the problem/solution, problem/cause/solution, modified comparative advantages, and Monroe's motivated sequence patterns.

Activities

1. **Identifying Your Target Audience.** Form small groups of four or five members each. As a group, come up with three different social issues that could be developed into a persuasive speech. Create a claim of fact or a claim of value for each

issue. Speculate as a group about where the target audience in the class probably stands on the issue. Next, poll the audience by anonymous ballot to discover whether you were right or wrong. Finally, decide how you might approach the speech based on what you learn about your audience.

2. **Debating with Comparative Advantages.** Form partners. Select one of the following topics and, using a comparative advantages pattern, debate in front of the class as to which is better. Recall that your goal is to show how the advantages of the alternative you advocate outweigh the disadvantages, as well as how the advantages of this particular alternative surpass the advantages of the other options. You might also show how the disadvantages of other options outweigh their advantages. Each person will have one to two minutes to speak. Ask the class to vote about which alternative seems better and discuss the reasons one speech was more persuasive.
   - **a.** *The Tonight Show* versus *Late Night with David Letterman.*
   - **b.** Coke versus Pepsi.
   - **c.** Macintosh versus IBM.
   - **d.** Going to the movie theater versus watching a movie on video.
   - **e.** Come up with your own.
3. **Invitational Impromptu Speaking.** Form small groups of four or five members each. Brainstorm several campus issues (parking, class size, tuition, alcohol, etc.). Select one issue and discuss it using the Invitational pattern:
   - **a.** Offer your perspective and how it works for you.
   - **b.** Create an atmosphere that encourages mutual understanding.
   - **c.** Focus on the positive aspects of a situation and persistence of them.
4. **Problems and Causes.** Form small groups of four or five members each. Brainstorm several problems on your campus, in your community, or in the country. Select one that continues to be a problem despite attempts to solve it. As a group, try to identify possible causes of the problem (reasons for its existence) that may, in fact, need to be dealt with in order to solve it.
5. **Group Commercial.** Form groups of five persons each. One person from each group selects an object from a bag of items the instructor brings to class. These items can be anything from the home or office. Each group develops a one- to two-minute "commercial" designed to sell the object to the class using Monroe's motivated sequence (attention, need, satisfaction, visualization, action). The object cannot be sold as what it actually is, but rather as fulfilling some need unique to college students. All students in the group must participate in the commercial, and all steps of Monroe's motivated sequence must be evident.
6. **Analyze an Advertisement.** Analyze a television, radio, or print advertisement you find particularly compelling using Monroe's motivated sequence. Identify all five elements of the sequence and explain why each was used effectively. Bring the advertisement with you to class to serve as supporting material as you discuss your analysis of it.

Key Terms

- Actuate
- Actuation persuasive speech
- Argument
- Attitude
- Belief
- Claim of fact
- Claim of policy
- Claim of value
- Coactive approach
- Comparative advantages pattern
- Dispositional persuasive speech
- Incremental change
- Invitational pattern
- Monroe's motivated sequence
- Persuasion
- Persuasive speaking
- Problem/cause/solution pattern
- Problem (no solution) pattern
- Problem/solution pattern
- Raised consciousness
- Refutative pattern
- Situational acceptance
- Sleeper effect
- Target audience
- Value

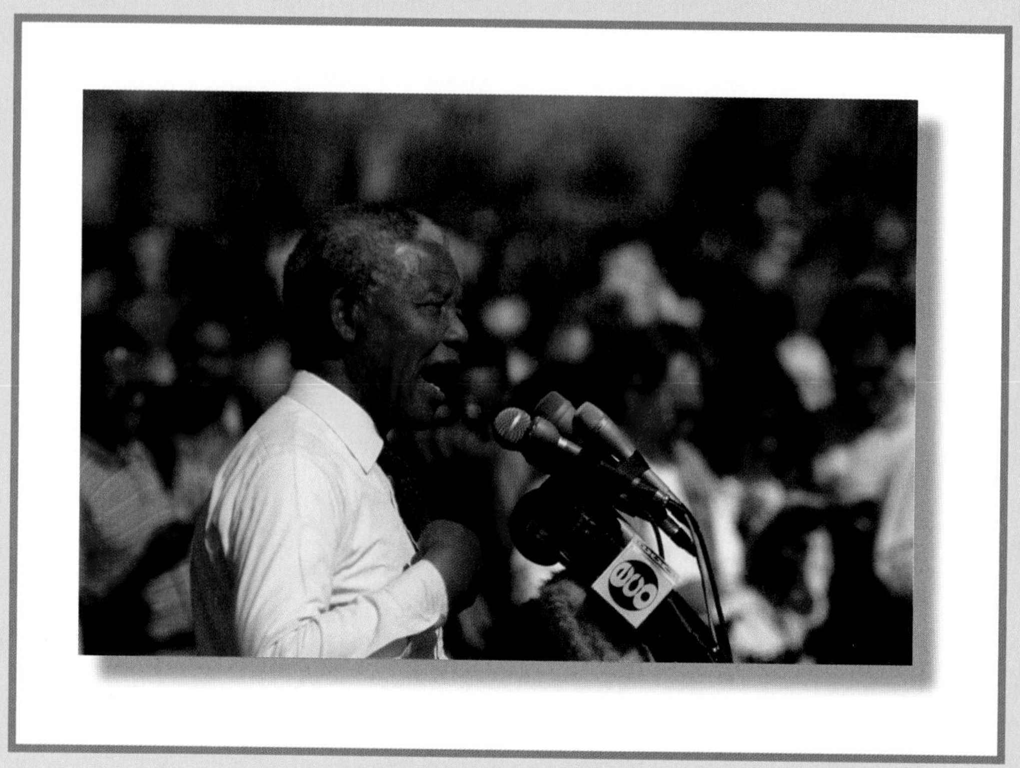

CHAPTER 16

Persuasive Strategies

Reflective Questions

1. Why is it important to cite credible sources during your persuasive speech?
2. Why is it so important to use respectful language in your persuasive speech?
3. Why would use of flawed logic make your persuasive speech less effective?
4. What do emotionally charged words do for your persuasive speech?

Last summer my husband and I bought a pickup truck. The fact that we bought this truck is interesting because I really didn't want one. Owning a truck just didn't make sense to me. You see both Tim and I work full-time outside the home. We are also the parents of two wonderful children. Each child attends a different school and is active in a number of extracurricular activities. We need two vehicles to juggle their transportation needs with our own work schedules. Because we try to carpool with other parents, it's also very important to drive vehicles that can accommodate more than one or two children at a time. Finally, we try to visit our extended families several times each year and they live in different states. So it just makes sense to own vehicles that have room for several people, are comfortable to ride in, and are economical for long-distance travel. Given our needs, owning a pickup truck rather than a car just didn't make sense to me. But we did buy one and I actually supported the decision when we did.

Teaching Tip
Refer students to the SpeechMaker CD-ROM. This software provides several tips for effective persuasive speaking. Consider assigning one of the scenarios to be completed before the class in which you will discuss this chapter.

Why did I change my mind? Quite honestly, I did so primarily as a result of several persuasive strategies Tim used during our discussions. More specifically, he used effective reasoning. With regard to carpooling, he demonstrated how a cab-and-a-half pickup truck can safely transport up to four children (with seat belts). He reasoned further that we ought to drive a four-wheel drive vehicle during the winter months, as well as when driving in the Montana and Wyoming mountains. Then he talked about the times we had to borrow a pickup truck to haul various things. If we owned a pickup, he reasoned, we would reduce some of our emotional stress in these situations.

He also bolstered his credibility by citing numerous sources that depicted cost comparisons between pickups and cars over the life of the vehicle. He offered facts and statistics regarding purchase price, mileage figures, repair estimates, and durability. He then took me to several dealerships to show me where the best deals were and why. He demonstrated that he'd really done his homework.

Teaching Tip
Have students complete the Analyzing a Speech assignment contained in the Activities section before you discuss this chapter in class. This activity will provide students with a solid foundation for a deeper in-class discussion of the material presented in this chapter.

Finally, he appealed to my emotions in a number of ways. He had me test-drive several of his favorite choices. He talked about how he was reaching an age when some men wanted to get a motorcycle or a convertible, but all he really wanted was a pickup truck. He talked about how much more practical his desire for a truck was. He asked me which one I liked the best and why. Doing so made me feel included. Finally, he brought the children along to look at and ride in these trucks. Afterward he asked them whether they would like to own a truck. Of course they did! You bet! Because Tim effectively employed a number of persuasive strategies, I agreed that we really ought to buy a pickup truck. And we did.

Discussion Tip
How were ethos, pathos, and logos defined in Chapter 6? According to Sellnow, why are these appeals particularly important to persuasive speeches?

The strategies of persuasion center on three types of appeals: appeals to ethos (speaker credibility), logos (logic and reasoning), and pathos (emotions). First articulated by the Greek philosopher Aristotle in his book *The Rhetoric,* these appeals continue to guide communicators today. Although they can be useful in any public speech, they are particularly important to persuasive speeches. By shaping the content, language, and delivery of your speech from the standpoint of these appeals, you can greatly increase your chances of successfully persuading listeners.

Ethos, logos, and pathos, as you may recall from Chapter 6, are motivational appeals—they attempt to compel listeners to believe you, to

What Do You Think?

Consider a time when you were convinced to purchase a product that you didn't necessarily want or need. What specifically persuaded you to do so?

agree with you, and to be impassioned about your topic. **Ethos,** or speaker credibility, is the sense of competence and character you convey. **Logos,** or logical appeals, is the systematic way you structure your argument, and the way you use reasoning to build your argument and support your claims with evidence. In Chapter 15, you learned about logos in terms of different ways to systematically structure your arguments. In this chapter, we look at logos in terms of reasoning and evidence. **Pathos,** or emotional appeals, refers to your attempts to evoke certain feelings in your listeners.

Teaching Tip
For a creative project that gives students a chance to explore ethos, pathos, and logos, see the Analyzing a News Report assignment located in the Activities section of this chapter

What Do You Think?

Identify a television commercial you've seen recently that compelled you in some way. What specific elements of the commercial "worked" for you? Which of those are actually related to ethos? Pathos? Logos?

Why are these motivational appeals crucial to the success of your persuasive speech? Keep in mind that you must motivate your listeners not only to listen and understand, but also to consider—and often reconsider—their attitudes, beliefs, values, and behaviors. Since your listeners have spent their lives developing and solidifying their attitudes, beliefs, values, and behaviors, how in the world can you influence these in a single speech? You do so by integrating motivational appeals throughout your speech, which encourage your listeners to believe in you, agree with you, and care about your topic. To influence your listeners, you must appeal to their minds and their hearts.

These appeals also allow you to round the cycle of learning, thereby addressing different learning styles. By incorporating all three kinds of appeals, you will make your speech more persuasive for example, to learners who prefer logical explanations and learners who prefer stories with emotional import. In addition, the resulting variety will help all listeners better retain your message (see Figure 16–1).

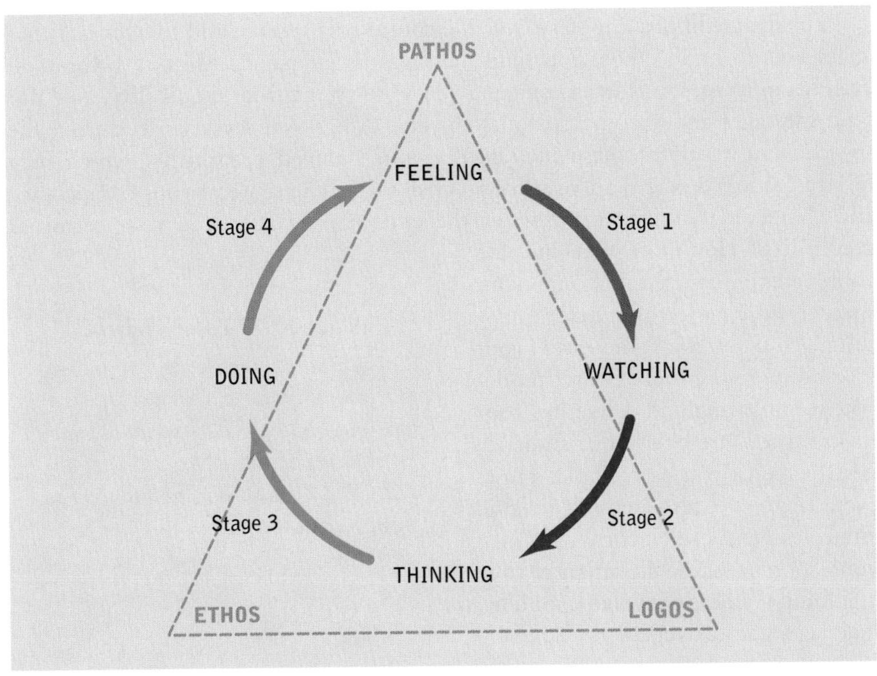

FIGURE 16–1 Rhetorical Appeals and the Learning Cycle

Strategies for Conveying Ethos

Discussion Tip
What two aspects of ethos does Sellnow discuss? In what ways might perceived credibility vary by topic and audience?

You probably were not surprised to read that public speakers are more compelling when they seem credible. The question is, what can you do to convey credibility (or ethos) in your speech? Keep in mind that there are two aspects of ethos, competence and character. **Competence** has to do with being perceived as well informed, skilled, or knowledgeable about your subject—in other words, as an expert of sorts. What academic credentials have you earned, personal or professional experience do you have, or research have you conducted that makes you knowledgeable about the topic of your speech? **Character** has to do with being perceived as trustworthy, honest, and sincere, as well as engaging, likable, and attractive (e.g., Booth-Butterfield & Gutowski, 1993; O'Keefe, 1990; Reardon, 1991). Notice that these definitions are in terms of listeners' perceptions. Your credibility depends, not on whether you are, in fact, knowledgeable and sincere, but on whether you can convince listeners that you are.

Our credibility can vary greatly. For instance, a speaker could be perceived as credible about one topic and not about another. If Madonna came to your campus to talk about some aspects of the popular music industry, you'd probably perceive her to be credible. If, for some unknown reason, she were to talk about pesticides, however, you'd probably question her credibility.

Credibility can also vary with one's audience—that is, the same speaker could be perceived as credible by one audience and not by another. For example, some friends told me that they voted for Jesse Ventura for governor of Minnesota, in part, because he does not have a college degree. For them, he seems credible because he represents common folk rather than aristocracy. Other friends, however, told me they were appalled when he was elected, in part, because he does not have a college degree. For them, he lacks credibility because he hasn't earned what they perceive to be a necessary fundamental education.

Finally, credibility can vary over the course of a speech, and it's this fact that enables us to build ethos. You send messages about your credibility before you even begin to speak. These messages give rise to your **initial credibility.** You also send messages about your credibility by the things you say and do during the speech. The result of these messages is your **derived credibility,** which may be stronger or weaker than your initial credibility. The sense of your competence and character that listeners have at the end of your speech is your **terminal credibility.** How can you increase your credibility throughout your speech? In a sense, of course, everything you do well increases your credibility, so the more effort you devote to preparing and delivering your speech, the more likely your audience is to perceive you as credible. However, there are also several specific strategies you can incorporate into your speech that will enhance your credibility; these involve content, language, and delivery.

> ***What Do You Think?***
>
> *Consider a television news reporter you perceive as credible. Why do you have this perception? What specific characteristics make him or her seem competent? What makes him or her seem to be of good character?*

Madonna would probably be perceived as a credible speaker on the topic of popular music, but not on pesticides.

Strategies Involving Content

When you develop your content, keep in mind three strategies you can use to enhance your credibility: explaining your competence, establishing common ground, and using strong evidence.

Teaching Tip
To provide students with an opportunity to practice these skills, see the Advertisements and Persuasive Appeals assignment contained in the Activities section of this chapter.

Explain Your Competence

Since competence is a crucial part of credibility, one way to enhance your credibility is to tell your listeners about your expertise. You should do this during your introductory comments and can also do it at appropriate places within the body of your speech. If you've done a good deal of research on the topic, tell your listeners. Don't assume they'll know. If you have personal experience related to your topic, tell your listeners. Don't make the mistake of thinking you'll sound arrogant or conceited. This strategy is especially important for student speakers, because you probably haven't yet established a reputation that can give you high initial credibility. It may also be especially important for women, because some research suggests that many women have been trained not to talk about their expertise and achievements (e.g., Murphy & Zorn, 1996). Let's consider Madonna once more. We saw that she would be a credible speaker about the music industry, but not about pesticides. Suppose, however, that at some point she had earned a degree in pest management and control. This experience would boost her credibility as a speaker about pesticides—but only if she tells listeners about it. In short, tell your listeners about your expertise: It can't hurt, and it might boost your credibility (Miller et al., 1992).

Establish Common Ground

The **common ground** strategy works by enhancing your character. This strategy has to do with identifying with your audience by talking about shared beliefs and values that are related to the argument you will address in your speech (Perloff, 1993). By talking about these shared values and beliefs, you demonstrate respect for your listeners and seem more likable to them. As with explaining your competence, it's especially important to create common ground at the beginning of your speech. This technique is particularly important when your topic is somewhat controversial or when your target audience is opposed to your position. In his speech arguing against the death penalty, for example, Lester used the common-ground technique when he said in his introduction, "I'm sure that you, like me, value human life." If you can get your listeners to nod their heads in agreement with you at the beginning, they are more likely to be receptive to the rest of your speech as well (McCroskey & Teven, 1999).

Use Strong Evidence

Background Tip
For an excellent discussion of the persuasive effects of evidence, see J. C. Reinard, "The Empirical Study of the Persuasive Effects of Evidence: The Status After 50 Years of Research," *Human Communication Research, 15* (1988): 3–59.

Teaching Tip
See Chapter 7 for a full discussion of supporting material.

Although you should use strong evidence in any speech you give, it is particularly important for persuasive speeches. Not only is it a crucial aspect of logos, but it also enhances credibility: The stronger your evidence, the stronger your credibility. You've demonstrated that you've researched well and, in a sense, you're borrowing the credibility of your sources. Later in the chapter we'll look at use of evidence to support your arguments. Here let's focus on three ways of using evidence to enhance credibility.

1. *Use varied supporting material.* By doing so, you'll address different learning styles and thus enhance your credibility and effectiveness with a range of listeners, as well as round the entire cycle of learning.
2. *Use qualified impartial sources.* Listeners are best persuaded by evidence that comes from qualified sources (Perloff, 1993; Reinard, 1988). By drawing on such sources, you demonstrate your competence. In addition, listeners are more persuaded by sources that seem impartial. For example, if you were presenting a persuasive speech on infant and toddler automobile safety standards, experts from the National Highway Traffic Safety Administration might be more persuasive than experts from the Ford Motor Company, whose remarks could be perceived as biased toward Ford products. By drawing on impartial sources and avoiding sources that could be perceived as biased, you demonstrate your character, particularly your fairness.
3. *Use new evidence.* You'll have a better chance of persuading your listeners effectively if you use supporting material that your listeners don't already know

(Morley & Walker, 1987). It stands to reason that commonly known facts and statistics will not persuade listeners during your speech if they haven't persuaded them before. New evidence will both get your listeners to rethink the issue and show them that you've researched it thoroughly.

Strategies Involving Language

You can enhance your character through your use of language. Always use language that is respectful to your listeners. In your introduction you might even express gratitude about the opportunity to speak to your listeners about the topic. This fosters a sense of goodwill that not only enhances your character, but also reduces potential barriers between you and your listeners. Humor can also enhance your character by making you seem likable and increasing listener receptivity to your message (Slan, 1998). However, be careful to avoid potentially offensive humor, which obviously would detract from your character.

Strategies Involving Delivery

Your delivery—that is, your attire, body language, and use of voice—can strengthen or weaken your credibility. For that reason, delivery is especially important to persuasive speaking and it's worth reviewing some of the suggestions made in Chapter 12.

In our culture, attractive people tend to be perceived as more competent, well organized, and confident (e.g., Buck & Tiene, 1989; Cherulnik, 1989; Drogosz & Levy, 1996; Robinson et al., 1989). Attire contributes to these perceptions, and research suggests that persuasive speakers dressed formally are perceived as more credible than those dressed casually or sloppily (Morris et al., 1996; Treinen, 1998). Thus, it's even more important for persuasive speakers than for other speakers to be neatly and professionally dressed.

Body language, in particular eye contact, can do a great deal to enhance your credibility at all stages of your speech. Research suggests that in our culture direct eye contact conveys both self-confidence and an interest in others (Beebe, 1974; Hall, 1959; Kelly, 1972). Walk in a confident way to the front of the room to give your speech, and before beginning, pause a few moments and make direct eye contact with a couple of listeners. Make an extra effort to look listeners in the eye throughout the speech. When you finish, pause and make eye contact again before returning to your seat. Similarly, if you're speaking to a large audience, pause and make audience contact before beginning and upon finishing your speech.

Research shows that your credibility is strongly influenced by your use of voice. If you can speak fluently, use a moderately fast rate, and express yourself with conviction, you'll appear more intelligent and confident than if you tend to lose your place, use a lot of "ums" and "uhs," speak too slowly, or sound monotonous or unconvinced (e.g., O'Keefe, 1990; Perloff, 1993). Make sure you rehearse your persuasive speech enough so that you can deliver it fluently and expressively, thus enhancing your credibility. Likewise, use stresses and pauses that convey a sincere sense of urgency about your topic. Your gestures and facial expressions should reinforce the sense of sincere conviction expressed in your voice.

Teaching Tip
Make sure that students fully understand the relationship between credibility and delivery. Even the most qualified experts in the field can undermine their credibility with poor delivery. In contradistinction, speakers who are not recognized experts can boost their perceived credibility with effective delivery.

Technology Tip
http://www.houckassociates.com/hint6.htm
The Houck Associates Web site summarizes research findings regarding the relationship between these nonverbal elements and speaker credibility. Have students visit this site and write a brief essay summarizing their findings.

Strategies for Conveying Ethos

- Explain your competence.
- Establish common ground.
- Use strong evidence.
- Use respectful language.
- Choose appropriate attire.
- Use direct eye contact.
- Speak fluently and with sincere conviction.

What Do You Think?

Consider a comedian you really dislike. In your opinion, what are some specific ways this person hurts his or her credibility in terms of content? Language? Delivery?

Strategies for Conveying Logos

Teaching Tip
Show an infomercial in class and have students identify the reasoning employed. Ask students to critique the infomercial using the guidelines for reasoning presented in this chapter.

Recall that logos refers to logical appeals—appeals to listeners' intellect. Thus, you convey logos by building a strong argument. More specifically, this means organizing your argument well, using strong evidence to support your claims, and using clear and effective reasoning to tie the evidence to your claims. By taking these steps, you make your argument persuasive to your audience. Hence, logos is conveyed in large part through structure—that is, through the organization of your main points, as discussed in Chapter 15. To some extent, you can also convey logos through language and delivery. For example, you can word your argument clearly and use transition words effectively, and you can use gestures and movement to reinforce the structure of your arguments. However, the most significant ways to convey logos lie in your content—that is, in your evidence and reasoning.

In the section on ethos, we saw that to boost your credibility your evidence should be strong, varied in type, and from reliable sources. Such evidence enhances credibility partly because it conveys logos: You are more credible because your evidence is sound. To convey logos, evidence must also be appropriate to the main points you're making. For each piece of evidence you consider, decide whether it makes your argument more compelling. If it doesn't, don't use it. You must also decide *how* it makes your argument more compelling—how it supports your main points.

Reasoning is the process of supporting your main points with evidence in a logical way. Rather than simply stating your evidence, you clarify for your listeners how it supports the point you are trying to make. Beginning speakers sometimes assume that these connections will be obvious. In fact, they probably won't be unless you articulate them (O'Keefe, 1990). When you do, you are essentially motivating your listeners to agree with you through logos. For each piece of evidence, you need to ask yourself the following questions:

- How does this piece of evidence support my main point?
- How can I make this connection clear to my listeners?

You'll find three types of reasoning to be particularly useful. These are inductive reasoning, deductive reasoning, and analogical reasoning. Which type of reasoning you use depends on the nature of your main point and of your evidence. In most persuasive speeches, you'll wind up using more than one type. When using these strategies, you must also be careful to avoid *reasoning fallacies,* or flawed reasoning.

Inductive Reasoning

Teaching Tip
Just as relying solely on one type of supporting material can be problematic, using only one type of argument can also be ineffective. Encourage students to combine argument types.

Inductive reasoning is the process of arriving at a general conclusion from a series of specific pieces of evidence. In our daily life, we often rely on inductive reasoning. For example, when I bought my Ford Escort, I reasoned as follows: (a) The previous two Escorts I owned were reliable. (b) *Consumer Reports* ranks Escorts consistently high across categories. (c) I see a lot of Escorts being driven around the city. Based on this evidence, I concluded the Escort is a reliable car. I have also noticed that college students often decide which classes to take (and *not* to take) based on inductive reasoning. That is, they form conclusions about particular classes—that they are fun, interesting, easy, boring, irrelevant, or difficult—based on what various people have told them and on course descriptions.

What Do You Think?

Is there a particular brand of laundry detergent, dish soap, pain killer, soda, or some other product that you typically purchase over others. Why? To what extent do your conclusions reflect inductive reasoning?

In a public speech, inductive reasoning can be an effective strategy for persuading others. You can base your conclusion on any kind of evidence—on examples, statistics, testimonies, and so on. Thus, if you discover a number of examples that support a main point, you can give these examples and show how they support the point. For example, Julie offered several examples of people who had been healed of different physical ailments with the help of chiropractors and without medication. These examples came from personal experiences, the experiences of friends and family members, and the experiences of people she learned about through library research. She used these examples to support her conclusion that chiropractors can heal physical ailments effectively.

When you reason inductively, the persuasiveness of your conclusion depends on the strength of the evidence on which it is based. To develop an effective inductive argument, therefore, you need to consider three key questions:

- Do I have enough specific items of evidence to support my conclusion?
- Are my items typical?
- Are my items recent enough?

Let's look at each question in turn.

It is generally not very effective to offer only one or two instances to support a conclusion. In her speech about chiropractors, Julie conducted library research because she realized that the few examples based on the experiences of people she knew would not be enough to persuade her listeners that chiropractors are effective.

Offering a lot of examples also isn't enough in itself. You've also got to show your listeners that your evidence is typical, not merely isolated incidents. One way to do this is by backing up examples with statistical evidence. This is what Ajay Krishnan (1998) did in his speech about auto repair fraud. After sharing some specific examples about people who had been victims of such fraud, he continued:

> The National Highway and Traffic Safety Administration reports that a whopping 40 percent of car repair costs last year were either fraudulent or unnecessary. But this 40 percent isn't just concentrated on a couple of gullible, exploitable consumers. Instead, as the *Orange County Register* of December 16, 1996, reveals, 90 percent of car owners are victims of such fraud (p. 120).

Once he included these statistics in his evidence, listeners couldn't dismiss the examples as aberrations and his conclusion was strengthened.

Depending on your topic, recency might be an issue as well. In a sense, this is related to the question of whether your evidence is typical: For many topics, if your evidence is old, it may no longer be typical. While it's fine to include older evidence, you should supplement it with newer evidence or otherwise show listeners that it is still valid.

Deductive Reasoning

Discussion Tip
How does deductive reasoning differ from inductive reasoning? Is it necessary to use evidence to make major and minor premises more compelling?

Deductive reasoning is the process of reaching a conclusion by showing how a general premise also applies to a specific case. Thus, whereas with inductive reasoning, you argue from specifics to reach a general conclusion, with deductive reasoning you argue from a general principle to reach a conclusion about something specific. Deductive reasoning works like this: You start with your **major premise,** a general principle that most people agree upon or that you provide support for. You move to your **minor premise,** establishing that the specific point or example you are concerned with fits within that general principle. You then give your conclusion, stating that the principle applies to your specific point or example. This three-part form of reasoning is called a **syllogism.** In its simplest form, deductive reasoning looks like this:

> ***Major premise:*** All opera singers can carry a tune.
>
> ***Minor premise:*** John is an opera singer.
>
> ***Conclusion:*** John can carry a tune.

Major premises often express commonly held beliefs, as in the previous example, or values, as in the following one:

> ***Major premise:*** It is wrong to censor speech or other forms of expression.
>
> ***Minor premise:*** Popular music is a form of expression.
>
> ***Conclusion:*** It is wrong to censor popular music.

Teaching Tip
Develop a series of overheads with several examples of inductive and deductive arguments. This will help students distinguish one from the other.

When you use deductive reasoning in your speech, you'll usually need to add supporting material to your major or minor premises to make your argument more compelling. For example, Tammy Frisby (1998) used deductive reasoning embellished in this way in her speech about the need to floss regularly:

> An obsession with killing the bacteria that live all around us has led us to buy antibacterial anything *(major premise).* But at the same time, according to the *Los Angeles Times* of June 15, 1997, 75 percent of us have enough bacteria in our mouths and inside infected pockets in our gums that if this oozing mess were out where it could be seen, it would be equivalent in size to a bone deep sore the size of both the palms of your hands *(minor premise).* More than just being disgusting, this load of bacteria is causing forty thousand Americans to die from heart attacks and forty-five thousand five hundred babies to be born prematurely each year *(minor premise is made more compelling by adding supporting material).* Yet the *Seattle Times* of April 10, 1996, reminds us that today six out of ten of us won't take the extra minute it would take to protect ourselves by practicing good dental hygiene *(conclusion).*

If we reduced Tammy's reasoning to its most basic syllogistic form, it would look like this:

Major premise: Bacteria is generally unhealthy.
Minor premise: Our mouths are full of bacteria.
Conclusion: Bacteria in our mouths is unhealthy.

To determine whether to embellish your major premise with supporting material, consider if your premise is something most listeners probably agree with. If not, provide evidence to support it before moving on to your minor premise. In Tammy's case, there was no need to offer supporting material for her major premise. Most listeners would agree that bacteria is generally unhealthy. If you think some listeners might doubt your major premise, however, offer supporting material for it. It certainly won't hurt your argument to do so, and it will probably help. Even for Tammy, adding a statement about the kinds of antibacterial products that pervade our markets would have embellished her major premise. After all, if listeners don't accept your major premise, they most definitely will not accept your conclusion. As with your major premise, bolstering your minor premise with supporting material cannot hurt your argument and will probably make it more compelling. Consider how much more persuasive Tammy's minor premise became when she bolstered the fact that a lot of bacteria grows in our mouths with evidence about some of its harmful effects.

When you reason deductively, the persuasiveness of your conclusion also depends on the truth of your premises. If the premises are true, the conclusion should be true. To develop an effective deductive argument, you need to consider three key questions:

Teaching Tip
Assign students to small groups and have them develop at least one inductive and deductive argument. Share these examples with the entire class.

- Is the major premise true?
- Is the minor premise true?
- Has anything been omitted from the premises that might affect the conclusion?

Consider this example:

Major premise: Calcium is an important part of a healthy diet.

Minor premise: Ice cream is high in calcium.

Conclusion: Ice cream is an important part of a healthy diet.

Although the major and minor premises are both true, the conclusion is not a valid one because of important facts that haven't been taken into account—namely, that ice cream is high in unhealthy saturated fats and that there are many other sources of calcium.

Analogical Reasoning

Analogical reasoning, or reasoning by comparison, links two things together and claims that what is true of one is therefore also true of the other. Advertisers use this strategy to motivate consumers to purchase a product when they claim "If you liked that other product, then you'll love this product." Movies are sometimes marketed this way as well: "If you liked *Ordinary People,* then you'll love *American Beauty,*" and so on. I even use this strategy to get my children to try a new food by telling them it tastes like something they like: "It's good. It tastes like chicken!"

Teaching Tip
Argument from analogy can enhance the style and wording of the speech. Have students review the material on language and style in Chapter 11.

This strategy is particularly useful in persuasive speeches in which you advocate or oppose a solution that has been tried elsewhere. You can use analogical reasoning to point to the successes or failures of these earlier programs as reasons to support or oppose the implementation of a similar program (Ziegelmueller et al., 1990). In her speech about personal watercraft safety, Rebecca Schwartz (1998) used analogical reasoning to argue in favor of certain safety rules by citing similar rules implemented by the Nebraska Games and Parks Commission and showing that they had been effective. Similarly, Stephanie Hamilton (1999) discussed policies implemented by the International Council of Cruise Lines to ensure justice for passengers who become victims of violent crimes while on board their ships. She then proposed that all cruise lines adopt such policies.

> ***What Do You Think?***
>
> *Consider a popular television program like* Who Wants to Be a Millionaire?, Survivor, *or* The Simpsons. *What other shows have imitated them in hopes of attracting viewers? To what degree are these producers using analogical reasoning?*

To develop an effective analogical argument, you need to consider two key questions:

- Are the similarities between the two cases relevant?
- Are any of the differences between them relevant?

First, think carefully about the similarities. Are these similarities relevant to the argument you are making, and are they strong enough? Both Rebecca's plea for personal watercraft safety policies and Stephanie's call for cruise line justice, for example, were very similar to their premises. Each was merely advocating that such policies be made more universal. The analogical argument becomes more compelling when more of these relevant comparisons are similar.

Second, think carefully about the differences. Are the differences that are irrelevant to your argument ones that can safely be ignored? Or are they differences that you should take into consideration in your speech, or even differences that might make an analogical argument impossible? Had Stephanie tried to argue that victims' rights programs that exist in the United States also be implemented on cruise ships, she would have failed because the differences are relevant. Cruise ships often sail on international waters and many cruise ships are registered in other countries, which makes U.S. laws and regulations inapplicable. For analogical reasoning to be compelling, then, you must consider the relevant similarities and differences between the two things being compared.

Avoiding Reasoning Fallacies

Teaching Tip
To give students an opportunity to analyze fallacies, see the Looking for Fallacies assignment in the Activities section of this chapter.

Reasoning fallacies are flawed reasoning of various kinds. They are sometimes used with the intent to deceive, but at other times they're simply the result of carelessness. Unfortunately, it is possible to persuade listeners based on flawed reasoning because the fallacies often appear reasonable. Since they are not valid, however, the consequences of persuading listeners based on them can be harmful. Hence, to be ethical as well as effective, you must avoid the use of flawed reasoning in your persuasive speeches. Fallacies can destroy the validity of an otherwise good argument (Ericson & Murphy, 1987). By knowing what they are and how they work, you can both avoid them in your speeches and identify them in the speeches of others. In this way, you'll improve your effectiveness as a persuasive speaker and as a listener of persuasive arguments. Although there are as many as 125 different fallacies, we'll focus on the 10 most common (*New York Public Library Desk Reference,* 1993). These are hasty generalization, false cause, slippery slope, either-or, straw man, bandwagon, appeal to tradition, red herring, ad hominem, and non sequitur (see Figure 16–2).

Hasty Generalization

The **hasty generalization** fallacy occurs when a speaker draws a conclusion based on too little evidence. In other words, people who jump to conclusions are

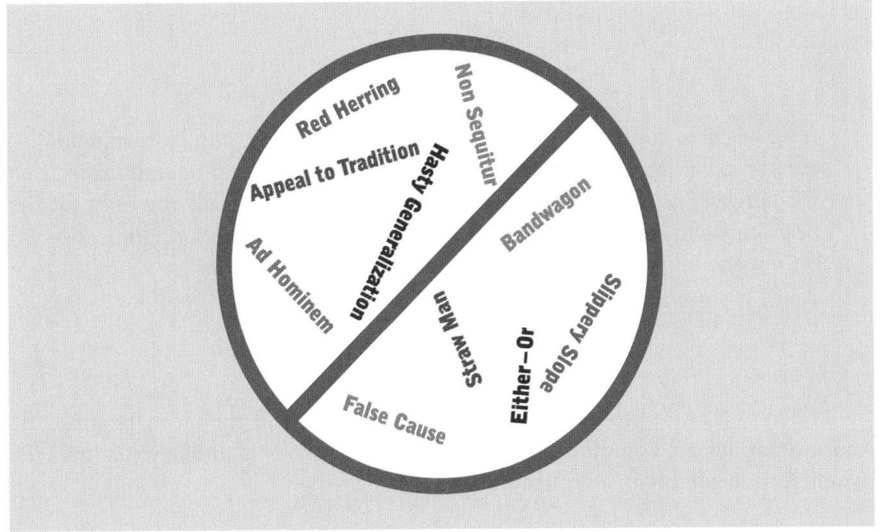

FIGURE 16–2
Reasoning Fallacies

Background Tip
For more information on fallacies, see S. M. Engel, *With Good Reason: An Introduction to Informal Fallacies*, 6th ed. (New York: St. Martin's Press, 2000).

committing hasty generalizations. Robin committed a hasty generalization when she said, "A child I know is being home schooled and can't read or write at grade level. Home schooling does not work." Robin was trying to use inductive reasoning, but did not offer enough evidence to support her conclusion. You might be wondering how much evidence is enough. You need not share every account you know of; however, you must let your listeners know that your examples are typical. Follow the guidelines discussed earlier regarding inductive reasoning.

False Cause

Discussion Tip
Have students discuss superstitions that exemplify the false cause fallacy. In addition, ask them to identify any instances in their own lives when they have committed this fallacy.

False cause occurs when a speaker claims that because one event follows another, the first event is the cause of the second. Another term for this fallacy is *post hoc, ergo propter hoc,* a Latin expression meaning "after this, therefore because of this." If after doing well on a test you didn't study for, you claimed that you did well because you didn't study, you would probably be engaging in a false cause fallacy. When my mother reasoned that I'd caught a head cold because I didn't dress warmly enough when it was chilly outside, she engaged in this fallacy. A virus caused my head cold, not chilly weather. If a speaker claims that violence among teenagers is caused by television violence, he or she is also engaging in this fallacy. In short, when one event follows another, there may be no connection at all between them, or the first event might be just one of many causes that are contributing to the second.

Slippery Slope

Like false cause, **slippery slope** is a fallacy involving cause and effect. Here, however, the focus is on how a particular action will set forth a chain of events that will inevitably lead to a certain result. For example, if you were to claim that offering free contraceptives to teenagers will lead to more sexual activity among teenagers, which will lead to the destruction of moral values, you would be committing the slippery slope fallacy. Likewise, Kathy's argument about gun control commits the slippery slope fallacy:

> If we begin to control the sale of guns by restricting the purchase of handguns, you can be certain that it won't end there. Next we'll be restricting the purchase of shotguns, and then hunting rifles. Eventually the right to bear arms will be eliminated from the Constitution altogether. Hunters—both men and women—will lose one of our basic freedoms.

There is a lot of ground between the initial event and the ultimate effect. Because situations are complex and involve many factors, it is unlikely that an event would lead inevitably to a certain result.

Either-Or

An **either-or** fallacy occurs when someone argues that there are only two alternatives when, in fact, others exist. In many such cases, the person is oversimplifying a complex issue. When Robert argued that "we'll either have to raise taxes or close the library," he committed an either-or fallacy. He reduced a complex issue to one oversimplified solution when, in fact, there were probably many other possible solutions as well. Moreover, speakers who use this fallacy usually make one of the alternatives so undesirable that supporting their position seems vital. One can assume that few, if any, of Robert's listeners would want to close the library; however, raising taxes is probably not the only way to keep its doors open.

Straw Man

The **straw man** fallacy is easy to refute. It occurs when a speaker weakens the opposing position by misrepresenting it in some way and then attacks that weaker (straw man) argument. That is, a speaker distorts an opposing view in a way that makes it seem trivial or silly and easy to refute. For example, in her speech advocating a seven-day waiting period to purchase handguns, Colleen favored regulation, not prohibition, of gun ownership. Kathy argued against her proposal by claiming that "it is our constitutional right to bear arms." Notice, however, that Colleen did not advocate abolishing the right bear arms at all. Hence, Kathy distorted her position, making it easier to refute. By doing so, she was guilty of using the straw man reasoning fallacy.

Teaching Tip
Make transparency masters of print ads that contain poor reasoning. Show these ads in class and ask students to identify the fallacies.

Bandwagon

The **bandwagon** fallacy occurs when a speaker presents something as being popular, and therefore good or desirable. The speaker might say that everyone is doing something so you should too, or that everyone believes something so it must be true. In other words, he or she is trying to get you to jump on the bandwagon. Some people might refer to this fallacy by its Latin name, ad populum. While it is not necessarily wrong to talk about how many people support your position, this support is no guarantee of the accuracy or worth of your position. It is your ethical responsibility to articulate *why* so many people support it. Doing so is not only ethical, it's what would make your claim persuasive. Advertisers and salespeople often use this fallacy to try to entice you to purchase a product. Also, politicians sometimes use polls in this way. Just because 61 percent of those polled (even assuming they're representative of the population) support a particular candidate does not necessarily mean that he or she is the best person for the job. In her speech, Julie talked about the growing number of people using chiropractors for a variety of physical ailments. Had she stopped there, she would have been guilty of using the bandwagon fallacy. She went on,

> ***What Do You Think?***
>
> *Think of a television commercial that tried to convince you to purchase a product simply because it's the "cool" thing to do or because "everyone else does it" (i.e., Gap, Dr. Pepper, Mountain Dew). Was this bandwagon appeal effective? Ethical? Why or why not?*

however, to discuss why more people are using chiropractors, citing research, for example, comparing the success rates of prescription drugs and chiropractic treatments.

Appeal to Tradition

Technology Tip
http://www.drury.edu/faculty/Ess/critthink.html
This Web page, developed by Dr. Charles Ess at Drury University, offers several useful suggestions for analyzing arguments. Have students visit this site and report their findings in class.

The **appeal to tradition** fallacy occurs when a speaker defends the way things are simply because that's the way they've always been. Traditions may or may not be good, but they cannot in themselves stand as solid reasons to oppose change. If things were best done as they were in the early days of our nation, only white males with property would be allowed to vote. Likewise, as more people telecommute today, some employers continue to maintain that work must occur in some office. They often support their position with an appeal to tradition fallacy: Since the advent of the modern office, people have always worked in offices. This tradition is not a solid reason for arguing against change, and in fact we see that many employees are more productive working from their homes. In other words, the old ways are not necessarily the best ways.

Red Herring

Also called a smoke screen, the **red herring** fallacy occurs when someone uses irrelevant evidence or arguments to try to divert listeners' attention from the real issue. It actually got its name from an English fox hunting practice: People would drag a fowl smelling smoked herring across a fox trail to divert the attention of the dogs who were trailing them. When political candidates avoid answering certain questions by talking about something altogether different, they are employing a red herring fallacy. They do this most often when questioned about their position on highly controversial issues, such as abortion, gun control, and censorship.

What Do You Think?

Consider the candidates running for the next election. Do you know where they stand on controversial issues like abortion, gun control, censorship, and so forth? Do you know where they stand on issues important to you?

Ad Hominem

Teaching Tip
Students often confuse verbal aggressiveness and argumentativeness. Explain that personal attacks are characteristic of verbally aggressive behavior.

Ad hominem is Latin for "at the person." This fallacy, also known as mudslinging or name-calling, occurs when a speaker attacks an opponent's character rather than dealing with the issue. Senator Joseph McCarthy used name-calling to build his own reputation after World War II, a time when many Americans feared Communism. He did so by accusing his opponents of being Communists with no rationale for his accusations. When Jon argued that Clara couldn't possibly understand political issues because "she's an airhead," he was employing an ad hominem fallacy. He attacked her personal character rather than her stand on the issues.

Non Sequitur

Non sequitur is Latin for "does not follow." This fallacy occurs when your conclusion doesn't follow from your evidence or when you support your argument with evidence that is not relevant. Advertisers sometimes encourage non sequitur fallacies, when, for example, they show beautiful models using their products in hopes that consumers will reason that using the products will make them look like the models. If a speaker were to argue that public school standards must be raised, and supported that position by citing the growing number of kids who are joining gangs, that speaker would be using a non sequitur fallacy. Although both statements might be true, the supporting material is not necessarily related to the particular argument.

In sum, to convey logos, you need to organize your argument well, use strong evidence to support its claims, and use clear and effective and ethical reasoning to tie the evidence to the claims. To do so, you can use inductive, deductive, and analogical reasoning. As you do, you must take care to avoid using reasoning fallacies.

What Do You Think?

Consider a friend or colleague who seems really smart. To what degree does that person's use of reasoning contribute to your perception of his or her intelligence?

Strategies for Conveying Pathos

Pathos involves a wide variety of emotional appeals—appeals to positive emotions like love, pride, compassion, and reverence, as well as to negative emotions like fear anger, jealousy, shame, and guilt. For example, you might appeal to listeners' compassion to persuade them to volunteer at the local center for domestic abuse. Or you might appeal to their fear of contracting a sexually transmitted disease to persuade them to practice safe sex. Often you'll combine positive and negative appeals. For example, to convince listeners to exercise and eat right, you might appeal to both fear and pride. Emotional appeals can be highly effective tools for a persuasive speaker because they touch the hearts of listeners, and listeners whose hearts are touched are far more likely to change their disposition or behavior (e.g., Eagly & Chaiken, 1993; Maloney, 1992). To add breadth, develop emotional appeals that address each level on Maslow's hierarchy of human needs (as discussed in Chapter 6).

Teaching Tip
As a homework assignment, have each student find at least three examples of emotional appeals. Instruct students to look for examples in speeches, newspaper articles, editorials, print advertisements, or television commercials. During the next class period, ask students to share their examples with the class.

Many of these emotional appeals come when you discuss positive and negative consequences related to your topic. You motivate listeners by demonstrating the desirable results of accepting your argument and the undesirable results of not accepting it. Weight loss programs, for example, often use a positive consequences motivational approach by showing before and after photographs of people who used the program. Environmentalists sometimes use a negative consequences motivational approach by describing what the world will be like if we continue to engage in destructive habits like polluting our air and water and depleting our natural resources.

Because appeals to pathos are directed at our emotions and because they can be very influential, they are susceptible to abuse. All too often, such appeals have been used to promote religious intolerance, ethnic and racial hatred, and so forth. A persuasive speaker must take extra care to use emotional appeals ethically. Keep two crucial points in mind as you prepare.

First, emotional appeals can be both effective and ethical when they are appropriate to your speech topic, goal, occasion, and audience. If they are inappropriate to any of these four aspects, don't use them. For example, don't share emotion-arousing photographs, videos, or music simply to get the attention of your listeners if they are not related directly to your topic and goal. Even if they are related to your topic and goal, don't appeal to disgust by showing vivid photographs of contaminated food products if you are speaking as part of a luncheon or dinner. Likewise, don't appeal to emotions by describing or showing graphic illustrations of illicit behaviors to a group of children. Simply put, consider what you're trying to accomplish, who your audience is, and where and when you'll be speaking; then integrate only those appeals to pathos that are appropriate to all four.

> **What Do You Think?**
>
> *Consider a time when a friend or family member shared a story or told a joke and you thought to yourself, "I can't believe she or he said that!" What made it inappropriate? Did it have to do with the topic, goal, occasion, audience, or something else?*

Discussion Tip
What guidelines does Sellnow offer for the effective and ethical use of emotional appeals? Should emotional appeals be used as a substitute for evidence and reasoning?

Second, emotional appeals can be both effective and ethical when they build on well-thought-out arguments. In other words, pathos can enhance an argument but should not itself make the argument (e.g., Waddell, 1990; White, 1992). Never substitute emotional appeals for evidence and reasoning. To ensure your appeals are ethical, ask yourself two questions before integrating each emotional appeal into your speech:

- Is this emotional appeal appropriate to my speech topic, goal, occasion, and audience?
- Does my emotional appeal complement a thoroughly supported argument rather than attempt to replace it?

That said, let's look at how you can incorporate emotional appeals into your content, language, and delivery.

Strategies Involving Content

When you develop the content of your speech, include supporting material that will appeal to listeners' emotions. Include appeals that address a variety of human needs. To do so, consider Maslow's hierarchy of human needs as discussed in Chapter 6 when developing your content. More specifically, include stories and testimonials that personalize and dramatize the issue for listeners. You can also use startling statistics, because listeners are more affected by emotions accompanied by surprise, and listener relevance links because emotions are stronger when listeners feel personally involved. When possible, strengthen the emotional impact by reinforcing this supporting material with presentational aids. Remember that appeals can be positive or negative.

Discussion Tip
What emotions does David Slater try to arouse in his audience? Can you give an example of an emotional appeal that you have used or heard in the past?

David Slater (1998), for example, used a story to appeal to emotions in his speech about becoming a bone marrow donor. He could have conveyed the content by simply saying something like: "By donating bone marrow—a simple procedure—you can help save lives." Instead, he shared a vivid story about Tricia, Tommy, and Daniel:

> When Tricia Matthews decided to undergo a simple medical procedure, she had no idea what impact it could have on her life. But more than a year later, when she saw five-year-old Tommy and his younger brother Daniel walk

> across the stage of the *Oprah Winfrey Show,* she realized that the short amount of time it took her to donate her bone marrow was well worth it. Tricia is not related to the boys who suffered from a rare immune deficiency disorder treated by a transplant of her marrow. Tricia and the boys found each other through the National Marrow Donor Program, or NMDP, a national network which strives to bring willing donors and needy patients together. Though the efforts Tricia made were minimal, few Americans made the strides she did. Few of us would deny anyone the gift of life, but sadly, few know how easily we can help (p. 63).

Notice how much more compellingly David Slater made his point by sharing this story that appealed to listeners' emotions. In addition to being moved, listeners could readily see that the procedure was simple and its benefits dramatic. They were thus far more likely to be persuaded to become donors.

You can often strengthen your emotional appeals by using different kinds of supporting material together. In his speech about Shaken Baby Syndrome, Ryan Labor (1998) began with the following vivid story:

> Last winter, two-year-old Cody Dannar refused to eat or play. He had a headache. Doctors said he just had the flu. After a couple weeks home with this mother, Cody felt better. Days later, according to *Woman's Day* of October 7, 1997, Cody's headaches returned. Coming home from work the next afternoon, his parents found the baby-sitter frantically calling 911 and Cody lying rigid and unconscious on the floor. He didn't have the flu; in fact, he wasn't sick at all. The baby-sitter had caused his headaches. To quiet Cody down, she had shaken him, damaging the base of Cody's brain that now risked his life as he lay on the ground (p. 70).

Ryan immediately followed with these startling statistics:

> Unfortunately, Cody isn't alone. Over one million infants and young children suffer from Shaken Baby Syndrome annually while thousands die. What's worse, these children are misdiagnosed by the majority of doctors. . . . The results are tragic. One quarter to one third of all SBS victims die within hours or days. Only 15 percent survive without damage. The remaining children suffer from blindness, learning disabilities, deafness, seizures, cerebral palsy, or paralysis (p. 70).

By first sharing a vivid story and then building on it with startling statistics, Ryan made the topic personal and then demonstrated its significance as a problem. Using the two kinds of supporting material led to a stronger emotional appeal. At a later point, he appealed to emotions through listener relevance:

Teaching Tip
Remind students that if they use stories to generate emotional appeal, the story needs to be delivered extemporaneously and with strong eye contact.

> Jacy Showers, Director of the first National Conference on Shaken Baby Syndrome, says "shaking occurs in families of all races, incomes, and education levels" and " . . . 81 percent of SBS offenders had no previous history of child abuse. The reason? The offenders were so young, either baby-sitters or new parents" (p. 71).

By making it clear to listeners that they couldn't dismiss the topic as irrelevant to themselves, he further strengthened the emotional appeal.

A personal testimonial, if appropriate, can also appeal effectively to emotions. Kristofer Kracht (1998) used a testimonial in his speech arguing for the inclusion of students with disabilities in all aspects of school life. In fact, as the following excerpts show, he threaded it throughout his speech:

> My brother, Joshua, who is mentally handicapped, is one of those born like a bird with a broken wing. . . . My parents have faced the problem of getting my brother included ever since he started school. . . . Just this year, my parents had to ask the physical education teacher if he would give Josh the opportunity to be in his class. The teacher's response was "no." . . . When *I* was in high school, my parents never had to ask a teacher if they wanted me in their classroom, so why should they have to ask for my brother? . . . It was easier in elementary school, but they are now faced with going to court. . . . I am holding a petition addressed to the NASSP [National Association of Secondary School Principals] and the NSBA [National School Board Association] as well as the North Central Accreditation Association and the Council of Chief State Officers . . . Please sign this petition (pp. 96–98).

By returning to this testimonial as one of the supports for successive main points, Kristofer Kracht gave his listeners an emotional motivation for signing the petition. Taken together with his arguments, this emotional appeal was compelling.

We're all aware of the potential emotional impact of photographs and other visuals and of music. For example, to reinforce her argument that television celebrities who embrace the "lollipop stick look" are contributing to the eating disorder epidemic among young girls, Jonna showed before and after photographs of Jennifer Aniston and Courtney Cox Arquette from *Friends,* as well as Calista Flockhart from *Ally McBeal.* These visuals clarified the dramatic weight loss of all three women in an emotional way that words could not convey. Look for opportunities to further reinforce the impact of your emotional appeals by using presentational aids.

Strategies Involving Language

Teaching Tip
Bring examples of both good and poor persuasive punch words to class. Have students identify the characteristics of effective persuasive punch words as well as the ways that poor language could be improved.

As we saw in Chapter 11, many language choices are available for conveying your content. In developing your speech, include **persuasive punch words**—words that evoke emotion. Persuasive punch words must be used selectively, however, or they'll lose their impact. Concentrate them in important parts of your speech, such as your preview, transitions, and summary, as well as the supporting material where you're making your emotional appeals.

Here's how Ryan Mulholland (1998) used evocative language in the preview of his speech, "Nuclear Scare: What's Happening Out There?"

> Today, let's *examine* the *dangers* that exist because of stolen nuclear material, the reasons *such a frightening situation* has arisen, and the steps we *must take* to protect ourselves from this, the *worst of all possible dangers* (p. 149).

Notice how much less compelling his preview would have been had he stated it like this:

> Today, let's *discuss what is happening* because of stolen nuclear material, why *this situation* has arisen, and what we *can do* to protect ourselves.

Presentational aids can reinforce the impact of your emotional appeals.

To see how persuasive punch words can be used to strengthen the emotional appeals in supporting material, consider this excerpt from Ryan Labor's (1998) speech:

> The *worst of all epidemics* is a silent one. With the majority of all *victims* either infants or young children, Shaken Baby Syndrome can be classified *a stealthy plague*. . . . When shaken, the brain is *literally ricocheted* inside the skull, *bruising the brain* and *tearing blood vessels* coming from the neck . . . *cutting off* oxygen and causing the *eyes to bulge* (p. 70).

In short, persuasive punch words can effectively appeal to the emotions of your listeners. The key is to use them strategically—where it matters.

Strategies Involving Delivery

Just as your language can reinforce emotional content, so can your delivery. Use stresses and pauses to signal to listeners the importance of content through which

Technology Tip
http://www.historychannel.com/historychannel/gspeech/archieve.html

The History Channel Web site contains several historically significant speeches. Have students select a speech and evaluate how the speaker uses delivery to convey emotions.

you make emotional appeals. Use vocal variety, and, as much as possible, convey with your voice the emotions you want your listeners to feel. Appropriate gestures and facial expressions can also help convey these emotions. Use gestures and facial expressions that emphasize a sense of urgency about the issue, for example, clenched fists, fist to palm, and furrowed brows. Convince your listeners that you feel the emotions yourself. Although effective use of delivery to convey emotions is subtle and far from easy, when done well it can truly heighten the impact of your speech. To achieve this, however, you must practice your delivery.

What Do You Think?

Consider a public service announcement you've seen on television (e.g., an appeal to listeners to send money to help starving children or to refrain from using tobacco, alcohol, or drugs). What are some specific ways the speaker's delivery (voice, facial expressions, gestures, etc.) helped convey conviction and reinforce emotional appeals?

Summary

To be a successful persuasive speaker, you must prepare and present a speech that employs effective rhetorical appeals to credibility, logic, and emotion. Doing so increases your chances to compel listeners to believe you, to agree with you, and to be impassioned about your topic. There are three types of appeals that can be integrated into your persuasive speech. Ethos, or speaker credibility, is the sense of competence and character you convey. Logos, or logical appeals, is your use of reasoning and evidence to build your argument. Pathos, or emotional appeals, involves evoking a range of emotions and feelings in your listeners.

You can bolster your ethos, or credibility, by ensuring that listeners will perceive you as competent—well informed, skilled, and knowledgeable about your subject—and as having character—as being trustworthy, honest, and sincere, as well as engaging and likable. To create a perception of high credibility—that is, high initial, derived, and terminal credibility—you can use several specific strategies in planning the content, language, and delivery of your speech. With regard to content, you can explain your competence, establish common ground, and use strong evidence. With regard to language, you can use respectful language and be gracious about the opportunity to speak to your audience. With regard to delivery, choose appropriate attire, pause before and after your speech, use direct eye contact, and speak fluently and with conviction.

You can convey logos by using strong evidence and logical reasoning. Reasoning is what makes your arguments and supporting material logical by showing listeners how your evidence supports your claim. You can do so by employing inductive, deductive, or analogical reasoning. Inductive reasoning is the process of arriving at a general conclusion from a series of specific pieces of evidence. Deductive reasoning is the process of reaching a conclusion by illustrating how a general premise applies to something specific. Analogical reasoning, or reasoning by comparison, links two things together and claims that what is true of one is therefore also true of the other. To be most effective as well as ethical, you must also avoid using fallacies, or flawed reasoning. Some of the most common errors to avoid are hasty generalization, false cause, slippery slope, either-or, straw man, bandwagon, appeal to tradition, red herring, ad hominem, and non sequitur.

You can convey pathos by appealing to listeners' emotions. Pathos can include appeals to positive emotions like pride and compassion and to negative emotions like anger and fear. Shape your content to generate emotional appeals by including vivid stories and testimonials, reinforced when possible by presentational aids. Startling statistics and listener relevance links can also effectively evoke emotions. You can also use persuasive punch words to evoke emotions. Use this language in the appropriate parts of your speech: in your preview, transitions, and summary, as well as in dramatic examples and stories you include as supporting material. In delivering your speech, you can use stresses and pauses, as well as gestures and facial expressions, to reinforce the emotions you want to evoke and to convey a sense of sincerity and urgency about your topic.

ACTIVITIES

1. **Analyzing a News Report.** Watch a television news human interest story. Listen carefully for strategies of ethos, logos, and pathos. What strategies within each type of appeal can you identify? Does the reporter rely more heavily on one type of appeal than the others? If so, how does this influence you? Consider these factors as you watch:
   - Regarding ethos, does the reporter explain his or her competence, establish common ground, use strong evidence, use respectful language, dress appropriately, use direct audience contact, speak fluently and with sincere conviction?
   - Regarding logos, does the reporter use inductive, deductive, or analogical reasoning or commit any reasoning fallacies?
   - Regarding pathos, does the reporter use positive or negative emotional appeals—such as stories, testimonials, statistics, persuasive punch words, presentational aids, and vocal variety—that are appropriate to the topic, goal, occasion, and audience?

2. **Advertisements and Persuasive Appeals.** Select two or three advertisements from a newspaper, magazine, or television that you find in some way compelling. Identify strategies of ethos, logos, and pathos used in them. Which strategies do you find most persuasive and why? Analyze the advertisements by considering these factors:
   - Regarding ethos, consider competence, common ground, strong evidence, and respectful language. If there are people in the advertisement, then also consider appropriate attire, audience contact, vocal fluency, and sense of sincere conviction?
   - Regarding logos, consider inductive, deductive, or analogical reasoning, and reasoning fallacies like hasty generalization, false cause, slippery slope,

either-or, straw man, bandwagon, appeal to tradition, red herring, ad hominem, or non sequitur.

- Regarding pathos, consider positive or negative emotional appeals—such as stories, testimonials, statistics, persuasive punch words, presentational aids, and vocal variety—that are appropriate or inappropriate to the topic, goal, occasion, and audience.

3. **Looking for Fallacies.** Read the letters-to-the-editor section of your local newspaper. See if you can identify examples of any of the ten reasoning fallacies discussed in this chapter (hasty generalization, false cause, either-or, slippery slope, straw man, bandwagon, appeal to tradition, red herring, ad hominum, and non sequitur).
4. **Analyzing a Speech.** What follows is the national championship speech from the 1998 Interstate Oratory competition held in Springfield, Illinois. In the speech, Clayton Johnson from Kansas State University argues that we must stop the practice of astroturf lobbying—a practice that is making a mockery of the democratic tradition of grassroots reform. He uses many of the strategies discussed in this chapter to argue his position. Try to identify places where he uses strategies of ethos, logos, and pathos in his speech. How does his use of these strategies make his speech more effective as well as ethical? Use the following questions to guide your analysis:
   - How does he establish a sense of competence about the subject?
   - How does he establish common ground?
   - What different kinds of supporting material does he use?
   - How does he help the reader/listener know his evidence is qualified and impartial?
   - Where does he use inductive reasoning, and how does he avoid committing a fallacy when he does?
   - Where does he use deductive reasoning, and how does he avoid committing a fallacy when he does?
   - Where does he use analogical reasoning, and how does he avoid committing a fallacy when he does?
   - Where does he use supporting material that appeals to emotions, for example, stories, testimonials, and statistics?
   - Where does he use persuasive punch words to appeal to emotions?

Astroturf Lobbying

Clayton Johnson, Kansas State University

When the citizens of Florida felt threatened by an onslaught of riverboat gambling, they took action. From the furnace of discontent rose Limited Casinos, Inc., a grassroots coalition proposing a law that would keep out new casinos. Ironically, the *Tampa Tribune* discovered that the primary source of funding for this antigambling grassroots coalition was Florida's own gambling industry. It seems the proposed law would have actually protected the state's casinos by keeping out competition.

Luckily, the February 19, 1997, *Tampa Tribune* reports that after discovering the organization's dubious intent, voters shot down the proposal.

But the public good isn't out of jeopardy yet, for the only thing rare about this case is that the deception failed. The June 19, 1997, *Sacramento Bee* explains that corporations have discovered an ethically questionable but extraordinarily effective way of impacting public policy—astroturf lobbying. By creating the illusion of a grassroots movement, astroturf lobbyists are convincing us to support legislation we don't understand and wouldn't support if we did. And it's all perfectly legal. When the March 22, 1997, *Public Relations Review* reports that astroturf lobbying is the fastest growing segment of the public relations field, we should take action.

To do so, we'll first clarify the mechanics of astroturf lobbying; second, discuss chief criticisms of this legal but controversial practice; and, finally, look at what can be done to ensure the legitimacy of grassroots reform.

In clarifying the mechanics of this practice, it will become clear that in both football and lobbying, astroturf has two main advantages over real grass. It's easier to maintain and it's a lot prettier.

On March 14, 1997, the AP [Associated Press] explained that astroturf coalitions are easier to maintain because they don't require actual members. In one version of this deceptive practice, corporations devise cool coalition names like "citizens against" or "the people for." Then they contact ordinary citizens, giving them a blatantly one-sided version of upcoming legislation, and many of us feel inclined to contact Congress even though we know nothing about the legislation or its impact on the community.

For example, since 1994, the "Coalition for Energy and Economic Revitalization" has been convincing Virginians to allow American Electric Power Company to build a massive power line across the state. The coalition insists that its only concern is the possibility of widespread electrical blackouts. Not so says the December 7, 1997, *Roanoke Times*, considering that the overwhelming majority of the coalition's funding, a whopping $700,00, comes from you guessed it, The American Electric Power Company. And it turns out that the Coalition for Energy and Economic Revitalization is nothing more than a trade name for a PR firm called Image Advertising.

Legitimate grassroots take time to coordinate and fund, but an astroturf movement bypasses those constraints. When you've got corporate funding and a PR spin doctor on your side, the movement's not only easier to maintain, it produces beautiful results. A well-run astroturf campaign can flood a legislator's desk with mail almost at will.

Ameritech, Indiana's largest phone company, used another version of astroturf lobbying to pass a controversial telecommunications bill. The March 17, 1997, *Indianapolis Star* reports that Ameritech cranked out computer-generated letters on behalf of some ten thousand Ameritech employees expressing their support for the bill. Presto! Bags of mail landed on the desks of legislators. With no references to the corporation on any of the stationery, it looked like thousands of independently frustrated citizens—the type of grassroots expression politicians respond to.

But Chief's running back Marcus Allen is quick to point out that astroturf might be prettier and easier to maintain than real grass, but it yields more injuries. And in the lobbying game, it's not the big-name players getting hurt. So let's, second, discuss chief criticisms of this legal but controversial practice.

First, it's a deceptive political tactic. After all, astroturf coalitions aren't really coalitions at all. They serve to mask the economic interest of private enterprise in the sheep's clothing of democratization. The March 22, 1997, *PR Review* asserts that when people get a phone call from an organization with a name like "Coalition for a Competitive Long Distance Service," they are likely to support the effort on its face without digging into the issue any further.

California Representative Nancy Pelosi told the May 12, 1997, *San Diego News-Tribune* that there's nothing more eloquent than having someone from your own district give you a call. But when those callers have been intentionally misled by an astroturf campaign, a violation of the public trust has occurred.

Second, critics worry that astroturf lobbying creates an environment where the law can literally be bought. *Fortune* magazine of December 8, 1997, explains that not long ago, real life lobbyists looked like their caricatures: fat, cigar-smoking men who shoved hundred dollar bills into the pockets of lawmakers. But now it's difficult to tell the lobbyist from the legitimate social reformer. With an arrogant public so willing to support grassroots campaigns, a well-funded corporate grassroots program can accomplish just about anything.

Third, astroturf lobbying preys on our most fragile citizens. If stories of astroturf lobbying sound horrible, consider that these are just the ones that get reported. According to the July 17, 1997, *Herald Sun,* without regulation this preferred means of lobbying yields untold exploitation, particularly of the elderly. When Blue Cross and Blue Shield of North Carolina wanted a bill passed which would allow them to convert to a for-profit entity, they called up their elderly subscribers and told them without the bill their premiums would skyrocket. The scared, confused senior citizens were then automatically patched through to their representatives. As the day wore on, it became clear that the callers knew nothing of the legislation and what looked like an outcry from the public was really an astroturf gimmick.

On the field of public policy, astroturf has caused enough damage. It's time to rip it up from the stadium floor and plant the seeds of authentic grass roots by finally looking at what can be done to ensure the legitimacy of grassroots reform.

In the governmental sphere we can do two things. First, law should require that lobbying campaigns disclose full corporate affiliation in every communication they have with the public. Second, PR agencies that offer astroturf services should be required to register as the lobbyists they are.

North Carolina's secretary of state Elaine Marshal echoed the views of many frustrated policy makers when she explained to the July 17, 1997, *Herald Sun* that while all citizens have a right to petition the government, all citizens also have the right to know when they are the target of professional persuasion. After all, the basic function of lobbying laws is to keep the public informed about who the hired guns are.

In the personal sphere, we can help institute these legislative changes by expressing our interest to congressional representatives. The December 26, 1997, *Wall Street Journal* argues that while national attempts at lobbying reform are at a stalemate, the climate is right for more localized reform. To speed up the process, I've started "Concerned Citizens Against Astroturf Lobbying." I've assembled a stack of postage paid envelopes containing a form letter you need only sign and place in the mail . . . just kidding. Before you express your interest in any legislation, research it yourself. Using "astroturf lobbying" and "corporate grass roots" as search terms should yield a plethora of information about this topic from a variety of sources. If after your close personal consideration you find this is one reform you'd like to be part of, write a handwritten letter to your congressional representatives expressing your opinion. It takes some effort, but nobody said democracy was easy. And while we'd like to blame the selfish corporate machine for the whole of this problem, let us not forget the second culprit behind astroturf lobbying—a citizenry that's politically apathetic enough to let it happen in the first place. Any one advertisement, telemarketing pitch, or even speech should only be a springboard for persuasion. The rest is up to us.

Today we've examined astroturf lobbying, discussed chief criticisms of this legal but controversial practice, and looked at what can be done to ensure the legitimacy of grassroots reform.

Grass roots has become quite the good term in American politics. It represents ordinary Americans organizing in the democratic tradition. When the people of Florida realized that Limited Casinos, Inc., was a mockery of that tradition, they stood up and vindicated themselves. Now it's our turn.

Key Terms

Ad hominem
Analogical reasoning
Appeal to tradition
Bandwagon
Character
Common ground
Competence
Deductive reasoning
Derived credibility
Either-or
Ethos
False cause
Hasty generalization
Inductive reasoning
Initial credibility
Logos
Major premise
Minor premise
Non sequitur
Pathos
Persuasive punch words
Reasoning fallacies
Red herring
Slippery slope
Straw man
Syllogism
Terminal credibility

CHAPTER 17

Speaking on Special Occasions

Reflective Questions

1. What makes special occasion speeches different from other types of speeches?
2. Why is it important to keep your speech of introduction short?
3. What is important to remember when giving a speech of acceptance?
4. When might a person give a speech of tribute?
5. What makes a speech to entertain different from merely speaking as entertainment?

Linda opened the envelope she had been waiting so anxiously for and read:

> The competition for this year's commencement address was extremely tough. All of the applicants were excellent. However, the committee has decided to ask you to represent the graduating class with your speech during the commencement ceremony.

Teaching Tip
Refer students to the SpeechMaker CD-ROM. This software exposes them to multiple speaking scenarios and helps them with every step of the speechmaking process. Consider assigning one of the scenarios to be completed before the class in which you will discuss this chapter.

It seemed too good to be true. The committee had chosen her!

Ben's grandfather had been more like a father than a grandfather to him. When Ben was growing up, he and his grandfather had spent hours playing ball, fishing, or simply watching television together. Although his grandfather had lived a long and fruitful life, Ben found it difficult to say goodbye. Still he wanted to do the eulogy. He only hoped that his words would do justice to his grandfather.

Kim could hardly believe she would have the opportunity to hear in person the scholar on whose work she had based her thesis paper. He had agreed to present a guest lecture on her campus. Not only that, but Kim had been asked to introduce him. What an honor! Kim wondered, "How do you introduce someone who is so distinguished? What should I say?"

What Is Special Occasion Speaking?

Throughout your life, you'll find that there are many different kinds of special occasions where you could be asked to speak. These occasions range from graduation ceremonies to awards banquets to wedding dinners to funerals. The particular speech you'd give on each of these occasions looks a bit different from the standard informative and persuasive speeches we've talked about in Chapters 14 through 16, as well as from the other special occasion speeches. Linda's commencement address, for example, adheres to guidelines that differ somewhat from Ben's eulogy and from Kim's speech of introduction. These types of speeches are different from one another because each is intended for a different type of occasion. Yet they are similar because in each case the occasion for giving it is special—that is, these are all **special occasion speeches.**

The situations Linda, Ben, and Kim face are far from uncommon. In fact, most people are at some point asked to present some type of special occasion speech. You'll therefore find it useful to know how to give such speeches effectively. Before looking at the different types of speeches, let's look at special occasion speeches in general.

When you give a special occasion speech, your goal lies somewhere in between informing and persuading. By this I mean that your goal is to *invite your listeners to agree with you* about the value of the person, object, event, or place the special occasion revolves around. Hence, special occasion speeches are essentially what we talked about as invitational speeches in Chapter 15. You do not merely inform, nor do you attempt to convince your audience. Rather, you invite them to agree. Another characteristic most special occasion speeches share is brevity: They are generally less than five minutes long. Some types, however, especially speeches of tribute like eulogies and keynote, commencement, and commemorative addresses, may be considerably longer.

Types of Special Occasion Speeches

In this chapter, we'll focus on seven of the most common types of special occasion speeches: (a) speeches of introduction, (b) speeches of welcome, (c) speeches of nomination, (d) speeches of presentation, (e) speeches of acceptance, (f) speeches of tribute, and (g) speeches to entertain.

Speeches of Introduction

A **speech of introduction** is a short speech, generally lasting three to five minutes, for the purpose of introducing the main speaker. To be effective, your introduction speech must achieve three goals: (a) establish a welcoming climate for the speaker, (b) highlight the speaker's credibility, and (c) generate enthusiasm for listening to the speaker and topic. These goals can essentially serve as guidelines as you prepare.

Teaching Tip
To give students an opportunity to analyze a speech of introduction, see the Professional Speaker Critique assignment located in the Activities section of this chapter.

First, it is important to both the main speaker and the listeners that you create a welcoming and friendly atmosphere. You can achieve this in several ways. Tell the audience how much you like or appreciate the speaker and why. Express your sincere pleasure at having the privilege of introducing the speaker. You might also say the speaker's name several times during your speech to help familiarize listeners with him or her. And you might share some personal facts about the speaker that audience members might identify with. (Of course, it is important not to share information that is too personal. If you are unsure about whether certain information is appropriate to share, ask the speaker in advance.) For example, Dr. Julia Wood, a noted scholar in interpersonal communication, spoke at North Dakota State University in April 1997 during a devastating flood. I'd asked her whether she was still willing to come, despite the flooding. During the speech of introduction, I shared her response. She'd said, "Of course. And I'll be sure to bring my boots!" This information, without being too personal, shared something about her that might have helped audience members relate to her as a person.

Second, you must establish and boost the speaker's credibility. In other words, you tell your listeners *why* they should listen to *this speaker* about *this topic.* Ask the speaker to provide you with a curriculum vita, resume, or biographical statement to help you generate this portion of your speech. (The most helpful resource is usually the curriculum vita, which details the speaker's educational background, professional experience, publications, awards and honors, and so forth. A resume is similar, but far briefer; and a biographical statement limits itself to the speaker's most notable accomplishments.) Select information that is relevant to the topic of the speech and will do the most to boost the speaker's credibility. Make sure that you do not set up unrealistic expectations on the part of the audience. That is, you want to arouse the audience's expectations, but not to the point that the speaker cannot live up to them.

Teaching Tip
Show a videotape of a sample speech of introduction and have students critique the speech using the guidelines presented in this chapter. Have students discuss what they liked about the speech as well as suggestions for improvement.

Finally, your speech of introduction should generate enthusiasm for the upcoming speech. If the speech has a title that is cleverly worded or intriguing, state the title. Share something unique about the speaker if it is something that might spark the audience's curiosity. Above all, you can generate enthusiasm through your own delivery by sounding excited yourself about what is to come.

Speech of Introduction Guidelines

- Create a friendly atmosphere.
- Establish the speaker's credibility.
- Generate enthusiasm for the speech.

What Do You Think?

When have you heard a speaker introduced? Did the introduction build enthusiasm for the speaker? Why or why not?

Teaching Tip
Have students prepare a speech of introduction for the person they most admire, assuming that person would then speak to the class.

Here is an example of a speech of introduction I delivered at the 1998 Red River Communication Conference. Notice how I attempted to establish a welcoming climate by expressing my pleasure at having the privilege of introducing the speaker and by mentioning the speaker's name several times during the short speech (Guideline 1). Also take note of the information I shared about the number of years he has taught and where, the books and journal articles he's published to date, and the awards and honors he's earned as a professor. I found this information on his curriculum vita and shared it to establish his credibility with the audience (Guideline 2). Finally, I stated the clever title at the beginning and the end, tried to sound excited myself, and asked the audience to join me in a welcoming applause as a clincher (Guideline 3). I used these strategies to generate enthusiasm for Professor Lawrence Grossberg:

Discussion Tip
Have students briefly look at this sample speech of introduction. How does the speaker create a friendly atmosphere? How does Dr. Sellnow establish the speaker's credibility? How does she generate enthusiasm for the speech?

Good evening and welcome to tonight's Red River Communication Conference keynote lecture, entitled "The Extraordinary Power of the Ordinary: On Taking Popular Culture Seriously." Tonight's keynote is the fourth in a series of four 1997–1998 Lyceums for the Liberal Arts, sponsored in part by the North Dakota Humanities Council.

I'm Deanna Sellnow, associate professor of communication here at NDSU. And I have the privilege of introducing our featured speaker, Professor Lawrence Grossberg, Morris Davis Professor of communication studies at the University of North Carolina at Chapel Hill.

Professor Grossberg earned his Ph.D. in 1976 from the University of Illinois at Urbana-Champaign, where he also taught for twenty years before moving to Chapel Hill. He has authored or coauthored thirteen books to date, with two more under contract at this time. His most recent books *Bringing It All Back Home: Essays on Cultural Studies* and *Dancing in Spite of Myself: Essays on Popular Culture,* both published in 1997, serve to ground much of his lecture this evening.

When he's not writing books, Professor Grossberg is publishing refereed journal articles (over one hundred to date), serving as international coeditor of *Cultural Studies,* and serving on the editorial review board for over a dozen refereed journals including *Culture and Policy, Critical Studies in Mass Communication, the Journal of Popular Music Studies,* and *Culture and Space,* as well as earning awards such as the B. Aubrey Fisher Mentorship Award from the International Communication Association in 1995

> and two grants from the National Endowment for the Humanities in support of Marxism and the Interpretation of Culture.
>
> When he's not actively pursuing his research agenda, Professor Grossberg is earning "outstanding teacher" honors for his efforts at both the undergraduate and graduate levels in courses such as "Communication and Culture," "Popular Culture," "Cultural Studies," and "Structuralism and Semiotics."
>
> We are certainly in for a treat tonight as we engage in intellectual exchange with Professor Grossberg as he challenges the current attacks on incorporating studies of popular culture into scholarly research and curricula. More specifically, he will demonstrate the enormous power that media and popular culture have on our lives and our culture in his address entitled "The Extraordinary Power of the Ordinary: On Taking Popular Culture Seriously." Please join me in welcoming Professor Lawrence Grossberg.

Speeches of Welcome

A **speech of welcome** is given as a formal, public greeting to a visiting person or group to make them feel comfortable and appreciated. Speeches of welcome are typically presented by a **master of ceremonies,** an individual who has been designated to set the mood of the program, introduce participants, and keep the program moving along. Most year-end honorary banquets as well as award ceremonies like the Academy Awards, the MTV Music Awards, the Emmy Awards, and the Tony Awards, use a master of ceremonies for this very purpose.

Teaching Tip
Have students write a one- to two-page paper in which they describe a speech of welcome they have given or observed. Ask them to evaluate how the speaker caught the attention of the audience, set a friendly tone, and provided important information.

In a speech of welcome, you invite listeners to agree that the occasion is friendly and their attendance is appreciated. You do this by respectfully catching their attention, graciously and thoughtfully setting a friendly tone, and providing information about the occasion and those in attendance. Typically, your speech of welcome is not more than two to four minutes long.

Speech of Welcome Guidelines

- Catch attention respectfully.
- Set a friendly tone.
- Provide information about the occasion and attendees.

The following example is taken from the National Sports Awards program aired on June 20, 1993. Tom Brokaw, *NBC Nightly News* anchor, was the master of ceremonies for this special event honoring five great athletes:

Teaching Tip
Remind students that these categories are not mutually exclusive. For example, a speech may be an introduction that includes a welcome and a nomination.

> Good evening and welcome. This is such a fitting national celebration because, after all, what would life be without the games that we play? The greatest athletes—the most memorable—are those who gave us a sense

> of exhilaration off the field as well as on. Heywood Hale Broun once said, "Sports don't build character; they reveal it." What you'll share here tonight is the essence of character as revealed by the lives of these great athletes.
>
> Sports are such an important part of our national culture, our language, our fantasies. Well, tonight the National Sports Awards honors those who played their games at the highest level—and lived their lives at the same heights. They lifted us all by their achievements and by their conduct. Four of them are here in Washington with us tonight; one of them, Ted Williams, has been asked by his doctor not to travel, so he's watching from his home. They were all nominated by a panel of leading sports journalists.
>
> The first that we honor tonight is a woman. When she was born, one of twenty-two children in a Tennessee family, no one could have guessed at that time that her story would echo over the decades, or that it would make even a big impression on the 1962 Middle Atlantic Conference High Jump Champion.

After Brokaw's brief speech of welcome, several individuals presented speeches of tribute to the first honoree, Wilma Rudolph. At that point, Brokaw presented her with the first National Sports Award.

Speeches of Nomination

Technology Tip
http://www.historychannel.com/speeches/index.html

The History Channel Web site contains several historically significant speeches. Have students visit the site, select a speech of nomination, and analyze the speech using the guidelines presented in this chapter.

A **speech of nomination** is given to propose an individual as a nominee for an elected office, honor, or award. Every four years, political parties do this at their national conventions. Although the speeches of nomination given at these conventions are rather long, most speeches of nomination are brief, lasting only about two to four minutes. Your goal is to highlight the qualities that make this person the most credible candidate for the position, honor, or award. To do so, you must do three specific things. First, clarify the importance of the position, honor, or award. You might describe the responsibilities involved in it, challenges or issues related to it, and the characteristics needed to fulfill it. Second, list your candidate's personal and professional qualifications that meet those criteria. Your goal in this step is to link your candidate with the position, honor, or award in ways that make him or her appear to be a natural choice. Third, formally place your candidate's name in nomination. Doing so at the end creates a dramatic climax to clinch your speech.

Speech of Nomination Guidelines

- Clarify the importance of the position, honor, or award.
- List your candidate's qualifications for it.
- Formally place your candidate's name in nomination.

Your speech of nomination could be as simple and brief as this:

I am very proud to place in nomination for president of our association the name of one of our most active members, Ms. Adrienne Lamb.

We all realize the demands of this particular post. It requires leadership. It requires vision. It requires enthusiasm and motivation. And, most of all, it requires a sincere love for our group and its mission.

This candidate meets and exceeds each one of these demands. It was Adrienne Lamb who chaired our visioning task force. She led us to articulate the mission statement we abide by today. It was Adrienne Lamb who chaired the fund-raising committee last year when we enjoyed a record drive. And it was Adrienne Lamb who acted as mentor to so many of us, myself included, when we were trying to find our place in this association and this community. This association and its members have reaped the benefits of Adrienne Lamb's love and leadership so many times and in so many ways. We now have the opportunity to benefit in even greater ways.

It is truly an honor and a privilege to place in nomination for president of our association, Ms. Adrienne Lamb!

Discussion Tip
In what ways are the skills of persuasive speaking relevant to the demands of speaking on special occasions? In what ways are the skills of informative speaking relevant to the demands of speaking on special occasions?

Speeches of Presentation

A **speech of presentation** is given when an individual or group receives an award, to present the award and recognize the recipient's accomplishments. If you have ever watched the Academy Awards, Grammy Awards, or the MTV Movie Awards, you have seen speeches of presentation. These speeches may be as brief as "And the winner is . . . ," but are usually a bit longer, however, generally not more than two to three minutes.

Teaching Tip
For a creative project that gives students an opportunity to construct speeches of presentation and acceptance, see The Awards assignment in the Activities section of this chapter.

Actor Tommy Lee Jones nominated Al Gore for president at the 2000 Democratic National Convention.

In a speech of presentation, you invite listeners to agree that the person or group is worthy of receiving the award. You do this by pointing out relevant achievements. If listeners aren't familiar with the award and its purpose, you should include an explanation in your speech. Sometimes special achievement awards are given at the Academy Awards, for example, and are usually explained during the ceremony. If the winner was chosen from a group of candidates, you should also acknowledge the worth of those not selected.

Speech of Presentation Guidelines

- Be brief (not more than two to three minutes).
- Point out relevant achievements.
- Explain unfamiliar awards.
- Acknowledge the worth of other candidates.

The following example is a speech given upon the presentation of an award for the Outstanding Graduate Teaching Assistant. Notice how the speaker explains the purpose of the award, acknowledges the other candidates, and points out the relevant achievements of the recipient all in a very short amount of time:

> Each year, the Department of Communication honors a graduating teaching assistant for truly outstanding achievements made while pursuing the graduate degree. The award is based on accomplishments in teaching, research, and service to the department and profession. Selection is made based on input from faculty members and peers.
>
> This year's award could have gone to any of the graduating teaching assistants, since all made contributions above and beyond what was required or expected: Shannon Scott, for his contributions to the Red River Communication Conference; Robin Smith and Mohan Dutta, for their contributions to the revised *Media Writing Workbook;* Pam Zaug, for her work with the integration of PowerPoint into the public speaking fundamentals curriculum; Kris Treinen, for her contributions as editorial assistant to the award-winning *North Dakota Journal of Speech and Theatre;* Jody Norri and Molly Bergstrom, for their presentations at regional and national conventions. Moreover, five of these seven graduating students have elected to go on to pursue the Ph.D. and have been accepted with assistantships across the country. The department is graduating a very fine group of winners this year.
>
> Based on the overwhelming response by her peers, this year's award goes to Ms. Pamela Zaug. Pam's student course evaluations indicate her ability to teach effectively to undergraduate students. Pam also has contributed to the department by helping infuse PowerPoint across the public speaking fundamentals curriculum. She has presented papers at several academic conferences. And, above all, she has acted as a true mentor for new graduate teaching assistants by answering their questions and helping them find their own answers throughout her tenure here.

Pam deserves special recognition for her outstanding achievements in teaching, research, and service. I am pleased to present Pam Zaug the 1997–1998 Outstanding Graduate Teaching Assistant in the Department of Communication at NDSU.

Speeches of Acceptance

A **speech of acceptance** is a speech to express appreciation for an award or gift received. Your goal is to sincerely convey to listeners your appreciation for the honor and the recognition. You might also thank individuals who contributed to your success. To be effective, your speech should be brief, humble, and gracious. This is not the time to call attention to some political cause. Nor would it be appropriate to in any way be offensive, as was U2's lead singer, Bono, who accepted the best album award at the 1994 Grammy Awards by saying "we shall continue to abuse our position and f_____ up the mainstream" (Bellafante, 1994, p. 109). Remember that your goal in a speech of acceptance is to convey appreciation in a way that makes your audience feel good about the fact that you are the one receiving the recognition.

Teaching Tip
Instruct students to prepare a hypothetical acceptance speech for an award they would like to receive.

What Do You Think?

Consider an acceptance speech you heard—for example, during an awards program on television or a ceremony you attended—that seemed inappropriate. Why did the speech seem inappropriate?

Discussion Tip
According to Sellnow, why is it important that speeches of acceptance not call attention to some political cause? Have you ever observed an inappropriate acceptance speech? What made the speech inappropriate?

Speech of Acceptance Guidelines

- Be brief (not more than one to two minutes).
- Acknowledge the competition.

Awards shows like the MTV Music Awards offer many speeches of presentation and acceptance throughout.

- Thank those who've contributed to your achievement.
- Thank those who gave the award.

Here is an example of a speech of acceptance given by a professor who was awarded the Outstanding Teaching Award for the College of Arts, Humanities, and Social Sciences. Notice how he briefly and humbly thanked those who gave him the award and those who contributed to his achievement, as well as acknowledged the competition:

> Thank you. You know, I've come to a lot of these banquets over the years and watched as others have accepted the awards for teaching, research, and service. And as I watched, I always thought to myself "*that's* the one [teaching] *I* want." There are so many excellent teachers in our college and I know I'm not the best, but I really care about my students and try to help them set goals for themselves, and then do what I can to assist them in achieving what they've set out to accomplish. This award means so much to me because it comes from them [students], and it comes from you [peers in the college]. Thank you for selecting me. It is truly an honor (Blanks Hindman, 1999).

Speeches of Tribute

Teaching Tip
For a creative project that gives students an opportunity to construct a speech of tribute, see the Eulogies assignment contained in the Activities section of this chapter.

A **speech of tribute** is a speech that praises or celebrates a person, a group, or an event. There are various types of speeches of tribute, including eulogies, toasts, farewells, dedications, commemorative addresses, and commencement addresses. Beyond informing your listeners, your goal is to invite them to truly appreciate the person, group, or event by arousing their sentiments. To do this, you need to focus your speech on the most notable aspects of the person, group, or event—that is, on the most notable characteristics, achievements, and influences on others. For example, if your speech of tribute focuses on a person, select a few key aspects of his or her personality to share, along with stories to illustrate them. You might also share some of his or her most outstanding achievements, and several things he or she has done to make a difference in the lives of others and the community. If you were to list a wide range of facts about the person, you would defeat your purpose. Listeners wouldn't be able to keep track of what you were saying. By being selective, you make your speech of tribute more compelling. With these basic guidelines in mind, let's look briefly at each type of speech of tribute.

Speech of Tribute Guidelines

- Focus on a few notable aspects.
- Acknowledge the sentiments of the audience.
- Arouse sentiments with vivid stories and examples.
- Arouse sentiments with emotional language and delivery.

A **eulogy** is a speech of tribute honoring someone who has recently died. Eulogies are often delivered at funerals but can also be public events in themselves. For example, former President Reagan presented a public eulogy after the *Challenger* space shuttle disaster in 1986. Notice how he focuses on a few notable aspects of those who died in the disaster by acknowledging each of them first by name and then as a group. He calls them heroes and brave and dedicated pioneers who are to be admired for their willingness to serve in spite of the dangers. Also take note of how he acknowledges the sentiments of the audience: "the families of the seven [who died]," "the schoolchildren of America who were watching the live coverage," "every man and woman who works for NASA or who worked on this mission," as well as "all the people of our country." Finally, notice his careful choice of stories, examples, and vivid language to arouse sentiments. He begins, for example, by talking about being "pained to the core by the tragedy," moves on to talk of "the courage it took

Teaching Tip
Assign a speech of tribute in which students honor someone who has had a major impact on their lives. The speech should focus on a few notable aspects, acknowledge the sentiments of the audience, and arouse sentiments with vivid stories, examples, emotional language, and delivery.

Tribute to the Challenger Astronauts

Ronald Reagan

Ladies and gentlemen, I'd planned to speak to you tonight to report on the State of the Union but the events of earlier today have led me to change those plans. Today is a day for mourning and remembering. Nancy and I are pained to the core by the tragedy of the shuttle *Challenger.* We know we share this pain with all of the people of our country. This is truly a national loss.

Nineteen years ago, almost to the day, we lost three astronauts in a terrible accident on the ground. But we've never lost an astronaut in flight; we've never had a tragedy like this. And perhaps we've forgotten the courage it took for the crew of the shuttle; but they, the *Challenger* Seven, were aware of the dangers, but overcame them and did their jobs brilliantly. We mourn seven heroes: Michael Smith, Dick Scobee, Judith Resnik, Ronald McNair, Ellison Onizuka, Gregory Jarvis, and Christa McAuliffe. We mourn their loss as a nation together.

[For] the families of the seven, we cannot bear, as you do, the full impact of this tragedy, but we feel the loss, and we're thinking about you so very much. Your loved ones were daring and brave, and they had that special grace, that special spirit that says, "Give me a challenge and I'll meet it with joy." They had a hunger to explore the universe and discover its truths. They wished to serve, and they did. They served all of us.

We've grown used to wonders in this century. It's hard to dazzle us, but for twenty-five years the United States space program has been doing just that. We've grown used to the idea of space, and perhaps we forget that we've only just begun. We're still pioneers. They, the members of the *Challenger* crew, were pioneers.

And I want to say something to the schoolchildren of America who were watching the live coverage of the shuttle's takeoff. I know it is hard to understand, but sometimes painful things like this happen. It's all part of the process of exploration and discovery. It's all part of taking a chance and expanding man's horizons. The future doesn't belong to the fainthearted; it belongs to the brave. The *Challenger* crew was pulling us into the future, and we'll continue to follow them.

I've always had great faith in and respect for our space program, and what happened today does nothing to diminish it. We don't hide our space program. We don't keep secrets and cover things up. We do it all up front and in public. That's the way freedom is, and we wouldn't change it for a minute.

We'll continue our quest in space. There will be more shuttle flights and more shuttle crews and, yes, more volunteers, more civilians, more teachers in space. Nothing ends here; our hopes and our journeys continue.

I wish to add that I wish I could talk to every man and woman who works for NASA or who worked on this mission and tell them: "Your dedication and professionalism have moved and impressed us for decades. And we know of your anguish. We share it."

There's coincidence today. On this day three hundred ninety years ago, the great explorer Sir Francis Drake died aboard ship off the coast of Panama. In his lifetime the great frontiers were the oceans, and an historian later said, "He lived by the sea, died on it, and was buried in it." Well, today we can say of the *Challenger* crew: Their dedication was, like Drake's, complete. The crew of the space shuttle *Challenger* honored us by the manner in which they lived their lives. We will never forget them, nor the last time we saw them, this morning, as they prepared for their journey and waved good-bye and "slipped the surly bonds of earth" to "touch the face of God." Thank you.

White House, Washington, D.C., January 28, 1986 (Transcribed from the video, Great Speeches, Volume V).

for the crew of the shuttle," and ends with the honorable "manner in which they lived their lives . . . waved good-bye and . . . to 'touch the face of God.'"

A **toast** is a very short speech of tribute, often delivered in impromptu fashion—that is, with little or no preparation time. Toasts are often given at wedding receptions, graduation dinners, awards luncheons, holiday dinners, and so forth. When you give a toast, your goal is to focus on some positive aspect of the person or group and to set a tone of goodwill.

Teaching Tip
Ask students to prepare a toast for a classmate who they feel has made the most progress as a speaker this semester.

A **farewell** is a speech of tribute honoring someone who is leaving, for example, someone who is retiring, resigning, relocating, or being promoted. Your goal is to create a sense of appreciation of the honoree's fellowship and accomplishments. If you are both the speaker and the person who is leaving, express gratitude for the opportunities your tenure provided you both professionally and personally.

A **dedication** is a speech of tribute that honors a worthy person or group by naming a structure like a building, monument, or park after the honoree. Your goal is to invite listeners to agree that the person or group deserves the honor. Many campus buildings are named after someone and have probably been dedicated at some point in time.

A **commemorative address** is a speech of tribute that inspires listeners by remembering accomplishments and setting new goals. Commemorative speeches might be given on occasions like an anniversary party, a family reunion, or an honor society's annual banquet. You should present some fact about the person, group, or event being celebrated and then build on that fact to create a desire for some new goal. Here is an excerpt from a commemorative speech I gave at a banquet of the Society of Women Engineers. Notice how I begin with the accomplishments that the group has achieved and then build on that to point to a new goal:

> When I was in high school, we used to shout a cheer to encourage our sports teams as they played. Perhaps some of you know it as well. It went something like this: "S-U-C-C-E-S-S. That's the way we spell success. Success! Success! Success!"
>
> Today, I've been asked to talk with you about success. First, I'd like to congratulate you for all your successes in life thus far. For example, you've graduated from high school. And you're in the process of earning your college degrees in a field that is not known for being welcoming to women, I might add! And you're learning about the joys of outreach and service to community, evidenced by your commitment to the goals of this organization. Congratulations on a job well done!
>
> Today, though, I want to move beyond the successes you've already achieved . . . to consider what it will mean to succeed tomorrow, next week, next year, and for the rest of your life. Actually, my specific goal is to challenge you to think differently about what "success" means. Then, I'll encourage you to live each day—no, each moment—of your life successfully (Sellnow, 1999).

Finally, a **commencement address** is a speech of tribute praising graduating students and congratulating them on their academic achievements. Commencement addresses are generally delivered by the class valedictorian or another student, or by a guest speaker. If you give a commencement address, begin by praising the graduating class. Then point graduates toward some future goals. Finally, inspire them to reach for those goals.

Commencement Address Guidelines

- Praise the graduating class.
- Point toward some future goals.
- Inspire graduating students to reach for those goals.

Notice how foreign correspondent Georgia Anne Geyer effectively includes each of these steps in her commencement address at the Saint Mary-of-the-Woods College.

JOY IN OUR TIMES: COMMENCEMENT ADDRESS, MAY 7, 1989

Georgia Anne Geyer

Three months ago, I walked into my condominium in downtown Washington and happened to see the great Russian/American conductor Mstislav Rostropovich, standing at our front desk. We are proud that he lives there. He is always a man filled with life and spirit, but this day he had the most marked look of pure joy on his face that I had ever had the . . . well . . . joy of seeing.

After greeting me, he stood for a few minutes at the desk and repeated several times, as if in sheer wonder, "Last night, I conducted two hundred fifty cellists. . . . Last night, I conducted two hundred fifty cellists. . . ." Ladies and gentlemen, at that moment I knew that I had seen as close to a beatific joy as I have ever seen, next to certain pictures of Christ. For I discovered then that this great musician, who is a cellist, had conducted at the world conference of five thousand cellists!

That magical moment—that blessed moment—made me think of our younger generation today—of your generation—and I wondered if any of them, of you, would understand that kind of joy. For when I go around to schools—and to the very best and most serious schools—what even our best young people ask me is things like, "Miss Geyer, what are they looking for out there?" In short, in place of that inner joy of Rostropovich's which knew his love for music and for his cello, many young people of your generation instead are looking and waiting for some elusive and fickle "someone" out there to tell them what they are.

"What are they looking for out there?" That is one phrase that will warn you if you let it of what *not* to be thinking, even in today's often treacherous world. Some others? "How can I get ahead? What's in it for me? Let's get him." And, "How can I stop being bored? What company can I take over today? How much will I make? What's in it for me?"

Let us, for a moment, consider "Joy." My dictionary says that it is the emotion excited by the acquisition or expectation of good." I like that. Not the acquisition of things, or of power, or of a handsome husband, or of the paltry fruit of any action. It is the magical and mystical act of discovering and finally knowing the God-given talents and the artistry that is inside yourself and nurturing and expressing them rather than trying vainly to find out what "society," whatever that is, fashionably at that moment, wants. Aristotle said that happiness is an activity that is "in accordance with virtue." Vince Lombardi, more in tune with our times, said that "happiness is winning." Donald Trump carried it to the zenith of our times' senselessness and anomie, saying that it's not "whether you win or lose, it's winning."

Let me say right off that I think the search for joy—and, remember, that only in America is the "pursuit of happiness" assured in the very Constitution itself—is very difficult for all Americans, young and old, today. Dr. Joseph Plummber, an authority on values, recently put out a study listing profound changes in our basic American values. He found that more people in the developed Western nations were seeking self-actualization rather than security or traditionally defined success. He found a self-fulfillment ethic, individualized definitions of success, a growing sense of limits. . . .

Now, this is all right so long as it is associated with principles, with "good," and with the courage to carry it through, for, as Churchill said, "Courage is the most important virtue, because it *guarantees* all the rest." Instead, I see many Americans terrified by risk, thinking apparently that a life without risk really *is* possible. We see the mother who drank half a bottle of Jim Beam whiskey every day during her pregnancy and is suing the company because her poor child is deformed. I see a remarkable amount of lack of joy, of gamesplaying instead of principle and of cases where the grand principle of equality has been debased to no more than equality of appetite.

And I see the warning of Alexis de Tocqueville about excessive individualism being realized. Two centuries ago the brilliant Frenchman warned of the democracy that he so admired that it held within it the seeds of its own demise. "Not only does democracy make every man forget his ancestors," he wrote, "but hides his descendants and separates his contemporaries from him, it throws him back forever upon himself alone and threatens in the end to confine him entirely within the solitude of his heart." That isolation, ladies and gentlemen, graduates and friends, is not democracy but a perverted democracy that looks to others desperately for approval, that looks not to a work one loves but to a lottery and to chance for succor, and that creates a person afraid to take the joy to live in one's arms, and equally incapable of living fully either in one's own self—or in community, for the common good.

Amidst all the good we have in our country, our churches and our lives, nevertheless today I also find this wanting. Where is joy? What is joy? Permit me to muse, modestly, on what I have learned through living an unorthodox life, about joy.

So I was the first woman foreign correspondent and syndicated columnist in our time. So I had to break ground and sometimes face barriers put up against me. So I lost a number of fiancés because of my love for understanding other countries, because of my liking for hotels and plane rides across the Red Seas of the world. So one of them once said in irk, "Gee Gee, the most beautiful words in the world to you are not 'I love you' but 'Room Service, Please.'"

That meant that everybody was always and is still asking me, "Didn't you feel bitter about it?" I have thought about that. Bitter? It never crossed my mind to be bitter. I was having so much fun, I was so filled with spirit and joy, I thanked God every day for the very privilege of being able to know everyone in the world and for being able to do this work I so loved. And if the Sisters of Providence will forgive me a wicked aside, I will add that the one thing your enemies can never forgive you of is, not money, not even success, but having so much fun in life!

My joys were often the little things: Interviewing a Khomeini or a Castro, Sadat or a Duarte, yes, those were good professionally, and afterwards I felt a great sense of satisfaction for breaking through . . . But I would often experience pure joy in odd and unexpected places. . . . Sitting at breakfast in Chile and quietly observing people and feeling so privileged to be there . . . being able to bring some message of truth about the world to my own people, something they didn't know . . . seeing an election in a war-torn El Salvador and watching the poor people dare everyone to go to vote . . . seeing Russia return to its own conscience—the inner conscience that was always there, waiting—as Gorbachev frees the Russian people these very days, before our eyes. . . .

I remember special messages that warmed me tremendously, like when I interviewed the late great Archbishop Oscar Romero of El Salvador in 1979. At one point, I asked this man, who seemed just to radiate goodness, whether it would not have been easier to have stayed out of all the fights for social justice he had entered. And his simple but profound words: "Well, I could have just stayed in the Archbishop's palace, but that would not have been very *easy,* would it?" It rang so very true. It would have been immeasurably harder, just as it will be immeasurably harder for you, if you choose to live a life without the components of joy.

But—what are those components? And why are they so hard to come by in our "fun-loving . . . non-risk taking . . . gamesplaying . . . world?"

—*Risk taking.* First and very important, being able to feel joy involves risk taking, and I do not mean juggling monies around frenziedly in the stock market. It means risking your popularity by taking a genuinely unpopular stand, risking your life to do what it is that *you* want to do in life. Risks are going to be there anyway. It's just street sense to take them on your terms, not theirs. In warfare, it is called being on the offensive. In life, it is called embracing life with all your heart.

Along these lines, I recall one spring day seven years ago when I was going to Central America—again. I just had a gut feeling that I did not want to go to El Salvador, because there had been so much fighting there. Usually I don't obey fearful feelings, having found that they pass and are not really accurate, but this time I did. So I took the plane to Nicaragua, and that week nothing at all happened in Salvador—and when I got to the Managua airport, I was standing second in line to pass through to the center of the airport . . . and the airport was blown up! I never tried to second-guess fate again after that!

—*Perspective.* What, you may ask, does perspective have to do with joy? Well, a whole lot!

Young people are always asking me how I "control" (a favorite word of your generation) my interviews. And I always answer, "Knowing more than they do." This is not, repeat not, a popular answer, but it is genuine and workable. I know history—so nothing surprises me. I know where things are, why and where they will be. The perspective of history—of all human life—gives me a terrifying confidence. Knowing the trajectory of mankind—its victories, its sordid defeats, its searchings for God and for meaning—I cannot be a utopian, which is dangerous anyway, but I also cannot be a pessimist. I see how far we have come; I can take joy in what we can accomplish in our lifetimes, because I know and understand the limits of what we can do.

Once I wrote a good friend, a Jesuit priest in Latin America, about how discouraged I was about how Latin America was going and he wrote back these very wise words, "Remember, Gee Gee, I am not responsible for the outcome, but I am responsible for my own fight." That's it. That's what I know. And that very simple perspective allows one to have joy in what one *is* able to do and not to moan and mourn over not being able to do the impossible. Because we cannot be perfect, that does not mean we cannot be good.

Perspective comes at you from the funniest, most unexpected places. In Finland last fall, I went to see this fine artist, Bjorn Weckstrom, and he explained to me, as no one else quite has, how we have come to this point, where so many search not for deeper meaning or for joy but "to do something, just to be someone for a moment." "A hundred years ago," Bjorn said, "people were living in small communities. Everyone had an identity known by the whole village. The group created the morals, the rules. . . . Even your name was taken from your father—you were 'son of . . .' Now the frames are eliminated. People are desperate, living in this super tribe. The village was an enormous security for people. In a way it gave people stability and a kind of harmony in life. The problem has been to create something new which would replace this. . . . Before, it was enough to be recognized for what you do before the village. But now the borders of the tribe have been moving out. Now to be somebody, you have to be on television. It is the problem of the identity of man today, the need to be someone even for a short moment. Even if man knows he's almost at the end of his rope. . . ." And, of course, the amorphous, unseen, cruelly judgmental audience of the TV is a harsh audience indeed, compared to the village—and the person never really knows, in this new audience, whether what he has done is good or not. And it really doesn't matter, for this audience more than likely has already long succumbed to the lowest value of the collective will.

—*Timing.* Understanding the right time for an idea, for a painting, for doing something—it is critical. It is an instinct; it comes from within people in whom street sense has been blended blessedly with intellectual searching. It is critical for work and it is critical for personal relationships. Too often today, we want to rush work, rush relationships, become managing editor at thirty-two, editor at thirty-five. . . . And later, we wonder where we have been, or whether we've been anywhere at all.

I talked with a young man the other day, who happened to be a fundamentalist Christian. He spoke of how important the three years before marriage to his wife had been, when they were not making love. "We got to know each other in a way at that time that we could never have known otherwise," he told me. "When you go to bed too soon, you lose all kinds of precious levels of the development of a relationship." He was so right. The Bible has a lot about this. "There is a time . . . and a time . . ."

—*Choices.* I have found through life that a truly joyful person is willing to make choices on the basis of what he knows, then stick with them, and change them if he must. It is a terribly unjoyful life not to be able to make choices, not to have the inner confidence.

That recalls the most interesting evening I had, four years ago, when I was asked to drive the late Clair Booth Luce to a dinner party. I was delighted, for here was one of the truly great women of our time, a woman who had done just about everything. . . . Mrs. Luce was not, repeat not, a woman you contradicted or, as I soon found out, even questioned. As soon as she got in the car, she was throwing very pointed and brilliant one-liners at me. She obviously had a message for me. In fact, she repeated it several times.

"You did it right," she said. "You spent twenty years doing what you do best." When I tried to remonstrate with this woman who had been ambassador, playwright, journalist, novelist, wife, mother, she disdained the suggestion. "No," she said, "I could have been a great playwright, I could have been a great playwright. . . ."

I am not suggesting that Mrs. Luce was right. Personally, I feel deeply what I have had to give up for what I wanted most. I am suggesting that wise people at different times in their lives realize that we all make choices, even when we think we are not making them; so, again, it is better to embrace them than to run from them. I dedicate that story to our noble older women graduates here today, who I know have had to make many, many choices and are still courageously making them, as their presence here attests.

And think, women of my generation—think of what we have seen! We have seen the first age when women have sought to define *themselves!* All through history, men have defined us. Finally, we are taking responsibility for ourselves! Easy? How could it be easy? And yet, we have finally arrived at trying to know and understand the ultimate political relationship, which is the ecstatic but endlessly bedeviling relationship between men and women and we have finally arrived at the moment, as the poet Louise Bogan puts it so beautifully, of women giving back to the world "half of its soul." Which brings me to . . .

—*Love.* Finally, love! There is really only one thing that I know to tell you graduates—only one thing—and that is to *follow what you love!* Follow it intellectually! Follow it sensuously! Follow it with generosity and nobility toward your fellow man! Don't deign to ask what "they" are looking for out there. Ask what you have inside. I was blessed—I was blessed because I knew what I loved—writing, my countries, being a courier between cultures—and I had dogged determination to follow it. Doing what you love, whether it is having children, working in a profession, being a nun, being a journalist, is all encompassing, all engrossing; it is like a very great love affair occurring every day. It is principle and creation; you know why you are here; your personal life and your professional life is all one. It is not fun, not games, not winning or losing, not making money or having your fifteen minutes on television; it is what no one can ever, ever take away from you, it is . . . pure joy.

In closing, I would like to ask you just to look around you today . . . to relish and preserve in your mind's eye and your memory this treasured moment at this quintessentially beautiful school.

Never again will you graduates be at this pure moment of your existence, when all the roads are open to you. Perhaps never again will you have friends and comrades, and teachers and sisters, as pure in their friendship because no one is yet what he or she is going to become. Never again probably will your families be quite so specially proud of you.

So, seize the moment joyfully. Follow not your interests, which change, but what you are and what you love, which will and should not change. And always remember these golden days.

God bless you all, and may the gods of the winds and the seas be with you on your voyage. Thank you.

Speeches to Entertain

A **speech to entertain** is a lighthearted speech that makes a serious point. Using humor, you invite listeners to agree with your opinion about an issue. Keep in mind that not all speaking to entertain qualifies as a speech to entertain. For example, a comedian's monologue that has no serious point cannot be considered a

Teaching Tip
To give students an opportunity to construct a speech to entertain, see the Pet Peeves assignment in the Activities section of this chapter.

Teaching Tip
Have students complete the Analyzing a Speech to Entertain assignment contained in the Activities section before you discuss this chapter in class. This activity will serve as a springboard for an in-class discussion of Chapter 17.

speech to entertain. There are five key guidelines to follow when preparing and presenting a speech to entertain.

First, make a point. In other words, like an informative or persuasive speech, a speech to entertain has a clear thesis statement or serious point. While you might not state your thesis as bluntly in your speech to entertain, by the end of the speech, your point should be clear. Kim Roe (1987), for example, offered this serious point, or thesis statement, in her speech to entertain: "Don't act upon assumptions" (p. 135). This serious point wasn't bluntly articulated in this way, however, until the concluding remarks of her speech.

Second, be creative and unique in your use of humor. You should avoid using stale jokes and clichés. Like your informative or persuasive speech, your speech to entertain should offer a new perspective.

Discussion Tip
Ask students to recall a speech to entertain they have heard. What made the speech memorable?

Third, use appropriate humor. To be appropriate, your humor must be related to the topic of your speech, should not offend or marginalize members of your audience, and should be positive in tone rather than, say, sarcastic. Some comedians make a pretty good living delivering sarcastic monologues that almost always offend someone or some group. They are not, however, considered effective public speakers. Since the occasions for most speeches to entertain are festive, you shouldn't bring that mood down with inappropriate, offensive, or sarcastic humor.

Fourth, be organized. Like any public speech, your speech to entertain should have a clear introduction, body, and conclusion. It cannot be merely a smattering of jokes or a stream-of-consciousness humorous monologue. All of the principles that guide effective public speech organization should guide this speech.

Teaching Tip
To give students an opportunity to analyze a speech to entertain, see the Analyzing a Speech to Entertain assignment in the Activities section of this chapter.

Finally, use a dynamic delivery style. This means your voice and body should convey an enthusiasm in keeping with your entertaining purpose. It also means you must use **comic timing**—that is, pause the right length of time to allow for applause and laughter. Generally, you need to listen for the peak of laughter or applause before moving on. If you don't wait long enough, listeners will be inhibited from laughing or applauding by fear of missing what you have to say next. If you wait too long, however, you'll create a sense of sluggishness, and you and your audience will lose momentum.

Speech to Entertain Guidelines

- Make a serious point.
- Be creative and unique.
- Use appropriate humor.
- Be organized.
- Use dynamic delivery.

What Do You Think?

Consider a comedian whom you consider offensive. Why? Can an offensive comedian still be funny? Why or why not?

Let's take a closer look at Kim Roe's speech to entertain.

National Championship Speech, 1987

Kim Roe

When I was about this tall, no, that was last year. [Laughter] When I was about this tall, my mom used to buy me story-records-with-*bing*-turn-the-page-go-along books. You know them, you loved them, you had them. Allow me to share with all of you one of my favorites. Three bears and a blonde bimbo meet in a bedroom. [Laughter] Goldilocks and the Three Bears.

"And Goldilocks, trembling with anticipation ran into her mother's arms and said, 'Bing, turn the page.'" [Laughter]

Naturally, I assumed that this was the ending, the climax, a Goldilocks catharsis. And even when I played it backwards it said: Mersh dea shea ner Goldilox is Satin. [Laughter and applause] Which wasn't as important to what I had done. I assumed.

And I am assuming that you're all assuming that my speech is on assuming. Can I make that assumption? I assume so. When an assumption is made it lays the foundation for disappointment. And I'm sure we've all heard that when we assume we make an ass out of you and well that's pretty much about it. [Laughter]

To better understand assumptions let's first take a look at, well, why we make asses out of ourselves, how it affects you, and ways to stop. Written, directed, and delivered by me. [Laughter]

Now I have to believe that each and every one of you here today already knows what an assumption is. And, if you don't, at least you have a good example of one. [Laughter] Some would go as far as to say, "What! Assumptions! Phaat." And if you're one of those you just might want to get that checked out. [Laughter] Or check out this true historical example. President Franklin Delano Roosevelt left a stack of papers on his desk with the top page saying, "Watch the borders." A presidential advisor, upon seeing this, quickly sent troops to secure the Mexican border. And, that wouldn't have been such a bad idea except that "Watch the borders" had been left for FDR's typist. And as my mother would've said, "Damn it to hell, somebody's going to get an ass-chewing." [Laughter]

One assumption. A potential disaster. One big question, why? Why do we make asses out of ourselves? Well, one reason is that we, for the most part being normal human beings, like very little surprise in our lives. [Not] knowing what is out there, or what's in store for the future, or what really goes into a hot dog, is frightening. We feel the need to fill the gaps in our lives with our assumptions.

Another reason why we assume is that there has been a lack of communication and understanding. Now, a prime example of this can be seen through the story of the Trojan Horse.

"Yo, fellow Trojans. A gift has been besto—A gift—We just got a present."

"Read the card, read the card!""

"Who's it from, who's it from?" [Laughter]

And as we all know that was one trick pony. [Laughter]

And finally, we assume because we rely on past experiences and knowledge. And it's fair to say that whenever Geraldo Rivera bursts on the screen to unveil another fast-breaking news story, the networks assume the ratings will go sky-high. So I too, like millions, tuned in to watch his riveting on-the-spot coverage of the uncovering of Al Capone's vault. Which turned out to be as entertaining as paste. [Laughter] But, tastes change. [Laughter] As did Geraldo's underwear when he opened that empty vault. [Laughter]

As children we are taught that monkeys live on bananas alone. But movies such as *Planet of the Apes* contradicted this assumption.

"Cornelius, [Laughter] would you like a Chicken McNugget?" [Laughter]

So right away we assume and fill in the gaps and probably don't know all the facts, and, hell, I like Roddy McDowell. [Laughter]

Now that we know why we assume let's see how it affects you, oh, what the heck, me too.

Usually, negatively. Assumptions can hurt us interpersonally, inside, right here where it counts, because we read into something because deep down we want it to turn out our way. And when that doesn't happen we feel hurt and disappointed. And believe me, I know, because I have always thought that I could sing, so I naturally assumed that I was going to get a part in my ninth grade variety show, especially singing this beautiful love ballad. [Laughter]

I'd like to dedicate this to my boyfriend Chuck. [Laughter]

"Some say love, [Laughter] it is a river that drowns a tender reed. [Laughter] But with the sun's love, in the spring becomes a rose." [Applause]

I ushered. [Laughter]

Now, assumptions can not only affect ourselves but others as well through stereotyping. There was this guy in my high school—some called him Pete. He was president of the chess club, math club, Eagle Scout Troop 411, and head hall monitor. I don't think you understand; you see Pete monitored everyone in the hall. [Laughter]

What do you assume? (A) Pete's athletic, and besides his chess knowledge, he's one lady-killer. (B) Well, Pete's a partier, and after a tough day in the hall, hey, it's Miller time. (C) Ha. Ha. Ha. Pete's hung like a horse. [Laughter]

Now, although stereotyping can be harmful, or gosh, pretty darn entertaining as well, misdirected conclusions can lead to disaster. To illustrate, let's look at a page in history. [Laughter] You might want to stand up in the back. Okay, let's talk about it. Well, it's an average size piece of paper and it's got some bold letters on it and a lot of words on it. The year, 1948. The event, the presidential election. The assumer, the *Chicago Tribune.* Now this newspaper released over one hundred thousand copies each with the headline, "DEWEY DEFEATS TRUMAN." I'm sorry. I don't care how charismatic he was, who would ever vote for Donald Duck's nephew? I mean Huey and Louie maybe, but Dewey? He was like Pete. He was a dork of a duck.

And from this example we can see that assuming can lead to big problems. And because I said it was a problem, you probably think there's going to be a solution. Well look, I don't want you to leave empty-handed so let me give you some simple solutions, and I'm not talking saline. [Laughter] Well, I guess that one just lends itself to it. [Laughter] Oh, they were written by me.

First of all, our assumptions come from an alternate source, and it's important for us to evaluate and validate our sources. For example, my Aunt Beulah told me that professional wrestling is real. Now do I consider my aunt, who is also an ex-roller derby queen, to be a reliable source? Well, yeh. She's toothless, but she's family. [Laughter] And besides, to see Aunt Beulah fly across the room and complete that flying-scissor-hook-combination-body-slam makes you want to believe.

So after you have considered the source, get accurate information. Because acting upon an assumption can lead to real disaster. I didn't want to be in that show anyway!!! [Laughter]

If they could see me now. [Laughter]

So what's the point? An assumption in itself is harmless. It's harmful when acted upon. Quite simply don't act upon assumptions. Consider the source, find out the information, get the facts, and act upon well-thought-out, educated information. And, hopefully, with this information we can turn our misplaced assumptions into directed conclusions. So that we no longer have to hear that when we assume we make an ass out of you and, oh all right, me too. But only once.

Well, my, Kimberly. You certainly have filled us in on assumptions. And all in less than ten minutes. Simply amazing.

Don't put me on the spot silly-artificial-story-telling voice; just turn the page. Bing. Kim's speech is over. [Applause]

Summary

Special occasion, or invitational, speeches are speeches people give for unique events. Your goal is to invite your listeners to agree with you about the value of a person, object, event, or place. There are various types of special occasion speeches; most are generally less than five minutes in length.

Speeches of introduction are short speeches that build enthusiasm for the main speaker and topic. To be effective, you must establish a welcoming climate, highlight the speaker's credibility, and generate enthusiasm for the speaker and topic.

Speeches of welcome are short speeches that invite listeners to agree that the occasion is friendly and their attendance is appreciated. To be effective, you must respectfully catch your listeners' attention, graciously and thoughtfully set a friendly tone, and provide information about the occasion and those in attendance.

Speeches of nomination are typically short speeches given to propose an individual as a nominee for an elected office, honor, or award. Your goal is to highlight the qualities that make this person the most credible candidate by clarifying the importance of the position, honor, or award and emphasizing the candidate's personal and professional qualifications. You then formally place your candidate's name in nomination.

Speeches of presentation are used to present an award and recognize the accomplishments of the person or group receiving it. Your goal is to invite listeners to agree that the person or group is worthy of the award. You do this by pointing out the achievements of the person or group. You might also explain the purpose of the award. You should also acknowledge the worth of those not selected.

Speeches of acceptance express appreciation for an award. In addition to expressing your appreciation for the honor and recognition, you might thank individuals who contributed to your success. To be effective, your speech should be brief, humble, and gracious.

Speeches of tribute praise or celebrate a person, group, or event. Eulogies, toasts, farewells, dedications, commemorative addresses, and commencement addresses are all speeches of tribute. Beyond informing your listeners, your goal is to invite them to appreciate the person, group, or event by arousing their sentiments. To achieve this goal, focus on the most notable characteristics, achievements, and influences.

Speeches to entertain are lighthearted speeches that make a serious point. Using humor, you invite listeners to agree with your opinion about an issue. When preparing and presenting a speech to entertain, be sure to make a point, use creative and unique humor, use appropriate humor, be organized, and use a dynamic delivery style.

At various times in your life, you'll be asked to give what we've called a special occasion speech. By knowing what these speeches are and following the basic guidelines presented, you can be effective when those times arise.

ACTIVITIES

1. **The Awards.** Form pairs. Then pick a favorite awards show (Oscars, MTV Awards, CMA Awards, Grammy Awards, Golden Globes, People's Choice Awards, etc.). Brainstorm together what the award is for. You can make up the name of the song, program, or film. One of you will give a speech of presentation based on the guidelines in this chapter:
   - Be brief (not more than two to three minutes).
   - Point out relevant achievements.
   - Explain unfamiliar awards.
   - Acknowledge the worth of other candidates.

   The other partner will give a speech of acceptance, following the guidelines:
   - Be brief (not more than one to two minutes).
   - Acknowledge the competition.
   - Thank those who've contributed to your achievement.
   - Thank those who gave the award.

   Develop short speeches and present them to the class.

2. **Professional Speaker Critique.** Attend a guest lecture on campus. Pay special attention to the speech of introduction. Critique the speech based on the guidelines provided in this chapter:
   - Establish a welcoming climate for the speaker.
   - Highlight the speaker's credibility.
   - Generate enthusiasm for listening to the speaker and topic.

   Be prepared to discuss your critique in class.
3. **Eulogies.** Form pairs. Interview each other to obtain information appropriate to a speech of tribute—that is, find out about your partner's most important characteristics, achievements, and influences on others. Prepare eulogies for each other and present them to the class.
4. **Pet Peeves.** Select a pet peeve that really bothers you. Prepare and present a speech to entertain, making a serious point about your pet peeve. Follow the five criteria for a speech to entertain:
   - Make a point.
   - Be creative and unique.
   - Use appropriate humor.
   - Be organized.
   - Use a dynamic delivery style.
5. **Commencement Address Analysis.** Analyze Georgia Anne Geyer's commencement address, "Joy in Our Times," which is included in this chapter. Examine the speech to discover how well she addresses the guidelines presented for speeches of tribute generally and commencement speeches specifically:
   - Praise the graduating class.
   - Point toward some future goals.
   - Inspire graduating students to reach for those goals.
6. **Analyzing a Speech to Entertain.** Analyze the speech to entertain by Kim Roe. Examine the speech according to the first four guidelines presented in this chapter. How well does she follow each guideline?
   - Make a serious point.
   - Be creative and unique.
   - Use appropriate humor.
   - Be organized.

Key Terms

Comic timing
Commemorative address
Commencement address
Dedication
Eulogy
Farewell
Master of ceremonies
Special occasion speeches
Speech of acceptance
Speech of introduction
Speech of nomination
Speech of presentation
Speech of tribute
Speech of welcome
Speech to entertain
Toast

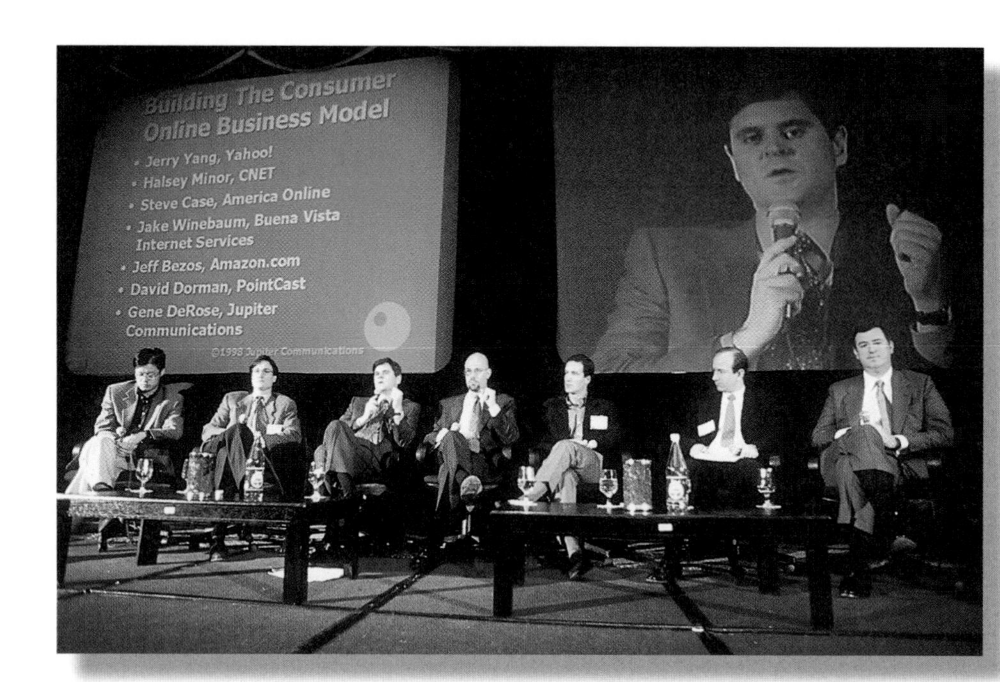
Building The Consumer Online Business Model
• Jerry Yang, Yahoo!
• Halsey Minor, CNET
• Steve Case, America Online
• Jake Winebaum, Buena Vista Internet Services
• Jeff Bezos, Amazon.com
• David Dorman, PointCast
• Gene DeRose, Jupiter Communications
©1998 Jupiter Communications

CHAPTER 18

Working and Speaking in Small Groups

Reflective Questions

1. What are the strengths you bring to a small group?
2. What are some reasons you might not like working in a small group?
3. What are some reasons for working in a small group?
4. How can you become a better group member?
5. Which leadership functions do you perform best?

*ork Session 1:* Julio, Kristi, Luke, and Bryn have been asked to work with Nick in a small group. The group must prepare a persuasive presentation that will account for one-third of their grade in the course. As the other members see it, Nick is a troublemaker in that he has contradicted the instructor on a number of occasions. Their impression might be compounded by the fact that Nick drives a Harley-Davidson motorcycle to school and wears black leather most days. Nick has also been absent more than most students and appears to be less than fully committed to earning a good grade. In short, the other members are worried that Nick will cause them to earn a lower grade than they would otherwise get.

Teaching Tip
To give students an opportunity to reflect on group roles, see the Group Member Role Self Reports assignment located in the Activities section of this chapter.

Work Session 2: After the instructor refused to move Nick into a different group, Julio, Kristi, Luke, and Bryn decide to restrict his participation and contributions. They agree not to ask him for any substantive help even though they realize he will earn a good grade for doing very little work. As they begin discussing their topic—the mandatory seat belt law—Nick explains that he has a lot of material on it since he is a fairly vocal opponent of the helmet law, which involves similar issues. Kristi and Luke become disgruntled because, as they suspected, whereas they plan to argue in support of the law, Nick actually opposes it. Kristi asks Bryn how she feels about this conflict, expecting to get her support. On the contrary, Bryn asks Nick to share some of his information. When he does, she discovers that much of it is highly relevant and can be used to strengthen the group's argument by enabling them to acknowledge and fairly treat objections. As Bryn explains this to the others, they begin to realize the hastiness of their judgments about Nick.

As suggested by this example, to which we'll return at various points throughout the chapter, working in small groups involves many complexities, which group members need to know how to handle. In this chapter, you will learn strategies that will enhance your ability to work and speak effectively in small groups. We begin by discussing the key characteristics of small groups, especially of problem-solving small groups. We then examine the nature of effective leadership and the responsibilities of group members. We look at the process of systematic problem solving, which groups can use as a plan to structure their work. Finally, we consider the process of preparing a group presentation, possible formats for the presentation, and approaches for evaluating group effectiveness.

Why Work in Small Groups?

When students are asked to work in small groups to complete a class project, whether for public speaking or for some other course, many often respond as Luke, Kristi, Julio, and Bryn did, with comments of frustration and resistance. The comments may, as in that case, focus on a group member or something else specific to the situation. Often, however, they reflect general concerns about group work. For example, students are concerned that a few people will end up doing most of the work, that it will be impossible to find mutually acceptable times to meet, that the group process will slow them down and might even lead to their getting a lower grade, or that they will be forced to compromise their ideas and values in order to reach a group consensus. Some students even go so far as to plead for the option of completing the assignment individually.

Although small group work undeniably has certain potential disadvantages, it is quickly becoming the preferred problem-solving approach in business and

> ***What Do You Think?***
>
> *Identify some of the small groups you've been part of. Did you enjoy working in them? Why or why not?*

industry (Ancona, 1990). Business and industry leaders have come to realize that the advantages of working in small groups far outweigh any disadvantages. Some of these advantages include deeper analysis of problems, greater breadth of ideas and of potential solutions, improved group morale, and increased productivity. Since small group participation is a reality we cannot avoid today or in years to come, it makes sense to learn more about how to make our participation effective. By learning techniques for effective participation and employing them in our small groups, we can maximize the advantages and minimize the potential disadvantages of working in small groups.

What Is a Small Group?

The **small group** can be difficult to define, especially because there are so many different types of small groups. For example, there are families and friendship groups, self-help and therapy groups, and problem-solving groups such as committees and task forces. What all these types of groups have in common is their limited size and the fact that their members aren't a random collection of people but, rather, have come together for a reason. In this chapter, we'll focus specifically on problem-solving groups, since that is the type of group you will participate in for this class assignment.

Teaching Tip
For a creative project that gives students an opportunity to develop a group presentation, see the Group Sales Pitch assignment in the Activities section of this chapter.

A **problem-solving group** has as its primary concern carrying out a task—more specifically, determining appropriate solutions to problems. What makes a group effective or ineffective at carrying out this task? It appears that several factors—group composition, group size, group goal, and group history—influence a group's likelihood of success.

Group Composition

Groups can be relatively homogeneous or heterogeneous. In other words, their members can be relatively similar to one another in cultural background, values and beliefs, age, and so on **(homogeneous groups)** or relatively different **(heterogeneous groups).** Research shows that heterogeneous groups can be more effective than homogeneous groups. The reason is that differences tend to lead to broader perspectives and more ideas, thereby facilitating creative problem solving (Porter & Samovar, 1992). In our ever-more-diverse society, group heterogeneity is increasingly possible.

> ***What Do You Think?***
>
> *Consider a group of which you are currently a member. Would you describe the group as relatively heterogeneous or homogeneous? Do you think the group is effective? How might this heterogeneity or homogeneity affect the group and its effectiveness?*

Under certain circumstances, however, heterogeneity can impede the group process: The group process is impeded when members cannot see beyond their own cultural perspectives to respect and value ideas and opinions that differ from their own. When Kristi and Luke became disgruntled with Nick's opinions about seat belt safety, they were allowing heterogene-

Discussion Tip
According to Sellnow, under what circumstances can heterogeneity impede the group process? Under what circumstances might heterogeneous groups be more effective than homogeneous groups?

ity to become a problem rather than an advantage. To ensure that heterogeneity proves advantageous, then, all members must agree to respect different perceptions and beliefs, including those arising from different cultural backgrounds. Ideally, all members must understand that multiple perspectives can enhance the quality of the group process and outcome.

Group Size

Discussion Tip
What is the ideal size for a problem-solving group? In what ways might hierarchies damage the group's chances for success?

A small group must have at least three members but can have as many as twenty. Most communication specialists agree that the ideal size for a problem-solving group ranges between four and seven people (Bales, 1955). Groups comprised of fewer than four people tend to lack diversity of perspectives. Groups with more than seven people tend to develop hierarchies and subgroups. **Hierarchies** occur when members of a group are seen as having different ranks. Hierarchies can damage the group's chances for success because, once they develop, members at the top of the hierarchy begin to dominate the discussion while those at the bottom become silent and dissatisfied with the group process (Wood et al., 1992). **Subgroups** are smaller groups within the group. For example, if three people in a group disagree with the others on the issue, they might form a subgroup, which could begin to disagree on other issues as well. Ongoing disagreement could ultimately lead to failure.

Group Goal

A **group goal** is a collective purpose that unifies members. This purpose could be specific, like persuading listeners to support coed dormitories on campus, or fairly vague, like improving campus safety. The more specific the goal, the more effective the group is likely to be. Thus, groups that begin with a vague goal work to make their goal more concrete. The students pursuing campus safety, for example, might decide to focus specifically on the possibility of a campus escort service between the hours of 11 P.M. and 6 A.M.

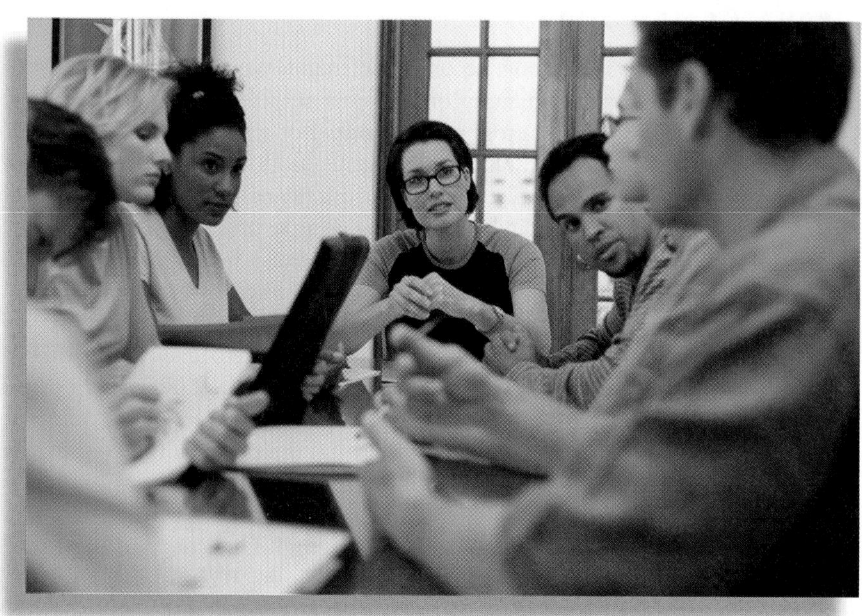

The ideal size for a problem-solving group ranges between four and seven people.

Your group goal might be partially imposed from outside the group. In your speech class, for example, your instructor might require you to present an informative or a persuasive speech or might require you to research a campus or community issue. Even in these cases, though, your group still determines its goal—and how specific the goal is. Keep in mind, then, that a group without a clear and specific purpose falters and ultimately fails. We've already seen, for individual presentations, the importance of narrowing your topic to arrive at a specific thesis statement. With groups, having a specific goal is only the first step. It's equally important to make certain that all members understand and are committed to the specific group goal.

> ***What Do You Think?***
>
> *Recall a small group you were involved in where members disagreed about what to do. Why couldn't members agree on the goal? What was the outcome and how satisfied were you with it?*

Group History

Group history refers to members' perceptions of the past work done by the group and its members. Every group begins developing a history from the first moment of the first meeting. In fact, in your speech class, each small group is a subset of a larger group—that is, the entire class—and so has a history that predates its first meeting. For example, Bryn, Julio, Kristi, and Luke's negative assumptions about Nick were based on Nick's behaviors in the group history of the class.

A positive group history, characterized by favorable perceptions, increases the group's likelihood of success. Success, in turn, leads to a more positive group history. For this reason, it's important to start off on the right foot. Research shows that initial successes lead members to have confidence in the group's capacity to meet future challenges (Krayer & Fiechtner, 1984).

Discussion Tip
Have students discuss situations in which favorable perceptions might increase the group's likelihood of success. Encourage students to discuss strategies for avoiding scapegoating.

A group's history doesn't always relate to reality. This can be a problem, especially when it takes the form of scapegoating. **Scapegoating** is the tendency to blame one or more members for the failure of the group. Since assigning blame is never as productive as seeking solutions, scapegoating is a recipe for certain failure for the group. If Nick's group had scapegoated Nick, rather than figuring out the contributions Nick had to offer, they would not have developed an effective presentation. In short, it's important to create a positive group history.

Many of the potential disadvantages of working in small groups can be reduced, avoided, or even turned into advantages by capitalizing on what we've discussed regarding group composition, group size, group goal, and group history. Following this advice will help make your small group experiences positive, both in the classroom and beyond it.

Discussion Tip
Ask students to list the strengths and weaknesses of working in a problem-solving group. Have students identify specific situations in which they have had positive and negative experiences.

Effective Leadership in Small Groups

To work effectively, a small group must have effective leadership. Traditionally, leadership was seen as a function that belonged to a single group member, the leader. Today, however, we perceive **leadership** as a range of diverse functions, which should ideally be shared by various group members. Have you ever been in

DILBERT reprinted by permission of United Feature Syndicate, Inc.

a small group that failed because the "leader" could not lead? The sharing of leadership functions avoids this problem and, as we'll see, makes it possible for functions to be done by those who can do them most effectively. To understand what makes for effective leadership, let's discuss the leadership functions, kinds of leaders, and leadership styles.

Functions of Leadership

Teaching Tip
Assign students to small groups and instruct them to create a definition of leadership and followership. Also, have students discuss effective leadership and followership traits.

There are three main kinds of leadership functions. Each kind meets a different set of group needs: task needs, relational needs, and housekeeping needs. It's because these needs are too diverse to be effectively met by a single person that leadership is usually most effective when it is shared. It follows that for effective leadership to occur, all group members must understand the different needs and functions of leadership, as well as their own leadership strengths.

Task Needs

Task needs concern substantive actions that must be taken in order for the group to achieve its goal. Task needs include all those things related to keeping the group on task—that is, moving toward the goal. These include:

- Setting and sticking to the agenda.
- Distributing the workload.
- Providing content for the discussion.
- Raising questions and posing alternative perspectives.
- Formulating criteria for evaluating possible solutions.
- Helping the group reach a decision on its final solution.

Technology Tip
http://www.nwlink.com/~donclark/leader/leadchr.html
This Web page contains a definition of leadership and describes several effective leadership traits. Have students visit this site and write a brief essay summarizing their findings.

As you can see, task needs cover a range of actions. The key is to meet each of these needs in some way—that is, someone usually assumes primary responsibility for each function. Consider which leadership functions you are particularly suited to fill as you read about group member roles related to task needs: initiator, expediter, information giver, information seeker, analyzer, and evaluator.

The **initiator** proposes new ideas and approaches, as well as distributes the initial workload. That is, you set the initial agenda in terms of what needs to be done and how to divide the workload into manageable pieces.

The **expediter** helps the group stick to the agenda. You perceive when the group is going astray and then lead them back to the problem at hand. In other words, you keep the group focused on the agenda, redirecting the discussion when necessary.

The **information giver** provides content for the discussion. More specifically, you might do research, organize your findings, and bring them to the group so they can provide a foundation for the group discussion and problem-solving process.

The **information seeker** raises questions and probes into the contributions of others. As you listen to the research and conclusions presented, you might pose alternative points of view and ask questions that will encourage group members to come up with yet other perspectives.

The **analyzer** helps the group relate the evidence provided by the information seeker to the issues that are at the core of the problem. Ultimately, the analyzer helps the group reach a decision about a conclusion, solution, or course of action.

The **evaluator** helps the group develop criteria for evaluating a conclusion, solution, or course of action and then makes an effort to apply those criteria to the group's decision.

Relational Needs

Relational needs are those involving interpersonal relationships among group members. Leadership functions that meet these needs essentially involve fostering and maintaining positive interpersonal relationships. These functions therefore include the following:

- Promoting self-esteem among members.
- Supporting divergent ideas.
- Encouraging reticent members to contribute to the discussion.
- Ensuring that all members feel satisfied with group outcomes.
- Dealing effectively with conflicts among members.

As with task needs, the key is to meet each of these relational needs in some way. Consider again which leadership functions you are particularly suited to fill as you read about group member roles related to relational needs: supporter, harmonizer, and gatekeeper.

The **supporter** responds favorably when good points are made. The response can be verbal (e.g., "good point" or "that's an interesting idea") or nonverbal (e.g., a smile or nod). All members should be supportive of course, but by being particularly diligent about recognizing contributions, you can improve the atmosphere in the group.

The **harmonizer** recognizes and deals with misunderstandings and disagreements as they occur. As harmonizer, you need to notice when someone appears upset and to be good at isolating the issues from the people and refocusing discussion accordingly.

The **gatekeeper** helps keep the communication channels open for everyone. For example, you notice when someone wants to talk, but can't break in to the conversation, and help them do so. You notice when someone is withdrawing from the conversation and try to bring them back in. And you realize when someone is monopolizing the conversation and are able to redirect it.

Housekeeping Needs

Housekeeping needs concern the many details that need to be kept. Leadership functions that meet housekeeping needs include the following:

- Deciding where and when the group will meet.
- Reserving a room for the meeting.
- Taking notes during the meeting.
- Summarizing the group's progress at the end of each meeting.

As with the task and relational needs, different members might be better suited to fill each of these leadership functions. Are you particularly suited to fill any of these functions? Consider them according to these group member roles related to housekeeping needs: administrator and recorder.

The **administrator** determines where and when the group will meet. To do so, you solicit and coordinate schedules in order to slate the meeting at a time when all members are available. You also make sure an appropriate room is available and do what is necessary to reserve it, as well as any equipment or special accommodations required for the meeting. And you communicate to all members in advance when and where the group will meet.

The **recorder** takes notes during the meeting and summarizes them for everyone at the end. This summary is often articulated both orally and in written form. You prepare and distribute the written summary after the meeting in preparation for the next meeting.

Discussion Tip
According to Sellnow, why are all three kinds of leadership discussed in this chapter essential to effective group process? What leadership functions are you most comfortable with?

All three kinds of leadership functions are essential to the effective group process. Clearly, a group can't function effectively unless necessary actions are taken, group members work together well, and details are attended to. Although everyone should do his or her part to fulfill the leadership functions to some degree, usually one person assumes primary responsibility for particular roles related to these needs. In fact, there may be a connection between excelling at a particular role and preferred learning style. If functions are divided, members can be responsible for those leadership functions they feel most capable of performing.

It is important that leadership functions be filled on this basis rather than on some arbitrary basis such as gender stereotypes. For example, although some studies have shown that women tend to meet the relational needs of a group slightly more effectively than men, it would be wrong to assume that the women in the group would be the best relational leaders (Helgesen, 1990). Nor would it be appropriate to assume that all the men would perform task-related leadership functions better than the women. In fact, some studies indicate that women in general are more adept at keeping the group focused on its task than are men (Shimanoff, & Jenkins, 1992). In short, each person should take on the leadership functions he or she can do best.

What Do You Think?

Consider the task, relational, and housekeeping leadership functions we've just discussed and the group member roles related to each of them. Which roles do you think you are particularly suited to fill? Are there any that you believe you are not so suited to fill? Why or why not?

Kinds of Leaders

Although in many small groups today leadership functions are shared, in some groups most of these functions are concentrated in a single leader. When we look at why this occurs, we can distinguish three kinds of leaders: designated leaders, emergent leaders, and implied leaders.

A **designated leader** is a person appointed as leader when the group is formed. Designated leaders can be effective for groups that meet once to perform a specific task. Under these circumstances, it's efficient to have a single leader, particularly one whose strengths lie in the area of task needs. However, designated leaders tend to be ineffective for other kinds of groups because, as we've seen, very rarely is one person most skilled at all the functions of leadership.

Teaching Tip
Have students complete the Leadership Analysis assignment contained in the Activities section before you discuss this chapter in class. This activity will serve as a springboard for an in-class discussion of leadership.

Sometimes a leader might emerge naturally during the group process. An **emergent leader** is someone who takes the initiative, stepping in to fill such functions as arranging the meetings, setting the agenda, and keeping the discussion focused. Notice that these actions concern task and housekeeping needs; typically, an emergent leader is someone whose strengths lie in meeting such needs. An emergent leader can be effective as long as he or she does not assume an authoritarian style, as discussed in the next section.

Most often, the emergent leader is also an implied leader. An **implied leader** is an individual who, in a workplace group, has the highest status or whom the other members perceive as having the highest status or the greatest expertise in the area. In a public speaking classroom, the implied leader might simply be the student who has delivered the best speeches or even the student who tends to talk the most during class discussions. Unfortunately, the group members' perception of the individual's status or expertise may, in fact, not be accurate. Someone who talks the most does not necessarily make the best leader.

> ***What Do You Think?***
>
> *Consider a group you have belonged to where the leader was designated. How effective was that group? Would the group have been more effective with shared leadership? Why or why not?*

Each of these leadership types has its limitations and risks. It becomes clear that designating a leader or allowing an implied leader to emerge may not be as effective as dividing leadership functions among group members.

Leadership Styles

Any small group, regardless of the kind of leader it has or if it operates using shared leadership, develops a **leadership style**—that is, a style of communicating and operating. Research reveals that there are three main leadership styles: authoritarian, laissez-faire, and democratic. The leadership style of your group can affect both its atmosphere and its productivity.

Teaching Tip
Develop a series of overheads illustrating the different leadership styles (authoritarianism, laissez-faire, and democratic) discussed in this chapter. This will help students distinguish one from another.

An **authoritarian leadership style** is directive, controlling, and dictatorial. This style tends to occur in groups where someone takes on the role of leader rather than in groups where leadership is shared. Directions for discussion are clearly set, and specific tasks are assigned to different members. Interaction among members is, explicitly or implicitly, discouraged. This style can be efficient and effective only under certain circumstances: It can work well for groups that meet one time to complete a specific task or for groups with a leader who is much more knowledgeable than the other members (White & Lippitt, 1968). For example, coaches can work effectively using this style as long as the players respect their superior knowledge. However, this efficiency may come at the expense of a positive climate, good morale among members, and the quality of the outcome. Apathy and resentment are common responses to this leadership style (Gibb, 1969; Lewin et al., 1939).

Teaching Tip
Remind students that leadership styles may need to change based on the situation or the nature of the task.

In contrast, a **laissez-faire leadership style** is nondirective and passive. In the groups that adopt this style, no one provides specific guidance or direction. The group moves toward its goal without working out the details of how it will get there. This style can be effective when a group consists of members who are mature, experienced, and self-directed. However, in most cases, groups need guidance in order to sustain a good atmosphere and be focused and productive. Hence, this style is not recommended (Bass, 1990; White & Lippitt, 1960). Its inefficiencies typically leave group members feeling frustrated.

Although the best leadership style for a group depends on various factors, most researchers agree that generally it's a democratic leadership style. A **democratic leadership style** is directive but not rigid. This style tends to encourage all members to take initiative and to participate in decision making. Since democratic leadership generally leads to good communication among members, it promotes group morale and positive results (Gibb, 1969; White & Lippitt, 1969).

Responsibilities of Group Members

Teaching Tip
For a creative project that gives students an opportunity to analyze group responsibilities, see the Responsibility Analysis assignment contained in the Activities section of this chapter.

Since we've seen that leadership functions are best shared, the following discussion is of groups where these functions are shared. In such a group, members, to be ethical, must do two things: respect and support the group and its goal, and value the contributions of each of its members. These things must be fulfilled by each member for the group to meet its task, relational, and housekeeping needs—that is, to function effectively. More specifically, each group member has five responsibilities:

- Being committed to the group goal.
- Keeping the discussion on track.
- Completing individual assignments.
- Managing interpersonal conflicts.
- Encouraging input from all members.

Be Committed to the Group Goal

Teaching Tip
If you are having students complete a group project, inform them that group interdependence should be a particularly salient concern. Students should be aware of the fact that their performance will affect the grade of every other member of the group.

In your public speaking class, being committed to the group goal means being committed to earning a good grade. It also means working together toward a solution and supporting that solution even if it doesn't fully fit your own position. Thus, in the example at the beginning of the chapter, the group took Nick's research and opinions into account and Nick agreed to support the group's ultimate recommendation—that seat belts be required. Being committed to the group goal, then, means finding a way to align your personal goals with the group goal as well as value the contributions of all members.

Keep the Discussion on Track

Although, as we discussed earlier, one member might most often perform the leadership function of keeping the discussion on track, this is a responsibility all members should share to a certain extent. It's irresponsible, unproductive, and ultimately unethical to get the discussion off track because you don't agree with what's being said, because you want to talk about personal matters, or for any other reason. It is your responsibility to make sure that your own input is relevant and to pitch in when necessary if other group members seem to be getting the discussion off track.

Complete Individual Assignments

A small group gives you the advantage of dividing up the work. The other side of this coin is that you are responsible to the group for completing your particular part of the work. This responsibility is more readily fulfilled if group members can volunteer for assignments rather than having assignments imposed upon them. By volunteering, members can choose the assignments that they feel most capable of doing. Bryn, for example, has high public speaking anxiety. As a graphic design major, she offered to prepare the visual materials for the presentation and do library research. Bryn and the group were more effective because she volunteered to complete assignments in areas where she was most competent.

Manage Conflict Among Group Members

All small groups experience some **conflict**—disagreement over issues or courses of action to be taken. Not only is conflict normal, but if managed appropriately, it can actually be beneficial to the group. Appropriately managed conflict can stimulate thinking, foster open communication, encourage diverse opinions, enlarge members' understanding of the issues, and ultimately make the group more productive. In fact, groups that *don't* experience some conflict run the risk of problems, especially of groupthink. **Groupthink** occurs when group members' desire to agree with one another and get along keeps them from fully discussing the issues, raising questions, or posing alternatives. Groups that succumb to groupthink are less likely to make the best decisions. Thus, it is the responsibility of all members to know the causes of conflict and not necessarily to avoid conflict, but rather help manage it when it appears.

Technology Tip
http://www.conflict-resolution.net/articles/

This Web site, hosted by the Conflict Resolution Resource Center, offers excellent information regarding conflict management. Have students visit this site and write a brief essay summarizing effective conflict management skills.

What, then, are some of the causes of conflict? Conflict in groups often stems directly from lack of agreement on issues and goals. A member may feel his or her views are incompatible with those of the other members. This is how Nick felt initially, since his opinions about seat belt laws were directly opposed to those of the others. Conflict may also stem from personal factors. For example, it might arise if a member feels his or her ego is being threatened, or is frustrated by the behavior of another member. Kristi and Luke initially felt frustrated because of Nick's behavior in previous class sessions.

Technology Tip
http://choo.fis.utoronto.ca/FIS/Courses/LIS2149/Groupthink.html

For a model of groupthink, see this Web page developed by Chun Wei Choo (faculty member of the faculty of information studies at the University of Toronto).

How should conflict be managed? The key is to shape the conflict so that it is constructive rather than destructive. Destructive conflict is marked by a competitive focus, self-interest, and a win-lose orientation (where people think in terms of "winners" and "losers"). Such conflict negatively affects the atmosphere and members may be reluctant to share their ideas because they are afraid of being personally attacked or criticized by others. Constructive conflict, on the other hand, occurs when all members understand that disagreements are a natural part of a productive group process. Hence, communication is cooperative. Members listen to opposing ideas openly and respectfully. There is a collective win-win attitude among members.

Teaching Tip
Group members must utilize effective listening skills to properly manage conflicts. Instruct students to revisit the material on listening in Chapter 4.

To shape conflict so that it is constructive, begin by separating the issues from the people involved. By focusing on issues rather than personalities, the group can clarify the issues and any misunderstandings that might have arisen. Once the issues are clarified, all members can offer input and the input can be more productive. To ensure that discussion is more productive, keep your emotions in check and phrase your comments in a descriptive, rather than judgmental, way. Finally, seek a win-win compromise rather than a win-lose solution. Whereas Kristi and Luke wanted to institute a win-lose solution by ignoring Nick's ideas, Bryn listened to his ideas and argued that they should be incorporated into the speech. In doing so, Bryn managed conflict ethically and effectively. Once you accept the fact that conflict in groups is natural, you can manage it in ways that enable you to better meet your goal.

Managing Conflict

1. Focus on issues, not personalities.
2. Try to clarify any misunderstandings.
3. Keep emotions in check.
4. Phrase comments descriptively, not judgmentally.
5. Seek ways to compromise.

Encourage Input From All Members

All too often in small group discussions, the more quiet members are overshadowed by the extroverts. If a member seems quiet, it is wrong to assume he or she has nothing to contribute. On the contrary, all members have valuable perspectives to share. If you are an extrovert, you have a special responsibility to refrain from dominating the discussion and ask others for their opinions as well. Bryn, for example, tends to be quiet during group discussions because of her speech anxiety, yet she was the one who realized how Nick's ideas could enhance the group's presentation. Because Kristi asked for Bryn's opinion, Bryn was able to offer the group a new perspective. Hence, it is the ethical responsibility of all members to both share their own ideas and encourage other members to participate in the discussion.

Each group member must adhere to these five responsibilities for a couple of reasons. First, doing so will ensure that the leadership functions are met, thus making the group more productive and effective. Second, doing so

What Do You Think?

Look over the five responsibilities of group members. Which of these responsibilities do you think come most naturally to you? Which should you pay special attention to and work at? Why? How?

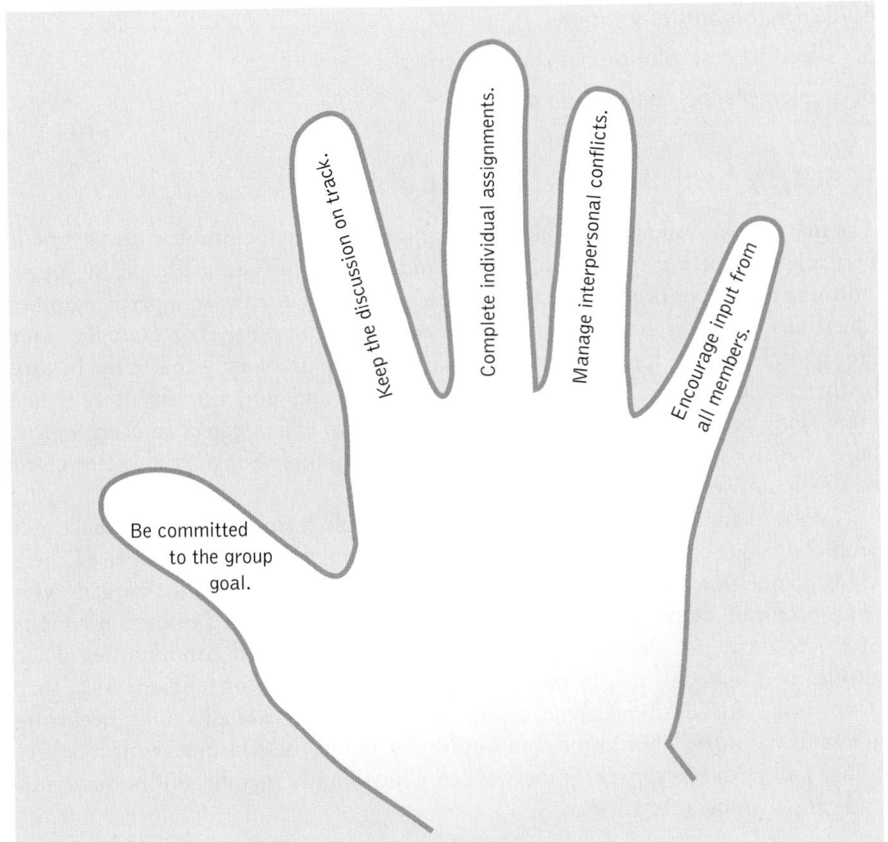

FIGURE 18–1
Group Member Responsibilities

demonstrates ethical behavior, both to the group as a whole and to the other individuals who are members of it. Adhering to these responsibilities makes you an ethical group member because doing so demonstrates that you respect and support the group and its goal, as well as value the contributions of each of the members (see Figure 18–1).

The Process of Systematic Group Problem Solving

A group needs a concrete approach to problem solving in order to come up with productive solutions in a short amount of time. The approach essentially gives the group a plan—or method to follow—for reaching its goal. When your group uses **systematic problem solving,** you identify a problem and, through a process of reasoning, attempt to discover the best way to solve it. After generating a host of potential solutions, you engage in a process of elimination until only the best solution remains. Essentially, your plan has six key steps (Dewey, 1933):

Teaching Tip
To give students an opportunity to practice systematic problem solving, see the Systematic Problem Solving assignment located in the Activities section of this chapter.

1. Identify and define the problem.
2. Analyze the problem.
3. Determine criteria for judging solutions.

4. Generate a host of solutions.
5. Select the best solution based on the criteria.
6. Implement the agreed-upon solution.

Identify and Define the Problem

Discussion Tip
Ask students to discuss the types of problem-solving groups they have participated in recently. How did these groups go about the process of problem solving? What problems did they encounter working in these groups? How might they avoid these problems in the future?

The first step in systematic problem solving is to identify the problem and define it in a way all group members understand and agree with. Groups begin by brainstorming a number of problems or felt needs and then narrow to a particular one. Questions can help groups identify and define the problem. For example, your group might ask the following questions: What is the problem? What is the history of the problem? Who is affected by this problem and how does it affect them? How many people are affected, in what ways, and to what degree? In other words, how extensive is the problem? Group members may find they must do research to be able to answer these questions.

Matt, Shannon, Pam, and Michelle, for example, identified gang violence as a problem in our country. In order to define the problem, however, they used these kinds of questions to guide their research. Hence, they discovered that gang violence occurs all across our nation. Gang violence is not isolated to certain regions of the country, nor does it occur only in densely populated communities. They also learned that victims can be of any age, race, ethnicity, or religion. And, they discovered statistics about the growing number of gang-related crimes occurring across the country. They also found out how many of these crimes result in severe injury and in death, as well as the ways in which family members of both victims and gang members are affected.

Analyze the Problem

Once the problem has been identified and defined, it can be analyzed. Again, questions can prove useful. They might include the following: Can the problem be subdivided into a series of smaller problems? Why has the problem occurred? What are the symptoms of the problem? What methods already exist for dealing with the problem? What are the limitations of those methods? Again, these questions are likely to lead group members to conduct additional research. Analyzing the problem in this way helps groups discover underlying causes of particular problems, causes that might need to be eliminated in order to successfully solve the problem.

Matt, Shannon, Pam, and Michelle discovered two important reasons why young people join gangs: for a sense of belonging and for something to do. Analyzing the problem revealed how many young gang members come from dysfunctional homes, as well as how many are enticed to join because they aren't involved in other kinds of group-related activities like sports, music, and so forth. They also discovered two underlying reasons why gang members commit more violent crimes than gangs did twenty years ago: easier access to guns and less ability to control anger. These causes proved very important to selecting a solution later.

Determine Criteria for Judging Solutions

Criteria are essentially standards you'll use for judging the merits of each proposed solution. In other words, criteria provide a blueprint for evaluating potential solutions. Without clear criteria, groups can easily select solutions that don't adequately address the real problem, or even select solutions that create a host of new problems. Questions you might ask when developing criteria include the following: Exactly what must your solutions achieve? Are there any factors that might limit your choice of solutions (cost, feasibility, location, complexity, expedience, risk/benefit ratio, etc.)? Once you've come up with criteria, you must prioritize your list. Which factors are most important? Which are least important? Which factors must be addressed for an ideal solution? Which must be addressed for an adequate solution?

After a good deal of discussion, Matt, Shannon, Pam, and Michelle decided on these criteria:

- *Expedience.* The solutions should be ones that can be implemented quickly, since lives are at stake.
- *Complexity.* The solutions should be simple to implement so they are more likely to be enacted.
- *Cost.* The solutions should not raise taxes.
- *Freedom.* The solutions should not infringe on the constitutional right to bear arms.

Generate a Host of Solutions

Having gained a better understanding as a result of the analysis, members brainstorm a host of possible solutions to the problem. At least one group member should record all these possible solutions as they are suggested. During this brainstorming phase, it is imperative that the group members withhold judgment and criticisms. To ensure that creativity is not stifled, no solution should be ignored or thrown out. Try to come up with at least six or seven solutions before you move on to the next step.

Teaching Tip
Groups may encounter problems when they rush too quickly to the solution before fully analyzing the problem. Remind students that such haste can seriously undermine the effectiveness of the group.

Matt, Shannon, Pam, and Michelle came up with these possible solutions:

- Make guns illegal.
- Make gang participation a felony punishable by law.
- Make parents accountable for the actions of their children.
- Offer anger management training to children.
- Provide alternative activities for youth.
- Crack down on the illegal gun market.

Select the Best Solution

It's at this point that judgments come into play. These judgments should be based on the criteria established by the group. You should consider each solution as it addresses the criteria and eliminate those solutions that do not meet them adequately. In addition to applying the criteria, your group might ask questions like the following as you discuss each potential solution: How will the solution solve the problem? How difficult will the solution be to implement? How likely is the solution to be successful? What additional benefits might result from implementing the solution? What problems might be caused? The group can use the criteria and questions to eliminate solutions. Once all the possible solutions have been considered, the group can decide on the best solution(s).

Teaching Tip
Ask students to generate a list of issues that may pose serious problems to the campus or community. Assign students to small groups and have them generate potential solutions using the problem-solving guidelines presented in this chapter.

Let's consider the solutions Matt, Shannon, Pam, and Michelle came up with based on their criteria and these kinds of questions:

- *Make guns illegal.* The group eliminated this solution because it infringes on the constitutional right to bear arms and because it would not be expedient to implement.
- *Make gang participation a felony punishable by law.* This solution was also eliminated because it would increase taxes, since more prisons would need to be built and because making it into a law would take a great deal of time.
- *Make parents accountable for the actions of their children.* Since Florida has a model program for making parents accountable, this solution was selected. It meets the criteria adequately.
- *Offer anger management training to children.* Although this seemed like a good idea, it was rejected because it failed to meet three of the four criteria: expedience, complexity, and cost.
- *Provide alternative activities for youth.* This solution was selected because it meets three of the four criteria. Although such programs might increase taxes, the group determined that they could propose programs that would not do so, as well. Hence, although it was not considered ideal in meeting the criteria, it did seem adequate.
- *Crack down on the illegal gun market.* Missouri has a program that could be modeled in other states. Hence, it could be expedient and fairly simply to duplicate. This solution was also accepted since it meets three of the four criteria. The only criterion that seemed questionable was cost.

The group members decided to develop a three-part solution. They would argue for parental accountability, a crackdown on the illegal gun market, and alternative programs and activities for adolescents.

Implement the Agreed-Upon Solution

Finally, the group can implement the agreed-upon solution or, if it is presenting the solution to others for implementation, can make recommendations for how the solution should be implemented. The group has already considered implementation in terms of deciding which solution(s) should be enacted, but must now fill in all the details. What tasks are required by the solution(s)? Who will carry out these tasks? What is a reasonable time frame for implementation generally and for each of the tasks specifically? These details are important factors to consider before any solution(s) will likely be enacted. Matt, Shannon, Pam, and Michelle created implementation plans both for parental accountability (based on Florida's documents) and cracking down on the illegal gun market (based on Missouri's documents), which could be duplicated in other states. They also provided concrete program ideas and clear strategies for churches, businesses, and service groups to implement for alternative programs for area youth. As such, they didn't merely offer solutions; they provided plans for implementing them.

Teaching Tip

Virtually any segment of the popular movie Apollo 13 can be used to illustrate a problem-solving group at work. Show a portion of this movie in class and follow it with a discussion of the guidelines presented in this chapter.

Systematic Problem Solving

- Identify and define the problem.
- Analyze the problem.

- Determine criteria for judging solutions.
- Generate a host of solutions.
- Select the best solution.
- Implement the agreed-upon solution(s).

Preparing Group Presentations

Once your group has successfully worked through the systematic problem-solving process, you are ready to prepare your group presentation. One effective way of doing this is to use the following five-step process:

1. Divide the topic into areas of responsibility.
2. Draft an outline of your topic area.
3. Combine member outlines to form a group outline.
4. Finalize the details of delivery.
5. Practice your presentation.

Divide the Topic into Areas of Responsibility

As a group, you should determine your thesis and main point design. Each member can then be responsible for researching and organizing the content necessary to develop a particular main point. If there are more people in your group than there are main points in your presentation, you might, for example, assign more than one person to a topic area or assign one person to develop and integrate presentational aids.

Draft an Outline of Your Topic Area

Each group member should construct an outline for his or her main point. Even though your outline is for only part of the presentation, it must still be thorough. Hence, you need to follow the steps for outline creation that were detailed in Chapter 10.

Teaching Tip
To facilitate this process, prepare and distribute an outline template for group members. Also, have the students turn outlines in early for constructive feedback.

Combine Member Outlines to Form a Group Outline

Once the individual outlines are completed, the group is ready to combine them into a single outline. Members should share their individual outlines and then, as a group, develop the transitions between main points and make any other changes needed for continuity and consistency. If no member was responsible for developing the introduction and conclusion, the group should create them now. Likewise, presentational aids should be integrated at this point.

Finalize the Details of Delivery

Because you're making a group presentation, you have more than the usual number of decisions to make about delivery. First and foremost, you need to decide who will speak and when. As we'll see in the next section, there are various presentation formats—oral reports, symposium presentations, and panel discussions. Which presentation format will you use? Also, various details need to be determined if your presentation is to flow smoothly. Who will introduce the speakers and when? Where will group members sit when they are not speaking? How will presentational aids be displayed and who will be responsible for displaying them?

Practice Your Presentation

It is crucial that you practice both individually and as a group. Of course, you'll use effective delivery skills as described in Chapter 12. However, as we've just discussed, group presentations pose some additional complexities. This means there is even more you and your group need to make sure you've gotten down, which means there is even more need for practice.

Discussion Tip
According to Sellnow, what are the key characteristics of the oral report, symposium, and panel discussion presentation formats? Which format is most appropriate for this class?

Group Presentation Formats

Many problem-solving groups are asked to present their findings in both written and oral reports. In your public speaking class, you will probably be asked to present your findings in the form of a formal typed outline and some sort of oral presentation. Let's look at the most common formats for oral group presentations.

Oral Report

Groups that give an **oral report** select one person to present all the group's information in an individual speech. In essence, one speaker represents the group, its work, and its results.

Symposium Presentation

In a **symposium presentation,** all members of the group typically present a portion of the information. All members are seated in front of the audience. One member acts as the moderator. He or she offers the introductory and concluding remarks and provides transitions between speakers. In a way, the moderator provides the structure for the presentation. When introduced, each speaker moves to the lectern to deliver a speech on the aspect he or she is covering. After all speakers have finished, the moderator returns to the lectern to offer concluding remarks and possibly open the floor for questions and discussion. Questions can be directed to the group as a whole or to individuals within the group.

The way your group divides the content among speakers will, of course, depend on how you've organized your material. For example, each speaker might focus on one step of the problem-solving process. Or each member might focus on one major issue related to the topic. If the presentation is persuasive, successive speakers might focus on the problem, the cause, and the solution; or if it's persuasive and you've used Monroe's motivated sequence, successive speakers might focus on demonstrating a need, offering a plan, and visualizing the future. Regardless of the organizational pattern your group chooses, it is important to carefully plan each speaker's segment of the presentation to ensure that all aspects of the group's project are covered.

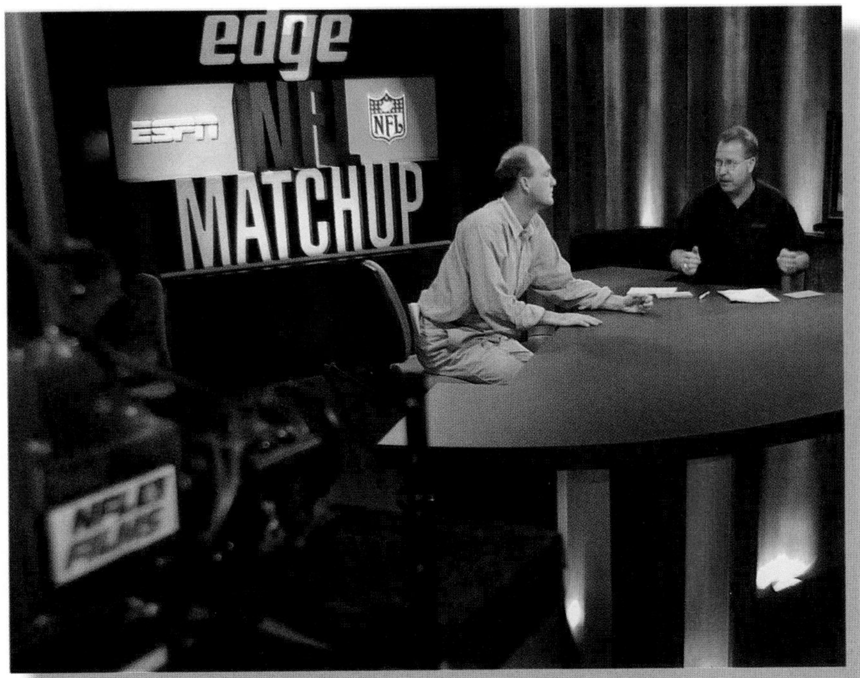

SportsCenter conducts panel discussions every time it is aired.

Panel Discussion

A **panel discussion** is actually a conversation among members of the group that takes place in front of an audience. Perhaps you've heard a panel of experts discuss a particular topic—for example, on radio or television talk shows like *Larry King Live* or *SportsCenter.* As in a symposium presentation, there is a moderator who introduces the topic and the speakers. The moderator's role is to interject questions and comments throughout the discussion, in order to clarify issues and keep the discussion on track. When the panelists speak, they use an impromptu style and keep their remarks brief. The panel discussion format is less formal than the oral report or symposium presentation. However, as with those formats, the topic is thoroughly researched in advance and the presentation is also planned and practiced, even if in a looser way.

Teaching Tip
To illustrate how panel discussions work, show students videotaped clips of such discussions on *Larry King Live.* Have students critique the panelists using the criteria presented in this chapter.

Evaluating Group Effectiveness

Just as the processes of preparing and presenting speeches are somewhat different for group speeches than for individual speeches, so is the process of evaluating effectiveness. Evaluations should focus on group dynamics during the preparation process as well as on the effectiveness of the presentation.

Evaluating Group Dynamics During the Preparation Process

To be effective, groups must work together as they define and analyze a problem, generate solutions, and select a course of action. They also need to work together

FIGURE 18–2
A Sample Evaluation Form for Group Dynamics

Directions: Use one form to evaluate each group member. Record meeting dates and attendance after each group meeting. Record summative evaluation and comments after all meetings have occurred.

Group Member Being Evaluated: ______________________________

Evaluator (your name): ______________________________

Meeting Dates and Attendance:

Meeting	Date	Present	Absent	Comments
1.				
2.				
3.				
4.				
5.				
etc.				

Responsibilities Summative Evaluation: Evaluate the effort made by the group member in terms of each of the five responsibilities as indicated below.

Rating Scale:

1 (poor)	2	3	4	5	6	7 (excellent)

(1) ____ **Committed to the goals of the group**
(rating) Critique (Provide a rationale for the rating you gave):

(2) ____ **Completes individual assignments**
(rating) Critique (Provide a rationale for the rating you gave):

(3) ____ **Avoids conflict and helps manage conflict**
(rating) Critique (Provide a rationale for the rating you gave):

(4) ____ **Encourages input from all members**
(rating) Critique (Provide a rationale for the rating you gave):

(5) ____ **Helps keep the discussion on track**
(rating) Critique (Provide a rationale for the rating you gave):

Overall critique of group dynamics as a whole:
_____ Critique:
(rating)

____

as they prepare their written report, which in some public speaking classrooms is the formal group outline, and practice the oral presentation.

Hence, it is important to evaluate group dynamics as it relates to the eventual outcome, which in most cases is the oral presentation. This can be done by obtaining from each group member written feedback on other members' efforts. Such evaluations can be based on the five responsibilities of group members, as in the sample evaluation form in Figure 18–2.

Like the evaluations business managers make of employees, these evaluations document the efforts of group members. They can be submitted to the instructor, just as they would be submitted to a supervisor. In business, these documents provide a basis for determining promotion, merit pay, and salary adjustments. In the classroom, they can provide a basis for determining one portion of each member's grade.

Teaching Tip
To heighten sensitivity to the problems of groupthink, make this issue a key factor in the evaluation of any group presentation. Also, remind students of the strategies for minimizing groupthink.

Evaluating Effectiveness of the Presentation

Effective group presentations depend on quality individual presentations as well as the overall effectiveness achieved collectively. Hence, evaluation of the presentation should be of each individual and of the group as a whole (see Figure 18–3). Again, this is not unlike the situation in business, where teams are evaluated on the basis of the usefulness of the team's solution and of individual team members' efforts toward developing and implementing that solution.

FIGURE 18–3
A Sample Evaluation Form for Group Presentations

Group Member Name: ______________________________

Critic (your name): ______________________________

Directions: Evaluate the effectiveness of each group member according to each of the following criteria for effective presentations individually and as a group.

Rating Scale:

1 (poor)	2	3	4	5	6	7 (excellent)

INDIVIDUAL PERFORMANCE CRITIQUE

______ **Delivery** (Use of voice and use of body)
(rating) Critique (Provide a rationale for the rating you gave):

______ **Structure** (Macrostructure and microstructure/language)
(rating) Critique (Provide a rationale for the rating you gave):

______ **Content** (Breadth and depth and listener relevance)
(rating) Critique (Provide a rationale for the rating you gave):

GROUP PERFORMANCE CRITIQUE

______ **Delivery** (Teamwork? Cooperation? Fluency? Use of aids?)
(rating) Critique (Provide a rationale for the rating you gave):

______ **Structure** (Balanced? Transitions? Flow? Attn/Clincher?)
(rating) Critique (Provide a rationale for the rating you gave):

______ **Content** (Thematic? Focused? Thorough? Construction of presentational aids?)
(rating) Critique (Provide a rationale for the rating you gave):

Overall Comments:

____

Teaching Tip
Remind students that group communication skills are likely to play a critical role in their success outside of academia. Have students write a brief essay linking the material in this chapter to their career interests.

Summary

Working in small groups is quickly becoming the preferred approach to solving problems and making decisions. It is therefore important to learn how to work and speak effectively in small groups.

The potential advantages of small group work far outweigh the disadvantages; the ultimate advantage is better solutions. To achieve these advantages it is important to understand leadership and group member functions as well as the processes of group problem solving and preparation of presentations. Your problem-solving small group will be more effective if it is heterogeneous, relatively small in size (five to seven members), and has a relatively focused specific goal.

Leadership in small groups consists of a range of diverse functions, which should ideally be shared by various group members. These functions are related to meeting task, relational, and housekeeping needs. Although leadership is usually most effective when shared among group members, sometimes a small group does have a specific leader that is designated, emergent, or implied. Leadership styles can be authoritarian, laissez-faire, or democratic. A democratic leadership style generally is the most effective for problem-solving small groups.

All members have certain responsibilities to the group. More specifically, all members need to be committed to the group goal, keep the discussion on track, complete individual assignments, manage conflicts among group members, and encourage input from all members.

Problem-solving small groups can also be most effective when they operate using a clear plan. The systematic problem-solving method consists of six steps designed for this purpose: Identify and define the problem, analyze the problem, determine criteria for judging solutions, generate a host of solutions, select the best solution based on the criteria, and implement the agreed-upon solution.

Group presentation formats include oral reports, symposium presentations, and panel discussions. Regardless of which format a group uses, several steps should be taken in preparing a presentation. Because group presentations differ from individual speeches, the evaluation process also differs to some degree: It looks at group dynamics during preparation and at both the group and the individual effectiveness of the presentation.

Finally, several essential steps must be taken when preparing and presenting group speeches, whether they take the form of an oral report, symposium, or panel discussion. Moreover, because group presentations differ from individual speeches, the means by which to evaluate group work also differ in certain ways. Working and speaking in small groups is becoming increasingly popular, in both personal and professional settings. When done effectively, it can increase productivity, improve morale, and even be fun. This chapter provides the groundwork for achieving those goals when working and speaking in small groups.

Activities

1. **Group Member Role Self Reports.** If you have formed a group for the purpose of working on a presentation, review the discussion of group member roles in this chapter. Each member should then write a self report indicating which

roles might be most appropriate, in view of his or her strengths and weaknesses. Discuss the reports and, as a group, identify which members will be most responsible for each of the roles.

2. **Group Sales Pitch.** Form groups of about five persons each. Pick an item that someone has with him or her (jewelry, school supply, chewing gum, etc.). As a group, devise a plan to sell that item to the class. To sell it, the group must generate a host of needs it may fulfill for their classmates and then convince the classmates of it. After about ten minutes or so, group members should discuss how the leadership functions were or were not met and by whom. Also discuss how responsibilities of group members were met and how they could be better met in the future. Present your findings to the rest of the class in the form of an oral report.
3. **Systematic Problem Solving.** Form groups of four or five persons. Choose a problem that's being debated on your campus. Once you have chosen a topic, work for about fifteen to twenty minutes to arrive at a solution and implementation plan using systematic problem solving. Present your solution to the class. Ask the class to evaluate your solution.
4. **Leadership Analysis.** Attend a meeting in your community. It can be a group to which you belong or one that is open to the public. Observe the group dynamics. Try to determine the degree to which each of the task, relational, and housekeeping needs are being met and by whom. Which roles are being played and by whom? (Task roles: initiator, expediter, information giver, information seeker, analyzer, evaluator. Relational roles: supporter, harmonizer, gatekeeper. Housekeeping roles: administrator, recorder.)
5. **Responsibilities Analysis.** Watch a group presentation on your campus, in your community, or on television (e.g., *Larry King Live, Point-Counterpoint, SportsCenter*, etc.). Evaluate each group member according to the responsibilities as detailed in Figure 18–2, as well as the presentation as detailed in Figure 18–3. Summarize your evaluations with a short paragraph indicating what you will and will not do in your own group presentation.

Key Terms

Administrator
Analyzer
Authoritarian leadership style
Conflict
Democratic leadership style
Designated leader
Emergent leader
Evaluator
Expediter
Gatekeeper
Group goal
Group history
Groupthink
Harmonizer
Heterogeous groups
Hierarchies
Homogeneous groups
Housekeeping needs
Implied leader
Information giver
Information seeker
Initiator
Laissez-faire leadership style
Leadership
Leadership style
Oral report
Panel discussion
Problem-solving group
Recorder
Relational needs
Scapegoating
Small group
Subgroups
Supporter
Symposium presentation
Systematic problem solving
Task needs

APPENDIX

Speeches for Analysis and Discussion

I Have a Dream

Martin Luther King, Jr.

Washington, D.C., August 28, 1963

I am happy to join with you today in what will go down in history as the greatest demonstration for freedom in the history of our nation.

Five score years ago, a great American, in whose symbolic shadow we stand today, signed the Emancipation Proclamation. This momentous decree came as a great beacon light of hope to millions of Negro slaves who had been seared in the flames of withering injustice. It came as a joyous daybreak to end the long night of captivity.

But one hundred years later, the Negro still is not free. One hundred years later, the life of the Negro is still sadly crippled by the manacles of segregation and the chains of discrimination. One hundred years later, the Negro lives on a lonely island of poverty in the midst of a vast ocean of material prosperity. One hundred years later, the Negro is still languishing in the corners of American society and finds himself an exile in his own land.

And so we've come here today to dramatize a shameful condition. In a sense we've come to our nation's Capitol to cash a check. When the architects of our republic wrote the magnificent words of the Constitution and the Declaration of Independence, they were signing a promissory note to which every American was to fall heir. This note was a promise that all men—yes, black men as well as white men—would be guaranteed the unalienable rights of life, liberty, and the pursuit of happiness.

It is obvious today that America has defaulted on this promissory note insofar as her citizens of color are concerned. Instead of honoring this sacred obligation, America has given the Negro people a bad check—a check which has come back marked "insufficient funds."

But we refuse to believe that the bank of justice is bankrupt. We refuse to believe that there are insufficient funds in the great vaults of opportunity of this nation. And so we've come to cash this check—a check that will give us upon demand the riches of freedom and the security of justice.

We have also come to this hallowed spot to remind America of the fierce urgency of now. This is no time to engage in the luxury of cooling off or to take the tranquilizing drug of gradualism. Now is the time to make real the promises of democracy. Now is the time to rise from the dark and desolate valley of segregation to the sunlit path of racial justice. Now is the time to lift our nation from the quicksands of racial injustice to the solid rock of brotherhood. Now is the time to make justice a reality for all of God's children.

It would be fatal for the nation to overlook the urgency of the moment. This sweltering summer of the Negro's legitimate discontent will not pass until there is an invigorating autumn of freedom and equality. Nineteen sixty-three is not an end, but a beginning. Those who hope that the

Negro needed to blow off steam and will now be content will have a rude awakening if the nation returns to business as usual. There will be neither rest nor tranquility in America until the Negro is granted his citizenship rights. The whirlwinds of revolt will continue to shake the foundations of our nation until the bright day of justice emerges.

But there is something that I must say to my people, who stand on the warm threshold which leads into the palace of justice. In the process of gaining our rightful place, we must not be guilty of wrongful deeds. Let us not seek to satisfy our thirst for freedom by drinking from the cup of bitterness and hatred.

We must forever conduct our struggle on the high plane of dignity and discipline. We must not allow our creative protest to degenerate into physical violence. Again and again we must rise to the majestic heights of meeting physical force with soul force.

The marvelous new militancy which has engulfed the Negro community must not lead us to a distrust of all white people. For many of our white brothers, as evidenced by their presence here today, have come to realize that their destiny is tied up with our destiny. They have come to realize that their freedom is inextricably bound to our freedom. We cannot walk alone.

As we walk, we must make the pledge that we shall always march ahead. We cannot turn back. There are those who are asking the devotees of civil rights, "When will you be satisfied?" We can never be satisfied as long as a Negro is the victim of the unspeakable horrors of police brutality. We can never be satisfied as long as our bodies, heavy with the fatigue of travel, cannot gain lodging in the motels of the highways and the hotels of the cities. We cannot be satisfied as long as a Negro in Mississippi cannot vote and a Negro in New York believes he has nothing for which to vote. No, no, we are not satisfied, and we will not be satisfied until justice rolls down like waters, and righteousness like a mighty stream.

I am not unmindful that some of you have come here out of great trials and tribulations. Some of you have come fresh from narrow jail cells. Some of you have come from areas where your quest for freedom left you battered by the storms of persecution and staggered by the winds of police brutality. You have been the veterans of creative suffering. Continue to work with the faith that unearned suffering is redemptive.

Go back to Mississippi, go back to Alabama, go back to South Carolina, go back to Georgia, go back to Louisiana, go back to the slums and ghettos of our Northern cities, knowing that somehow this situation can and will be changed. Let us not wallow in the valley of despair.

I say to you today, my friends, so even though we face the difficulties of today and tomorrow, I still have a dream. It is a dream deeply rooted in the American dream.

I have a dream that one day this nation will rise up and live out the true meaning of its creed: "We hold these truths to be self-evident: that all men are created equal."

I have a dream that one day on the red hills of Georgia the sons of former slaves and the sons of former slave owners will be able to sit down together at the table of brotherhood.

I have a dream that one day even the state of Mississippi, a state sweltering with the heat of injustice, sweltering with the heat of oppression, will be transformed into an oasis of freedom and justice.

I have a dream that my four little children will one day live in a nation where they will not be judged by the color of their skin but by the content of their character. I have a dream today.

I have a dream that one day, down in Alabama, with its vicious racists, with its governor having his lips dripping with the words of interposition and nullification, one day right there in Alabama little black boys and black girls will be able to join hands with little white boys and white girls as sisters and brothers. I have a dream today.

I have a dream that one day every valley shall be exalted, every hill and mountain shall be made low, the rough places will be made plain and the crooked places will be made straight, and the glory of the Lord shall be revealed, and all flesh shall see it together.

This is our hope. This is the faith that I go back to the South with. With this faith we will be able to hew out of the mountain of despair a stone of hope. With this faith we will be able to transform the jangling discords of our nation into a beautiful symphony of brotherhood. With this faith we will be able to work together, to pray together, to struggle together, to go to jail together, to stand up for freedom together, knowing that we will be free one day.

This will be the day—this will be the day when all of God's children will be able to sing with a new meaning, "My country 'tis of thee, sweet land of liberty, of thee I sing. Land where my fathers died, land of the pilgrim's pride, from every mountainside, let freedom ring." And if America is to be a great nation, this must become true.

So let freedom ring from the prodigious hilltops of New Hampshire. Let freedom ring from the mighty mountains of New York. Let freedom ring from the heightening Alleghenies of Pennsylvania!

Let freedom ring from the snowcapped Rockies of Colorado! Let freedom ring from the curvaceous peaks of California!

But not only that. Let freedom ring from Stone Mountain of Georgia!

Let freedom ring from Lookout Mountain of Tennessee!

Let freedom ring from every hill and every molehill of Mississippi. From every mountainside, let freedom ring.

And when this happens, when we allow freedom to ring—when we let it ring from every village and every hamlet, from every state and every city—we will be able to speed up that day when all of God's children, black men and white men, Jews and Gentiles, Protestants and Catholics, will be able to join hands and sing in the words of the old Negro spiritual, "Free at last! free at last! Thank God Almighty, we are free at last!"

Source: Delivered on the steps of the Lincoln Memorial in Washington, D.C. on August 28, 1963. Reprinted by arrangement with The Heirs to the Estate of Martin Luther King, Jr., c/o Joan Daves Agency as agent for the proprietor.

WHO THEN WILL SPEAK FOR THE COMMON GOOD?: DEMOCRATIC CONVENTION KEYNOTE ADDRESS

Barbara Jordan, Congresswoman

New York, July 12, 1976

One hundred and forty-four years ago, members of the Democratic Party first met in convention to select a presidential candidate. Since that time, Democrats have continued to convene once every four years and draft a party platform and nominate a presidential candidate. And our meeting this week is a continuation of that tradition.

But there is something different about tonight. There is something special about tonight. What is different? What is special? I, Barbara Jordan, am a keynote speaker.

A lot of years passed since 1832, and during that time it would have been most unusual for any national political party to ask that a Barbara Jordan deliver a keynote address . . . but tonight here I am. And I feel that notwithstanding the past that my presence here is one additional bit of evidence that the American dream need not forever be deferred.

Now that I have this grand distinction what in the world am I supposed to say?

I could easily spend this time praising the accomplishments of this party and attacking the Republicans, but I don't choose to do that.

I could list the many problems which Americans have. I could list the problems which cause people to feel cynical, angry, frustrated: problems which include lack of integrity in government; the feeling that the individual no longer counts; the reality of material and spiritual poverty; the feeling that the grand American experiment is failing or has failed. I could recite these problems and then I could sit down and offer no solutions. But I don't choose to do that either.

The citizens of America expect more. They deserve and they want more than a recital of problems.

We are a people in a quandary about the present. We are a people in search of our future. We are a people in search of a national community.

We are a people trying not only to solve the problems of the present: unemployment, inflation . . . but we are attempting on a larger scale to fulfill the promise of America. We are attempting to fulfill our national purpose; to create and sustain a society in which all of us are equal.

Throughout our history, when people have looked for new ways to solve their problems, and to uphold the principles of this nation, many times they have turned to political parties. They have often turned to the Democratic Party.

What is it, what is it about the Democratic Party that makes it the instrument that people use when they search for ways to shape their future? Well, I believe the answer to that question lies in our concept of governing. Our concept of governing is derived from our view of people. It is a concept deeply rooted in a set of beliefs firmly etched in the national conscience of all of us.

Now what are these beliefs?

First, we believe in equality for all and privileges for none. This is a belief that each American regardless of background has equal standing in the public forum, all of us. Because we believe this idea so firmly, we are inclusive rather than an exclusive party. Let everybody come.

I think it no accident that most of those emigrating to America in the 19th century identified with the Democratic Party. We are a heterogeneous party made up of Americans of diverse backgrounds.

We believe that the people are the source of all governmental power; that the authority of the people is to be extended, not restricted. This can be accomplished only by providing each citizen with every opportunity to participate in the management of the government. They must have that.

We believe that the government which represents the authority of all the people, not just one interest group, but all the people, has an obligation to actively underscore, actively seek to remove those obstacles which would block individual achievement . . . obstacles emanating from race, sex, economic condition. The government must seek to remove them.

We are a party of innovation. We do not reject our traditions, but we are willing to adapt to changing circumstances, when change we must. We are willing to suffer the discomfort of change in order to achieve a better future.

We have a positive vision of the future founded on the belief that the gap between the promise and reality of America can one day be finally closed. We believe that.

This, my friends, is the bedrock of our concept of governing. This is a part of the reason why Americans have turned to the Democratic Party. These are the foundations upon which a national community can be built.

Let's all understand that these guiding principles cannot be discarded for short-term political gains. They represent what this country is all about. They are indigenous to the American idea. And these are principles which are not negotiable.

In other times, I could stand here and give this kind of exposition on the beliefs of the Democratic Party and that would be enough. But today that is not enough. People want more. That is not sufficient reason for the majority of the people of this country to vote Democratic. We have made mistakes. In our haste to do all things for all people, we did not foresee the full consequences of our actions. And when the people raised their voices, we didn't hear. But our deafness was only a temporary condition, and not an irreversible condition.

Even as I stand here and admit that we have made mistakes I still believe that as the people of America sit in judgment on each party, they will recognize that our mistakes were mistakes of the heart. They'll recognize that.

And now we must look to the future. Let us heed the voice of the people and recognize their common sense. If we do not, we not only blaspheme our political heritage, we ignore the common ties that bind all Americans.

Many fear the future. Many are distrustful of their leaders and believe that their voices are never heard. Many seek only to satisfy their private work wants. To satisfy private interests.

But this is the great danger America faces. That we will cease to be one nation and become instead a collection of interest groups: city against suburb, region against region, individual against individual. Each seeking to satisfy private wants.

If that happens, who then will speak for America?

Who then will speak for the common good?

This is the question which must be answered in 1976.

Are we to be one people bound together by common spirit sharing in a common endeavor or will we become a divided nation?

For all of its uncertainty, we cannot flee the future. We must not become the new puritans and reject our society. We must address and master the future together. It can be done if we restore the belief that we share a sense of national community, that we share a common national endeavor. It can be done.

There is no executive order; there is no law that can require the American people to form a national community. This we must do as individuals and if we do it as individuals, there is no president of the United States who can veto that decision.

As a first step, we must restore our belief in ourselves. We are a generous people so why can't we be generous with each other? We need to take to heart the words spoken by Thomas Jefferson:

> Let us restore to social intercourse the harmony and that affection without which liberty and even life are but dreary things.

A nation is formed by the willingness of each of us to share in the responsibility for upholding the common good.

A government is invigorated when each of us is willing to participate in shaping the future of this nation.

In this election year we must define the common good and begin again to shape a common good and begin again to shape a common future. Let each person do his or her part. If one citizen is unwilling to participate, all of us are going to suffer. For the American idea, though it is shared by all of us, is realized in each one of us.

And now, what are those of us who are elected public officials supposed to do? We call ourselves public servants but I'll tell you this: we as public servants must set an example for the rest of the nation. It is hypocritical for the public official to admonish and exhort the people to uphold the common good. More is required of public officials than slogans and handshakes and press releases. More is required. We must hold ourselves strictly accountable. We must provide the people with a vision of the future.

If we promise as public officials, we must deliver. If we as public officials propose, we must produce. If we say to the American people it is time for you to be sacrificial; sacrifice. If the public official says that, we (public officials) must be the first to give. We must be. And again, if we make mistakes, we must be willing to admit them. We have to do that. What we have to do is strike a balance between the idea, the belief, that government ought to do nothing. Strike a balance.

Let there be no illusions about the difficulty of forming this kind of a national community. It's tough, difficult, not easy. But a spirit of harmony will survive in America only if each of us remembers that we share a common destiny.

I have confidence that we can form this kind of national community.

I have confidence that the Democratic Party can lead the way. I have confidence. We cannot improve on the system of government handed down to us by the founders of the Republic; there is no way to improve upon that. But what we can do is to find new ways to implement that system and realize our destiny.

Now, I began this speech by commenting to you on the uniqueness of a Barbara Jordan making the keynote address. Well, I am going to close my speech by quoting a Republican president and I ask you that as you listen to these words of Abraham Lincoln, relate them to the concept of national community in which every last one of us participates:

> As I would not be a slave, so I would not be a master. This expresses my idea of Democracy. Whatever differs from this, to the extent of the difference is no Democracy.

INAUGURAL ADDRESS

John F. Kennedy

Washington, D.C., January 20, 1961

Vice President Johnson, Mr. Speaker, Mr. Chief Justice, President Eisenhower, Vice President Nixon, President Truman, reverend clergy, fellow citizens, we observe today not a victory of party but a celebration of freedom—symbolizing an end, as well as a beginning—signifying renewal, as well as change. For I have sworn before you and Almighty God the same solemn oath our forebears prescribed nearly a century and three-quarters ago.

The world is very different now. For man holds in his mortal hands the power to abolish all forms of human poverty and all forms of human life. And yet the same revolutionary beliefs for which our forebears fought are still at issue around the globe—the belief that the rights of man come not from the generosity of the state, but from the hand of God.

We dare not forget today that we are the heirs of that first revolution. Let the word go forth from this time and place, to friend and foe alike, that the torch has been passed to a new generation of Americans—born in this century, tempered by war, disciplined by a hard and bitter peace, proud of our ancient heritage—and unwilling to witness or permit the slow undoing of those human rights to which this nation has always been committed, and to which we are committed today at home and around the world.

Let every nation know, whether it wishes us well or ill, that we shall pay any price, bear any burden, meet any hardship, support any friend, oppose any foe, in order to assure the survival and the success of liberty.

This much we pledge—and more.

To those old allies whose cultural and spiritual origins we share, we pledge the loyalty of faithful friends. United, there is little we cannot do in a host of cooperative ventures. Divided, there is little we can do—for we dare not meet a powerful challenge, at odds, and split asunder.

To those new states whom we welcome to the ranks of the free, we pledge our word that one form of colonial control shall not have passed away merely to be replaced by a far more iron tyranny. We shall not always expect to find them supporting our view. But we shall always hope to find them strongly supporting their own freedom—and to remember that, in the past, those who foolishly sought power by riding the back of the tiger ended up inside.

To those peoples in the huts and villages across the globe struggling to break the bonds of mass misery, we pledge our best efforts to help them help themselves, for whatever period is required—not because the Communists may be doing it, not because we seek their votes, but because it is right. If a free society cannot help the many who are poor, it cannot save the few who are rich.

To our sister republics south of our border: we offer a special pledge—to convert our good words into good deeds—in a new alliance for progress—to assist free men and free governments in casting off the chains of poverty. But this peaceful revolution of hope cannot become the prey of hostile powers. Let all our neighbors know that we shall join with them to oppose aggression or subversion anywhere in the Americas. And let every other power know that this hemisphere intends to remain the master of its own house.

To that world assembly of sovereign states, the United Nations, our last best hope in an age where the instruments of war have far outpaced the instruments of peace, we renew our pledge of support—to prevent it from becoming merely a forum for invective—to strengthen its shield of the new and the weak—and to enlarge the area in which its writ may run.

Finally, to those nations who would make themselves our adversary, we offer not a pledge but a request: that both sides begin anew the quest for peace, before the dark powers of destruction unleashed by science engulf all humanity in planned or accidental self-destruction.

We dare not tempt them with weakness. For only when our arms are sufficient beyond doubt can we be certain beyond doubt that they will never be employed.

But neither can two great and powerful groups of nations take comfort from our present course—both sides overburdened by the cost of modern weapons, both rightly alarmed by the steady spread of the deadly atom, yet both racing to alter that uncertain balance of terror that stays the hand of mankind's final war.

So let us begin anew—remembering on both sides that civility is not a sign of weakness, and sincerity is always subject to proof. Let us never negotiate out of fear. But let us never fear to negotiate.

Let both sides explore what problems unite us instead of belaboring those problems which divide us.

Let both sides, for the first time, formulate serious and precise proposals for the inspection and control of arms—and bring the absolute power to destroy other nations under the absolute control of all nations.

Let both sides seek to invoke the wonders of science instead of its terrors. Together let us explore the stars, conquer the deserts, eradicate disease, tap the ocean depths, and encourage the arts and commerce.

Let both sides unite to heed in all corners of the earth the command of Isaiah—to "undo the heavy burdens . . . and to let the oppressed go free."

And if a beachhead of cooperation may push back the jungle of suspicion, let both sides join in creating, not a new balance of power, but a new world of law, where the strong are just and the weak secure and the peace preserved.

All this will not be finished in the first one hundred days. Nor will it be finished in the first one thousand days, nor in the life of this administration, nor even perhaps in our lifetime on this planet. But let us begin.

In your hands, my fellow citizens, more than mine, will rest the final success or failure of our course. Since this country was founded, each generation of Americans has been summoned to give testimony to its national loyalty. The graves of young Americans who answered the call to service surround the globe.

Now the trumpet summons us again—not as a call to bear arms, though arms we need; not as a call to battle, though embattled we are—but a call to bear the burden of a long twilight struggle, year in and year out, "rejoicing in hope, patient in tribulation"—a struggle against the common enemies of man: tyranny, poverty, disease, and war itself.

Can we forge against these enemies a grand and global alliance, North and South, East and West, that can assure a more fruitful life for all mankind? Will you join in that historic effort?

In the long history of the world, only a few generations have been granted the role of defending freedom in its hour of maximum danger. I do not shrink from this responsibility—I welcome it. I do not believe that any of us would exchange places with any other people or any other generation. The energy, the faith, the devotion which we bring to this endeavor will light our country and all who serve it—and the glow from that fire can truly light the world.

And so, my fellow Americans: ask not what your country can do for you—ask what you can do for your country.

My fellow citizens of the world: ask not what America will do for you, but what together we can do for the freedom of man.

Finally, whether you are citizens of America or citizens of the world, ask of us here the same high standards of strength and sacrifice which we ask of you. With a good conscience our only sure reward, with history the final judge of our deeds, let us go forth to lead the land we love, asking His blessing and His help, but knowing that here on earth God's work must truly be our own.

Address to the National Women's Rights Convention, 1855

Lucy Stone

The last speaker alluded to this movement as being that of a few disappointed women. From the first years to which my memory stretches, I have been a disappointed woman. When, with my brothers, I reached forth after the sources of knowledge, I was reproved with "It isn't fit for you; it doesn't belong to women." Then there was but one college in the world where women were admitted, and that was in Brazil. I would have found my way there, but by the time I was prepared to go, one was opened in the young state of Ohio—the first in the United States where women and negroes could enjoy opportunities with white men. I was disappointed when I came to seek a profession worthy of an immortal being—every employment was closed to me, except those of the teacher, the seamstress, and the housekeeper. In education, in marriage, in religion, in everything, disappointment is the lot of a woman. It shall be the business of my life to deepen this disappointment in every woman's heart until she bows down to it no longer. I wish that women, instead of being walking showcases, instead of begging of their fathers and brothers the latest and gayest new bonnet, would ask of them their rights.

The question of Women's Rights is a practical one. The notion has prevailed that it was only an ephemeral idea: that it was but women claiming the right to smoke cigars in the streets, and to frequent barrooms. Others have supposed it a question of comparative intellect; others still, of sphere. Too much has already been said and written about woman's sphere. Trace all the doctrines to their source and they will be found to have no basis except in the usages and prejudices of the age. This is seen in the fact that what is tolerated in woman in one country is not tolerated in another. In this country women may hold prayer-meetings, etc., but in Mohammedan countries it is written upon their mosques, "Women and dogs, and other impure animals, are not permitted to enter." Wendell Phillips says, "The best and greatest thing one is capable of doing, that is his sphere." I have confidence in the Father to believe that when He gives us the capacity to do anything He does not make a blunder. Leave women, then, to find their sphere. And do not tell us before we are born even, that our province is to cook dinners, darn stockings, and sew on buttons. We are told woman has all the rights she wants; and even women, I am ashamed to say, tell us so. They mistake the politeness of men for rights—seats while men stand in this hall tonight, and their adulations; but these are mere courtesies. We want rights. The flour-merchant, the house-builder, and the postman charge us no less on account of our sex; but when we endeavor to earn money to pay all these, then, indeed, we find the difference. Man, if he have energy, may hew out for himself a path where no mortal has ever trod, held back by nothing but what is in himself; the world is all before him, there to choose; and we are glad for you, brothers, men, that it is so. But the same society that drives forth the young man keeps woman at home—a dependent—working little cats on worsted, and little dogs on punctured paper; but if she goes heartily and bravely to give herself to some worthy purpose, she is out of her sphere and she loses caste. Women working in tailor-shops are paid one-third as much as men. Someone in Philadelphia has stated that women make fine shirts for twelve and a half cents apiece; that no woman can make more than nine a week, and the sum thus earned, after deducting rent, fuel, etc., leaves her just three and a half cents a day for bread. Is it a wonder that women are driven to prostitution? Female teachers in New York are paid fifty dollars a year, and for every such situation there are five hundred applicants. I know not what you believe of God, but I believe He gave yearnings and longings to be filled, and that He did not mean all our time should be devoted to feeding and clothing the body. The present condition of woman causes a horrible perversion of the marriage relation. It is asked of a lady, "Has she married well?" "Oh, yes, her husband is rich." Woman must marry for a home, and you men are the sufferers by this; for a woman who loathes you may marry you because you have the means to get money which she can not have. But when woman can enter the lists with you and make money for herself, she will marry you only for deep and earnest affection.

I am detaining you too long, many of you standing, that I ought to apologize, but women have been wronged so long that I may wrong you a little. [*Applause*]. A woman undertook in Lowell to sell shoes to ladies. Men laughed at her, but in six years she has run them out, and has a monopoly of the trade. Sarah Tyndale, whose husband was an importer of china, and died bankrupt, continued his business, paid off his debts, and has made a fortune and built the largest china warehouse in the world. [*Mrs. Mott here corrected Lucy. Mrs. Tyndale has not the largest china warehouse, but the largest assortment of china in the world.*] Mrs. Tyndale, herself, drew the plan of her warehouse, and it is the best plan ever drawn. A laborer to whom the architect showed it, said: "Don't she know e'en as much as some men?" I have seen a woman at manual labor turning out chair-legs in a cabinet-shop with a dress short enough not to drag in the shavings. I wish other women would imitate her in this. It made her hands harder and broader, it is true, but I think a hand with a dollar and a quarter a day in it, better than one with a crossed ninepence. The men in the shop didn't use tobacco, nor swear—they can't do those things where there are women, and we owe it to our brothers to go wherever they work to keep them decent. The widening of woman's sphere is to improve her lot. Let us do it, and if the world scoff, let it scoff—if it sneer, let it sneer—but we will go on emulating the example of the sisters Grimke and Abby Kelly. When they first lectured against slavery they were not listened to as respectfully as you listen to us. So the first female physician meets many difficulties, but to the next the path will be made easy.

Lucretia Mott has been a preacher for years; her right to do so is not questioned among friends. But when Antoinette Brown felt that she was commanded to preach, and to arrest the progress of thousands that were on the road to hell; why, when she applied for ordination they acted as though they had rather the whole world should go to hell, than that Antoinette Brown should be allowed to tell them how to keep out of it. She is now ordained over a parish in the state of New York, but when she meets on the Temperance platform the Rev. John Chambers, or your own Gen. Carey [*Applause*] they greet her with hisses. Theodore Parker said: "The acorn that the schoolboy carries in his pocket and the squirrel stows in his cheek, has in it the possibility of an oak, able to withstand, for ages, the cold winter and the driving blast." I have seen the acorn men and women, but never the perfect oak; all are but abortions. The young mother, when first the newborn babe nestles in her bosom, and a heretofore unknown love springs up in her heart, finds herself unprepared for this new relation in life, and she sends forth the child scarred and dwarfed by her own weakness and imbecility, as no stream can rise higher than its fountain.

Glory and Hope: Let There Be Work, Bread, Water, and Salt for All

Nelson Mandela, President of South Africa

Pretoria, South Africa, May 10, 1994

Your Majesties, Your royal highnesses, distinguished guests, comrades, and friends: Today, all of us do, by our presence here, and by our celebrations in other parts of our country and the world, confer glory and hope to newborn liberty.

Out of the experience of an extraordinary human disaster that lasted too long must be born a society of which all humanity will be proud.

Our daily deeds as ordinary South Africans must produce an actual South African reality that will reinforce humanity's belief in justice, strengthen its confidence in the nobility of the human soul, and sustain all our hopes for a glorious life for all.

All this we owe both to ourselves and to the peoples of the world who are so well represented here today.

To my compatriots, I have no hesitation in saying that each one of us is as intimately attached to the soil of this beautiful country as are the famous jacaranda trees of Pretoria and the mimosa trees of the bushveld.

Each time one of us touches the soil of this land, we feel a sense of personal renewal. The national mood changes as the seasons change.

We are moved by a sense of joy and exhilaration when the grass turns green and the flowers bloom.

That spiritual and physical oneness we all share with this common homeland explains the depth of the pain we all carried in our hearts as we saw our country tear itself apart in a terrible conflict, and as we saw it spurned, outlawed, and isolated by the peoples of the world, precisely because it has become the universal base of the pernicious ideology and practice of racism and racial oppression.

We, the people of South Africa, feel fulfilled that humanity has taken us back into its bosom, that we, who were outlaws not so long ago, have today been given the rare privilege to be host to the nations of the world on our own soil.

We thank all our distinguished international guests for having come to take possession with the people of our country of what is, after all, a common victory for justice, for peace, for human dignity.

We trust that you will continue to stand by us as we tackle the challenges of building peace, prosperity, nonsexism, nonracialism, and democracy.

We deeply appreciate the role that the masses of our people and their democratic, religious, women, youth, business, traditional, and other leaders have played to bring about this conclusion. Not least among them is my Second Deputy President, the Honorable F. W. de Klerk.

We would also like to pay tribute to our security forces, in all their ranks, for the distinguished role they have played in securing our first democratic elections and the transition to democracy, from bloodthirsty forces which still refuse to see the light.

The time for the healing of the wounds has come.

The moment to bridge the chasms that divide us has come.

The time to build is upon us.

We have, at last, achieved our political emancipation. We pledge ourselves to liberate all our people from the continuing bondage of poverty, deprivation, suffering, gender, and other discrimination.

We succeeded to take our last steps to freedom in conditions of relative peace. We commit ourselves to the construction of a complete, just, and lasting peace.

We have triumphed in the effort to implant hope in the breasts of the millions of our people. We enter into a covenant that we shall build the society in which all South Africans, both black and white, will be able to walk tall, without any fear in their hearts, assured of their inalienable right to human dignity—a rainbow nation at peace with itself and the world.

As a token of its commitment to the renewal of our country, the new Interim Government of National Unity will, as a matter of urgency, address the issue of amnesty for various categories of our people who are currently serving terms of imprisonment.

We dedicate this day to all the heroes and heroines in this country and the rest of the world who sacrificed in many ways and surrendered their lives so that we could be free.

Their dreams have become reality. Freedom is their reward.

We are both humbled and elevated by the honor and privilege that you, the people of South Africa, have bestowed on us, as the first president of a united, democratic, nonracial, and nonsexist South Africa, to lead our country out of the valley of darkness.

We understand it still that there is no easy road to freedom.

We know it well that none of us acting alone can achieve success.

We must therefore act together as a united people, for national reconciliation, for nation building, for the birth of a new world.

Let there be justice for all.

Let there be peace for all.

Let there be work, bread, water, and salt for all.

Let each know that for each the body, the mind, and the soul have been freed to fulfill themselves.

Never, never, and never again shall it be that this beautiful land will again experience the oppression of one by another and suffer the indignity of being the skunk of the world.

The sun shall never set on so glorious a human achievement!

Let freedom reign. God bless Africa!

THE SHAME OF HUNGER

Elie Wiesel

Brown University

Providence, Rhode Island, April 5, 1990

A survivor of the concentration camps at Auschwitz and Buchenwald, Elie Wiesel has won a congressional medal and the 1986 Nobel Prize for Peace. He delivered the following speech at Brown University on April 5, 1990.

I have been obsessed with the idea of hunger for years and years because I have seen what hunger can do to human beings. It is the easiest way for a tormenter to dehumanize another human being. When I think of hunger, I see images: emaciated bodies, swollen bellies, long bony arms pleading for mercy, motionless skeletons. How can one look at these images without losing sleep?

And eyes, my God, eyes. Eyes that pierce your consciousness and tear your heart. How can one run away from those eyes? The eyes of a mother who carries her dead child in her arms, not knowing where to go, or where to stop. At one moment you think that she would keep on going, going, going—to the end of the world. Except she wouldn't go very far, for the end of the world, for her, is there. Or the eyes of the old grandfather, who probably wonders where creation had gone wrong, and whether it was all worthwhile to create a family, to have faith in the future, to transmit misery from generation to generation, whether it was worth it to wager on humankind.

And then the eyes of all eyes, the eyes of children, so dark, so immense, so deep, so focused and yet at the same time, so wide and so vague. What do they see? What do hungry children's eyes see? Death? Nothingness? God? And what if their eyes are the eyes of our judges?

Hunger and death, death and starvation, starvation and shame. Poor men and women who yesterday were proud members of their tribes, bearers of ancient culture and lore, and who are now wandering among corpses. What is so horrifying in hunger is that it makes the individual death an anonymous death. In times of hunger, the individual death has lost its uniqueness. Scores of hungry people die daily, and those who mourn for them will die the next day, and the others will have no strength left to mourn.

Hunger in ancient times represented the ultimate malediction to society. Rich and poor, young and old, kings and servants, lived in fear of drought. They joined the priests in prayer for rain. Rain meant harvest, harvest meant food, food meant life, just as lack of food meant death. It still does.

Hunger and humiliation. A hungry person experiences an overwhelming feeling of shame. All desires, all aspirations, all dreams lose their lofty qualities and relate to food alone. I may testify to something I have witnessed, in certain places at certain times, those people who were reduced by hunger, diminished by hunger, they did not think about theology, nor did they think about God or philosophy or literature. They thought of a piece of bread. A piece of bread was, to them, God, because a piece of bread then filled one's universe. Diminished by hunger, man's spirit is diminished as well. His fantasy wanders in quest of bread. His prayer rises toward a bowl of milk.

Thus the shame.

In Hebrew, the word *hunger* is linked to shame. The prophet Ezekiel speaks about "Kherpat raav," the shame of hunger. Of all the diseases, of all the natural diseases and catastrophes, the only one that is linked to shame in Scripture is hunger—the shame of hunger. Shame is associated neither with sickness nor even with death, only with hunger. For man can live with pain, but no man ought to endure hunger.

Hunger means torture, the worst kind of torture. The hungry person is tortured by more than one sadist alone. He or she is tortured, every minute, by all men, by all women. And by all the elements surrounding him or her. The wind. The sun. The stars. By the rustling of trees and the silence of night. The minutes that pass so slowly, so slowly. Can you imagine time, can you imagine time, when you are hungry?

And to condone hunger means to accept torture, someone else's torture.

Hunger is isolating; it may not and cannot be experienced vicariously. He who never felt hunger can never know its real effects, both tangible and intangible. Hunger defies imagination; it even defies memory. Hunger is felt only in the present.

There is a story about the great French–Jewish composer Daniel Halevy who met a poor poet: "Is it true," he asked, "that you endured hunger in your youth?" "Yes," said the poet. "I envy you," said the composer, "I never felt hunger."

And Gaston Bachelard, the famous philosopher, voiced his view on the matter, saying, "My prayer to heaven is not, 'Oh God, give us our daily bread,' but give us our daily hunger."

I don't find these anecdotes funny. These anecdotes were told about and by people who were not hungry. There is no romanticism in hunger, there is no beauty in hunger, no creativity in hunger. There is no aspiration in hunger. Only shame. And solitude. Hunger creates its own prison walls; it is impossible to demolish them, to avoid them, to ignore them.

Thus, if hunger inspires anything at all, it is, and must be, only the war against hunger.

Hunger is not a matter of choice. Of course, you may say, but what about the hunger striker? Haven't they chosen to deprive themselves of nourishment, aren't they hungry? Yes, but not the same way. First, they suffer alone; those around them do not. Second, they are given the possibility to stop any time they so choose, any time they will, any time their cause is attained. Not so [with] the people in Africa. Not so [with] the people in Asia. Their hunger is irrevocable. And last, hunger strikers confer a meaning, a purpose, upon their ordeal. Not so [with] the victims in Ethiopia or Sudan. Their hunger is senseless. And implacable.

The worst stage in hunger is to see its reflection in one's brother, one's father, one's child. Hunger renders powerless those who suffer its consequences. Can you imagine a mother unable, helpless, to alleviate her child's agony? There is the abyss in shame. There, suffering and hunger and shame multiply.

In times of hunger, family relations break down. The father is impotent, his authority gone, the mother is desperate, and the children, the children, under the weight of accumulated suffering and hunger, grow older and older, and soon, they will be older than their grandparents.

But then, on the other hand, perhaps of all of the woes that threaten and plague the human condition, hunger alone can be curtailed, attenuated, appeased, and ultimately vanquished, not by destiny, nor by the heavens, but by human beings. We cannot fight earthquakes, but we can fight hunger. Hence our responsibility for its victims. *Responsibility* is the key word. Our tradition emphasizes the question, rather than the answer. For there is a "quest" in question, but there is "response" in responsibility. And this responsibility is what makes us human, or the lack of it, inhuman.

Hunger differs from other cataclysms such as floods in that it can be prevented or stopped so easily. One gesture of generosity, one act of humanity, may put an end to it, at least for one person. A piece of bread, a bowl of rice or soup makes a difference. And I wonder, what would happen, just imagine, what would happen, if every nation, every industrialized or non-industrialized nation, would simply decide to sell one aircraft, and for the money, feed the hungry. Why shouldn't they? Why shouldn't the next economic summit, which includes the wealthiest, most powerful, the richest nations in the world, why shouldn't they decide that since there are so many aircrafts, why shouldn't they say: "Let's sell just one, just one, to take care of the shame and the hunger and the suffering of millions of people."

So the prophet's expression, "the shame of hunger," must be understood differently. When we speak of our responsibility for the hungry, we must go to the next step and say that the expression "shame of hunger" does not apply to the hungry. It applies to those who refuse to help the hungry. Shame on those who could feed *the hungry*, but are too busy to do so.

Millions of human beings constantly are threatened in Africa and Asia, and even in our own country, the homeless and the hungry. Many are going to die of starvation, and it will be our fault. For we could save them, and if we do not, we had better have a good reason why we don't.

If we could airlift food and sustenance and toothpaste to Berlin in 1948, surely we could do as much for all the countries, Ethiopia and Sudan and Mozambique and Bangladesh, in the year 1990. Nations capable of sending and retrieving vehicles in space must be able to save human lives on earth.

Let our country, and then other countries, see in hunger an emergency that must be dealt with right now. Others, our allies, will follow. Private relief often has been mobilized in the past: Jews and Christians, Moslems and Buddhists have responded to dramatic appeals from the African desert. One of my most rewarding moments was when I went to the Cambodian border ten years ago and saw there the misery, the weakness, the despair, the resignation, of the victims.

But I also saw the extraordinary international community motivated by global solidarity to help them. And who were they? They represented humankind at its best: There were Jews and Christians and Moslems and Buddhists from all over the world. And if ever I felt proud of the human condition, it was then. It is possible to help, but private help is insufficient. Government-organized help is required; only governments can really help solve this tragedy that has cosmic repercussions.

We must save the victims of hunger simply because they can be saved. We look therefore at the horror-filled pictures, when we dare to look, day after day. And I cannot help but remember those who had surrounded us elsewhere, years and years ago. Oh, I do not wish to make comparisons. I never do. But I do have the right to invoke the past, not as a point of analogy, but as a term of reference. I refuse to draw analogies with the Jewish tragedy during the era of darkness; I still believe and will always believe that no event ought to be compared to that event. But I do believe that human tragedies, all human tragedies, are and must be related to it. In other words, it is because one people has been singled out for extinction that others were marked for slavery. It is because entire communities were wiped out then that others were condemned to die later in other parts of the planet. All events are intertwined.

And it is because we have known hunger that we must eliminate hunger. It is because we have been subjected to shame that we must now oppose shame. It is because we have witnessed humanity at its worst that we must now appeal to humanity at its best.

Civility without Censorship: The Ethics of the Internet — Cyberhate

Raymond W. Smith, Chairman of Bell Atlantic Corporation
Los Angeles, California, December 1, 1998

Thank you, Rabbi Cooper, for the gracious introduction . . . and let me acknowledge the tremendous contributions the Museum and the Center have made toward harmonizing race relations and advancing equality and justice. We're truly honored that you would include us in today's program.

For the past two years, I've been using the "bully pulpit" to alert various civil rights leaders and organizations (like Martin Luther King III and the NAACP) of the dangers posed by cyberhate. If not for the early groundbreaking work by the Simon Wiesenthal Center, I doubt whether I would have even known of this growing threat. Thank you for warning us — and now, for showing us — how extremists are using the Internet for their own purposes.

When thinking about this morning's topic, I can't help but mention a cartoon that recently appeared in the newspapers. Through the doorway, a mother calls out to her teenager — who is surrounded by high-tech equipment — "I hope you're not watching sex stuff on the Internet!" To which her son replies, "Naw, I'm getting it on TV!"

Until recently, the chief concern of parents was pornography — kids' access to it over the Web and the fear of sexual predators cruising cyberspace. Now, we're worried about hate mongers reaching out to our children in digital space.

As we have just seen and heard, Neo-Nazis and extremists of every political stripe who once terrorized people in the dead of night with burning crosses and painted swastikas are now sneaking up on the public — especially our kids — through the World Wide Web.

As cyberhate is nothing less than the attempt to corrupt public discourse on race and ethnicity via the Internet, many people see censorship of Web sites and Net content as the only viable way to meet this growing threat.

I disagree.

Instead of fearing the Internet's reach, we need to embrace it — to value its ability to connect our children to the wealth of positive human experience and knowledge. While there is, to quote one critic, "every form of diseased intelligence" in digital space, we must remember that it comprises only a small fraction of cyberspace. The Internet provides our children unlimited possibilities for learning and education — the great libraries, cities, and cultures of the world also await them at just the click of a mouse key.

In short, we need to think about ways to keep cyberhate off the screen, and more about ways to meet it head on: which translates into fighting destructive rhetoric with constructive dialogue — hate speech with truth — restrictions with greater Internet access.

This morning then, I would like to discuss with you the options that are available to combat cyberhate that don't endanger our First Amendment guarantees—and that remain true to our commitment to free speech.

That people and institutions should call for a strict ban on language over the Web that could be considered racist, anti-Semitic, or bigoted is totally understandable. None of us was truly prepared for the emergence of multiple hate-group Web sites (especially those geared toward children), or the quick adoption of high-technology by skinheads and others to market their digital cargo across state lines and international datelines at the speed of light.

One possible reason some people feel inclined to treat the Internet more severely than other media is that the technology is new and hard to understand. Also, the Internet's global reach and ubiquitous nature make it appear ominous. As Justice Gabriel Bach, of Israel, noted, this ability makes it especially dangerous. "I'm frightened stiff by the Internet," he said. "Billions of people all over the world have access to it."

My industry has seen all this before.

The clash between free speech and information technology is actually quite an old one. Nearly a century ago, telephone companies, courts, and the Congress debated whether "common earners" (public phone companies) were obligated to carry all talk equally, regardless of content. And in the end—though some believed that the phone would do everything from eliminate Southern accents and increase Northern labor unrest—free speech won out in the courts.

Whatever the technology, be it the radio or the silver screen, history teaches us that white supremacists, anti-Semites, and others will unfortunately come to grasp, relatively early on, a new medium's potential.

We simply can't condemn a whole technology because we fear that a Father Coughlin or a Leni Riefenstahl (early pioneers in the use of radio and film to advance anti-Semitism or Hitler's Reich) is waiting in the wings to use the latest technology to their own advantage. Nor can we expect the Congress, the federal government, or an international regulatory agency to tightly regulate cyberspace content in order to stymie language we find offensive.

The wisdom of further empowering such organizations and agencies like the FCC or the United Nations aside, it is highly doubtful even if they had the authority, that they would have the ability to truly stem the flow of racist and anti-Semitic language on the World Wide Web.

Anybody with a phone line, computer, and Internet connection can set up a Web site—even broadcast over the Net.

Even if discovered, and banned, online hate groups can easily jump Internet service providers and national boundaries to avoid accountability. I think cyber guru, Peter Huber, got it right when he said, "To censor Internet filth at its origins, we would have to enlist the Joint Chiefs of Staff, who could start by invading Sweden and Holland."

Then there is the whole matter of disguise. Innocent sounding URLs (handles or Web site names) can fool even the most traveled or seasoned "cybernaut."

As for efforts on Capitol Hill and elsewhere to legislate all so-called "offensive" language off the Internet, here again, we can expect the courts to knock down any attempts to curtail First Amendment rights on the Internet. As the Supreme Court ruled last year when it struck down legislation restricting the transmission of "indecent" material online: (To Quote) "Regardless of the strength of the government's interest, the level of discourse reaching a mailbox simply cannot be limited to what is suitable for a sandbox."

In short, although the temptation is great to look to legislation and regulation as a remedy to cyberhate, our commitment to free speech must always take precedent over our fears.

So, cyberhate will not be defeated by the stroke of a pen.

Now, this is not to say that, because we place such a high value on our First Amendment rights, we can't do anything to combat the proliferation of hate sites on the Internet or protect young minds from such threatening and bigoted language.

Law enforcement agencies and state legislators can use existing laws against stalking and telephone harassment to go after those who abuse e-mail . . . parents can install software filtering programs (such as the Anti-Defamation League's HateFilter, or the one Bell Atlantic uses, CyberPatrol) to block access to questionable Internet sites . . . schools and libraries can protect children by teaching them how to properly use the Internet and challenge cyberhate . . . and Internet Service Providers can voluntarily decline to host hate sites. (Bell Atlantic Internet Services, for instance, reserves the right to decline or terminate service which "espouses, promotes, or incites bigotry, hatred, or racism.")

Given that today's panel has representatives from state government, law enforcement, the courts, and the Internet industry, we can discuss these initiatives later in more detail. The point is, there are other ways besides empowering national or international oversight agencies, or drafting draconian legislation, to lessen the impact of cyberhate.

Freedom, not censorship, is the only way to combat this threat to civility. In short, more speech—not less—is needed on the World Wide Web.

In fact, the best answer to cyberhate lies in the use of information technology itself. As a reporter for the *Boston Globe* recently concluded, (quote) "The same technology that provides a forum for extremists, enables civil rights groups and individuals to mobilize a response in unprecedented ways."

We totally agree.

Our prescription to cyberhate is therefore rather simple, but far-reaching in its approach:

The first component is access: if we're to get to a higher level of national understanding on racial and ethnic issues—and strike at the very roots of cyberhate—we must see that no minority group or community is left out of cyberspace for want of a simple Internet connection or basic computer.

At Bell Atlantic, we've been working very hard to provide the minority communities we serve with Internet access. Across our region, thousands of inner-city schools, libraries, colleges, and community groups are now getting connected to cyberspace through a variety of our foundation and state grant programs. Also, our employees have been in the forefront of volunteering their time and energy to wire schools to the Internet during specially designated "Net" days.

Internet access alone, however, won't build bridges of understanding between people—or level the playing field between cyber-haters and the targets of their hate.

The second thing we must do is make sure the Web's content is enriched by minority culture and beliefs, and that there are more Web sites and home pages dedicated to meeting head-on the racist caricatures and pseudo history often found in cyberspace.

While cyberhate cannot be mandated or censored out of existence, it can be countered by creating hundreds of chatlines, home pages, bulletin boards, and Web sites dedicated to social justice, tolerance, and equality—for all people regardless of race, nationality, or sexual orientation.

Over the past two years, Bell Atlantic has helped a number of minority and civil rights groups launch and maintain their Web sites (like the NAACP, the Leadership Council on Civil Rights, and the National Council of La Raza), and we've done the same for dozens of smaller cultural organizations (like the Harlem Studio Museum and El Museo del Barrio).

We believe that kind of moral leadership can have a tremendous impact. Quite simply, we need more Simon Wiesenthal Centers, Anti-Defamation Leagues, and Southern Poverty Law Centers monitoring and responding to cyberhate.

If we're to bring the struggle for human decency and dignity into cyberspace, we must see that the two most powerful revolutions of the twentieth century—those of civil rights and information technology—are linked even closer together.

Finally, we need to drive real-time, serious dialogue on the religious, ethnic, and cultural concerns that divide us as a nation—a task for which the Internet is particularly suited.

Precisely because it is anonymous, the Internet provides a perfect forum to discuss race, sexual orientation, and other similar issues. On the

Internet, said one user, "you can speak freely and not have fears that somebody is going to attack you for what comes out of your heart." It's the kind of open and heart-felt discussion that we need to advance and sponsor online.

Already, a number of small groups and lone individuals are meeting the cyberhate challenge through simple dialogue between strangers. I'm talking about Web sites run by educators to inform parents about online hate materials . . . sites operated by "recovering" racists to engage skinheads and other misguided kids in productive debate . . . Web sites run by concerned citizens to bridge the gap in ignorance between ethnic, racial, and other communities.

The "Y? forum," also known as the National Forum on People's Differences, is a wonderful example of a Web site where readers can safely ask and follow discussions on sensitive cross-cultural topics without having to wade through foul language or "flame wars."

As a columnist from the *Miami Herald* described the appeal of these kinds of sites: "As long as we are mysteries, one to another, we face a perpetuation of ignorance and a feeding of fear. I'd rather people ask the questions than try to make up the answers. I'd rather they ask the questions than turn to myth and call it truth."

In closing, my company recognizes that the Internet doesn't operate in a vacuum. We agree that those who profit from information technology have a special responsibility to see that its promise is shared across class, race, and geographic boundaries.

That's why we're working with the public schools and libraries in our region to see that they're all equipped with the pens, pencils, and paper of the twenty-first century . . . why we're helping to further distance learning and telemedicine applications that serve the educational and health needs of the disabled and isolated . . . why we're helping minority groups and civil rights organizations use information technology to spread their vision and their values to the millions of people electronically linked to the global village.

And that's the way it should be.

Let me leave you with a personal story. . . .

When growing up, my Jewish friends and I often swapped theology tales from the Hassidic Masters for stories from the Lives of the Saints. I remember from these discussions that one of the great Rabbis noted that the first word of the Ten Commandments is "I" and the last word is "neighbor." In typical Talmundic fashion, the Rabbi was telling us that if we want to incorporate the Commandments into our lives, we must move from a focus on ourselves to others.

At Bell Atlantic, the more we grow—in both scale and scope—the greater the emphasis we place on being a good corporate citizen, and the more we're driven to see that digital technology is used for purposes of enlightenment and education.

The Internet will fundamentally transform the way we work, learn, do commerce. It will also, if properly used and rightly taught, help bridge the gap in understanding between communities—becoming not a tool of hate, but one of hope.

Thank you again for the invitation to join you this morning.

Delivered at the Simon Wiesenthal Center/Museum of Tolerance, Los Angeles, California, December 1, 1998.

GLOSSARY

Academic journals: publish articles by professional researchers and educators

Accommodators: learners who tend to prefer concrete experience (feeling) and active experimentation (doing)

Accuracy: using words that most precisely convey the meaning you intend

Active sentence: the subject *performs* the action

Actual example: a short story about an event that actually occurred

Actuate: move to action

Actuation persuasive speech: designed to influence behavior

Ad hominem: fallacy in which a speaker attacks personal characteristics of the opponent rather than the issue at hand

Administrator: determines where and when the group will meet

Alliteration: the repetition of sounds at the beginnings of words that are near one another

Analogical reasoning: strategy that links two concepts together and claims that what is true of one will—by comparison—also be true of the other

Analogy: an extended metaphor; a comparison drawn between two essentially unrelated concepts or objects

Analyzer: helps the group relate the evidence provided by the information giver to the issues that are at the core of the problem

Antithesis: combining contrasting ideas in the same sentence

Apathy barrier: the tendency of listeners to be indifferent toward a speech

Appeal to tradition: fallacy in which a speaker opposes change and defends the status quo simply because that's the way it's always been done

Appreciative listening: listening for enjoyment through the works and experiences of others

Argument: articulating a position with the support of evidence and reasoning

Assimilators: learners who tend to prefer abstract conceptualization (thinking) and reflective observation (watching and listening)

Assonance: the repetition of vowel sounds in the words of a phrase or sentence

Attention catcher: material in the introduction that grabs listeners' attention and relates to the topic

Attitude: a predisposition to respond favorably or unfavorably to something, to like or dislike it

Audience analysis: a process of finding out who your listeners are and adapting your speech to their needs and interests

Audience-based communication apprehension: a tendency to feel anxious about communicating with a certain person or group of people

Audience-centered: considering who your audience members are and tailoring your message to their interests, desires, and needs

Audience contact: a way of establishing eye contact in a large auditorium; you must create a sense of looking listeners in the eye even though you cannot actually do so

Audio aids: audiotaped excerpts of music, conversations, environmental sounds, speeches, and so on

Audiovisual aids: presentational aids that combine sight and sound

Auditory channel: what the receivers hear

Auditory distraction: associated with something someone hears

Authoritarian leadership style: directive, controlling, and dictatorial

Bandwagon: fallacy in which a speaker assumes that because something is popular, it is also good or desirable

Bar graphs: consist of parallel bars with lengths proportional to specific quantities; they highlight comparisons between two or more items

Belief: something one accepts as true or false, even though neither can be shown

Brainstorming: a process of generating as many ideas as possible; used in the topic selection and narrowing process to generate ideas for potential topics

Breadth: the variety of different pieces of evidence used to explain your main points

Brief example: short, specific instance offered to illustrate a point

Browsers: a doorway into the World Wide Web, for example, Netscape Navigator, Internet Explorer, and Mosaic

Card playing: a process of brainstorming in which you put each idea on a separate index card or slip of paper

Causal pattern: main points are organized in a way that shows a cause and effect relationship

Channels: pathways through which messages are communicated between sender and receiver

Character: being perceived as trustworthy, honest, and sincere, as well as engaging, likable, and attractive

Chronemics: socially constructed perceptions about time

Chronological pattern: the main points follow a time sequence

Claim of fact: focuses on whether something is true—that is, it takes a position on something that is not known but can be argued for

Claim of policy: states a position about whether a specific course of action should be taken

Claim of value: makes a judgment about whether some concept or action is good, right, moral, fair, or better than some other concept or action

Cliché: an overused expression

Clincher: a final statement that reinforces your main ideas, provides closure to the speech, and ties back to the introduction

Closed-ended question: question that elicits a small range of specific answers

Coactive approach: a strategic method for confronting reluctant audiences intelligently and constructively

Cognitive distortions: unrealistic negative statements about yourself that lead you to judge your public speaking experience harshly, even if the experience goes well

Cognitive restructuring: a process to help you systematically rebuild your thoughts about public speaking

Comic timing: pause the right length of time to allow for applause and laughter

Commemorative address: a speech of tribute that inspires listeners by remembering accomplishments and setting new goals

Commencement address: a speech of tribute praising graduating students and congratulating them on their academic achievements

Common ground: a technique for bolstering ethos by identifying with your audience by talking about shared beliefs and values related to your argument

Communication: the process of sending and receiving verbal and nonverbal messages to create shared meaning

Communication apprehension: the fear or anxiety associated with real or anticipated communication with others

Communication orientation: approaching a public speech as a message you are trying to get across to listeners rather than as a performance

Communication rules: guides for what is appropriate in a situation based on place, time, occasion, and cultural context

Communication situation: the particular context within which communication occurs

Comparative advantages pattern: a main point arrangement that leads your audience to agree with your disposition that one of two or more alternatives is better than the others

Competence: perception of being well informed, skilled, or knowledgeable about your subject

Comprehensive listening: listening for understanding

Concept mapping: a visual means of exploring connections between a topic and related ideas

Concrete words: refer to tangible people, places, and things

Conflict: disagreement over issues or courses of action to be taken

Connectives: words or phrases that serve as glue to hold the speech together

Connotation: what a word suggests or implies

Constructive criticism: criticism in which comments are specific, are about the speech rather than the speaker, are accompanied by a rationale, and are phrased as personal opinions using "I" language

Content: the actual ideas in your speech

Context-based communication apprehension: a tendency to feel anxious about communication in a particular setting

Controlled nervousness: to control anxiety and turn it into positive energy that can actually enhance delivery

Convergers: learners who tend to prefer abstract conceptualization (thinking) and active experimentation (doing)

Conversational: you sound and look as though you are *talking with* your listeners rather than presenting in front of them or reading to them

Credentials: pieces of evidence that qualify you as an authority

Credible evidence: information that seems both believable and reliable

Critical listening: listening that includes hearing, understanding, evaluating, and assigning worth to a message

Current evidence: information that is not outdated

Decoding: attaching meanings to symbols

Dedication: a speech of tribute that honors a worthy person or group by naming a structure like a building, monument, or park after that person or group

Deductive reasoning: strategy that starts with a generally agreed-upon major premise and then demonstrates how a point or example—or minor premise—fits within that general principle

Definition: statement that clarifies the meaning of a word or phrase

Delivery: the way speakers communicate messages orally and visually through their voice, face, and body

Democratic leadership style: directive but not rigid

Demographic characteristics: characteristics of an audience such as age, sex, gender, sexual orientation, race, ethnicity, and sociocultural background

Denotation: the dictionary definition of a word

Depth: the level of detail of the evidence

Derived credibility: perception of credibility attained by what a speaker says and does during the speech itself

Description: statement that attempts to create a picture of something for listeners

Designated leader: a person who is appointed as leader

Diagram: a type of drawing used to show a whole and its parts

Dialect: a regional variety of a language

Direct question: a question that requests an overt response from listeners

Direct quotation: material lifted verbatim from a particular document

Directory: a human-edited Web search index

Discriminative listening: listening "between the lines"

Dispositional persuasive speech: designed to influence listeners' beliefs, attitudes, or values toward your topic

Divergers: learners who tend to prefer concrete experience (feeling) and reflective observation (watching and listening)

Either-or: fallacy in which a speaker argues that there are only two approaches to a problem when, in fact, more exist

Emergent leader: someone who takes the initiative to act as leader

Empathic listening: listening to support, help, and empathize with the speaker

Encoding: putting ideas into symbols

Enunciation: the act of speaking distinctly and clearly; how crisply vowel and consonant sounds are formed

Environmental characteristics: factors that influence why listeners attend and what they expect from a particular public speech

Ethics: our principles about what is right and wrong, moral and immoral, honest or dishonest, fair or unfair

Ethnocentrism: the tendency to assume one's own cultural values and beliefs are better than the values and beliefs of other groups

Ethos: appeals to speaker credibility, in the sense of competence and character

Eulogy: a speech of tribute honoring someone who has recently died

Evaluator: helps the group develop criteria for evaluating decisions

Evidence: any information that clarifies, explains, or in some way adds breadth or depth to your topic (also called *supporting material*)

Example: specific case used to illustrate or represent a concept, condition, experience, or group of some sort

Expanded personal inventory: a list of topics that interest you and why

Expediter: helps the group stick to the agenda

Expert testimony: a quotation or paraphrase from a recognized professional in a field related to your topic

Explanation: goes beyond definition to provide details about how and why

Extemporaneous method: speaking from a key word outline

Extended example: story or narrative developed at some length to illustrate a point

External interference: any distraction that originates in the communication situation

Eye contact: looking at your audience during the presentation

Facial expressions: facial movements that can reinforce a wide range of verbal messages

Fact: information established as accurate, usually concerning events, times, people, and places

Factual example: instance that actually occurred

False cause: fallacy in which a speaker claims that because one event follows another, the first event is the cause of the second

Farewell: a speech of tribute honoring someone who is leaving, for example, retiring, resigning, relocating, or being promoted

Feedback: those messages that listeners send back to a speaker about the clarity and acceptability of the speech

Figures of speech: language strategies that make striking comparisons between things or ideas that are not obviously alike

Flip charts: large pads of paper displayed on easels

Flowcharts: illustrate a sequence of steps

Focus group: a communication transaction with a small group of individuals for the purpose of gathering information from them

Formal outline: a typed outline, which labels and applies all macrostructural elements of your speech, using complete sentences and a complete reference list

Frame of reference: the listener's goals, knowledge, experience, values, and attitudes through which the message is filtered

Gatekeeper: helps keep the communication channels open

Gender: socialized tendencies of men and women to perceive, believe, and behave in the world

Gender-linked terms: words that somehow imply exclusion of either males or females

General purpose: to inform, to persuade, or to entertain

Government documents: documents and academic journals published by the federal government, often unavailable elsewhere

Graphs: representations intended to make statistics, statistical trends, and statistical relationships clearer

Group density: how crowded the room feels to audience members

Group goal: a collective purpose that unifies members

Group history: members' perceptions about the past work done by the group and its members

Groupthink: when a group opts for consensus over opposing alternative perspectives

Harmonizer: recognizes and deals with misunderstandings and disagreements among members

Hasty generalization: fallacy in which a speaker attempts to draw a conclusion based on too little evidence

Hearing: a physiological process

Heterogeneous groups: comprised of members with different cultural identities

Hierarchies: members of a group are seen as having different ranks

Homogeneous groups: comprised of members with similar cultural identities

Housekeeping needs: concern the many details that need to be kept

Human-edited index: Web search index edited by a human being (directory)

Hyperlinks: connections between two Web documents

Hypothetical example: a short story about a plausible event that never occurred; imaginary or fictitious instance or illustration

Impersonal communication: communication between two people about general information

Implied leader: an individual whom the other members perceive as having the highest status or greatest expertise

Impression formation and management: tendency to prejudge a speaker based on manner and appearance

Impromptu method: speaking with limited preparation

Inclusion: language choices that show your respect for your audience and for all types of people in general

Incremental change: small movement in the direction of your ultimate goal

Inductive reasoning: strategy of arriving at a general conclusion from a series of specific facts or examples

Information giver: provides content for the discussion

Information seeker: raises questions and probes into the contributions of others

Informative speaking: a public speech in which one shares knowledge to create mutual understanding

Initial credibility: perception of credibility before one even begins to speak

Initial ethos: opening credibility of a speaker, achieved with a planned pause and taking a moment to establish eye contact with the listeners

Initiator: proposes new ideas and approaches, as well as distributes the initial workload

Intelligibility: to be understood

Intelligible: able to be understood

Interactive model of communication: accounts for the feedback receivers return to senders

Interference: anything that acts as a barrier to the communication of a message

Internal interference: any distraction that originates in the thoughts of the sender or receiver

Internal previews and summaries: connect pieces of supporting material to the main point or subpoints they address

Internet: a worldwide network of computers that links resources and people at colleges and universities, government agencies, libraries, corporations, and homes

Interpersonal communication: communication between two people who have a relationship

Interview: a communication transaction with one individual for the purpose of gathering information

Introduction: announces your topic and provides a brief road map of how you will proceed

Invitational pattern: a main point arrangement designed to invite rather than convince listeners to agree with your position

Irrational beliefs: beliefs that project harm onto events that are not harmful

Jargon: particular terminology of a trade or profession that is not generally understood by outsiders

Kinesics: how the body communicates through facial expressions, gestures, posture, and movement

Laissez-faire leadership style: nondirective and passive

LCD panel: a device connected to a computer and placed on top of an overhead projector that projects what is on the computer monitor to a screen in the front of the room

LCD projector: a unit that can be connected to a VCR or computer, which projects the images onto a screen

Leadership: a range of diverse functions, which should ideally be shared by various group members

Leadership style: group's overall style of communicating and operating

Leading questions: questions phrased in such a way as to prompt a certain response

Learning style: a preferred way of receiving, organizing, and interpreting information

Line graphs: used to represent trends over time and sometimes compare trends over time

Linear model of communication: conceives of communication as a one-way process

Listener relevance link: a statement that reveals how and why the ideas you offer might benefit your listeners

Listening: multidimensional psychological process of receiving, attending to, constructing meaning from, and responding to spoken or nonverbal messages

Logos: appeals to logic, conveyed through structure, evidence, and reasoning

Macrostructure: the general framework for your ideas

Main point summary: a brief statement in the conclusion that reminds listeners of the main points

Main topic: the subject of your speech

Major premise: a general principle that most people agree upon or for which you provide support

Manuscript method: reading a speech that has been written out in its entirety

Maps: schematic representations of real or imaginary geographic areas

Marginalize: ignore or render illegitimate the experiences and values of some people

Mass communication: the mediated process whereby messages are transmitted to large publics

Master of ceremonies: an individual who has been designated to set the mood of the program, introduce participants, and keep the program moving along

Media: the equipment used to display presentational aids

Memorized method: presenting from memory a script that was originally written out in its entirety

Mental distractions: wandering thoughts that occur while listening to a message

Message: any signal sent by one person and interpreted by another

Metaphor: an implied comparison between two unlike things made without using *like* or *as*

Metasearch engine: an Internet tool that searches for a key word through several search engines at once

Microstructure: language and style choices you make to convey your ideas

Minor premise: a specific point or example that fits within your major premise

Modeling: a learned response arising from watching the behaviors and reactions of those whom we admire

Models: scaled-down or scaled-up versions of actual objects

Monroe's motivated sequence: a five-step approach for arranging your main points consisting of attention, need, satisfaction, visualization, and action

Motivated movement: reinforces the verbal message by emphasizing important points, referencing presentational aids, or clarifying structure

Non sequitur: fallacy in which a speaker offers supporting material that is not related to the argument

Nonverbal communication: all those elements of a speech other than the words themselves that can contribute to the message

Nonverbal messages: those messages we send using nonlinguistic means

Object language: the concept of appearance as it communicates

Onomatopoeia: the use of words that sound like the things they stand for

Open-ended question: asks respondents to reply in their own words

Oral footnotes: oral references to the original source of particular information at the point of presenting it during the speech

Oral report: one person presents the findings of the group in the form of an individual speech

Oral style: language and style choices unique to oral communication, characterized by use of personal pronunciation, simple language and sentence structure, repetition, and superlatives

Organization: the process of putting ideas and information together in a way that will make sense to listeners

Organizational charts: illustrate hierarchical relationships among positions in organizations

Organizational mapping: a process

of brainstorming in which you record as many ideas as you can think of related to your thesis as well as to each other

Outlining: a systematic process of placing your ideas in a recognizable pattern that listeners can easily follow

Panel discussion: a prepared conversation among group members that takes place in front of an audience

Paralanguage: use of voice to communicate

Parallel treatment: to provide similar labels for the genders when referring to them together

Parallelism: repeating words or grammatical structures within or across sentences

Passive sentence: the subject *experiences* the action

Pathos: appeals to listeners' emotions

Pauses: wait time before, during, or after a phrase to add emotional impact

Peer testimony: a quotation or paraphrase from someone who has firsthand experience related to a topic

Performance orientation: approaching a public speech as a performer, in which a perfect speech must be delivered flawlessly to a hypercritical audience

Personal inventory: a list of topics that interest you

Personification: attributing human qualities to a concept or to an inanimate object

Persuasion: the process of influencing other people's attitudes, beliefs, values, or behaviors

Persuasive punch words: language choices that evoke emotion

Persuasive speaking: the process of influencing attitudes, beliefs, values, or behaviors through a public speech

Physical distractions: distractions associated with body aches, pains, and feelings

Pie graphs: show what proportions of a whole are represented by each of its parts

Pitch: the highness or lowness of the voice on the musical staff

Plagiarism: presenting another person's ideas as your own

Political correctness: to demonstrate through language choices a concern for fairness and respect for different groups, based on race, gender, or ethnicity, as well as different identities and worldviews

Poll: a quick method to find out where your listeners stand on a topic

Posterboards: large pieces of tag board or foam core displayed on easels

Posture: conveying confidence and commitment through the way you stand and carry yourself

Preparation outline: a working rough draft of your speech

Presentational aids: visual, audio, and audiovisual supporting materials that help explain the ideas in your speech

Preview: a statement in the introduction that alerts listeners to the main points of the speech

Primacy-recency effect: the tendency to remember the first and last items conveyed orally in a series more than the items in between

Problem/cause/solution pattern: a main point arrangement with the first main point articulating the problem, the second analyzing its causes, and the third presenting multifaceted solutions

Problem (no solution) pattern: a main point arrangement that focuses on the depth and breadth of a problem in order to convince listeners that it is, in fact, a significant problem

Problem/solution pattern: a two-main points arrangement where the first main point examines the problem and the second presents solutions

Problem-solving group: small group primarily concerned with carrying out a task of determining appropriate solutions to problems

Progressive muscle relaxation therapy: when one systematically tenses and releases certain muscle groups while focusing on what a relaxed state feels like

Pronunciation: how the sounds of a word are said and which parts are stressed

Proxemics: the way in which space and distance communicate

Psychological characteristics: characteristics that motivate audience members to listen and retain ideas presented in a message

Public communication: the process of sending messages to large audiences

Public speaking: a sustained formal presentation made by a speaker to an audience

Questionnaire: a series of questions designed to elicit particular information about a topic

Raised consciousness: sensitizing your listeners to an issue and making them more receptive to persuasion in the future

Rate: the speed at which the speech is delivered

Reasoning fallacies: flawed reasoning

Receiver: a person to whom a sender communicates

Recorder: takes notes during meetings and summarizes them for everyone

Red herring: fallacy in which a speaker attacks an issue using irrelevant evidence or arguments as distractions

Refutative pattern: a main point arrangement that persuades by both disproving the opposing position and bolstering your own

Reinforcement: a learning process in which the responses one gets shape future expectations and behavior

Relational needs: involve interpersonal relationships among group members

Relevant evidence: information that is directly related to your topic

Repetition: restating words, phrases, or sentences for emphasis

Research: the process of locating supporting material

Research interview: an interview conducted to gather information for a speech

Rhetorical question: a question phrased in a way that stimulates thought, but not an overt response

Rhetorical situation: the specific circumstances in which the speech is to be delivered—the speaker (you), the audience (your classmates), and the occasion

Robot-generated index: comprehensive Web computer program that automatically visits a multitude of Web sites based on key words (search engine)

Scapegoating: the tendency to blame one or more members for the failure of a group

Search engine: robot-generated Web computer program that automatically visits a multitude of sites based on key words

Self-disclosure: sharing of personal information that is not generally known by others

Self-talk: those thoughts that go through our minds about our perceived success or failure in particular situations

Sender: a person who initiates communication

Sensory aids: appeal to senses such as sight, sound, taste, touch, or smell

Sex: biological differences between males and females

SIER model: a four-step process for understanding the dynamics of critical listening

Signposts: words or short phrases that mark where you are in a speech or help move the speech forward

Simile: a comparison between two unlike things using the words *like* or *as*

Situational acceptance: agreement that a certain policy, approach, or behavior is acceptable in some instances

Situational communication apprehension: a short-lived feeling of anxiety that occurs during a specific encounter

Skills training: a systematic method of breaking the speechmaking process into specific skills that can be mastered first in isolation and then together

Slang: a meaning that is arbitrarily assigned to a word by a particular social group or subculture

Sleeper effect: the change emerges later after listeners absorb your ideas into their own belief systems

Slide transition: means for moving from one slide to the next in a computerized slide show

Slippery slope: fallacy that is similar to false cause, but the speaker focuses on how a particular action will set forth a chain of events that will inevitably lead to a certain result

Small group: three to twenty people who come together for a reason

Small group communication: when three to twenty people meet to perform a task, reach a common goal, share ideas, or engage in a social experience

Socialization: a process of learning to fit within the rules of a society

Sociocultural background: differences in listeners' backgrounds such as ethnicity, culture, and even region

Spatial pattern: main points help create a mental picture of what an object, person, place looks like based on location or direction

Speaker credibility statement: one or more sentences indicating what makes you an authority on the topic of your speech

Speaking outline: a brief outline used solely as a memory aid while presenting the actual speech

Special occasion speeches: designed to fit the needs of some special occasion

Specific purpose: what you hope to accomplish in the speech

Speech of acceptance: a speech to express appreciation for an award or gift received

Speech of demonstration: a type of speech in which the goal is to clarify a process or a procedure

Speech of description: a type of speech in which the goal is to paint a clear picture in the minds of listeners

Speech of explanation: a type of speech in which the goal is to generate a clear interpretation in the minds of listeners

Speech of introduction: a short speech, generally lasting three to five minutes, for the purpose of introducing the main speaker

Speech of nomination: a speech given to propose an individual as a nominee for an elected office, honor, or award

Speech of presentation: a speech given when an individual or group receives an award, to present the award and recognize the recipient's accomplishments

Speech of tribute: a speech that praises or celebrates a person, a group, or an event

Speech of welcome: a formal public greeting to a visiting person or group to make the honoree feel comfortable and appreciated

Speech to entertain: a light-hearted speech that makes a serious point

Standard English: the language preferences described in the dictionary

Startling fact or statistic: a piece of information that is both little known and shocking

Statistics: the collection and arrangement of numerical facts

Stereotype: an assumption that all members of a certain group behave or believe a certain way solely because they belong to that particular group

Straw man: fallacy in which a speaker weakens some aspect of the opposing position by misrepresenting it and then attacks that weaker (straw man) argument

Stress: emphasis placed on words to indicate the importance of the ideas expressed

Structure: the overall framework used to organize your content

Structures of speech: sentence strategies that combine ideas in a particular way

Subgroups: smaller groups within the primary group

Supporter: responds favorably, whether verbally or nonverbally, when good points are made

Supporting material: any information that clarifies, explains, or in some way adds breadth or depth to your topic (also called *evidence*)

Survey: a general or comprehensive view of a particular issue; a method of obtaining information from a large pool of people in a short amount of time

Syllogism: a three-part form of deductive reasoning

Symposium presentation: all members of the group present orally a portion of the findings in mini speeches

Systematic desensitization: a series of techniques focused around progressive relaxation, visualization, and participation

Systematic problem-solving: the process of identifying a problem and, through a process of reasoning, attempting to discover the best way to solve it

Target audience: the portion of your audience you most want to persuade

Task needs: substantive actions that must be taken in order for the group to achieve its goal

Terminal credibility: perception of a speaker's credibility at the end of the speech

Terminal ethos: closing credibility of a speaker, achieved with a planned pause and taking a moment to establish eye contact with listeners

Testimony: quotations or paraphrases used to support a point

Thesaurus: a book of synonyms

Thesis restatement: a reiteration of the thesis statement in the conclusion, usually offered in past tense

Thesis statement: a one-sentence summary of the speech

Timbre: what distinguishes your voice from other voices (also known as vocal quality)

Toast: a very short speech of tribute, usually delivered in impromptu fashion, often given at wedding receptions, graduation dinners, awards luncheons, holiday dinners, and so forth

Topical pattern: main point arrangement used when a topic is divided into subtopics or categories

Traitlike communication apprehension: a tendency to feel anxious about speaking in most situations

Transactional model of communication: concept of communication as a complex, multifaceted, and interactive process of creating shared meaning

Transition: a word or phrase that shows the relationship between two main points and lets the audience know you have completed one main point and are moving on to another

Values: the enduring set of principles that shape your beliefs and attitudes

Verbal immediacy: use of language to reduce the psychological distance between you and your audience

Verbal messages: the words we use

Visual aids: pictures, drawings and diagrams, charts, graphs, and models

Visual channel: what the receivers see

Visual distractions: distractions associated with something someone sees

Vivid language and style: evokes feelings and images in the listeners' minds and thus invites them to internalize your ideas

Vocal quality: what distinguishes your voice from other voices (also known as timbre)

Vocal variety: changing rate, pitch, and volume in ways that reinforce the emotional meaning of the message

Vocalized pauses: unnecessary words that disrupt the fluency of your message, making your message less clear to listeners

Volume: how loudly or softly one speaks

Worldview: your way of looking at the world

World Wide Web: a software system that makes accessing information on the Internet simple

REFERENCES

Chapter 1

Adler, R., & Towne, N. (1996). *Looking out, looking in* (8th ed.). Fort Worth, TX: Harcourt Brace College Publishers.

Ancona, D. (1990). Outward bound: Strategies for team survival in an organization. *Academy of Management Journal, 33,* 334–365.

Astor, D. (1999, October 30). Cartoonists drawing more topical comics as century draws to a close. *Editor and Publisher,* 37.

Bakos, J. D., Jr. (1997). Communication skills for the 21st century. *Journal of Professional Issues in Engineering Education and Practice, 123*(1), 14–16.

Barbe, W., & Swassing, R. H. (1979). *The Swassing-Barbe modality index.* Columbus, OH: Waner-Bloser.

Brinson, S. L. (1992). TV fights: Women and men in interpersonal arguments on prime time television dramas. *Argumentation and Advocacy, 29*(2), 89–105.

Brown, T. (1997). The front line: Dilbert's message hits home. *HR Focus, 72*(2), 13.

Canfield, A. A. (1980). *Learning styles inventory manual.* Ann Arbor, MI: Humanics, Inc.

Capowski, G. (1997). We have seen Dilbert, and he is us. *HR Focus, 74*(2), 16.

Coffey, R. (1987, September 18). Biden's borrowed eloquence beats the real thing. *Chicago Tribune,* sec. 1, 23.

DeVito, J. (1993). *Messages: Building interpersonal communication skills* (2nd ed.). New York: Harper Collins.

Douglas, W. (1996). The fall from grace?: The modern family on television. *Communication Research, 23*(6), 675–703.

Dunn, R., Dunn, K., & Price, G. E. (1975). *Learning style inventory.* Lawrence, KS: Price Systems.

Ford, W. S. Z., & Wolvin, A. D. (1993). The differential impact of a basic communication course on perceived communication competencies in class, work, and social contexts. *Communication Education, 42*(3), 215–223.

Gardner, H. (1983). *Frames of mind: The theory of multiple intelligences.* New York: Basic Books.

Greenberg, B. S., Sherry, J. L., Busselle, R. W., Hnilo, L. R., & Smith, S. W. (1997). Daytime television talk shows: Guests, content and interactions. *Journal of Broadcasting and Electronic Media, 41*(3), 412–426.

Hahner, Jeffrey C., Sokoloff, M. A., & Salisch, S. L. (1993). *Speaking clearly: Improving voice and diction* (4th ed.). New York: McGraw-Hill.

Halone, K. K., Cunconan, T. M., Coakley, C. G., & Wolvin, A. D. (1998). Toward the establishment of general dimensions underlying the listening process. *International Journal of Listening, 12,* 12–28.

Honeycutt, J. M., Wellman, L. B., & Larson, M. S. (1997). Beneath family role portrayals: An additional measure of communication influence using time series analyses of turn at talk on a popular television program. *Journal of Broadcasting and Electronic Media, 41*(1), 40–57.

Jhally, S. (1995). *Dreamworlds II* [Video]. North Hampton, MA: The Media Education Foundation.

Job outlook 2000: What employers want. (2000, July 19).

National Association of Colleges and Employers [Online]. Available: **http://www.jobweb.org/Pubs/joboutlook/sv/svpg5.html/**

Johannesen, R. (1990). *Ethics in human communication* (3rd ed.). Prospect Heights, IL: Waveland Press.

Kaus, M. (1987, September 28). Biden's belly flop. *Newsweek,* 23–24.

Kellermann, K. (1992). Communication: Inherently strategic and primarily automatic. *Communication Monographs, 59,* 288–300.

Kramer, M. W., & Hinton, J. S. (1996). The differential impact of a basic public speaking course on perceived communication competencies in class, work, and social contexts. *Basic Communication Course Annual, 8,* 1–25.

Kolb, D. (1984). *Experiential learning: Experience as the source of learning and development.* Englewood Cliffs, NJ: Prentice-Hall.

Landay, L. (1999). Millions "Love Lucy": Commodification and the Lucy phenomenon. *NWSA Journal, 11*(2), 25.

Larson, M. S. (1991). Sibling interactions in 1950s versus 1980s sitcoms: A comparison. *Journalism Quarterly, 68*(3), 381–388.

Littlejohn, S. (1989). *Theories of human communication* (3rd ed.). Belmont, CA: Wadsworth.

McCarthy, B. (1980). *The 4MAT system: Teaching to learning styles with right/left mode techniques.* Barrington, IL: Excel.

McCroskey, J. C. (1993). *An introduction to rhetorical communication* (6th ed.). Englewood Cliffs, NJ: Prentice-Hall.

Maes, J. D. (1997). A managerial perspective: Oral communication competency is most important for business students in the workplace. *The Journal of Business Communication, 34*(1), 67–80.

Margolis, J. (1987, September 17). Biden threatened by accusations of plagiarism in his speeches. *Chicago Tribune,* sec. 1, 3.

Nagle, R. A. (1987). The ideal job candidate of the 21st century. *Journal of Career Planning and Employment,* 40.

New York Times. (1994, September 6), A12, A14.

Nilsen, T. (1974). *Ethics of speech communication* (2nd. ed.). Indianapolis, IN: Bobbs-Merrill.

Nineteen-nineties: As the 20th century comes to a close, the TV nation has grown into one big unhappy family. (1999, February 19). *Entertainment Weekly,* 96+.

Peterson, M. S. (1997). Personnel interviewers' perceptions of the importance and adequacy of applicants' communication skills. *Communication Education, 46*(4), 287–291.

Poole, M. (1998). The small group should be the fundamental unit of communication research. In Judith Trent (Ed.), *Communication: Views from the Helm for the 21st Century.* Needham Heights, MA: Allyn & Bacon, 94–97.

Renzulli, J. S., & Smith, L. H. (1978). *The learning styles inventory: A measure of student preference for instructional techniques.* Mansfield Center, CT: Creative Learning Press.

Richmond, V., & McCroskey, J. C. (1995). *Communication: Apprehension, avoidance, and effectiveness* (4th ed.). Scottsdale, AZ: Gorsuch Scarisbrick.

Seinfeld, J. (1993). *SeinLanguage.* New York: Bantam.

Shaw, M. (1981). *Group dynamics: The psychology of small group behavior.* New York: McGraw-Hill.

Stinson, L. M., & Asquith, J. (1997). Excellent communication skills are an essential part of being an accountant. *Journal of Technical Writing and Communication, 27*(4), 385–390.

Trank, D. M. (1990). Directing multiple sections of the basic course. In Friedrich, G. & Vangelisti, A. (Eds.), *Teaching Communication: Theory, Research, Methods.* Hillsdale, NJ: Erlbaum, 403–413.

Trank, D. M., & Lewis, P. (1991). The introductory communication course: Results of a national survey. *Basic Communication Course Annual, 3,* 106–122.

Trenholm, S., & Jenson, A. (1992). *Interpersonal Communication* (2nd ed.). Belmont, CA: Wadsworth.

Ulmer, R., & Sellnow, T. (1997). Strategic ambiguity and the ethic of significant choice in the tobacco industry. *Communication Studies, 48*(3), 215–233.

Wallace, K. (1955). An ethical basic of communication. *The Speech Teacher, 4,* 1–9.

Wasserstein, W. (December, 1988). Streeping beauty: A rare interview with cinema's first lady. *Interview,* 90.

Wattenberg, B. J. (1991). *The first universal nation: Leading indicators and ideas about the surge of America in the 1990s.* New York: The Free Press.

Weitzel, A. R. (1987). *Careers for speech communication graduates.* Salem, WI: Sheffield.

Willis, E. (1996). Bring in the noise. *The Nation, 262*(13), 19–21.

Wilson, T . (1996). Television's everyday life: Towards a phenomenology of the "televised subject." *Journal of Communication Inquiry, 20*(1), 49–67.

Wolvin, A. D. (1998a). The basic course and the future of the workplace. *Basic Communication Course Annual, 10,* 1–6.

Wolvin, A. D. (1998b). Careers in communication: An update. *Journal of the Association for Communication Administration, 27,* 71–73.

Wolvin, A. D., Berko, R. M., & Wolvin, D. R. (1999). *The public speaker/The public listener* (2nd ed.). Los Angeles: Roxbury.

Chapter 2

Ayres, J. (1986). Perceptions of speaking ability: An explanation of stage fright. *Communication Education, 35,* 275–287.

Bandura, A. (1973). *Social learning theory.* Englewood Cliffs, NJ: Prentice-Hall.

Behnke, R. R., & Beatty, L. W. (1981). A cognitive–physiological model of speech anxiety. *Communication Monographs, 48,* 158–163.

Bello, R. (1995, April 5–9). Public speaking apprehension and gender as predictors of speech competence. New Orleans, LA: Paper presented at the annual conference of the Southern States Communication Association.

Bourhis, J., & Berquist, C. (1990). Communication apprehension in the basic course: Learning styles and preferred instructional strategies of high and low apprehensive students. *Basic Communication Course Annual, 3,* 27–46.

Bourhis, J., & Stubbs, J. (1991, April). *Communication apprehension, learning styles, and academic achievement.* Chicago, IL: Paper presented at the Central States Communication Association annual meeting.

Bourne, E. J. (1990). *The anxiety and phobia workbook.* Oakland, CA: New Harbinger Publications.

Daly, J. A., & Buss, A. H. (1984). The transitory causes of audience anxiety. In J. A. Daly & J. C. McCroskey (Eds.), *Avoiding communication.* Beverly Hills, CA: Sage.

Daly, J. A., & Stafford, L. (1984). Implications of quietness: Some facts and speculation. In J. A. Daly & J. C. McCroskey (Eds.), *Avoiding communication.* Beverly Hills, CA: Sage.

Davis, M., Echelon, E., & McKay, M. (1988). *The relaxation and stress workbook.* Oakland, CA: New Harbinger Publications.

Desberg, P., & Marsh, G. (1988). *Controlling stagefright: Presenting yourself from one to one thousand.* Oakland, CA: New Harbinger Publications.

Dwyer, K. (1998a). Communication apprehension and learning style preference: Correlations and implications for teaching. *Communication Education, 47,* 137–150.

Dwyer, K. (1998b). *Conquer your speechfright.* Orlando, FL: Harcourt Brace College Publishers.

Ellis, A., & Dryden, W. (1987). *The practice of rational emotive therapy.* New York: Springer.

Friedrich, G., & Goss, B. (1984). Systematic desensitization. In J. A. Daly & J. C. McCroskey (Eds.). *Avoiding communication.* Beverly Hills, CA: Sage.

Griffin, K. (1995, July). Beating performance anxiety. *Working Woman,* 62–65, 76.

Hahner, J., Sokoloff, M., & Salisch, S. (1993). *Speaking clearly: Improving voice and diction* (4th ed). New York: McGraw-Hill.

Hoffman, J., & Sprague, J. (1982). A survey of reticence and communication apprehension treatment programs at U.S. colleges and universities. *Communication Education, 31,* 185–193.

Jacobson, E. (1938). *Progressive relaxation.* Chicago, IL: Chicago University Press.

McCarthy, B. (1987). *The 4MAT system: Teaching to learning styles with right/left mode techniques.* Barrington, IL: Excel.

McCroskey, J. C. (1972). The implementation of a large-scale program of systematic desensitization for communication apprehension. *Speech Teacher, 21,* 255–264.

McCroskey, J. C. (1977). Oral communication apprehension: A review of recent theory and research. *Human Communication Research, 4,* 78–96.

McCroskey, J. C. (1982). Oral communication apprehension: A reconceptualization. In M. Burgoon (Ed.), *Communication Yearbook 6.* Beverly Hills, CA: Sage.

McCroskey, J. C. (1984). The communication apprehension perspective. In J. A. Daly & J. C. McCroskey (Eds.), *Avoiding communication.* Beverly Hills, CA: Sage.

McCroskey, J. C., Ralph, D. C., & Barrick, J. E. (1970). The effect of systematic desensitization on speech anxiety. *Speech Teacher, 19,* 32–36.

Motley, M. (1991). Public speaking anxiety qua performance anxiety: A revised model and an alternative therapy. In M. Booth–Butterfield (Ed.) *Communication, cognition, and anxiety.* Newbury Park, CA: Sage.

Neer, M. R., & Kircher, W. F. (1991). Classroom interventions for reducing public speaking anxiety. *Basic Communication Course Annual, 3,* 202–223.

Pucel, J., & Stocker, G. (1983). A nonverbal approach to communication: A cross–cultural study of stress behaviors. *Communication, 12,* 53–65.

Richmond, V., & McCroskey, J. C. (1995). *Communication: Apprehension, avoidance, and effectiveness* (4th ed.). Scottsdale, AZ: Gorsuch Scarisbrick.

Rolfson, K. (1995). An experiential learning group as treatment for high communication apprehensive students at NDSU. Unpublished master's thesis. Fargo, ND: North Dakota State University.

White, D. (1998, September). Smile when you say that. *Working Woman,* 94–95.

Wolpe, J. (1958). *Psychotherapy by reciprocal inhibition.* Stanford, CA: Stanford University Press.

Chapter 4

Active listening (1997). *Public Management, 79*(12), 25–28.

Adler, R., & Towne, N. (1996). *Looking out, looking in* (8th ed.). Fort Worth, TX: Harcourt Brace College Publishers.

Barker, L., Edwards, C., Gaines, K., & Holley, F. (1980). An investigation of proportional time spent in various communication activities by college students. *Journal of Applied Communication Research, 8,* 101–109.

Bostrom, R. N. (1990). *Listening behavior: Measurement and application.* New York: The Guilford Press.

Cissna, K., & Sieburg, E. (1981). Patterns of interactional confirmation and disconfirmation. In C. Wilder-Mott & J. H. Weakland (Eds.), *Rigor and imagination: Essays from the legacy of Gregory Bateson.* New York: Praeger, 253–282.

Coakley, C., & Wolvin, A. (1991). Listening in the educational environment. In D. Borisoff & M. Purdy (Eds.), *Listening in everyday life: A personal and professional approach.* Lanham, MD: University Press of America.

DeWine, S., & Daniels, T. (1993). Beyond the snapshot: Setting a research agenda in organizational communication. In S. A. Deetz (Ed.), *Communication Yearbook 16.* Thousand Oaks, CA: Sage, 252–330.

Gitomer, J. (2000). Good listening skills open doors to closing sales. *The Business Journal—Serving Phoenix and the Valley of the Sun, 20*(32), 33.

Gunderson, T. (1999). Listen and learn. *Restaurant Hospitality, 83*(3), 26.

Halone, K. K., Cunconan, T. M., Coakley, C. G., & Wolvin, A. D. (1998). Toward the establishments of general dimensions underlying the listening process. *International Journal of Listening, 12,* 12–28.

Hiam, A. (1997). Is anybody listening? *Workforce, 76*(8), 92.

Horowitz, A. (1996). Hey! Listen up! *Computerworld, 30*(27), 64–67.

Hunsaker, R. (1991, November). Critical listening—a neglected skill. Presentation to the 77th annual meeting of the Speech Communication Association.

International Listening Association (1996). An ILA definition of listening.

International Listening Association Web page [Online]. Available: **http://www.listen.org/**

Kaye, S. (1998). Effective communication skills for engineers. *IIE Solutions, 30*(9), 44–47.

Kiewitz, C. (1997). Cultural differences in listening style preferences: A comparison of young adults in Germany, Israel, and the United States. *International Journal of Public Opinion Research, 9*(3), 233–248.

Kiewra, K., DuBois, N., Christian, J., & McShane, A. (1988). Providing Study Notes: Comparison of three types of notes for review. *Journal of Educational Psychology, 80,* 595–598.

Legge, W. (1971). Listening, intelligence, and school achievement. In S. Duker (Ed.), *Listening: Related readings*. Netuchen, NJ: Scarecrow Press, 121–133.

Linowes, J. G. (1998). Listening between the lines. *Journal of Management in Engineering, 14*(6), 21–23.

Luiten, J., Ames, W., & Ackerson, G. (1980). A meta–anlaysis of the effects of advance organizers on learning and retention. *American Educational Research, 17,* 211–218.

Mayer, L. (1996). *Fundamentals of Voice and Articulation* (11th ed.). Madison, WI: Brown & Benchmark.

Messmer, M. (1998, March). Improving your listening skills. *Management Accounting,* 14.

Miccinati, J. L. (1988). Mapping the terrain: Connecting reading with academic writing. *Journal of Reading, 31,* 542–552.

Morgan, G. (1983, August). Therapeutic listening: A communication tool. *Training and Development Journal,* 44.

Mulvaney, S. (1998). Improving listening skills. *Journal of Property Management, 63* (4), 20.

Ritts, V., Patterson, M., & Tubbs, M. (1992). Expectations, impressions, and judgments of physically attractive students: A review. *Review of Educational Research, 62,* 413–426.

Ross, R. (1983). *Speech communication: Fundamentals and practice* (6th ed.). Englewood Cliffs, NJ: Prentice-Hall.

Salopek, J. J. (1999). Is anyone listening? *Training and Development, 53*(9), 58–60.

Steil, L. K., Barker, L. L., & Watson, K. W. (1983). *Effective listening.* Reading, MA: Addison-Wesley.

Temple, L., & Loewen, K. (1993). Perceptions of power: First impressions of a woman wearing a jacket. *Perceptual and Motor Skills, 76,* 339–348.

Treinen, K. (1998). *The effects of gender and physical attractiveness on peer critiques of a persuasive speech.* Unpublished master's thesis. Fargo, ND: North Dakota State University.

Watson K., & Barker, L. (1984). Listening behavior: Definition and measurement. In R. N. Bostrom & B. Westley (Eds.), *Communication Yearbook 8.* Beverly Hills, CA: Sage.

Wolvin, A., & Coakley, C. (1991). A survey of the status of listening training in some Fortune 500 corporations. *Communication Education, 40,* 152–164.

Wolvin, A., & Coakley, C. (1992) *Listening* (4th ed.). Dubuque, IA: William C. Brown.

Chapter 5

Lamb, M. (1991). Animal behavior processes. *Journal of Experimental Psychology, 17,* 45–54.

Richmond, V. P., & McCroskey, J. C. (1995). *Communication: Apprehension, avoidance, and effectiveness* (4th ed.). Scottsdale, AZ: Gorsuch Scarisbrick.

Suskind, R., & Lublin, J. (1995, January 26). Critics are succinct: Long speeches tend to get short interest. *Wall Street Journal,* A1–A5.

Weiten, W. (1986). *Psychology applied to modern life* (2nd ed.). Belmont, CA: Wadsworth.

Chapter 6

Aristotle. (1954). *Rhetoric* (W. Rhys Roberts, Trans.). New York: Modern Library, 1954.

Bashi, V., & McDaniel, A. (1997). A theory of immigration and racial stratification. *Journal of Black Studies, 27*(5), 668–683.

Berko, R., Wolvin, A., & Ray, R. (1997). *Business communication in a changing world.* New York: St. Martin's Press.

Brumfit, C. (1993). Simplification in pedagogy. In M. L. Tickoo (Ed.), *Simplification: Theory and application.* Anthology Series 31.

Canary, D. J., & Dindia, K. (1998). *Sex differences and similarities in communication.* Mahwah, NJ: Erlbaum.

Canary, D. J., & Hause, K. S. (1993). Is there any reason to research sex differences in communication? *Communication Quarterly, 41,* 129–144.

Caplan, S. E. (1999). Acquisition of message–production skill by younger and older adults: Effects of age, task complexity, and practice. *Communication Monographs, 66*(1), 31–48.

De Ciantis, S. M., & Kirton, M. J. (1996). A psychometric reexamination of Kolb's experiential learning cycle construct: A separation of level, style, and process. *Educational and Psychological Measurement, 56*(5), 809–821.

DiMartino, E. C. (1989). Understanding children from other cultures. *Childhood Education, 66,* 30–32.

Di Santa Ana, J. (1996). Cultures in tension and dialogue. *International Review of Mission, 85*(336), 93–103.

Donavan, J. M., & Rundle, B. A. (1997). Psychic unity constraints upon successful intercultural communication. *Language and Communication, 17*(3), 219–236.

Dunn, R. S., & Dunn, K. J. (1979). Learning styles/teaching styles: Should they . . . can they . . . be matched? *Educational Leadership, 36,* 238–244.

Faludi, S. (1991). *Backlash: The undeclared war against American women.* New York: Doubleday.

Gudykunst, W. B., Matsumoto, Y., Ting-Toomey, S., Nishida, T., Kim, K., & Heyman, S. J. (1996). The influence of cultural individualism-collectivism, self construals, and individual values on communication styles across cultures. *Human Communication Research, 22*(4), 510–544.

Hummert, M. L., Shaner, J. L., Garstka, T. A., & Henry, C. (1998). Communication with older adults: The influence of age stereotypes, context, and communicator age. *Human Communication Research, 25*(1), 124–153.

Hummert, M. L., Wieman, J. M., & Nussbaum, J. F. (Eds.). (1994). *Interpersonal communication in older adulthood: Interdisciplinary theory and research.* Thousand Oaks, CA: Sage.

Iino, M. (1993). The trap of generalization: A case of encountering a new culture. *Working Papers in Educational Linguistics, 9,* 21–45.

Kemper, S., & Harde, T. (1999). Experimentally disentangling what's beneficial about elderspeak from what's not. *Psychology and Aging, 14*(4), 656.

Kim, M., Hunter, J. E., Miyahara, A., Horvath, A., Bresnahan, M., & Yoon, H. (1996). Individual- vs. culture-level dimensions of individualism and collectivism: Effects on preferred conversational styles. *Communication Monographs, 63*(1), 29–50.

Kirtley, M. D., & Weaver, J. B. (1999). Exploring the impact of gender role self-perception on communication style. *Women's Studies in Communication, 22*(2), 190.

Kolb, D. (1984). *Experiential learning: Experience as the source of learning and development.* Englewood Cliffs, NJ: Prentice-Hall.

Lee, M. (1993, July 27). Asian Americans don't fit their monochrome image. *Christian Science Monitor, 85*(168), 9–10.

Lee, W. B. (1990, March 22–25). Cultural differences and decision making: The example of support to primary education project in Cameroon. Anaheim, CA: Paper presented to the National Conference of the Comparative and International Education Society.

Lustig, M. W., & Koester, J. (1993). *Intercultural competence: Interpersonal communication across cultures.* New York: Harper Collins, 37–50.

McAdoo, L. (1999). Gender and student critiques. Unpublished master's thesis, Fargo, ND; North Dakota State University.

McGuire, W. (1985). Attitudes and attitude change. In G. Lindzey & E. Aronson (Eds.). *The handbook of social psychology* (2nd ed.). New York: Random House.

Magolda, M. B. (1989). Gender differences in cognitive development: An analysis of cognitive complexity and learning styles. *Journal of College Student Development, 30,* 213–220.

Marshall, C. (1990, October). The power of the learning styles philosophy. *Educational Leadership, 48,* 62.

Maslow, A. (1970). A theory of human motivation. *Psychological Review, 50,* 370–396.

Masterson, J., Watson, N., & Cichon, E. (1991). Cultural differences in public speaking. *World Communication, 20,* 39–47.

Merriam, A. H. (1982, April 6–9). Comparative chronemics and diplomacy: American and Iranian perspectives on time. Hot Springs, AR: Paper presented at the Annual Meeting of the Southern Speech Communication Association.

Nussbaum, J. F., & Coupland, J. (Eds.). (1995). *Handbook of communication and aging research.* Mahwah, NJ: Erlbaum.

Petronio, S., Ellemers, N., Giles, H., & Gallois, C. (1998). (Mis)communicating across boundaries. *Communication Research,* 571.

Plotnik, R. (1993). *Introduction to psychology* (3rd ed.). Belmont, CA: Wadsworth.

Reeder, H. M. (1996). A critical outlook at gender difference in communication research. *Communication Studies, 47*(4), 318–331.

Reinard, J. C. (1988). The empirical study of the persuasive effects of evidence. *Human Communication Research, 15,* 3–59.

Reisman, J. (1990). Intimacy in same-sex friendships. *Sex Roles, 23,* 65–82.

Richmond, V. P., & McCroskey, J. C.(1995). *Communication: Apprehension, avoidance, and effectiveness* (4th ed.). Scottsdale, AZ: Gorsuch Scarisbrick.

Rogers, C. (1983). *Freedom to learn for the '80s.* Columbus, OH: Merrill.

Sellnow, D., & Golish, T. (2000). The relationship between a required self-disclosure speech and public speaking anxiety: Considering gender equity. *Basic Communication Course Annual, 12,* 28–59.

Sprague, J. (1993). Why teaching works: The transformative power of pedagogical communication. *Communication Education, 42,* 349–366.

Suzuki, S. (1998). In-group and out-group communication patterns in international organizations: Implications for social identity theory. *Communication Research, 25*(2), 154–184.

Tannen, D. (1992). *You just don't understand.* New York: Ballentine Books.

Thimm, C. (1998). Age stereotypes and patronizing messages: Features of age-adapted speech in technical instructions to the elderly. *Journal of Applied Communication Research, 26*(1), 66–83.

Weatherall, A. (1998). Re-visioning gender and language research. *Women and Language, 21*(1), 1–9.

Williams, A. (1997). Young people's beliefs about intergenerational communication: An initial cross-cultural comparison. *Communication Research, 24*(4), 370–394.

Wood, J. (1994). *Gendered lives: Communication, gender, and culture.* Belmont, CA: Wadsworth.

Chapter 7

American Psychological Association. (1994). *Publication manual of the American Psychological Association* (4th ed.). Washington, DC. Author.

Basch, R. (1996). *Secrets of the super net searchers: The reflections, revelations, and hard-won wisdom of 35 of the world's top Internet researchers.* Wilton, CT: Pemberton Press.

Kent, P. (1998). *The complete idiot's guide to the Internet* (5th ed.). Indianapolis, IN: Alpha Books.

Munger, D., Anderson, D., Benjamin, B., Busiel, C., & Paredes-Holt, B. (1999). *Researching online* (2nd ed.). New York: Longman.

Quaratiello, A. R. (1997). *The college student's research companion.* New York: Neal Schuman.

Reddick, R., & King, E. (1996). *The online student: Making the grade on the Internet.* Fort Worth, TX: Harcourt Brace College Publishers.

Reinard, J. (1991). *Foundations of argument.* Dubuque, IA: William C. Brown.

Shalala, D. (1994, May 15). Domestic terrorism: An unacknowledged epidemic. *Vital Speeches of the Day,* 451.

Whitely, S. (Ed.). (1994). *The American Library Association guide to information access.* New York: Random House.

Young, G. (Ed.). (1998). *The Internet.* New York: H. W. Wilson.

Chapter 8

Connor, U., & McCagg, P. (1987). A contrastive study of English expository prose paraphrases. In U. Connor & R. B. Kaplan (Eds.), *Writing across languages: Analysis of L2 text.* Reading, MA: Addison-Wesley, 73–86.

Darnell, D. (1963). The relation between sentence-order and comprehension. *Speech Monographs, 30,* 97–100.

Dwyer, K. K. (1998). *Conquer your speechfright.* Fort Worth, TX: Harcourt Brace College Publishers.

Foss, S., & Foss, K., (1994). *Inviting transformation: Presentational speaking for a changing world.* Prospect Heights, IL: Waveland Press.

Hoffman, R. (1992). Temporal organization as a rhetorical resource. *Southern Communication Journal, 57,* 194–204.

Smith, R. (1951). Effects of speech organization upon attitudes of college students. *Speech Monographs, 18,* 292–301.

Thompson, E. (1967). Some effects of message structure on listening comprehension. *Speech Monographs, 34,* 51–57.

Chapter 9

Humes, J. C. (1988). *Standing ovation: How to be an effective speaker and communicator.* New York: Harper & Row.

Slan, J. (1998). *Using stories and humor to grab your audience.* Needham Heights, MA: Allyn & Bacon.

Trenholm, S. (1989). *Persuasion and social influence.* Englewood Cliffs, NJ: Prentice-Hall.

Chapter 11

Beard, H., & Cerf, C. (1993). *The officially politically correct dictionary and handbook.* New York: Villard Books.

Braithwaite, D., & Braithwaite, C. (1997). Viewing persons with disabilities as a culture. In L. Samovar & R. Porter (Eds.), *Intercultural communication: A reader* (8th ed.). Belmont, CA: Wadsworth, 154–164.

Browner, C. M. (1998). Cleaner air and economic progress. Cited in C. M. Logue & J. DeHart (Eds.), *Representative American speeches: 1997–1998.* New York: H. W. Wilson, 187–192.

Duck, S. W. (1994). *Meaningful relationships.* Thousand Oaks, CA: Sage.

Fisher, M. (1992). A whisper of AIDS. In M. Fisher, *Sleep with the angels: A mother challenges AIDS* (1994). Wakefield, MA: Moyer Bell.

Gastil, J. (1990). Generic pronouns and sexist language: The oxymoronic character of masculine generics. *Sex Roles, 23,* 629–643.

Gorham, J. (1988). The relationship between verbal teacher immediacy behaviors and student learning. *Communication Education, 37,* 40–53.

Grabmeier, J. (1992, November). Clashing over political correctness. *USA Today,* 60–61.

Hamilton, M. C. (1991). Masculine bias in the attribution of personhood: People = male, male = people. *Psychology of Women Quarterly, 15,* 393–402.

Legette, G., Mead, C., Kramer, M., & Beal, R. (1991). *Prentice-Hall handbook for writers* (11th ed.). Englewood Cliffs, NJ: Prentice-Hall.

Maggio, R. (1988). *The nonsexist word finder: A dictionary of gender-free usage.* Boston, MA: Beacon.

Miller, C., & Swift, K. (1991). *Words and women: New language in new times.* New York: Harper Collins.

Motley, M. (1991). Public speaking anxiety qua performance anxiety: A revised model and an alternative therapy. In M. Booth-Butterfield (Ed.), *Communication, cognition, and anxiety.* Newbury Park, CA: Sage.

Powell, R. G., & Harville, B. (1990). The effects of teacher immediacy and clarity on instructional outcomes: An intercultural assessment. *Communication Education, 39,* 369–379.

Shotter, J. (1993). *Conversational realities: The construction of life through language.* Newbury Park, CA: Sage.

Strossen, N. (1992, November), The controversy over politically correct speech. *USA Today,* 57–59.

Switzer, J. Y. (1990). The impact of generic word choices: An empirical investigation of age- and sex-related differences. *Sex Roles, 22,* 69–82.

Treinen, K., and Warren, J. (2001). Antiracist pedagogy in the basic course: Teaching cultural communication as if whiteness matters. *Basic Communication Course Annual 13.* Boston, MA: American Press, 46–75.

Wood, J. (1994). Gendered lives: Communication, gender, and culture. Belmont, CA: Wadsworth.

Chapter 12

Barker, L. L., Cegala, D. J., Kibler, R. J., & Wahlers, K. J. (1979). *Groups in process.* Englewood Cliffs, NJ: Prentice-Hall.

Bate, B. (1992). *Communication and the sexes.* Prospect Heights, IL: Waveland Press.

Blouin, D., Summers, T., Kelley, E., Glee, R., Sweat, S., & Arledge, L. (1982). Recruiter and student evaluation of career appearance. *Adolescence, 17*(68), 821–830.

Cherulnik, P. D. (1989). *Physical attractiveness and judged suitability for leadership* (Report No. CG 021 893). Chicago, IL: Annual Meeting of the Midwestern Psychological Association. (ERIC Document Services No. ED 310 317).

Decker, B. (1992). *You've got to be believed to be heard.* New York: St. Martin's Press.

Drogosz, L. M., & Levy, P. E. (1996). Another look at the effects of appearance, gender and job type on performance-based decisions. *Psychology of Women Quarterly, 20,* 437–445.

Hall, E. T. (1968). Proxemics. *Current Anthropology, 9,* 83–108.

Lawrence, S. G., & Watson, M. (1991). Getting others to help: The effectiveness of professional uniforms in charitable fund raising. *Journal of Applied Communication Research, 19,* 170–185.

Lustig, M. W., & Koester, J. (1993). *Intercultural competence: Interpersonal communication across cultures.* New York: Harper Collins.

Mayer, L. V. (1994). *Fundamentals of voice and diction* (10th ed.). Madison, WI: William C. Brown.

Molloy, J. T. (1975). *Dress for success.* New York: Warner.

Morris, T. L., Gorham, J., Cohen, S. H., & Huffman, D. (1996). Fashion in the classroom: Effects of attire on student perceptions of instructors in college classes. *Communication Education, 45,* 135–148.

Phillips, P. A., & Smith, L. R. (1992). *The effects of teacher dress on student perceptions* (Report No. SP 033 944). (ERIC Document Services No. ED 347 151).

Temple, L. E., & Loewen, K. R. (1993). Perceptions of power: First impressions of a woman wearing a jacket. *Perceptual and Motor Skills, 76,* 339–348.

Watzlawick, Bavelas, & Jackson. (1967). *Pragmatics of human communication.* New York: W. W. Norton.

Chapter 13

Currid, C. (1995). *Make your point: The complete guide to successful business presentations using today's technology.* Rocklin, CA: Prima Publishing.

Hotch, R. (1992, August). Making the best of presentations. *Nation's Business,* 37–38.

Mitchell, G. (1987). *The trainer's handbook.* New York: American Management Association.

Vogel, D. R., Dickson, G. W., & Lehman, J. A. (1986). Persuasion and the role of visual presentation support: The UM/3M Study. Commissioned by Visual Systems Division of 3M.

Zayes-Baya, E. P. (1977–1978). Instructional media in the

total language picture. *International Journal of Instructional Media, 5,* 145–150.

Chapter 14

Baker, L. (1998). The Illongot headhunters. Used by permission.

Banach, W. J. (1991, March 15). Are you too busy to think? *Vital Speeches of the Day, 57*(11): 351–353.

Foss, S., & Foss, K. (1994). *Inviting transformation: Presentational speaking for a changing world.* Prospect Heights, IL: Waveland Press.

Ledbetter, C. (1995, July 1). Take a test drive on the Information Superhighway: Unmasking the jargon. *Vital Speeches of the Day,* 565–569.

Sev'er, A., & Ungar, S. (1997). No laughing matter: Boundaries of gender-based humor in the classroom. *Journal of Higher Education, 68*(1): 87–105.

Swift, W. B., & Swift, A. T. (1994, March). Humor experts jazz up the workplace. *HR Magazine on Human Resources, 39*(3): 72–76.

Wallinger, L. (May 1997). Don't smile before Christmas: The role of humor in education. *NASSP Bulletin, 81,* 27–34.

Wanzer, M., & Frymier, A. (1999). The relationship between student perceptions of instructor humor and students' reports of learning. *Communication Education, 48,* 48–62.

Chapter 15

Anton, M. L. R. (1994). Sexual assault policy a must. *Winning Orations.* Mankato, MN: Interstate Oratorical Association.

Cook, J. S. (1989). *The elements of speechwriting and public speaking.* New York: Collier Books.

Foss, S. K., & Foss, K. A. (1994). *Inviting transformation: Presentational speaking for a changing world.* Prospect Heights, IL: Waveland Press.

Foss, S. K., Foss, K. A., & Griffin, C. L. (1999). *Feminist rhetorical theories.* Thousand Oaks, CA: Sage.

Frisby, T. (1998). Floss or die. *Winning Orations.* Mankato, MN: Interstate Oratorical Association.

Johannesen, R. L. (1990). *Ethics in human communication* (3rd ed.). Prospect Heights, IL: Waveland Press.

Lewis, H. (1998). I spy, with my high tech eye. *Winning Orations.* Mankato, MN: Interstate Oratorical Association.

McCombs, M. E. (1981). The agenda-setting approach. In D. D. Nimmo & K. R. Sanders (Eds.), *Handbook of political communication.* Beverly Hills, CA: Sage.

Perloff, R. M. (1993). *The dynamics of persuasion.* Hillsdale, NJ: Erlbaum.

Simons, H. W. (1986). *Persuasion: Understanding, practice, and analysis.* New York: Random House.

Sonnenberg, F. K. (1988, September/October). Presentations that persuade. *The Journal of Business Strategy,* 55.

Ziegelmueller, G. W., Kay, J., & Dause, C. A. (1990). *Argumentation: Inquiry and advocacy* (2nd ed.). Englewood Cliffs, NJ: Prentice-Hall.

Chapter 16

Beebe, S. A. Eye contact: A nonverbal determinant of speaker credibility. *Speech Teacher, 23,* 21–25.

Booth-Butterfield, S., & Gutowski, C. (1993). Message modality and source credibility can interact to affect argument processing. *Communication Quarterly, 41,* 77–89.

Buck, S., & Tiene, D. C. (1989). The impact of physical attractiveness, gender, and teaching philosophy on teacher evaluations. *Journal of Educational Research, 82,* 172–177.

Cherulnik, P. D. (1989). *Physical attractiveness and judged stability for leadership* (Report No. CG 021 893). Chicago, IL: Annual Meeting of the Midwestern Psychological Association. (ERIC Document Services No. ED 310 317).

Drogosz, L. M. & Levy, P. E. (1996). Another look at the effects of appearance, gender and job type on performance-based decisions. *Psychology of Women Quarterly, 20,* 437–445.

Eagly, A. H. & Chaiken, S. (1993). *The psychology of attitudes.* Fort Worth, TX: Harcourt Brace Jovanovich.

Ericson, J. M., Murphy, J. J., & Zeuschner, R. B. (1987). *The debater's guide* (revised edition). Carbondale, IL: Southern Illinois University Press.

Frisby, T. (1998). Floss or die. *Winning Orations.* Mankato, MN: Interstate Oratorical Association, 67–70.

Hall, E. (1959). *The silent language.* Garden City, NY: Doubleday.

Hamilton, S. (1999). Cruise ship violence. *Winning Orations.* Mankato, MN: Interstate Oratorical Association, 92–94.

Kelly, F. D. (1972). Communicational significance of therapist proxemic cues. *Journal of Consulting and Clinical Psychology, 39,* 345.

Kracht, K. (1998). Including Joshua: What's the big deal? *Winning Orations.* Mankato, MN: Interstate Oratorical Association, 96–98.

Krishnan, A. (1998). Is Mr. Goodwrench really Mr. Rip Off? *Winning Orations.* Mankato, MN: Interstate Oratorical Association.

Labor, R. (1998). Shaken Baby Syndrome: The silent epidemic. *Winning Orations.* Mankato, MN: Interstate Oratorical Association, 70–72.

Maloney, S. R. (1992). *Talk your way to the top.* Englewood Cliffs, NJ: Prentice-Hall.

McCroskey, J. C. & Teven, J. (1999). Goodwill: A reexamination of the construct and its measurement. *Communication Monographs, 66,* 90–103.

Morley, D. D. & Walker, K. (1987). The role of importance, novelty, and plausibility in producing belief change. *Communication Monographs, 54,* 436–442.

Miller, L. C., Cook, L. L., Tsang, J., & Morgan, F. (1992). Should I brag? Nature and impact of positive and boastful disclosures for women and men. *Human Communication Research, 18,* 364–399.

Mulholland, R. (1998). Nuclear scare: What's happening out there? *Winning Orations.* Mankato, MN: Interstate Oratorical Association, 149–152.

Murphy, B. O. & Zorn, T. (1996). Gendered interaction in professional relationships. In Wood, J. (Ed.). *Gendered relationships.* Mountain View, CA: Mayfield, 213–232.

O'Keefe, D. (1990). *Persuasion: Theory and research.* Newbury Park, CA: Sage.

Perloff, R. M. (1993). *Dynamics of persuasion.* Hillsdale, NJ: Lawrence Erlbaum, 145–149.

Reardon, K. K. (1991). *Persuasion in practice* (2nd ed.). Newbury Park, CA: Sage.

Reinard, J. C. (1988). The empirical study of the persuasive effects of evidence: The status after fifty years of research. *Human Communication Research, 15,* 3–59.

Roberts, W. Rhys (trans.). 1954). *The Rhetoric* (Aristotle). New York: Modern Library.

Robinson, D. L., Stack, D. W., & Nelson, W. H. (1989). *The effect of physical attractiveness and spokesperson sex on perceived source and organization credibility* (Report No. CS 506 642). San Francisco, CA: Annual meeting of the International Communication Association. (ERIC Document Services No. ED 306 622).

Schwartz, R. (1998). Personal watercraft safety. *Winning Orations.* Mankato, MN: Interstate Oratorical Association, 60–63.

Slan, J. (1998). *Using stories and humor: Grab your audience.* Boston, MA: Allyn & Bacon.

Slater, D. (1998). Sharing life. *Winning Orations.* Mankato, MN: Interstate Oratorical Association, 63–66.

The New York Public Library Desk Reference (2nd ed.). (1993). New York: Stonesong-Simon.

Waddell, C. (1990). The role of pathos in the decision-making process: A study in the rhetoric of science policy. *Quarterly Journal of Speech, 76,* 381–400.

Witte, K. (1992). Putting the fear back into fear appeals: The extended parallel model. *Communication Monographs, 59,* 329–349.

Ziegelmueller, G. W., Kay, J., & Dause, C. A. (1990). *Argumentation and advocacy* (2nd ed.). Englewood Cliffs, NJ: Prentice-Hall.

Chapter 17

Bellefante, G. (1994, March 14). People. *Time,* 109.

Foss, S. & Foss, K. (1994). *Inviting transformation: Presentational speaking for a changing world.* Prospect Heights, IL: Waveland Press.

Geyer, G. A. (1989, August 15). Joy in our times. *Vital Speeches of the Day,* 666–668.

Reagan, R. (1986, January 28). Tribute to the CHALLENGER astronauts. In Rohler, L. E., & Cook, R. (Eds). 1993. *Great Speeches for Criticism and Analysis* (2nd ed.). Greenwood, IN: Alistair Press, 314–315.

Roe, K. (1987). After dinner speaking final round winner. In John K. Boaz and James R. Brey (Eds.). *1987 Championship Debates and Speeches (Vol. 2).* Normal, IL: American Forensic Association.

Sellnow, D. (1999). Success. Speech delivered to the Society of Women Engineers at their Spring Banquet, April 17, 1999.

Chapter 18

Ancona, D. G. (1990). Outward bound: Strategies for team survival in an organization. *Academy of Management Journal, 33,* 334–365.

Bass, B. M. (1990). *Bass and Stodgill's handbook of leadership: Theory, research, and managerial applications* (3rd Ed). New York: Free Press.

Dewey, J. (1933). *How we think.* Boston, MA: D. C. Heath and Company.

Gibb, C. (1969). Leadership. In G. Lindsey & E. Aronson (Eds.). *The Handbook of Social Psychology* (2nd ed.). Reading, MA: Addison-Wesley.

Helgesen, S. (1990). *The female advantage: Women's ways of leadership.* New York: Doubleday.

Lewin, K., Lippitt, R., & White, R. K. (1939). Patterns of aggressive behavior in experimentally created "social climates." *Journal of Social Psychology, 10,* 271–299.

Porter, R. E. & Samovar, L. A. (1992). Communication in the multicultural group. In Cathcart and Samovar (Eds.). *Small group communication* (6th ed.). Dubuque, IA: William C. Brown.

Shimanoff, S. B. & Jenkins, M. M. (1992). Leadership and gender: Challenging assumptions and recognizing resources. In Cathcart and Samovar (Eds.). *Small group communication* (6th ed.). Dubuque, IA: William C. Brown.

White, R. & Lippitt, R. (1960). *Autocracy and democracy.* New York: Harper & Row.

White, R. & Lippitt, R. (1969). Leader behavior and member reaction in three social climates. In Cartwright, D. & Zander, A. (Eds.). *Group Dynamics* (3rd ed.). New York: Harper & Row.

CREDITS

Chapter 1 Page xxvi (AIE, page xxxiv): © James Steinfeldt/Shooting Star; **Page 6:** © Bob Daemmrich/Stock Boston; **Page 9:** © Bob Daemmrich/Stock Boston; **Page 25:** © David Wells/The Image Works.

Chapter 2 Page 32: © Journal Courier/Steve Warmowski/The Image Works; **Page 34:** ©Courtesy The Boston Globe; **Page 43:** © Milton L. Howell, Jr.; **Pages 49–50:** "Personal Report of Communication Apprehension" from *Communication: Apprehension, Avoidance & Effectiveness 4/e,* by Virginia P. Richmond and James C. McCroskey. Copyright © 1995 Allyn & Bacon. Reprinted/adapted by permission; **Pages 50–52:** "Personal Report of Public Speaking Anxiety" from *Communication: Apprehension, Avoidance & Effectiveness 4/e,* by Virginia P. Richmond and James C. McCroskey. Copyright © 1995 Allyn & Bacon. Reprinted/adapted by permission.

Chapter 3 Page 56: © Richard Pasley/Stock Boston; **Page 60:** © AP/Wide World Photos; **Page 67:** © Richard Lord/The Image Works.

Chapter 4 Page 72: © Paul S. Howell/Liaison Agency; **Page 74:** © Werner Krutein/Liaison Agency; **Page 78:** © Rhoda Sidney/Stock Boston.

Chapter 5 Page 96: © AP/Wide World Photos; **Page 98:** © Bob Daemmrich/Stock Boston; **Page 101:** Reproduced with permission of Yahoo! Inc. © 2000 by Yahoo! Inc. YAHOO! And the YAHOO! Logos are trademarks of Yahoo! Inc.; **Page 108:** © Michael Newman/PhotoEdit.

Chapter 6 Page 114: © Syracuse Newspapers/John Berry/The Image Works; **Page 118:** © Bob Daemmrich/The Image Works; **Page 121:** © Suzanne Dunn/The Image Works; **Page 123:** © Chromosohm/Sohm/Stock Boston; **Page 128:** From *Motivation and Personality, 3/e* by Maslow. Copyright © 1998. Reprinted by permission of Prentice-Hall, Inc., Upper Saddle River, NJ.; **Page 135:** Used with permission by Amazon.com. All rights reserved.

Chapter 7 Page 138: © Bob Kramer/Stock Boston; **Page 150:** © Journal-Courier/Steve Warmowski/The Image Works; **Page 154:** Used with permission from WWW Virtual Library at http://vlib.org. All rights reserved.

Chapter 8 Page 168: © Peter Southwick/Stock Boston; **Page 175:** © Jim Zuckerman/CORBIS; **Page 176:** © Bruce Burkhardt/CORBIS.

Chapter 9 Page 184: © Richard Hutchings/PhotoEdit/Picture Quest; **Page 191:** © Francoise de Mulder/CORBIS.

Chapter 10 Page 204: © Steve Chenn/CORBIS; **Page 211:** © Stacy Pick/Stock Boston.

Chapter 11 Page 226: © Traver/Liaison Agency; **Page 242:** © Jeroboam; **Page 245:** © Ken Redding/CORBIS; **Pages 249–252:** "Whisper of Aids," the following has been used with the express permission of the Republican National Committee. All rights reserved. (Mary Fisher "Aids" speech to Republican National Convention members.)

Chapter 12 Page 254: © Bettmann/CORBIS; **Page 261:** © AP/Wide World; **Page 268:** © Seth Resnick/Stock Boston.

Chapter 13 Page 282: © Spencer Grant/PhotoEdit; **Page 285:** © Bob Daemmrich/Stock Boston; **Page 289:** © Raoul Minsart/CORBIS; **Page 302:** © Will Hart/PhotoEdit.

Chapter 14 Page 308: © Dean C. Worcester/NGS Image Collection; **Page 314:** © Bettmann/CORBIS; **Page 321:** © Milton L. Howell, Jr.

Chapter 15 Page 328: © Julian Calder/CORBIS; **Page 333:** © Bob Daemmrich/The Image Works; **Page 349:** © Steve Jay Crise/CORBIS.

Chapter 16 Page 360: © Paul Velasco: Gallo Images/ CORBIS; **Page 365:** © Barry King/Liaison Agency; **Page 381:** © Barry King/Liaison Agency; **Pages 384–387:** "Astroturf Lobbying" by Clayton Johnson, *Winning Orations,* 1998. Permission granted by Interstate Oratorical Association, Mankato, MN.

Chapter 17 Page 388: © Michael Newman/PhotoEdit; **Page 395:** © Newsmakers/ Liaison Agency; **Page 397:** © Reuters NewMedia Inc./ CORBIS; **Pages 402–407:** Georgia Ann Geyer "Joy in our Times" Commencement Address, *Vital Speeches of the Day,* August 15, 1989. Reprinted by permission of Vital Speeches and the author.

Chapter 18 Page 414: ©Fabian Falcon/Stock Boston; **Page 418:** © RNT Productions/ CORBIS; **Page 433:** © AP/Wide World Photo.

Appendix Pages A-2–A-5: "I Have A Dream" by Martin Luther King, Jr. Reprinted by arrangement with The Heirs to the Estate of Martin Luther King, Jr., c/o The Writer's House, agent for the proprietor. Copyright © 1963 Martin Luther King Jr., copyright renewed 1991 by Coretta Scott King; **Pages A-18–A-21:** "The Shame of Hunger" by Elie Wiesel. Copyright © 1990 by Elie Wiesel. Reprinted by permission of Georges Borchardt, Inc., for the author; **Pages A-22–A-27:** Address delivered 12/1/98 by Bell Atlantic Corporation Chairman, Raymond Smith at Wiesenthal Center in Los Angeles, CA. Reprinted by permission from Vital Speeches.

INDEX

Page numbers appearing in italics refer to figures and tables. Entries appearing in boldface refer to Key Terms.